America's Healthy Cooking

America's Healthy Cooking

more than 800 easy-to-follow recipes

JG PRESS

Published by World Publications Group, Inc.
455 Somerset Avenue
North Dighton, MA 02764
www.wrldpub.net

All photographs courtesy of Sunset Books

ISBN 1-57215-347-4

Editors: Joel Carino and Emily Zelner
Designer: Lynne Yeamans/Lync
Production Director: Ellen Milionis

Printed and bound in China by SNP Leefung Printers Limited.

1 2 3 4 5   06 05 03 02

contents

introduction

Stuffed Trout, Kung Pao Chicken, Spicy Pork Tenderloin, Stuffed Shells with Roasted Red Pepper Sauce, Peach Shortcake—sound like too much work to prepare and too many calories? Not so! In fact, just the opposite is true. These dishes will not require an excessive amount of time in the kitchen and they are all low in fat and high in nutrition. And they are just a few examples of the many irresistible recipes that we have compiled for you.

Light cuisine has become the cooking style of choice for people concerned with healthy eating. Simply stated, the basis of this type of cooking is that the food you prepare should look good, taste good, and be good for you. Fresh ingredients prepared with a minimum of fuss, served in sensible-size portions, nutritionally well-balanced and nourishing—this is healthy American cooking.

As you peruse the recipes in this book, you'll notice that we recommend a variety of foods, with an emphasis on fresh fruits and vegetables, low-fat or non-fat dairy products, and a variety of techniques for lighter cooking. Everything is fresh and fresh-tasting. Since we take the light approach to ingredients whenever possible, you'll find, for example, foods sautéed in reduced amounts of butter, and soups and sauces enriched with low-fat yogurt.

No matter how low the recipe's calorie count, though, the food you prepare has to taste good in order for you to commit to a lighter style of eating. With that in mind, the recipes in this book have been selected as much for their imaginative and tempting flavors as for their good nutrition. Herbs and spices, offered simply or in intriguing combinations, deftly season many of these dishes. Often, familiar ingredients are used in exciting new ways to produce some unexpectedly delicious results.

The recipes in this book make use of familiar rather than exotic foods, carefully selected for freshness, prepared using familiar techniques, and flavored creatively. As every good cook knows, fine cooking begins with fresh ingredients. Cooking with a light touch enhances the natural flavor of the food. And with fresh ingredients, you have control over exactly what goes into a dish.

The best cooking techniques for healthy cooking are those that use the least fat. Besides being lower in calories and cholesterol, these methods bring out the natural flavor of the food. Most people know that steaming is an excellent way to cook vegetables to tender, nutrition-filled perfection. But it's also an ideal fat-free technique for cooking fish and chicken. Simmering is another fat-free method, one that infuses food with the flavors of the cooking liquid—wine, perhaps, or broth. Sautéing can be light, if you use a minimum of fat, as recommended in the recipes in this book. Stir-frying is another wonderful method of cooking meat or seafood and vegetables quickly. Grilling, broiling, baking, and roasting also can produce a variety of delicious dishes. In short— the options for cooking with both good taste and good nutrition are far from limited.

You can add flavor to these cooking methods without adding many calories or a lot of salt. Instead, reach for herbs, spices, lemon or lime, and other naturally light flavorful boosters. From pea pods to sole, food gains in flavor when you add a pinch of basil, coriander, parsley, or other herbs. And don't forget the spices—exotic ones, such as turmeric and curry, as well as cinnamon, nutmeg, and other traditional favorites. Soups and sauces gain body and flavor from chopped or puréed vegetables, or even yogurt.

Your choices in seasoning and cooking healthy meals are limited only by your imagination— so experiment and enjoy!

appetizers

cucumber & jicama salsa

preparation time: about 25 minutes

1 medium-size cucumber, peeled, seeded, and diced

About 1 pound jicama, peeled, rinsed, and diced

1/3 cup chopped fresh basil

1/3 cup sliced green onions

1/4 cup lemon juice

1/4 cup plain nonfat yogurt

1 small fresh jalapeño chile, seeded and minced

Salt

In a nonmetal bowl, mix cucumber, jicama, basil, onions, lemon juice, yogurt, and chile; season to taste with salt. (At this point, you may cover and refrigerate the salsa for up to 6 hours.)

makes about 6 cups

per 1/4 cup: 11 calories, 0.5 g protein, 2 g carbohydrates, 0.03 g total fat, 0 mg cholesterol, 4 mg sodium

barley sushi scoops

preparation time: about 50 minutes

2 cups water

3/4 cups pearl barley, rinsed and drained

1 large carrot, finely diced

1/3 cup seasoned rice vinegar (or 1/3 cup distilled white vinegar plus 2 tablespoons sugar)

1 medium-size cucumber, finely sliced

1/3 cup sliced green onions

2 tablespoons drained pickled ginger, chopped

4 ounces small cooked shrimp

Fish sauce (*nuoc mam* or *nam pla*) or salt

1 green onion

40 to 48 medium-size butter lettuce leaves (about 1 1/2 lbs. *total*), rinsed and crisped

1 In a 1 1/2- to 2-quart pan, bring water to a boil. Add barley; reduce heat to low, cover, and simmer for 20 minutes. Sprinkle carrot over barley. Cover and continue to simmer until barley is tender to bite (about 10 more minutes).

2 Remove barley from heat; drain. Let cool, uncovered, in pan; then transfer to a medium-size bowl and mix in vinegar, cucumber, sliced onions, ginger, and shrimp. Season to taste with fish sauce and spoon into a serving bowl. Garnish with whole onion.

3 To eat, spoon barley mixture onto lettuce; wrap to enclose, then eat out of hand.

makes 10 to 12 servings

per serving: 85 calories, 5 g protein, 17 g carbohydrates, 0.4 g total fat, 20 mg cholesterol, 40 mg sodium

tomato-crab quesadillas

preparation time: about 45 minutes

4 medium-size fresh green Anaheim chiles or other large mild chiles

1/4 cup dry white wine

2 small shallots

1 tablespoon lemon juice

1 cup firmly pocked cilantro leaves

1/2 cup peeled, coarsely chopped jicama

1/4 cup fat-free reduced-sodium chicken broth

1 tablespoon honey

2 medium-size firm-ripe tomatoes, finely chopped

4 ounces cooked crabmeat

3/4 cup shredded jack cheese

1 cup sliced green onions

10 flour tortillas (*each* 7 to 9 inches in diameter)

Cilantro sprigs

1 To prepare chile sauce, place chiles on a baking sheet. Broil 4 to 6 inches below heat, turning often, until charred all over (about 8 minutes). Cover with foil and let cool on baking sheet; then remove and discard skins, stems and seeds.

2 In a blender or food processor, whirl chiles, wine, shallots, and lemon juice until smooth. Pour into a 2- to 3-quart pan. Bring to a boil, stirring, until reduced to 1/3 cup (5 to 10 minutes).

3 Return mixture to blender or food processor. Add cilantro leaves and jicama. Whirl until smooth; scrape sides of container several times. With motor running, slowly add broth and honey and whirl to blend. Serve sauce cool or cold. (At this point, you may cover and refrigerate for up to 4 hours. It makes about 1 cup).

4 Place tomatoes in a fine wire strainer and let drain well; discard juice.

5 In a bowl, mix crab, cheese, and onions. Gently mix in tomatoes. Place 5 tortillas in a single layer on 2 lightly-oiled large baking sheets. Evenly top tortillas with crab mixture, covering tortillas to within 3/4 inch of edges. Top each tortilla with one of the remaining tortillas.

6 Bake in a 450° oven until tortillas are lightly browned (7 to 9 minutes), switching positions of baking sheets halfway through baking.

7 Slide quesadillas onto a serving board; cut each quesadilla into 6 wedges. Garnish with cilantro sprigs. Add chile sauce to taste.

makes 8 to 10 servings

per serving: 209 calories, 9 g protein, 29 g carbohydrates, 6 g total fat, 23 mg cholesterol, 308 mg sodium

PLAN AHEAD, THEN RELAX: You'll appreciate special occasions more—and so will your guests—if you're out of the kitchen and part of the party. Careful planning allows you the luxury of relaxing and enjoying the event. Choose recipes that are delicious and easy to make; prepare as much as possible ahead of time. If any dishes do require last-minute attention, make sure you have time to finish them easily.

curry beef in lettuce

preparation time: about 30 minutes

1 teaspoon cornstarch

6 tablespoons cider vinegar

3 large firm-ripe pears

12 ounces lean ground beef

4 ounces mushrooms, chopped

1/2 cup golden raisins

1/4 cup firmly packed brown sugar

2 tablespoons curry powder

2 tablespoons tomato paste

1/2 teaspoon ground cinnamon

1/4 cup sliced green onions

2 tablespoons chopped parsley

1/2 cup plain nonfat yogurt

1 head butter lettuce, separated into leaves, rinsed, and crisped

Salt

1 In a large bowl, blend cornstarch with 2 tablespoons of the vinegar. Peel, core, and finely chop pears; gently stir into vinegar mixture and set aside.

2 Crumble beef into a wide nonstick frying pan or wok; add mushrooms and raisins. Stir-fry over medium-high heat until meat is browned (8 minutes). Add water, 1 tablespoon at a time, if pan appears dry. Spoon off and discard fat from pan.

3 Stir in sugar, 1/4 cup water, remaining 1/4 cup vinegar, curry powder, tomato paste, and cinnamon. Bring to a boil; then stir until almost all liquid has evaporated (about 3 minutes).

4 Add pear mixture; stir until mixture boils and thickens slightly. Transfer to a serving bowl; stir in onions and parsley.

5 To serve, spoon meat mixture and yogurt into lettuce leaves; season to taste with salt.

makes 4 to 6 servings

per serving: 319 calories, 18 g protein, 50 g carbohydrates, 8 g total fat, 43 mg cholesterol, 129 mg sodium

scorched corn & chile salsa

preparation time: about 30 minutes

2 medium-size ears corn

1 small tomato, seeded and finely chopped

1 medium-size fresh green Anaheim or other mild green chile, seeded and finely chopped

2 cloves garlic, minced or pressed

2 tablespoons lime juice

1 tablespoon ground dried California or New Mexico chiles

Salt

1 Remove and discard husks and silk from corn. Place corn on a lightly oiled grill 4 to 6 inches above a solid bed of medium-hot coals. Cook, turning as needed, until kernels are browned (about 8 minutes). Meanwhile, in a medium-size bowl, combine tomato, chopped chile, garlic, lime juice, and ground chiles; set aside.

2 Cut corn kernels from cobs and stir into tomato mixture; season to taste with salt. If made ahead, let cool; then cover and refrigerate for up to 4 hours. Serve at room temperature.

makes about 3 cups

per 1/4 cup: 14 calories, 0.5 g protein, 3 g carbohydrates, 0.2 g total fat, 0 mg cholesterol, 3 mg sodium

garlic chicken bites with tomato-raisin sauce

preparation time: about 30 minutes

3 tablespoons minced cilantro

2 teaspoons coarsely ground pepper

8 cloves garlic, minced

1 pound skinless, boneless chicken thighs, cut into 1 ¹/₂-inch chunks

¹/₃ cup tomato sauce

1 tablespoon firmly packed brown sugar

1 tablespoon distilled white vinegar or cider vinegar

¹/₂ cup raisins

1 In a small bowl, mix cilantro, pepper, and three-fourths of the garlic; rub mixture over chicken. Place chicken pieces well apart in a lightly-oiled 10- by 15-inch rimmed baking pan.

2 Bake in a 500° oven until chicken is lightly browned and no longer pink in center; cut to test (18 to 20 minutes).

3 Meanwhile, in a food processor or blender, whirl remaining garlic, tomato sauce, sugar, vinegar, and raisins until raisins are chopped. Serve chicken hot, with tomato-raisin sauce.

makes 4 servings

per serving: 221 calories. 24 g protein, 22 g carbohydrates, 5 g total fat, 194 mg cholesterol, 225 mg sodium

north beach bruschetta

preparation time: about 30 minutes

²/₃ cup nonfat ricotta cheese

¹/₄ cup shredded carrot

¹/₄ cup dried currants or raisins

2 tablespoons thinly sliced green onion

1 tablespoon Dijon mustard

¹/₂ teaspoon dried basil

8 ounces unsliced crusty bread

4 ounces thinly sliced pastrami

¹/₃ cup shredded part-skim mozzarella cheese

1 In a medium-size bowl, combine ricotta, carrot, currants, onion, mustard, and basil. Set aside.

2 Cut bread in half horizontally. Set halves crust side down; if needed, cut a thin slice from cut side of halves to make each piece about 1 inch thick. Trim crust side of each piece so bread sits steadily. Then cut each piece in half crosswise.

3 Spread cut sides of bread with ricotta mixture. Loosely pleat pastrami over ricotta mixture, covering bread. Sprinkle with mozzarella. Arrange bread on a 12- by 15-inch baking sheet and bake in a 400° oven until mozzarella is melted (about 7 minutes).

makes 4 servings

per serving: 271 calories, 19 g protein, 38 g carbohydrates, 3 g total fat, 15 mg cholesterol, 880 mg sodium

cherry tomatoes with smoked oysters

preparation time: about 10 minutes

2 baskets cherry tomatoes

1 can (3 oz.) tiny smoked oysters, drained

Italian parsley sprigs (optional)

Frisée (optional)

1 Remove stems from tomatoes. Slice each tomato vertically to within about ¼ inch of base; spread apart and slip in a smoked oyster and, if desired, parsley.

2 Arrange on a platter and garnish with frisée, if desired.

makes about 40 appetizers

per appetizer: 4 calories, 0.3 g protein, 0.6 g carbohydrates, 0.1 g total fat, 2 mg cholesterol, 14 mg sodium

crostini with fresh tomatoes

preparation time: about 20 minutes

1 pound very ripe pear-shaped tomatoes, seeded and chopped

⅓ cup chopped red onion

2 tablespoons chopped fresh basil leaves or 1 tablespoon dry basil leaves

2 tablespoons olive oil

6 slices (about 3 ½ by 5 inches and about ½ inches thick *each*) crusty Italian or French bread

Freshly ground pepper

1 Place about two-thirds of the tomatoes in a clean towel or cheese-cloth. Wring tightly to remove juice. Set crushed tomatoes aside. Mix remaining tomatoes with onion, basil, and oil; set aside.

2 Place bread in a single layer on a baking sheet. Broil about 5 inches below heat, turning once, until golden on both sides (about 4 minutes total).

3 Spread slices with crushed tomatoes. Mound onion mixture on top. Season to taste with pepper.

makes 6 servings

per serving: 188 calories, 5 g protein, 31 g carbohydrates, 5 g total fat, 0.5 mg cholesterol, 282 mg sodium

cherry pepper shooters

preparation time: 20 minutes

2 jars (about 1 lb. *each*) mild cherry peppers, drained

1 can (about 8 oz.) pineapple chunks packed in juice, drained

2 ounces thinly sliced prosciutto, cut into 1 ½-inch squares

1 Cut off and discard pepper stems. With a small spoon, scoop out and discard seeds.

2 Cut each pineapple chunk in half; wrap each half in a piece of prosciutto. Stuff wrapped pineapple chunks into peppers.

makes 12 servings

per serving: 44 calories, 1 g protein, 8 g carbohydrates, 0.7 g total fat, 4 mg cholesterol, sodium information not available

chicken satay

preparation time: about 2 hours

1 clove garlic, minced or pressed

2 tablespoons soy sauce

1 tablespoon salad oil

1 teaspoon *each* **ground cumin and ground coriander**

2 whole chicken breasts (about 2 lbs. *total***), split, skinned, and boned**

Basting Sauce (recipe follows)

Peanut Sauce (recipe follows)

1 Mix garlic, soy, oil, cumin, and coriander. Cut chicken into ¾-inch chunks. Add to marinade, stirring to coat evenly. Cover and refrigerate for at least 1 ½ hours or up to 2 hours.

2 Meanwhile, prepare Basting Sauce and Peanut Sauce; set aside. Also, soak 16 bamboo skewers in hot water to cover for 30 minutes.

3 Thread 4 or 5 cubes of chicken on each skewer. Place on a rack in a broiler pan; brush with half the baste. Broil 4 to 6 inches below heat, turning once and brushing with remaining baste, until no longer pink in center when cut (about 10 minutes).

4 Offer with sauce for dipping.

makes about 16 appetizers

BASTING SAUCE

Mix 3 tablespoons lemon juice, 2 tablespoons soy sauce, and ¼ teaspoon *each* ground cumin and ground coriander.

per appetizer: 94 calories, 17 g protein, 1 g carbohydrates, 2 g total fat, 43 mg cholesterol, 435 mg sodium

PEANUT SAUCE

In a 1- to 1 ½-quart pan, boil 1 cup water, ⅔ cup creamy or crunchy peanut butter, and 2 cloves garlic, minced or pressed, over medium-high heat, stirring, until thickened (about 4 minutes). Remove from heat and stir in 2 tablespoons firmly packed brown sugar, 1 ½ tablespoons lemon juice, 1 tablespoon soy sauce, and ¼ to ½ crushed red pepper. Let cool to room temperature.

makes 1 ½ cups

per tablespoon: 57 calories, 3 g protein, 3 g carbohydrates, 4 g total fat, 0 mg cholesterol, 93 mg sodium

STAPLES FOR QUICK MEALS: Always keep your kitchen well-stocked and replenish your supplies before they run out. These foods should always be in stock: sugar, flour, salt, and rice in your pantry; a variety of spices and herbs conveniently arranged in a cool place away from direct light; and eggs, dairy products, mustard, and mayonnaise in the refrigerator. You'll also want to keep basic vegetables like onions, carrots, and potatoes on hand.

baked vegetables provençal

preparation time: about 1 hour

4 tablespoons olive oil

1 large eggplant, ends trimmed, cut in half lengthwise

1 large red bell pepper cut in half, stemmed, and seeded

1 medium-size onion, cut in half

2 large pear shaped tomatoes, coarsely chopped

2 tablespoons white wine vinegar

1/4 cup chopped Italian parsley

Salt and pepper

Niçoise olives (optional)

Italian parsley sprigs (optional)

1 Pour 2 tablespoons of the oil into a 10- by 15-inch baking pan. Lay eggplant, bell pepper, and onion, cut sides down, in oil. Bake in a 350° oven until eggplant is very soft when pressed (about 50 minutes). Let cool briefly.

2 Trim off and discard skin from eggplant. Coarsely chop eggplant, bell pepper, and onion. Place in a strainer along with tomatoes; gently press out excess liquid. Transfer to a bowl. Stir in vinegar, chopped parsley, and remaining 2 tablespoons oil. Season to taste with salt and pepper.

3 If made ahead, cover and refrigerate until next day. Serve at room temperature, stirring before serving.

4 Garnish with olives and parsley sprigs, if desired.

makes about 4 cups

per tablespoon: 11 calories, 0.1 g protein, 0.9 g carbohydrates, 0.8 g total fat, 0 mg cholesterol, 0.8 mg sodium

black beans & fresh corn nachos

preparation time: about 45 minutes

About 1 1/2 cups Lime Salsa (page 67)

1 can (about 15 oz.) refried beans

4 cups cooked yellow or white corn kernels (from 4 large ears corn); or 2 packages (about 10 oz. *each*) frozen corn kernels, thawed

1 cup shredded jalapeño jack cheese

About 12 cups water-crisped corn tortilla chips or purchased tortilla chips

Cilantro leaves

1 Prepare Lime Salsa and refrigerate.

2 Prepare Refried Black Beans. Spoon beans onto a large, oven-proof rimmed platter; spread out evenly to make an oval. Top beans evenly to make an oval. Top beans evenly with corn, then sprinkle with cheese. Bake in a 400 ° oven until hot in center (about 10 minutes).

3 Remove bean mixture from oven. Tuck some of the tortilla chips around edge of platter; serve remaining chips alongside. Garnish with cilantro.

4 To serve, spoon bean mixture onto plates; top with some of the Lime Salsa. To eat, scoop bean mixture onto chips; add more salsa to taste.

makes 12 appetizer or 8 main-dish servings

per serving: 423 calories, 18 g protein, 67 g carbohydrates, 12 g total fat, 22 mg cholesterol, 668 mg sodium

nachos with pita chips

preparation time: about 45 minutes

4 whole wheat pita breads (*each* about 5 inches in diameter), cut crosswise into halves

1 pound carrots (about 8 small carrots), cut into 1-inch lengths

2 cans (about 15 oz. *each*) garbanzo beans, drained and rinsed

1/4 cup lemon juice

3 or 4 cloves garlic, peeled

4 teaspoons Asian sesame oil

Salt

1 jar (about 7 oz.) roasted red peppers, drained, rinsed, and chopped

1 cup shredded reduced-fat jack cheese

Lemon wedges

1 cup plain nonfat yogurt

1 Carefully peel pita bread halves apart, stack halves, then cut stack into 3 equal wedges. Spread wedges in a single layer on 2 large baking sheets. Bake in a 350° oven until browned and crisp (about 15 minutes), switching positions of baking sheets halfway through baking. Let cool on baking sheets on racks.

2 Meanwhile, in a 2- to 3-quart pan, combine carrots and 4 cups water. Bring to a boil over medium-high heat; then reduce heat, cover, and simmer, stirring occasionally, until carrots are tender when pierced but still bright in color (about 15 minutes). Drain well.

3 Pour carrots into a food processor or blender and add lemon juice, garlic and oil. Whirl until smoothly puréed. Season to taste with salt. Spoon bean mixture onto a large ovenproof rimmed platter; spread out to make an oval. Top with red peppers and sprinkle with cheese.

4 Bake in a 400° oven until bean mixture is hot in center (about 10 minutes). Remove from oven. Tuck some of the pita chips around edge of platter; serve remaining chips alongside. Serve with lemon wedges to squeeze to taste, and offer yogurt to spoon over nachos to taste.

makes 8 servings

per serving: 267 calories, 14 g protein, 38 g carbohydrates, 7 g total fat, 10 mg cholesterol, 491 mg sodium

bell pepper & oyster boats

preparation time: about 20 minutes

4 medium-size red bell peppers, stemmed and seeded

1 can (3 3/4 oz.) small smoked oysters, drained

2 small packages (3 oz. *each*) cream cheese, at room temperature

2 tablespoons lemon juice

1 teaspoon celery seeds

64 chive pieces (*each* 4 in. long)

1 Cut each bell pepper lengthwise into 8 equal strips. If necessary, cut larger oysters in half so you have 32 pieces.

2 Beat cream cheese, lemon juice, and celery seeds until smooth. Spread about 1 teaspoon of the mixture over end of each pepper strip. Top with 1 oyster piece and 2 chives. If made ahead, cover and refrigerate until the next day.

makes 32 appetizers

per appetizer: 26 calories, 09 g protein, 1 g carbohydrates, 2 g total fat, 9 mg cholesterol, 38 mg sodium

spinach-bean roll-ups

preparation time: about 25 minutes

1 package (about 10 oz.) frozen chopped spinach, thawed and squeezed dry

1 large package (about 8 oz.) nonfat cream cheese or Neufchatel cheese, at room temperature

1/2 cup grated Parmesan cheese

2 tablespoons nonfat mayonnaise

1 teaspoon prepared horseradish, or to taste

1/8 teaspoon ground allspice, or to taste

1 can (about 15 oz.) cannellini (white kidney beans)

1 tablespoon seasoned rice vinegar (or 1 tablespoon) distilled white vinegar plus 1/2 teaspoon sugar)

2 teaspoons honey

3/4 teaspoon chopped fresh thyme or 1/4 teaspoon dried thyme

1/3 cup thinly sliced green onions

1/3 cup finely chopped parsley

6 reduced-fat flour tortillas (*each* about 7 inches in diameter)

About 48 whole fresh spinach leaves, rinsed and crisped

Thyme sprigs (optional)

1 In a medium-size bowl, combine chopped spinach, cream cheese, Parmesan cheese, mayonnaise, horseradish, and allspice. Mix well; set aside.

2 Drain beans, reserving liquid. Rinse beans well, place in another medium-size bowl, and add vinegar, honey, and chopped thyme. Coarsely mash beans with a spoon; add enough of the reserved bean liquid to give mixture a spreadable consistency (do not make it too thin). Set aside. In a small bowl, combine onions and parsley; set aside.

3 To assemble roll-ups, divide spinach mixture equally among tortillas. With a spatula, spread spinach mixture to cover tortillas evenly; then top tortillas equally with bean filling; carefully spread to cover spinach mixture. Sprinkle with onion mixture. Roll up each tortilla tightly to enclose filling. (At this point, you may cover tightly and refrigerate for up to 3 hours.)

4 Line 6 individual plates with spinach leaves. With a serrated knife, carefully cut each tortilla diagonally into 4 equal slices (wipe knife clean between cuts, if desired.); arrange on spinach-lined plates. Garnish with thyme sprigs, if desired.

makes 6 servings

per serving: 230 calories, 15 g protein, 33 g carbohydrates, 4 g total fat, 9 mg cholesterol, 964 mg sodium

watermelon pico de gallo

preparation time: about 35 minutes

1 medium-large orange

1 1/2 cups seeded, diced watermelon

3/4 cup peeled, diced jicama

1 fresh jalapeño chile, seeded and minced

1 tablespoon lime juice

1 tablespoon minced cilantro

1 Finely grate 2 teaspoons peel (colored part only) from orange; place in a non-metal bowl.

2 Cut off remaining peel and all white membrane from orange. Holding fruit over bowl to catch juice, cut between membranes to release orange segments; then dice segments and drop into bowl.

3 Add watermelon, jicama, chile, lime juice, and cilantro to bowl; mix gently. If made ahead, cover and refrigerate for up to four hours.

makes about 3 cups

per serving: 17 calories, 0.3 g protein, 4 g carbohydrates, 0.1 g total fat, 0 mg cholesterol, 1 mg sodium

picadillo-stuffed empanadas

preparation time: about 1 ³/₄ hours

Cornmeal-Cumin Pastry (recipe follows)

2 tablespoons slivered almonds

1 teaspoon salad oil

1 large onion, finely chopped

2 cloves garlic, minced or pressed

6 ounces ground turkey or chicken breast

1 can (about 8 oz.) tomato sauce

¹/₂ teaspoon ground cinnamon

¹/₈ teaspoon ground cloves

2 tablespoons dried currants or raisins

2 teaspoons cider vinegar

Salt

1 Prepare Cornmeal-Cumin Pastry.

2 Toast almonds in a small frying pan over medium heat until golden (5 to 7 minutes), stirring often. Transfer almonds to a bowl and let cool; then coarsely chop and set aside.

3 In a wide nonstick frying pan, combine oil, onion, garlic, and 1 tablespoon water. Cook over medium heat, stirring often, until mixture is deep golden (about 20 minutes); if onion sticks to pan bottom or pan appears dry, add more water, 1 tablespoon at a time. Crumble turkey into pan and cook over medium-high heat, stirring often, until well browned (about 10 minutes); if pan appears dry, add more water, 1 tablespoon at a time.

4 Stir in tomato sauce, cinnamon, and currants. Bring mixture to a boil; then reduce heat and simmer, uncovered, until almost all liquid has evaporated and mixture is slightly thickened (about 10 minutes). Remove from heat, stir in almonds and vinegar, and season to taste with salt.

5 On a floured board, roll out pastry ¹/₈ inch thick. Cut into 3 ¹/₂-inch rounds. Spoon equal amounts of filling onto half of each pastry round. Moisten edges of rounds with water; fold plain half of each round over filling. Press edges together with a fork.

6 Arrange empanadas on a lightly oiled 12- by 15-inch baking sheet. Bake in a 400° oven until lightly browned (about 20 minutes).

CORNMEAL-CUMIN PASTRY

In a food processor (or a bowl), combine 1 cup all-purpose flour, ¹/₂ cup yellow cornmeal, 1 ¹/₂ teaspoons baking powder, ¹/₄ teaspoon salt, and 2 tablespoons butter or margarine. Whirl (or rub with your fingers) until mixture resembles coarse crumbs. Add ¹/₃ cup milk, 1 large egg white, and ¹/₂ teaspoon cumin seeds; whirl (or stir with a fork) until dough holds together (add 1 table-spoon more milk if needed). With lightly floured hands, pat dough into a ball. Wrap airtight and refrigerate until ready to use or for up to 1 hour.

makes about 16 empanadas

per serving: 96 calories, 5 g protein, 13 g carbohydrates, 3 g total fat, 11 mg cholesterol, 192 mg sodium

creamy guacamole

preparation time: less than 20 minutes

1 teaspoon grated lemon peel

2 tablespoons lemon juice

1 medium-size soft-ripe avocado

1 cup low-fat (1%) cottage cheese

2 to 4 cloves garlic, peeled

1/8 teaspoon salt

2 tablespoons minced cilantro

1 fresh jalapeño or serrano chile, seeded and
   minced

1 tablespoon thinly sliced green onion

2 small tomatoes, finely chopped and drained well

Cilantro sprigs

1 About 8 cups tortilla chips or bite-size pieces of raw vegetables.

2 Place lemon peel and lemon juice in a blender or food processor. Pit and peel avocado; transfer avocado to blender along with cottage cheese, garlic, and salt. Whirl until smoothly puréed.

3 Spoon guacamole into a serving bowl and gently stir in minced cilantro, chile, onion, and half the tomatoes. (At this point, you may cover and refrigerate for up to 2 hours; stir before serving.)

4 To serve, garnish with remaining tomatoes and cilantro sprigs. Scoop guacamole onto tortilla chips.

makes about 3 cups, about 8 servings

per serving: 138 calories, 6 g protein, 21 g carbohydrates, 4 g total fat, 1 mg cholesterol, 215 mg sodium

mussel & clam appetizer

preparation time: about 1 1/2 hours

1 cup Salsa Fresca (recipe on page 67)

1 1/2 cups Tomatillo Salsa (recipe on page 63)

3 pounds mussels, scrubbed

1 cup *each* dry white wine and water

2 tablespoons lemon juice

1 pound clams (suitable for steaming), scrubbed

3 small French baguettes (8 oz. *each*), sliced
   1/2-inch thick, lightly toasted

Lime wedges

1 Prepare Salsa Fresca and Tomatillo Salsa; set aside.

2 Discard any mussels that don't close when tapped. Pull beard (clump of fibers along side of shell) off each mussel with a quick tug.

3 In a 6- to 8-quart pan, simmer mussels, wine, water, and lemon juice, covered, over medium-high heat just until shells open (about 5 minutes). Lift out with a slotted spoon, discarding any mussels that don't open. Let cool. Meanwhile, add clams, about a third at a time, to pan, cover, and simmer just until open (about 8 minutes). Lift out with a slotted spoon, discarding any clams that don't open. Let cool.

4 Remove mussels and clams from shells and pile in a large plate. Spoon shellfish onto bread slices; top with salsas and a squeeze of lime.

makes about 3 dozen appetizers

per appetizer: 83 calories, 5 g protein, 12 g carbohydrates, 1 g total fat, 9 mg cholesterol, 161 mg sodium

water-crisped tortilla chips

preparation time: about 10 minutes

6 corn tortillas (*each* 6 inches in diameter) or
   6 flour tortillas (*each* 7 to 9 inches in diameter)

Salt (optional)

1 Dip tortillas, one at a time, in hot water; drain briefly: Season tortillas to taste with salt if desired. Stack tortillas; then cut the stack unto 6 to 8 wedges.

2 Arrange wedges in a single layer on large baking sheets. Do not overlap wedges. Bake in a 500° oven for 4 minutes. With a metal spatula, turn wedges over; continue to bake until crisp and browned, about 2 more minutes. (At this point, you may let cool; then store airtight at room temperature for up to 5 days.)

makes about 4 cups corn chips

per cup of corn chips: 83 calories, 2 g protein, 17 g carbohydrates, 0.9 g total fat, 0 mg cholesterol, 60 mg sodium

makes about 6 cups flour chips

per cup of flour chips: 114 calories, 3 g protein, 19 g carbohydrates, 2 g total fat, 0 mg cholesterol, 167 mg sodium

sweet potatoes with caviar

preparation time: about 40 minutes

2 pounds sweet potatoes, scrubbed

Vegetable oil cooking spray

1/4 cup caviar

1/3 to 1/2 cup light sour cream

1 Cut off and discard ends of unpeeled potatoes, then cut potatoes crosswise into 1/4-inch-thick slices. Spray two 10- by 15-inch rimmed baking pans with cooking spray. Arrange potato slices in a single layer in pans. Spray with cooking spray.

2 Bake in a 400° oven until slices are golden brown on bottom (about 15 minutes); turn slices over and continue to bake until browned on top (about 10 more minutes). Potatoes at edges of pans brown faster, so move these to centers of pans when you turn slices.

3 While sweet potatoes are baking, place caviar in a fine wire strainer and rinse under cool running water; drain well, then refrigerate until ready to use.

4 Lift potato slices onto a platter in a single layer. Dot each slice with sour cream, then with caviar.

makes about 60 appetizers

per appetizer: 22 calories, 4 g carbohydrates, 0.6 g total fat, 7 mg cholesterol, 19 mg sodium

yogurt cheese & tomato torta

preparation time: about 1 hour
chilling time: at least 13 hours

Yogurt Cheese (recipe follows)

Tomato Pesto (recipe follows)

Rosemary sprigs

Toasted French bread baguette slices or bite-size pieces of raw vegetables

1 Prepare Yogurt Cheese and Tomato Pesto.

2 Smoothly line a tall, wide-mouth 2-cup container (such as a bowl, a basket without finish or dye, or a clean new flowerpot) with muslin or a double layer of cheesecloth. Press a fourth of the Yogurt Cheese evenly into bottom of container. Evenly distribute a third of the Tomato Pesto over cheese. Repeat layers to use remaining cheese and pesto, finishing with cheese.

3 Fold edges of cloth over cheese. Press gently to compact. If using a basket or flowerpot, set it in a rimmed pair to catch liquid. Cover airtight and refrigerate for at least 1 hour or up to 6 hours; occasionally pour off liquid as it accumulates.

4 Fold back cloth; invert torta onto a serving plate. Lift off cloth. Garnish with rosemary sprigs. To eat, spread torta on toast slices.

makes about 2 cups (8 to 10 servings)

YOGURT CHEESE

Line a fine strainer with muslin or a double layer of cheesecloth. Set strainer over a deep bowl (bottom of strainer should sit at least 2 inches above bottom of bowl). Spoon 4 cups plain nonfat yogurt into cloth. Cover airtight and refrigerate until yogurt is firm (at least 12 hours) or for up to 2 days; occasionally pour off liquid that drains into bowl. Gently press cheese to remove excess liquid.

TOMATO PESTO

Soak 1 cup dried tomatoes in boiling water to cover until soft (about 30 minutes). Drain; squeeze out excess liquid. Whirl tomatoes in a food processor or blender (or chop with a knife) until minced. Mix tomatoes with 2 tablespoons grated Parmesan cheese, 1 clove garlic (minced or pressed), and 1 teaspoon minced fresh rosemary or $\frac{1}{2}$ teaspoon dry rosemary. Season to taste with salt.

per serving: 64 calories, 6 g protein, 9 g carbohydrates, 0.6 g total fat, 0.9 mg cholesterol, 66 mg sodium

hot artichoke appetizer

preparation time: 1 hour 15 minutes

1 long, slender baguette (about 25 inches long), cut diagonally into 24 slices

1/2 cup grated Parmesan cheese

1 large package (about 8 oz.) Neufchatel cheese or regular cream cheese, at room temperature

3/4 cup low-fat (2%) cottage cheese

1 cup nonfat sour cream

1/8 teaspoon dried dill weed (or to taste)

2 cans (about 14 oz. *each*) artichoke hearts, drained and chopped

1 Arrange bread slices in a single layer (overlapping as little as possible) in shallow 10- by 15-inch baking pans. Bake in a 325° oven until crisp and tinged with brown (15 to 20 minutes). Transfer toast to a rack to cool.

2 In a large bowl, combine Parmesan cheese, Neufchatel cheese, cottage cheese, sour cream, and dill weed. Beat with an electric mixer until smooth (or whirl in a food processor or blender until smooth).

3 Reserve about a fourth of the artichokes. With a spoon, stir remaining artichokes into cheese mixture until evenly distributed.

4 Transfer cheese-artichoke mixture to a shallow 4- to 5-cup baking dish; bake in a 325° oven until lightly browned (about 30 minutes).

5 Sprinkle with reserved artichokes and return to oven for about 5 minutes. Serve with toast.

makes 12 servings

per serving: 212 calories, 11 g protein, 25 g carbohydrates, 7 g total fat, 19 mg cholesterol, 452 mg sodium

pickled vegetables

preparation time: about 30 minutes

8 oz. small carrots (each 4 to 5 inches long)

1 package (about 10 oz.) frozen tiny onions, thawed

1 large red bell pepper seeded and cut into strips about 1/2 inch wide

1 package (about 9 oz.) frozen artichoke hearts, thawed

2 cups white wine vinegar

3/4 cup sugar

2 tablespoons drained capers

2 small dried hot red chiles

2 cloves garlic, peeled and crushed

1 In a 2- to 3-quart pan, bring 4 cups water to a boil over high heat. Add carrots and boil, uncovered, until barely tender when pierced (about 3 minutes); drain well.

2 In a clean, dry wide-mouth 1 1/2- to 2-quart jar (or in two 1-quart jars), layer carrots, onions, bell pepper, and artichokes. Set aside.

3 In pan used to cook carrots, stir together vinegar, sugar, capers, chiles, and garlic. Bring to a boil over high heat, stirring until sugar is dissolved. Pour hot vinegar mixture over vegetables. Cover and refrigerate for at least 1 day or up to 2 weeks. To serve, lift vegetables from marinade.

makes about 6 cups

per 1/4 cup: 42 calories, 0.5 g protein, 10 g carbohydrates, 0.1 g total fat, 0 mg cholesterol, 28 mg sodium

white bean & roasted garlic bruschetta

preparation time: about 1 1/2 hours

1 large head garlic

1/2 teaspoon olive oil

8 slices crusty bread, such as Italian ciabatta or sourdough (*each* about 1/2 inch)

2 cans (about 15 oz. *each*) cannellini (white kidney beans)

1/2 cup lightly packed fresh basil leaves

1/4 cup chopped Italian or regular parsley

1/4 cup lemon juice

4 teaspoons Asian sesame oil

1/2 teaspoon salt

1 pound pear-shaped (Roma-type) tomatoes thinly sliced

4 to 6 teaspoons drained capers (or to taste)

Fresh basil leaves

About 12 canned mild cherry peppers, drained (optional)

Pepper

1 Slice 1/4 inch off top of garlic head. Then rub garlic with olive oil. Wrap garlic in foil and bake in a 375° oven until soft when pressed (about 1 1/4 hours). Carefully remove garlic from foil; transfer to a rack and let stand until cool enough to touch (about 10 minutes).

2 Meanwhile, arrange bread slices slightly apart in a large, shallow baking pan. Broil about 6 inches below heat, turning once, until golden on both sides (about 5 minutes). Let cool on a rack.

3 Squeeze garlic cloves from skins into a food processor or blender. Drain beans, reserving liquid. Rinse beans and add to processor along with the 1/2 cup basil leaves, parsley, lemon juice, sesame oil, and salt. Whirl until coarsely puréed. If necessary, add enough of the reserved bean liquid to make mixture spreadable (do not make it too thin). Discard remaining liquid.

4 Top toast slices equally with bean mixture; arrange tomato slices, capers, and basil leaves over bean mixture. Serve with cherry peppers, if desired. Season to taste with pepper.

makes 4 servings

per serving: 445 calories, 19 g protein, 77 carbohydrates, 8 g total fat, 0 mg cholesterol, 1,455 mg sodium

spicy pepper relish

preparation time: about 45 minutes

2 large red bell peppers

2 large yellow bell peppers

8 fresh red or green serrano chiles

1 cup sugar

2/3 cup distilled white vinegar

1 Seed bell peppers and chiles; cut into thin strips. In a large bowl, mix peppers, chiles, sugar, and vinegar; pour into a wide frying pan.

2 Place pan over medium to medium-high heat. Cook, uncovered, stirring often, until almost all liquid has evaporated (about 30 minutes). Let cool slightly before serving. If made ahead, cover and refrigerate for up to 3 days.

makes about 1 1/2 cups

per serving: 168 calories, 1 g protein, 43 g carbohydrates, 0.2 g total fat, 0 mg cholesterol, 4 mg sodium

roasted sausage & onion with pita breads

preparation time: about 1 hour

12 ounces mild turkey Italian sausages, cut diagonally into 1-inch lengths

2 large onions, cut into wedges about ¹/₂-inch thick

5 tablespoons balsamic vinegar

12 miniature pita breads (*each* about 3 inches in diameter), cut into halves

1 In a 9- by 13-inch baking pan, combine sausages, onions, and ¼ cup of the vinegar. Bake in a 425° oven until sausage is well browned and almost all liquid has evaporated (about 45 minutes); stir occasionally and add water, ¼ cup at a time, if drippings begin to scorch.

2 Remove pan from oven and add 1 tablespoon water and remaining 1 tablespoon vinegar. Let stand for about 3 minutes; then stir to scrape browned bits free from pan bottom.

3 Transfer sausage-onion mixture to a serving dish and keep hot. To serve, spoon mixture into pita bread halves.

makes 12 serving

per serving: 140 calories, 8 g protein, 20 g carbohydrates, 3 g total fat, 15 mg cholesterol, 339 mg sodium

jicama & fresh fruit platter

preparation time: 30 minutes

1 small jicama, peeled and rinsed

Fresh Fruit (directions follow)

²/₃ cup lime juice

¹/₂ teaspoon salt

1 tablespoon chill powder

1 Cut jicama in half lengthwise; then slice each half thinly.

2 Prepare Fresh Fruit. Coat jicama and fruit with lime juice; arrange separately on a platter. If made ahead, cover and refrigerate for up to 2 hours.

3 In a small bowl, combine salt and chili powder; sprinkle over jicama and fruit.

FRESH FRUIT

Remove rinds from 1 large slice watermelon and 1 small honeydew melon; then cut fruit into chunks. Peel, seed, and slice 1 large papaya. Peel 3 medium-size oranges, remove white membrane, and separate into sections.

makes 8 servings

per serving: 88 calories, 2 g protein, 21 g carbohydrates, 0.6 g total fat, 0 mg cholesterol, 155 mg sodium

grilled vegetable appetizer

preparation time: about 1 3/4 hours

2 long, slender baguettes (*each* about 25 inches long), cut diagonally into slices about 1 inch thick

4 medium-size slender eggplants, such as Asian or Italian

3 medium-size sweet potatoes or yams

1 large onion

3 tablespoons olive oil

2 large red bell peppers, seeded

3 large heads garlic, unpeeled (leave heads whole)

1 1/2 teaspoons chopped fresh rosemary or 1/2 teaspoon dried rosemary, crumbled

1 1/2 teaspoons chopped fresh sage or 1/2 teaspoon dried rubbed sage

Rosemary sprigs and fresh sage leaves

Salt and pepper

1 Arrange bread slices in a single layer (overlapping as little as possible) in shallow 10- by 15-inch baking pans. Bake in a 325° oven until crisp and tinged with brown (15 to 20 minutes). Transfer toast to a rack to cool.

2 While bread is toasting, ignite 70 charcoal briquettes in a large barbecue with dampers open. Spread coals out in a solid layer and let burn until medium-low to low; if fire is too hot, vegetables will scorch.

3 Cut ends from eggplants and sweet potatoes; cut unpeeled onion into quarters. Brush cut surfaces of onion with a little of the oil. Place eggplants, sweet potatoes, onion, bell peppers and garlic on a greased grill 4 to 6 inches above coals. Cover barbecue. Cook until vegetables are very tender when pressed, watching carefully to prevent scorching; allow about 40 minutes for eggplant and peppers, 50 to 60 minutes for onion and garlic, and 1 hour for sweet potatoes. During the first 30 minutes of grilling, turn vegetables every 5 minutes; after 30 minutes, add 10 more briquettes to the fire and turn vegetables every 10 minutes. Remove vegetables from grill as they are cooked.

4 Remove peel from sweet potatoes, onion and bell peppers. Cut heads of garlic in half horizontally. Coarsely chop eggplants, peppers and sweet potatoes. Squeeze half the garlic cloves from skins and finely chop.

5 On a platter, arrange chopped eggplants, peppers, and sweet potatoes; onion quarters; and whole garlic cloves. Place chopped garlic in center of platter.

6 Drizzle vegetables with remaining oil; sprinkle with chopped rosemary and sage. Garnish with rosemary sprigs and sage leaves. Place toast in a basket. Serve; or, if made ahead, cover lightly and let stand for up to 2 hours.

7 To serve, top toast with garlic (either chopped or whole cloves), then spoon other vegetables on top. Season to taste with salt and pepper.

makes 8 servings

per serving: 376 calories, 10 g protein, 70 g carbohydrates, 7 g total fat, 0 mg cholesterol, 365 mg sodium

wild mushroom polenta boards

preparation time: 2 hours

1/2 cup all-purpose flour

1/2 cup polenta or yellow cornmeal

1/4 cup instant nonfat dry milk

1 1/2 teaspoons baking powder

1 tablespoon butter or margarine

2 tablespoons olive oil or salad oil

1 medium-size head garlic

8 ounces *each* fresh shiitake, chanterelle, and oyster mushrooms

1 tablespoon *each* chopped fresh rosemary and chopped fresh sage; or 1 teaspoon *each* dried rubbed sage and dried rosemary

2 teaspoons cornstarch mixed with 3/4 cup fat-free reduced-sodium chicken broth

2 tablespoons grated Parmesan cheese

Rosemary and sage sprigs

1 In a food processor or a medium-size bowl, whirl or stir together flour, polenta, dry milk, and baking powder: Add butter; whirl or rub with your fingers until mixture resembles coarse crumbs. Add 1/3 water; whirl or stir with a fork until dough begins to form a ball. Turn dough out onto a lightly floured board and pat into a ball; then knead briefly, just until dough holds together smoothly.

2 Divide dough into 6 equal portions; cover with plastic wrap. Flour board well; then, working with one piece of dough at a time, roll each piece into an irregular 6- to 7-inch round. As rounds are shaped, arrange them, slightly apart, on large baking sheets; cover with plastic wrap. When all rounds have been shaped, remove plastic wrap and bake polenta boards in a 350° oven until lightly browned (12 to 14 minutes). If made ahead, let cool completely on racks; then store airtight until next day.

3 Pour 1 tablespoon of the oil into a small baking pan. Cut garlic head in half crosswise (through cloves). Place garlic, cut side down, in pan; bake in a 350° oven until cut side is golden brown (about 45 minutes). Using a thin spatula, lift garlic from pan and transfer to a rack; let stand until cool enough to touch (about 10 minutes). Squeeze garlic cloves from skins into a small bowl; mash garlic thoroughly.

4 While garlic is baking, trim and discard stems from shiitake mushrooms. Thinly slice shiitake mushroom caps and whole chanterelles. Place sliced shiitake and chanterelle mushrooms and whole oyster mushrooms in a 5- to 6-quart pan; add remaining 1 tablespoon oil, chopped rosemary, and chopped sage. Cover and cook over medium-high heat until mushrooms are juicy (about 8 minutes). Uncover; cook, stirring often, until almost all liquid has evaporated and mushrooms are browned (15 to 20 more minutes). Add cornstarch mixture and mashed garlic; stir until mixture boils and thickens slightly.

5 Lay polenta boards, side by side, on 2 large baking sheets. Spoon hot mushroom sauce into center of each; sprinkle evenly with cheese. Broil 4 to 6 inches below heat until sizzling (about 2 minutes). With a spatula, transfer to individual plates; garnish with rosemary and sage sprigs.

makes 6 servings

per serving: 202 calories, 7 g protein, 29 g carbohydrates, 7 g total fat, 7 mg cholesterol, 276 mg sodium

curried spinach dip

preparation time: about 15 minutes
chilling time: at least 2 hours

2 cups lowfat cottage cheese

1/4 cup nonfat milk

2 tablespoons lemon juice

1 package (about 10 oz.) frozen chopped spinach,
  thawed and squeezed dry

3 green onions, thinly sliced

2 teaspoons curry powder

Raw vegetable strips or spears

1 In a food processor or blender, combine cottage cheese, milk, and lemon juice. Whirl until smooth and glossy. Add spinach, onions, and carry powder; whirl until blended.

2 Pour into a bowl; cover and refrigerate for at least 2 hours or up to 1 day. Serve with vegetables.

makes about 2 ³/4 cups

per tablespoon: 12 calories , 2 g protein, 0.8 g carbohydrates, 0.2 g total fat, 0.8 mg cholesterol, 48 mg sodium

texas caviar

preparation time: about 1 1/4 hours

Water-Crisped Tortilla Chips or packaged
  tortilla chips

1 1/2 cups dried black-eyed peas

2 large tomatoes, seeded and chopped

1/2 cup chopped cilantro

1 or 2 jalapeño or other small hot chiles,
  stemmed and seeded

2 tablespoons white wine vinegar

Salt

Cilantro sprigs (optional)

1 Prepare Water-Crisped Tortilla Chips and set aside.

2 In a 2- to 3-quart pan, bring 1 quart water to a boil. Add peas; reduce heat, cover, and simmer until tender (about 50 minutes). Drain, rinse well with cold water, and drain again. Transfer to a bowl and set aside.

3 In a blender or food processor, combine tomatoes, chopped cilantro, and chiles. Whirl until finely chopped; stir in vinegar: Add mixture to peas and stir well; season to taste with salt. Garnish with cilantro sprigs, if desired, and offer with tortilla chips.

makes 8 to 10 servings

per serving: 104 calories, 7 g protein, 19 g carbohydrates, 0.4 g total fat, 0 mg cholesterol, 130 mg sodium

chili shrimp

preparation time: 35 minutes

1 bottle or can (about 12 oz.) beer

$^1/_2$ cup finely chopped onion

$^3/_4$ teaspoon celery seeds

1 dried bay leaf

1 pound large raw shrimp (31 to 35 per lb.), shelled and deveined

$^1/_2$ cup tomato-based chili sauce

1 tablespoon honey-flavored mustard

About 20 large fresh spinach leaves, rinsed and crisped

2 tablespoons drained capers

1 In a wide frying pan, combine beer, onion, celery seeds, and bay leaf. Bring to a boil over high heat; boil for 2 minutes. Add shrimp. Reduce heat, cover, and simmer, stirring occasionally, until shrimp are just opaque in center; cut to test (about 3 minutes). With a slotted spoon, lift shrimp from pan and transfer to a large bowl.

2 Bring shrimp cooking liquid to a boil over high heat; then boil until reduced to $^1/_3$ cup. Remove and discard bay leaf. Add chili sauce and mustard to reduced liquid; blend well. Serve; or cover shrimp and dressing separately and refrigerate until cool (at least 1 hour) or until next day.

3 To serve, line 4 individual plates with spinach leaves; top equally with shrimp, then with dressing. Sprinkle with capers.

makes 4 servings

per serving: 171 calories, 21 g protein, 17 g carbohydrates, 2 g total fat, 140 mg cholesterol, 731 mg sodium

thai chicken in pitas

preparation time: about 25 minutes, plus 1 hour for Cilantro Mustard to stand

Cilantro Mustard (recipe follows)

4 cloves garlic, minced

3 tablespoons minced cilantro

$^1/_2$ teaspoon coarsely ground pepper

1 pound boneless, skinless chicken breast, cut into $^1/_2$-inch pieces

1 teaspoon olive oil or salad oil

4 pita breads (*each* about 6 inches in diameter), cut into quarters

1 Prepare Cilantro Mustard; set aside.

2 In a large bowl, mix garlic, cilantro, pepper and chicken. Heat oil in a wide nonstick pan or wok over medium-high heat. When oil is hot, add chicken mixture. Stir-fry until meat is no longer pink in center; cut to test (3 to 4 minutes). Add water, 1 tablespoon at a time, if pan appears dry.

3 With a slotted spoon, transfer chicken to a serving bowl. To eat, spoon chicken into pita breads; drizzle chicken with Cilantro Mustard.

CILANTRO MUSTARD

1 In a 1- to 1 $^1/_2$-quart pan, stir together 3 tablespoons dry mustard, 3 tablespoons distilled white vinegar or white wine vinegar, and 2 tablespoons water; cover and let stand for 1 hour.

2 Mix 3 tablespoons sugar and 1 tablespoon all-purpose flour, add to mustard mixture along with 5 tablespoons butter or margarine, cut into chunks. Bring just to a boil over medium- high heat, stirring. Remove from heat and let cool. If made ahead, cover airtight and refrigerate for up to 4 days. Just before serving, stir in 1 to 2 tablespoons chopped cilantro.

makes 6 to 8 servings

per serving: 255 calories, 19 g protein, 27 g carbohydrates, 8 g total fat, 51 mg cholesterol, 277 mg sodium

turkey jerky

preparation time: about 10 minutes
marinating time: at least 1 hour
baking time: at least 4 to 6 hours (in a conventional oven)

**1 pound skinless, boneless turkey breast;
  or 1 pound turkey breast tenderloins**

1 tablespoon salt

1/2 cup water

2 tablespoons firmly packed brown sugar

**2 cloves garlic, minced or pressed; or 1/4 teaspoon
  garlic powder**

**1/2 small onion, minced; or 1/4 teaspoon onion
  powder**

1 teaspoon pepper

1/2 teaspoon liquid smoke

Vegetable oil cooking spray

1 Rinse turkey and pat dry. Pull off and discard any fat and connective tissue. For easier slicing, freeze meat until it's firm but not hard. Cut into 1/8- to 1/4-inch slices slices (cut breast piece with or across the grain, tenderloins lengthwise).

2 In a nonmetal bowl, stir together salt, water, sugar, garlic, onion, pepper, and liquid smoke. Add turkey and mix well. Cover and refrigerate for at least 2 hours or up to 24 hours; turkey will absorb almost all liquid.

3 You may dry turkey in a dehydrator or a conventional oven. Depending upon drying method, evenly coat dehydrator racks (you need 3, each about 10 by 13 inches or metal racks (to cover a 10- by 15-inch rimmed baking pan) with cooking spray. Lift turkey strips from bowl and shake off any excess liquid; lay strips close together, but not overlapping, on racks.

4 If using a dehydrator, arrange trays as manufacturer directs and dry at 140° until jerky cracks and breaks when bent (4 1/2 to 6 hours; remove a strip of jerky from dehydrator and let stand for about 5 minutes before testing). If using an oven, place pan on center rack of a 150° to 200° oven; prop door open about 2 inches. Dry until jerky cracks and breaks when bent (4 to 6 hours; remove a strip of jerky from oven and let stand for about 5 minutes before testing).

5 Let jerky cool on racks. Serve; or package airtight and store in a cool, dry place for up to 3 weeks, in the refrigerator for up to 4 months (freeze for longer storage).

makes about 7 ounces

per ounce: 93 calories, 16 g protein, 5 g carbohydrates, 0.8 g total fat, 40 mg cholesterol, 975 mg sodium

pineapple salsa

preparation time: about 20 minutes

1 cup diced fresh or canned pineapple

1/2 cup chopped, peeled, seeded cucumber

1 fresh jalapeño chile, seeded and minced

1 teaspoon grated lime peel

3 tablespoons lime juice

2 tablespoons minced cilantro

In a nonmetal bowl, mix pineapple, cucumber, chile, lime peel, lime juice, and cilantro. If made ahead, cover and refrigerate for up to 4 hours.

makes about 1 3/4 cups

per serving: 14 calories, 0.2 g protein, 4 g carbohydrates, 0.1 g total fat, 0 mg cholesterol, 2 mg sodium

swordfish with lemon relish

preparation time: about 1¼ hours

Lemon Peel Relish (recipe follows)

32 French bread baguette slices (*each* about 2 inches wide and ¼ inch thick)

1 pound boneless, skinless swordfish steaks (about ½ inch thick)

¼ cup dry white wine

Salt and pepper

2 small pear-shaped (Roma-type) tomatoes, seeded and cut into thin strips

1 Prepare Lemon Peel Relish and set aside.

2 Arrange bread slices in a single layer on baking sheets. Bake in a 350° oven until lightly toasted (about 10 minutes). Let cool. (At this point, you may store airtight at room temperature for up to 2 days.)

3 Rinse fish, pat dry, and cut into 16 equal pieces, each about 1 inch square. Then cut each piece in half horizontally so that pieces are about ¼-inch thick. Arrange fish in a single layer in a foil-lined 10- by 15-inch rimmed baking pan. Drizzle with wine; season to taste with salt and pepper. Cover loosely with additional foil.

4 Bake in a 375° oven until fish is just opaque but still moist in center, cut to test (about 6 minutes). Let cool in pan. (At this point, you may cover and refrigerate for up to 4 hours.)

5 Up to 30 minutes before serving, spoon equal amounts of Lemon Peel Relish onto each bread slice. Just before serving, drain fish and pat dry; set a piece atop relish on each bread slice. Top with tomatoes.

LEMON PEEL RELISH

With a vegetable peeler, pare yellow peel (including a little white pith) from 6 large lemons. Mince peel. Cut off and discard remaining pith from 2 of the lemons (reserve remaining 4 lemons for other uses). Cut the 2 lemons into chunks; remove and discard seeds. Chop fruit coarsely. Heat 1 tablespoon salad oil in a medium-size frying pan over medium high heat. Add ½ cup finely chopped onion, cook, stirring often, until onion is soft but not browned (about 5 minutes). Add lemon peel, chopped lemons, ½ cup dry white wine, ⅓ cup sugar, and 1 teaspoon pepper. Cook, stirring often, until almost all liquid has evaporated and mixture is syrupy (15 to 18 minutes). Let cool. If made ahead, cover and refrigerate for up to 2 weeks.

makes 32 appetizers

per appetizer: 56 calories, 4 g protein, 8 g carbohydrates, 1 g total fat, 6 mg cholesterol, 60 mg sodium

baked shrimp with garlic

preparation time: about 25 minutes
marinating time: at least 4 hours

1/2 cup olive oil

1 clove garlic, minced or pressed

1/4 teaspoon salt

1 pound medium-size raw shrimp (about 36 per lb.), shelled and deveined

1 tablespoon finely minced parsley

Parsley sprigs (optional)

1 Mix oil, garlic, and salt. Add shrimp, turning to coat; sprinkle with minced parsley. Cover and refrigerate for at least 4 hours or until next day.

2 Transfer to a 10- to 15-inch baking pan. Bake in a 375° oven until shrimp are opaque when cut (about 10 minutes). Arrange in a bowl. Garnish with parsley sprigs, if desired. Offer with wooden picks.

makes about 3 dozen appetizers

per appetizer: 37 calories, 2 g protein, 0.1 g carbohydrates, 3 g total fat, 16 mg cholesterol, 30 mg sodium

miso grilled mushrooms

preparation time: about 20 minutes
marinating time: at least 6 hours

3 tablespoons miso

1/4 cup sake or dry sherry

1 teaspoon grated fresh ginger

2 teaspoons honey

2 tablespoons lemon juice

2 tablespoons rice vinegar or distilled white vinegar

16 medium-size to large mushrooms (about 1 lb. *total*)

1 green onion (including top), thinly sliced

1 Mix miso, sake, ginger, honey, lemon juice, and vinegar until blended. Add mushrooms, stirring to coat. Cover and refrigerate for at least 6 hours or until next day.

2 Soak 8 bamboo skewers in hot water to cover for 30 minutes. Drain marinade into a small pan and set aside. Thread 2 mushrooms on each skewer and place on a lightly greased grill 4 to 6 inches above a solid bed of low-glowing coals. (Or place on a rack in a broiler pan and broil about 6 inches below heat.) Cook, brushing occasionally with marinade and turning once or twice, until browned (about 5 minutes).

3 Remove mushrooms from skewers. Heat remaining marinade, pour into a small bowl, and top with onion. Offer mushrooms with wooden picks.

makes 16 appetizers

per appetizer: 79 calories, 1 g protein, 4 g carbohydrates, 0.3 g total fat, 0 mg cholesterol, 119 mg sodium

TIME-SAVING TOOLS: Using well-designed utensils correctly and appropriately increases our efficiency in the kitchen. Sharp knives are a must; store them in a protected place, such as a wooden block or on a magnetic rack. Hone your chopping and slicing skills so you can use knives to the greatest advantage—and save time.

roasted tomato-eggplant crostini

preparation time: about 1 1/4 hours

Olive oil cooking spray

1 large real onion, cut into 1/2-inch-thick slices

2 tablespoons balsamic or red wine vinegar

1 1/2 pounds firm pear-shaped (Roma-type) tomatoes, cut into 1/4-inch-thick slices

1 medium-size eggplant, unpeeled, cut crosswise into 1/2-inch-thick slices

Salt and pepper

16 slices crusty Italian or French bread (*each about 3 1/2 inches wide*)

1 Coat two 10- by 15-inch rimmed baking pans with cooking spray. Arrange onion slices in a single layer in one of the pans; drizzle with vinegar. Arrange tomato slices in same pan, overlapping slightly. Arrange eggplant slices in a single layer in second pan. Coat all vegetables lightly with cooking spray. Bake in a 450° oven until eggplant is browned and very soft where pressed (about 30 minutes) and tomatoes are well browned on edges (about 50 minutes).

1 Transfer all vegetables to a food processor or blender; whirl until coarsely puréed. Season to taste with salt and pepper. (At this point, you may cover and refrigerate for up to 3 days; bring to room temperature before serving.)

2 Place bread in a single layer on a baking sheet. Broil about 5 inches below heat, turning once, until golden on both sides (about 4 minutes).

3 To serve, spread toast with vegetable purée, using about 2 tablespoons purée for each slice.

makes 16 appetizers

per appetizer: 94 calories, 3 g protein, 18 g carbohydrates, 2 g total fat, 0 mg cholesterol, 152 mg sodium

mushroom pâté with wheat toast points

preparation time: about 30 minutes

Wheat Toast Points (recipe follows)

2 tablespoons butter or margarine

1 pound mushrooms, chopped

3/4 cup chopped shallots

1 small carrot, chopped

1 clove garlic, minced or pressed

Ground white pepper

Chopped parsley

1 Prepare Wheat Toast Points and set aside.

2 Melt butter in a wide frying pan over medium-high heat. Add mushrooms, shallots, carrot, and garlic. Cook, stirring often, until liquid has evaporated and mushrooms are browned (10 to 15 minutes). Transfer mixture to a food processor or blender and whirl until puréed. Season to taste with white pepper. Mound on a plate and sprinkle with parsley. Serve warm or at room temperature, surrounded by Wheat Toast Points.

WHEAT TOAST POINTS

Stack 10 slices whole wheat bread; trim off crusts. Cut stack in half diagonally. Arrange triangles in a single layer on a baking sheet and broil about 5 inches below heat, turning once, until browned on both sides (2 to 3 minutes).

makes 10 servings

per serving: 99 calories, 4 g protein, 15 g carbohydrates, 3 g total fat, 6 mg cholesterol, 148 mg sodium

norwegian meatballs

preparation time: about 45 minutes

¹/₄ cup low-sodium chicken broth or water

6 tablespoons all-purpose flour

2 pounds ground skinless chicken or turkey breast

2 large egg whites (about ¹/₄ cup)

1 teaspoon *each* pepper and dry sage

¹/₂ teaspoon *each* fennel seeds and salt

Gjetost Sauce (recipe follows)

1 In a bowl, smoothly mix broth and flour; then add chicken, egg whites, pepper, sage, fennel seeds, and salt. Mix well. Shape meat mixture into 1-tablespoon mounds (you will have about 48); set slightly apart in 2 nonstick or lightly oiled 10- by 15-inch rimmed baking pans.

2 Bake meatballs in a 500° oven for 10 minutes. Meanwhile, prepare Gjetost Sauce; keep hot. Turn meatballs over with a wide spatula and continue to bake until well browned on outside and no longer pink in center; cut to test (about 2 more minutes).

3 To serve, add meatballs to hot Gjetost Sauce; stir gently to mix. Keep hot on a warming tray. Spear meatballs with small skewers to eat.

GJETOST SAUCE

In a wide frying pan, combine 1 large onion, chopped, and ¹/₄ cup low-sodium chicken broth. Cook over medium-high heat, stirring, until liquid evaporates and onion begins to brown. To deglaze, add ¹/₄ cup more low-sodium chicken broth and stir to scrape browned bits free. Then continue to cook, stirring occasionally, until onion is richly browned. Stir in 2 tablespoons cornstarch, smoothly mix in 2 cups low-sodium chicken broth: Bring to a rapid boil over high heat, stirring. Reduce heat to low and add 1 cup (about 4 oz.) shredded gjetost cheese; stir until cheese is melted. Pour into a serving bowl; use hot (sauce thins if reheated).

makes about 24 servings

per serving: 82 calories, 10 g protein, 5 g carbohydrates, 2 g total fat, 22 mg cholesterol, 110 mg sodium

shrimp with tart dipping sauce

preparation time: about 30 minutes

35 medium-size shrimp (about 1 lb. *total*), shelled and deveined

35 whole chives (about 7 inches long *each*)

¹/₄ cup *each* dry white wine and white wine vinegar

1 tablespoon *each* minced shallots and minced chives

¹/₂ teaspoon pepper

1 In a 4- to 6-quart pan, bring about 1 quart water to a boil over high heat. Add shrimp; reduce heat, cover, and simmer until opaque in center; cut to test (3 to 4 minutes). Lift out and immerse in ice water until cool. Drain and set aside.

2 Drop whole chives into pan and cook just until wilted (about 5 seconds). Remove immediately with tongs. Tie a chive around center of each shrimp.

3 In a small bowl, stir together wine, vinegar, shallots, minced chives, and pepper. Arrange shrimp on a platter and offer with sauce.

makes 8 servings (about 4 appetizers each)

per serving: 57 calories, 10 g protein, 1 g carbohydrates, 0.8 g total fat, 70 mg cholesterol, 69 mg sodium

layered bean dip

preparation time: about 50 minutes

Pita Crisps (recipe follows)

1 can (about 15 oz.) garbanzo beans or 2 cups cooked garbanzo beans

3 tablespoons tahini (sesame-seed paste)

1/4 cup lemon juice

1/2 teaspoon ground cumin

1 clove garlic, minced or pressed

1/2 cup plain nonfat yogurt

1 tablespoon minced fresh mint

1/2 cup *each* thinly sliced cucumber and thinly sliced radishes

1/4 cup crumbled feta cheese

1 Prepare Pita Crisps; set aside.

2 Drain beans, reserve 1/4 cup of the liquid, then rinse beans. In a food processor or blender, whirl beans, the reserved cup of liquid, tahini, lemon juice, cumin and garlic until smooth. Spoon mixture onto a large platter and spread out to make an 8-inch circle.

3 In a bowl, stir together yogurt and mint; spread over bean mixture. Sprinkle cucumber, radishes, and cheese over yogurt mixture. Tuck Pita Crisps around edge of bean mixture; scoop mixture onto crisps to eat.

PITA CRISPS

Split 6 pita breads (each about 6 inches in diameter) horizontally to make 12 rounds. In a small bowl, stir together 2 tablespoons olive oil and 1 clove garlic (minced or pressed). Brush split sides of bread with oil mixture, then sprinkle with pepper. Cut each round into 6 wedges. Arrange in a single layer on baking sheets. Bake in a 350° oven until crisp and golden (12 to 15 minutes) Serve at room temperature.

makes 12 servings

per serving: 183 calories, 6 g protein, 27 g carbohydrates, 6 g total fat, 3 mg cholesterol, 312 mg sodium

smoky tuna spread

preparation time: about 10 minutes

1 can (about 9 1/4 oz.) water packed albacore tuna, drained

1/3 cup low-fat cottage cheese

3 tablespoons lemon juice

1/2 teaspoon liquid smoke

Pepper

About 1 tablespoon drained capers

Parsley sprig and 1 thin strip of lemon peel

French bread baguette slices

1 In a food processor, combine tuna, cottage cheese, lemon juice, and liquid smoke; whirl until very smooth (or beat with an electric mixer). Season to taste with pepper.

2 Spoon mixture into a small bowl. If made ahead, cover and refrigerate for up to 1 day.

3 Just before serving, garnish with capers, parsley sprig, and lemon peel. Serve with bread.

makes about 1 1/3 cups

per tablespoon: 19 calories, 4 g protein, 0.3 g carbohydrates, 0.3 g total fat, 5 mg cholesterol, 71 mg sodium

steeped shrimp

preparation time: about 50 minutes

chilling time: at least an hour

1/3 cup vinegar

1 tablespoon *each* mustard seeds and cumin seeds

2 teaspoons black peppercorns

8 thin quarter-size slices fresh ginger

10 cilantro sprigs (*each* about 4 in. long)

10 fresh mint sprigs (*each* about 4 in. long) or 2 tablespoons dry mint leaves

2 tablespoons olive oil

2 pounds medium-size raw shrimp (about 36 per lb.)

Mint Ginger Vinegar (recipe follows)

Seeded Mayonnaise (recipe follows)

1 In an 11- to 12-quart pan, combine 5 quarts water, vinegar, mustard seeds, cumin seeds, peppercorns, ginger, cilantro, mint, and oil. Cover and bring to a boil over high heat.

2 Add shrimp to pan. Cover and remove from heat. Let steep until shrimp are opaque when cut (about 2 minutes). Lift out shrimp and drain. Pour cooking liquid through a fine strainer; reserve seeds but discard liquid, ginger, mint sprigs, and cilantro. Let shrimp cool; then shell and devein. Cover and refrigerate for at least 1 hour or until next day.

3 Prepare Mint-Ginger Vinegar and Seeded Mayonnaise. Offer with shrimp for dipping.

makes about 6 dozen appetizers

per appetizer: 11 calories, 2 g protein, 0.1 g carbohydrates, 0.2 g total fat, 16 mg cholesterol, 15 mg sodium

MINT-GINGER VINEGAR

Mix 1 ½ cups rice or cider vinegar and 3 tablespoons sugar until sugar is dissolved. Up to 2 hours before serving, add 2 tablespoons minced cilantro and 2 tablespoons minced fresh mint or dry mint leaves. Makes about 2 cups.

per tablespoon: 6 calories, 0 g protein, 2 g carbohydrates, 0 g total fat, 0 mg cholesterol, 0.1 mg sodium

SEEDED MAYONNAISE

Mix 2 cups mayonnaise, 3 tablespoons lemon juice, and reserved seeds from cooking liquid.

makes about 2 cups

per tablespoon: 101 calories, 0.3 g protein, 0.7 g carbohydrates, 11 g total fat, 8 mg cholesterol, 79 mg sodium

salsa verde

preparation time: about 25 minutes

---

1 1/4 pounds tomatillos, husks removed

1/3 cup chopped cilantro

1 jalapeño or other small hot chile, stemmed and seeded

3/4 cup low-sodium chicken broth

1/3 cup lime juice

1 Rinse tomatillos to remove sticky film; arrange in a single layer on a baking sheet and roast in a 500° oven until slightly singed (about 15 minutes). Let cool. Place in a blender or food processor with cilantro and chile; whirl until puréed. Stir in chicken broth and lime juice.

2 If made ahead, cover and refrigerate for up to 2 days.

makes 3 cups

per tablespoon: 4 calories, 0.2 g protein, 0.6 g carbohydrates, 0.1 g total fat, 0 mg cholesterol, 1 mg sodium

caesar cream with parmesan toast

preparation time: about 35 minutes

Parmesan Toast (recipe follows)

¹/₂ cup freshly grated Parmesan cheese

1 clove garlic

¹/₂ cup lightly packed parsley

2 to 3 tablespoons lemon juice

1 cup light or regular sour cream

Parsley sprig

1 to 2 quarts small inner green or rest romaine
lettuce leaves or a combination, rinsed and
crisped

1 Prepare Parmesan Toast.

2 Combine cheese, garlic, the ¹/₂ cup parsley, and 2 tablespoons of the lemon juice in a blender or food processor; whirl until smooth, adding 3 to 4 tablespoons of the sour cream if necessary to form a purée.

3 Transfer to a bowl and stir in remaining sour cream. Add additional lemon juice to taste, if desired. If made ahead, cover and refrigerate for up to a day.

4 Place dip on a serving tray, garnish with parsley sprig. Arrange lettuce and Parmesan Toast alongside.

PARMESAN TOAST

Slice half an 8-ounce baguette about ³/₈ inch thick. Arrange bread on a large baking sheet. Bake in a 350° oven, turning slices once or twice, until lightly toasted (about 10 minutes). Remove from oven and brush with olive oil (about 1 tablespoon total); sprinkle lightly with freshly grated Parmesan cheese (about 2 tablespoons total). Return to oven and bake until golden brown (3 to 5 more minutes). Serve warm or at room temperature. If made ahead, package airtight and let stand at room temperature for up to a day.

makes 8 to 10 servings (about 1 ¹/₄ cups)

per serving: 134 calories, 6 g protein, 11 g carbohydrates, 8 g total fat, 15 mg cholesterol, 205 mg sodium

calico fish salad

preparation time: about 30 minutes

1 pound orange roughy or sole fillets

3 tablespoons coarse-grained mustard

¹/₄ cup celery leaves (optional)

²/₃ cup *each* diced yellow bell pepper, tomato,
and celery

2 tablespoons lemon juice

2 teaspoons minced fresh tarragon leaves or
¹/₂ teaspoon dry tarragon leaves

Salt and pepper

16 inner romaine lettuce leaves, washed and
crisped

1 Rinse fish and pat dry. Arrange in a single layer in an 8- to 9-inch square pan. Spread fillets with mustard and, if desired, top with celery leaves. Cover pan with foil.

2 Bake in a 400° oven just until fish looks just slightly translucent or wet inside when cut in thickest part (about 10 minutes). Let cool; discard celery leaves, if used. Add bell pepper, tomato, diced celery, lemon juice, and tarragon to fish, mixing gently with a fork and breaking fish into bite-size pieces. Season to taste with salt and pepper. If made ahead, cover and refrigerate until next day.

3 Place fish salad in a small bowl and surround with lettuce leaves for scooping.

makes 16 appetizers

per appetizer: 44 calories, 5 g protein, 1 g carbohydrates, 2 g total fat, 6 mg cholesterol, 52 mg sodium

quick cuke chips

preparation time: about 20 minutes

3 large cucumbers

1 large red bell pepper, seeded and cut into
¹/₂-inch-wide strips

1 large onion, thinly sliced

1 tablespoon each salt and dill seeds

³/₄ cup sugar

¹/₂ cup white wine vinegar

1 Cut unpeeled cucumbers crosswise into ¼-inch-thick slices. In a large bowl, combine cucumbers, bell pepper, and onion. Add salt and dill seeds; stir well. Let stand, uncovered, for 1 to 2 hours; stir occasionally.

2 In a small bowl, combine sugar and vinegar; stir until sugar is dissolved. Pour over vegetables and mix gently. Spoon into glass or ceramic containers, cover, and refrigerate for at least 1 day or up to 3 weeks. Drain before serving.

makes about 8 cups

per ¹/₄ cup: 18 calories, 0.3 g protein, 4 g carbohydrates, 0.1 g total fat, 0 mg cholesterol, 104 mg sodium

crabby potatoes

preparation time: about 1¹/₂ hours

12 small red thin-skinned potatoes, scrubbed

1 teaspoon olive oil

4 ounces flaked cooked crabmeat

2 tablespoons *each* plain nonfat yogurt and
reduced-calorie mayonnaise

2 tablespoons minced chives or thinly sliced
green onion

2 teaspoons lemon juice

1 tablespoon chopped parsley

2 tablespoons grated Parmesan cheese

Pepper

1 Pierce each potato in several places with a fork. Arrange potatoes in a single layer in a shallow baking pan; add oil and turn potatoes to coat. Bake in a 375° oven until tender throughout when pierced (45 to 55 minutes). Let cool slightly. (At this point, you may cover and refrigerate for up to 1 day.)

2 Cut potatoes in half crosswise. Using a small melon baller, scoop out centers of potato halves, leaving about a ¼-inch shell. Reserve centers for other uses. Set potato halves, cut side up, in a shallow baking pan (if necessary, trim a sliver from rounded side of potato halves to steady them in the pan).

3 In a small bowl, stir together crab, yogurt, mayonnaise, chives, lemon juice, parsley, and cheese until evenly blended. Season to taste with pepper. Spoon mixture into potato shells. Broil about 4 inches below heat until golden (3 to 5 minutes).

makes 24 appetizers

per appetizer: 32 calories, 2 g protein, 0.8 g total fat, 4 g carbohydrates, 5 mg cholesterol, 31 mg sodium

QUICK COOKING INGREDIENTS: Supermarket produce sections are becoming an increasingly good source of quick-cooking ingredients. Today it's no trick to find peeled pineapple, sliced mushrooms, shredded carrots, prewashed spinach and salad greens, and broccoli flowerets.

beef rillettes

preparation time: about 4 1/2 hours
chilling time: at least 7 hours

About 1 ¼ pounds beef shanks (about 1 inch thick)

1 clove garlic, peeled

½ teaspoon *each* pepper and dry thyme

1 dry bay leaf

2 cups water

Salt

2 small French bread baguettes, thinly sliced

2 heads Belgian endive, separated into spears, rinsed, and crisped (optional)

Dijon Mustard (optional)

1 Place beef in a 1 ¼- to 1 ½-quart casserole; add garlic, pepper, thyme, and bay leaf. Pour in water; cover tightly and bake in a 250° oven until meat is so tender it falls apart in shreds when prodded with a fork (about 4 hours).

2 Lift meat from casserole, reserving liquid. Let meat stand until cool enough to touch, then remove and discard all fat, bones, and connective tissue. Tear meat into fine shreds, cover, and refrigerate.

3 Refrigerate cooking liquid separately until surface fat has hardened (about 4 hours). Lift off and discard fat. Measure liquid (it should be softly jelled); you need 1 ½ cups. (If liquid is still fluid, transfer to a small pan and boil until reduced to 1 ½ cups; if it is rigid, add enough water to make 1 ½ cups.) Heat liquid until hot, then add meat and heat until warm. Season to taste with salt. Pour into a 2 ½- to 3-cup crock or jar. Cover and refrigerate until firm (at least 3 hours) or for up to 3 days (gelatin may weep if mixture is kept for longer than 3 days).

4 To serve, spread on bread slices or, if desired, spoon into endive spears. Add mustard to taste, if desired.

makes about 2 ¼ cups

per 1-tablespoon serving on bread: 48 calories, 3 g protein, 7 g carbohydrates, 0.8 total fat, 4 mg cholesterol, 83 mg sodium

pickled herring

preparation time: about 10 minutes
marinating time: at least 1 day

1 ½ cups or 2 jars (6 to 8 oz. *each*) marinated or wine-flavored herring fillet pieces

1 carrot, thinly sliced

1 small red onion, thinly sliced

1 teaspoon whole allspice, slightly crushed

⅓ cup distilled white vinegar

1 cup water

2/3 cup sugar

1 bay leaf

1 Drain liquid from herring. Alternate layers of herring, carrot, onion, and allspice in a deep 4-cup container until all are used.

2 In a small bowl, stir together vinegar, water, and sugar; pour over herring. Tuck in bay leaf. Cover and refrigerate for at least a day or up to 4 days.

makes about 2 ½ dozen appetizers

per appetizer: 44 calories, 1 g protein, 6 g carbohydrates, 2 g total fat, 1 mg cholesterol, 83 mg sodium

dry-roasted potato chips

preparation time: about 3 hours

1 pound white thin-skinned potatoes

Nonstick cooking spray

Salt

1 With narrow blade of a food dicer (mandolin) or food processor, cut potatoes into very thin slices. In a 3- to 4-quart pan, bring 2 quarts water to a boil. Cook potatoes, about a third at a time, until slightly translucent (about 1 ½ minutes). Lift out with a slotted spoon; let drain.

2 Place wire racks on large baking sheets (you'll need about 4 sheets, or use them in sequence). Lightly coat racks with cooking spray.

3 Arrange potato slices on racks in a single layer. Season to taste with salt. Bake in a 200° oven until chips are crisped (2 to 2 ½ hours). Serve hot or at room temperature. If made ahead, let cool; store airtight at room temperature for up to 1 week.

makes about 1 quart

per cup: 91 calories, 2 g protein, 20 g carbohydrates, 0.3 g total fat, 0 mg cholesterol, 7 mg sodium

ricotta roquefort cheesecake

preparation time: about 1 hour
chilling time: at least 2 hours

4 cups part-skim or whole-milk ricotta cheese

1 cup packed Roquefort cheese

1 teaspoon freshly ground pepper

Salt

6 large egg whites

¼ cup freshly grated Parmesan cheese

36 to 48 radishes

Chopped parsley

Crisp rye or whole wheat crackers

1 Combine ricotta, Roquefort, and pepper in a food processor or bowl; whirl or mix until blended. Season to taste with salt. Beat in egg whites.

2 Spread mixture in a 10-inch spring-form pan. Sprinkle evenly with Parmesan cheese.

3 Bake in a 325° oven until cheesecake is firm in center when pan is gently shaken (35 to 45 minutes). Let cool; cover and refrigerate for at least 2 hours or up to a day. Meanwhile, trim and discard root ends of radishes; rinse well and drain. Pinch off and discard all but 1 or 2 pretty leaves from each radish. Wrap radishes in a damp towel, place in a plastic bag, and refrigerate for at least 30 minutes or up to a day.

4 Remove pan rim and set cake on a platter. Slice a few radishes. Surround cake with whole radishes. Garnish with radishes and parsley. Serve with crackers.

makes 16 to 18 servings

per serving: 131 calories, 119 g protein, 4 g carbohydrates, 8 g total fat, 28 mg cholesterol, 302 mg sodium

mini-calzones

preparation time: about 2 1/2 hours

Whole Wheat Dough (recipe follows)

2 tablespoons olive oil

2 tablespoons minced shallot

2 ounces Black Forest ham, chopped

4 cups coarsely chopped, lightly packed spinach

1/4 cup part-skim ricotta cheese

1/2 teaspoon ground nutmeg

1 Prepare Whole Wheat Dough.

2 While dough is rising, prepare filling. Heat 1 tablespoon of the oil in a wide frying pan over medium high heat. Add shallot and ham; cook, stirring occasionally, until shallot is soft (about 5 minutes). Add spinach and cook, stirring often, until liquid has evaporated (about 5 minutes). Remove from heat. Add ricotta cheese and nutmeg; mix well. Let cool.

3 Punch Whole Wheat Dough down and knead briefly on a lightly floured board to release air. Shape dough into a ball, then roll out 1/8 inch thick. Cut dough into 3-inch rounds. Place about 1 teaspoon of the spinach filling on half of each round. Fold plain half of each round over filling; press edges together to seal. Transfer calzones to oiled, cornmeal-dusted baking sheets. Brush tops with remaining 1 tablespoon oil; prick tops with a fork.

4 Bake calzones in a 425° oven until lightly browned (about 15 minutes). Serve warm. If made ahead, let cool, then cover and refrigerate for up to 1 day. To reheat, arrange on baking sheets and heat, uncovered, in a 425° oven for about 5 minutes.

WHOLE WHEAT DOUGH

In a large bowl, combine 1 package active dry yeast and 3/4 cup warm water (about 110°); let stand until yeast is softened (about 5 minutes). Add 1 teaspoon each salt and sugar; stir in 1 cup all-purpose flour. Beat with a heavy spoon or an electric mixer until smooth. Then mix in about 1 cup whole wheat flour or enough to make dough hold together. Turn dough out onto a lightly floured board and knead until smooth and elastic (about 5 minutes), adding more flour as needed to prevent sticking. Place dough in an oiled bowl and turn over to oil top; cover with plastic wrap and let rise in a warm place until almost doubled (about 1 hour).

makes about 36 calzones

per calzone: 40 calories, 2 g protein, 6 g carbohydrates, 1 g total fat, 1 mg cholesterol, 93 mg sodium

COOKING WITH EGG WHITES In order to lower your fat intake, use more egg whites and fewer whole eggs or egg yolks. The whites serve much the same function as whole eggs in many recipes, and omitting all or most of the yolks reduces fat, calories, and cholesterol.

chili chicken chunks with blender salsa

preparation time: about 30 minutes

Blender Salsa (recipe follows)

³/₄ cup soft whole wheat bread crumbs

¹/₄ cup yellow cornmeal

2 teaspoons chili powder

¹/₂ teaspoon *each* paprika, ground cumin, and dry oregano

Vegetable oil cooking spray or salad oil

1 ¹/₂ pounds boneless, skinless chicken breast halves

2 large egg whites (about ¹/₄ cup)

1 Prepare Blender Salsa and refrigerate.

2 Spread bread crumbs in a shallow baking pan and bake in a 350° oven; stirring once, until lightly browned (about 5 minutes). Add cornmeal, chili powder, paprika, cumin, and oregano; stir well. Set aside.

3 Lightly coat a baking sheet with cooking spray. Rinse chicken and pat dry; then cut each breast half into 8 equal pieces. Place egg whites in a small bowl and beat lightly with a fork. Dip chicken pieces into egg whites; lift out and drain briefly. Then roll in crumb mixture to coat, place on baking sheet, and bake until meat in center is no longer pink; cut to test (about 15 minutes). Serve with salsa.

BLENDER SALSA

In a blender or food processor, combine 12 ounces tomatoes, cut into chunks; ¹/₂ small onion, cut into chunks; 3 tablespoons canned diced green chiles; 4 teaspoons distilled white vinegar; and 1 tablespoon chopped cilantro. Whirl until smooth.

makes 8 servings

per serving: 142 calories, 22 g protein, 9 g carbohydrates, 2 g total fat, 49 mg cholesterol, 124 mg sodium

apricot-orange glazed chicken

preparation time: about 55 minutes

6 boneless, skinless chicken breast halves (about 2 lbs. *total*)

1 cup apricot jam

2 tablespoons *each* prepared horseradish, minced fresh ginger, grated orange peel, and firmly packed brown sugar

¹/₄ cups orange juice

1 Soak thirty-six 6- to 8-inch bamboo skewers in hot water to cover for at least 30 minuutes.

2 Rinse chicken and pat dry. Cut each breast half lengthwise into 6 equal slices, then weave each slice onto a skewer. Place skewers on a lightly oiled rack in a broiler pan.

3 In a 1- to 1 ¹/₂-quart pan, combine jam, horseradish, ginger, orange peel, sugar, and orange juice. Stir over medium-high heat until jam is melted; keep mixture warm.

4 Brush chicken with some of the jam mixture. Broil 6 inches below heat, turning once and brushing 2 or 3 times with remaining jam mixture, until meat in thickest part is no longer pink; cut to test (about 8 minutes). Brush with any remaining jam mixture; serve hot.

makes 36 appetizers

per appetizer: 54 calories, 6 g protein, 7 g carbohydrates, 0.3 g total fat, 15 mg cholesterol, 21 mg sodium

hummus with pita crisps

preparation time: about 25 minutes

Pita Crisps (directions follow)

1 can (about 15 ¹/₂ oz.) garbanzo beans

2 tablespoons sesame tahini

2 cloves garlic

3 tablespoons lemon juice

¹/₈ teaspoon ground red pepper (cayenne)

¹/₂ small onion

2 tablespoons minced parsley

1 Prepare Pita Crisps and set aside.

2 Meanwhile, drain beans, reserving liquid. Rinse beans well and place in a blender or food processor with tahini, garlic, lemon juice, red pepper, onion, and 3 tablespoons of the reserved bean liquid. Whirl until smooth. With motor running, add more of the bean liquid, a little at a time, until mixture is smooth and thick.

3 Transfer to a shallow bowl and sprinkle with parsley. Offer with pita triangles.

makes 8 to 10 servings

PITA CRISPS

Cut 6 whole wheat pita breads (6-inch diameter) in half crosswise. Peel halves apart; stack and cut into 3 wedges. Place in a single layer on baking sheets and bake in a 350° oven until browned and crisped (12 to 15 minutes).

makes 72 pieces

per serving: 175 calories, 6 g protein, 32 g carbohydrates, 3 g total fat, 0 mg cholesterol, 354 mg sodium

asian guacamole with pot sticker crisps

preparation time: about 40 minutes

Pot Sticker Crisps (recipe follows)

1 tablespoon black or white (regular) sesame seeds

1 large firm-ripe avocado

1 tablespoon shredded pickled ginger

3 tablespoons seasoned rice vinegar, or 3 tablespoons cider vinegar plus 1 teaspoon sugar

¹/₂ teaspoon wasabi powder or prepared horseradish

1 Prepare Pot Sticker Crisps.

2 Toast sesame seeds in a small frying pan over medium-high heat, stirring often, until seeds begin to pop (3 to 4 minutes). Remove from pan and set aside.

3 Pit and peel avocado; dice into a bowl. Add ginger, vinegar, wasabi, and ¹/₂ teaspoon of the sesame seeds; mix gently.

4 Transfer to a serving bowl and sprinkle with remaining sesame seeds. Serve with Pot Sticker Crisps.

POT STICKER CRISPS

Dip 12 round pot sticker wrappers, one at a time, in water, shaking off excess. Place in a single layer on a large greased baking sheet. Bake in a 450° oven until browned and crisp (4 to 8 minutes, depending on thickness of wrappers). Let cool on racks. If made ahead, package airtight and store at room temperature for up to 2 days.

makes 4 to 6 servings

per serving: 194 calories, 6 g protein, 25 g carbohydrates, 9 g total fat, 0 mg cholesterol, 220 mg sodium

barbecued shrimp

preparation time: about 30 minutes

1 can (about 8 oz.) tomato sauce

$1/2$ cup light molasses

1 teaspoon dry mustard

Dash of liquid hot pepper seasoning

1 clove garlic, minced or pressed

1 tablespoon salad oil

$1/8$ teaspoon dry thyme

Pepper

2 pounds medium-size raw shrimp (about 36 per lb.), shelled and deveined

1 In a large glass bowl, mix tomato sauce, molasses, mustard, hot pepper seasoning, garlic, oil, and thyme. Season to taste with pepper. Add shrimp and stir to coat. Cover and refrigerate for at least 4 hours or until next day.

2 Meanwhile, soak about twenty-four 6- to 8-inch bamboo skewers in hot water to cover for at least 30 minutes.

3 Lift shrimp from bowl, reserving marinade; thread about 3 shrimp on each skewer. Place on a lightly oiled grill about 6 inches above a solid bed of low coals. (Or place on a rimmed baking sheet and broil about 6 inches below heat.) Cook, turning once and brushing often with marinade, until shrimp are opaque in center; cut to test (about 4 minutes).

makes about 24 appetizers

Per appetizer: 41 calories, 6 g protein, 2 g carbohydrates, 0.7 g total fat, 47 mg cholesterol, 65 mg sodium

glazed onions with corn, peppers & shrimp

preparation time: about 25 minutes

3 tablespoons olive oil

1 package (10 oz.) frozen tiny whole onions

1 cup whole-kernel corn, fresh or frozen

3 tablespoons balsamic or red wine vinegar

1 teaspoon sugar

1 jar (7 oz.) roasted peppers, drained and cut into $1/2$-inch slivers

$1/4$ pound small cooked shrimp

$1/4$ cup chopped green onions (including some tops)

Salt and pepper

1 small French baguette, sliced $1/4$ inch thick

1 Heat 1 tablespoon of the oil in an 8- to 10-inch frying pan over medium-high heat. Add whole onions and cook, stirring occasionally, until lightly browned (about 10 minutes). Reduce heat to medium; add corn, vinegar, and sugar. Cook, shaking pan often, until liquid has evaporated and onions are slightly browner (about 5 more minutes). Add roasted peppers and remaining 2 tablespoons oil, stirring until hot. Transfer to a bowl.

2 Scatter shrimp and green onions over vegetable mixture. Season to taste with salt and pepper. Offer with baguette slices.

makes about 2 dozen appetizers

per appetizer: 60 calories, 2 g protein, 8 g carbohydrates, 2 g total fat, 10 mg cholesterol, 70 mg sodium

CREATIVITY WITH LEFTOVERS: Leftovers of many kinds are easily transformed into tempting sandwiches. Cold cooked chicken, turkey, ham, beef, lamb, and meat loaf are all popular sandwich fillings; mild fish or hard-cooked eggs, chopped and mixed with mayonnaise and seasonings, are delicious as well. And if you have a bit of sour cream, cream cheese, or thick salad dressing to use up, try it as a sandwich spread in place of the usual butter, margarine, or mayonnaise. To add juiciness, color, and crunch to your sandwiches, add lettuce, sliced tomatoes, and alfalfa sprouts.

roasted eggplant marmalade

preparation time: about 2 ½ hours

**4 medium-size eggplants, unpeeled, cut into
½-inch cubes**

**¼ cup *each* minced garlic and minced fresh
ginger**

⅓ cup firmly packed brown sugar

¼ cup red wine vinegar

2 tablespoons Asian sesame oil

**2 tablespoons chopped fresh tarragon or
2 teaspoons dry tarragon**

2 teaspoons fennel seeds

1 cup low-sodium chicken broth

1 In a 10- by 15- by 2-inch baking; pan, mix eggplant, garlic, ginger, sugar, vinegar, oil, tarragon, and fennel seeds. Bake in a 400° oven, stirring occasionally, until liquid evaporates and eggplant browns and begins to stick to pan (about 1 ½ hours).

2 To deglaze, add ½ cup of the broth and stir to scrape browned bits free. Then continue to bake until eggplant begins to brown again (about 20 minutes). Repeat deglazing and browning steps, using remaining ½ cup broth.

3 Serve marmalade warm or cool. If made ahead, let cool; then cover and refrigerate for up to 10 days (freeze for longer storage).

makes about 4 cups

per ¼ cup: 70 calories, 2 g protein, 13 g carbohydrates, 2 g total fat, 0 mg cholesterol, 11 mg sodium

corn salsa

preparation time: about 30 minutes

**3 medium-size ears corn, about 8 inches long,
husks and silk removed**

½ cup finely chopped European cucumber

⅓ cup lime juice

¼ cup thinly sliced green onions

1 tablespoon grated orange peel

3 tablespoons orange juice

**2 tablespoons chopped fresh mint or 1 teaspoon
dried mint**

1 teaspoon cumin seeds

1 or 2 fresh jalapeño chiles, seeded and minced

Salt

1 In a 5- to 6-quart pan, bring about 3 quarts water to a boil over high heat. Add corn, cover, and cook until hot (4 to 6 minutes). Drain, then let cool. With a sharp knife, cut kernels from cobs.

2 In a nonmetal bowl, mix corn, cucumber, lime juice, onions, orange peel, orange juice, mint, cumin seeds, and chiles; season to taste with salt. (At this point, you may cover and refrigerate for up to 4 hours.)

makes about 3 cups

per ¼ cup: 32 calories, 1 g protein, 7 g carbohydrates, 0.4 g total fat, 0 mg cholesterol, 6 mg sodium

roasted potatoes parmesan

preparation time: about 1 1/2 hours

16 small red thin-skinned potatoes, scrubbed

1/3 cup *each* grated Parmesan cheese and plain lowfat yogurt

2 tablespoons minced green onion or chives

Paprika

1 Pierce each potato in several places with a fork. Arrange in a single layer in a shallow baking pan. Bake in a 375° oven until tender when pierced (about 1 hour). Let cool slightly. (At this point, you may cover and refrigerate for up to a day)

2 In a small bowl, mix cheese, yogurt, and onion.

3 To fill potatoes, cut each in half. Scoop out a small depression from center of cut side of each potato half. Set halves, cut sides up, in a shallow rimmed baking pan (if necessary, trim a sliver from rounded side of potato halves to steady them). Spoon cheese mixture into potato halves. Sprinkle generously with paprika. Bake in a 350° oven until heated through (about 15 minutes). Serve hot.

makes 32 appetizers

per appetizer: 23 calories, 1 g protein, 4 g carbohydrates, 0.3 g total fat, 0.8 mg cholesterol, 19 mg sodium

black bean salsa with crisp vegetables

preparation time: about 35 minutes

1 can (about 15 oz.) black beans

2 tablespoons lime juice

1/3 cup coarsely chopped cilantro

1/2 cup thinly sliced green onions

3 small pear-shaped (Roma-type) tomatoes, seeded and chopped

Salt and pepper

1 small jicama

1 small cucumber, thinly sliced

Cilantro sprigs

1 Drain beans, reserving 1 tablespoon of the liquid. Place reserved liquid and half the beans in a medium-size bowl. Add lime juice, then mash beans with a fork or potato masher until smooth. Stir in remaining beans, chopped cilantro, onions, and tomatoes. Season to taste with salt and pepper. (At this point, you may cover and refrigerate for up to 4 hours.)

2 Peel and rinse jicama; cut in half lengthwise, then thinly slice each half. Arrange jicama and cucumber slices on a platter and set aside. If made ahead, cover and refrigerate for up to 2 hours.

3 Spoon bean salsa into a serving bowls; garnish with cilantro sprigs. Serve bean salsa with jicama and cucumber slices to taste.

makes about 30 servings

per serving: 20 calories, 1 g protein, 4 g carbohydrates, 0.1 g total fat, 0 mg cholesterol, 46 mg sodium

turkey-broccoli bundles

preparation time: about 20 minutes

1 pound broccoli

10 thin slices (²/₃ lb. *total*) cooked skinless
  turkey breast

³/₄ cup part-skim ricotta cheese

¹/₃ cup plain lowfat yogurt

¹/₄ cup prepared horseradish

1 teaspoon pepper

1 Trim broccoli, leaving about 2 inches of stalk below flowerets; peel stalks, if desired. Cut broccoli lengthwise into 20 spears. Place spears on a rack in a pan above 1 inch boiling water; cover and steam over high heat until tender-crisp (about 3 minutes). Lift out and immerse in ice water until cool. Drain and set aside.

2 Cut turkey slices in half lengthwise. Wrap each spear of broccoli with a piece of turkey, leaving top of floweret exposed. In a small bowl, beat ricotta, yogurt, horseradish, and pepper.

3 Arrange bundles on a platter. Offer with yogurt mixture.

makes 10 servings (2 appetizers each)

per serving: 88 calories, 12 g protein, 4 g carbohydrates, 3 g total fat, 27 mg cholesterol, 62 mg sodium

lamb shish kebabs

preparation time: about 55 minutes
marinating time: at least 4 hours

¹/₂ cup blackberry syrup

¹/₄ cup red wine vinegar

2 tablespoons *each* reduced-sodium soy sauce
  and chopped fresh mint leaves

2 cloves garlic, minced or pressed

¹/₂ teaspoon pepper

2 cans (about 8 oz. *each*) whole water chestnuts,
  drained

1 ¹/₂ pounds lean boneless lamb (leg or shoulder),
  fat trimmed, cut into 1-inch cubes

1 Mix syrup, vinegar, soy sauce, paint, garlic, and pepper. Add water chestnuts and lamb, stirring to coat. Cover and refrigerate for at least 4 hours or until next day, stirring several times.

2 Soak 12 bamboo skewers in hot water to cover for 30 minutes. Drain meat and water chestnuts and thread alternately on skewers (to avoid splitting water chestnuts, rotate skewer as you pierce them).

3 Place skewers on a lightly greased grill 4 to 6 inches above a solid bed of medium coals. (Or place on a rack in a broiler pan and broil about 4 inches below heat.) Cook, turning occasionally, until meat is browned but still pink in center; cut to test (about 8 minutes).

makes 6 servings (2 skewers each)

per serving: 238 calories, 25 g protein, 19 g carbohydrates, 7 g total fat, 76 mg cholesterol, 164 mg sodium

FILL IN WITH WATER You can give sauces a velvety quality without using much fat; just replace some or all of the butter, margarine, or oil with slightly thickened water or other liquid (as appropriate to the dish). For each cup of liquid, use 1 tablespoon flour for a thin sauce, 2 tablespoons for a medium sauce, and 3 to 4 tablespoons for a thick sauce. If you use cornstarch, arrowroot, or potato starch, you'll need just half the amount of starch for the same thickening effect after cooking.

oysters with tomatillo salsa

preparation time: 20 minutes

Tomatillo Salsa (recipe follows)

48 small Pacific oysters in shells (*each* 2 to 3 inches in diameter)

1 Prepare Tomatillo Salsa; set aside.

2 Scrub oysters with a stiff brush under cool running water. Then set oysters, cupped sides down, on a grill 4 to 6 inches above a solid bed of hot coals. When shells begin to open, carefully remove oysters from grill; shells and juices are hot, so use tongs or hot pads. Cut oysters free from shells, discarding top shells.

3 To serve, spoon 1 tablespoon salsa over each oyster; serve oysters in the shell.

makes 4 dozen appetizers

TOMATILLO SALSA

Drain 2 cans (13 oz. each) tomatillos and discard juice. Chop tomatillos, place in a large bowl, and mix in 1 can (4 oz.) diced green chiles, ½ cup each minced green onions (including tops) and minced fresh cilantro, and 2 tablespoons lime juice. Season to taste with salt. If made ahead, cover and refrigerate for up to 2 days.

makes 3 cups

per appetizer: 34 calories, 4 g protein, 3 g carbohydrates, 1 g total fat, 21 mg cholesterol, 54 mg sodium

pickled maui onions

preparation time: about 15 minutes

1 large Maui onion or other mild white onion

³/₄ cup water

6 tablespoons distilled white vinegar

3 tablespoons sugar

2 cloves garlic, peeled and crushed

1 small dried hot red chile

1 ½ teaspoons salt

1 Cut onion lengthwise into 1-inch-wide wedges. Place in a 3-to 4-cup heatproof wide-mouth jar.

2 In a 1- to 1 ½-quart pan, combine water, vinegar, sugar, garlic, chile, and salt. Bring to a boil over high heat, stirring until sugar is dissolved.

3 Pour hot liquid over onion; cover tightly. Let cool; then refrigerate for at least 3 days or up to 1 month.

makes about 2 cups

per ¼ cup: 33 calories, 0.5 g protein, 8 g carbohydrates, 0.1 g total fat, 0 mg cholesterol, 415 mg sodium

miso-marinated pork with apple and onion

preparation time: about 35 minutes
marinating time: at least 1 hour

1 pound pork tenderloin, trimmed of fat

1/3 cup *each* aka miso and maple syrup

1/4 cup sake, dry white wine, or water

2 tablespoons minced fresh ginger

2 medium-size apples such as McIntosh or Fuji

Lemon juice

1 large onion, cut into wedges, layers separated

1 Cut pork into 1/8-inch-thick, 6- to 7-inch-long slices; place in a 1-quart heavy-duty plastic bag. Add miso, syrup, sake, and ginger; mix well. Seal bag and refrigerate for at least 1 hour or until next day.

2 Core apples, cut into 1/2-inch wedges, and brush with lemon juice to prevent darkening. Lift pork slices from bag, reserving marinade in bag.

3 To assemble each skewer, thread tip of a thin metal skewer through end of a pork slice; thread on a piece of onion and an apple wedge, then thread skewer through pork again. Repeat process until skewer is full; you should have 8 skewers total.

4 Place skewers on a grill 4 to 6 inches above a solid bed of medium coals. Cook, basting with marinade and turning often, until meat is no longer pink in center; cut to test (about 10 minutes).

makes 8 servings

per serving: 165 calories, 15 g protein, 19 g carbohydrates, 3 g total fat, 42 mg cholesterol, 446 mg sodium

cherry tomato salsa

preparation time: about 25 minutes

2 cups red cherry tomatoes, cut into halves

1/3 cup lightly packed cilantro leaves

2 fresh jalapeño chiles, seeded

1 clove garlic, peeled

2 tablespoons lime juice

2 tablespoons thinly sliced green onion

Salt and pepper

1 Place tomatoes, cilantro, chiles, and garlic in a food processor; whirl just until coarsely chopped (or chop coarsely with a knife).

2 Turn mixture into a nonmetal bowl; stir in lime juice and onion. Season to taste with salt and pepper. (At this point, you may cover and refrigerate for up to 4 hours.)

makes about 2 cups

per 1/4 cup: 12 calories, 0.5 g protein, 3 g carbohydrates, 0.1 g total fat, 0 mg cholesterol, 5 mg sodium

asian eggplant dip

preparation time: about 1 1/4 hours

1 large eggplant, trimmed

2 cloves garlic

2 tablespoons soy sauce

2 tablespoons rice wine (mirin) or dry vermouth

1 tablespoon *each* minced fresh ginger, minced cilantro and sesame oil

1/2 teaspoon crushed dried hot red chiles

Salt

1 With a fork, pierce eggplant deeply in 10 to 12 places. Set in an 8- to 9-inch baking pan. Bake in a 350° oven until very soft when pressed (about 1 hour). Let cool. If desired, trim off and discard skin. Cut eggplant into large chunks.

2 Place eggplant, garlic, soy, wine, ginger, cilantro, oil, and chiles in a blender or food processor and whirl until fairly smooth; scrape container sides often. Season to taste with salt.

3 If made ahead, cover and refrigerate for up to 4 days. Serve at room temperature.

makes about 2 cups

per tablespoon: 13 calories, 0.3 g protein, 2 g carbohydrates, 0.4 g total fat, 0 mg cholesterol, 65 mg sodium

scallop ceviche

preparation time: about 25 minutes

1/2 pound sea or bay scallops

1/3 cup lime or lemon juice

1/4 cup diced white onion

1 or 2 fresh jalapeño or serrano chiles, stemmed, seeded, and finely diced

2 tablespoons salad oil

1/2 teaspoon chopped fresh oregano leaves or 1/8 teaspoon dry oregano leaves

1/2 cup chopped yellow, green, or red bell pepper

2 teaspoons minced cilantro

Salt

Oregano sprigs

Lime halves or wedges

1 large head Belgian endive, separated into leaves, washed and crisped (optional)

1 Rinse scallops and pat dry. If using sea scallops, cut into 1/2-inch pieces.

2 In a large nonmetal bowl, stir together scallops, lime juice, onion, chiles, oil, and chopped oregano. Cover and refrigerate, stirring occasionally, for at least 8 hours or until next day.

3 Stir bell pepper and cilantro into scallop mixture; season to taste with salt. Pour into a serving bowl and garnish with oregano sprigs. Offer with lime halves and, if desired, endive leaves for scooping.

makes about 6 servings

per serving: 82 calories, 7 g protein, 3 g carbohydrates, 5 g total fat, 12 mg cholesterol, 64 mg sodium

CHOOSE REDUCED-FAT, LOW-FAT OR NONFAT DAIRY PRODUCTS:

lime salsa

Preparation time: about 25 minutes

1 large ripe red or yellow tomato, finely diced

8 medium-size tomatillos, husked, rinsed, and chopped

¼ cup minced red or yellow bell pepper

2 tablespoons minced red onion

1 teaspoon grated lime peel

1 tablespoon lime juice

In a nonmetal bowl, mix tomato, tomatillos, bell pepper, onion, lime peel, and lime juice. (At this point, you may cover and refrigerate for up to 4 hours before serving.)

makes about 4 cups

per ¼ cup: 9 calories, 0.4 g protein, 2 g carbohydrates, 0.1 g total fat, 0 mg cholesterol, 2 mg sodium

salsa fresca

preparation time: about 20 minutes

2 medium-size ripe tomatoes, coarsely chopped

2 large tomatillos, husked, rinsed, and chopped; or 1 medium-size ripe tomato, coarsely chopped

¼ cup chopped cilantro

⅓ cup chopped onion or thinly sliced green onions

2 tablespoons lime juice

2-6 tablespoons minced fresh or canned hot chiles

Salt

In a medium-size bowl, combine tomatoes, tomatillos, cilantro, onion, lime juice, and chiles. Stir to mix well; then season to taste with salt. If made ahead, cover and refrigerate for up to 4 hours.

makes 2 ½ to 3 cups

per ¼ cup: 14 calories, 0.6 g protein, 3 g carbohydrates, 0.2 g total fat, 0 mg cholesterol, 4 mg sodium

pineapple salsa

preparation time: about 20 minutes

1 cup diced fresh or canned pineapple

½ cup chopped, peeled, seeded cucumber

1 fresh jalapeño chile, seeded and minced

1 teaspoon grated lime peel

3 tablespoons lime juice

2 tablespoons minced cilantro

In a nonmetal bowl, mix pineapple, cucumber, chile, lime peel, lime juice, and cilantro. If made ahead, cover and refrigerate for up to 4 hours.

makes about 1 ¾ cups

per serving: 14 calories, 0.2 g protein, 4 g carbohydrates, 0.1 g total fat, 0 mg cholesterol, 2 mg sodium

soup

salsa fish soup

preparation time: about 25 minutes

6 cups fat-free reduced-sodium chicken broth

²/₃ cup regular or quick-cooking rice

2 cups frozen corn kernels

1 pound skinned, boned mild flavored
white-fleshed fish (such as rockfish or
Lingcod), cut into 1-inch chunks

1 cup refrigerated or canned tomato-based
chunk-style salsa; or 1 cup canned
Mexican-style stewed tomatoes

Lime wedges

1 In a 5- to 6-quart pan, combine broth and rice. Bring to a boil over high heat. Reduce heat, cover, and simmer until rice is tender to bite (about 15 minutes; about 5 minutes for quick-cooking rice).

2 Add corn, fish, and salsa to pan. Cover and simmer soup until fish is just opaque in thickest part; cut to test (about 5 minutes). Offer lime wedges to squeeze into soup to taste.

makes 4 servings

per serving: 338 calories, 31 g protein, 48 g carbohydrates, 3 g total fat, 40 mg cholesterol, 1,679 mg sodium

fish & pea soup

preparation time: about 35 minutes

3 large leeks

2 tablespoons vegetable oil

1 clove garlic, minced or pressed

1 large carrot, finely chopped

1 cup dry white wine or fat-free reduced-sodium
chicken broth

6 cups fat-free reduced-sodium chicken broth

1 dried bay leaf

1 teaspoon dried tarragon

1½ to 2 pounds skinless rockfish or lingcod fillets

1 package frozen tiny peas, broken apart

Salt and pepper

1 Cut off and discard root ends and green tops of leeks; discard coarse outer leaves. Split leeks lengthwise and rinse well; thinly slice crosswise.

2 Heat oil in a 5- to 6-quart pan over medium heat. Add leeks, garlic, and carrot; cook, stirring occasionally, until leeks are soft but not browned (6 to 8 minutes). Add wine, broth, bay leaf, and tarragon. Bring to a boil; then reduce heat to medium-low and cook for 5 minutes.

3 Meanwhile, rinse fish, pat dry, and cut into 1-inch chunks. To pan, add fish and peas. Cover and cook until fish is just opaque but still moist in thickest part; cut to test (about 6 minutes). Season to taste with salt and pepper.

makes 6 servings

per serving: 285 calories, 32 g protein, 17 g carbohydrates, 7 g total fat, 46 mg cholesterol, 808 mg sodium

asparagus, shrimp & watercress soup

preparation time: about 30 minutes

12 ounces asparagus

7 cups fat-free reduced-sodium chicken broth

1 teaspoon grated lemon peel

1 teaspoon dried tarragon

1/8 teaspoon ground white pepper

1 ounce dried capellini

12 ounces medium-size raw shrimp (40 to 45 per lb.), shelled and deveined

2 cups lightly packed watercress sprigs, rinsed and drained

3 tablespoons lemon juice

1 Snap off and discard tough ends of asparagus, then cut spears into 1/2-inch-thick diagonal slices. Set aside.

2 In a 4- to 5-quart pan, combine broth, lemon peel, tarragon, and white pepper; bring to a boil over high heat. Add capellini; when broth returns to a boil, reduce heat and boil gently for 4 minutes. Add shrimp and asparagus. Continue to cook just until shrimp are opaque in center; cut to test (about 3 minutes). Stir in watercress, then lemon juice. Serve immediately (greens will lose their bright color as soup stands).

makes 4 to 6 servings

per serving: 121 calories, 19 g protein, 9 g carbohydrates, 1 g total fat, 84 mg cholesterol, 996 mg sodium

gingered shrimp & capellini soup

preparation time: about 40 minutes

6 cups fat-free reduced-sodium chicken broth

2 tablespoons minced fresh ginger

12 ounces extra-large shrimp (26 to 30 per lb.), shelled and deveined

2 ounces dried capellini, broken into 2-inch pieces

1 package (about 10 oz.) frozen tiny peas, thawed

1/2 cup thinly sliced green onions

Fish sauce (*nam pla* or *nuac mam*), oyster sauce, or reduced-sodium soy sauce

1 Combine broth and ginger in a 4- to 5-quart pan. Cover and bring to a boil over high heat. Stir in shrimp and pasta; cover, immediately remove pan from heat, and let stand for 4 minutes (do not uncover). Check shrimp for doneness (shrimp should be opaque but moist-looking in center of thickest part; cut to test). If shrimp are still translucent, cover and let stand until done, checking at 2-minute intervals.

2 Add peas, cover, and let stand until heated through (about 3 minutes).

3 Stir in onions and ladle soup into bowls. Offer fish sauce to add to taste.

makes 4 to 6 servings

per serving: 172 calories, 19 g protein, 18 g carbohydrates, 4 g total fat, 84 mg cholesterol, 299 mg sodium

shrimp & white bean soup

preparation time: about 45 minutes

1 tablespoon vegetable oil

2 large onions, chopped

1 cup thinly sliced celery

3 cloves garlic, minced or pressed

2 cans (about 15 oz. *each*) white kidney beans (canellini), drained and rinsed

4 cups fat-free reduced-sodium chicken broth

¼ cup catsup

⅓ pound small cooked shrimp

¼ cup chopped parsley

Salt and pepper

1 Heat oil in a 4- to 5-quart pan over medium-high heat. Add onions, celery, and garlic; cook, starring often, until all vegetables are browned (about 20 minutes).

2 Transfer vegetable mixture to a food processor or blender; add half the beans and 2 cups of the broth. Whirl until smoothly puréed, then return to pan. Purée remaining beans with remaining 2 cups broth; add to pan. Stir in catsup. (At this point, you may cover and refrigerate until next day.)

3 To serve, stir soup over medium heat until hot. Ladle soup into 4 bowls; top equally with shrimp and parsley. Season to taste with salt and pepper.

makes 4 servings

per serving: 297 calories, 21 g protein, 38 g carbohydrates, 7 g total fat, 73 mg cholesterol, 1,172 mg sodium

sweet potato soup

preparation time: about 45 minutes

4 medium-large sweet potatoes, peeled and diced

About 6 cups fat-free reduced-sodium chicken broth

1 ½ tablespoons curry powder

¼ cup tomato paste

2 tablespoons lemon juice

¼ cup dry sherry

Salt and pepper

Cilantro leaves

1 In a 4- to 5-quart pan, combine potatoes and 6 cups of the broth. Bring to a boil over medium-high heat; reduce heat, cover, and boil gently until potatoes are soft enough to mash readily (about 20 minutes). With a slotted spoon, transfer potatoes to a food processor or blender; add curry powder and about ½ cup of the cooking broth. Whirl until puréed.

2 Return sweet potato purée to pan; stir in tomato paste, lemon juice, and sherry. (At this point, you may cover and refrigerate for up to a day.)

3 To serve, reheat soup over medium heat, stirring often, until hot. If soup is too thick, thin with a little more broth. Season to taste with salt and pepper. Garnish with cilantro.

makes 8 to 10 servings

per serving: 146 calories, 5 g protein, 30 g carbohydrates, 0.5 g total fat, 0 mg cholesterol, 503 mg sodium

italian sausage & bow-tie soup

preparation time: about 1 hour

Low-fat Italian Sausage (recipe follows)

2 large onions, chopped

2 cloves garlic minced or pressed

5 cups beef broth

1 can (about 28 oz.) pear-shaped tomatoes

1 1/2 cups dry red wine

1 tablespoon each dried basil and sugar

1 medium-size green bell pepper, seeded and chopped

2 medium-size zucchini, sliced 1/4 inch thick

5 ounces (about 2 1/2 cups) dried farafalle (about 1 1/2-inch size)

1/2 cup chopped parsley

Salt and pepper

1 Prepare Low Fat Italian Sausage.

2 Combine onions, garlic, and 1 cup of the broth in a 5- to 6-quart pan. Bring to a boil over medium-high heat and cook, stirring occasionally, until liquid has evaporated and onion mixture begins to brown (about 10 minutes). To deglaze pan, add 3 tablespoons water, stirring to loosen browned bits. Continue to cook, stirring often, until liquid has evaporated and onion mixture begins to brown again (about 1 minute). Repeat deglazing step, adding 3 tablespoons more water each time, until onion mixture is richly browned.

3 Stir in sausage and 1/2 cup more water. Cook, stirring gently, until liquid has evaporated and meat begins to brown (8 to 10 minutes).

4 Add remaining 4 cups broth, stirring to loosen browned bits. Stir in tomatoes (break up with a spoon) and their liquid, wine, basil, sugar, bell pepper, zucchini, and pasta. Bring to a boil over high heat; reduce heat, cover, and simmer just until pasta is tender to bite (about 15 minutes).

5 Sprinkle soup with parsley. Offer salt and pepper to add to taste.

makes 6 servings

LOW FAT ITALIAN SAUSAGE

Cut 1 pound pork tenderloin or boned pork loin, trimmed of fat, into 1-inch chunks. Whirl in a food processor, about half at a time, until coarsely chopped (or put through a food chopper fitted with a medium blade). In a large bowl, combine pork, 1/4 cup dry white wine, 2 tablespoons chopped parsley, 1 1/2 teaspoons crushed fennel seeds, 1/2 teaspoon crushed red pepper flakes, and 2 cloves garlic, minced or pressed. Mix well. Cover and refrigerate. If made ahead, refrigerate for up to a day.

per serving: 327 calories, 23 g protein, 37 g carbohydrates, 4 g total fat, 49 mg cholesterol, 1,632 mg sodium

turkey albóndigas soup

preparation time: about 45 minutes

1 pound lean ground turkey

1/2 cup cooked brown or white rice

1/4 cup all-purpose flour

1/4 cup water

1 teaspoon ground cumin

1 can (about 14 1/2 oz.) pear-shaped (Roma-style) tomatoes

6 cups fat-free reduced-sodium chicken broth

4 cups beef broth

2 cups chopped onions

6 medium-size carrots, thinly sliced

1 teaspoon dried oregano

2 teaspoons chili powder

12 ounces stemmed spinach leaves, rinsed well and drained (about 3 cups lightly packed)

1/3 cup chopped cilantro

1 or 2 limes, cut into wedges

1 To prepare turkey meatballs, in a bowl, mix the turkey, rice, flour, water, and cumin. Shape mixture into 1- to 1 1/2-inch balls and place, slightly apart, in a 10- by 15-inch rimmed baking pan. Bake in a 450° oven until well browned (about 15 minutes). Pour off fat; set aside. (At this point, you may make ahead, let cool; then cover and refrigerate until next day.)

2 Pour tomatoes and their liquid into an 8- to 10-quart pan; break tomatoes up with a spoon. Add chicken broth, beef broth, onions, carrots, oregano, and chili powder.

3 Bring to a boil over high heat; then reduce heat to low. Add meatballs and simmer for 10 minutes. Stir in spinach and cilantro and cook until greens are wilted (about 3 more minutes).

4 To serve, ladle soup into bowls; serve with lime wedges to squeeze into soup to taste.

makes 6 to 8 servings

per serving: 235 calories, 19 g protein, 28 g carbohydrates, 8 g total fat, 47 mg cholesterol, 341 mg sodium

maritata soup

preparation time: about 25 minutes

12 cups beef broth

8 ounces dried vermicelli, broken into short lengths

1/2 cup freshly grated Parmesan cheese

1/3 cup Neufchatel or nonfat cream cheese

3 large egg whites

1 Bring broth to a boil in a 5- to 6-quart pan over high heat. Stir in pasta; reduce heat, cover, and simmer just until pasta is tender to bite (8 to 10 minutes).

2 Meanwhile, beat Parmesan cheese, Neufchatel cheese, and egg whites with an electric mixer or in a blender until well combined.

3 Slowly pour about 1 cup of the simmering broth into cheese mixture, mixing to combine. Then return cheese-broth mixture to pan, stirring constantly until hot (2 to 3 minutes).

makes 8 servings

per serving: 188 calories, 9 g protein, 22 g carbohydrates, 5 g total fat, 11 mg cholesterol, 2,613 mg sodium

lamb, lentil & couscous soup

preparation time: about 1 1/4 hours

1 large onion, chopped

1 tablespoon minced fresh ginger

1 teaspoon cumin seeds

1 tablespoon curry powder

10 cups low-sodium chicken broth

8 ounces (about 1 1/4 cups) lentils, rinsed and drained

1 pound lean ground lamb

1 teaspoon *each* ground coriander and chili powder

4 ounces (about 2/3 cup) dried couscous

1/4 cup cilantro

Plain nonfat yogurt

1 Combine onion, ginger, cumin, and 1/4 cup water in a 5- to 6-quart pan. Cook over medium-high heat, stirring often, until liquid has evaporated and onion begins to brown. To deglaze pan, add 2 tablespoons water, stirring to loosen browned bits. Continue to cook, stirring often, until liquid has evaporated and onion begins to brown again. Repeat deglazing step, adding 2 tablespoons more water each time, until onion is light golden.

2 Reduce heat to low and add curry powder; cook, stirring, until fragrant (about 1 minute). Add broth and lentils; stir to loosen browned bits. Bring to a boil over high heat; reduce heat, cover, and simmer just until lentils are almost tender to bite (20 to 30 minutes). Meanwhile, mix lamb, coriander, and chili powder in a bowl; shape into 3/4-inch balls.

3 Drop meatballs into soup. Stir in pasta. Cover and continue to simmer just until lamb is no longer pink in center (cut to test) and pasta is tender to bite (about 5 minutes). Ladle into bowls. Sprinkle with cilantro. Offer yogurt to add to taste.

makes 6 to 8 servings

per serving: 322 calories. 29 g protein, 38 g carbohydrates, 9 g total fat, 43 mg cholesterol, 220 mg sodium

shell & bean soup

preparation time: about 40 minutes

1 small red onion, chopped

1 teaspoon olive oil

1 cup chopped celery

4 cloves garlic, chopped

10 cups fat free reduced-sodium chicken broth

1 1/2 cups dried small pasta shells

3 to 4 cups cooked or canned white beans, drained and rinsed

1 cup shredded carrots

1 package (about 10 oz.) frozen tiny peas

1/2 cup grated Parmesan cheese

1 Set aside 1/3 cup of the chopped onion. In a 6- to 8-quart pan, combine remaining onion, oil, celery and garlic. Cook over medium-high heat, stirring often, until onion is lightly browned (5 to 8 minutes). Add broth and bring to a boil. Stir in pasta and beans; reduce heat, cover, and simmer until pasta is almost tender to bite (5 to 7 minutes). Add carrots and peas; bring to a boil.

2 Ladle soup into individual bowls; sprinkle equally with cheese and reserved onion.

makes 6 to 8 servings

per serving: 324 calories, 22 g protein, 53 g carbohydrates, 3 g total fat. 5 mg cholesterol, 1,113 mg sodium

tortellini & escarole soup

preparation time: 45 minutes

1 tablespoon olive oil

1 large onion, chopped

2 large carrots, chopped

1 strip lemon zest, about $1/4$ inch by 4 inches

10 cups fat-free reduced-sodium chicken broth;

1 package (about 9 oz.) fresh cheese or meat tortellini or ravioli

1 package (about 10 oz.) frozen tiny peas, thawed

8 ounces (about 6 cups) shredded escarole

Freshly grated or ground nutmeg

Lemon wedges

Salt

1 Heat oil in a 5- to 6-quart pan over medium-high heat. Add onion, carrots, and lemon zest. Cook, stirring, until onion is soft (5 to 8 minutes).

2 Add broth and bring to a boil over high heat. Add pasta; reduce heat and boil gently, stirring occasionally, just until pasta is tender to bite (4 to 6 minutes; or according to package directions).

3 Stir in peas and escarole; cook just until escarole is wilted (1 to 2 minutes). Remove and discard zest.

4 Ladle soup into bowls. Dust generously with nutmeg. Offer lemon and salt to add to taste.

makes 8 servings

per serving: 193 calories, 11 g protein, 27 g carbohydrates, 7 g total fat, 13 mg cholesterol, 316 mg sodium

spring vegetable soup with shells

preparation time: about 40 minutes

8 cups low-sodium chicken broth

2 cups diced carrots

4 ounces (about 1 cup) dried small shell-shaped pasta

2 cups thinly sliced asparagus

1 package (about 10 oz.) frozen tiny peas

$1 1/4$ to $1 1/2$ pounds tiny cooked shrimp.

$1/2$ cup thinly sliced green onions

$1/4$ cup minced parsley

Parsley sprigs (optional)

Salt and pepper

1 Bring broth to a boil in a 5- to 6-quart pan over high heat. Stir in carrots and pasta; reduce heat, cover, and boil gently just until carrots and pasta are tender to bite 8 to 10 minutes; or according to package directions).

2 Add asparagus and peas; cook until heated through (about 2 minutes). Remove from heat and keep warm.

3 Combine shrimp, onions, and minced parsley in a small bowl. Ladle soup into bowls and spoon in shrimp mixture, dividing evenly. Garnish with parsley sprigs, if desired. Offer salt and pepper to add to taste.

makes 8 to 10 servings

per serving: 178 calories, 22 g protein, 18 g carbohydrates, 3 g total fat, 136 mg cholesterol, 312 mg sodium

black bean soup

preparation time: about 40 minutes

SOUP:

2 teaspoons vegetable oil

1 large onion, chopped

**1 ³/₄ or 2 ³/₄ cups fat-free reduced-sodium
chicken broth**

1 large can (about 28 oz.) tomatoes

**3 cans (about 15 oz. *each*) black beans,
drained, rinsed, and puréed; or 1 package
(about 7 oz.) instant refried black bean mix**

1 fresh jalapeño chile, seeded and minced

2 teaspoons cumin seeds

CONDIMENTS:

Cheddar cheese

Plain nonfat yogurt

Cilantro leaves

Lime wedges

1 In a 5- to 6-quart pan, combine oil and onion. Cook over medium heat, stirring often, until onion is deep golden (about 20 minutes). Add 1 ¾ cups broth (or 2 ¾ cups if using instant beans).

2 Add tomatoes and their liquid to pan; break tomatoes up with a spoon. Stir in beans, chile, and cumin seeds. Bring to a boil; then reduce heat and simmer, uncovered, until soup is thick and flavors are blended (7 to 10 minutes).

3 To serve, ladle soup into bowls. Add condiments to taste.

makes 4 servings

per serving: 327 calories , 21 g protein, 51 g carbohydrates, 6 g total fat, 0 mg cholesterol, 795 mg sodium

chilled cucumber & cilantro soup

preparation time: about 10 minutes
chilling time: at least 2 hours

1 very large cucumber, peeled and cut into chunks

1 ¹/₄ cups low-sodium chicken broth

³/₄ cup firmly packed cilantro leaves

¹/₂ cup nonfat or low-fat milk

¹/₂ cup lemon juice

Salt

1 In a food processor or blender, combine cucumber, broth, cilantro, milk, and lemon juice; whirl until smoothly puréed, Season purée to taste with salt.

2 Cover and refrigerate until cold (at least 2 hours) or until next day.

3 To serve, ladle into bowls.

makes 4 servings

per serving: 36 calories, 3 g protein, 6 g carbohydrates, 1 g total fat, 0.6 mg cholesterol, 62 mg sodium

tomato, beef & orzo soup

preparation time: about 1 3/4 hours

1 teaspoon olive oil or salad oil

1 pound lean boneless beef cut into 3/4-inch chunks

About 5 cups beef broth

1 small onion, chopped

1 1/2 teaspoons dried thyme

1 can (about 6 oz.) tomato paste

4 ounces (about 2/3 cup) dried orzo or other rice-shaped pasta

1 large tomato, chopped

2 tablespoons dry red wine (or to taste)

Cilantro

Salt and pepper

1 Heat oil in a 4- to 5-quart pan over medium heat. Add beef and cook, stirring, until browned (about 10 minutes); if pan appears dry, stir in water, 1 tablespoon at a time. Add 1 cup of the broth; stir to loosen browned bits. Bring to a boil over high heat; reduce heat, cover, and simmer for 30 minutes.

2 Add onion and thyme. Cook, uncovered, over medium-high heat, stirring often, until liquid has evaporated and pan drippings are richly browned (about 10 minutes). Add 4 cups more broth and tomato paste. Bring to a boil over high heat, stirring to loosen browned bits; reduce heat, cover, and boil gently for 20 more minutes.

3 Add pasta, cover, and continue to cook, stirring often, just until pasta is tender to bite (8 to 10 minutes; or according to package directions). Stir in tomato. If soup is too thick, add a little broth or water; if too thin, continue to simmer until thickened. Remove from heat and add wine. Ladle into bowls. Garnish with cilantro. Offer salt and pepper to add to taste.

makes 4 or 5 servings

per serving: 300 calories, 23 g protein, 28 g carbohydrates, 9 g total fat, 59 mg cholesterol, 1,985 mg sodium

mushroom barley soup

preparation time: about 1 1/2 hours

1 tablespoon salad oil or olive oil

1 pound mushrooms, thinly sliced

1 large onion, chopped

2 medium-size carrots, thinly sliced

10 cups vegetable broth

1 cup pearl barley, rinsed and drained

1 tablespoon finely chopped fresh oregano or 1 teaspoon dried oregano

8 ounces red or green Swiss chard

Pepper

1 Heat oil in a 5- to 6-quart pan over medium-high heat. Add mushrooms, onion, and carrots. Cook, stirring often, until vegetables are soft and almost all liquid has evaporated (about 25 minutes). Add broth, barley, and oregano. Bring to a boil over high heat; then reduce heat, cover, and simmer until barley is tender to bite (about 30 minutes).

2 Meanwhile, trim and discard discolored stem ends from chard. Rinse chard and drain well; then coarsely chop leaves and stems.

3 Stir chard into soup and simmer, uncovered, until leaves are limp and bright green (5 to 10 minutes). Ladle soup into bowls; season to taste with pepper:

makes 6 to 8 servings

per serving: 196 calories, 5 g protein, 37 g carbohydrates, 4 g total fat, 0 mg cholesterol, 1,512 mg sodium

chicken noodle soup

preparation time: about 45 minutes

1 teaspoon vegetable oil

1 large onion, chopped

8 cups fat-free reduced-sodium chicken broth

3 cloves garlic, minced or pressed

1/2 teaspoon dried thyme

1/2 teaspoon pepper

2 large carrots, thinly sliced

1/2 cup chopped celery

5 ounces dried wide egg noodles

3 cups shredded cooked chicken

1 small zucchini, chopped

1 medium-size tomato, peeled, seeded, and chopped

2 tablespoons chopped parsley

1 Heat oil in a 5- to 6-quart pan over medium-high heat. Add onion and soak, stirring often, until onion is soft (about 5 minutes); if pan appears dry or onion sticks to pan bottom, stir in water, 1 tablespoon at a time.

2 Add broth, garlic, thyme, and pepper; bring to a boil. Stir in carrots, celery, and noodles; reduce heat, cover, and boil gently just until carrots are barely tender to bite (about 10 minutes).

3 Stir in chicken, zucchini, and tomato; heat until steaming. Garnish with parsley.

makes 6 servings

per serving: 276 calories, 29 g protein, 24 g carbohydrates, 7 g total fat, 91 mg cholesterol, 955 mg sodium

garlic soup with ravioli

preparation time: about 55 minutes

1 head garlic

1 teaspoon salad oil

6 cups low-sodium chicken broth

1 package (about 9 oz.) fresh low fat or regular cheese ravioli or tortellini

3 tablespoons each finely chopped red bell pepper and green onions

1/4 teaspoon Asian sesame oil (optional)

Cilantro

1 Peel garlic; thinly slice cloves. Heat salad oil in a nonstick frying pan over medium-low heat. Add garlic and cook, stirring often, until golden brown (about 10 minutes; do not scorch); if pan appears dry or garlic sticks to pan bottom, stir in water, 1 tablespoon at a time. Meanwhile, bring broth to a boil in a 4- to 5-quart pan over high heat. When garlic is done, pour about 1/2 cup of the broth into frying pan, stirring to loosen browned bits. Return garlic mixture to broth; reduce heat, cover, and simmer for 15 minutes.

2 Increase heat to high and bring to a boil. Separating any ravioli that are stuck together, add pasta to broth. Reduce heat and boil gently, stirring occasionally, just until pasta is tender to bite (4 to 6 minutes; or according to package directions).

3 Add bell pepper, onions, and, if desired, sesame oil and cook just until heated through (about 2 minutes). Garnish with cilantro.

makes 6 servings

per serving: 164 calories, 10 g protein, 23 g carbohydrates, 6 g total fat, 26 mg cholesterol, 268 mg sodium

pozole

preparation time: about 2 hours

1 pound pork tenderloin, trimmed of fat and silvery membrane and cut into 1 1/2-inch chunks

1 pound skinless, boneless chicken or turkey thighs, cut into 1 1/2-inch chunks

3 quarts low-sodium chicken broth

2 large onions, cut unto chunks

1 teaspoon dry oregano

1/2 teaspoon cumin seeds

2 cans (about 14 oz. *each*) yellow hominy, drained

Salt and pepper

Lime slices or wedges

1 1/2 cups crisp corn tortilla strips

1 Place pork and chicken in a 6- to 8-quart pan. Add broth, onions, oregano, and cumin seeds to pan. Bring to a boil over high heat; then reduce heat, cover, and simmer until meat is tender when pierced (about 1 1/2 hours). Lift out meat with a slotted spoors; place in a bowl to cool.

2 Pour cooking broth into a strainer set over a bowl. Press residue to remove liquid; discard residue. Return broth to pan and bring to a boil over high heat.

3 Add hominy and reduce heat; simmer, uncovered, until flavors are blended (about 10 minutes). Coarsely shred meat and return to broth. Serve soup hot or warm. If made ahead, let cool; then cover and refrigerate until next day. Reheat before serving.

4 To serve, ladle into bowls. Season to taste with salt and pepper and serve with lime slices and tortilla strips.

makes 8 to 10 servings

per serving: 265 calories, 27 g protein, 25 g carbohydrates, 8 g total fat. 75 mg cholesterol. 429 mg sodium

golden tomato-papaya gazpacho

preparation time: 20 minutes
chilling time: at least 2 hours

2 pounds ripe yellow regular or cherry tomatoes

1 large ripe papaya, peeled, seeded, and diced

1 cup diced cucumber

1/4 cup minced onion

2 tablespoons white wine vinegar

2 cups low sodium chicken broth

2 tablespoons minced fresh basil

1/8 teaspoon liquid hot pepper seasoning

Salt

Basil sprigs

1 Dice tomatoes; place in a large nonmetal bowl. Stir in papaya, cucumber, onion, vinegar, broth, minced basil, and hot pepper seasoning. Season to taste with salt.

2 Cover and refrigerate until cold (at least 2 hours) or until next day. Garnish with basil sprigs.

makes 10 to 12 servings

per serving: 37 calories, 2 g protein, 8 g carbohydrates, 0.7 g total fat, 0 mg cholesterol, 30 mg sodium

sherried lentil bisque

preparation time: about 1 1/2 hours

2 packages (about 12 oz. *each*, about 3 1/2 cups *total*) lentils

11 cups vegetable broth

3 cups chopped celery

3 cups chopped carrots

3 large onions, chopped

1 small red or green bell pepper, seeded and finely chopped

1 medium-size zucchini, finely chopped

3 tablespoons dry sherry

4 1/2 teaspoons cream sherry

1 cup reduced-fat sour cream

Thinly sliced green onions

Salt and pepper

1 Sort through lentils, discarding any debris. Rinse and drain lentils; place in an 8- to 10-quart pan and add broth, celery, carrots, chopped onions, bell pepper, and zucchini. Bring to a boil over high heat; then reduce heat, cover, and simmer until lentils are very soft to bite (about 50 minutes).

2 In a food processor or blender, whirl hot lentil mixture, a portion at a time, until smoothly puréed. Return purée to pan and stir in dry sherry and cream sherry. If made ahead, let cool; then cover and refrigerate until next day.

3 To serve, stir soup often aver medium-high heat until steaming; ladle into bowls. Top with sour cream and green onions; season to taste with salt and pepper.

makes 12 servings

per servings: 293 calories, 19 g protein, 47 g carbohydrates, 4 g total fat, 7 mg cholesterol, 959 mg sodium

mexican beef & pork birria

preparation time: about 2 1/2 hours

1 pound boneless beef top round, trimmed of fat

1/2 pound lean boneless pork, trimmed of fat

1 medium-size onion, thinly sliced

1 medium-size carrot, coarsely shredded

2 cloves garlic, minced or pressed

3 tablespoons chili powder

1 teaspoon *each* ground cumin and salad oil

4 cups water

2 cans (14 1/2 oz. *each*) regular-strength beef broth

Salt

About 1/2 cup sliced green onions (including tops)

1 large lime, cut into 6 wedges

1 Cut beef and pork into 1-inch cubes. In a 3 1/2- to 4-quart pan, combine meat with onion, carrot, garlic, chili powder, cumin, oil, and 1/2 cup of the water. Cover and simmer over medium-low heat for 30 minutes.

2 Uncover; increase heat to medium and cook, stirring often, until liquid has evaporated (20 to 25 minutes). Add 1 cup more of the water, stirring to loosen any browned bits in pan. Blend in remaining 2 1/2 cups water and beef broth. Bring to a boil; then cover, reduce heat, and simmer until meat is very tender (about 1 1/2 hours). Skim and discard surface fat, if necessary. Season to taste with salt. Garnish with green onions and lime.

makes 6 servings

per serving: 207 calories, 28 g protein, 7 g carbohydrates, 36 g total fat, 67 mg cholesterol, 608 mg sodium

golden pepper bisque

preparation time: about 1 hour

Garlic croutons

2 large yellow bell peppers

1 tablespoon salad oil or olive oil

1 large onion, chopped

2 large thin-skinned potatoes, peeled and cut into 1/2-inch chunks

2 large carrots, cut into 1/2-inch slices

1 large stalk celery, thinly sliced

6 cups low-sodium chicken broth

Extra-virgin olive oil

Salt and pepper

Shredded cotija or Parmesan cheese

1 Prepare garlic croutons; set aside.

2 Cut bell peppers in half lengthwise. Set halves, cut side down, in a 10- by 15 inch rimmed baking pan. Broil 4 to 6 inches below heat until charred all over (about 8 minutes). Cover with foil and let cool in pan. Remove and discard skins, stems, and seeds; cut peppers into chunks.

3 In a 5- to 6-quart pan, combine salad oil and onion. Cook over medium-high heat, stirring occasionally, until onion is lightly browned (about 10 minutes). Add roasted bell peppers, potatoes, carrots, celery, and broth, bring to a boil; then reduce heat, cover, and simmer until carrots are very soft to bite (20 to 25 minutes).

4 In a blender or food processor, whirl vegetable mixture, a portion at a time, until smoothly puréed. If made ahead, let cool; then cover and refrigerate until next day. Reheat, covered, before serving.

5 To serve, ladle soup into wide bowls. Add olive oil, salt, pepper, cheese, and garlic croutons to taste.

makes 6 to 8 serving.

per serving: 132 calories, 5 g protein, 23 g carbohydrates, 4 g total fat, 0 mg cholesterol, 126 mg sodium

peas & lettuce in mint broth

preparation time: about 40 minutes

4 cups low-sodium chicken broth

1 1/4 cups firmly packed fresh mint leaves

Peel (colored part only) pared from 1 medium-size lemon

2 cups frozen tiny peas

1 teaspoon lemon juice

1 tablespoon slivered fresh mint

1 teaspoon shredded lemon peel

4 butter lettuce leaves, rinsed and crisped

1 In a 2- to 3-quart pan, combine broth, the 1 1/4 cups mint leaves, and peel of 1 lemon. Bring to a boil over high heat. Cover, remove from heat, and let stand for at least 15 minutes to allow mint to flavor broth (or refrigerate for up to 1 day). With a slotted spoon, remove mint from broth; discard mint and lemon peel.

2 Return broth to a boil over high heat. Add peas and stir until hot (1 to 2 minutes). Stir in lemon juice. Pour broth through a strainer equally into each of 4 wide, shallow bowls. Quickly mix peas with slivered mint and shredded lemon peel. Place a lettuce leaf in each bowl; spoon pea mixture into leaves, dividing equally. Eat with a knife, fork, and spoon.

makes 4 servings

per serving: 100 calories, 7 g protein, 14 g carbohydrates, 2 g total fat, 0 mg cholesterol, 181 mg sodium

fresh tomato soup with homemade pasta

preparation time: about 1 ¼ hours

1 tablespoon salad oil

2 large onions, chopped

3 pounds firm-ripe tomatoes (about 6 large), peeled, seeded, and chopped

3 cups low-sodium chicken broth

1 can (about 8 oz.) tomato sauce

1 tablespoon chopped fresh oregano or 1 teaspoon dried oregano

½ teaspoon ground cumin

4 ounces egg pasta cut for fettuccine, or purchased fresh fettuccine

2 tablespoons dry sherry (or to taste)

Oregano sprigs

Freshly grated Parmesan cheese

Salt and pepper

1 Heat oil in a 4- to 5- quart pan over medium-high heat. Add onions and cook, stirring often, until soft (about 10 minutes); if pan appears dry or onions stick to pan bottom, stir in water, 1 tablespoon at a time.

2 Add tomatoes, broth, tomato sauce, chopped oregano, and cumin. Bring to a boil; reduce heat, cover, and simmer until tomatoes are soft (about 15 minutes).

3 Remove 4 cups of the mixture and whirl in a blender or food processor, a portion at a time, until puréed. Return to pan, bring to a boil over high heat. Meanwhile, cut pasta into 3-inch lengths.

4 Stir in pasta; reduce heat, cover, and boil gently just until pasta is tender to bite (1 to 3 minutes; or according to package directions).

5 Remove pan from heat and add sherry. Ladle soup into bowls. Garnish with oregano sprigs. Offer cheese, salt, and pepper to add to taste.

makes 6 servings

per serving: 172 calories, 6 g protein, 29 g carbohydrates, 5 g total fat, 19 mg cholesterol, 313 mg sodium

roasted eggplant soup

preparation time: about 1 ½ hours

1 large eggplant

1 small onion

3 cups low-sodium chicken broth

2 tablespoons lemon juice

Pepper

12 thin red bell pepper strips

4 teaspoons finely chopped parsley

1 Pierce eggplant in several places with a fork; then place eggplant and unpeeled onion in a small, shallow baking pan. Bake in a 350° oven until vegetables are very soft when squeezed (about 1 ¼ hours). Let stand until cool enough to handle. (At this point, you may cover and refrigerate for up to 8 hours.)

2 Peel eggplant and onion; then transfer to a food processor or blender and add ½ cup of the broth. Whirl until puréed. Add remaining 2 ½ cups broth and whirl until blended. Pour into a 2- to 3-quart pan and bring to a boil over high heat, stirring occasionally. Remove from heat; stir in lemon juice and season to taste with pepper.

3 To serve, ladle soup into 4 bowls; top each serving with 3 bell pepper strips and 1 teaspoon of the parsley.

makes 4 servings

per serving: 79 calories, 4 g protein, 15 g carbohydrates, 1 g total fat, 0 mg cholesterol, 49 mg sodium

roasted vegetable and cheese soup

preparation time: 55 minutes

2 medium-size leeks

1 large ear corn, husk and silk removed

1 small red onion, cut in half

1 large red bell pepper

1 large yellow or green bell pepper

2 cloves garlic, peeled

4 cups fat free reduced-sodium chicken broth

1 cup shredded reduced-fat sharp Cheddar cheese

½ cup nonfat sour cream

1 Trim and discard roots and tough tops from leeks; remove and discard coarse outer leaves. Split leeks lengthwise; thoroughly rinse leek halves between layers. In a large, shallow baking pan, arrange leeks, corn, onion halves, and whole bell peppers.

2 Broil 4 to 6 inches below heat, turning vegetables as needed to brown evenly, for 10 minutes. Add garlic. Continue to broil, turning as needed, until vegetables are well charred (about 5 more minutes); remove vegetables from pan as they are charred. Cover vegetables loosely with foil and let stand until cool enough to handle (about 10 minutes).

3 With a sharp knife, cut corn kernels from cob. Remove and discard skins, seeds, and stems from bell peppers. Coarsely chop peppers, leeks, onion, and garlic.

4 In a 4- to 5-quart pan, combine vegetables and broth. Bring to a boil over high heat; then reduce heat, cover, and simmer for 10 minutes to blend flavors. Ladle soup into individual bowls; sprinkle with cheese, top with sour cream, and serve.

makes 4 servings

per serving: 231 calories, 18 g protein, 30 g carbohydrates, 8 g total fat, 30 mg cholesterol; 901 mg sodium

spinach & buttermilk soup

preparation time: about 20 minutes

1 package (about 10 oz.) frozen chopped spinach

4 cups low-sodium chicken broth

2 tablespoons grated lemon peel

2 tablespoons cornstarch

2 cups lowfat buttermilk

Salt and pepper

1 In a 3- to 4-quart pan, combine spinach and 2 cups of the broth. Bring to a boil over high heat, using a spoon to break spinach apart. As soon as you have broken spinach into chunks, pour broth-spinach mixture into a food processor or blender; add 2 tablespoon of the lemon peel and whirl until smoothly puréed.

2 In pan, mix remaining 2 cups broth with cornstarch until smooth; add spinach mixture. Bring to a boil over high heat, sharing often. Stir in buttermilk, season to taste with salt and pepper, and serve at once. (Do not heat soup after adding buttermilk; the color will change for the worse.)

3 To serve, pour soup into bowls or mugs; sprinkle with remaining 1 tablespoon lemon peel.

makes 4 servings

per serving: 114 calories, 8 g protein, 14 g carbohydrates, 3 g total fat, 5 mg cholesterol, 235 mg sodium

white gazpacho

preparation time: about 15 minutes
chilling time: at least 2 hours

1 cucumber, peeled and coarsely chopped

2 cups plain nonfat yogurt

2 tablespoons lemon juice

1 clove garlic, peeled

2 cups low sodium chicken broth

2 tablespoons minced cilantro

2 tablespoons sliced green onion

Thin cucumber slices

Thinly slivered green onion tops

1 In a blender or food processor, whirl chopped cucumber, yogurt, lemon juice, and garlic until puréed (if using a blender, add about ½ cup of the broth). Pour into a 2-quart container and stir in broth.

2 Cover and refrigerate until cold (at least 2 hours). Then stir in cilantro and sliced onion.

3 Pour mixture into a nonmetal serving bowl or pitcher. To serve, ladle or pour into bowls or glasses; garnish with cucumber slices and slivered onion.

makes 4 servings

per serving: 100 calories, 9 g protein, 15 g carbohydrates, 2 g total fat, 2 mg cholesterol, 155 mg sodium

garden gazpacho

preparation time: about 30 minutes
chilling time: at least 1 hour

1 large cucumber

2 large tomatoes, peeled, seeded, and chopped

1 large red or green bell pepper, seeded and chopped

1/3 cup sliced ripe olives

1/4 cup lime juice

4 cups low-sodium chicken broth or spicy tomato cocktail

1 clove garlic, minced or pressed

1/2 cup thinly sliced green onions

1 tablespoon minced fresh thyme or 2 teaspoons dry thyme.

Liquid hot pepper seasoning

Lime wedges

1 Peel cucumber and cut in half lengthwise; scoop out and discard seeds. Chop cucumber; place in a large bowl and add tomatoes, bell pepper, olives, lime juice, broth, garlic, onions, and thyme. Stir well; season to taste with hot pepper seasoning. Cover and refrigerate until cold (at least 1 hour) or for up to 1 day.

2 To serve, stir gazpacho well. Ladle into bowls and serve with lime wedges.

makes 8 servings

per serving: 47 calories, 2 g protein, 7 g carbohydrates, 2 g total fat, 0 mg cholesterol, 84 mg sodium

leek soup with brie

preparation time: about 1 1/4 hours

Toasted French Bread (recipe follows)

6 to 9 large leeks

2 tablespoons butter or margarine

8 ounces mushrooms, thinly sliced

1 clove garlic, minced or pressed

1/2 teaspoon dry tarragon

1/4 teaspoon ground white pepper

2 1/2 tablespoons unbleached all-purpose flour

1 quart homemade or canned vegetable broth

1/3 cup whipping cream

6 ounces Brie cheese

1 Prepare Toasted French Bread.

2 Cut off and discard root ends of leeks. Trim tops, leaving about 3 inches of green leaves. Discard coarse outer leaves. Split leeks in half lengthwise and rinse well. Thinly slice (you should have about 2 quarts).

3 Melt butter in a 4- to 5-quart pan over medium heat. Add leeks, mushrooms, garlic, tarragon, and pepper. Cook, stirring occasionally, until vegetables are very soft and most of the liquid has evaporated (about 15 minutes).

4 Add flour and cook, stirring, until bubbly. Remove from heat and gradually stir in broth and cream. Return to heat and bring to a boil, stirring constantly.

5 Ladle soup into 6 heatproof 1 1/2- to 2-cup soup bowls. Top each serving with a piece of Toasted French Bread buttered side up.

6 Slice Brie 1/2 inch thick; place a cheese slice on each toast slice. Bake in a 425° oven until bubbly (about 10 minutes). Then broil about 6 inches below heat until lightly browned (1 to 2 minutes).

makes 6 servings

TOASTED FRENCH BREAD

Cut 6 slices (each about 1/2 inch thick) from a loaf of French bread. Arrange slices in a single layer on a baking sheet. Bake in a 325° oven until dry (20 to 25 minutes). Spread one side with butter or margarine, using 1/2 teaspoon for each slice. (At this point, you may wrap in foil and let stand at room temperature for up to a day.)

per serving: 357 calories, 11 g protein, 37 g carbohydrates, 20 g total fat , 59 mg cholesterol, 1,048 mg sodium

cream beet borscht

preparation time: 10 minutes

2 cans (about 15 oz. *each*) pickled beets

About 4 cups plain nonfat yogurt

1 cup vegetable broth

Dill sprigs

Pepper

1 Drain beets, reserving 1 1/2 cups of the liquid. In a large bowl, combine beets, reserved liquid, 4 cups of the yogurt, and broth. In a food processor or blender, whirl beet mixture, about a third at a time, until smoothly puréed. If made ahead, cover and refrigerate until next day.

2 Serve borscht cool or cold. To serve, ladle into wide bowls. Add yogurt to taste and garnish with dill sprigs. Season to taste with pepper.

makes 6 to 8 servings

per serving: 113 calories, 8 g protein, 19 g carbohydrates, 0.5 g total fat, 3 mg cholesterol, 582 mg sodium

ruote & meatball soup

preparation time: about 1 hour

Herbed Meatballs (recipe follows)

14 cups fat-free reduced-sodium chicken broth

1/3 cup reduced-sodium soy sauce

1/3 cup lightly packed brown sugar

3 tablespoons smooth peanut butter

1/4 cup distilled white vinegar (or to taste)

10 ounces (about 4 1/2 cups) dried ruote or other medium-size pasta shape

12 ounces spinach (about 3 cups lightly packed), coarse stems removed, rinsed, and drained

1/2 cup chopped red bell pepper

1 teaspoon Asian sesame oil (or to taste)

Cilantro

Crushed red pepper flakes

1 Prepare Herbed Meatballs.

2 Combine broth, soy sauce, sugar, peanut butter, and vinegar in a 6- to 8-quart pan. Bring to a boil over high heat, stirring occasionally with a whisk. Stir in meatballs and pasta; reduce heat and boil gently just until pasta is tender to bite (8 to 10 minutes; or according to package directions).

3 Add spinach and bell pepper. Cook just until heated through (about 3 minutes). Add sesame oil and ladle into bowls. Garnish with cilantro. Offer pepper flakes to add to taste.

makes 8 to 10 servings

HERBED MEATBALLS

In a large bowl, combine 1 pound fresh ground turkey breast, 1/2 cup cooked couscous, 1/4 cup all-purpose flour, 1/4 cup water, and 1/2 teaspoon ground coriander or dried basil. Mix well. Shape into 1- to 1 1/2-inch balls. Place balls slightly apart in a lightly oiled 10- by 15-inch baking pan. Bake in a 450° oven until well browned (about 15 minutes). Pour off any fat. Keep warm.

per serving: 276 calories, 20 g protein, 40 g carbohydrates, 5 g total fat, 29 mg cholesterol, 444 mg sodium

leek & green onion chowder

preparation time: about 50 minutes

3 pounds leeks

1 tablespoon butter or margarine

2 tablespoons all-purpose flour

1/2 teaspoon ground white pepper

6 cups low-sodium chicken broth

3 cups thinly sliced green onions

3 tablespoons lemon juice

Salt

Thin lemon slices

Reduced-fat sour cream

1 Trim ends and all but 3 inches of green tops from leeks; remove tough outer leaves. Split leeks lengthwise; rinse well, then thinly slice crosswise.

2 Melt butter in a 5- to 6-quart pan over medium-high heat. Add leeks; cook, stirring often, until soft (8 to 10 minutes). Stir in flour and white pepper; then stir in broth, bring to a boil over high heat, stirring. Add onions, cook, stirring, just until onions turn bright green (about 2 minutes). Stir in lemon juice and season to taste with salt.

3 To serve, ladle soup into bowls. Garnish each serving with lemon slices and a dollop of sour cream.

makes 6 servings

per serving: 136 calories, 5 g protein, 22 g carbohydrates, 4 g total fat, 5 mg cholesterol, 102 mg sodium

minestrone genovese

preparation time: about 1 hour

Pesto (recipe follows)

2 large leeks

12 cups fat-free reduced-sodium chicken broth

2 large carrots, thinly sliced

2 large stalks celery, thinly sliced

2 cans (about 15 oz. *each*) cannellini (white kidney beans), drained

10 ounces (about 2 1/2 cups) dried medium-size elbow macaroni

3/4 pound yellow crookneck squash or zucchini, cut into 1/2-inch chunks

1 large red bell pepper, seeded and cut into 1/2-inch pieces

2 packages (about 10 oz. *each*) frozen tiny peas

Basil sprigs

Salt and pepper

1 Prepare Pesto.

2 Cut off and discard root ends and green tops of leeks. Discard coarse outer leaves. Split leeks in half lengthwise and rinse well; thinly slice crosswise.

3 Combine leeks, broth, carrots, and celery in an 8- to 10-quart pan. Bring to a boil over high heat; reduce heat, cover, and simmer for 10 minutes.

4 Stir in beans, pasta, squash, and bell pepper; cover and simmer just until pasta is tender to bite (about 10 more minutes).

4 Add peas and bring to a boil. Stir in 1/2 cup of the Pesto into soup. Serve hot or at room temperature if made ahead, let cool and then cover and refrigerate for up to a day; bring to room temperature or reheat before serving. Garnish with basil. Offer salt, pepper, and remaining Pesto to add to taste.

makes 12 servings

PESTO

In a food processor or blender, combine 2 cups lightly packed fresh basil, 1 cup freshly grated Parmesan cheese, 1/4 cup olive oil, 2 tablespoons pine nuts or slivered almonds, and 1 or 2 cloves garlic. Whirl until smooth. Season to taste with salt. If made ahead, cover and refrigerate for up to a day.

makes 1 cup

per serving: 322 calories, 17 g protein, 46 g carbohydrates, 9 g total fat, 5 mg cholesterol, 957 mg sodium

homemade chicken broth

preparation time: about 20 minutes
cooking time: about 3 hours
chilling time: at least 4 hours

5 pounds bony chicken pieces

2 large onions, cut into chunks

2 large carrots, cut into chunks

6 to 8 parsley sprigs

1/2 teaspoon whole black peppercorns

1 Rinse chicken and place in a 6- to 8-quart pan. Add onions, carrots, parsley sprigs, peppercorns, and 3 1/2 quarts water. Bring to a boil over high heat; then reduce heat, cover, and simmer for 3 hours. Let cool.

2 Pour broth through a fine strainer into a bowl; discard residue. Cover broth; refrigerate for at least 4 hours or up to 2 days. Lift off and discard fat. To store, freeze in 1- to 4-cup portions.

makes about 10 cups

per cup: Due to variations in ingredients and cooking time, precise nutritional data is not available. The nutritional value of this broth is similar to that of canned low-sodium chicken broth.

creamy garbanzo soup with barley

preparation time: about 1 hour

2 tablespoons salad oil

1 medium-size onion, chopped

1/3 cup pearl barley

1 teaspoon cumin seeds

5 cups low-sodium chicken broth

2 cans (about 15 1/2 oz. *each*) garbanzo beans, drained and rinsed

1/4 cup sesame seeds

6 green onions (including tops), thinly sliced

1 Heat 1 tablespoon of the oil in a 5- to 6-quart pan over medium-high heat. Add chopped onion, barley, and cumin. Cook, stirring often, until barley is opaque and onion is soft (about 5 minutes).

2 Add chicken broth and bring to a boil; reduce heat, cover, and simmer until barley is tender (about 25 minutes). Add beans; cover and simmer until hot (about 10 minutes). Pour half the bean mixture into a blender; whirl until puréed. Return to pan.

3 Meanwhile, heat remaining oil in a small frying pan over medium-high heat. Add sesame seeds and cook, stirring often, until golden (about 4 minutes). Add green onions and cook, stirring, until bright green (about 1 minute). Ladle soup into bowls and offer with sesame mixture.

makes 6 servings

per serving: 322 calories, 12 g protein, 46 g carbohydrates, 11 g total fat, 0 mg cholesterol, 485 mg sodium

tomato & roasted pepper gazpacho

preparation time: about 25 minutes
chilling time: at least 2 hours

3 medium-size red bell peppers

1 1/2 cups low-sodium chicken broth

1/4 cup lime juice

3 green onions, thinly sliced

3 medium-size firm-ripe pear-shaped (Rome- type) tomatoes, diced

1 *each* small yellow and green bell pepper, seeded and diced

Salt and pepper

1 Cut red bell peppers in half lengthwise. Set halves, cut side down, in a 10- by 15-inch rimmed baking pan. Broil 4 to 6 inches below heat until charred all over (about 8 minutes). Cover with foil and let cool in pan. Remove and discard skins, stems, and seeds.

2 In a food processor or blender, whirl roasted peppers, broth, and lime juice until smoothly puréed. Stir in onions, tomatoes, and yellow and green bell peppers; season to taste with salt and pepper.

3 Cover and refrigerate until cold (at least 2 hours) or until next day.

makes 4 servings

per serving: 75 calories, 3 g protein, 16 g carbohydrates, 1 g total fat, 0 mg cholesterol, 56 mg sodium

vegetable soup with couscous

preparation time: about 1 1/2 hours

1 tablespoon olive oil

2 ounces pancetta or bacon, chopped

2 cloves garlic, minced or pressed

1 large onion, chopped

8 cups low-sodium chicken broth

1 large russet potato, peeled and diced

2 tablespoons chopped fresh mint or
   1 tablespoon dried mint

1/2 teaspoon dried oregano

1/4 teaspoon mashed red pepper flakes
   (or to taste)

2 cans (about 15 oz. *each*) garbanzo beans,
   drained

1 1/2 pounds pear-shaped (Roma-type) tomatoes,
   diced

5 ounces (about 3/4 cup) dried couscous

1 pound escarole, ends trimmed, cut into
   3-inch slivers

Freshly grated Parmesan cheese

Salt and pepper

1 Heat oil in a 5- to 6-quart pan over medium-high heat (omit oil if using bacon). Add pancetta browned (about 5 minutes). Add garlic and onion; cook, stirring, until onion is soft (about 5 more minutes). Drain off fat.

2 Add broth, potato, mint, oregano, and red pepper flakes. Bring to a boil; reduce heat, cover, and simmer for 30 minutes.

3 Add beans and tomatoes; return to a boil. Stir in pasta; reduce heat, cover, and summer just until pasta is tender to bite (about 5 minutes).

4 Stir in escarole and cook just until wilted (about 1 minute). Serve hot or at room temperature, if made ahead, let cool and then cover and refrigerate for up to a day; bring to room temperature or reheat before serving.

5 Offer cheese, salt, and pepper to add to taste.

makes 6 to 8 servings

per serving: 298 calories, 14 g protein, 44 g carbohydrates, 10 g total fat, 5 mg cholesterol, 347 mg sodium

double pea soup

preparation time: about 1 hour

2 pounds dried yellow or green split peas

1 tablespoon butter or margarine

4 cloves garlic, minced

10 cups low-sodium chicken broth

1 package (about 10 oz.) frozen tiny peas

Salt and pepper

1 Rinse and sort split peas, discarding any debris. Drain peas; set aside.

2 Melt butter in a 5- to 6-quart pan over medium-high heat; add garlic and cook, stirring, until golden (about 2 minutes). Add split peas and broth; increase heat to high. Bring broth to a boil; then reduce heat, cover, and simmer until split peas are very tender to bite (about 45 minutes). Add frozen peas and continue to simmer, stirring often, until heated through (about 5 more minutes). Season to taste with salt and pepper.

makes 8 servings

per serving: 463 calories, 32 g protein, 75 g carbohydrates, 5 g total fat, 4 mg cholesterol, 146 mg sodium

curried corn shrimp soup

preparation time: about 45 minutes

chilling time: at least 3 hours

2 cups low-sodium chicken broth

2 large tart apples, peeled, cored, and chopped

1 large onion, chopped

1/2 teaspoon curry powder

1 large red bell pepper

4 cups cold buttermilk

1/4 cup lime juice

1 1/2 cups cooked yellow or white corn kernels
(from 2 medium-size ears corn); or
1 package (about 10 oz.) frozen corn kernels,
drained

1/2 cup minced cilantro

1/3 pound tiny cooked shrimp

Cilantro sprigs

1 In a 4- to 5-quart pan, combine broth, apples, onion and curry powder. Bring to a boil over high heat; then reduce heat, cover, and simmer until apples mash easily (about 30 minutes).

2 Let cool; then cover and refrigerate until cold (at least 3 hours) or until next day. Pour mixture into a blender or food processor and whirl until smoothly puréed.

3 Seed bell pepper and cut a few thin slivers from it; set slivers aside. Dice remaining pepper. Put diced pepper in a tureen and stir in apple-onion purée, buttermilk, lime juice, 1 1/4 cups of the corn, and minced cilantro. (At this point, you may cover and refrigerate soup, pepper slivers, and remaining 1/4 cup corn until next day.)

4 To serve, ladle soup into bowls and top equally with shrimp, remaining corn, bell pepper slivers, and cilantro sprigs.

makes 6 servings

per serving: 211 calories, 14 g protein, 36 g carbohydrates, 3 g total fat, 55 mg cholesterol, 277 mg sodium

red onion borscht

preparation time: about 1 hour

1 1/2 tablespoons salad oil

2 1/2 to 3 pounds red onions, thinly sliced

1/2 cup red wine vinegar

2 medium-size beets, peeled and shredded

2 1/2 tablespoons all-purpose flour

6 cups low-sodium chicken broth

1/3 cup port

Salt and pepper

Reduced fat sour cream (optional)

1 Heat oil in a 5- to 6-quart pan over medium-low heat. Reserve several onion slices for garnish; then add remaining onions to pan along with vinegar and beets. Cook, stirring often, until onions are very soft but not browned (25 to 30 minutes). Add flour and stir until bubbly. Remove pan from heat and gradually stir in broth. (At this point, you may cover and refrigerate for up to 2 days.)

2 Return soup to medium heat and bring to a boil, stirring occasionally; then reduce heat and simmer for 10 minutes. Stir in port. Season to taste with salt and pepper.

3 To serve, ladle soup into bowls. Garnish each serving with a dollop of sour cream, if desired, and a few of the reserved onion slices.

makes 8 servings

per serving: 144 calories, 5 g protein, 21 g carbohydrates, 4 g total fat, 0 mg cholesterol, 73 mg sodium

hot & sour tofu soup

preparation time: 55 minutes

8 medium-size dried shiitake mushrooms

1 teaspoons salad oil

1 clove garlic, minced or pressed

1 tablespoon minced fresh ginger

10 cups fat-free reduced-sodium chicken broth

4 ounces dried linguine, broken into 3-inch pieces

1 pound regular reduced-fat tofu, rinsed and
   drained, cut into 1/2-inch cubes

3 tablespoons seasoned rice vinegar; or
   3 tablespoons distilled white vinegar and
   2 teaspoons sugar (or to taste)

5 teaspoons reduced-sodium soy sauce
   (or to taste)

3 tablespoons cornstarch mixed with
   1/4 cup water

4 green onions, thinly sliced

Chili oil

1 Soak mushrooms in boiling water to cover until soft (about 20 minutes). Drain; cut off and discard coarse stems. Cut caps into thin strips; Set aside.

2 Heat salad oil in a 5- to 6-quart pan over medium heat. Add garlic and ginger. Cook, stirring, until garlic is light golden (about 2 minutes); if pan appears dry or garlic sticks to pan bottom, stir in water, 1 tablespoon (15 ml) at a time. Add broth and mushrooms; bring to a boil over high heat. Stir in pasta; reduce heat, cover, and boil gently just until pasta is tender to bite (8 to 10 minutes; or according to package directions).

3 Add tofu, vinegar, and soy sauce. Stir cornstarch mixture; add to soup, stirring until smooth. Cook over medium-high heat, stirring, just until soup comes to a boil and thickens slightly. Add onions; ladle into bowls. offer chili oil to add to taste.

makes 6 to 8 servings

per serving: 151 calories, 12 g protein, 22 g carbohydrates, 2 g total fat, 0 mg cholesterol, 1,248 mg sodium

cantaloupe-tangerine soup

preparation time: about 10 minutes

1 large cantaloupe, chilled

1 small can (about 6 oz.) frozen tangerine or
   orange juice concentrate, partially thawed

Mint sprigs

1 Cut cantaloupe in half; scoop out and discard seeds. Scoop fruit from rind and place in a food processor or blender; add tangerine juice concentrate and whirl until smoothly puréed. If made ahead, cover and refrigerate for up to 1 day; whirl again to blend before serving.

2 To serve, pour soup into bowls and garnish with mint sprigs.

makes 4 servings

per serving: 146 calories, 2 g protein, 35 g carbohydrates, 0.7 g total fat, 0 mg cholesterol, 17 mg sodium

tomato fava soup

preparation time: 55 minutes

2 tablespoons olive oil

1 large onion, chopped

1 1/2 pounds ripe tomatoes, quartered

2 tablespoons finely chopped fresh savory or
  1 teaspoon dried savory

3/4 teaspoon sugar

1/4 teaspoon pepper

2 cups shelled fava beans; see Note

4 cups fat-free reduced-sodium chicken broth

1 Heat oil in a 3- to 4-quart pan over medium-high heat. Add onion and cook, stirring often, until it begins to brown (5 to 10 minutes). Add tomatoes, savory, sugar, and pepper. Bring to a boil; then reduce heat and simmer, uncovered, until tomatoes are very soft when pressed (about 15 minutes).

2 Meanwhile, in a 2- to 3-quart pan, bring 4 cups water to a boil over high heat. Add beans and simmer, uncovered, until just tender when pierced (3 to 5 minutes). Drain, then let stand until cool enough to touch. With your fingers, slip skins from beans; discard skins and set beans aside.

3 In a food processor or blender, whirl tomato mixture until coarsely puréed. Return to pan and add broth; stir over high heat until hot. Ladle soup into individual bowls; sprinkle beans equally over each serving.

makes 6 servings

per serving: 261 calories, 17 g protein, 39 g carbohydrates, 6 g total fat, 0 mg cholesterol, 447 mg sodium

Note: A few people, typically of Mediterranean descent, have a severe allergic reaction to fava beans and their pollen. If favas are new to you, check your family history before eating them.

warm-up vegetable soup

preparation time: about 1 hour

1 tablespoon olive oil or salad oil

1 medium-size onion, finely chopped

8 ounces mushrooms, thinly sliced

1 teaspoon *each* dry oregano, dry basil, and
  dry marjoram

6 cups low-sodium chicken broth

1 medium-size thin-skinned potato, peeled and
  cut into 1/2-inch cubes

1 pound banana squash, peeled and cut into
  1/2-inch cubes

3/4 cup dry small shell-shaped pasta

1 cup diced pear-shaped (Roma-type) tomatoes

Salt and pepper

1 Heat oil in a 5- to 6-quart pan over medium heat. Add onion, mushrooms, oregano, basil, and marjoram. Cook, stirring often, until vegetables are tinged with brown (about 10 minutes). Stir in broth, potato, and squash. Bring to a boil; reduce heat, cover, and boil gently until potato is tender to bite (about 15 minutes).

2 Add pasta, cover, and continue to cook until pasta is just tender to bite (10 to 12 minutes). Stir in tomatoes; simmer until heated through (about 2 minutes). Season to taste with salt and pepper.

makes 6 servings

per serving: 171 calories, 7 g protein, 27 g carbohydrates, 5 g total fat, 0 mg cholesterol, 65 mg sodium

squash & yam soup with prosciutto

preparation time: about 1 hour

1 ³/4 pounds butternut or other yellow-fleshed squash, peeled, seeded, and cut into 1-inch chunks

1 ³/4 pounds yams or sweet potatoes, peeled and cut into 1-inch chunks

7 cups low-sodium chicken broth

¹/4 cup balsamic vinegar

2 tablespoons firmly packed brown sugar

1 tablespoon minced fresh ginger

¹/4 to ¹/2 teaspoon crushed red pepper flakes

1 tablespoon butter or margarine

6 ounces thinly sliced prosciutto, cut into thin slivers

1 In a 5- to 6-quart pan, combine squash, yams, broth, vinegar, sugar, ginger, and red pepper flakes. Bring to a boil over high heat; then reduce heat, cover, and simmer gently until squash and yams are soft enough to mash easily (about 30 minutes).

2 In a food processor or blender, whirl vegetable broth mixture, a portion at a time, until smoothly puréed. Return to pan; cook over high heat, stirring often, until steaming (about 5 minutes).

3 Meanwhile, melt butter in a wide frying pan over medium-high heat. Add prosciutto and cook, stirring often, until lightly browned and crisp (6 to 8 minutes). Drain prosciutto well on paper towels.

4 To serve, ladle soup into bowls; top with prosciutto.

makes 6 to 8 servings

per serving: 276 calories, 12 g protein, 44 g carbohydrates, 7 g total fat, 24 mg cholesterol, 533 mg sodium

tortellini & chicken soup

preparation time: about 25 minutes

3 large cans (about 49 ¹/2 oz. *each*) chicken broth; or 4 ¹/2 quarts homemade chicken broth

1 package (about 9 oz.) fresh cheese-filled spinach tortellini

1 pound spinach, stems removed, leaves rinsed and coarsely chopped

1 pound boneless, skinless chicken breasts, cut into ¹/2-inch chunks

8 ounces mushrooms, sliced

1 medium-size red bell pepper, seeded and diced

1 cup cooked rice

2 teaspoons dry tarragon

Salt and pepper

Grated Parmesan cheese

1 In an 8- to 10-quart pan, bring broth to a boil over high heat. Add tortellini; reduce heat and boil gently, uncovered, until just tender to bite (about 6 minutes).

2 Add spinach, chicken, mushrooms, bell pepper, rice, and tarragon to broth; return to a boil over high heat. Then reduce heat, cover, and simmer until chicken is no longer pink in center; cut to test (about 2 minutes). Season soup to taste with salt and pepper; serve with cheese to add to taste.

makes 10 to 12 servings

per serving: 200 calories, 20 g protein, 21 g carbohydrates, 4 g total fat, 37 mg cholesterol, 1,824 mg sodium

chard soup with beans & orzo

preparation time: about 1 1/2 hours

1 pound pear-shaped (Roma-type) tomatoes

2 tablespoons olive oil

1 large onion, chopped

1 clove garlic, minced or pressed

2 medium-size stalks celery, diced

2 ounces thinly sliced prosciutto or cooked ham, slivered

12 cups beef broth

2 large carrots, diced

1 tablespoon minced fresh rosemary or
   1 teaspoon dried rosemary

1 pound Swiss chard, coarse stems removed

3 cans (about 15 oz. *each*) pinto beans, drained and rinsed

8 ounces green beans, cut into 1-inch lengths

1 pound zucchini, cut into 3/4-inch chunks

4 ounces (about 2/3 cup) dried orzo or other rice-shaped pasta

Freshly grated Parmesan cheese

Salt and pepper

1 Bring 4 cups water to a boil in an 8- to 10-quart pan over high heat. Drop tomatoes into water and cook for 1 minute. Lift out; peel and discard skin. Chop tomatoes and set aside. Discard water.

2 Heat oil in pan over medium-high heat. Add onion, garlic, celery, and prosciutto. Cook, stirring often, until onion is soft (5 to 8 minutes). Add broth, carrots, and rosemary. Bring to a boil; reduce heat, cover, and simmer for 10 minutes. Meanwhile, cut chard crosswise into 1/2-inch strips. Mash 1 can of the pinto beans.

3 Add mashed and whole pinto beans, green beans, zucchini, and tomatoes to pan; stir well. Cover and simmer for 5 more minutes.

4 Stir in chard and pasta; simmer, uncovered, just until pasta is tender to bite (about 10 more minutes). Serve hot or at room temperature. If made ahead, let cool and then cover and refrigerate for up to a day; bring to room temperature or reheat before serving.

5 Offer cheese, salt, and pepper to add to taste.

makes 10 to 12 servings

per serving: 210 calories, 11 g protein, 30 g carbohydrates, 5 g total fat, 4 mg cholesterol, 2,179 mg sodium

STORING HOMEMADE SOUP:

goulash soup

preparation time: about 2 ½ hours

1 pound boneless beef round tip, trimmed of fat

2 medium-size onions, finely chopped

1 clove garlic, minced or pressed

1 teaspoon salad oil

1 tablespoon sweet Hungarian paprika

½ teaspoon dry marjoram leaves

5 cups water

2 tablespoons all-purpose flour

3 beef bouillon cubes

2 small thin-skinned potatoes, cut into ½-inch cubes

1 medium-size red bell pepper, seeded and finely chopped

Salt and white pepper

¼ cup chopped parsley

1 Cut beef into ½-inch cubes. In a 3 ½- to 4-quart pan, combine beef, onions, garlic, oil, paprika, marjoram, and ½ cup of the water. Cover and simmer over medium-low heat for 30 minutes. Uncover and increase heat to medium; cook, stirring often, until liquid has evaporated and onions are browned (20 to 25 minutes).

2 Stir in flour until smoothly blended. Add 1 cup more of the water and bouillon cubes, stirring to dissolve bouillon and loosen any browned bits in pan. Gradually blend in remaining 3 ½ cups water and bring to a boil. Add potatoes and bell pepper. Reduce heat, cover, and simmer, stirring occasionally, until meat is very tender (1 to 1 ½ hours). Skim and discard surface fat, if necessary. Season to taste with salt and pepper. Stir in parsley.

makes 4 servings

per serving: 264 calories, 27 g protein, 24 g carbohydrates, 6 g total fat, 68 mg cholesterol, 664 mg sodium

caribbean corn chowder

preparation time: about 30 minutes

1 tablespoon salad oil

1 large onion, finely chopped

1 large red bell pepper, seeded and chopped

3 large fresh green Anaheim or other large mild chiles, seeded and chopped

5 ½ cups low-sodium chicken broth

2 tablespoons minced fresh tarragon or 1 teaspoon dry tarragon

¼ teaspoon pepper

5 large ears corns, husks and silk removed

Tarragon sprigs (optional)

1 Heat oil in a 5- to 6-quart pan over medium-high heat. Add onion, bell pepper, and chiles. Cook, stirring often, until onion is soft (about 5 minutes). Add broth, minced tarragon, and pepper; bring to a boil. Meanwhile, cut corn kernels from cobs.

2 Add corn to boiling broth mixture. Reduce heat, cover, and simmer until corn is hot (about 5 minutes). If made ahead, let cool; then cover and refrigerate for up to 1 day. Serve hot or cool.

3 To serve, ladle soup into bowls; garnish with tarragon sprigs, if desired.

makes 6 servings

per serving: 165 calories, 6 g protein, 28 g carbohydrates, 5 g total fat, 0 mg cholesterol, 67 mg sodium

harvest turkey soup

preparation time: about 1 hour

Vegetable oil cooking spray

1 pound ground skinless turkey

1 medium-size onion, chopped

1 teaspoon dry oregano

1 teaspoon Italian herb seasoning; or ¼ teaspoon *each* dry basil, dry marjoram, dry oregano, and dry thyme

3 large firm-ripe tomatoes, chopped

3 large carrots, thinly sliced

1 large potato, peeled and diced

6 cups beef broth

1 cup *each* tomato juice and dry red wine

1 tablespoon Worcestershire

½ cup dry tiny pasta bow ties (tripolini) or other small shapes

2 medium-size zucchini, coarsely diced

Liquid hot pepper seasoning

1 Coat a wide 4- to 5-quart pan with cooking spray. Crumble turkey into pan; add onion, oregano, and herb seasoning. Cook over medium heat, stirring often, until turkey is no longer pink and onion is soft but not browned (about 5 minutes). Stir in tomatoes, carrots, potato, broth, tomato juice, wine, and Worcestershire. Increase heat to medium-high and bring to a boil; then reduce heat, cover, and boil gently for 20 minutes.

2 Add pasta; cover and cook for 5 minutes. Stir in zucchini and boil gently, uncovered, until pasta and zucchini are just tender to bite (8 to 10 minutes). Season to taste with hot pepper seasoning.

makes 6 to 8 servings

per serving: 241 calories, 18 g protein, 29 g carbohydrates, 7 g total fat, 47 mg cholesterol, 949 mg sodium

cold cucumber & dill bisque

preparation time: about 15 minutes

2 large cucumbers, peeled

1 cup low-sodium chicken broth

1 cup plain lowfat yogurt

¼ cup lightly packed chopped fresh dill

3 tablespoons lime juice

½ pound small cooked shrimp

Dill sprigs (optional)

1 Cut cucumbers into 1 ½-inch chunks. Place in a blender or food processor with chicken broth; whirl until puréed. Add yogurt, chopped dill, and lime juice; whirl until blended. (For a smoother texture, rub bisque through a fine sieve.)

2 Ladle into bowls and top with shrimp. Garnish with dill sprigs, if desired.

makes 4 servings

per serving: 132 calories, 17 g protein, 12 g carbohydrates, 2 g total fat, 114 mg cholesterol, 196 mg sodium

curried fish chowder

preparation time: about 50 minutes

1 tablespoon margarine

1 large onion, chopped

2 tablespoons minced fresh ginger

1 clove garlic, minced or pressed

1 1/2 tablespoons curry powder

6 cups regular-strength chicken broth or chicken-vegetable stock

1 pound thin-skinned potatoes, unpeeled, cut into 1/2-inch cubes

1/2 pound carrots, cut into 1/2-inch cubes

3 strips (*each* 1/2 by 4 inches) lemon peel (yellow part only)

2 small dried hot red chiles

1 pound rockfish fillets, cut into 1/2-inch cubes

1/4 cup thinly sliced green onions (including tops)

1 cup nonfat plain yogurt

1 lemon, cut into wedges

1 Melt margarine in a 5- to 6-quart pan over medium-high heat. Add chopped onion, ginger, and garlic; cook, stirring occasionally, until onion is soft (about 7 minutes). Add curry powder; stir for 2 minutes. Add broth, potatoes, carrots, lemon peel, and chiles; bring to a boil over high heat. Reduce heat, cover, and simmer until potatoes are tender when pierced (about 20 minutes).

2 Add fish. Cover and simmer until fish is opaque (about 2 minutes). If desired, remove and discard chiles. Ladle soup into a tureen and sprinkle with green onions; top with yogurt. Serve with lemon wedges.

makes 4 to 6 servings

per serving: 246 calories, 21 g protein, 28 g carbohydrates, 6 g total fat, 29 mg cholesterol, 1,120 mg sodium

sausage-barley soup with swiss chard

preparation time: about 1 1/2 hours

1 pound turkey kielbasa, cut into 1/4-inch-thick slices

1 large onion, chopped

2 large carrots, thinly sliced

10 cups beef broth

1 cup pearl barley, rinsed and drained

1 tablespoon minced fresh oregano or 1 teaspoon dry oregano

8 ounces Swiss chard

Prepared horseradish and Dijon mustard

1 In a 5- to 6-quart pan, combine sausage, onion, and carrots. Cook over medium heat, stirring often, until sausage and vegetables are lightly browned (about 15 minutes). Discard any fat from pan.

2 To pan, add broth, barley, and oregano. Bring to a boil; then reduce heat, cover, and simmer until barley is tender to bite— about 30 minutes. (At this point, you may let cool, then cover and refrigerate for up to 1 day. Reheat before continuing.)

3 Trim and discard stem ends from chard; rinse chard well, then coarsely chop and stir into soup. Simmer, uncovered, until chard stems are tender-crisp to bite (6 to 8 minutes). Serve soup with horseradish and mustard to add to taste.

makes 6 servings

per serving: 298 calories, 21 g protein, 37 g carbohydrates, 8 g total fat, 52 mg cholesterol, 2,134 mg sodium

black & white bean soup

preparation time: about 45 minutes

1 large onion, chopped

1 clove garlic, peeled and sliced

3 ½ cups vegetable broth

⅓ cup oil-packed dried tomatoes, drained and finely chopped

4 green onions, thinly sliced

¼ cup dry sherry

2 cans (about 15 oz. *each*) black beans, drained and rinsed well

2 cans (about 15 oz. *each*) cannellini (white kidney beans), drained and rinsed

Slivered green onions (optional)

1 In a 5- to 6-quart pan, combine chopped onion, garlic, and ½ cup water. Cook over medium-high heat, stirring often, until liquid evaporates and browned bits stick to pan bottom (about 10 minutes). To deglaze pan, add 2 tablespoons of the broth, stirring to loosen browned bits from pan; continue to cook until browned bits form again. Repeat deglazing step, using 2 tablespoons more broth. Then stir in ½ cup more broth and pour mixture into a food processor or blender.

2 In same pan, combine tomatoes and sliced green onions. Cook over high heat, stirring, until onions are wilted (about 2 minutes). Add sherry and stir until liquid has evaporated. Remove from heat.

3 To onion mixture in food processor, add black beans. Whirl, gradually adding 1 ¼ cups of the broth, until smoothly puréed. Pour into a 3- to 4-quart pan.

4 Rinse processor; add cannellini and whirl until smoothly puréed, gradually adding remaining 1 ½ cups broth. Stir puréed cannellini into pan with tomato mixture. Place both pans of soup over medium-high heat and cook, stirring often, until steaming.

5 To serve, pour soup into 6 wide 1 ½- to 2-cup bowls as follows. From pans (or from 2 lipped containers such as 4-cup pitchers, which are easier to handle), pour soups simultaneously into opposite sides of each bowl so that soups flow together but do not mix. Garnish with slivered green onions, if desired.

makes 6 servings

per serving: 283 calories, 14 g protein, 38 g carbohydrates, 8 g total fat, 0 mg cholesterol, 996 mg sodium

cool scallop soup

preparation time: about 20 minutes
chilling time: at least 4 hours

1 pound bay or sea scallops

2/3 cup lemon juice

About 1 3/4 pounds cucumbers

1/3 cup firmly packed watercress sprigs

1/3 cup thinly sliced green onions

1 cup plain low-fat yogurt

Salt

2 medium-size pear-shaped (Roma-type) tomatoes, seeded and diced

1 Rinse scallops and pat dry. If using sea scallops, cut them into ½-inch pieces. Place scallops in a nonmetal bowl, add lemon juice, and stir to combine.

2 Cover and refrigerate, stirring occasionally, for at least 4 hours or up to 1 day. With a slotted spoon, lift out scallops, reserving lemon juice. Cover scallops and return to refrigerator.

3 Cut off a third of one of the cucumbers; score its skin lengthwise with a fork, then thinly slice. Set cucumber slices aside. Also reserve 4 of the watercress sprigs.

4 Coarsely chop remaining cucumbers. Place in a food processor or blender with reserved lemon juice, remaining watercress sprigs, onions, and yogurt; whirl until smooth. Season purée to taste with salt.

5 Drain scallops, reserving any liquid; stir liquid into cucumber purée. To serve, pour purée into bowls; add scallops, tomatoes, and reserved cucumber slices to each serving. Garnish with reserved watercress sprigs.

makes 4 servings

per serving: 181 calories, 24 g protein, 18 g carbohydrates, 2 g total fat, 41 mg cholesterol, 241 mg sodium

chinese chicken & shrimp soup

preparation time: about 20 minutes

5 cups low-sodium chicken broth

2 tablespoons finely chopped fresh ginger

2 to 3 teaspoons reduced-sodium soy sauce

12 ounces boneless, skinless chicken breasts, cut into 1/2-inch cubes

6 ounces mushrooms, sliced

3 cups thinly sliced bok choy

1 cup cubed firm tofu (about 1/2-inch cubes)

1/2 cup sliced green onions

8 ounces small cooked shrimp

1/4 cup chopped cilantro

Ground red pepper (cayenne) or chili oil (optional)

1 In a 4- to 5-quart pan, combine broth, ginger, and soy sauce; bring to a boil over high heat. Add chicken, mushrooms, bok choy, tofu, and onions. Reduce heat, cover, and simmer until chicken is no longer pink in center; cut to test (about 2 minutes).

2 Remove pan from heat and stir in shrimp and cilantro. Season to taste with red pepper, if desired.

makes 4 to 6 servings

per serving: 244 calories, 37 g protein, 8 g carbohydrates, 7 g total fat, 128 mg cholesterol, 409 mg sodium

faux-fresh tomato soup

preparation time: about 1 ¼ hours

Herbed Cheese Croutons (recipe follows)

1 teaspoon olive oil

1 medium-size onion, chopped

1 large carrot, chopped

5 cups, low-sodium chicken broth

1 can (about 15 oz.) tomato purée

3 tablespoons dry basil or ⅓ cup chopped
   fresh basil

¾ teaspoon sugar

½ teaspoon ground white pepper

1 Prepare Herbed Cheese Croutons and set aside.

2 In a 3- to 4-quart pan, combine oil, onion, carrot, and 1 cup of the broth. Bring to a boil over high heat; then boil, uncovered, stirring occasionally, until liquid evaporates and vegetables began to brown (about 10 minutes). To deglaze, add 3 tablespoons water and stir to scrape browned bits free. Then continue to cook, stirring occasionally, until mixture begins to brown again. Repeat deglazing and browning steps about 2 more times, using 3 table-spoons water each time; vegetable mixture should be golden brown.

3 Add remaining 4 cups broth. Stir to scrape browned bits free. Stir in tomato purée, basil, sugar, and white pepper. Bring to a boil over high heat; then reduce heat, cover, and simmer until vegetables are very tender to bite (about 20 minutes). Whirl mixture, a portion at a time, in a food processor or blender until smoothly puréed. Return purée to pan; bring to a simmer over medium heat.

4 To serve, ladle soup into bowls; top each serving with 2 croutons. Accompany with remaining croutons.

makes 4 servings

HERBED CHEESE CROUTONS

Slice 1 small French bread baguette (about 8 oz.) crosswise into ¼-inch-thick slices. Sprinkle slices with 2 tablespoons grated Romano or Parmesan cheese; then sprinkle lightly with about 1 teaspoon dry basil and about ¼ teaspoon coarse salt. Place bread slices in a single layer on large baking sheets. Bake in a 300° oven until toasted and golden brown (about 20 minutes), switching positions of baking sheets after 20 minutes. Serve croutons warm or at room temperature.

per serving: 297 calories, 12 g protein, 51 g carbohydrates, 6 g total fat, 3 mg cholesterol, 968 mg sodium

potato, cauliflower & watercress soup

preparation time: about 1 hour

1 ¹/₂ cups cauliflower flowerets, cut into bite-size
   pieces

2 ¹/₂ cups nonfat milk

2 tablespoons butter or margarine

¹/₂ cup slivered shallots

¹/₈ teaspoon ground nutmeg

2 large russet potatoes, peeled and diced

1 ³/₄ cups low-sodium chicken broth

8 cups lightly packed watercress sprigs

Salt and ground white pepper

¹/₄ to ¹/₃ cup plain low-fat yogurt or reduced-fat
   sour cream

1 In a 2- to 3-quart pan, combine cauliflower and milk. Bring to a boil over medium heat; then reduce heat to medium-low and cook until cauliflower is tender when pierced (8 to 10 minutes). Place a strainer over a large bowl and pour cauliflower mixture through it; then set cauliflower and milk aside.

2 Rinse pan; set over medium heat and add butter. When butter is melted, add shallots and nutmeg; cook, stirring occasionally, until shallots are soft but not browned (3 to 5 minutes). Add potatoes and broth; increase heat to medium-high and bring to a boil. Reduce heat, cover, and simmer until potatoes are very tender when pierced (15 to 20 minutes). Reserve several watercress sprigs for garnish, then stir remaining watercress into potato mixture and cook, uncovered, for 5 minutes. Add cauliflower to pan and cook until heated through (about 3 minutes).

3 In a food processor or blender, whirl potato mixture, a portion at a time, until smooth. Return to pan, add reserved strained milk, and heat just until steaming (do not boil). Season to taste with salt and white pepper.

4 To serve, ladle soup into bowls. Garnish each serving with a dollop of yogurt and a watercress sprig.

makes 4 to 6 servings

per serving: 195 calories, 10 g protein, 27 g carbohydrates, 6 g total fat, 16 mg cholesterol, 179 mg sodium

beef stock

preparation time: about 45 minutes
cooking time: about 2 ¹/₂ hours
chilling time: at least 4 hours

4 pounds beef and veal shanks, cut up

2 carrots, cut into chunks

2 medium-size onions, quartered

2 stalks celery, cut into pieces (include leaves)

1 dry bay leaf

2 cloves garlic, peeled

2 whole cloves

6 whole black peppercorns

¹/₄ teaspoon dry thyme

1 Place meat in a roasting pan and bake in a 450° oven until browned (20 to 25 minutes). Transfer to a 6-to 8-quart pan. Add 1 cup water to roasting pan and stir to scrape browned bits free; then pour over beef along with 11 more cups water. Add carrots, onions, celery, bay leaf, garlic, cloves, peppercorns, and thyme.

2 Bring to a boil over high heat; reduce heat, cover, and simmer until meat falls from bones (about 2 ¹/₂ hours). Let cool.

3 Pour stock through a fine strainer into a bowl; discard residue. Cover stock; refrigerate for at least 4 hours or up to 2 days. Lift off and discard fat. To store, freeze in 1- to 4-cup portions.

makes about 3 quarts

per cup: Due to variations in ingredients and cooking time, precise nutritional data is not available. The nutritional value of this broth is similar to that of canned beef broth, but the homemade version is lower in sodium.

winter minestrone

preparation time: about 20 minutes
cooking time: about 1 hour and 5 minutes

2 tablespoons olive oil

1 large onion, finely chopped

1 large celery stalk, finely chopped

2 large cloves garlic, minced or pressed

1 teaspoon dry basil leaves

$^1/_2$ teaspoon *each* dry rosemary, dry oregano
  leaves, and dry thyme leaves

$^1/_4$ cup pearl barley

2 large thin-skinned potatoes, diced

3 large carrots, diced

8 cups low-sodium chicken broth

1 large turnip, peeled and diced

1 can (about 15 oz.) cannellini (white kidney beans)
  or red kidney beans, drained and rinsed

$^2/_3$ cup small shell pasta or elbow macaroni

$^1/_4$ cup tomato paste

2 cups finely shredded green cabbage

Grated Parmesan cheese

1 Heat oil in a 5- to 6-quart pan over medium-high heat. Add onion, celery, garlic, basil, rosemary, oregano, and thyme. Cook, stirring, until onion is soft (about 5 minutes). Add barley, potatoes, carrots, and chicken broth; bring to a boil over high heat. Reduce heat, cover, and simmer for 20 minutes. Add turnip. Cover and simmer for 20 more minutes.

2 Stir in beans, pasta, and tomato paste. Bring to a boil over high heat; reduce heat, cover, and simmer until pasta is al dente (about 15 minutes). Add cabbage and simmer, uncovered, until tender-crisp (about 5 more minutes). Ladle into bowls and offer with Parmesan.

makes 8 to 10 servings

per serving: 241 calories, 9 g protein, 41 g carbohydrates, 5 g total fat, 0 mg cholesterol, 314 mg sodium

SOUP GARNISHES ADD PIZZAZZ:

jamaican black bean & rice soup

preparation time: about 15 minutes
cooking time: about 2 1/4 hours

1 pound (about 2 1/2 cups) dried black beans

6 cups water

4 cups low-sodium chicken broth

2 tablespoons salad oil

1 large onion, finely chopped

5 cloves garlic, minced or pressed

1 1/2 teaspoons *each* ground cumin and dry oregano leaves

1 1/2 cups cooked brown rice

2 tablespoons red wine vinegar

Salt

1 cup plain lowfat yogurt

4 green onions (including tops), thinly sliced

6 radishes, thinly sliced

Lime or lemon wedges

1 Rinse beans and sort through, discarding any debris; drain well. Place in a 4- to 5-quart pan with water and bring to a boil over high heat. Reduce heat, cover, and simmer until beans swell, absorbing most of the water (about 45 minutes). Add chicken broth. Cover and simmer until beans are tender (about 1 1/2 more hours).

2 Meanwhile, heat oil in a small frying pan over medium heat. Add chopped onion, garlic, cumin, and oregano and cook, stirring, until onion is limp (about 7 minutes). Set aside.

3 In a blender or food processor, whirl about 2 cups of the beans and a little of the broth until smooth; return to bean mixture. Stir in onion mixture, rice, and vinegar; season to taste with salt. Cook over medium heat until steaming.

4 Ladle into bowls and offer with yogurt, green onions, radishes, and lime.

makes 8 to 10 servings

per serving: 280 calories, 15 g protein, 45 g carbohydrates, 5 g total fat, 2 mg cholesterol, 46 mg sodium

fish pot-au-feu

preparation time: about 45 minutes

5 cups low-sodium chicken broth

1 cup dry white wine; or 1 cup low-sodium chicken broth plus 3 tablespoons white wine vinegar

1/2 teaspoon dry tarragon

4 small red thin-skinned potatoes, scrubbed

4 medium-size carrots, cut into halves

4 medium-size leeks

1 1/2 pounds firm-textured white-fleshed fish fillets such as lingcod or sea bass

1 In a 5- to 6-quart pan, combine broth, wine, and tarragon; bring to a boil over high heat. Add potatoes and carrots; return to a boil. Then reduce heat, cover, and boil gently for 10 minutes.

2 Meanwhile, trim ends and all but 3 inches of green tops from leeks; remove tough outer leaves. Split leeks lengthwise; rinse well. Add leeks to pan, cover, and boil gently until leeks and potatoes are tender when pierced (about 10 more minutes). Lift leeks from broth with a slotted spoon, cover, and keep warm.

3 Rinse fish and pat dry; then cut into 4 equal portions. Add fish to soup, cover, and simmer until carrots are tender when pierced and fish is just opaque but still moist in thickest part; cut to test (7 to 10 minutes).

3 With a slotted spatula, carefully lift fish from pan and arrange in 4 wide, shallow bowls. Evenly distribute vegetables alongside fish and ladle broth over all.

makes 4 servings

per serving: 316 calories, 36 g protein, 32 g carbohydrates, 4 g total fat, 89 mg cholesterol, 219 mg sodium

winter vegetable lentil chowder

preparation time: about 1 1/2 hours

10 cups low-sodium chicken broth

1 teaspoon *each* whole white peppercorns and coriander seeds

1/2 teaspoon whole allspice

3 strips lemon peel (yellow part only; *each* about 1/2 by 3 inches)

1 cup lentils, rinsed and drained

3 medium-size leeks (about 1 lb. total)

1 1/2 pounds banana squash, peeled and cut into 1/2-inch cubes

12 ounces Swiss chard

Salt and pepper

1 In a 5- to 6-quart pan, combine broth, white peppercorns, coriander seeds, allspice, and lemon peel. Bring to a boil over high heat; then reduce heat, cover, and simmer until flavors are blended (20 to 30 minutes). Remove and discard lemon peel. Add lentils to broth; cover and simmer for 15 minutes.

2 Trim ends and all but 3 inches of green tops from leeks; remove tough outer leaves. Split leeks lengthwise; rinse well, then thinly slice crosswise.

3 Add leeks and squash to lentil mixture. Cover; simmer until squash is tender to bite (about 15 minutes). Trim and discard stem ends from chard; rinse chard well, drain, and cut crosswise into 1/4-inch-wide strips. Add chard to broth; simmer, uncovered, until wilted (about 5 minutes). Season to taste with salt and pepper.

makes 6 servings

per serving: 221 calories, 16 g protein, 34 g carbohydrates, 3 g total fat, 0 mg cholesterol, 215 mg sodium

beef & pumpkin soup

preparation time: about 1 1/4 hours

1 tablespoon salad oil

1 large onion, chopped

1 stalk celery, thinly sliced

8 cups low-sodium chicken broth

8 ounces boneless beef chuck, trimmed of fat and cut into 1/2-inch cubes

3 1/2 pounds Hubbard or banana squash, peeled, seeded, and cut into 1/2-inch cubes (you should have about 10 cups)

2 large carrots, coarsely chopped

8 ounces spinach, stems removed, leaves rinsed and cut crosswise into 1/4-inch-wide strips

Salt and pepper

1 Heat oil in a 6- to 8-quart pan over medium-high heat. Add onion and celery; cook, stirring often, until onion is soft (about 5 minutes). Add broth and beef. Bring to a boil; then reduce heat, cover, and simmer for 30 minutes. Add squash and carrots. Bring to a boil; then reduce heat, cover, and simmer until squash and beef are very tender when pierced (about 15 more minutes).

2 With a slotted spoon, lift about three-fourths of the squash from pan; mash coarsely. Return mashed squash to pan, then stir in spinach. Bring to a boil over high heat; then reduce heat and simmer, uncovered, until spinach is wilted (about 3 minutes). Skim and discard fat from soup, if necessary; season soup to taste with salt and pepper.

makes 6 to 8 servings

per serving: 183 calories, 14 g protein, 21 g carbohydrates, 6 g total fat, 19 mg cholesterol, 127 mg sodium

split pea & lamb soup

preparation time: about 30 minutes
cooking time: about 1 ¾ hours

12 ounces dried green or yellow split peas

4 cups thinly sliced celery

1 large onion, chopped

8 ounces boneless lamb shoulder or neck, trimmed of fat and cut into ½-inch chunks

2 cloves garlic, minced

1 large dry bay leaf

About 7 cups low-sodium chicken broth

1 Rinse and sort peas, discarding any debris; then drain peas and set aside.

2 In a 5- to 6-quart pan, combine celery, onion, lamb, garlic, bay leaf, and ½ cup water. Cover and boil gently over medium-high heat for 10 minutes. Then uncover and continue to cook, stirring often, until liquid evaporates and vegetables and meat begin to brown. To deglaze, add ⅓ cup water and stir to scrape browned bits free. Then continue to cook, stirring occasionally, until mixture begins to brown again. Repeat deglazing and browning steps several more times, using about ⅓ cup water each time; mixture should be richly browned (about 30 minutes total).

3 To pan, add split peas and 7 cups of the broth; bring to a boil over high heat. Reduce heat, cover, and simmer until peas are very tender to bite (about 1 hour). Remove and discard bay leaf. (At this point, you may let cool, then cover and refrigerate for up to 1 day. Reheat before continuing.)

4 Transfer 3 cups of the soup (but no meat) to a food processor or blender. Whirl until smoothly puréed; return to pan. If desired, thin soup with a little more broth. Stir over high heat until steaming.

makes 4 to 6 servings

per serving: 375 calories, 30 g protein, 51 g carbohydrates, 6 g total fat, 30 mg cholesterol, 202 mg sodium

spiced cream of pumpkin soup

preparation time: about 1 hour

3 large leeks

1 tablespoon olive oil or salad oil

½ cup currants

½ pound carrots, thinly sliced

3 cups regular-strength chicken broth or chicken-vegetable stock

2 cups nonfat milk

1 can (1 lb.) solid-pack pumpkin

¼ teaspoon ground nutmeg

Toasted pumpkin seeds

1 Trim ends and all but 3 inches of green tops from leeks; remove tough outer leaves. Split leeks lengthwise; rinse well, then thinly slice crosswise. Set aside.

2 Heat oil in a 3- to 4-quart pan over medium heat; add currants and stir until puffed (about 2 minutes). Lift from pan with a slotted spoon; set aside. Add leeks and carrots to pan; stir often until leeks are golden (about 10 minutes). Add 1 cup of the broth; bring to a boil, then reduce heat, cover and simmer until carrots are very tender to bite (about 10 minutes).

3 In a blender or food processor, whirl leek mixture until smooth. Return to pan and add remaining 2 cups broth, milk, pumpkin, and nutmeg. Cook over medium heat, stirring often, until soup is hot (about 15 minutes). Stir in currants. Offer pumpkin seeds to add to taste.

makes 6 servings

per serving: 165 calories, 6 g protein, 29 g carbohydrates, 4 g total fat, 2 mg cholesterol, 570 mg sodium

lamb meatball & lentil soup

preparation time: about 45 minutes
cooking time: about 1 1/2 hours

Olive oil cooking spray

1 large onion, finely chopped

2 cups plus 2 tablespoons water

2 cloves garlic, minced or pressed

1 teaspoon *each* dry thyme and ground cumin

1/4 teaspoon whole allspice

1 dry bay leaf

1 cinnamon stick (about 3 inches long)

1 cup finely chopped celery

2 medium-size carrots, thinly sliced

1 1/2 cups lentils, rinsed and drained

1 can (about 15 oz.) tomato purée

6 cups low-sodium chicken broth

Lamb Meatballs (recipe follows)

4 cups coarsely shredded spinach

Salt and pepper

1 Coat a 5- to 6-quart pan with cooking spray. Add onion and 2 tablespoons of the water. Cook over medium heat, stirring often, until onion is soft but not browned (about 5 minutes). Stir in garlic, thyme, cumin, allspice, bay leaf, cinnamon stick, celery, and carrots. Add lentils, tomato purée, broth, and remaining 2 cups water. Bring to a boil over high heat; then reduce heat, cover, and boil gently until lentils and vegetables are very tender to bite (about 1 hour).

2 Meanwhile, prepare Lamb Meatballs.

3 Add Lamb Meatballs to soup. Cover, increase heat to medium, and simmer until meatballs are cooked through; cut into one meatball to test (about 20 minutes). Stir in spinach and continue to cook, uncovered, just until spinach is wilted and bright green (2 to 3 minutes). Remove and discard bay leaf and cinnamon stick. Skim and discard fat from soup, if necessary. Season to taste with salt and pepper.

makes 6 servings

LAMB MEATBALLS

In a medium-size bowl, beat 1 large egg white (about 2 tablespoons) slightly. Mix in 1/4 cup finely chopped onion, 12 ounces ground lamb loin or leg, 1/4 teaspoon each pepper and ground cinnamon, 1/2 teaspoon salt, and 3 tablespoons chopped parsley. Shape mixture into 1-inch balls. Arrange meatballs in a single layer, cover, and refrigerate until ready to use.

per serving: 351 calories, 31 g protein, 46 g carbohydrates, 6 g total fat, 37 mg cholesterol, 629 mg sodium

SOUP SERVING IDEAS: Though the classic soup server is a lidded tureen, any handsome pot, bowl, or casserole will do if the size is appropriate. For a small, pourable soup, a pitcher is a handy dispenser.

chicken, shiitake & bok choy soup

preparation time: about 1 hour

Ginger-Garlic Paste (recipe follows)

1 1/2 tablespoons Asian sesame oil or salad oil

5 to 6 ounces fresh shiitake or regular mushrooms, thinly sliced

8 green onions, sliced

3 cups low-sodium chicken broth

4 boneless, skinless chicken breast halves (about 1 1/2 lbs. *total*)

2 large carrots, cut into thin slanting slices

8 baby bok choy, coarse outer leaves removed

2 cups hot cooked short- or medium-grain rice

3 tablespoons minced cilantro

1 Prepare Ginger-Garlic Paste and set aside.

2 Heat oil in a 4- to 5-quart pan over medium heat. Add mushrooms and half the onions; cook, stirring often, until mushrooms are lightly browned (about 10 minutes). Add broth and stir to scrape browned bits free. Cover pan and bring broth to a boil over high heat.

3 Rinse chicken; pat dry. Add chicken and carrots to boiling broth, making sure meat and vegetables are covered with liquid. Reduce heat to low, cover, and simmer until meat in thickest part of chicken breasts is no longer pink; cut to test (about 15 minutes).

4 Lift chicken to a cutting board. Add bok choy and remaining onions to pan; cover and simmer over medium heat until bok choy is bright green and just tender when pierced (about 5 minutes). Meanwhile, cut chicken across the grain into 1/2-inch-wide slanting slices.

5 Place a 1/2-cup scoop of rice off center in each of 4 wide, shallow soup bowls. Arrange a sliced chicken breast around each mound of rice. With a slotted spoon, distribute vegetables evenly among bowls. Stir cilantro into broth; then gently pour broth into bowls over chicken and vegetables. Offer Ginger-Garlic Paste to stir into soup to taste.

makes 4 servings

GINGER-GARLIC PASTE

In a blender or food processor, combine 3/4 cup coarsely chopped fresh ginger, 3 cloves garlic (peeled), and 3 tablespoons seasoned rice vinegar (or 3 tablespoons distilled white vinegar plus 1 tablespoon sugar). Whirl until very smooth. Spoon into a small bowl. If made ahead, cover and refrigerate for up to 4 hours.

makes about 1/2 cup.

per serving of soup: 441 calories, 47 g protein, 9 g total fat, 42 g carbohydrates, 99 mg cholesterol, 230 mg sodium

per teaspoon of ginger-garlic paste: 4 calories, 0.1 g protein, 0.9 g carbohydrates, 0 g total fat, 0 mg cholesterol, 38 mg sodium

pistou soup with split peas

preparation time: about 35 minutes
cooking time: about 1 1/2 hours

1 pound large leeks

2 tablespoons olive oil

1 cup chopped carrots

1/8 to 1/4 teaspoon ground red pepper (cayenne)

2 medium-size thin-skinned potatoes, peeled and diced

2/3 cup green split peas, rinsed and drained

1 1/2 quarts homemade or canned vegetable broth

1 1/2 quarts water

Pistou (recipe follows)

1 cup frozen cut green beans

2/3 cup 2-inch pieces dry spaghetti

Grated Parmesan cheese (optional)

1 Cut off and discard root ends of leeks. Trim tops, leaving about 3 inches of green leaves. Discard coarse outer leaves. Split leeks in half lengthwise and rinse well. Thinly slice.

2 Heat oil in a 6- to 8-quart pan over medium heat. Stir in leeks, carrots, and ground red pepper. Cook, stirring often, until leeks are soft but not browned (6 to 8 minutes).

3 Stir in potatoes, split peas, broth, and water. Bring to a boil; reduce heat, cover, and simmer until peas are tender to bite (about 1 hour). Meanwhile, prepare Pistou.

4 Stir beans, spaghetti, and Pistou into soup. Increase heat to medium-high and boil gently, uncovered, until spaghetti is just tender to bite (8 to 10 minutes). Serve with cheese to add to taste, if desired.

makes 6 to 8 servings

PISTOU

In a medium-size bowl, combine 4 cloves garlic, minced or pressed; 1 can (about 6 oz.) tomato paste; 3/4 cup grated Parmesan cheese; 1/4 cup minced parsley; 1 1/2 tablespoons dry basil; and 1/4 cup olive oil. Stir well.

per serving: 359 calories, 13 g protein, 44 g carbohydrates, 16 g total fat, 7 mg cholesterol, 1,241 mg sodium

spirited cherry soup

preparation time: about 25 minutes

4 cups pitted light or dark sweet cherries (or use some of each)

3 1/2 cups white grape juice

2 teaspoons grated lemon peel

2 tablespoons lemon juice

3 tablespoons orange-flavored liqueur or 1 1/2 teaspoons grated orange peel

Mint sprigs and thin strips of orange peel (optional)

1 Divide cherries among 4 bowls.

2 In a 2- to 3-quart pan, combine grape juice and lemon peel; bring to a boil over high heat. Stir in lemon juice and liqueur; then pour juice mixture equally over cherries. Garnish each serving with mint sprigs and orange peel, if desired.

makes 4 servings

per serving: 278 calories, 2 g protein, 63 g carbohydrates, 1 g total fat, 0 mg cholesterol, 79 mg sodium

citrus chicken soup

preparation time: about 1 ½ hours

4 chicken breast halves (about 2 lbs. *total*)

6 cups low-sodium chicken broth

1 medium-size onion, finely chopped

1 can (about 14 ½ oz.) diced tomatoes

1 teaspoon grated lemon peel

½ teaspoon dry oregano

¼ teaspoon pepper

2 medium-size thin-skinned potatoes, scrubbed and diced

1 medium-size ear corn

⅓ cup coarsely chopped cilantro

2 medium-size fresh red or green Anaheim or other large mild chiles, seeded and finely chopped

1 small firm-ripe avocado

2 tablespoons lime juice

Lime wedges

1 Rinse chicken, pat dry, and place in a 5- to 6-quart pan. Add broth, onion, tomatoes, lemon peel, oregano, and pepper; bring to a boil over medium-high heat. Then reduce heat, cover, and simmer until meat in thickest part of chicken breasts is no longer pink; cut to test (about 25 minutes). Lift out chicken and set aside until cool enough to handle.

2 While chicken is cooling, add potatoes to pan; cover and cook over medium-low heat until tender when pierced (about 25 minutes). Meanwhile, remove and discard skin and bones from chicken; tear meat into bite-size pieces and set aside.

3 Remove and discard husk and silk from corn; cut corn kernels from cob.

4 Skim and discard fat from soup. Add chicken, corn, cilantro, and chiles. Cook just until meat and vegetables are heated through (3 to 5 minutes). Pit, peel, and dice avocado; mix gently with lime juice.

5 To serve, ladle soup into bowls. Offer avocado to sprinkle atop soup and lime wedges to squeeze into each serving.

makes 6 servings

per serving: 270 calories, 28 g protein, 24 g carbohydrates, 7 g total fat, 57 mg cholesterol, 241 mg sodium

vegetable broth

preparation time: about 20 minutes
cooking time: about 2 hours

1 pound leeks

1 large onion, chopped

3 cloves garlic, minced

2 cups chopped parsley

8 ounces mushrooms, coarsely chopped

1 large can (about 28 oz.) crushed tomatoes

1 teaspoon *each* salt and dry thyme

1 dry bay leaf

½ teaspoon whole black peppercorns

¼ teaspoon whole cloves

1 Cut ends and all but 3 inches of green tops from leeks. Discard tough outer leaves. Split leeks in half lengthwise; rinse well, then thinly slice crosswise.

2 In a 5 ½- to 6-quart pan, combine leeks, onion, garlic, parsley, mushrooms, tomatoes, salt, thyme, bay leaf, peppercorns, cloves, and 10 cups water. Bring to a boil; then reduce heat, cover, and simmer until broth is richly flavored (about 2 hours).

3 Pour broth through a fine strainer into a bowl, pressing down on solids to remove as much liquid as possible. Discard residue. If made ahead, let cool; then cover and refrigerate for up to 3 days.

makes about 10 cups

per cup: 30 calories, 1 g protein, 0.3 g total fat, 6 g carbohydrates, 0 mg cholesterol, 355 mg sodium

tuna bean soup

preparation time: about 45 minutes

1 large onion, chopped

4 ounces mushrooms, sliced

5 cups low-sodium chicken broth

2 cans (about 15 oz. *each*) pinto beans, drained and rinsed; or 4 cups cooked pinto beans, drained and rinsed

2 cans (about 15 oz. *each*) red kidney beans, drained and rinsed; or 4 cups cooked red kidney beans, drained and rinsed

1 large can (about 28 oz.) chopped tomatoes

1 can (about 8 oz.) tomato sauce

½ teaspoon dry oregano

2 cans (about 6 oz. *each*) water-packed albacore tuna, drained

Thinly sliced green onions (optional)

1 In a 5- to 6-quart pan, combine chopped onion and mushrooms. Cover and cook over medium-high heat until vegetables release their liquid (5 to 8 minutes). Uncover. Bring to a boil over high heat; then boil, stirring often, until liquid evaporates and vegetables begin to brown. To deglaze, add ¼ cup of the broth and stir to scrape browned bits free. Continue to cook, stirring occasionally, until vegetables begin to brown again.

2 Add pinto and kidney beans to pan; then add remaining 4 ¾ cups broth, tomatoes, tomato sauce, and oregano. Stir to combine. Bring to a boil over high heat; then reduce heat, cover, and simmer for 15 minutes. (At this point, you may let cool, then cover and refrigerate for up to 1 day. Reheat before continuing.)

3 Stir tuna into soup; heat through. Ladle soup into bowls and top with green onions, if desired.

makes 8 to 10 servings

per serving: 223 calories, 21 g protein, 28 g carbohydrates, 3 g total fat, 15 mg cholesterol, 738 mg sodium

green & gold melon soup

preparation time: about 20 minutes

Honeydew Melon Soup (recipe follows)

Cantaloupe Soup (recipe follows)

Plain lowfat yogurt (optional)

Mint sprigs (optional)

1 Prepare Honeydew Melon Soup and Cantaloupe Soup.

2 Pour each into a separate small pitcher. With a pitcher in each hand, simultaneously and gently pour soups into wide bowls. Top with a dollop of yogurt and with mint, if desired.

makes 6 to 8 servings

HONEYDEW MELON SOUP

In a blender or food processor, smoothly purée 5 cups chopped honeydew melon and ⅓ cup lime juice. Stir in 2 tablespoons sugar. (At this point, you may cover and refrigerate until next day.) Stir in 2 teaspoons minced fresh mint leaves before serving.

CANTALOUPE SOUP

In a blender or food processor, smoothly purée 5 cups chopped cantaloupe and ⅓ cup lemon juice. Stir in 2 tablespoons sugar. (At this point, you may cover and refrigerate until next day.) Stir before serving.

per serving: 115 calories, 2 g protein, 29 g carbohydrates, 0.5 g total fat, 0 mg cholesterol, 27 mg sodium

salads

melon, papaya & cucumber salad

preparation time: about 25 minutes

3 small cantaloupes

1 medium-size firm-ripe papaya, peeled, seeded, and diced

1 medium-size cucumber, peeled, seeded, and diced

About 2 tablespoons minced fresh mint or 1 teaspoon dried mint, or to taste

3 tablespoons lime juice

1 tablespoon honey

Mint sprigs

1 Cut 2 of the melons in half lengthwise. Scoop out and discard seeds. If a melon half does not sit steadily, cut a very thin slice from the base so the melon half does sit steadily. Set melon halves aside.

2 Peel, seed, and dice remaining melon. Transfer to a large nonmetal bowl. Add papaya, cucumber, minced mint, lime juice, and honey. Mix gently to combine.

3 Set a melon half in each of 4 bowls (or on each of 4 dinner plates). Spoon a fourth of the fruit mixture into each melon half. (At this point, you may cover and refrigerate for up to 4 hours.) Just before serving, garnish each melon half with mint sprigs.

makes 4 servings

per serving: 135 calories, 3 g protein, 33 g carbohydrates, 0.8 g total fat, 0 mg cholesterol, 28 mg sodium

red & yellow pepper salad

preparation time: about 25 minutes

5 large yellow bell peppers

1 large red bell pepper, seeded and diced

²/₃ cup peeled, minced jicama

2 tablespoons minced cilantro

1 ¹/₂ tablespoons distilled white vinegar

1 teaspoon honey

About ¹/₈ teaspoon ground red pepper (cayenne), or to taste

1 Set 4 of the yellow bell peppers upright, then cut off the top quarter of each. Remove and discard seeds from pepper shells; set shells aside. Cut out and discard stems from top pieces of peppers; then dice these pieces and transfer to a large nonmetal bowl.

2 Seed and dice remaining yellow bell pepper and add to bowl. Then add red bell pepper, jicama, cilantro, vinegar, honey, and ground red pepper; mix gently.

3 Spoon pepper mixture equally into pepper shells. (At this point, you may cover and refrigerate salad for up to 4 hours.).

makes 4 servings

per serving: 90 calories, 3 g protein, 21 g carbohydrates, 0.6 g total fat, 0 mg cholesterol, 7 mg sodium

warm chinese chicken salad

preparation time: about 25 minutes

1/3 cup seasoned rice vinegar (or 1/3 cup distilled white vinegar plus 2 teaspoons sugar)

1 tablespoon reduced-sodium soy sauce

1 1/2 teaspoons sugar

1 1/2 teaspoons Asian sesame oil

7 cups (about 7 oz.) finely shredded iceberg lettuce

3 cups (about 3 oz.) bite-size pieces of radicchio

1/3 cup lightly packed cilantro leaves

1/4 cup sliced green onions

1 pound skinless, boneless chicken breast, cut into thin strips

2 cloves garlic, minced or pressed

Cilantro sprigs

1 In a small bowl, stir together vinegar, 1 tablespoon water, soy sauce, sugar, and oil; set aside.

2 In a large serving bowl, combine lettuce, radicchio, cilantro leaves, and onions; cover and set aside.

3 In a wide nonstick frying pan or wok, combine chicken, 1 tablespoon water, and garlic. Stir-fry over medium-high heat until chicken is no longer pink in center; cut to test (3 to 4 minutes). Add water, 1 tablespoon at a time, if pan appears dry. Add vinegar mixture to pan and bring to a boil. Quickly pour chicken and sauce over greens, then mix gently but thoroughly. Garnish with cilantro sprigs and serve immediately.

makes 4 servings

per serving: 185 calories, 28 g protein, 10 g carbohydrates, 3 g total fat, 66 mg cholesterol, 626 mg sodium

nectarine, plum & basil salad-salsa

preparation time: under 20 minutes

2 large firm-ripe nectarines, pitted and diced

2 large firm-ripe plums, pitted and diced

1/4 cup firmly packed fresh basil leaves (minced) or about 1 tablespoon dried basil, or to taste

1 1/2 tablespoons red wine vinegar

1 tablespoon honey

4 to 8 large butter lettuce leaves, rinsed and crisped

1 In a large nonmetal bowl, mix nectarines, plums, basil, vinegar, and honey. (At this point, you may cover and refrigerate for up to 4 hours.)

2 To serve, place 1 or 2 lettuce leaves on each of 4 dinner plates. Spoon a fourth of the fruit mixture onto each plate.

makes 4 servings

per serving: 83 calories, 1 g protein, 20 g carbohydrates, 0.7 g total fat, 0 mg cholesterol, 2 mg sodium

warm spinach, pear & sausage salad

preparation time: about 30 minutes

3 green onions

8 ounces spinach, stems removed, leaves rinsed and crisped

1 large yellow or red bell pepper, seeded and cut lengthwise into thin strips

5 medium-size firm-ripe pears

1 teaspoon olive oil or vegetable oil

8 to 10 ounces mild or hot turkey Italian sausages, casings removed

1/3 cup balsamic vinegar

3/4 teaspoon fennel seeds

1 Trim and discard ends of onions. Cut onions into 2-inch lengths; then cut each piece lengthwise into slivers. Tear spinach into bite-size pieces. Place onions, spinach, and bell pepper in a large serving bowl, cover, and set aside.

2 Peel and core pears; slice thinly. Heat oil in a wide nonstick frying pan or wok over medium-high heat. When oil is hot, add pears and stir-fry until almost tender to bite (about 5 minutes). Lift pears from pan with a slotted spoon; transfer to a bowl and keep warm.

3 Crumble sausage into pan and stir-fry over medium-high heat until browned (5 to 7 minutes); add water, 1 tablespoon at a time, if pan appears dry. Add pears, vinegar, and fennel seeds to pan. Stir gently to mix, scraping browned bits free from pan bottom. Immediately pour hot pear mixture over spinach mixture; toss gently but thoroughly until spinach is slightly wilted.

makes 4 servings

per serving: 155 calories, 3 g protein, 36 g carbohydrates, 2 g total fat, 0 mg cholesterol, 36 mg sodium

cucumber & green onion salad

preparation time: about 40 minutes

3 cucumbers, thinly sliced

1 tablespoon salt

1/2 cup thinly sliced green onions

1/3 cup seasoned rice vinegar; or 1/3 cup distilled white vinegar plus 2 1/2 teaspoons sugar

1 tablespoon sugar

Pepper

1 In a bowl, lightly crush cucumbers and salt with your hands. Let stand for 20 to 30 minutes; then turn into a colander, squeeze gently, and let drain. Rinse with cool water, squeeze gently, and drain well again. (At this point, you may cover and refrigerate until next day)

2 In a nonmetal bowl, mix cucumbers, onions, vinegar, and sugar. Season to taste with pepper. Serve in bowl or transfer with a slotted spoon to a platter. Serve cold or at room temperature.

makes 8 servings

per serving: 38 calories, 1 g protein, 9 g carbohydrates, 0.2 g total fat, 0 mg cholesterol, 337 mg sodium

stir-fried pork & escarole salad

preparation time: about 30 minutes

3 quarts lightly packed rinsed, crisped escarole or spinach leaves

²/₃ cup cider vinegar

3 tablespoons honey

2 large Red Delicious apples, cored and thinly sliced

4 teaspoons cornstarch

1 cup fat-free reduced-sodium chicken broth

2 teaspoons Dijon mustard

¹/₂ teaspoon dried thyme

2 teaspoons olive oil

2 large shallots, chopped

1 pound lean boneless pork loin, loin end, or leg, trimmed of fat and cut into paper-thin ¹/₂- by 3-inch slices

1 cup raisins

1 Place escarole on a wide serving platter. In a medium-size bowl, stir together vinegar, honey, and apples. Then remove apples with a slotted spoon and scatter over escarole. Add cornstarch, broth, mustard, and thyme to vinegar mixture in bowl; stir well and set aside.

2 Heat oil in a wide nonstick frying pan or wok over medium-high heat. When oil is hot, add shallots and pork and stir-fry until meat is lightly browned (about 3 minutes). Push meat to one side of pan. Stir vinegar mixture well, pour into pan, and stir just until boiling (about 1 minute). Stir meat into sauce; then quickly spoon meat mixture over escarole and sprinkle with raisins.

makes 4 servings

per serving: 443 calories, 28 g protein, 67 g carbohydrates, 9 g total fat, 67 mg cholesterol, 305 mg sodium

watercress, butter lettuce & shrimp salad

preparation time: about 35 minutes

1 tablespoon mustard seeds

¹/₄ cup boiling water

Olive oil cooking spray

2 ¹/₂ cups ¹/₂-inch cubes sourdough French bread

¹/₄ cup balsamic or red wine vinegar

2 teaspoons Dijon mustard

1 tablespoon olive oil

2 ¹/₂ quarts torn butter lettuce leaves, rinsed and crisped

2 ¹/₂ quarts lightly packed watercress sprigs, rinsed and crisped

8 ounces small cooked shrimp

1 Place mustard seeds in a small bowl; pour boiling water over them. Let stand for at least 10 minutes or up to 8 hours; drain well.

2 Spray a shallow rimmed baking pan with cooking spray. Spread bread cubes in pan; spray with cooking spray. Bake in a 350° oven until crisp and golden brown (12 to 15 minutes). Let cool in pan on a rack. (At this point, you may store airtight at room temperature for up to 2 days.)

3 In a small bowl, stir together mustard seeds, vinegar, mustard, and oil. Arrange lettuce, watercress, and shrimp in a large salad bowl; add mustard seed dressing and mix lightly until greens are coated. Top salad with croutons.

makes 6 servings

per serving: 123 calories, 12 g protein, 10 g carbohydrates, 4 g total fat, 74 mg cholesterol, 229 mg sodium

litchi, penne & chicken salad

preparation time: about 40 minutes

5 ounces (about 1 1/2 cups) dried penne

1 can (about 11 oz.) litchis

3/4 cup plain low-fat yogurt

3/4 teaspoon grated lemon peel

4 teaspoons lemon juice

1 1/2 teaspoons dried thyme

2 cups bite-size pieces cooked chicken

1/2 cup finely diced celery

8 large butter lettuce leaves, rinsed and crisped

1/3 cup chopped green onions

Salt and pepper

1 Bring 8 cups water to a boil in a 4- to 5-quart pan over medium-high heat. Stir in pasta and cook just until tender to bite (8 to 10 minutes); or cook according to package directions. Drain, rinse with cold water until cool, and drain well.

2 Drain litchis, reserving 1/3 cup of the syrup; set fruit aside. In a large nonmetal bowl, mix reserved 1/3 cup litchi syrup, yogurt, lemon peel, lemon juice, and thyme. Add pasta, chicken, and celery. Mix thoroughly but gently. (At this point, you may cover pasta mixture and fruit separately and refrigerate for up to 4 hours; stir pasta occasionally.)

3 Arrange lettuce on individual plates. Top with pasta mixture and litchis. Sprinkle with onions. Offer salt and pepper to add to taste.

makes 4 servings

per serving: 358 calories, 28 g protein, 47 g carbohydrates, 7 g total fat, 65 mg cholesterol, 136 mg sodium

roasted bell pepper & black bean salad

preparation time: about 25 minutes

2 large red bell peppers

1/2 cup seasoned rice vinegar; or 1/2 cup distilled white vinegar plus 1 tablespoon sugar

1 tablespoon olive oil

1 tablespoon honey

1/2 teaspoon chili oil

3 cans (about 15 oz. *each*) black beans, drained and rinsed; or 6 cups cooked (about 3 cups dried) black beans, drained and rinsed

1/4 cup minced cilantro

2 tablespoons thinly sliced green onion

Salt

Cilantro sprigs

1 Cut peppers in half lengthwise. Set pepper halves, cut side down, in a 10- by 15-inch rimmed baking pan. Broil 4 to 6 inches below heat until charred all over (about 8 minutes). Cover with foil and let cool in pan. Then remove and discard skins, stems, and seeds; cut peppers into strips or chunks.

2 In a bowl, mix vinegar, 1 tablespoon water, olive oil, honey, and chili oil. Add beans and roasted peppers; mix gently but thoroughly. (At this point, you may cover and refrigerate until next day.)

3 To serve, stir minced cilantro and green onion into bean mixture. Season to taste with salt and garnish with some cilantro sprigs.

makes 6 servings

per serving: 295 calories, 16 g protein, 52 g carbohydrates, 4 g total fat, 0 mg cholesterol, 400 mg sodium

kidney cobb salad

preparation time: about 25 minutes

DRESSING:

1/3 cup non-fat mayonnaise

1/3 cup nonfat sour cream

2 tablespoons balsamic vinegar

2 tablespoons smooth unsweetened applesauce

1 tablespoon olive oil

1 tablespoon Dijon mustard

1 tablespoon chopped fresh dill or 1 teaspoon dried dill weed

1 teaspoon sugar, or to taste

Dill sprigs (optional)

SALAD:

2 cans (about 15 oz. *each*) red kidney beans

1 large yellow or red bell pepper

6 ounces feta cheese

1 very small red onion

1 large head red leaf lettuce, separated Into leaves, rinsed, and crisped

1 package (about 10 oz.) frozen tIny peas, thawed and drained

1 For dressing, in a small bowl, combine mayonnaise, sour cream, vinegar, applesauce, oil, mustard, chopped dill, and sugar. Beat until smoothly blended. If a thinner dressing is desired, add water, 1 tablespoon at a time, until dressing has the desired consistency. Spoon into a small serving bowl; garnish with dill sprigs, if desired. Cover lightly and refrigerate while you prepare salad.

2 Drain beans and rinse well. Seed and finely chop bell pepper. Crumble cheese. Thinly slice onion; separate slices into rings.

3 To assemble salad, line a rimmed platter or a wide salad bowl with large lettuce leaves, then break remaining leaves into bite-size pieces and arrange atop whole leaves. Mound peas, beans, bell pepper, and cheese separately on lettuce; place onion in center. Offer dressing to add to taste.

makes 6 servings

per serving: 256 calories, 16 g protein, 32 g carbohydrates, 7 g total fat, 25 mg cholesterol, 718 mg sodium

ginger oil

preparation time: about 10 minutes

1/4 cup ground ginger

1 cup vegetable oil or olive oil

1 In a small pan, whisk together ginger and 1/4 cup of the oil until well blended. Gradually whisk in remaining 3/4 cup oil. Heat over medium heat, stirring often, just until warm (not hot or boiling). Remove from heat and let cool slightly.

2 Carefully pour oil into a clean, dry glass bottle or jar, leaving ginger sediment behind; discard sediment. (Or strain oil, if desired.) Cover airtight and store for up to 6 months.

makes about 1 cup

per tablespoon: 124 calories, 0.1 g protein, 1 g carbohydrates, 14 g total fat, 0 mg cholesterol, 0.4 mg sodium

split pea & green pea salad

preparation time: about 45 minutes

1 cup green split peas

2 cups vegetable broth

1/2 teaspoon dried thyme

1 package (about 10 oz.) frozen tiny peas (do not thaw)

4 ounces (about 10 tablespoons) dried orzo or other rice-shaped pasta

1/4 cup thinly sliced green onions

1/4 cup chopped fresh mint

1/4 cup vegetable oil

1 teaspoon finely shredded lemon peel

2 tablespoons lemon juice

About 24 large butter lettuce leaves, rinsed and crisped

Mint sprigs

Thyme sprigs

Salt and pepper

1 Sort through split peas, discarding any debris; then rinse and drain peas. In a 1 ½- to 2-quart pan, bring broth to a boil over high heat. Add split peas and dried thyme. Reduce heat, cover, and simmer until split peas are tender to bite (about 25 minutes); drain and discard any remaining cooking liquid. Transfer split peas to a large bowl, add frozen peas, and mix gently but thoroughly. Let stand, stirring occasionally, until mixture is cool (about 3 minutes).

2 Meanwhile, in a 4- to 5-quart pan, bring about 8 cups water to a boil over medium-high heat; stir in pasta and cook until just tender to bite, about 5 minutes. (Or cook pasta according to package directions.) Drain, rinse with cold water, and drain well again. Transfer pasta to bowl with peas. Add onions and chopped mint; mix gently. In a small bowl, beat oil, lemon peel, and lemon juice until blended. Add to pea mixture; mix gently but thoroughly.

3 To serve, line 4 individual plates with lettuce leaves; top each plate equally with pea mixture. Garnish salads with mint and thyme sprigs. Season to taste with salt and pepper.

makes 4 servings

per serving: 458 calories, 19 g protein, 62 g carbohydrates, 15 g total fat, 0 mg cholesterol, 607 mg sodium

cilantro slaw

preparation time: about 15 minutes

8 ounces green cabbage, very finely shredded (about 3 cups)

8 ounces red cabbage, very finely shredded (about 3 cups)

1 cup firmly packed cilantro leaves, minced

1/4 cup lime juice

1 tablespoon *each* water and honey

1/2 teaspoon cumin seeds

Salt and pepper

In a large nonmetal bowl, mix green cabbage, red cabbage, cilantro, lime juice, water, honey, and cumin seeds. Season to taste with salt and pepper. If made ahead, cover and refrigerate for up to 4 hours.

makes 6 servings

per serving: 33 calories, 1 g protein, 8 g carbohydrates, 0.2 g total fat, 0 mg cholesterol, 14 mg sodium

fruited quinoa salad

preparation time: about 45 minutes

2 tablespoons pine nuts or slivered almonds

1 1/4 cups dried apricots

1 1/2 cups quinoa or 1 cup bulgur

2 teaspoons olive oil or vegetable oil

2 or 3 cups fat-free reduced-sodium chicken broth

2 teaspoons grated lemon peel

2 tablespoons lemon juice

1 cup dried currants

Salt

1 Toast pine nuts in a small frying pan over medium heat until golden brown (3 to 5 minutes), stirring often. Transfer nuts to a bowl; set aside. Coarsely chop 1/2 cup of the apricots; set aside.

2 Place quinoa in a fine strainer; rinse thoroughly with water (bulgur needs no rinsing). Heat oil in a 3- to 4-quart pan over medium heat. Add quinoa or bulgur; cook, stirring often, until grain turns a slightly darker brown (8 to 10 minutes).

3 To pan, add broth (3 cups for quinoa, 2 cups for bulgur), lemon peel, and lemon juice. Bring to a boil over high heat. Reduce heat, cover, and simmer until grain is just tender to bite (10 to 15 minutes). Drain and discard any liquid from grain. Stir chopped apricots and 1/2 cup of the currants into grain. Let stand until warm; or let cool, then cover and refrigerate until next day.

4 To serve, season quinoa mixture to taste with salt. Mound mixture in center of a serving dish or large rimmed serving platter. Garnish with remaining 3/4 cup apricots, remaining 1/2 cup currants, and pine nuts.

Makes 6 servings.

per serving: 349 calories, 10 g protein, 70 g carbohydrates, 7 g total fat, 0 mg cholesterol, 81 mg sodium

wilted spinach salad with oranges

preparation time: about 35 minutes

2 medium-size oranges

2 quarts lightly packed spinach leaves, rinsed and crisped

1 large onion, thinly sliced and separated into rings

1/4 cup balsamic or red wine vinegar

2 teaspoons vegetable oil

1 teaspoon dried tarragon

1 Grate 1 teaspoon peel (colored part only) from one of the oranges; set aside. With a sharp knife, cut remaining peel and all white membrane from both oranges. Holding fruit over a bowl to catch juice, cut between membranes to free segments; place segments in bowl with juice and set aside. Place spinach in a large salad bowl.

2 In a wide frying pan, combine onion, vinegar, oil, tarragon, and grated orange peel. Place over medium-low heat, cover, and cook until onions are tender-crisp when pierced (6 to 8 minutes). Gently stir in orange segments and juice. Pour orange mixture over spinach. Mix lightly, then serve at once.

makes 4 servings

per serving: 103 calories, 4 g protein, 18 g carbohydrates, 3 g total fat, 0 mg cholesterol, 70 mg sodium

black bean & jicama salad

preparation time: under 20 minutes

1 can (about 15 oz.) black beans, drained and rinsed; or 2 cups cooked (about 1 cup dried) black beans, drained and rinsed

1 cup peeled, finely chopped jicama

1/4 cup crumbled panela or feta cheese

3 tablespoons lime juice

1/3 cup minced cilantro

2 tablespoons thinly sliced green onion

2 teaspoons honey

1/4 teaspoon crushed red pepper flakes

4 to 8 butter lettuce leaves, rinsed and crisped

1 In a bowl, combine beans, jicama, cheese, lime juice, cilantro, onion, honey, and red pepper flakes. Mix well. (At this point, you may cover and refrigerate for up to 4 hours.)

2 To serve, spoon bean mixture into lettuce leaves.

makes 4 servings

per serving: 164 calories, 9 g protein, 28 g carbohydrates, 2 g total fat, 8 mg cholesterol, 100 mg sodium

mizuna, fennel & crab salad

preparation time: under 20 minutes

12 ounces fennel

2/3 pound mizuna, bare stems trimmed, leaves rinsed and crisped

2/3 cup plain nonfat yogurt

1/4 cup reduced-fat sour cream

2 tablespoons lemon juice

1 tablespoon Dijon mustard

1 teaspoon dried tarragon

1/2 teaspoon sugar

1 1/2 pounds cooked crabmeat

1 Cut feathery tops from fennel; chop tops and set aside for dressing. Cut root ends and any bruised spots from fennel head; then thinly slice (you should have 2 cups) and place in a large bowl.

2 Reserve 3/4 cup of the mizuna for dressing. Cut remaining mizuna into 2- to 3-inch long pieces; add to bowl with fennel.

3 To prepare dressing, in a blender or food processor, combine the 3/4 cup reserved mizuna, yogurt, sour cream, lemon juice, mustard, 1 tablespoon of the reserved chopped fennel tops, tarragon, and sugar. Whirl until puréed; set aside.

4 Mound crab on mizuna mixture, placing the most attractive crab pieces on top. At the table, add dressing to salad; mix gently.

makes 6 servings

per serving: 172 calories, 27 g protein, 7 g carbohydrates, 4 g total fat, 117 mg cholesterol, 460 mg sodium

white bean & tomato salad

preparation time: about 1 1/2 hours

1 large red onion, cut into 3/4-inch chunks

2 1/2 teaspoons olive oil

2 tablespoons balsamic or red wine vinegar

12 to 14 medium-size firm-ripe pear-shaped (Roma-type) tomatoes, cut lengthwise into halves

Salt

3 cans (about 15 oz. *each*) cannellini (white kidney beans)

2 tablespoons *each* chopped fresh thyme and chopped fresh basil; or 2 teaspoons *each* dry thyme and dry basil

Pepper

1 In a lightly oiled square 8- to 10-inch baking pan, mix onion, 1/2 teaspoon of the oil, and vinegar. Arrange tomatoes, cut side up, in a lightly oiled 9- by 13-inch baking pan; rub with remaining 2 teaspoons oil, then sprinkle with salt.

2 Bake onion and tomatoes in a 475° oven until edges of onion chunks and tomato halves are dark brown (40 to 50 minutes for onion, about 1 hour and 10 minutes for tomatoes); switch positions of baking pans halfway through baking.

3 Pour beans and their liquid into a 2- to 3-quart pan. Add fresh thyme (or both dry thyme and dry basil). Bring to a boil; reduce heat and simmer for 3 minutes, stirring. Pour beans into a fine strainer set over a bowl; reserve liquid. Place beans in a serving bowl; tap herbs from strainer into beans.

4 Chop 8 tomato halves; stir into beans along with fresh basil (if used) and onion. Add some of the reserved liquid to moisten, if desired. Season to taste with salt and pepper. Arrange remaining 16 to 20 tomato halves around edge of salad.

makes 8 side dish or 4 main-dish servings

per serving: 179 calories, 10 g protein, 32 g carbohydrates, 2 g total fat, 0 mg cholesterol, 566 mg sodium

autumn pear salad

preparation time: 20 minutes

1/4 cup red wine vinegar

2 tablespoons extra virgin olive oil

1 tablespoon drained capers

1 tablespoon lemon juice

1/4 teaspoon *each* pepper and honey

4 large firm-ripe red pears

1 package prewashed spinach leaves, coarse stems and any yellow or bruised leaves discarded, remaining leaves rinsed and crisped

8 ounces mushrooms, thinly sliced

3/4 cup dried cranberries

4 ounces sliced pancetta or bacon, crisply cooked, drained, and crumbled

1 In a large bowl, combine vinegar, oil, capers, lemon juice, pepper, and honey; beat until well blended. Set aside.

2 Core pears and cut each into about 16 wedges. As pears are cut, transfer them to bowl with dressing; mix gently to coat with dressing. Add spinach, mushrooms, and cranberries; mix until coated with dressing. Then divide salad among individual plates and sprinkle with pancetta.

makes 8 servings

per serving: 160 calories, 3 g protein, 27 g carbohydrates, 6 g total fat, 5 mg cholesterol, 163 mg sodium

warm cioppino salad

preparation time: about 30 minutes

1/4 cup lemon juice

1 teaspoon dried basil

1 teaspoon dried oregano

2 cloves garlic, minced or pressed

3 quarts lightly packed rinsed, crisped spinach leaves, torn into bite-size pieces

1 tablespoon olive oil

8 ounces extra-large raw shrimp (26 to 30 per lb.), shelled and deveined

2 cups thinly sliced mushrooms

2 cups thinly sliced zucchini

1 can (about 14 1/2 oz.) tomatoes, drained and chopped

12 pitted ripe olives

8 ounces cooked crabmeat

1 To prepare lemon dressing, in a small bowl, stir together lemon juice, basil, oregano, and garlic; set aside.

2 Place spinach in a wide serving bowl, cover, and set aside.

3 Heat oil in a wide nonstick frying pan or wok over medium-high heat. When oil is hot, add shrimp and stir-fry until just opaque in center; cut to test (3 to 4 minutes). Remove from pan with tongs or a slotted spoon and set aside.

4 Add mushrooms and zucchini to pan; stir-fry until zucchini is just tender to bite (about 3 minutes). Return shrimp to pan; add tomatoes, olives, and lemon dressing. Stir until mixture is heated through. Pour shrimp mixture over spinach, top with crab, and mix gently but thoroughly.

makes 6 servings

per serving: 149 calories, 18 g protein, 10 g carbohydrates, 15 g total fat, 85 mg cholesterol, 380 mg sodium

tomatillo & tomato salad

preparation time: about 15 minutes

3 pounds (about 10 cups) ripe cherry tomatoes (red, yellow, yellow-green, orange); include some that are 1/2 inch or less in diameter

10 medium-size tomatillos, husked, rinsed, and thinly sliced

1 fresh jalapeño chile, seeded and minced

1/2 cup lightly packed cilantro leaves

1/4 cup lime juice

Salt and pepper

Lime wedges

1 Cut any tomatoes larger than 3/4 inch in diameter into halves; then place tomatoes in a nonmetal bowl.

2 Add tomatillos, chile, cilantro, and lime juice; mix gently. Season to taste with salt and pepper; serve with lime wedges.

makes 8 to 10 servings

per serving: 39 calories, 2 g protein, 8 g carbohydrates, 0.6 g total fat, 0 mg cholesterol, 14 mg sodium

PREPARING SALAD GREENS: Putting salads together is simpler if you rinse and crisp the greens in advance (up to a few days before use). Each time you make a tossed salad, try to prepare several meals' worth of greens. First discard the coarse outer leaves and stems; then rinse the remaining leaves and dry them in a lettuce spinner (or drain on paper towels or a clean dishtowel). Wrap the leaves loosely in dry paper towels; store in a plastic bag in the crisper of your refrigerator. When you're ready for salad, your greens will be clean, chilled, and crisp. You can even store salad ready-made: just fill plastic bags with torn greens and crisp vegetables such as sliced radishes, celery, and bell pepper.

asian salad

preparation time: about 40 minutes

6 cups lightly packed rinsed, crisped spinach leaves

¹/₄ cup unseasoned rice vinegar or white wine vinegar

2 tablespoons reduced-sodium soy sauce

2 teaspoons honey

1 teaspoon Asian sesame oil

2 teaspoons sesame seeds

2 teaspoons vegetable oil

5 cups broccoli flowerets

1 pound carrots, cut into ¹/₄-inch diagonal slices

1¹/₂ cups thinly sliced celery

1 medium-size onion, thinly sliced

1 Arrange spinach leaves on a large platter; cover and set aside. In a small bowl, stir together vinegar, soy sauce, honey, and sesame oil; set aside.

2 In a wide nonstick frying pan or wok, stir sesame seeds over medium heat until golden (about 3 minutes). Pour out of pan and set aside. Heat 1 teaspoon of the vegetable oil in pan over medium-high heat. When oil is hot, add half of the broccoli, carrots, celery, and onion. Stir-fry until vegetables are hot and bright in color (about 3 minutes). Add ¹/₃ cup water to pan, cover, and cook until vegetables are just tender to bite (about 3 minutes). Uncover and continue to cook, stirring, until liquid has evaporated (1 to 2 more minutes). Remove vegetables from pan and set aside. Repeat to cook remaining broccoli, carrots, celery, and onion, using remaining 1 teaspoon vegetable oil and adding ¹/₃ cup water after the first 3 minutes of cooking.

3 Return all cooked vegetables to pan and stir in vinegar mixture. Spoon vegetables onto spinach-lined platter and sprinkle with sesame seeds.

makes 6 servings

per serving: 118 calories, 6 g protein, 20 g carbohydrates, 3 g total fat, 0 mg cholesterol, 297 mg sodium

hot chile oil

preparation time: about 10 minutes

6 to 12 small dried hot red chiles (use the greater number of chiles for more heat)

1 cup vegetable oil or olive oil

1 Place 3 whole chiles in a small pan; add oil. Split each of the remaining 3 to 9 chiles in half; add to pan. Heat over medium heat, stirring gently, just until warm (not hot or boiling). Remove from heat and let cool slightly.

2 With a slotted spoon, remove split chiles and seeds from oil; discard. Remove whole chiles; set aside. Carefully (watch that you don't splatter) pour oil into a clean, dry glass bottle or jar. (Or strain oil, if desired.) Add whole chiles to bottle; cover airtight and store for up to 6 months.

makes about 1 cup

per tablespoon: 121 calories, 0.1 g protein, 0.4 g carbohydrates, 14 g total fat, 0 mg cholesterol, 0.2 mg sodium

shrimp & spinach slaw

preparation time: about 25 minutes

4 cups finely shredded green cabbage

3 cups thinly sliced spinach leaves

1 medium-size cucumber, peeled and sliced

2 medium-size celery stalks, sliced

²/₃ cup plain nonfat yogurt

3 tablespoons reduced-calorie mayonnaise

¹/₂ cup thinly sliced green onions

1 teaspoon grated lemon peel

2 tablespoons lemon juice

1 tablespoon sugar

About 12 large spinach leaves, rinsed and crisped (optional)

³/₄ to 1 pound small cooked shrimp

Lemon wedges

Salt and pepper

1 To prepare salad, in a large bowl, combine cabbage, sliced spinach leaves, cucumber, and celery.

2 To prepare yogurt-lemon dressing, in a small bowl, combine yogurt, mayonnaise, onions, lemon peel, lemon juice, and sugar. (At this point, you may cover and refrigerate the salad and dressing separately until next day.)

3 Add dressing to salad and mix well. If using large spinach leaves, use them to garnish salad in bowl; or arrange them around rim of a large platter and mound salad in center. Sprinkle shrimp over salad. Offer lemon wedges to squeeze over salad to taste; season to taste with salt and pepper.

makes 8 servings

per serving: 107 calories, 13 g protein, 9 g carbohydrates, 3 g total fat, 100 mg cholesterol, 189 mg sodium

red slaw

preparation time: 15 minutes

1 medium-size head red cabbage

3 tablespoons *each* balsamic vinegar and salad oil

2 cans (about 15 oz. *each*) red kidney beans, drained and rinsed

1 can (about 15 oz.) pickled beets, drained and coarsely chopped

2 tablespoons finely chopped crystallized ginger

2 ¹/₂ cups pitted sweet cherries, fresh or thawed frozen

1 Remove 4 to 8 large outer cabbage leaves and set aside. Then core cabbage and finely shred enough of it to make 5 cups; set aside. Reserve any remaining cabbage for other uses.

2 In a large bowl, beat vinegar and oil until blended. Stir in beans, beets, and ginger. Gently mix in shredded cabbage and cherries. (At this point, you may cover and refrigerate slaw and whole cabbage leaves separately for up to 4 hours.)

3 To serve, stir sliced onions into slaw. Arrange 1 or 2 of the whole cabbage leaves on each of 4 individual plates. Divide slaw equally among plates; garnish with whole green onions, if desired. Season to taste with salt and pepper.

makes 4 servings

per serving: 468 calories, 16 g protein, 13 g total fat, 78 g carbohydrates, 0 mg cholesterol, 577 mg sodium

mixed greens with pesto dressing

preparation time: 35 minutes

1 tablespoon pine nuts

2 teaspoons Asian sesame oil

1 clove garlic, minced or pressed

3 slices Italian or sourdough sandwich bread, cut into 1/2-inch cubes

1/4 cup chopped fresh basil

1/4 cup chopped Italian or regular parsley

1 cup nonfat sour cream

1 tablespoon white wine vinegar

1 teaspoon honey

1 or 2 cloves garlic, peeled

Salt and pepper

8 ounces (about 8 cups) mixed salad greens, rinsed and crisped

1 Toast pine nuts in a wide nonstick frying pan over medium heat until golden (about 3 minutes), stirring often. Pour out of pan and set aside. In same pan (with pan off heat), combine 1 teaspoon of the oil, garlic, and 1 tablespoon water. Add bread cubes and toss gently to coat. Place pan over medium heat; cook, stirring occasionally, until croutons are crisp and tinged with brown (about 10 minutes). Remove from pan and set aside.

2 In a food processor or blender, combine basil, parsley, sour cream, vinegar, honey, remaining 1 teaspoon oil, and garlic; whirl until smoothly puréed. Season to taste with salt and pepper; set aside.

3 Place greens in a large bowl; add dressing and mix gently but thoroughly Add croutons and mix again. Sprinkle with pine nuts.

makes 4 servings

per serving: 154 calories, 8 g protein, 20 g carbohydrates, 4 g total fat, 0 mg cholesterol, 177 mg sodium

fennel & orange salad

preparation time: 20 minutes

2 large heads fennel

1/4 cup seasoned rice vinegar

2 tablespoons olive oil

1 tablespoon grated orange peel

1 teaspoon anise seeds

4 large oranges

Seeds from 1 pomegranate

Salt

1 Trim stems from fennel, reserving the feathery green leaves. Trim and discard any bruised areas from fennel; then cut each fennel head into thin slivers. Place slivered fennel in a large bowl.

2 Finely chop enough of the fennel leaves to make 1 tablespoon (reserve remaining leaves); add to bowl along with vinegar, oil, orange peel, and anise seeds. Mix well.

3 Cut off and discard peel and all white membrane from oranges. Cut fruit crosswise into slices about 1/4 inch thick; discard seeds.

4 Divide fennel mixture among individual plates. Arrange oranges alongside fennel mixture; sprinkle salads equally with pomegranate seeds. Garnish with reserved fennel leaves. Season to taste with salt.

makes 6 servings

per serving: 147 calories, 2 g protein, 26 g carbohydrates, 5 g total fat, 0 mg cholesterol, 290 mg sodium

garbanzo antipasto salad

preparation time: about 50 minutes

chilling time: at least 1 hour

8 ounces sourdough bread, cut into about
¹/₂-inch cubes

¹/₂ cup white wine vinegar

2 tablespoons olive oil

1 tablespoon chopped fresh oregano or 1 teaspoon
dried oregano

2 teaspoons honey (or to taste)

2 cloves garlic, minced or pressed

¹/₈ to ¹/₄ teaspoon pepper

2 cans (about 15 oz. *each*) garbanzo beans,
drained and rinsed

2 large tomatoes, chopped and drained well

¹/₄ cup slivered red onion, in about 1-inch lengths

¹/₄ cup oil-cured olives, pitted and sliced

3 to 4 tablespoons drained capers

¹/₃ cup *each* nonfat mayonnaise and nonfat sour
cream

2 tablespoons chopped fresh dill or 2 teaspoons
dried dill weed

8 to 12 butter lettuce leaves, rinsed and crisped

1 Spread bread cubes in a single layer in a shallow 10- by 15-inch baking pan. Bake in a 325° oven, stirring occasionally, until crisp and tinged with brown (15 to 20 minutes). Set aside. If made ahead, let cool completely in pan on a rack, then store airtight for up to 2 days.

2 In a large bowl, combine vinegar, oil, oregano, honey, garlic, and pepper. Beat until blended. Add beans, tomatoes, onion, olives, and capers; mix gently but thoroughly. Cover and refrigerate for at least 1 hour or up to 4 hours.

3 Meanwhile, in a small bowl, beat mayonnaise, sour cream, and dill until smoothly blended; cover and refrigerate.

4 To serve, line 4 individual rimmed plates or shallow bowls with lettuce leaves. Add croutons to salad and mix gently but thoroughly, being sure to coat croutons with marinade. Then, using a slotted spoon, transfer salad to plates; top each serving with a dollop of dill dressing.

makes 4 servings

per serving: 466 calories, 16 g protein, 67 g carbohydrates, 15 g total fat, 0 mg cholesterol, 1,234 mg sodium

green chile dressing

preparation time: about 10 minutes

1 small can (about 4 oz.) diced green chiles

¹/₃ cup lime juice

¹/₄ cup water

¹/₄ cup chopped cilantro

1 clove garlic, peeled

1 or 2 fresh jalapeño chiles, seeded and chopped

1 ¹/₂ teaspoons sugar

In a blender or food processor, combine green chiles, lime juice, water, cilantro, garlic, jalapeño chiles, and sugar; whirl until smoothly puréed. (At this point, you may cover and refrigerate dressing for up to 4 hours.)

makes about 1 cup

per tablespoon: 5 calories, 0.1 g protein, 1 g carbohydrates, 0.01 g total fat, 0 mg cholesterol, 44 mg sodium

pesto pasta salad

preparation time: 35 minutes

1 cup dried tomatoes (not packed in oil)

2 tablespoons pine nuts

1 pound dried medium-size pasta shells or elbow macaroni

1 cup firmly packed chopped fresh spinach

3 tablespoons dried basil

1 or 2 cloves garlic, peeled

⅓ cup grated Parmesan cheese

¼ cup olive oil

1 teaspoon Asian sesame oil

Salt and pepper

1 Place tomatoes in a small bowl and add boiling water to cover. Let stand until soft (about 10 minutes), stirring occasionally. Drain well; gently squeeze out excess liquid. Cut tomatoes into thin slivers and set aside.

2 While tomatoes are soaking, toast pine nuts in a small frying pan over medium heat until golden (about 3 minutes), stirring often. Pour out of pan and set aside.

3 In a 6- to 8-quart pan, bring 4 quarts water to a boil over medium-high heat; stir in pasta and cook until just tender to bite, 8 to 10 minutes. (Or cook pasta according to package directions.) Drain, rinse with cold water until cool, and drain well again. Pour into a large serving bowl.

4 In a food processor or blender, whirl spinach, basil, garlic, cheese, olive oil, sesame oil, and 1 teaspoon water until smoothly puréed; scrape sides of container as needed and add a little more water if pesto is too thick.

5 Add tomatoes and spinach pesto to pasta; mix well. Sprinkle with pine nuts; season to taste with salt and pepper.

makes 8 servings

per serving: 332 calories, 11 g protein, 49 g carbohydrates, 10 g total fat, 3 mg cholesterol, 78 mg sodium

capellini chinese style

preparation time: about 35 minutes
chilling time: at least 30 minutes

3 tablespoons seasoned rice vinegar; or 3 tablespoons distilled white vinegar and 2 teaspoons sugar

3 tablespoons lime juice

4 teaspoons Asian sesame oil (or to taste)

1 tablespoon reduced-sodium soy sauce

1/16 teaspoon ground red pepper (cayenne)

8 ounces dried capellini

½ cup thinly sliced green onions

⅓ cup chopped red bell pepper

Lime wedges

1 Combine vinegar, lime juice, oil, soy sauce, and ground red pepper in a large nonmetal serving bowl; mix until blended. Set aside.

2 Bring 8 cups water to a boil in a 4- to 5-quart pan over medium-high heat. Stir in pasta and cook just until tender to bite (about 4 minutes); or cook according to package directions. Drain, rinse with cold water until cool, and drain well.

3 Add pasta to vinegar mixture. Mix thoroughly but gently. Cover and refrigerate until cool (at least 30 minutes) or for up to 4 hours; stir occasionally.

4 Stir in onions and bell pepper just before serving. Offer lime wedges to add to taste.

makes 4 to 6 servings

per serving: 217 calories, 6 g protein, 38 g carbohydrates, 4 g total fat, 0 mg cholesterol, 305 mg sodium

cool beans & bows

preparation time: about 30 minutes
chilling time: at least 30 minutes

4 ounces (about 2 cups) dried farfalle

$1/2$ cup seasoned rice vinegar; or $1/2$ cup distilled white vinegar and 4 teaspoons sugar

$1/4$ cup minced parsley

1 tablespoon each olive oil, water, and honey

$1/4$ teaspoon chili oil

1 can (about 15 oz.) kidney beans, drained and rinsed

1 can (about 15 oz.) black beans, drained and rinsed

1 large pear-shaped (Roma-type) tomato, diced

$1/4$ cup thinly sliced green onions

1 Bring 8 cups water to a boil in a 4- to 5-quart pan over medium-high heat. Stir in pasta and cook just until tender to bite (8 to 10 minutes); or cook according to package directions. Drain, rinse with cold water until cool, and drain well.

2 Combine vinegar, parsley, olive oil, water, honey, and chili oil in a large nonmetal bowl. Mix well. Add kidney and black beans, pasta, and tomato. Mix thoroughly but gently. Cover and refrigerate until cool (at least 30 minutes) or for up to 4 hours; stir occasionally.

3 Stir onions into pasta mixture just before serving. Transfer to a large serving bowl.

makes 4 to 6 servings

per serving: 256 calories, 11 g protein, 44 g carbohydrates, 4 g total fat, 0 mg cholesterol, 724 mg sodium

couscous tabbouleh

preparation time: about 25 minutes
chilling time: at least 30 minutes

10 ounces (about 1 $2/3$ cups) dried couscous

1 $1/2$ cups firmly packed fresh mint, minced

2 tablespoons olive oil

$1/2$ cup lemon juice (or to taste)

Salt and pepper

6 to 8 large butter lettuce leaves, rinsed and crisped

2 large tomatoes, thinly sliced

Mint sprigs

1 Bring 2 $1/4$ cups water to a boil in a 3- to 4-quart pan over high heat. Stir in pasta; cover, remove from heat, and let stand until liquid is absorbed (about 5 minutes). Transfer pasta to a large nonmetal bowl and let cool, fluffing occasionally with a fork.

2 Add minced mint, oil, and lemon juice to pasta. Season to taste with salt and pepper. Mix well. Cover and refrigerate until cool (at least 30 minutes) or for up to 4 hours; fluff occasionally with a fork.

3 Line a platter with lettuce leaves. Mound tabbouleh in center; arrange tomatoes around edge. Garnish with mint sprigs.

makes 6 to 8 servings

per serving: 210 calories, 6 g protein, 36 g carbohydrates, 5 g total fat, 0 mg cholesterol, 14 mg sodium

lentil & pappardelle salad

preparation time: about 1 hour
chilling time: at least 30 minutes

2 cups beef broth

6 ounces (about 1 cup) lentils, rinsed and drained

1 teaspoon dried oregano

6 ounces dried pappardelle or extra-wide egg
   noodles

1/3 cup lemon juice

3 tablespoons chopped fresh mint or 1 teaspoon
   dried mint

2 tablespoons olive oil

1 teaspoon honey (or to taste)

6 cups shredded red leaf lettuce leaves

1 or 2 cloves garlic, minced or pressed

2/3 cup crumbled feta cheese (or to taste)

Mint sprigs

1 Bring broth to a boil in a 1 ½- to 2-quart pan over high heat. Add lentils and oregano; reduce heat, cover, and simmer just until lentils are tender to bite (20 to 30 minutes). Drain, if necessary. Transfer to a large nonmetal bowl and let cool. Meanwhile, bring 8 cups water to a boil in a 4- to 5-quart pan over medium-high heat. Stir in pasta and cook just until tender to bite (8 to 10 minutes); or cook according to package directions. Drain, rinse with cold water until cool, and drain well.

2 Add pasta, lemon juice, chopped mint, oil, and honey to lentils. Mix thoroughly but gently. Cover and refrigerate until cool (at least 30 minutes) or for up to 4 hours; stir occasionally.

3 Arrange lettuce on a platter. Stir garlic into pasta mixture and spoon onto lettuce. Sprinkle with cheese. Garnish with mint sprigs.

makes 6 to 8 servings

per serving: 273 calories, 14 g protein, 37 g carbohydrates, 8 g total fat, 34 mg cholesterol, 619 mg sodium

melon, basil & bacon salad

preparation time: 25 minutes
cooling time: about 20 minutes

6 ounces sliced bacon

1 1/2 tablespoons firmly packed brown sugar

8 cups peeled, seeded melon wedges; use any soft,
   aromatic melon, such as honeydew, cantaloupe,
   and/or crenshaw

1/4 cup lime juice

1/3 cup finely slivered fresh basil

Basil sprigs

1 Line a shallow 10- by 15-inch baking pan with foil. Arrange bacon in pan in a single layer; bake in a 350° oven for 10 minutes. Spoon off and discard drippings. Evenly pat sugar onto bacon; bake until bacon is deep golden (about 10 more minutes).

2 Lift bacon to a board; let cool slightly, then cut diagonally into ½-inch slices. In a large, shallow bowl, combine melon, lime juice, and slivered basil. Top with bacon; garnish with basil sprigs.

makes 4 servings

per serving: 210 calories, 6 g protein, 36 g carbohydrates, 7 g total fat, 10 mg cholesterol, 226 mg sodium

macaroni salad

preparation time: about 45 minutes
chilling time: at least 30 minutes

Tofu Mayonnaise (recipe follows)

8 ounces (about 2 cups) dried elbow macaroni

1 large hard-cooked egg, chopped

1/2 cup thinly sliced celery

1 jar (about 2 oz.) chopped pimentos, drained

1/2 cup chopped dill pickles

1/4 cup thinly sliced green onions

Green leaf lettuce leaves, washed and crisped

Tomato slices

Thyme or parsley sprigs

1 Prepare Tofu Mayonnaise; cover and refrigerate.

2 Bring 8 cups water to a boil in a 4- to 5-quart pan over medium-high heat. Stir in pasta and cook just until tender to bite (8 to 10 minutes); or cook according to package directions. Drain, rinse with cold water until cool, and drain well.

3 Transfer pasta to a large nonmetal bowl. Add Tofu Mayonnaise, egg, celery, pimentos, and pickles. Mix well. Cover and refrigerate until cool (at least 30 minutes) or for up to 2 hours; stir occasionally. Just before serving, stir in onions. Arrange lettuce and tomatoes on individual plates. Top with pasta. Garnish with thyme sprigs.

Makes 8 servings

TOFU MAYONNAISE

Rinse 8 ounces soft tofu in a colander. Coarsely mash tofu; let drain for 10 minutes. Transfer to a blender or food processor. Add 1/4 cup low-sodium chicken or vegetable broth, 3 tablespoons lemon juice, 2 tablespoons olive oil or salad oil, 2 teaspoons each prepared horseradish and sugar, and 1 teaspoon each dried thyme and Dijon mustard. Whirl until smooth. Season to taste with salt. If made ahead, cover and refrigerate for up to an hour. Stir before using.

per serving: 173 calories, 6 g protein, 25 g carbohydrates, 5 g total fat, 27 mg cholesterol, 165 mg sodium

ginger pear & hazelnut salad

preparation time: about 30 minutes

1/3 cup hazelnuts

1/2 cup balsamic or red wine vinegar

3 tablespoons *each* honey and minced crystallized ginger

8 small or 4 large firm-ripe Bartlett pears

2 tablespoons lemon juice

Leaf lettuce leaves, rinsed and crisped

1 Spread hazelnuts in a shallow baking pan and toast in a 350° oven until pale golden beneath skins (about 10 minutes). Let cool slightly; then rub off as much of skins as possible with your fingers. Chop nuts coarsely and set aside.

2 In a small bowl, stir together vinegar, honey, and ginger; set aside. Halve and core pears; brush cut sides with lemon juice. Line a platter with lettuce leaves; arrange pear halves, cut side up, on lettuce. Spoon dressing over pears, then sprinkle with hazelnuts.

makes 8 servings

per serving: 138 calories, 1 g protein, 29 g carbohydrates, 3 g total fat, 0 mg cholesterol, 4 mg sodium

chicken & citrus pasta salad

preparation time: about 1 1/2 hours
chilling time: at least 30 minutes

2 large oranges

Citrus Pasta Salad (recipe follows)

Orange Cream (recipe follows)

1/4 cup orange marmalade

1 teaspoon prepared horseradish

6 skinless, boneless chicken breast halves
    (about 1 1/2 lbs. *total*)

2 large blood oranges or 1 small pink grapefruit

2 medium-size avocados, optional

2 tablespoons lemon juice (optional)

Basil sprigs

Finely shredded orange peel

1 Grate 4 teaspoons peel from oranges. Prepare Citrus Pasta Salad and Orange Cream, using grated peel; cover and refrigerate.

2 Mix marmalade and horseradish in a large bowl. Add chicken and stir to coat. Place chicken in a lightly oiled 10- by 15-inch baking pan. Bake in a 450° oven until meat in thickest part is no longer pink; cut to test (12 to 15 minutes). Let cool. Meanwhile, cut peel and white membrane from oranges and blood oranges; slice fruit crosswise into rounds 1/4 inch thick. (For grapefruit, cut segments from membrane; discard membrane.)

3 Arrange pasta salad and chicken on a platter. Place fruit around edge. If desired, pit, peel, and slice avocados; coat with lemon juice and place on platter. Garnish with basil sprigs and shredded orange peel. Offer Orange Cream to add to taste.

makes 6 servings

CHICKEN & CITRUS PASTA SALAD

1 Bring 12 cups water to a boil in a 5- to 6-quart pan over medium-high heat. Stir in 12 ounces (about 5 cups) dried rotini or other corkscrew-shaped pasta. Cook just until tender to bite (8 to 10 minutes); or cook according to package directions. Drain, rinse with cold water until cool, and drain well. In a large nonmetal bowl, combine 1 tablespoon grated orange peel; 3/4 cup orange juice; 1 small orange, peeled and coarsely chopped; 3 tablespoons white wine vinegar or distilled white vinegar; 3 tablespoons chopped fresh basil; 1 tablespoon each honey and Dijon mustard; 1 1/2 teaspoons ground cumin; and 1 fresh jalapeño chile, seeded and finely chopped. Mix until blended. Add pasta and mix thoroughly but gently. Cover and refrigerate until cool (at least 30 minutes) or for up to 4 hours; stir occasionally. Just before serving, stir in 1/4 cup chopped parsley and 2 or 3 cloves garlic, minced or pressed.

per serving: 463 calories, 38 g protein, 70 g carbohydrates, 4 g total fat, 74 mg cholesterol, 158 mg sodium

ORANGE CREAM

In a small nonmetal bowl, combine 1 cup nonfat or reduced-fat sour cream, 3 tablespoons orange marmalade, 2 teaspoons prepared horseradish, and 1 teaspoon grated orange peel. Mix until blended. Season to taste with ground white pepper. If made ahead, cover and refrigerate for up to a day. Stir before serving.

makes about 1 1/4 cups

per serving: 16 calories, 1 g protein, 3 g carbohydrates, 0 g total fat, 0 mg cholesterol, 10 mg sodium

quinoa & spinach salad

preparation time: about 50 minutes

1/2 cup quinoa

1 cinnamon stick (about 3 inches long)

1/2 teaspoon cumin seeds

1/2 cup *each* unsweetened apple juice and water

3 tablespoons dried currants

2 cans (about 15 oz. *each*) cannellini (white kidney beans), drained and rinsed

8 cups bite-size pieces rinsed, crisped fresh spinach

1 large red-skinned apple, cored and thinly sliced

1/3 cup cider vinegar

3 tablespoons honey

2 tablespoons salad oil

1 Place quinoa in a fine strainer and rinse thoroughly with cool water; drain well. Then place quinoa in a 1 1/2- to 2-quart pan and cook over medium heat, stirring often, until darker in color (about 8 minutes). Add cinnamon stick, cumin seeds, apple juice, and water. Increase heat to medium-high and bring mixture to a boil; then reduce heat, cover, and simmer until almost all liquid has been absorbed and quinoa is tender to bite (about 15 minutes). Discard cinnamon stick; stir in currants and half the beans. Use quinoa mixture warm or cool.

2 In a large serving bowl, combine spinach, remaining beans, and apple. Mound quinoa mixture atop spinach mixture. In a small bowl, beat vinegar, honey, and oil until blended; pour over salad and mix gently but thoroughly.

makes 4 servings

per serving: 422 calories, 16 g protein, 72 g carbohydrates, 10 g total fat, 0 mg cholesterol, 336 mg sodium

ceviche with radishes & peas

preparation time: about 40 minutes
cooking time: at least 1 1/2 hours

3/4 cup each unseasoned rice vinegar and water; or 1 cup distilled white vinegar plus 1/2 cup water

2 tablespoons minced crystallized ginger

1/2 teaspoon coriander seeds

1 pound skinless, boneless lean, firm-textured fish such as halibut, mahi-mahi, or swordfish, cut into 1/2-inch chunks

1 cup frozen tiny peas, thawed

1 cup sliced red radishes

Salt and pepper

1 In a wide nonstick frying pan, bring vinegar, water, ginger, and coriander seeds to a boil over high heat. Add fish. Reduce heat, cover, and simmer until fish is just opaque but still moist in thickest part; cut to test (3 to 4 minutes). With a slotted spoon, transfer fish to a bowl.

2 Boil cooking liquid over high heat, uncovered, until reduced to 1 cup; pour over fish. Cover and refrigerate until cool (at least 1 1/2 hours) or for up to 8 hours.

3 Gently mix peas and radish slices with fish. Spoon into 4 or 6 shallow soup bowls; distribute liquid equally among bowls. Season to taste with salt and pepper.

makes 4 main-dish or 6 first-course servings

per serving: 196 calories, 26 g protein, 16 g carbohydrates, 3 g total fat, 36 mg cholesterol, 137 mg sodium

wheat berry satay salad

preparation time: 15 minutes, plus about 30 minutes for salad to cool
cooking time: about 1 3/4 hours

2 large yellow or white onions, thinly sliced

2 cups wheat berries, rinsed and drained

3 cups vegetable broth

About 1/8 teaspoon crushed red pepper flakes (or to taste)

1 tablespoon finely chopped fresh ginger

2 tablespoons creamy peanut butter

2 tablespoons fruit or berry jam or jelly

2 tablespoons seasoned rice vinegar or
    2 tablespoons distilled white vinegar plus
    1/2 to 1 teaspoon sugar

About 1 tablespoon reduced-sodium soy sauce (or to taste)

1 cup chopped cilantro

1 cup sliced green onions

1/4 cup finely chopped salted roasted peanuts

1 In a 4- to 5-quart pan, combine yellow onions and 1/2 cup water. Cook over medium-high heat, stirring often, until liquid evaporates and browned bits stick to pan bottom (10 to 15 minutes). To deglaze pan, add 1/4 cup more water, stirring to loosen browned bits from pan; continue to cook until browned bits form again. Repeat deglazing step 3 or 4 more times or until onions are dark brown, using 1/4 cup water each time.

2 Add wheat berries, broth, red pepper flakes, and ginger to pan. Bring to a boil; then reduce heat, cover, and simmer, stirring occasionally, until wheat berries are just tender to bite (50 to 60 minutes). Remove from heat; drain and reserve cooking liquid.

3 In a small bowl, beat 1/4 cup of the reserved cooking liquid, peanut butter, and jam until smoothly blended. Stir peanut butter mixture, vinegar, and soy sauce into wheat berry mixture. Cover salad and let stand until cool (about 30 minutes).

4 Add two-thirds each of the cilantro and green onions to salad; mix gently but thoroughly. If a moister texture is desired, mix in some of the remaining cooking liquid. Transfer salad to a serving bowl; sprinkle with remaining cilantro, remaining green onions, and peanuts.

makes 4 servings

per serving: 517 calories, 19 g protein, 92 g carbohydrates, 12 g total fat, 0 mg cholesterol, 1,136 mg sodium

pineapple, strawberry & apple salad

preparation time: about 25 minutes

1 medium-size pineapple

1 small tart green-skinned apple

1 cup coarsely chopped strawberries

1/3 cup plain low-fat yogurt

8 to 16 butter lettuce leaves, rinsed and crisped

8 whole strawberries

1 cup small-curd cottage cheese

1 Cut peel and eyes from pineapple. Slice off top third of pineapple; cut out and discard core, then chop fruit. Place chopped pineapple in a medium-size bowl and set aside. Cut remaining pineapple lengthwise into 8 wedges; cut off and discard core from each wedge. Core apple and cut into 1/2-inch chunks. Add apple, chopped strawberries, and yogurt to chopped pineapple; mix lightly.

2 On each of 8 individual plates, arrange 1 or 2 lettuce leaves, a pineapple wedge, a whole strawberry, an eighth of the cottage cheese, and an eighth of the fruit mixture.

makes 8 servings

per serving: 92 calories, 4 g protein, 16 g carbohydrates, 2 g total fat, 4 mg cholesterol, 115 mg sodium

smoked salmon pasta salad

preparation time: about 30 minutes

8 ounces (about 3 cups) dried radiatorre or rotini

¼ cup seasoned rice vinegar; or ¼ cup distilled white vinegar and 2 teaspoons sugar

1 tablespoon chopped fresh dill or ½ teaspoon dried dill weed

1 tablespoon olive oil

8 cups bite-size pieces green leaf lettuce leaves

¼ cup thinly sliced red onion

2 to 4 ounces sliced smoked salmon or lox, cut into bite-size pieces

Dill sprigs

Freshly grated Parmesan cheese

1 Bring 8 cups water to a boil in a 4- to 5-quart pan over medium-high heat. Stir in pasta and cook just until tender to bite (8 to 10 minutes); or cook according to package directions. Drain, rinse with cold water until cool, and drain well.

2 Combine vinegar, chopped dill, and oil in a large nonmetal serving bowl. Mix until blended. Add pasta, lettuce, and onion. Mix thoroughly but gently. Stir in salmon. Garnish with dill sprigs. Offer cheese to add to taste.

makes 6 servings

per serving: 194 calories, 8 g protein, 32 g carbohydrates, 4 g total fat, 3 mg cholesterol, 316 mg sodium

cherry salad with orange dressing

preparation time: about 30 minutes

Orange Dressing (recipe follows)

1 medium-size head iceberg lettuce

1 small pineapple, peeled, cored, and cut into 1-inch chunks

2 ½ cups dark sweet cherries, stemmed and pitted

1 Prepare Orange Dressing; set aside.

2 Remove 4 of the largest lettuce leaves; set aside. Break remaining lettuce into bite-size pieces and place in a large bowl. Add pineapple and cherries. Pour dressing over salad and mix to coat evenly.

3 Line a salad bowl with reserved lettuce leaves; spoon in salad.

makes 6 servings

ORANGE DRESSING

Toast 2 tablespoons sesame seeds in a wide frying pan over medium-high heat until golden (2 to 4 minutes), stirring often. Pour out of pan and set aside. In a bowl, stir together 1 cup plain nonfat yogurt, 3 tablespoons each frozen orange juice concentrate (thawed) and lime juice, and ¼ teaspoon salt. Add sesame seeds; stir until well blended.

per serving: 162 calories, 5 g protein, 33 g carbohydrates, 3 g total fat, 0.8 mg cholesterol, 130 mg sodium

sweet & sour ravioli salad

preparation time: about 40 minutes
chilling time: at least 30 minutes

1 package (about 9 oz.) fresh low-fat or regular cheese ravioli or tortellini

2 pounds pear-shaped (Roma-type) tomatoes (about 10 large)

1/2 cup seasoned rice vinegar; or 1/2 cup distilled white vinegar and 4 teaspoons sugar

2 tablespoons firmly packed brown sugar

1/2 teaspoon *each* coriander seeds, cumin seeds, and mustard seeds

1/16 teaspoon ground red pepper (cayenne)

Parsley sprigs

1 Bring 12 cups water to a boil in a 5- to 6-quart pan over medium-high heat. Separating any ravioli that are stuck together, add pasta. Reduce heat to medium and boil gently, stirring occasionally, just until pasta is tender to bite (4 to 6 minutes); or cook according to package directions. Lift out pasta, rinse with cold water until cool, and drain well. Transfer to a large nonmetal serving bowl and set aside.

2 Bring water in pan back to a boil. Drop in tomatoes and cook for 1 minute. Drain and let cool. Peel and discard skin; cut into bite-size pieces. Set aside.

3 Combine vinegar, brown sugar, coriander seeds, cumin seeds, mustard seeds, and ground red pepper in a 1- to 1 1/2-quart pan. Bring to a simmer over low heat. Cook, stirring, just until sugar is dissolved (about 1 minute).

4 Add tomatoes and vinegar mixture to pasta. Mix thoroughly but gently. Let cool briefly; then cover and refrigerate until cool (at least 30 minutes) or for up to 4 hours; stir occasionally.

5 Garnish with parsley.

makes 6 to 8 servings

per serving: 153 calories, 6 g protein, 27 g carbohydrates, 3 g total fat, 22 mg cholesterol, 481 mg sodium

strawberry tarragon dressing

preparation time: about 20 minutes

1 1/2 cups strawberries, hulled

About 1/4 cup lemon juice

1 tablespoon sugar

1 tablespoon finely chopped shallot

1 teaspoon chopped fresh tarragon or 1/2 teaspoon dried tarragon

1/2 teaspoon cornstarch

2 tablespoons orange juice

1 Whirl strawberries in a blender or food processor until puréed. Rub through a fine wire strainer into a 2-cup glass measure. Add 1/4 cup of the lemon juice and enough water to make 1 cup. Transfer to a small pan and add sugar, shallot, and tarragon.

2 Smoothly mix cornstarch and orange juice; stir into strawberry mixture. Bring to a boil over high heat, stirring constantly. Set pan in a bowl of ice water to chill mixture quickly; then taste and add more lemon juice, if needed. (At this point, you may cover and refrigerate for up to a day.)

makes about 1 cup

per tablespoon: 10 calories, 0.1 g protein, 2 g carbohydrates, 0.1 g total fat, 0 mg cholesterol, 1 mg sodium

indonesian brown rice salad

preparation time: about 1 1/2 hours

BROWN RICE SALAD:

2 cups long-grain brown rice

2 cups Chinese pea pods

1 medium-size red bell pepper

5 green onions

1 can (about 8 oz.) water chestnuts, drained

1/4 cup cilantro leaves

1 cup raisins

1 cup roasted peanuts

CILANTRO SAUCE:

2 cups plain nonfat yogurt

1/2 cup cilantro leaves

1 teaspoon Asian sesame oil

1/2 teaspoon finely chopped garlic

1/4 teaspoon salt (or to taste)

LIME DRESSING:

2/3 cup unseasoned rice vinegar or cider vinegar

2 tablespoons *each* lime juice and reduced-sodium soy sauce

1 tablespoon minced fresh ginger

2 teaspoons finely chopped garlic

1 teaspoon honey

1 In a 2 1/2- to 3-quart pan, bring 4 1/2 cups water to a boil over medium-high heat. Stir in rice; then reduce heat, cover, and simmer until liquid has been absorbed and rice is tender to bite (about 45 minutes). Transfer to a large bowl and let cool, stirring occasionally.

2 Meanwhile, remove and discard ends and strings of pea pods; thinly slice pea pods. Seed and chop bell pepper. Thinly slice onions; chop water chestnuts.

3 To cooled rice, add pea pods, bell pepper, onions, water chestnuts, the 1/4 cup cilantro, raisins, and peanuts. Mix gently but thoroughly; set aside.

4 In a small serving bowl, combine yogurt, the 1/2 cup cilantro, oil, the 1/2 teaspoon garlic, and salt. Stir until blended; set aside.

5 In another small bowl, combine vinegar, lime juice, soy sauce, ginger, the 2 teaspoons garlic, and honey. Beat until blended; pour over salad and mix gently but thoroughly. Serve salad with cilantro sauce.

makes 8 servings

per serving: 545 calories, 18 g protein, 90 g carbohydrates, 15 g total fat, 2 mg cholesterol, 560 mg sodium

PLAN-AHEAD SALADS: Advance planning can provide you with leftover meat and poultry for main-dish salads. If you're roasting one chicken for Sunday dinner, roast a second one alongside—and use the extra meat in a salad later in the week. Keep in mind that a 3-pound frying chicken will yield about 3 cups meat; a 1-pound whole chicken breast will yield about 1 1/2 cups meat. A half pound of cooked boneless ham, beef, or turkey will yield about 2 cups meat. Keep hard-cooked eggs in the refrigerator (marked to distinguish them from raw eggs). A common ingredient in main-dish salads, they also add extra flavor and a protein boost to side-dish salads. Slice or chop the eggs coarsely and toss them with the salad; or cut into wedges and use as a garnish.

steak, couscous & greens with raspberries

preparation time: about 1 1/4 hours
marinating time: at least 30 minutes
chilling time: at least 30 minutes

1 pound lean boneless top sirloin steak (about 1 inch thick), trimmed of fat

1/2 cup dry red wine

5 tablespoons raspberry vinegar or red wine vinegar

1/4 cup chopped green onions

2 tablespoons reduced-sodium soy sauce

1 tablespoon sugar

2 teaspoons chopped fresh tarragon or 1/2 teaspoon dried tarragon

1 tablespoon raspberry or apple jelly

3/4 cup low-sodium chicken broth

2/3 cup low-fat milk

1/4 teaspoon ground coriander

6 1/2 ounces (about 1 cup) dried couscous

1 tablespoon olive oil

8 cups bite-size pieces red leaf lettuce leaves

2 cups raspberries

Tarragon sprigs (optional)

1 Slice steak across grain into strips about 1/8 inch thick and 3 inches long. Place meat, wine, 1 tablespoon of the vinegar, 2 tablespoons of the onions, soy sauce, 2 teaspoons of the sugar, and chopped tarragon in a large heavy-duty resealable plastic bag or large nonmetal bowl. Seal bag and rotate to coat meat (or stir meat in bowl and cover airtight). Refrigerate for at least 30 minutes or up to a day, turning (or stirring) occasionally.

2 Cook jelly in a 2- to 3-quart pan over low heat, stirring, until melted. Add broth, milk, and coriander; increase heat to medium-high and bring to a gentle boil. Stir in couscous. Cover, remove from heat, and let stand until liquid is absorbed (about 5 minutes).

3 Transfer couscous mixture to a large nonmetal bowl; let cool briefly, fluffing occasionally with a fork. Cover and refrigerate until cool (at least 30 minutes) or for up to 2 hours, fluffing occasionally. Meanwhile, heat 1 teaspoon of the oil in a wide nonstick frying pan over medium-high heat. Add meat and its juices and cook, stirring, until browned and done to your liking; cut to test (3 to 5 minutes). Transfer to a large nonmetal bowl and let cool.

4 Combine remaining 2 teaspoons oil, remaining 4 tablespoons vinegar, and remaining 1 teaspoon sugar in a large nonmetal bowl. Mix until blended. Add lettuce and turn to coat. Arrange lettuce on individual plates. Stir remaining 2 tablespoons onions into couscous mixture. Spoon onto lettuce, top with meat, and sprinkle with raspberries. Garnish with tarragon sprigs, if desired.

makes 4 servings

per serving: 456 calories, 34 g protein, 55 g carbohydrates, 10 g total fat, 71 mg cholesterol, 273 mg sodium

creamy herb dressing

1 cup plain nonfat yogurt

3 tablespoons balsamic vinegar

1 1/2 teaspoons chopped fresh oregano or 1/4 teaspoon dried oregano

1 teaspoon Dijon mustard

2 to 3 teaspoons sugar

In a nonmetal bowl, mix yogurt, vinegar, oregano, mustard, and sugar. If made ahead, cover and refrigerate for up to 3 days.

makes 1 1/4 cups

per tablespoon: 9 calories, 0.6 g protein, 1 g carbohydrates, 0 g total fat, 0.2 mg cholesterol, 15 mg sodium

curried shrimp & shell salad

preparation time: about 25 minutes
cooking time: about 15 minutes
chilling time: at least 30 minutes

Curry Dressing (recipe follows)

2 ounces (about ¹/₂ cup) dried small shell-shaped pasta

12 ounces tiny cooked shrimp

1 cup coarsely chopped cucumber

3 tablespoons dried tomatoes packed in oil, drained well and coarsely chopped

Salt

4 to 8 large butter lettuce leaves, rinsed and crisped

Lemon wedges

1 Prepare Curry Dressing; cover and refrigerate.

2 Bring 4 cups water to a boil in a 3- to 4-quart pan over medium-high heat. Stir in pasta and cook just until tender to bite (8 to 10 minutes); or cook according to package directions. Drain, rinse with cold water until cool, and drain well. Transfer pasta to a large nonmetal bowl. Add shrimp, cucumber, tomatoes, and dressing. Mix thoroughly but gently. Season to taste with salt. Cover and refrigerate until cool (at least 30 minutes) or for up to 4 hours; stir occasionally.

3 Arrange lettuce on individual plates. Spoon pasta mixture onto lettuce. Offer lemon to add to taste.

CURRY DRESSING

In a small nonmetal bowl, combine ¹/₄ cup nonfat or reduced-calorie mayonnaise, 1 tablespoon Dijon mustard, ¹/₂ teaspoon grated lemon peel, 1 tablespoon lemon juice, 1 teaspoon each dried dill weed and honey, ¹/₂ teaspoon curry powder, and ¹/₄ teaspoon pepper. Mix until blended. If made ahead, cover and refrigerate for up to an hour. Stir before using.

makes 4 servings

per serving: 226 calories, 21 g protein, 19 g carbohydrates, 7 g total fat, 166 mg cholesterol, 395 mg sodium

green & white sesame salad

preparation time: about 25 minutes

¹/₃ cup seasoned rice vinegar (or ¹/₃ cup distilled white vinegar plus 1 tablespoon sugar)

1 tablespoon *each* sugar, hoisin sauce, and Dijon mustard

3 tablespoons sesame seeds

1 pound slender asparagus, tough ends removed

10 to 12 ounces slender green beans, ends removed

12 ounces jicama, peeled and cut into long matchstick strips

1 In a small bowl, stir together vinegar, sugar, hoisin sauce, and mustard. Set aside.

2 Toast sesame seeds in a wide frying pan over medium-high heat until golden (2 to 4 minutes), stirring often. Add to dressing and stir to mix.

3 Pour water into frying pan to a depth of ¹/₂-inch and bring to a boil over high heat. Add asparagus and beans. Cover and cook just until vegetables are tender-crisp to bite (2 to 3 minutes). Drain, immerse in cold water until cool, and drain again.

4 Arrange asparagus, beans, and jicama on a platter. Stir dressing well; drizzle over vegetables.

makes 6 servings

per serving: 100 calories, 4 g protein, 17 g carbohydrates, 3 g total fat, 0 mg cholesterol, 429 mg sodium

shrimp & orzo with pesto dressing

preparation time: about 35 minutes

Pesto Dressing (recipe follows)

6 cups low-sodium chicken broth

8 ounces (about 1 1/3 cups) dried orzo or other rice-shaped pasta

1 pound tiny cooked shrimp

1 cup chopped green onions

1 tablespoon grated lemon peel

1/2 cup lemon juice

1 small head iceberg lettuce, rinsed and crisped

3 cups tiny cherry tomatoes

1 Prepare Pesto Dressing; cover and refrigerate.

2 Bring broth to a boil in a 4- to 5-quart pan over medium-high heat. Stir in pasta and cook just until barely tender to bite (about 5 minutes). Drain well, reserving liquid for other uses. Let cool completely.

3 Transfer pasta to a large bowl. Add shrimp, onions, lemon peel, and lemon juice. Mix thoroughly but gently.

4 Shred lettuce and place in a shallow serving bowl. Spoon pasta mixture into bowl. Arrange tomatoes around edge of bowl. Offer dressing to add to taste.

makes 5 or 6 servings

per serving: 274 calories, 26 g protein, 38 g carbohydrates, 4 g total fat, 148 mg cholesterol, 305 mg sodium

PESTO DRESSING

In a blender or food processor, combine 1/2 cup each chopped fresh basil and chopped cilantro, 1 cup plain nonfat yogurt, and 1 tablespoon white wine vinegar. Whirl until smooth. If made ahead, cover and refrigerate for up to 4 hours. Stir before serving.

makes about 1 1/4 cups

per serving: 8 calories, 0.7 g protein, 1 g carbohydrates, 0 g total fat, 0.2 mg cholesterol, 9 mg sodium

carrot slaw

preparation time: about 20 minutes
chilling time: at least 1 hour

1 1/2 pounds carrots, shredded

1 teaspoon grated lime peel

1/3 cup lime juice

2 tablespoons *each* distilled white vinegar and honey

1 tablespoon Dijon mustard

1 teaspoon caraway seeds

1/4 teaspoon crushed red pepper flakes

Salt

In a medium-size bowl, combine carrots, lime peel, lime juice, vinegar, honey, mustard, caraway seeds, and red pepper flakes. Mix gently; then season to taste with salt. Cover and refrigerate until cold (at least 1 hour) or for up to 2 days. To serve, lift to individual plates with a slotted spoon.

makes 4 to 6 servings

per serving: 94 calories, 2 g protein, 23 g carbohydrates, 0.5 g total fat, 0 mg cholesterol, 141 mg sodium

spinach salad with garlic croutons

preparation time: about 25 minutes

1 1/2 **pounds spinach, stems removed, leaves rinsed and crisped**

1 medium-size red onion, thinly sliced and separated into rings

8 ounces mushrooms, thinly sliced

1 large red bell pepper, seeded and thinly sliced

2 ounces feta cheese, crumbled

1/2 **cup lemon juice**

4 teaspoons olive oil

1/2 **teaspoon dry oregano**

2 cloves garlic, peeled

1 small French bread baguette, cut into 1/2**-inch-thick slices**

1 Tear spinach leaves into bite-size pieces, if desired. Place spinach, onion, mushrooms, and bell pepper in a large bowl; set aside.

2 In a blender, whirl cheese, lemon juice, oil, oregano, and 1 clove of the garlic until smoothly blended; set aside.

3 Place baguette slices in a single layer on a baking sheet and broil about 5 inches below heat, turning once, until golden on both sides (about 4 minutes). Let toast slices cool briefly. Rub remaining garlic clove evenly over top of each toast slice; then discard garlic clove.

4 Pour dressing over salad and mix gently. Spoon salad onto individual plates. Arrange toasted baguette slices atop salads (or arrange toast on a plate and serve on the side).

makes 6 servings

per serving: 208 calories, 9 g protein, 31 g carbohydrates, 7 g total fat, 8 mg cholesterol, 410 mg sodium

chili potato salad

preparation time: about 45 minutes
cooling time: about 30 minutes

1 1/2 **pounds large thin-skinned potatoes, scrubbed**

1 can (about 17 oz.) corn kernels, drained

1/2 **cup** *each* **sliced celery and chopped red onion**

2/3 **cup chopped red bell pepper**

2 tablespoons salad oil

1/4 **cup cider vinegar**

2 teaspoons chili powder

1 clove garlic, minced or pressed

1/2 **teaspoon liquid hot pepper seasoning**

Salt and pepper

1 Place unpeeled potatoes in a 5- to 6-quart pan and add enough water to cover. Bring to a boil over high heat; then reduce heat, partially cover, and boil gently until potatoes are tender when pierced (25 to 30 minutes). Drain, immerse in cold water until cool, and drain again. Cut into 3/4-inch cubes.

2 In a large bowl, combine potatoes, corn, celery, onion, and bell pepper. Add oil, vinegar, chili powder, garlic, and hot pepper seasoning; mix gently, then season to taste with salt and pepper. If made ahead, cover and refrigerate for up to 1 day. Serve cold or at room temperature.

makes 6 servings

per serving: 210 calories, 5 g protein, 39 g carbohydrates, 5 g total fat, 0 mg cholesterol, 257 mg sodium

golden pepper salad

preparation time: about 25 minutes

Golden Dressing (recipe follows)

1 head red leaf lettuce

1 small head red oak leaf lettuce

1 small head chicory

1 large bunch watercress

1 head Belgian endive

1 *each* medium-size yellow and red bell pepper

1 can (about 15 oz.) garbanzo beans, drained and rinsed; or 2 cups cooked garbanzo beans, drained and rinsed

1 Prepare Golden Dressing; set aside.

2 Separate lettuces into leaves (tear larger leaf lettuce leaves in half). Discard outer leaves from chicory. Discard tough stems from watercress. Rinse and crisp lettuces, chicory, and watercress; then place all greens in a 3- to 4-quart bowl.

3 Cut endive in half lengthwise, then cut each half crosswise into thin strips. Cut bell peppers in half lengthwise; remove seeds, then cut each pepper half crosswise into thin strips. Add endive, bell peppers, and beans to bowl of greens.

4 Stir Golden Dressing to blend, pour over salad, and mix gently.

makes 8 servings

GOLDEN DRESSING

In a blender or food processor, combine 1 tablespoon olive oil, ½ cup diced yellow bell pepper, 1 tablespoon minced shallot, and ⅛ teaspoon each salt and ground red pepper (cayenne). Whirl until mixture is smoothly puréed. (At this point, you may cover dressing and refrigerate for up to 1 day.) Just before using, add 2 tablespoons white wine vinegar and stir until thoroughly blended.

per serving: 84 calories, 4 g protein, 12 g carbohydrates, 3 g total fat, 0 mg cholesterol, 125 mg sodium

green pea salad

preparation time: 15 minutes
chilling time: at least 3 hours

⅓ cup plain low-fat yogurt

1 ½ tablespoons Dijon mustard

⅛ teaspoon pepper

1 package (about 10 oz.) frozen tiny peas, thawed

1 hard-cooked large egg, chopped

½ cup finely chopped red or green bell pepper

⅓ cup thinly sliced green onions

¼ cup thinly sliced celery

Butter lettuce leaves, rinsed and crisped

1 In a large bowl, stir together yogurt, mustard, and pepper. Add peas, egg, bell pepper, onions, and celery. Mix gently. Cover and refrigerate for at least 3 hours or up to 1 day.

2 To serve, line a platter or individual plates with lettuce; spoon salad onto lettuce.

makes 6 servings

per serving: 61 calories, 4 g protein, 8 g carbohydrates, 2 g total fat, 36 mg cholesterol, 201 mg sodium

beef & bow-tie salad

preparation time: about 50 minutes
marinating time: at least 30 minutes
chilling time: at least 30 minutes

1 pound lean boneless top sirloin steak (about 1 inch thick), trimmed of fat

2 tablespoons dry sherry

Blue Cheese Dressing (recipe follows)

6 to 8 ounces (3 to 4 cups) dried farfalle (about 1 1/2-inch size)

1/4 cup red wine vinegar

1 tablespoon olive oil or salad oil

1 tablespoon chopped fresh thyme or 1 teaspoon dried thyme

1 teaspoon sugar

Salt and pepper

8 cups bite-size pieces butter lettuce leaves

Thyme sprigs

1 Slice steak across grain into strips about 1/8-inch thick and 3 inches long. Place meat and sherry in a large heavy-duty resealable plastic bag or nonmetal bowl. Seal bag and rotate to coat meat (or stir meat in bowl and cover airtight). Refrigerate for at least 30 minutes or up to a day, turning (or stirring) occasionally.

2 Prepare Blue Cheese Dressing; cover and refrigerate.

3 Bring 8 cups water to a boil in a 4- to 5-quart pan over medium-high heat. Stir in pasta and cook just until tender to bite (8 to 10 minutes); or cook according to package directions. Drain, rinse with cold water until cool, and drain well.

4 Combine vinegar, 2 teaspoons of the oil, chopped thyme, and sugar in a large nonmetal bowl. Stir until blended. Add pasta and mix thoroughly but gently. Cover and refrigerate until cool (at least 30 minutes) or for up to 2 hours; stir occasionally. Meanwhile, heat remaining 1 teaspoon oil in a wide nonstick frying pan over medium-high heat. Add steak and its juices and cook, stirring, until browned and done to your liking; cut to test (3 to 5 minutes). Transfer to a large nonmetal bowl and let cool. Season to taste with salt and pepper.

5 Combine lettuce and dressing in a large serving bowl; turn to coat. Add beef to pasta mixture and stir gently. Spoon onto greens. Garnish with thyme sprigs.

makes 4 to 6 servings

BLUE CHEESE DRESSING

In a blender or food processor, combine 4 ounces low-fat (1%) or soft tofu, rinsed and drained; 1/4 cup low-fat buttermilk; 1 tablespoon white wine vinegar; 2 teaspoons each sugar and olive oil; 1 teaspoon Dijon mustard; and 1 clove garlic. Whirl until smooth. Season to taste with salt and pepper. Gently stir in 1/4 cup crumbled blue-veined cheese. (At this point, you may cover and refrigerate for up to an hour.) Stir in 1 tablespoon chopped green onion before using.

per serving: 376 calories, 28 g protein, 36 g carbohydrates, 12 g total fat, 61 mg cholesterol, 210 mg sodium

chicken salad with kumquats

preparation time: about 35 minutes
standing time: about 20 minutes

1 ½ **pounds chicken breast halves, skinned**

Ginger-Mint Dressing (recipe follows)

³/₄ **cup kumquats, thinly sliced, seeds and ends discarded**

1 small cucumber, cut in half lengthwise, then thinly sliced crosswise

16 Belgian endive spears or 8 large radicchio leaves, rinsed and crisped

Mint sprigs (optional)

1 In a 5- to 6-quart pan, bring about 3 quarts water to a boil over high heat. Rinse chicken and add to water; return to a boil. Then cover pan tightly, remove from heat, and let stand until meat in thickest part is no longer pink; cut to test (about 20 minutes). If chicken is not done after 20 minutes, return it to water, cover pan; and let stand longer, checking at 2- to 3-minute intervals. Remove chicken from water and let cool; then tear meat into shreds and discard bones. (At this point, you may cover and refrigerate until next day.)

2 Prepare Ginger-Mint Dressing

3 Add kumquats to bowl with dressing; mix gently. Mix in cucumber and chicken. On each of 4 individual plates, place 4 endive spears or 2 radicchio leaves; top equally with chicken mixture. Garnish with mint sprigs, if desired.

makes 4 servings

GINGER-MINT DRESSING

In a large bowl, combine ½ cup lemon juice, ¼ cup finely shredded fresh mint or 2 tablespoons dry mint, 2 tablespoons each water and minced crystallized ginger, 2 ½ teaspoons sugar, and 1 tablespoon fish sauce (*nam pla* or *nuoc mam*) or reduced-sodium soy sauce.

per serving: 211 calories, 28 g protein, 21 g carbohydrates, 2 g total fat, 65 mg cholesterol, 90 mg sodium

golden potato salad

preparation time: about 50 minutes
cooling time: about 30 minutes

3 ½ **pounds small red thin-skinned potatoes, scrubbed**

8 ounces slender green beans, ends removed

³/₄ **cup chopped yellow bell pepper**

About ¹/₃ **cup low-sodium chicken broth**

3 tablespoons red wine vinegar

1 tablespoon *each* balsamic vinegar and olive oil

1 teaspoon *each* ground turmeric, crushed anise seeds, and dry tarragon

Salt and pepper

1 Place unpeeled potatoes in a 5- to 6-quart pan and add enough water to cover. Bring to a boil; reduce heat, partially cover, and boil gently until potatoes are tender when pierced (about 25 minutes). Lift out with a slotted spoon and let stand until cool (about 30 minutes). Meanwhile, return water in pan to a boil over high heat. Add beans and cook, uncovered, just until tender-crisp to bite (2 to 3 minutes). Drain, immerse in cold water until cool, and drain again. Cut potatoes into ½-inch-thick slices; cut beans into 1-inch lengths.

2 In a large bowl, combine bell pepper, ¹/₃ cup of the broth, red wine vinegar, balsamic vinegar, oil, turmeric, anise seeds, and tarragon. Add potatoes and beans; mix gently. For a moister salad, add a little more broth. Season to taste with salt and pepper.

makes 8 servings

per serving: 190 calories, 5 g protein, 39 g carbohydrates, 2 g total fat, 0 mg cholesterol, 19 mg sodium

gingered pork & ziti salad

preparation time: about 45 minutes
chilling time: at least 30 minutes

6 ounces (about 2 cups) dried ziti or penne

²/₃ cup mango or pear nectar

1 tablespoon minced fresh ginger

2 teaspoons olive oil

1 or 2 cloves garlic, minced or pressed

1 teaspoon Asian sesame oil

1 ¹/₂ cups roasted or Chinese-style barbecued pork, cut into thin ¹/₂-inch pieces

¹/₃ cup chopped red bell pepper

4 to 8 red leaf lettuce leaves, rinsed and crisped

¹/₄ cup thinly sliced green onions

4 whole green onions (optional)

Salt and pepper

1 Bring 8 cups water to a boil in a 4- to 5-quart pan over medium-high heat. Stir in pasta and cook just until tender to bite (8 to 10 minutes); or cook according to package directions. Drain, rinse with cold water until cool, and drain well.

2 Combine mango nectar, ginger, olive oil, garlic, and sesame oil in a large nonmetal bowl. Mix until blended. Add pasta, pork, and bell pepper. Mix thoroughly but gently. Cover and refrigerate until cool (at least 30 minutes) or for up to 3 hours; stir occasionally.

3 Arrange lettuce on individual plates. Stir sliced onions into pasta mixture and spoon onto lettuce. Garnish with whole onions, if desired. Offer salt and pepper to add to taste.

makes 4 servings

per serving: 346 calories, 24 g protein, 40 g carbohydrates, 10 g total fat, 50 mg cholesterol, 51 mg sodium

shrimp & jicama with chile vinegar

preparation time: about 35 minutes

Chile Vinegar (recipe follows)

2 cups shredded jicama

1 pound small cooked shrimp

4 large ripe tomatoes, sliced

4 large tomatillos, husked, rinsed, and sliced

Cilantro sprigs

1 Prepare Chile Vinegar. Place jicama and shrimp in separate bowls. Add ¹/₄ cup of the Chile Vinegar to each bowl; mix gently. Reserve remaining vinegar.

2 On each of 4 individual plates, arrange tomatoes and tomatillos, overlapping slices slightly. Mound jicama over or beside tomato slices. Spoon shrimp over jicama; spoon remaining Chile Vinegar over all. Garnish with cilantro sprigs.

CHILE VINEGAR

In a small bowl, stir together ²/₃ cup white wine vinegar, ¹/₄ cup sugar, 2 to 3 tablespoons seeded, minced fresh hot green chiles, and 3 to 4 tablespoons chopped cilantro.

makes 4 servings

per serving: 261 calories, 28 g protein, 34 g carbohydrates, 2 g total fat, 221 mg cholesterol, 279 mg sodium

pork & rotini salad with oranges

preparation time: 1 hour
chilling time: at least 30 minutes

8 ounces (about 3 ¹/₂ cups) dried rotini or other corkscrew-shaped pasta

1 teaspoon salad oil

1 pound pork tenderloin or boned pork loin, trimmed of fat, sliced into thin strips ¹/₂ inch wide

1 tablespoon minced garlic

1 teaspoon *each* chili powder and dried oregano

³/₄ cup lime juice

3 tablespoons sugar

1 teaspoon reduced-sodium soy sauce

¹/₃ cup chopped cilantro

6 large oranges

About 40 large spinach leaves, coarse stems removed, rinsed and crisped

1 Bring 8 cups water to a boil in a 4- to 5-quart pan over medium-high heat. Stir in pasta and cook just until tender to bite (8 to 10 minutes); or cook according to package directions. Drain, rinse with cold water until cool, and drain well; set aside.

2 Heat oil in a wide nonstick frying pan over medium-high heat. Add pork, garlic, chili powder, and oregano. Cook, stirring, until pork is no longer pink in center; cut to test (about 5 minutes). Remove pan from heat and add lime juice, sugar, and soy sauce; stir to loosen browned bits. Transfer to a large nonmetal bowl and let cool briefly. Add pasta and cilantro. Mix thoroughly but gently. Cover and refrigerate until cool (at least 30 minutes) or for up to 2 hours; stir occasionally.

3 Cut peel and white membrane from oranges; thinly slice fruit crosswise. Arrange spinach on individual plates. Top with orange slices and pasta mixture.

makes 6 servings

per serving: 362 calories, 23 g protein, 59 g carbohydrates, 5 g total fat, 49 mg cholesterol, 99 mg sodium

pesto-orange potato salad

preparation time: about 25 minutes

2 medium-size oranges

¹/₂ cup *each* lightly packed parsley sprigs and cilantro leaves

¹/₄ cup grated Parmesan cheese

³/₄ cup plain low-fat yogurt

1 teaspoon sugar

2 pounds russet potatoes, cooked, peeled, and cut into ¹/₂-inch cubes

Salt and pepper

¹/₂ cup walnut halves

1 Grate 2 teaspoons peel (colored part only) from oranges; set peel aside. Cut remaining peel and all white membrane from oranges. Holding fruit over a bowl to catch juice, cut between membranes to release orange segments; set segments aside.

2 Pour juice in bowl into a blender or food processor; add the 2 teaspoons grated orange peel, parsley, cilantro, cheese, yogurt, and sugar. Whirl until smooth.

3 Place potatoes in a large bowl; pour yogurt mixture over potatoes and mix gently. Season to taste with salt and pepper. Garnish with orange segments and walnuts.

makes 6 to 8 servings

per serving: 196 calories, 6 g protein, 31 g carbohydrates, 6 g total fat, 4 mg cholesterol, 82 mg sodium

chef's salad with fruit

preparation time: about 25 minutes

Honey-Mustard Dressing (recipe follows)

12 cups bite-size pieces red leaf lettuce, rinsed and crisped

2 large red Bartlett or other firm-ripe pears

4 kiwi fruit, peeled and thinly sliced crosswise

2 large carrots, coarsely grated

3 ounces part-skin mozzarella cheese, finely shredded

1/4 pound thinly sliced cooked skinless turkey breast, cut into julienne strips

1 Prepare Honey-Mustard Dressing and set aside.

2 Place lettuce in a large shallow bowl or on a platter. Core and slice pears. Arrange pears, kiwis, carrots, mozzarella, and turkey in separate mounds on lettuce. Offer with dressing.

HONEY-MUSTARD DRESSING

Mix ½ cup cider vinegar, 3 tablespoons each salad oil and honey, and 2 teaspoons dry mustard. If made ahead, cover and refrigerate for up to 2 days.

makes 6 servings

per serving: 286 calories, 12 g protein, 40 g carbohydrates, 11 g total fat, 21 mg cholesterol, 110 mg sodium

---

caesar salad

preparation time: about 15 minutes

Garlic Croutons (recipe follows)

2/3 cup nonfat or reduced fat sour cream

1 or 2 cloves garlic, minced or pressed

2 tablespoons lemon juice

1 teaspoon Worcestershire (optional)

6 to 8 canned anchovy fillets, rinsed, drained, patted dry, and finely chopped

8 cups lightly packed bite-size pieces of rinsed, crisped romaine lettuce

About 1/4 cup grated Parmesan cheese

1 Prepare Garlic Croutons; set aside.

2 In a large nonmetal bowl, beat sour cream, garlic, lemon juice, and Worcestershire (if desired) until blended. Stir in anchovies.

3 Add lettuce to bowl with dressing; mix gently but thoroughly to coat with dressing. Spoon salad onto individual plates and add cheese and croutons to taste.

makes 4 to 6 servings

GARLIC CROUTONS

In a small bowl, combine 1 tablespoon olive oil, 1 tablespoon water, and 1 clove garlic, minced or pressed. Cut 3 ounces (about 3 slices) French bread into ¾-inch cubes and spread in a 10- by 15-inch nonstick rimmed baking pan. Brush oil mixture evenly over bread cubes. Bake in a 350° oven until croutons are crisp and golden (10 to 12 minutes). If made ahead, let cool; then store airtight for up to 2 days.

makes about 3 cups

per serving: 70 calories, 7 g protein, 5 g carbohydrates, 2 g total fat, 6 mg cholesterol, 311 mg sodium

orange & olive patio salad

preparation time: about 20 minutes
cooling time: about 1 hour

1/2 cup water

1 teaspoon arrowroot

4 teaspoons honey

2 tablespoons finely chopped fresh mint

1 small mild red onion, thinly sliced crosswise

1/4 cup red wine vinegar

6 cups lightly packed mixed bite-size pieces of butter lettuce and radicchio (or all butter lettuce), rinsed and crisped

6 cups lightly packed watercress sprigs, rinsed and crisped

2 medium-size oranges, peeled and thinly sliced crosswise

1/4 cup small pitted ripe or Niçoise olives

1/4 cup lime juice

About 1/4 cup mixed fresh basil and fresh mint leaves (optional)

Salt and pepper

1 In a small pan, combine water, arrowroot, honey, and chopped mint. Bring to a boil over high heat, stirring constantly. Remove from heat and let stand until cold (about 1 hour).

2 Meanwhile, in a large salad bowl, combine onion and vinegar. Let stand for at least 15 minutes or up to 3 hours. Drain, discarding vinegar; separate onion slices into rings.

3 In same salad bowl, combine onion rings, lettuce, radicchio, and watercress; mix lightly. Top with orange slices and olives.

4 Stir lime juice into honey-mint mixture, then pour through a fine wire strainer over salad; discard residue. Garnish with basil and mint leaves, if desired; season to taste with salt and pepper.

makes 8 to 10 servings

per serving: 49 calories, 2 g protein, 11 g carbohydrates, 0.6 g total fat, 0 mg cholesterol, 49 mg sodium

curry oil

preparation time: About 10 minutes

1/4 cup curry powder

1 cup vegetable oil or olive oil

1 to 3 cinnamon sticks (*each* about 3 inches long)

1 In a small pan, whisk together curry powder and 1/4 cup of the oil until well blended. Gradually whisk in remaining 3/4 cup oil. Add cinnamon stick(s). Heat over medium heat, stirring often, just until warm (not hot or boiling). Remove from heat and let cool slightly.

2 With a clean, dry slotted spoon, lift out cinnamon stick(s); set aside. Carefully pour oil into a clean, dry glass bottle or jar, leaving curry sediment behind; discard sediment. (Or strain oil, if desired.) Add cinnamon stick(s) to bottle; cover airtight and store for up to 6 months.

makes about 1 cup

per tablespoon: 125 calories, 0.2 g protein, 1 g carbohydrates, 14 g total fat, 0 mg cholesterol, 0.8 mg sodium

thai coleslaw

preparation time: about 40 minutes

$^1/_3$ **cup** *each* **unseasoned rice vinegar and lime juice**

$^1/_4$ **cup slivered red pickled ginger**

2 small fresh serrano or jalapeño chiles, seeded and finely chopped

1 tablespoon *each* **sugar and Asian sesame oil**

1 tablespoon fish sauce (*nam pla* or *nuoc mam*)

$^1/_2$ **teaspoon wasabi (green horseradish) powder**

2 teaspoons sesame seeds

About 1 pound bok choy (coarse outer leaves removed), rinsed and crisped

1 small red onion, cut into thin slivers

2 medium-size carrots, thinly sliced

8 cups finely slivered Savoy or green cabbage

1 small head radicchio, cut into thin slivers

1 In a small bowl, stir together vinegar, lime juice, ginger, chiles, sugar, oil, fish sauce, and wasabi powder; set aside.

2 Toast sesame seeds in small frying pan over medium-high heat until golden (2 to 4 minutes), stirring often. Pour out of pan and set aside.

3 Thinly slice bok choy and place in a large bowl. Add onion, carrots, cabbage, radicchio, and dressing; mix gently. Sprinkle with sesame seeds.

makes 8 to 12 servings

per serving: 62 calories, 3 g protein, 10 g carbohydrates, 2 g total fat, 0 mg cholesterol, 64 mg sodium

viennese potato salad

preparation time: about 1 hour

2 $^1/_2$ pounds small red thin-skinned potatoes, scrubbed

$^1/_2$ **cup pecan or walnut pieces**

3 large red-skinned apples

$^1/_2$ **cup sliced green onions cup raisins**

$^1/_3$ **cup late-harvest gewürztraminer or Johannesburg Riesling**

$^1/_3$ **cup cider vinegar**

2 tablespoons salad oil

1 tablespoon grated lemon peel

2 teaspoons poppy seeds

1 Place unpeeled potatoes in a 5- to 6-quart pan and add enough water to cover. Bring to a boil over high heat; then reduce heat, partially cover, and boil gently until potatoes are tender when pierced (about 25 minutes). Drain, immerse in cold water until cool, and drain again. Cut into 1-inch cubes and set aside.

2 Toast pecans in a wide frying pan over medium-high heat until lightly browned and fragrant (about 3 minutes), stirring often. Pour out of pan and let cool; chop coarsely and set aside.

3 Core 2 of the apples and cut fruit into 1-inch chunks (set remaining apple aside to use for garnish). In a large bowl, combine apple chunks, potatoes, pecans, onions, raisins, wine, vinegar, oil, lemon peel, and poppy seeds; mix gently. If made ahead, cover and refrigerate for up to 6 hours.

4 To serve, mound salad on a large rimmed platter. Core remaining apple and cut into slices; fan slices out next to salad along one side of platter.

makes 6 to 8 servings

per serving: 307 calories, 4 g protein, 51 g carbohydrates, 10 g total fat, 0 mg cholesterol, 15 mg sodium

sweet potato & ginger salad

preparation time: about 30 minutes

¹/₂ **pound sweet potatoes**

2 **tablespoons lemon juice**

1 **medium-large pineapple**

1 **cup finely shredded peeled jicama**

2 **tablespoons salad oil**

2 **teaspoons honey**

1 **teaspoon** *each* **minced fresh ginger and grated lemon peel**

Finely chopped parsley

Red leaf lettuce leaves

1 In a 5-quart pan, bring about 3 quarts water to a boil over high heat. Peel and shred sweet potatoes; immediately add to boiling water. Cook for 30 seconds, then drain well and mix with lemon juice.

2 Cut off pineapple peel. Cut about half the pineapple into 4 crosswise slices, cover, and refrigerate. Core and finely chop remaining pineapple; drain briefly in a colander.

3 Squeeze excess liquid from jicama. Mix jicama, chopped pineapple, oil, honey, ginger, and lemon peel with sweet potatoes. (At this point, you may cover and let stand at room temperature for up to 4 hours.)

4 To serve, place an equal portion of jicama mixture atop each pineapple slice. Sprinkle with parsley and present on a lettuce-lined platter.

makes 4 servings

per serving: 244 calories, 2 g protein, 45 g carbohydrates, 8 g total fat, 0 mg cholesterol, 11 mg sodium

summer fruit & almond salad

preparation time: about 50 minutes

¹/₂ **cup sliced almonds**

8 **ounces jicama, peeled and cut into matchstick pieces**

¹/₄ **cup orange juice**

2 **tablespoons lemon juice**

1 **teaspoon each poppy seeds and sugar**

¹/₄ **teaspoon almond extract**

2 **cups cubed, seeded watermelon**

2 **cups cubed cantaloupe**

1 **cup seedless grapes, halved**

1 **cup strawberries, hulled and sliced**

12 **to** 16 **large lettuce leaves, rinsed and crisped**

1 **large kiwi fruit, peeled and thinly sliced**

1 Toast almonds in a wide frying pan over medium-high heat until golden (about 3 minutes), stirring often. Pour out of pan and set aside.

2 In a large bowl, mix jicama, orange juice, lemon juice, poppy seeds, sugar, and almond extract. Add watermelon, cantaloupe, grapes, and strawberries; mix gently.

3 Arrange lettuce leaves on 6 to 8 individual plates; evenly mound fruit mixture on lettuce. Garnish salad with kiwi fruit and almonds.

makes 6 to 8 servings

per serving: 128 calories, 3 g protein, 21 g carbohydrates, 4 g total fat, 0 mg cholesterol, 12 mg sodium

potato salad with seed vinaigrette

preparation time: about 50 minutes

Seed Vinaigrette (recipe follows)

5 large red thin-skinned potatoes, scrubbed

1 cup thinly sliced celery

1/2 cup thinly sliced green onions

1 small red bell pepper, seeded and finely chopped

Salt

1 Prepare Seed Vinaigrette and set aside.

2 Place unpeeled potatoes in a 5- to 6-quart pan and add enough water to cover. Bring to a boil over high heat; then reduce heat, partially cover, and boil gently until potatoes are tender when pierced (25 to 30 minutes). Drain, immerse in cold water until cool, and drain again. Cut into 3/4-inch cubes.

3 In a large bowl, gently mix potatoes, celery, onions, bell pepper, and Seed Vinaigrette. Season to taste with salt. If made ahead, cover and refrigerate for up to 1 day. Serve cold or at room temperature.

makes 6 to 8 servings

SEED VINAIGRETTE

In a wide frying pan, combine 1 teaspoon each mustard seeds, cumin seeds, and fennel seeds. Cook over medium heat until fragrant (3 to 5 minutes), stirring often. Using the back of a heavy spoon, coarsely crush seeds. Remove from heat and mix in 2 tablespoons salad oil, 1/3 cider vinegar, 1/2 teaspoon coarsely ground pepper, and 1 clove garlic (minced or pressed).

per serving: 169 calories, 3 g protein, 30 g carbohydrates, 4 g total fat, 0 mg cholesterol, 29 mg sodium

sweet potato & apple salad

preparation time: about 1 hour
cooling time: about 30 minutes

2 pounds small sweet potatoes or yams

1/2 cup walnuts

2 tablespoons honey

1 teaspoon grated lemon peel

1 tablespoon lemon juice

3/4 teaspoon ground ginger

1/2 teaspoon ground cinnamon

1 cup plain nonfat yogurt

2 large red-skinned apples, cored and cut into 3/4-inch cubes

3/4 cup thinly sliced celery

Salt

1 Place unpeeled potatoes in a 5- to 6-quart pan and add enough water to cover. Bring to a boil over high heat; then reduce heat, partially cover, and boil gently until potatoes are tender when pierced (25 to 30 minutes). Drain and let stand until cool (about 30 minutes). Meanwhile, toast walnuts in a wide frying pan over medium-high heat until lightly browned and fragrant (about 3 minutes), stirring often. Pour out of pan and let cool.

2 In a large bowl, stir together honey, lemon peel, lemon juice, ginger, cinnamon, and yogurt. Peel potatoes and cut into 3/4-inch cubes; then add potatoes, apples, celery, and 1/3 cup of the walnuts to dressing in bowl. Mix gently. Season to taste with salt. Transfer to a serving bowl and garnish with remaining walnuts.

makes 8 to 10 servings

per serving: 207 calories, 4 g protein, 39 g carbohydrates, 5 g total fat, 0.5 mg cholesterol, 42 mg sodium

black bean, corn & pepper salad

preparation time: about 15 minutes
chilling time: at least 1 hour

2 cans (about 15 oz. *each*) black beans or cannellini (white kidney beans), drained and rinsed; or 4 cups cooked black beans or cannellini, drained and rinsed

1 1/2 cups cooked fresh yellow or white corn kernels (from 2 medium-size ears corn); or 1 package (about 10 oz.) frozen corn kernels, thawed

1 large red bell pepper, seeded and finely chopped

2 small fresh jalapeño chiles, seeded and finely chopped

1/2 cup firmly packed chopped cilantro

1/4 cup lime juice

2 tablespoons salad oil

Salt and pepper

Lettuce leaves, rinsed and crisped

1 In a large bowl, combine beans, corn, bell pepper, chiles, cilantro, lime juice, and oil; mix lightly. Season to taste with salt and pepper. Cover and refrigerate for at least 1 hour or for up to 1 day.

2 To serve, line a serving bowl with lettuce leaves; spoon in bean mixture.

makes 6 servings

per serving: 197 calories, 9 g protein, 29 g carbohydrates, 6 g total fat, 0 mg cholesterol, 186 mg sodium

orzo with spinach & pine nuts

preparation time: about 35 minutes

8 ounces dry orzo or tiny shell-shaped pasta

2 tablespoons pine nuts

1 tablespoon olive oil

1/2 cup minced red onion

4 ounces stemmed spinach leaves, rinsed and chopped

2 medium-size pear-shaped (Roma-type) tomatoes, seeded and diced

3 ounces feta cheese, crumbled

1/4 cup chopped parsley

Pepper

1 In a 5- to 6-quart pan, cook orzo in about 3 quarts boiling water until just tender to bite (about 5 minutes); or cook according to package directions. Drain, rinse with cold water until cool, and drain again.

2 Toast pine nuts in a medium-size frying pan over medium heat until golden (3 to 5 minutes), stirring often. Pour out of pan and set aside.

3 Heat oil in pan. Add onion; cook, stirring often, until soft (about 5 minutes). Add spinach and cook, stirring, just until wilted (about 2 more minutes).

4 In a large bowl, gently mix pasta, pine nuts, and spinach mixture. Add tomatoes, cheese, and parsley. Mix again; season to taste with pepper. If made ahead, cover and refrigerate for up to 4 hours. Serve at room temperature.

makes 6 servings

per serving: 229 calories, 9 g protein, 32 g carbohydrates, 8 g total fat, 13 mg cholesterol, 181 mg sodium

poultry

lemon chicken

preparation time: about 30 minutes

5 or 6 large lemons

¾ cup plus 1 tablespoon cornstarch

⅓ cup fat-free reduced-sodium chicken broth

¼ cup sugar

2 tablespoons light corn syrup

2 tablespoons distilled white vinegar

1 tablespoon plus 1 teaspoon vegetable oil

½ teaspoon salt (optional)

2 cloves garlic, minced or pressed

2 large egg whites

¼ cup all-purpose flour

1 teaspoon baking powder

1 teaspoon finely minced fresh ginger

⅛ teaspoon ground white pepper

1 pound skinless, boneless chicken breast, cut into ½- by 3-inch strips

Finely shredded lemon peel

Cilantro sprigs

1 To prepare sauce, finely shred enough peel (colored part only) from 1 or 2 of the lemons to make ½ teaspoon; set aside. Squeeze enough juice to measure 3 tablespoons. In a small bowl, stir together lemon juice and 1 tablespoon of the cornstarch until blended. Stir in lemon peel, broth, sugar, corn syrup, vinegar, 1 tablespoon water, 1 teaspoon of the oil, ¼ teaspoon of the salt (if using), and garlic. Set sauce aside.

2 Thinly slice the remaining lemons and place slices on a rimmed platter, overlapping them, if necessary; cover and set aside.

3 In a large bowl, beat egg whites and ½ cup water to blend. Add remaining ¾ cup cornstarch, flour, baking powder, ginger, remaining ¼ teaspoon salt (if using), and white pepper; stir until smoothly blended.

4 Heat remaining 1 tablespoon oil in a wide nonstick frying pan or wok over medium-high heat. Meanwhile, dip chicken pieces in egg-white batter. Lift out and drain briefly to let excess batter drip off; discard remaining batter.

5 When oil is hot, add chicken and stir-fry gently, separating pieces, until meat is lightly browned on outside and no longer pink in center; cut to test (5 to 7 minutes; if any pieces brown too much, remove them from pan and keep warm). Arrange chicken over lemon slices on platter; keep warm.

6 Wipe pan clean (be careful; pan is hot). Stir reserved lemon sauce well; pour into pan. Stir over medium-high heat until sauce boils and thickens slightly (1 to 2 minutes). Pour sauce over chicken and sprinkle with additional shredded lemon peel. Garnish with cilantro sprigs.

makes 4 servings

per serving: 368 calories, 30 g protein, 56 g carbohydrates, 6 g total fat, 66 mg cholesterol, 245 mg sodium

THAWING CHICKEN IN THE MICROWAVE: Unwrap a frozen 3- to 3 ½- pound cut-up chicken, then place on a microwave-safe plate; cover loosely with heavy-duty plastic wrap. Microwave on MEDIUM (50%) for 10 minutes, turning chicken over and giving plate a quarter turn after 5 minutes. Let stand for 10 minutes. Repeat, microwaving and standing; as soon as possible, separate pieces and arrange in a single layer, with meatiest portions toward edge of plate. Wings should be thawed after second 10-minute period. Microwave remaining pieces on MEDIUM (50%) for 5 more minutes; let stand for 5 minutes. If needed, microwave on MEDIUM (50%) for 2 more minutes. Thawed chicken should be flexible, but still very cold.

peanut chicken with rice

preparation time: about 40 minutes

1 cup long-grain white rice

1 package (about 10 oz.) frozen tiny peas, thawed and drained

3 tablespoons crunchy or smooth peanut butter

3 tablespoons plum jam or grape jelly

1 1/2 teaspoons lemon juice

1 1/2 teaspoons reduced-sodium soy sauce

1 teaspoon Asian sesame oil

2 teaspoons vegetable oil mixed with teaspoon ground ginger

1 pound skinless, boneless chicken breast, cut into 54-inch pieces

2 tablespoons sliced green onion

Lemon wedges

1 In a 3- to 4-quart pan, bring 2 cups water to a boil over high heat; stir in rice. Reduce heat, cover, and simmer until liquid has been absorbed and rice is tender to bite (about 20 minutes). Stir peas into rice; remove from heat and keep warm. Fluff occasionally with a fork.

2 While rice is cooking, prepare sauce. In a small bowl, stir together peanut butter, jam, 2 tablespoons water, lemon juice, soy sauce, and sesame oil. Set aside.

3 Heat ginger oil in a wide nonstick frying pan or wok over medium-high heat. When oil is hot, add chicken and stir-fry until no longer pink in center; cut to test (4 to 6 minutes). Remove chicken from pan with a slotted spoon and keep warm. Discard drippings from pan and wipe pan clean (be careful; pan is hot).

4 Stir sauce well and pour into pan. Stir over medium heat just until smoothly blended and heated through. Add chicken and onion; remove pan from heat and stir to coat chicken and onion with sauce.

5 Spoon rice mixture onto a rimmed platter and top with chicken mixture. Offer lemon wedges to squeeze over stir-fry to taste.

makes 4 servings

per serving: 481 calories, 36 g protein, 58 g carbohydrates, 11 g total fat, 66 mg cholesterol, 312 mg sodium

chicken breasts calvados

preparation time: about 45 minutes

1 large Golden Delicious apple, peeled, cored, and thinly sliced

1/4 cup apple brandy, brandy, or apple juice

1/4 teaspoon ground nutmeg

2 skinless, boneless chicken breast halves (about 6 oz. *each*)

2 slices Havarti cheese (about 1 oz. *each*)

Chopped parsley

1 Divide apple slices between 2 shallow ovenproof 1 1/2- to 2-cup ramekins. Pour 2 tablespoons of the brandy into each ramekin, then sprinkle 1/8 teaspoon of the nutmeg evenly over apples. Cover ramekins tightly with foil and bake in a 400° oven until apples are tender when pierced (about 20 minutes).

2 Rinse chicken and pat dry. Place one piece in each ramekin; baste with cooking juices, then sprinkle evenly with remaining 1/8 teaspoon nutmeg. Bake, uncovered, until meat in thickest part is no longer pink; cut to test (about 12 minutes).

3 Top each chicken piece with a cheese slice. Broil 6 inches below heat until cheese is bubbly (about 2 minutes). Sprinkle with parsley.

makes 2 servings

per serving: 413 calories, 46 g protein, 15 g carbohydrates, 10 g total fat, 128 mg cholesterol, 324 mg sodium

mediterranean baked chicken & vegetables

preparation time: about 40 minutes

4 chicken breast halves (about 1 ³/₄ lbs. *total*), skinned and trimmed of fat

8 ounces mushrooms, sliced

1 pound zucchini, cut into ¹/₄-inch-thick slices

1 tablespoon olive oil

1 teaspoon *each* pepper and dry oregano

1 teaspoon fennel seeds, crushed

1 tablespoon dry basil

1 can (about 14 ¹/₂ oz.) pear-shaped tomatoes

Parsley sprigs

Grated Parmesan cheese

1 Rinse chicken, pat dry, and place in a 12- by 15-inch broiler pan. Arrange mushrooms and zucchini around chicken. Drizzle with oil. Sprinkle with pepper, oregano, fennel seeds, and basil; mix to coat chicken and vegetables with seasonings.

2 Cover pan tightly and bake in a 425° oven for 15 minutes. Cut up tomatoes, then stir tomatoes and their liquid into pan. Cover and continue to bake until meat near bone is no longer pink; cut to test (5 to 10 more minutes). Garnish with parsley sprigs; offer cheese to add to taste.

makes 4 servings

per serving: 230 calories , 34 g protein, 12 g carbohydrates, 6 g total fat 75 mg cholesterol, 258 mg sodium

apple country chicken

preparation time: about 55 minutes

1 teaspoon curry powder

1 large Golden Delicious apple, cored and chopped

1 large yellow onion, finely chopped

1 tablespoon lemon juice

4 ounces mushrooms, sliced

1 teaspoon chicken-flavored instant bouillon

2 cups apple juice or cider

3 ¹/₄ to 3 ¹/₂ pounds chicken thighs, skinned and trimmed of fat

1 tablespoon all-purpose flour

2 tablespoons sliced green onion

Plain low-fat yogurt or reduced-fat sour cream (optional)

1 Place curry powder in a wide frying pan and stir over medium heat until slightly darker in color (3 to 4 minutes). Add apple, yellow onion, lemon juice, mushrooms, bouillon, and 1 ¹/₂ cups of the apple juice. Increase heat to high and bring juice mixture to a boil.

2 Rinse chicken, pat dry, and add to pan. Then reduce heat, cover, and simmer until meat near bone is no longer pink; cut to test (about 30 minutes). Transfer chicken to a platter and keep warm.

3 In a small bowl, smoothly blend flour and remaining ¹/₂ cup apple juice. Gradually add to sauce in pan, stirring constantly; increase heat to high and cook, stirring, until sauce is thickened. Pour over chicken. Garnish with green onion; offer yogurt to add to taste, if desired.

makes 4 to 6 servings

per serving: 314 calories, 36 g protein, 25 g carbohydrates, 7 g total fat, 146 mg cholesterol, 380 mg sodium

raspberry-glazed turkey sauté

preparation time: about 35 minutes

3 green onions

1/3 cup seedless red raspberry jam or jelly

3 tablespoons raspberry or red wine vinegar

1 tablespoon Dijon mustard

1/2 teaspoon grated orange peel

3/4 teaspoon chopped fresh tarragon or
1/4 teaspoon dried tarragon

8 ounces dried eggless spinach fettuccine or plain fettuccine

1 teaspoon olive oil or vegetable oil

2 turkey breast tenderloins (about 1 lb. *total*), cut into 1/4- by 2-inch strips

About 1 cup fresh raspberries

Tarragon sprigs

1 Trim and discard ends of onions. Cut onions into 2-inch lengths; then cut each piece lengthwise into slivers. Set aside. In a small bowl, stir together jam, vinegar, mustard, orange peel, and chopped tarragon; set aside.

2 In a 4- to 5-quart pan, cook fettuccine in about 8 cups boiling water until just tender to bite (8 to 10 minutes); or cook according to package directions.

3 Meanwhile, heat oil in a wide nonstick frying pan or wok over medium-high heat. When oil is hot, add turkey and 1 tablespoon water. Stir-fry just until turkey is no longer pink in center; cut to test (about 2 minutes). Add water, 1 table-spoon at a time, if pan appears dry. Remove turkey from pan with a slotted spoon and keep warm. Discard drippings from pan; wipe pan clean (be careful; pan is hot).

4 Add jam mixture to pan and bring to a boil over medium-high heat; then boil, stirring, just until jam is melted and sauce is smooth (about 1 minute). Remove from heat and stir in turkey and onions.

5 Drain pasta well and divide among 4 warm individual rimmed plates or shallow bowls; top with turkey mixture. Sprinkle each with raspberries and garnish with tarragon sprigs.

makes 4 servings

per serving: 435 calories, 36 g protein, 64 g carbohydrates, 3 g total fat, 70 mg cholesterol, 178 mg sodium

baked chicken with pears

preparation time: about 40 minutes

Vegetable oil cooking spray or salad oil

6 boneless, skinless chicken breast halves (about 2 1/4 lbs. *total*)

3 tablespoons lemon juice

4 teaspoons cornstarch

1 cup pear-flavored brandy or apple juice

2 large red Bartlett or other firm-ripe pears (about 1 lb. *total*)

1 Lightly coat a 9- by 13-inch baking pan with cooking spray. Rinse chicken and pat dry; then rub with lemon juice and arrange, skinned side up, in pan. Bake in a 425° oven until meat in thickest part is no longer pink; cut to test (15 to 20 minutes).

2 Meanwhile, in a medium-size pan, smoothly blend cornstarch and brandy. Halve and core pears; cut lengthwise into 1/2-inch-thick slices. Add to brandy mixture and stir gently. Bring to a boil over medium-high heat; then reduce heat, cover, and simmer until pears are tender when pierced (about 5 minutes).

3 When chicken is done, pour pear mixture into baking pan; shake pan to mix gently. Transfer chicken and pears to individual plates; drizzle with sauce.

makes 6 servings

per serving: 348 calories, 40 g protein, 25 g carbohydrates, 3 g total fat, 99 mg cholesterol, 112 mg sodium

chicken chutney burgers

preparation time: about 15 minutes

²/₃ cup Major Grey chutney, large pieces chopped

1 ¹/₂ tablespoons lemon juice

1 tablespoon Dijon mustard

³/₄ pound ground chicken

¹/₄ cup sliced green onion

¹/₂ teaspoon ground cumin

8 slices (*each* ¹/₂ in. thick) sourdough French bread

4 thin slices red onion

20 pre-washed spinach leaves

1 Combine chutney, lemon juice, and mustard; set two-thirds of mixture aside. Combine remaining chutney mixture with chicken, green onion, and cumin. Shape into 4 patties, each about 4 inches wide, and place on a rack in a broiler pan. Broil 3 inches below heat until well browned on both sides, turning as needed (6 to 7 minutes).

2 Meanwhile, brown bread in a toaster, then spread one side of each slice with reserved chutney mixture.

3 Separate red onion into rings and place between bread with burgers and spinach.

makes 4 servings

per serving: 387 calories, 23 g protein, 61 g carbohydrates, 4 g total fat, 60 mg cholesterol, 948 mg sodium

ground turkey chili mole

preparation time: about 1 hour

1 medium-size onion, chopped

1 pound ground skinless turkey

2 cloves garlic, minced or pressed

1 can (about 8 oz.) tomato sauce

1 can (about 14 ¹/₂ oz.) stewed tomatoes

1 can (about 15 oz.) red kidney beans, drained and rinsed; or 2 cups cooked red kidney beans, drained and rinsed

1 tablespoon molasses

¹/₄ teaspoon liquid hot pepper seasoning

1 tablespoon unsweetened cocoa

1 teaspoon *each* paprika and ground cumin

¹/₂ teaspoon *each* dry oregano and dry basil

1 In a 4- to 5-quart pan, combine onion and ¹/₄ cup water. Bring to a boil over medium-high heat; then boil, stirring occasionally, until liquid evaporates and onion begins to brown (about 5 minutes). To deglaze, add ¹/₄ cup more water and stir to scrape browned bits free. Then continue to cook, stirring occasionally, until onion begins to brown again. Repeat deglazing and browning steps, using ¹/₄ cup more water.

2 Crumble turkey into pan; add garlic. Cook, stirring, until meat is no longer pink and liquid has evaporated. Stir in tomato sauce, tomatoes, beans, molasses, hot pepper seasoning, cocoa, paprika, cumin, oregano, and basil. Bring to a boil; reduce heat, cover, and simmer until flavors are well blended (about 30 minutes).

makes 4 to 6 servings

per serving: 256 calories, 22 g protein, 25 g carbohydrates, 8 g total fat, 66 mg cholesterol, 685 mg sodium

chicken and apple stir-fry

preparation time: about 35 minutes

4 teaspoons butter or margarine

2 large tart apples, peeled, cored, and cut into
¼-inch-thick slices

1 pound skinless, boneless chicken breast, cut into
½- by 2-inch strips

1 large onion, finely chopped

⅔ cup dry sherry or apple juice

½ cup half-and-half

1 Melt 1 tablespoon of the butter in a wide nonstick frying pan or wok over medium heat. Add apples and stir-fry just until tender to bite (about 2 minutes). Remove apples from pan with a slotted spoon and keep warm.

2 Increase heat to medium-high and melt remaining 1 teaspoon butter in pan. Add chicken and stir-fry until no longer pink in center; cut to test (3 to 4 minutes). Remove chicken from pan with a slotted spoon and keep warm.

3 Add onion and 2 tablespoons of the sherry to pan; stir-fry until onion is soft (about 3 minutes). Add remaining sherry and bring to a boil; boil, stirring, for 1 minute. Add half-and-half and boil, stirring, until sauce is slightly thickened (about 2 minutes). Return apples and chicken to pan and mix gently but thoroughly.

makes 4 servings

per serving: 309 calories, 28 g protein, 21 g carbohydrates, 8 g total fat, 84 mg cholesterol, 126 mg sodium

braised chicken with green chile sauce

preparation time: about 55 minutes

1 large onion, chopped

2 cloves garlic, minced or pressed

1 cup low-sodium chicken broth

1 teaspoon dry oregano

½ teaspoon ground cumin

1 tablespoon red wine vinegar

3 pounds boneless, skinless chicken or turkey
thighs, trimmed of fat and cut into 1-inch chunks

2 large green bell peppers, seeded and chopped

½ cup chopped cilantro

1 large can (about 7 oz.) diced green chiles

Salt and pepper

Hot cooked rice or warm flour tortillas

Tomato wedges, plain nonfat yogurt or reduced-
fat sour cream, and lime wedges

1 In a 5- to 6-quart pan, combine onion, garlic, broth, oregano, and cumin. Bring to a boil over high heat; boil, stirring occasionally, until liquid evaporates and onion begins to brown (about 10 minutes). To deglaze, add 2 tablespoons water and stir to scrape browned bits free. Then continue to cook, stirring occasionally, until onion begins to brown again. Repeat deglazing and browning steps, using 2 tablespoons water each time, until onion is richly browned. Then deglaze one last time with vinegar and 1 tablespoon water.

2 Stir in chicken, bell peppers, cilantro, chiles, and 1 tablespoon water. Cover and cook over low heat, stirring often, until chicken chunks are no longer pink in center; cut to test (about 15 minutes). Skim and discard fat from sauce; season to taste with salt and pepper.

3 Spoon chicken mixture into a bowl. Serve over rice; offer tomato wedges, yogurt, and lime wedges to season each serving.

makes 6 to 8 servings

per serving: 273 calories, 40 g protein, 9 g carbohydrates, 8 g total fat, 161 mg cholesterol, 351 mg sodium

fig-stuffed turkey roast

preparation time: 1 ½ hours

1 turkey breast half (about 3 ½ lbs.), boned and skinned

3 tablespoons Dijon mustard

1 tablespoon chopped fresh rosemary or 1 teaspoon dried rosemary

12 dried Calimyrna or Mission figs, finely chopped

1 tablespoon honey

1 tablespoon olive oil

2 cloves garlic, minced

Pepper

Rosemary sprigs

1 Rinse turkey and pat dry. Then slice lengthwise down middle, cutting meat almost but not quite through. Push cut open and press turkey to make it lie as flat as possible. Spread turkey with mustard and sprinkle with half the chopped rosemary; set aside.

2 In a bowl, mix figs with honey. Mound fig mixture evenly down center of turkey. Starting from a long side, lift turkey and roll over filling to enclose. Tie roll snugly with cotton string at 2- to 3-inch intervals. Rub roll with oil, then with garlic; pat remaining chopped rosemary onto roll and sprinkle generously with pepper.

3 Place roll on a rack in a 9- by 13-inch baking pan; add ⅓ cup water to pan. Bake in a 375° oven until a meat thermometer inserted in thickest part of roll (insert thermometer in meat, not filling) registers 160° to 165°, about 1 ¼ hours. Add water, ¼ cup at a time, if pan appears dry.

4 Remove roll from oven and let stand for 10 minutes; then snip and discard strings and cut roll crosswise into thick slices. Garnish with rosemary sprigs. Serve with pan juices, if desired.

makes 6 to 8 servings

per serving: 308 calories, 44 g protein, 24 g carbohydrates, 3 g total fat, 117 mg cholesterol, 232 mg sodium

plum chicken

preparation time: about 35 minutes

4 boneless, skinless chicken breast halves (about 1 ½ lbs. *total*)

1 cup Asian plum sauce

¼ cup minced onion

1 teaspoon grated lemon peel

2 tablespoons lemon juice

1 tablespoon reduced-sodium soy sauce

½ teaspoon *each* dry mustard and ground ginger

¼ teaspoon *each* pepper and liquid hot pepper seasoning

¼ teaspoon anise seeds, crushed

1 Rinse chicken and pat dry; then place, skinned side up, in a 9- by 13-inch baking pan. In a small bowl, stir together plum sauce, onion, lemon peel, lemon juice, soy sauce, mustard, ginger, pepper, hot pepper seasoning, and anise seeds.

2 Pour sauce evenly over chicken. Bake in a 400° oven, basting halfway through baking, until meat in thickest part is no longer pink; cut to test (about 25 minutes).

3 To serve, transfer chicken to a platter and spoon sauce over top.

makes 4 servings

per serving: 278 calories, 41 g protein, 23 g carbohydrates, 2 g total fat, 99 mg cholesterol, 581 mg sodium

salsa chicken

preparation time: about 30 minutes

2 medium-size tomatoes, chopped and drained well

¼ cup thinly sliced green onions

¼ cup lime juice

1 small fresh jalapeño chile, seeded and finely chopped

1 tablespoon chopped cilantro

1 clove garlic, minced or pressed

About 8 cups finely shredded iceberg lettuce

2 large egg whites

½ cup yellow cornmeal

1 ½ teaspoons chili powder

½ teaspoon ground cumin

1 pound skinless, boneless chicken breast, cut into 1-inch pieces

2 teaspoons olive oil or vegetable oil

½ cup nonfat sour cream

Cilantro sprigs

1 To prepare tomato salsa, in a large bowl, combine tomatoes, onions, lime juice, jalapeño, chopped cilantro, and garlic; set aside. (At this point, you may cover and refrigerate for up to 3 hours.) Divide lettuce among 4 individual plates; cover and set aside.

2 In a shallow bowl, beat egg whites to blend; set aside. In a large bowl, combine cornmeal, chili powder, and cumin. Add chicken and turn to coat. Then lift chicken from bowl, shaking off excess coating. Dip chicken into egg whites, then coat again with remaining cornmeal mixture.

3 Heat oil in a wide nonstick frying pan or wok over medium-high heat. When oil is hot, add chicken and stir-fry gently until no longer pink in center; cut to test (5 to 7 minutes). Remove from pan and keep warm. Pour reserved salsa into pan; reduce heat to medium and cook, stirring, until salsa is heated through and slightly thickened (1 to 2 minutes).

4 Arrange chicken over lettuce; top with salsa and sour cream. Garnish with cilantro sprigs.

makes 4 servings

per serving: 284 calories, 34 g protein, 26 g carbohydrates, 5 g total fat, 66 mg cholesterol, 152 mg sodium

chicken with pumpkin seeds

preparation time: about 35 minutes

4 chicken breast halves (about 1 ¾ lbs. *total*), skinned and trimmed of fat

⅓ cup roasted pumpkin seeds

1 can (about 4 oz.) diced green chiles

½ cup shredded jack cheese

Lime wedges

1 Rinse chicken and pat dry; then place, skinned side up, in a 9- by 13-inch baking pan. In a small bowl, mix pumpkin seeds, chiles, and cheese; pat evenly onto chicken.

2 Bake chicken in a 450° oven until meat near bone is no longer pink; cut to test (20 to 25 minutes). Serve with lime wedges.

makes 4 servings

per serving: 226 calories, 35 g protein, 5 g carbohydrates, 7 g total fat, 90 mg cholesterol, 334 mg sodium

spicy chicken tortas

preparation time: about 35 minutes

TORTAS:

1 pound skinless, boneless chicken thighs

2 cups fat-free reduced-sodium chicken broth

¼ cup chili powder

¼ cup firmly packed brown sugar

2 teaspoons dried oregano

1 teaspoon anise seeds

About 1 tablespoon red wine vinegar, or to taste

2 tablespoons chopped cilantro

2 tablespoons thinly sliced green onion

4 French rolls

8 to 12 butter lettuce leaves, rinsed and crisped

CONDIMENTS:

avocado slices

asadero or string cheese

1 Rinse chicken and pat dry; set aside. In a 4- to 5-quart pan with a tight-fitting lid, combine 4 cups water, broth, chili powder, sugar, oregano, and anise seeds. Bring to a rolling boil over high heat. Remove pan from heat and immediately add chicken. Cover pan and let stand until meat in thickest part is no longer pink; cut to test (15 to 20 minutes; do not uncover until ready to test). If chicken is not done, return it to hot water, cover, and let steep for 2 to 3 more minutes.

2 Drain chicken, reserving 2 cups of the cooking liquid. Return reserved liquid to pan. Bring to a boil over high heat; boil until reduced to ½ cup, watching closely to prevent scorching.

3 Serve chicken and sauce warm or cold. To serve, stir vinegar, cilantro, and onion into sauce. Cut chicken diagonally across the grain into thin slices; set aside. Cut rolls in half lengthwise and moisten cut surfaces evenly with sauce. Fill rolls with chicken and lettuce. Offer additional sauce and condiments to add to taste.

makes 4 servings

per serving: 464 calories, 33 g protein, 68 g carbohydrates, 7 g total fat, 94 mg cholesterol, 1,819 mg sodium

greek chicken pockets

preparation time: about 30 minutes

Herb Dressing (recipe follows)

4 to 6 pita breads (*each* about 6 inches in diameter)

3 small firm-ripe tomatoes, thinly sliced

2 small green bell peppers, seeded and thinly sliced

3 cups shredded cooked chicken

¼ cup crumbled feta cheese

1 Prepare Herb Dressing.

2 Cut each pita bread in half; gently open halves and fill equally with tomatoes, bell peppers, chicken, and cheese. Then spoon dressing into each sandwich.

makes 4 to 6 servings

HERB DRESSING

In a small bowl, stir together 1 cup plain nonfat yogurt, ½ cup minced peeled cucumber, and 1 tablespoon each minced fresh dill and minced fresh mint (or 1 teaspoon each dry dill weed and dry mint).

per serving: 397 calories, 34 g protein, 44 g carbohydrates, 9 g total fat, 82 mg cholesterol, 512 mg sodium

chicken yakitori

preparation time: about 1 hour
marinating time: 1 to 8 hours

2 tablespoons sesame seeds

3 whole chicken breasts (about 1 lb. *each*), skinned, boned, and split

Sherry-Soy Marinade (recipe follows)

6 medium-size Asian eggplants

18 large fresh shiitake mushrooms or regular button mushrooms

1 In a small frying pan, toast sesame seeds over medium heat, shaking pan often, until golden (about 3 minutes). Set aside.

2 Cut each breast half into 6 equal-size chunks; place in a medium-size bowl, Prepare Sherry-Soy Marinade. Pour ¼ cup of the marinade over chicken, turning gently to coat; reserve remaining marinade. Cover and refrigerate chicken and reserved marinade separately for at least 1 hour or up to 8 hours.

3 Lift chicken from marinade and let drain briefly, discarding marinade in bowl. Thread chicken on skewers. Set aside.

4 Evenly slash each eggplant lengthwise in 4 or 5 places, making cuts about ⅓ inch deep. Cut mush room stems flush with caps. Place eggplants on a lightly greased grill 4 to 6 inches above a solid bed of hot coals. Cook, turning often, until very soft when pressed (about 35 minutes).

5 About 20 minutes before eggplants are done, dip mushrooms in reserved marinade, drain briefly, and place on grill. Cook, turning once, until lightly browned (about 10 minutes total). Meanwhile, place chicken on grill and cook, turning occasionally, until meat in center is no longer pink; cut to test (10 to 12 minutes).

6 Arrange chicken and vegetables on separate platters. Moisten with some of the remaining marinade and sprinkle with sesame seeds. Offer with remaining marinade.

makes 6 servings

SHERRY-SOY MARINADE

Stir together ⅓ cup dry sherry, 3 tablespoons *each* sesame oil and reduced sodium soy sauce, and 1 ½ teaspoons finely minced fresh ginger.

per serving: 295 calories, 39 g protein, 16 g carbohydrates, 9 g total fat, 86 mg cholesterol, 332 mg sodium

chicken and mushrooms with couscous

preparation time: about 40 minutes

1 pound skinless, boneless chicken thighs, trimmed of fat

1 tablespoon margarine

1 large onion, finely chopped

12 ounces mushrooms, sliced

2 teaspoons cornstarch

1 cup fat-free reduced-sodium chicken broth

3 tablespoons dry sherry

2 tablespoons soy sauce

1/8 teaspoon ground red pepper (cayenne)

2 cups low-fat (2%) milk

1 1/2 cups couscous

Vegetable oil cooking spray

Cilantro sprigs

1 Rinse chicken; pat dry. Place pieces between sheets of plastic wrap and pound with a flat-surfaced mallet until about 1/4 inch thick; then cut chicken into 1/2-inch-wide strips. Set aside.

2 Melt margarine in a wide nonstick frying pan over medium-high heat. Add onion and mushrooms; cook, stirring often, until liquid has evaporated and onion is golden and sweet tasting (10 to 12 minutes).

3 Meanwhile, in a bowl, blend cornstarch and 1/4 cup of the broth; stir in sherry, soy sauce, and red pepper. Set aside. In a 2-quart pan, bring milk and remaining 3/4 cup broth to a boil. Stir in couscous; cover, remove from heat, and let stand for 10 minutes.

4 Remove onion mixture from frying pan and set aside. Spray pan with cooking spray and place over high heat. Add chicken and cook, lifting and stirring, until meat is tinged with brown and is no longer pink in center; cut to test (4 to 5 minutes). Return onion mixture to pan; add cornstarch mixture and cook, stirring constantly, until sauce is bubbly (about 1 minute). Fluff couscous with a fork, then mound on a warm platter; spoon chicken beside couscous. Garnish with cilantro sprigs.

makes 4 to 6 servings

per serving: 446 calories, 31 g protein, 57 g carbohydrates, 9 g total fat, 83 mg cholesterol, 705 mg sodium

turkey chorizo sausage

preparation time: about 40 minutes
cooling time: at least 8 hours

1 large onion, chopped

2 teaspoons *each* chili powder and dried oregano

1 teaspoon *each* cumin seeds and crushed red pepper flakes

1 cup low-sodium chicken broth

1 pound ground turkey or chicken breast

1/2 cup cider vinegar

1 In a wide frying pan, combine onion, chili powder, oregano, cumin seeds, red pepper flakes, and broth. Bring to a boil over high heat; boil, stirring occasionally, until liquid has evaporated and browned bits stick to pan. Add 2 tablespoons water, stirring to scrape browned bits free; cook until mixture begins to brown again. Repeat this deglazing step, adding 2 tablespoons of water each time, until onion is a rich brown color.

2 Add 2 tablespoons more water, then crumble turkey into pan; cook, stirring, until browned bits stick to pan. Repeat deglazing step, adding vinegar in 2-tablespoon portions, until mixture is a rich brown color. If made ahead, let cool; then cover and refrigerate until next day.

makes about 3 1/2 cups

per serving: 48 calories, 8 g protein, 2 g carbohydrates, 0.5 g total fat, 20 mg cholesterol, 92 mg sodium

sautéed turkey with provolone & sage

preparation time: about 15 minutes

1 pound thinly sliced turkey breast

2 teaspoons finely chopped fresh sage or
   1 teaspoon dried sage

2 teaspoons olive oil

1/2 cup finely shredded provolone or part-skim
   mozzarella cheese

Pepper

Sage sprigs

Lemon wedges

Salt

1 Rinse turkey and pat dry. Sprinkle one side of each slice with chopped sage; set aside.

2 Heat 1 teaspoon of the oil in a wide nonstick frying pan over medium-high heat. Add half the turkey, sage-coated side down, and cook until golden on bottom (about 1 1/2 minutes). Then turn pieces over and continue to cook until no longer pink in center; cut to test (30 to 60 more seconds). Transfer cooked turkey to a platter and sprinkle with half the cheese. Cover loosely with foil and keep warm.

3 Repeat to cook remaining turkey; using remaining 1 teaspoon oil; add water, 1 tablespoon at a time, if pan appears dry. Transfer turkey to platter; sprinkle with remaining cheese.

4 Sprinkle turkey with pepper; garnish with sage sprigs. Season to taste with lemon and salt.

makes 4 servings

per serving: 184 calories, 31 g protein, 0.3 g carbohydrates, 6 g total fat, 78 mg cholesterol, 149 mg sodium

garlic chicken

preparation time: 15 minutes
cooking time: about 1 1/2 hours

1 large head garlic

1/2 teaspoon olive oil

4 boneless, skinless chicken breast halves
   (1 1/2 lbs. *total*)

1 tablespoon chopped fresh thyme or 1 teaspoon
   dried thyme

1/4 teaspoon coarsely ground pepper

1/8 teaspoon salt

1/2 cup shredded fontina cheese

4 small thyme sprigs

1 Slice 1/2 inch off top of garlic head. Then rub garlic with oil. Wrap garlic in foil and bake in a 375° oven until very soft when pressed (about 1 1/4 hours). Carefully remove garlic from foil; transfer to a rack and let stand until cool enough to touch (about 10 minutes).

2 Meanwhile, rinse chicken, pat dry, and sprinkle with chopped thyme and pepper. Place, skinned side up, in a lightly oiled 9-inch baking pan. Bake in a 450° oven until meat in thickest part is no longer pink; cut to test (12 to 15 minutes). Meanwhile, squeeze garlic cloves from skins into a small bowl. Add salt; mash garlic thoroughly with a fork, incorporating salt.

3 Spread a fourth of the garlic mixture over each chicken piece; then sprinkle chicken with cheese. Return to oven; continue to bake just until cheese is melted and bubbly (about 3 more minutes). Press a thyme sprig into cheese on each piece of chicken.

makes 4 servings

per serving: 258 calories, 43 g protein, 9 g carbohydrates, 5 g total fat, 107 mg cholesterol, 241 mg sodium

chicken in a squash shell

preparation time: about 1 hour

Nonstick cooking spray

2 small acorn squash

Soy-Ginger Sauce (recipe follows)

1 tablespoon salad oil

1 pound boneless and skinless chicken breasts, cut into $1/2$-inch cubes

$1/2$ cup *each* finely diced red bell pepper and jicama

1 small onion, finely chopped

2 small firm-ripe tomatoes, peeled and finely diced

1 teaspoon Szechuan peppercorns, coarsely ground, or $1/2$ teaspoon pepper

$1/4$ cup chopped green onions (including tops)

Plain lowfat yogurt (optional)

1 Lightly coat a 9- by 13-inch baking pan with cooking spray. With a sharp, heavy knife, cut squash in half lengthwise and scoop out seeds. Arrange squash, cut sides down, in pan. Bake in a 400° oven until tender when pierced (about 40 minutes).

2 Meanwhile, prepare Soy-Ginger Sauce and set aside.

3 About 15 minutes before squash is done, heat oil in a wide frying pan or wok over medium-high heat. Add chicken and cook, stirring, until meat in center is no longer pink; cut to test (2 to 3 minutes). Lift out with a slotted spoon and set aside. Add bell pepper, jicama, onion, tomatoes, and peppercorns to pan; cook, stirring, for 5 minutes. Add sauce; boil until thickened. Return chicken and any juices to pan, remove from heat, and keep warm.

4 Place squash in individual bowls and fill with chicken mixture. Sprinkle with green onions. Offer with yogurt, if desired.

makes 4 servings

SOY-GINGER SAUCE

Stir together 2 tablespoons each reduced-sodium soy sauce and dry sherry, $3/4$ cup low-sodium chicken broth, 1 tablespoon each cornstarch and firmly packed brown sugar, and 1 teaspoon finely minced fresh ginger.

per serving: 282 calories, 29 g protein, 30 g carbohydrates, 6 g total fat, 66 mg cholesterol, 396 mg sodium

chicken enchilada bake

preparation time: about 50 minutes

12 corn tortillas (7-inch diameter)

5 medium-size tomatoes, peeled and thinly sliced

2 cups skinless and boneless shredded cooked chicken breast

1 cup thinly sliced green onions (including tops)

1 tablespoon margarine

2 tablespoons all-purpose flour

2 cups low-sodium chicken broth

1 cup plain lowfat yogurt

1 can (4 oz.) diced green chiles

2 ounces (about $1/2$ cup) grated Cheddar cheese

1 Dip tortillas, one at a time, in water; let drain briefly. Stack and cut into 8 wedges. Spread a third of the tortillas in a 9- by 13-inch baking pan. Top with half the tomatoes; cover with half the chicken and onions. Repeat layers, ending with tortillas. Set aside.

2 In a 2- to 3-quart pan, melt margarine over medium heat. Add flour and cook, stirring, for 20 seconds. Whisk in chicken broth and bring to a boil. Remove from heat and add yogurt and chiles, whisking until smooth. Pour over tortilla mixture.

3 Cover and bake in a 375° oven for 20 minutes. Remove cover, sprinkle with Cheddar, and continue baking, uncovered, until cheese is melted (about 10 more minutes).

makes 8 servings

per serving: 254 calories, 19 g protein, 28 g carbohydrates, 8 g total fat, 39 mg cholesterol, 293 mg sodium

curried turkey & coconut rice

preparation time: about 45 minutes

1 cup low-fat (1%) milk

1 cup long-grain white rice

¼ cup sweetened shredded coconut

2 tablespoons lemon juice

1 clove garlic, minced or pressed

½ teaspoon ground cumin

¼ teaspoon chili powder

2 turkey breast tenderloins (about 1 lb. *total*), cut into 1-inch pieces

½ cup golden raisins

¼ cup dry white wine

2 medium-size carrots, cut into ¼-inch slanting slices

1 large onion, thinly sliced

2 teaspoons olive oil or vegetable oil

2 to 3 teaspoons curry powder

1 to 2 tablespoons chopped fresh mint

2 tablespoons salted roasted cashews, chopped

Mint or parsley sprigs

1 To prepare coconut rice, in a 3- to 4-quart pan, combine 1 cup water and milk. Bring just to a boil over medium-high heat. Stir in rice. Reduce heat, cover, and simmer until liquid has been absorbed and rice is tender to bite (about 20 minutes). Stir in coconut. Keep warm until ready to serve, fluffing occasionally with a fork.

2 Meanwhile, in a large bowl, combine 1 tablespoon water, lemon juice, garlic, cumin, and chili powder. Add turkey and stir to coat. Set aside; stir occasionally. In a small bowl, combine raisins and wine; let stand until raisins are softened (about 10 minutes), stirring occasionally.

3 In a wide nonstick frying pan or wok, combine carrots, onion, and ¼ cup water. Cover and cook over medium-high heat until carrots are tender-crisp to bite (about 5 minutes). Uncover and stir-fry until liquid has evaporated. Remove vegetables from pan with a slotted spoon and keep warm.

4 Heat oil in pan. When oil is hot, add turkey mixture. Stir-fry just until meat is no longer pink in center; cut to test (3 to 4 minutes). Add water, 1 tablespoon at a time, if pan appears dry. Add curry powder and stir-fry just until fragrant (about 30 seconds; do not scorch).

5 Add raisins (and soaking liquid) to pan; return vegetables to pan. Bring to a boil; boil, stirring, until liquid has evaporated (about 2 minutes). Remove from heat; stir in chopped mint and cashews. Spoon coconut rice into 4 wide bowls; top with turkey mixture and garnish with mint sprigs.

makes 4 servings

per serving: 506 calories, 36 g protein, 70 g carbohydrates, 8 g total fat, 73 mg cholesterol, 156 mg sodium

BUYING AND STORING POULTRY: Fresh poultry should never be left at room temperature for long. If you buy your chicken and turkey at a supermarket, make it one of the last items you pick up; then get it home and into the refrigerator as quickly as possible. Cook fresh poultry within 3 days of purchase. If you can't use it that soon, enclose it securely in heavy-duty foil, freezer paper, or plastic bags, then freeze for up to 6 months.

turkey fajitas

preparation time: about 25 minutes

1/4 cup lime juice

1 tablespoon balsamic vinegar or red wine vinegar

1 clove garlic, minced or pressed

1/2 teaspoon ground coriander

1/2 teaspoon ground cumin

1/2 teaspoon honey

2 turkey breast tenderloins (about 1 lb. *total*), cut into 1/2- by 2-inch strips

4 reduced-fat flour tortillas (*each* 7 to 9 inches in diameter)

1 tablespoon olive oil

1 large green bell pepper, seeded and cut into thin strips

1 large red onion, thinly sliced

Lime wedges

1 In a large bowl, stir together lime juice, vinegar, garlic, coriander, cumin, and honey. Add turkey and stir to coat. Set aside to marinate, stirring occasionally.

2 Brush tortillas lightly with hot water; then stack tortillas, wrap in foil, and heat in a 350° oven until warm (10 to 12 minutes).

3 Meanwhile, heat 2 teaspoons of the oil in a wide nonstick frying pan or wok over medium-high heat. When oil is hot, add bell pepper and onion and stir-fry until vegetables are lightly browned (2 to 3 minutes). Remove vegetables from pan with a slotted spoon and keep warm.

4 Heat remaining 1 teaspoon oil in pan. When oil is hot, lift turkey from marinade and drain briefly (reserve marinade). Add turkey to pan and stir-fry until no longer pink in center; cut to test (2 to 3 minutes). Add marinade and bring to a boil; return vegetables to pan and mix gently. Spoon mixture onto a platter.

5 Offer tortillas and lime wedges alongside turkey mixture. Fill tortillas with turkey mixture; add a squeeze of lime, roll up, and eat out of hand.

makes 4 servings

per serving: 280 calories, 31 g protein, 23 g carbohydrates, 6 g total fat, 70 mg cholesterol, 356 mg sodium

turkey & mushroom burgers

preparation time: about 25 minutes

1 egg white

1/4 cup dry white wine

1/3 cup soft French bread crumbs

1/4 teaspoon salt

1/8 teaspoon pepper

1/4 cup finely chopped shallots

1 pound lean ground turkey breast

4 ounces mushrooms, finely chopped

Olive oil cooking spray

6 onion hamburger rolls, split and warmed

1 In a medium-size bowl, beat egg white and wine until blended. Stir in bread crumbs, salt, pepper, and shallots; then lightly mix in turkey and mushrooms. Shape turkey mixture into 6 patties, each about 1/2 inch thick.

2 Spray a wide nonstick frying pan with cooking spray. Place over medium-high heat; add turkey patties. Cook, turning once, until patties are lightly browned on both sides and juices run clear when a knife is inserted in center (8 to 10 minutes). Serve on warm rolls.

makes 6 servings

per serving: 235 calories, 24 g protein, 25 g carbohydrates, 3 g total fat, 47 mg cholesterol, 394 mg sodium

stuffed chicken breasts with chutney

preparation time: about 50 minutes

1 tablespoon olive oil

2 cloves garlic, minced or pressed

1 large onion, chopped

2 ¼ cups chopped spinach leaves

4 whole chicken breasts, skinned, boned, and split

1 tablespoon balsamic vinegar

½ cup low-sodium chicken broth

¼ cup chutney

1 Heat oil in a 12- to 14-inch frying pan over medium-high heat. Add garlic and onion and cook, stirring occasionally, until onion is soft (about 7 minutes). Add 2 cups of the spinach; let cool.

2 Rinse chicken; pat dry. Place each breast half between 2 sheets of plastic wrap. Pound with a flat-surfaced mallet to a thickness of about ¼ inch.

3 In center of each breast half, mound an equal portion of the spinach mixture. Roll meat around filling to enclose; fasten with wooden picks. Place chicken rolls in pan used for spinach.

4 In a small bowl, mix vinegar, broth, and chutney. Pour over chicken. Bring to a simmer over medium heat. Cover and simmer until meat is no longer pink and filling is hot in center; cut to test (about 8 minutes). Remove chicken from pan; remove wooden picks and keep chicken warm.

5 Increase heat to high and bring chutney mixture to a boil. Cook, stirring occasionally, until reduced to ½ cup (about 5 minutes); then pour over chicken. Garnish with remaining ¼ cup spinach.

makes 8 servings

per serving: 174 calories, 27g protein, 8 g carbohydrates, 3 g total fat, 66 mg cholesterol, 107 mg sodium

sherried chicken with onion marmalade

preparation time: about 35 minutes
marinating time: at least 30 minutes

6 small boneless, skinless chicken breast halves (1 ½ to 1 ¾ lbs. *total*)

3 tablespoons cream sherry

2 small red onions

½ cup dry red wine

1 tablespoon *each* red wine vinegar and honey

Italian or regular parsley sprigs

Salt and pepper

1 Rinse chicken, pat dry, and place in a heavy-duty plastic food-storage bag; add 2 tablespoons of the sherry. Seal bag and rotate to coat chicken with sherry Refrigerate for at least 30 minutes or up to 6 hours, turning bag over several times.

2 Thinly slice onions; wrap several slices airtight and refrigerate. In a wide frying pan, combine remaining onion slices, wine, vinegar, and honey. Cook over medium-high heat, stirring often, until liquid has evaporated. Remove from heat and stir in remaining 1 tablespoon sherry. Set aside.

3 Turn chicken and its marinade into a 9- by 13-inch baking pan; arrange chicken, skinned side up, in a single layer. Bake in a 450° oven until meat in thickest part is no longer pink; cut to test (12 to 15 minutes). With a slotted spoon, transfer chicken to a platter. Top with onion mixture. Garnish with reserved onion slices and parsley sprigs. Season to taste with salt and pepper.

makes 6 servings

per serving: 200 calories, 30 g protein, 9 g carbohydrates, 2 g total fat, 74 mg cholesterol, 91 mg sodium

mediterranean turkey with couscous

preparation time: about 25 minutes

2 turkey breast tenderloins (about 1 lb. *total*), cut into ¹/₂-inch pieces

2 cloves garlic, minced or pressed

1 teaspoon paprika

¹/₂ teaspoon grated lemon peel

¹/₈ teaspoon salt (optional)

¹/₈ teaspoon pepper

2 teaspoons cornstarch

2 tablespoons balsamic vinegar

1 ¹/₂ cups fat-free reduced-sodium chicken broth

²/₃ cup low-fat (1%) milk

1 ¹/₂ teaspoons chopped fresh oregano or ¹/₂ teaspoon dried oregano

1 cup couscous

1 medium-size red bell pepper, seeded and cut into thin strips

2 teaspoons olive oil

¹/₃ to ¹/₂ cup chopped pitted calamata olives

¹/₄ cup finely chopped parsley

Oregano sprigs

1 In a large bowl, mix turkey, garlic, paprika, ¹/₄ teaspoon of the lemon peel, salt (if used), and pepper; set aside.

2 To prepare sauce, in a bowl, smoothly blend cornstarch and vinegar. Stir in ¹/₂ cup of the broth. Set aside.

3 In a 3- to 4-quart pan, combine remaining 1 cup broth, milk, chopped oregano, and remaining ¹/₄ teaspoon lemon peel. Bring just to a boil over medium-high heat; stir in couscous. Cover, remove from heat, and let stand until liquid has been absorbed (about 5 minutes). Transfer to a rimmed platter and keep warm; fluff occasionally with a fork.

4 While couscous is standing, in a wide nonstick frying pan or wok, combine bell pepper and 2 tablespoons water. Stir-fry over medium-high heat until pepper is just tender-crisp to bite (about 2 minutes); add water, 1 tablespoon at a time, if pan appears dry. Remove from pan with a slotted spoon and keep warm.

5 Heat oil in pan. When oil is hot, add turkey mixture and stir-fry just until meat is no longer pink in center; cut to test (2 to 3 minutes). Stir reserved sauce well; pour into pan. Then add bell pepper and olives; cook, stirring, until sauce boils and thickens slightly (1 to 2 minutes). Pour turkey mixture over couscous. Sprinkle with parsley and garnish with oregano sprigs.

makes 4 servings

per serving: 415 calories, 37 g protein, 44 g carbohydrates, 9 g total fat, 72 mg cholesterol, 823 mg sodium

CHECKING TO SEE IF YOUR CHICKEN IS DONE: For a whole chicken or turkey, insert a meat thermometer in thickest part of the thigh (not touching bone) after turning bird breast up. (For turkey breast, insert in thickest part, not touching bone.) Begin checking thermometer three-quarters of the way through cooking; when it registers the correct temperature (consult a temperature chart), the bird is done.

light cassoulet

preparation time: 30 minutes
cooking time: about 1 1/2 hours

1 large onion, chopped

2 medium-size carrots, thinly sliced

1 medium-size red bell pepper, seeded and thinly sliced

3 cloves garlic, minced or pressed

1 can (about 14 1/2 oz.) low-sodium stewed tomatoes

2/3 cups vegetable broth

2/3 cup dry red wine

1 teaspoon dried thyme

1 dried bay leaf

1/4 teaspoon *each* pepper and liquid hot pepper seasoning

2 cans (about 15 oz. *each*) cannellini (white kidney beans), drained and rinsed

1 1/2 pounds boneless, skinless chicken breasts, cut into 1-inch pieces

4 ounces turkey kielbasa (Polish sausage), thinly sliced

1/4 cup finely chopped parsley

1 In a 5- to 6-quart pan, combine onion, carrots, bell pepper, garlic, and 1/2 cup water. Cook over medium-high heat, stirring often, until liquid evaporates and browned bits stick to pan bottom (about 10 minutes). To deglaze pan, add 1/3 cup water, stirring to loosen browned bits from pan; continue to cook until browned bits form again. Repeat deglazing step about 2 more times or until vegetables are browned, using 1/3 cup water each time.

2 Stir in tomatoes and their liquid, broth, wine, thyme, bay leaf, pepper, and hot pepper seasoning. Bring to a boil; then reduce heat, cover, and simmer for 45 minutes.

3 Stir in beans; simmer, uncovered, for 10 minutes. Stir in chicken and sausage. Continue to simmer, uncovered, until chicken is no longer pink in center; cut to test (about 10 more minutes). Just before serving, remove and discard bay leaf. To serve, ladle mixture into bowls and sprinkle with parsley.

makes 8 servings

per serving: 240 calories, 29 g protein, 24 g carbohydrates, 3 g total fat, 59 mg cholesterol, 557 mg sodium

chicken jambalaya

preparation time: about 1 1/2 hours

1 tablespoon salad oil

1/2 pound Canadian bacon, diced

1 1/2 pounds skinned and boned chicken breasts, cut into bite-size chunks

1 large onion, chopped

3 cloves garlic, minced or pressed

2 large green bell peppers, seeded and chopped

1 cup chopped celery

6 large tomatoes, chopped

1 large can (15 oz.) no-salt-added tomato sauce

2 bay leaves, crumbled

1 teaspoon dry thyme leaves

2 teaspoons ground white pepper

1 teaspoon ground red pepper (cayenne)

1/2 cup chopped parsley

1 1/2 cups long-grain white rice

3 cups low-sodium chicken broth

1 Heat oil in a 12- to 14-inch frying pan over medium heat. Add Canadian bacon and chicken; cook, stirring often, until browned on all sides (about 6 minutes). Transfer chicken to a 4- to 5-quart casserole.

2 Add onion, garlic, bell peppers, and celery to pan. Cook, stirring occasionally, until onion is soft (about 10 minutes). Add tomatoes, tomato sauce, bay leaves, thyme, white pepper, red pepper, and parsley; cook, stirring occasionally, until sauce boils. Boil gently, uncovered, for 5 minutes.

3 Pour sauce over chicken; stir in rice and broth. Cover and bake in a 375° oven until rice is tender to bite (about 45 minutes).

makes 6 servings

per serving: 471 calories, 42 g protein, 57 g carbohydrates, 8 g total fat, 85 mg cholesterol, 685 mg sodium

apricot-mustard chicken

preparation time: about 30 minutes

1 can (12 oz.) apricot nectar

3 tablespoons Dijon mustard

3 whole chicken breasts (about 1 lb. *each*), skinned, boned, and split

2 1/2 cups low-sodium chicken broth

10 ounces (about 1 3/4 cups) couscous

2 tablespoons minced fresh basil leaves

Basil sprigs and lime wedges (optional)

1 In a wide frying pan, combine apricot nectar and mustard. Bring to a boil over high heat. Arrange chicken breasts, skinned sides down, in pan. Reduce heat, cover, and simmer for 10 minutes. Turn chicken and continue cooking until meat in thickest part is no longer pink; cut to test (5 to 8 more minutes).

2 Meanwhile, bring chicken broth to a boil in a 2- to 3-quart pan over high heat; stir in couscous. Cover, remove from heat, and let stand until broth is completely absorbed (about 5 minutes).

3 With a fork, fluff couscous; transfer to a platter. Lift out chicken with a slotted spoon and arrange over couscous; keep warm.

4 Boil apricot mixture over high heat, stirring often, until reduced to 1 cup (about 5 minutes). Pour over chicken and sprinkle with minced basil. Garnish with basil sprigs and lime, if desired.

makes 6 servings

per serving: 380 calories, 41 g protein, 46 g carbohydrates, 3 g total fat, 86 mg cholesterol, 352 mg sodium

turkey curry with soba

preparation time: about 50 minutes

1 tablespoon salad oil

1 pound boneless, skinless turkey breast, cut into
    1 1/2-inch chunks

1 large onion, thinly sliced

1 clove garlic, minced or pressed

1 tablespoon grated fresh ginger

1 teaspoon *each* crushed red pepper flakes,
    ground coriander, ground cumin, and
    ground turmeric

1/2 teaspoon fennel seeds

1 cup low-sodium chicken broth

1 package (about 7 oz.) dry soba noodles

1 cup plain nonfat yogurt

1/4 cup unsalted dry-roasted cashews

1 Heat oil in a wide frying pan over medium heat. Add turkey and cook, stirring often, until browned on all sides (about 6 minutes). Using a slotted spoon, remove turkey from pan.

2 Add onion and garlic to pan; cook, stirring occasionally, until onion is soft (about 10 minutes). Add ginger, red pepper flakes, coriander, cumin, turmeric, and fennel seeds; cook, stirring, for 1 minute.

3 Return turkey to pan. Add broth and bring to a boil. Then reduce heat, cover, and simmer until meat is no longer pink in center; cut to test (about 20 minutes). Remove from heat.

4 While turkey is simmering, cook noodles in boiling water according to package directions until just tender to bite; drain well and pour into a large, shallow serving bowl.

5 Stir yogurt into turkey mixture, then pour mixture over noodles. Sprinkle with cashews.

makes 6 servings

per serving: 294 calories, 6 g total fat, 34 g carbohydrates, 27 g protein, 48 mg cholesterol, 340 mg sodium

turkey & lima bean stew

preparation time: about 20 minutes
cooking time: about 1 hour

1 large onion, chopped

2 cups sliced mushrooms

1 cup thinly sliced carrots

1 teaspoon dry thyme

3 cups low-sodium chicken broth

2 tablespoons lemon juice

2 pounds boneless, skinless turkey or chicken
    thighs, trimmed of fat and cut into 1-inch chunks

1 tablespoon cornstarch

1 package (about 10 oz.) frozen baby lima beans,
    thawed

1 In a 5- to 6-quart pan, combine onion, mushrooms, carrots, thyme, and 1 cup of the broth. Bring to a boil over high heat; then boil, stirring occasionally, until liquid evaporates and vegetables begin to brown (about 10 minutes). To deglaze, add 1/4 cup more broth and stir to scrape browned bits free. Then continue to cook, stirring occasionally, until vegetables begin to brown again. Repeat deglazing and browning steps, using 1/4 cup more broth each time, until vegetable mixture is richly browned. Then deglaze one last time with lemon juice.

2 Stir turkey and 1/2 cup more broth into vegetable mixture. Bring to a boil over high heat. Then reduce heat to low, cover, and simmer until turkey chunks are no longer pink in center; cut to test (about 40 minutes; about 25 minutes for chicken). Skim and discard fat from sauce.

3 Smoothly blend cornstarch with 3/4 cup of the broth. Add cornstarch mixture and beans to pan; bring to a boil over medium-high heat, stirring. Continue to boil, stirring, until beans are tender to bite.

makes 6 servings

per serving: 299 calories, 36 g protein, 20 g carbohydrates, 7 g total fat, 114 mg cholesterol, 182 mg sodium

kung pao chicken

preparation time: about 50 minutes

1 cup long-grain white rice

Cooking Sauce (recipe follows)

1 ¹/₂ cups Chinese pea pods (also called snow or sugar peas) or sugar snap peas, ends and strings removed

1 tablespoon cornstarch

1 tablespoon dry white wine

¹/₂ teaspoon sugar

1 pound boneless, skinless chicken breast, cut into ³/₄-inch chunks

2 cloves garlic, minced or pressed

1 cup peeled, shredded jicama

2 tablespoons salted roasted peanuts, chopped

1 In a 3- to 4-quart pan, bring 2 cups water to a boil over high heat; stir in rice. Reduce heat, cover, and simmer until liquid has been absorbed and rice is tender to bite (about 20 minutes). Meanwhile, prepare Cooking Sauce; set aside. Cut pea pods diagonally into ³/₄-inch pieces; set aside.

2 In a large bowl, dissolve cornstarch in wine; stir in sugar. Add chicken and stir to coat. Then turn chicken mixture into a wide nonstick frying pan or wok; add garlic and 1 tablespoon water. Stir-fry over medium-high heat until meat is no longer pink in center; cut to test (4 to 6 minutes). Remove from pan with a slotted spoon and keep warm.

3 Add pea pods, jicama, and 1 tablespoon water to pan; stir-fry until pea pods are tender-crisp to bite (about 1 minute). Stir Cooking Sauce well; pour into pan and bring to a boil. Remove from heat and stir in chicken.

4 Spoon rice onto a rimmed platter; top with chicken mixture and sprinkle with peanuts.

makes 4 servings

COOKING SAUCE

Mix 1 tablespoon each sugar and chili paste with garlic; 1 tablespoon unseasoned rice vinegar or distilled white vinegar; and 1 tablespoon *each* hoisin sauce and Asian sesame oil.

per serving: 425 calories, 33 g protein, 51 g carbohydrates, 9 g total fat, 66 mg cholesterol, 122 mg sodium

lemon turkey scaloppine

preparation time: about 25 minutes

1 pound skinned and boned turkey breast, sliced ¹/₂ inch thick

2 tablespoons all-purpose flour

1 tablespoon salad oil

¹/₂ cup lemon juice

2 tablespoons drained capers

1 lemon, thinly sliced

1 Rinse turkey, pat dry, and cut into serving-size pieces. Place between sheets of plastic wrap. With a flat-surfaced mallet, pound turkey to a thickness of about ¹/₄ inch. Dust with flour.

2 Heat oil in a 12- to 14-inch frying pan over medium-high heat. Add turkey and cook, turning once, until golden brown on both sides (about 4 minutes). With a slotted spoon, transfer turkey to a platter; keep warm.

3 Add lemon juice and capers to pan. Bring to a boil and cook, stirring, until thickened (about 2 minutes). Pour sauce over turkey; garnish with lemon slices.

makes 4 servings

per serving: 186 calories, 27 g protein, 8 g carbohydrates, 5 g total fat, 70 mg cholesterol, 193 mg sodium

grilled turkey with peaches

preparation time: about 30 minutes
grilling time: about 1 hour

---

1 teaspoon minced fresh ginger

²/₃ cup peach chutney or Major Grey's chutney

1 turkey breast half (about 3 lbs.), boned and skinned

3 large firm-ripe peaches; or 6 canned peach halves, drained

2 tablespoons lemon juice (if using fresh peaches)

6 green onions

1 At least 30 minutes before cooking, prepare a barbecue for indirect grilling.

2 In a blender or food processor, combine ginger and ⅓ cup of the chutney. Whirl until puréed. Coarsely chop remaining ⅓ cup chutney and set aside. Rinse turkey, pat dry, and brush all over with some of the chutney-ginger mixture.

3 Place turkey on grill directly above drip pan. Cover barbecue and open vents. Cook turkey, brushing occasionally with chutney mixture, until a meat thermometer inserted in thickest part registers 165° (about 1 hour).

4 Meanwhile, immerse fresh peaches in boiling water for 30 seconds; lift out and let cool for 1 minute. Peel, halve, and pit; coat with lemon juice. Peel off outer layer of onions; trim tops, leaving about 4 inches of green leaves.

5 About 10 minutes before turkey is done, lay peach halves (cut side down) and onions on grill directly above coals. Cook, turning once and brushing several times with chutney mixture, until peaches are hot and onion tops are wilted (about 10 minutes).

6 To serve, thinly slice turkey across the grain. Arrange on a platter and surround with peaches and onions. Offer reserved chopped chutney to add to taste.

makes 6 servings

per serving: 324 calories, 45 g protein, 31 g carbohydrates, 1 g total fat, 111 mg cholesterol, 406 mg sodium

layered turkey enchiladas

preparation time: about 15 minutes
baking time: about 1 hour and 20 minutes

---

1 cup shredded extra-sharp Cheddar cheese

1 pound ground skinned turkey breast

1 large can (7 oz.) diced green chiles

1 medium-size onion, chopped

1 cup mild green salsa

1 ½ cups chopped pear-shaped (Roma-type) tomatoes

8 corn tortillas (*each* 6 to 7 inches in diameter)

1 Mix ¾ cup of the cheese with turkey, chiles, onion, ½ cup of the salsa, and 1 cup of the tomatoes. Divide into 7 equal portions.

2 Place 1 tortilla in a shallow 9- to 10-inch diameter baking pan; cover evenly with one portion of the turkey mixture. Repeat to use remaining tortillas and turkey mixture; top stack with a tortilla. Cover with remaining ¼ cup cheese, ½ cup salsa, and ½ cup tomatoes.

3 Cover with foil and bake in a 400° oven for 40 minutes. Uncover and continue to bake until turkey is no longer pink; cut to center of stack to test (about 40 more minutes). Let stand for 5 minutes, then cut into wedges.

makes 4 to 6 servings

per serving: 284 calories, 26 g protein, 25 g carbohydrates, 9 g total fat, 67 mg cholesterol, 684 mg sodium

stuffed chicken legs with capellini

preparation time: about 1 1/2 hours

1/2 cup *each* cilantro leaves and fresh basil

1/2 cup freshly grated Parmesan cheese

3 whole chicken legs (about 1 1/2 lbs. *total*)

3 large red bell peppers

4 slices bacon

12 ounces dried capellini

1/2 cup seasoned rice vinegar; or 1/2 cup distilled white vinegar and 4 teaspoons sugar

1/4 cup capers, drained

1 tablespoon grated lemon peel

Finely shredded lemon peel

Cilantro sprigs

Salt and pepper

1 Combine cilantro leaves, basil, and cheese in a food processor or blender. Whirl until minced.

2 Cut a slit just through skin at joint on outside of each chicken leg. Slide your fingers between skin and meat to separate, leaving skin in place. Tuck cilantro mixture under skin, spreading evenly. Set aside.

3 Place bell peppers on a lightly greased grill 4 to 6 inches above a solid bed of hot coals. Grill, turning as needed, until charred all over (about 10 minutes). Cover with foil and let cool. Pull off and discard skin, stems, and seeds. Cut into strips and set aside.

4 Lay chicken on grill when coals have cooled down to medium heat and cook, turning as needed, until meat near thighbone is no longer pink; cut to test (about 40 minutes). Meanwhile, cook bacon in a wide nonstick frying pan over medium heat until crisp (about 5 minutes). Lift out, drain well, and crumble; set aside. Discard all but 2 teaspoons of the drippings; set pan with drippings aside.

5 Bring 12 cups water to a boil in a 5- to 6-quart pan over medium-high heat. Stir in pasta and cook just until tender to bite (about 4 minutes); or cook according to package directions. Drain well and keep warm.

6 Add vinegar, capers, and grated lemon peel to pan with drippings. Bring just to a boil over medium heat. Add pasta and bacon. Cook, stirring, just until warm. Transfer to a platter. Cut chicken legs apart. Place chicken and bell peppers on platter. Garnish with shredded lemon peel and cilantro sprigs. Offer salt and pepper to add to taste.

makes 6 servings

per serving: 457 calories , 28 g protein, 52 g carbohydrates, 15 g total fat, 64 mg cholesterol, 858 mg sodium

shredded chicken filling

preparation time: about 1 hour

6 dried ancho or pasilla chiles

1 teaspoon salad oil

2 large onions, chopped

2 cloves garlic, minced or pressed

1 can (about 14 ½ oz.) tomatoes

2 teaspoons sugar

1 teaspoon dried oregano

½ teaspoon ground cumin

2 cups finely shredded cooked chicken or turkey
breast

Salt and pepper

1 Place chiles on a baking sheet and toast in a 300° oven until fragrant (3 to 4 minutes). Remove from oven; let cool. Discard stems, seeds, and veins; then place chiles in a bowl, cover with 1 ½ cups boiling water, and let stand until pliable (about 30 minutes).

2 While chiles are soaking, place oil, onions, garlic, and 1 tablespoon water in a wide nonstick frying pan. Cook over medium heat, stirring often, until mixture is deep golden (20 to 30 minutes); if onions stick to pan or pan appears dry, add more water, 1 tablespoon at a time.

3 Drain chiles, discarding liquid. In a blender or food processor, whirl chiles, tomatoes and their liquid, sugar, oregano, and cumin until smoothly puréed.

4 Stir chicken and chile-tomato mixture into onion mixture. Reduce heat and simmer, uncovered, stirring occasionally, until mixture is thick and flavors are blended (about 10 minutes). Season to taste with salt and pepper.

makes about 3 cups

per serving: 90 calories, 9 g protein, 10 g carbohydrates, 3 g total fat, 20 mg cholesterol, 75 mg sodium

mu shu sandwiches

preparation time: about 20 minutes

1 tablespoon salad oil

3 cups thinly sliced onions

2 cups thinly sliced green or red bell peppers

1 pound boneless, skinless chicken breast, cut into
½- by 2-inch strips

¼ cup hoisin sauce

Whole green onions (ends trimmed)

4 pita breads (*each* about 6 inches in diameter),
cut crosswise into halves

Pickled scallions and pickled sliced ginger
(optional)

1 Heat 2 teaspoons of the oil in a wide nonstick frying pan or wok over medium-high heat. When oil is hot, add onions and peppers; stir-fry until vegetables are lightly browned (2 to 3 minutes). Remove from pan with a slotted spoon; keep warm.

2 Heat remaining 1 teaspoon oil in pan. When oil is hot, add chicken and stir-fry until no longer pink in center; cut to test (3 to 4 minutes). Add hoisin sauce to pan; then return vegetables to pan and stir to mix well.

3 Pour into a bowl and garnish with green onions. Fill bread halves with chicken mixture and, if desired, pickled scallions and pickled ginger.

makes 4 servings

per serving: 379 calories, 33 g protein, 45 g carbohydrates, 6 g total fat, 66 mg cholesterol, 400 mg sodium

summer turkey stir-fry

preparation time: about 30 minutes

Cooking Sauce (recipe follows)

1 ³/₄ cups water

1 cup bulgur

1 tablespoon salad oil

3 cloves garlic, minced or pressed

1 pound boneless, skinless turkey breast, cut into ³/₄-inch chunks

3 cups thinly sliced carrots

2 small zucchini, sliced

2 tablespoons minced fresh ginger

¹/₂ cup thinly sliced green onions

1 Prepare Cooking Sauce and set aside.

2 In a 2- to 3-quart pan, bring 1 ¹/₂ cups of the water to a boil over high heat; stir in bulgur. Reduce heat, cover, and simmer until bulgur is tender to bite and water has been absorbed (about 15 minutes).

3 Meanwhile, heat oil in a wide frying pan or wok over high heat. Add garlic and turkey and cook, stirring, until meat is no longer pink in center; cut to test (about 5 minutes). Add carrots, zucchini, ginger, and remaining ¹/₄ cup water. Cover and continue to cook, stirring occasionally, until vegetables are tender-crisp to bite (about 5 more minutes). Uncover, bring to a boil, and boil until almost all liquid has evaporated. Stir in Cooking Sauce; boil, stirring, until sauce is bubbly and thickened.

4 To serve, spoon bulgur onto individual plates and top with turkey mixture. Sprinkle with onions.

makes 4 servings

COOKING SAUCE

In a small bowl, mix ¹/₂ cup low-sodium chicken broth, 2 tablespoons reduced-sodium soy sauce, and 1 tablespoon cornstarch.

per serving: 345 calories, 35 g protein, 41 g carbohydrates, 5 g total fat, 70 mg cholesterol, 402 mg sodium

apricot-stuffed turkey roast

preparation time: about 15 minutes
roasting time: about 1 ¹/₄ hours

1 turkey breast half (about 3 ¹/₂ lbs.), boned and skinned

3 tablespoons Dijon mustard

1 teaspoon dry rosemary

10 to 12 dried apricots

1 tablespoon olive oil

1 teaspoon minced or pressed garlic

Pepper

1 Rinse turkey and pat dry; then place, skinned side down, on a board. Make a lengthwise cut down center of thickest part of turkey, being careful not to cut all the way through. Push cut open and press meat to make it lie as flat as possible.

2 Spread turkey with mustard and sprinkle with ¹/₂ teaspoon of the rosemary; then top evenly with apricots. Starting at a long edge, roll up turkey firmly jelly roll style, enclosing filling. Tie roll snugly with cotton string at 2- to 3-inch intervals. Rub turkey with oil, then garlic; pat remaining ¹/₂ teaspoon rosemary over turkey and sprinkle generously with pepper.

3 Place turkey on a rack in a 9- by 13-inch baking pan. Roast in a 375° oven until a meat thermometer inserted in thickest part registers 165° and meat in center is no longer pink; cut to test (1 hour and 15 to 20 minutes). Let stand for about 10 minutes; then remove strings and cut roll crosswise into thick slices.

makes 6 to 8 servings

per serving: 238 calories, 44 g protein, 4 g carbohydrates, 4 g total fat, 111 mg cholesterol, 282 mg sodium

roast turkey with apple orzo

preparation time: about 20 minutes
cooking time: about 2 ¼ hours

2 tablespoons chopped pecans

1 boned turkey breast half (3 to 3 ½ lbs.), trimmed of fat

⅓ cup apple jelly

1 tablespoon raspberry vinegar or red wine vinegar

¼ teaspoon ground sage

2 cups apple juice

about 2 ¾ cups low-sodium chicken broth

10 ounces (about 1 ⅔ cups) dried orzo or other rice-shaped pasta

½ cup dried cranberries or raisins

¼ teaspoon ground coriander

1 tablespoon cornstarch mixed with 3 tablespoons cold water

⅓ cup chopped parsley or green onions

Sage sprigs

Salt and pepper

1 Toast nuts in a small frying pan over medium heat, shaking pan often, until golden (about 4 minutes). Remove from pan and set aside.

2 Place turkey skin side up. Fold narrow end under breast; pull skin to cover as much breast as possible. Tie snugly lengthwise and crosswise with cotton string at 1-inch intervals. Place in a nonstick or lightly oiled square 8-inch pan.

3 Combine jelly, vinegar, and ground sage in a 1- to 1 ½-quart pan. Cook over medium-low heat, stirring, until jelly is melted. Baste turkey with some of the mixture, reserving remaining mixture.

4 Roast turkey in a 375° oven, basting with pan drippings and remaining jelly mixture, until a meat thermometer inserted in thickest part registers 160° (about 2 hours); if drippings start to scorch, add ⅓ cup water to pan, stirring to loosen browned bits. Meanwhile, combine apple juice and 1 ⅓ cups of the broth in a 4- to 5-quart pan. Bring to a boil over high heat. Stir in pasta, cranberries, and coriander. Reduce heat, cover, and simmer, stirring occasionally, until almost all liquid is absorbed (about 15 minutes); do not scorch. Remove from heat and keep warm, stirring occasionally.

5 Transfer turkey to a warm platter; cover and let stand for 10 minutes. Meanwhile, pour pan drippings and accumulated juices into a 2-cup glass measure; skim off and discard fat. Stir cornstarch mixture and blend into drippings. Add enough of the remaining broth to make 1 ½ cups. Pour into a 1- to 1 ½-quart pan and cook over medium-high heat, stirring, until boiling. Pour into a serving container.

6 Remove strings from turkey. Slice meat and arrange on individual plates. Stir parsley into pasta and mound beside turkey; sprinkle with nuts. Garnish with sage sprigs. Offer gravy, salt, and pepper to add to taste.

makes 8 to 10 servings

per serving: 456 calories, 41 g protein, 45 g carbohydrates, 12 g total fat, 93 mg cholesterol, 104 mg sodium

chicken chimichangas

preparation time: about 15 minutes
cooking time: about 40 minutes

Shredded Chicken Filling (page 222)

About 1 ¹/₂ cups salsa of your choice

5 cups shredded lettuce

1 ¹/₂ cups shredded carrots

8 flour tortillas (7- to 9-inch diameter)

About 1/3 cup nonfat milk

¹/₂ cup shredded Cheddar cheese

Plain nonfat yogurt

1 Prepare Shredded Chicken Filling; set aside. In a small bowl, mix lettuce and carrots; set aside.

2 To assemble each chimichanga, brush both sides of a tortilla liberally with milk; let stand briefly to soften tortilla. Spoon an eighth of the filling down the center of tortilla; top with 1 table-spoon of the cheese. Lap ends of tortilla over filling; then fold sides to center to make a packet. Place chimichanga, seam side down, on a lightly oiled 12- by 15-inch baking sheet and brush with milk. Repeat to make 7 more chimichangas.

3 Bake in a 500° oven, brushing with milk after 5 minutes, until golden brown (8 to 10 minutes).

4 To serve, divide lettuce mixture among 8 plates; place 1 chimi-changa on each plate. Add salsa and yogurt to taste.

makes 8 servings

per serving: 291 calories, 19 g protein, 37 g carbohydrates, 9 g total fat, 38 mg cholesterol, 338 mg sodium

oregano-rubbed turkey

preparation time: about 20 minutes
marinating time: at least 2 hours

1 tablespoon salt

1 ¹/₂ teaspoons sugar

1 ¹/₂ pounds thinly sliced turkey breast

¹/₄ cup sliced green onions

2 tablespoons finely chopped Italian or regular parsley

3 cloves garlic, minced

1 teaspoon chopped fresh oregano or ¹/₂ teaspoon dried oregano

¹/₂ teaspoon *each* coarsely ground pepper and grated lemon peel

2 teaspoons olive oil

Italian or regular parsley sprigs

Lemon wedges

1 In a large bowl, combine salt and sugar. Rinse turkey and pat dry; then add to bowl and turn to coat evenly with salt mixture. Cover and refrigerate for at least 2 hours or up to 3 hours. Rinse turkey well, drain, and pat dry.

2 In a small bowl, combine onions, chopped parsley, garlic, oregano, pepper, and lemon peel. Rub onion mixture evenly over both sides of each turkey slice.

3 Heat 1 teaspoon of the oil in a wide nonstick frying pan over medium-high heat. Add half the turkey and cook until golden on bottom (about 1 ¹/₂ minutes). Then turn pieces over and continue to cook until no longer pink in center; cut to test (30 to 60 more seconds). Transfer cooked turkey to a platter, cover loosely with foil, and keep warm.

4 Immediately cook remaining turkey, using remaining 1 teaspoon oil; add water, 1 tablespoon at a time, if pan appears dry. Transfer turkey to platter and garnish with parsley sprigs. Serve at once. Season to taste with lemon.

makes 6 servings

per serving: 148 calories, 28 g protein, 2 g carbohydrates, 2 g total fat, 70 mg cholesterol, 1,155 mg sodium

chili & anise chicken tortas

preparation time: about 35 minutes

1 pound skinless, bone less chicken thighs

4 cups water

2 cups low-sodium chicken broth

1/4 cup chili powder

4 cup firmly packed brown sugar

2 teaspoons dried oregano

1 teaspoon anise seeds

About 1 tablespoon red wine vinegar, or to taste

2 tablespoons *each* chopped cilantro and thinly sliced green onion

4 French rolls (*each* about 6 inches long)

8 to 12 butter lettuce leaves, rinsed and crisped

CONDIMENTS:

Avocado slices and asadero or string cheese

1 Rinse chicken and pat dry; set aside. In a 4- to 5-quart pan with a tight-fitting lid, combine water, broth, chili powder, sugar, oregano, and anise seeds. Bring to a rolling boil over high heat. Remove pan from heat and immediately add chicken. Cover pan and let stand until meat in thickest part is no longer pink; cut to test (15 to 20 minutes; do not uncover until ready to test). If chicken is not done, return it to hot water, cover, and let steep for 2 to 3 more minutes.

2 Drain chicken, reserving 2 cups of the cooking liquid. Return reserved liquid to pan. Bring to a boil over high heat; boil until reduced to 1/2 cup, watching closely to prevent scorching.

3 Serve chicken and sauce warm or cold. To serve, stir vinegar, cilantro, and onion into sauce. Cut chicken across the grain into thin slanting slices; set aside. Cut rolls in half lengthwise and moisten cut surfaces evenly with sauce. Fill rolls with chicken and lettuce. Offer additional sauce and condiments to add to taste.

makes 4 servings

per serving: 464 calories, 33 g protein, 68 g carbohydrates, 7 g total fat, 94 mg cholesterol, 1,819 mg sodium

brunch paella

preparation time: about 55 minutes

1 pound turkey Italian sausages (casings removed), crumbled into 1/2-inch pieces

1 cup long-grain white rice

1 large onion (about 8 oz.), chopped

2 cloves garlic, minced or pressed

2 cups fat-free reduced sodium chicken broth

1 1/2 cups chopped tomatoes

1/4 teaspoon saffron threads

1 package (about 9 oz.) frozen artichoke hearts, thawed and drained

1/4 cup chopped parsley

Lemon wedges

1 In a wide nonstick frying pan or wok, stir-fry sausage over medium-high heat until browned (7 to 10 minutes). Remove sausage from pan with a slotted spoon; set aside. Pour off and discard all but 1 teaspoon fat from pan.

2 Add rice to pan; stir-fry until rice begins to torn opaque (about 3 minutes). Add onion, garlic, and 2 tablespoons water; stir-fry for 5 more minutes. Add more water, 1 tablespoon at a time, if pan appears dry.

3 Stir in broth, tomatoes, saffron, artichokes, and parsley; then return sausage to pan. Bring to a boil; reduce heat, cover, and simmer until liquid has been absorbed and rice is tender to bite (about 20 minutes). Serve with lemon wedges.

makes 4 to 6 servings

per serving: 195 calories, 7 g protein, 41 g carbohydrates, 0.7 g total fat, 0 mg cholesterol, 294 mg sodium

yucatan tamale pie

preparation time: about 1 ½ hours

3 ounces achiote condiment or substitute
(recipe follows)

2 cups low-sodium chicken broth

2 tablespoons minced fresh mint or 1 teaspoon
dry mint

¹/₈ teaspoon anise seeds

3 cups bite-size pieces of cooked chicken

2 large onions, chopped

2 large tomatoes, cored and cut into wedges

2 tablespoons cornstarch mixed with ¹/₄ cup
cold water

Masa Topping (recipe follows)

Cilantro sprigs

1 Place achiote condiment (or substitute) in a 2-quart pan; stir in ½ cup of the broth. With a heavy spoon, work mixture into a smooth paste. Stir in remaining 1 ½ cups broth, mint, and anise seeds. Bring to a boil over high heat. Then reduce heat and simmer, uncovered, for 5 minutes, stirring often to prevent sticking. (At this point, you may let cool, then cover and refrigerate until next day.)

2 Stir chicken, onions, tomatoes, and cornstarch mixture into achiote mixture; pour into a deep 2- to 3-quart casserole and spread evenly. Prepare Masa Topping; drop in spoonfuls over chicken mixture.

3 Bake on bottom rack of a 400° oven until filling is bubbly in center and topping is well browned (about 45 minutes). Remove from oven and let stand for 5 minutes before serving. Garnish with cilantro sprigs.

makes 6 servings

ACHIOTE SUBSTITUTE

In a small bowl, mix 3 tablespoons paprika, 2 tablespoons distilled white vinegar, 1 ½ teaspoons dry oregano, 3 cloves garlic (minced), and ½ teaspoon ground cumin.

MASA TOPPING

In a small bowl, combine ½ cup each masa harina (dehydrated masa flour) and all-purpose flour. Stir in 1½ teaspoons baking powder. Add 1 large egg white, 1½ tablespoons salad oil, and ½ cup nonfat milk; stir just until blended.

per serving: 316 calories, 26 g protein, 30 g carbohydrates, 10 g total fat, 63 mg cholesterol, 215 mg sodium

honeyed chicken

preparation time: about 30 minutes

2 tablespoons sesame seeds

3 tablespoons honey

¹/₄ cup *each* dry sherry and Dijon mustard

1 tablespoon lemon juice

3 whole chicken breasts (about 1 lb. *each*),
skinned, boned, and split

1 In a small frying pan, toast sesame seeds over medium heat, shaking pan often, until golden (about 3 minutes). Transfer to a small bowl and add honey, sherry, mustard, and lemon juice; stir until blended.

2 Arrange chicken breasts, slightly apart, in a 9- by 13-inch baking pan. Drizzle with honey mixture. Bake in a 400° oven, basting several times with sauce, until meat in thickest part is no longer pink; cut to test (15 to 20 minutes). Transfer chicken to individual plates. Offer with any remaining sauce.

makes 6 servings

per serving: 229 calories, 35 g protein, 12 g carbohydrates, 4 g total fat, 86 mg cholesterol, 398 mg sodium

chicken-yogurt enchilada casserole

preparation time: about 1 hour

1 cup plain nonfat yogurt

1 cup low-fat (1%) cottage cheese

2 cloves garlic, peeled

2 teaspoons *each* chili powder, sugar, and cornstarch

1 tablespoon butter or margarine

1/4 cup all-purpose flour

2 cups low-sodium chicken broth

1 large can (about 7 oz.) diced green chiles

12 corn tortillas (6-inch diameter)

2 cups bite-size pieces of cooked chicken

1 small onion, chopped

1/2 cup shredded jack cheese

1 In a blender or food processor, whirl yogurt, cottage cheese, garlic, chili powder, sugar, and cornstarch until smoothly puréed. Set aside.

2 Melt butter in a 1 1/2- to 2-quart pan over medium-high heat. Add flour and 1/3 cup water; stir just until bubbly. Whisk in broth; bring to a boil, stirring. Remove from heat; let cool for 5 minutes. Whisk yogurt mixture into flour mixture; stir in chiles. Cover bottom of a 9- by 13-inch baking dish with a third of the yogurt-flour mixture.

3 Dip tortillas, one at a time, in hot water. Drain briefly; cut into strips 1 inch wide. Scatter half the tortilla strips over yogurt-flour mixture in baking dish; cover with all the chicken and onion, half the jack cheese, and half the remaining yogurt-flour mixture. Top with remaining tortilla strips, yogurt-flour mixture, and jack cheese.

4 Cover dish tightly with foil and bake in a 400° oven for 30 minutes. Uncover; continue to bake until mixture is golden brown on top and appears firm in center when dish is gently shaken (15 to 20 more minutes).

makes 8 servings

per serving: 261 calories, 20 g protein, 29 g carbohydrates, 8 g total fat, 41 mg cholesterol, 465 mg sodium

oven fried chicken

preparation time: about 35 minutes
marinating time: 20 minutes

2 tablespoons dry sherry

2 cloves garlic, minced or pressed

4 boneless, skinless chicken breast halves (about 1 1/2 lbs. *total*)

1/2 cup soft whole wheat bread crumbs

2 tablespoons cornmeal

1 teaspoon paprika

1/2 teaspoon *each* salt, pepper, dry sage, dry thyme, and dry basil

Vegetable oil cooking spray

1 In a shallow bowl, stir together sherry and garlic. Rinse chicken and pat dry; add to sherry mixture, turn to coat, and let stand for 20 minutes.

2 In another shallow bowl, mix bread crumbs, cornmeal, paprika, salt, pepper, sage, thyme, and basil. Lift chicken from marinade and drain briefly; discard marinade. Turn each chicken piece in crumb mixture to coat.

3 Lightly coat a shallow baking pan with cooking spray; arrange chicken pieces in pan. Bake in a 450° oven until meat in thickest part is no longer pink; cut to test (15 to 20 minutes). Serve hot or cold.

makes 4 servings

per serving: 231 calories, 40 g protein, 8 g, carbohydrates, 3 g total fat, 99 mg cholesterol, 418 mg sodium

stir-fried turkey with coconut rice

preparation time: about 45 minutes

Coconut Rice (recipe follows)

2 tablespoons lemon juice

1 clove garlic, minced or pressed

1/2 teaspoon ground cumin

1/4 teaspoon chili powder

2 turkey breast tenderloins (about 1 lb. *total*), cut into 1-inch pieces

1/2 cup golden raisins

1/4 cup dry white wine

2 medium-size carrots, cut into 1/4-inch slanting slices

1 large onion (about 8 oz.), thinly sliced

2 teaspoons olive oil or salad oil

2 to 3 teaspoons curry powder

1 to 2 tablespoons chopped fresh mint or parsley

2 tablespoons salted roasted cashews, chopped

Mint or parsley sprigs

1 Prepare Coconut Rice. Meanwhile, in a large bowl, combine 1 tablespoon water, lemon juice, garlic, cumin, and chili powder. Add turkey and stir to coat. Set aside; stir occasionally. In a small bowl, combine raisins and wine; let stand until raisins are softened (about 10 minutes), stirring occasionally.

2 In a wide nonstick frying pan or wok, combine carrots, onion, and 1/4 cup water. Cover and cook over medium-high heat until carrots are tender-crisp to bite (about 5 minutes). Uncover and stir-fry until liquid has evaporated. Remove vegetables from pan with a slotted spoon and keep warm.

3 Heat oil in pan. When oil is hot, add turkey mixture. Stir-fry just until meat is no longer pink in center; cut to test (3 to 4 minutes). Add water, 1 tablespoon at a time, if pan appears dry. Add curry powder and stir-fry just until fragrant (about 30 seconds; do not scorch).

4 Add raisins (and soaking liquid) to pan; return vegetables to pan. Bring to a boil; then boil, stirring, until liquid has evaporated (about 2 minutes). Remove from heat; stir in chopped mint and cashews. Spoon Coconut Rice into 4 wide bowls; top with turkey mixture and garnish with mint sprigs.

makes 4 servings

COCONUT RICE

In a 3- to 4-quart pan, combine 1 cup each water and low-fat milk. Bring just to a boil over medium- high heat. Stir in 1 cup long-grain white rice. Reduce heat, cover, and simmer until liquid has been absorbed and rice is tender to bite (about 20 minutes). Stir in 1/4 cup sweetened shredded coconut. Keep warm until ready to serve, fluffing occasionally with a fork.

per serving: 502 calories, 36 g protein, 70 g carbohydrates, 7 g total fat, 72 mg cholesterol, 158 mg sodium

jalapeño chicken with mole poblano

preparation time: about 45 minutes

1 tablespoon sesame seeds

1 large onion, chopped

4 cloves garlic, minced or pressed

1 small very ripe banana, chopped

1/4 cup chopped pitted prunes

2 tablespoons raisins

1 tablespoon creamy peanut butter

5 tablespoons unsweetened cocoa powder

3 tablespoons chili powder

2 teaspoons sugar

1/2 teaspoon ground cinnamon

1/8 teaspoon ground coriander

1/8 teaspoon ground cumin

1/8 teaspoon ground cloves

1/8 teaspoon anise seeds, crushed

2 cups fat-free reduced-sodium chicken broth

1 small can (about 6 oz.) tomato paste

8 skinless, boneless chicken breast halves
(about 6 oz. *each*)

1 Toast sesame seeds in a wide nonstick frying pan over medium heat until golden (about 4 minutes), stirring often. Transfer to a bowl; set aside.

2 To pan, add onion, garlic, banana, prunes, raisins, peanut butter, and 3 tablespoons water. Cook over medium heat, stirring often, until mixture is richly browned (10 to 15 minutes); if pan appears dry, add more water, 1 tablespoon at a time. Stir in cocoa, chili powder, sugar, cinnamon, coriander, cumin, cloves, anise seeds, and 3/4 cup of the broth. Bring mixture to a boil over medium-high heat.

3 Transfer hot onion mixture to a food processor or blender and add tomato paste, 2 teaspoons of the anise seeds, and a little of the remaining broth. Whirl until smoothly puréed; then stir in remaining broth. Cover and keep warm. (At this point, you may let cool; then cover and refrigerate for up to 3 days; freeze for longer storage. Reheat before continuing.)

4 While onion mixture is browning, rinse chicken and pat dry. Place jelly in a bowl and stir to soften; add chicken in a lightly oiled 10- by 15-inch rimmed baking pan. Bake in a 450° oven until meat in thickest part is no longer pink; cut to test (12 to 15 minutes).

5 To serve, spoon some of the warm mole sauce onto dinner plates; top with chicken, then more mole sauce. Sprinkle with remaining 1 teaspoon sesame seeds. Season to taste with salt; serve with lime wedges to squeeze over chicken to taste.

makes 8 servings

per serving: 264 calories, 34 g protein, 23 g carbohydrates, 6 g total fat, 74 mg cholesterol, 322 mg sodium

MICROWAVE A WHOLE FRYING CHICKEN: Remove neck and giblets; reserve for other uses, if desired. Discard lumps of fat. Rinse chicken inside and out, and pat dry. Stuff, if desired and close stuffed cavities with string and wooden picks (not metallic skewers). Place, breast down, on a nonmetallic rack in a 7 by 11-inch microwave-proof baking dish. Cover with heavy-duty plastic wrap or wax paper. For a 3- to 3 1/2-pound bird, microwave on HIGH for 6 to 7 minutes per pound, turning chicken over and rotating dish a quarter turn halfway through cooking.

turkey chili

preparation time: about 55 minutes

1 tablespoon salad oil

1 pound skinned and boned turkey breast, cut into 1 ¹/₂-inch chunks

1 medium-size onion, chopped

1 small green bell pepper, seeded and chopped

1 clove garlic, minced or pressed

1 small can (about 8 oz.) tomatoes, drained and chopped

2 cans (about 15 oz. *each*) kidney beans, drained

1 large can (15 oz.) no-salt-added tomato sauce

2 tablespoons reduced-sodium soy sauce

1 ¹/₂ tablespoons chili powder

¹/₂ teaspoon *each* ground cumin, dry sage leaves, and dry thyme leaves

Garnishes (optional; suggestions follow)

1 Heat oil in a 12- to 14-inch frying pan over medium heat. Add turkey and cook, stirring often, until browned on all sides (about 6 minutes).

2 Remove turkey from pan. Add onion, bell pepper, and garlic; cook, stirring occasionally, until onion is soft (about 10 minutes). Add tomatoes, beans, tomato sauce, soy, chili powder, cumin, sage, and thyme. Bring to a boil. Then reduce heat, cover, and simmer until chili is thick and meat is no longer pink in center; cut to test (about 20 minutes; uncover for last 5 minutes).

3 Serve in bowls and accompany with garnishes.

makes 4 servings

GARNISHES

In separate bowls, offer 8 green onions (including tops), sliced; 1 cup chopped tomatoes; and ¹/₂ cup shredded jack cheese, if desired.

per serving: 407 calories, 40g protein, 47g carbohydrates, 7g total fat, 70 mg cholesterol, 1259 mg sodium

chicken kebabs shanghai

preparation time: about 40 minutes
marinating time: at least 30 minutes

³/₄ teaspoon grated orange peel

¹/₃ cup orange juice

3 tablespoons firmly packed brown sugar

2 tablespoons reduced-sodium soy sauce

4 teaspoons *each* minced fresh ginger and red wine vinegar

1 tablespoon Asian sesame oil or salad oil

¹/₂ teaspoon ground coriander

1 ¹/₂ pounds skinned, boned chicken breasts, cut into 1 ¹/₂-inch chunks

1 medium-size pineapple, peeled, cored, and cut into 1-inch chunks

1 In a medium-size bowl, mix orange peel, orange juice, sugar, soy sauce, ginger, vinegar, oil, and coriander. Stir in chicken. Cover and refrigerate for at least 30 minutes or up to 2 hours.

2 Lift chicken from marinade and drain briefly; reserve marinade. Thread chicken and pineapple chunks on thin metal skewers, alternating 2 chicken chunks and one pineapple chunk. Brush reserved marinade over pineapple. Place skewers on a rack in a 12- by 15-inch broiler pan. Broil about 4 inches below heat, turning once, until chicken is no longer pink in center; cut to test (about 12 minutes).

makes 4 to 6 servings

per serving: 299 calories, 33 g protein, 319 carbohydrates, 5 g total fat, 79 mg cholesterol, 333 mg sodium

picadillo stew

preparation time: about 40 minutes

2 tablespoons slivered almonds

1/4 cup dry red wine

2 tablespoons reduced sodium soy sauce

1 tablespoon lemon juice

2 teaspoons sugar

1 teaspoon *each* ground cumin, ground coriander, and chili powder

1/8 teaspoon ground cinnamon

4 teaspoons cornstarch

1 teaspoon salad oil

1 pound boneless turkey breast, cut into 1-inch chunks

1 large onion, chopped

2 cloves garlic, minced or pressed

1 can (about 14 1/2 oz.) tomatoes

2/3 cup raisins

Pepper

1 Toast almonds in a small flying pan over medium heat until golden (5 to 7 minutes), stirring often. Transfer almonds to a bowl and set aside.

2 In a small bowl, mix wine, soy sauce, lemon juice, sugar, cumin, coriander, chili powder, cinnamon, and cornstarch until smooth. Set aside.

3 Heat oil in a wide nonstick frying pan or 5-quart pan over high heat. Add turkey, onion, and garlic. Cook, stirring, until meat is no longer pink in thickest part; cut to test (10 to 15 minutes). Add water, 1 tablespoon at a time, if pan appears dry. Add tomatoes and their liquid (break tomatoes up with a spoon), wine mixture, and raisins to pan. Bring to a boil; boil, stirring, just until thickened.

4 To serve, ladle stew into bowls and sprinkle with almonds. Season to taste with pepper.

makes 4 servings

per serving: 317 calories, 32 g protein, 36 g carbohydrates, 5 g total fat, 70 mg cholesterol, 538 mg sodium

strawberry chicken

preparation time: about 10 minutes
baking time: about 45 minutes

1 can (about 8 oz.) tomato sauce

1 cup strawberry jam

2 tablespoons red wine vinegar

1 tablespoon chili powder

1/2 teaspoon *each* dry thyme and ground ginger

12 skinless chicken thighs (2 to 2 1/4 lbs. *total*) trimmed of fat

Salt

3 cups hot cooked a short-grain rice

1/2 cup thinly sliced green onions

1 In a shallow 3-quart casserole, mix tomato sauce, jam, vinegar, chili powder, thyme, and ginger.

2 Rinse chicken and pat dry; then add to sauce and turn to coat. Bake in a 400° oven, basting occasionally, until meat near bone is no longer pink; cut to test (about 45 minutes). Season to taste with salt.

3 Spoon rice onto a platter. Top with chicken, sauce, and onions.

makes 4 to 6 servings

per serving: 505 calories, 33 g protein, 81 g carbohydrates, 6 g total fat, 118 mg cholesterol, 441 mg sodium

chicken curry in pita bread

preparation time: about 40 minutes

1/2 cup raisins or dried currants

1 cup plain nonfat yogurt

2 tablespoons cornstarch

2 teaspoons olive oil

12 ounces skinless, boneless chicken breast, cut into 1/2-inch pieces

1 medium-size onion, chopped

2 cloves garlic, minced or pressed

2 teaspoons curry powder

1/2 cup apricot jam or preserves

Salt and pepper

1 medium-size cucumber, very thinly sliced

4 pita breads (*each* about 6 inches in diameter), cut crosswise into halves

1 In a small bowl, combine raisins and 1/4 cup water; let stand until raisins are softened (about 10 minutes), stirring occasionally. Meanwhile, in another small bowl, stir together yogurt and cornstarch until smoothly blended; set aside.

2 Heat oil in a wide nonstick frying pan or wok over medium-high heat. When oil is hot, add chicken and 1 tablespoon water. Stir-fry until meat is no longer pink in center; cut to test (3 to 4 minutes). Remove chicken from pan with a slotted spoon and keep warm. Discard drippings from pan.

3 Add onion, garlic, curry powder, and 1/4 cup water to pan; stir-fry until onion is soft (about 4 minutes; do not scorch). Add water, 1 tablespoon at a time, if pan appears dry. Add raisins (and soaking water) and jam. Bring to a boil; then boil, stirring, until almost all liquid has evaporated (5 to 7 minutes). Reduce heat to medium-low; stir in chicken and yogurt mixture. Simmer gently, stirring constantly, until sauce is slightly thickened (do not boil). Season to taste with salt and pepper.

4 To serve, divide cucumber slices equally among pita halves; fill pitas equally with chicken mixture.

makes 4 servings

per serving: 506 calories, 30 g protein, 88 g carbohydrates, 5 g total fat, 51 mg cholesterol, 442 mg sodium

chicken-stuffed melon with raspberries

preparation time: about 45 minutes

Lime-Honey Dressing (recipe follows)

1 1/2 pounds skinned and boned chicken breasts

4 cups water

2 large cantaloupes

1 cup seedless green grapes

2 kiwi fruit, peeled and sliced

1 cup raspberries

1 Prepare dressing; set aside. Rinse and drain chicken. In a 4- to 5-quart pan, bring water to a boil over high heat. Add chicken, cover pan, and remove from heat. Let stand, covered, until chicken is no longer pink in thickest part; cut to test (about 20 minutes). Drain chicken and place in ice water until cool; drain again. Cut into 1/2-inch chunks.

2 Cut each cantaloupe in half, making zigzag cuts. Scoop out and discard seeds. With a curved grapefruit knife, cut fruit from rind, then cut into 1/2-inch chunks. Drain melon pieces and shells.

3 In a bowl, combine melon, chicken, and grapes; spoon into shells. Top with kiwi slices, raspberries, and dressing.

makes 4 servings

LIME-HONEY DRESSING

Stir together 1/2 cup each lime juice and honey with 1/2 teaspoon each ground coriander and ground nutmeg.

per serving: 340 calories, 29 g protein, 55 g carbohydrates, 3 g total fat, 66 mg cholesterol, 101 mg sodium

saffron & honey chicken

preparation time: about 1 hour

²/₃ cup low-sodium chicken broth

2 tablespoons *each* lime juice and honey

¹/₄ teaspoon saffron threads

1 teaspoon white Worcestershire

2 teaspoons curry powder

¹/₂ teaspoon dry oregano

¹/₄ teaspoon paprika

¹/₈ teaspoon pepper

2 teaspoons reduced-sodium soy sauce

2 tablespoons white rice flour blended with
   ¹/₄ cup cold water

6 *each* chicken drumsticks and thighs (about
   3 lbs. *total*), skinned and trimmed of fat

Chopped parsley

1 In a 1 ¹/₂- to 2-quart pan, stir together broth, lime juice, honey, saffron, Worcestershire, curry powder, oregano, paprika, pepper, and soy sauce. Bring to a boil over high heat; then reduce heat and simmer, uncovered, stirring occasionally, until reduced to ¹/₂ cup (about 15 minutes). Stir in rice flour mixture; bring to a boil over high heat, stirring. Remove from heat.

2 Rinse chicken, pat dry, and arrange, skinned side up, in a 9- by 13-inch baking pan. Spoon sauce evenly over chicken. Cover and bake in a 375° oven until meat near bone is no longer pink; cut to test (about 35 minutes).

3 Transfer chicken to a platter; stir sauce to blend, then spoon over chicken. Sprinkle with parsley.

makes 6 servings

per serving: 198 calories, 27 g protein, 10 g carbohydrates, 5 g total fat, 104 mg cholesterol, 193 mg sodium

chicken and black bean bake

preparation time: about 35 minutes

1 package (about 7 oz.) or 1 ²/₃ cups instant
   refried black bean mix

2 cups boiling water

¹/₃ to ¹/₂ cup dry sherry or water

4 boneless, skinless chicken breast halves (about
   1 ¹/₂ lbs. total)

8 cups shredded iceberg lettuce

¹/₂ cup shredded jack cheese

1 fresh red or green jalapeño chile, thinly sliced
   crosswise (optional)

Cherry tomatoes

Reduced-fat sour cream

1 In a shallow 2- to 2 ¹/₂-quart baking dish, combine refried bean mix, boiling water, and sherry (use the ¹/₂-cup amount if you prefer a saucelike consistency). Rinse chicken and pat dry; then arrange, skinned side up, atop beans. Bake in a 400° oven until meat in thickest part is no longer pink; cut to test (about 20 minutes). Stir any liquid that accumulates around chicken into beans.

2 Mound lettuce equally on 4 individual plates; top with beans and chicken. Sprinkle with cheese and chile (if used); garnish with cherry tomatoes. Offer sour cream to add to taste.

makes 4 servings

per serving: 469 calories, 54 g protein, 36 g carbohydrates, 8 g total fat, 114 mg cholesterol, 597 mg sodium

sake-steamed chicken

preparation time: about 30 minutes
marinating time: at least 30 minutes

$^1/_2$ **cup sake or unseasoned rice vinegar**

$^1/_2$ **teaspoon salt**

**6 boneless, skinless chicken breast halves
(about 2 $^1/_4$ lbs. total)**

1 small head iceberg lettuce

About $^1/_3$ cup reduced-sodium soy sauce

1 tablespoon prepared horseradish

Lemon wedges

3 cups hot cooked rice

$^1/_2$ **cup thinly sliced green onions**

1 In a medium-size bowl, stir together sake and salt until salt is dissolved. Rinse chicken and pat dry; add to marinade and turn to coat. Cover and refrigerate for at least 30 minutes or up to 2 hours.

2 Lift chicken from bowl and drain briefly; discard marinade. Arrange chicken, with thickest parts toward outside, in a single layer in a 10- to 11-inch round heatproof nonmetal dish. Cover with wax paper or foil and set on a rack in a large pan above 1 inch of boiling water. Cover and steam, keeping water at a steady boil, until meat in thickest part is no longer pink; cut to test (about 12 minutes).

3 Meanwhile, place 1 or 2 large lettuce leaves on each of 6 individual plates. Finely shred remaining lettuce; mound atop leaves. Divide soy sauce among 6 tiny dipping bowls; add $^1/_2$ teaspoon of the horseradish to each, then place bowls on plates. Place a few lemon wedges on each plate.

4 Cut chicken crosswise into $^1/_2$-inch-wide strips. Spoon rice and chicken over lettuce; sprinkle with onions. To eat, squeeze lemon into soy mixture. Dip chicken into sauce. Or tear lettuce leaves into pieces and fill with chicken, rice, and shredded lettuce; season with sauce and eat out of hand.

makes 6 servings

per serving: 360 calories, 44 g protein, 35 g carbohydrates, 3 g total fat, 99 mg cholesterol, 742 mg sodium

apple turkey loaf

preparation time: about 25 minutes
baking time: about 1 hour

1 tablespoon butter or margarine

**2 medium-size tart green-skinned apples,
cored and chopped**

1 medium-size onion, chopped

1 $^1/_2$ pounds ground skinless turkey breast

1 $^1/_2$ teaspoons dry marjoram

1 teaspoon each dry thyme, dry sage, and pepper

$^1/_2$ **cup chopped parsley**

2 large egg whites (about $^1/_4$ cup)

$^1/_2$ **cup each fine dry bread crumbs and
nonfat milk**

1 Melt butter in a wide frying pan over medium heat. Add apples and onion. Cook, stirring occasionally, until onion is soft (about 7 minutes). Remove from heat and let cool; then spoon into a large bowl. Add turkey, marjoram, thyme, sage, pepper, parsley, egg whites, bread crumbs, and milk; mix lightly.

2 Pat turkey mixture into a 5- by 9-inch loaf pan. Bake in a 350° oven until browned on top and no longer pink in center; cut to test (about 1 hour). Drain and discard fat from pan, then invert pan and turn loaf out onto a platter. Serve loaf hot; or let cool, then cover and refrigerate for up to 1 day.

makes 6 servings

per serving: 237 calories, 32 g protein, 19 g carbohydrates, 3 g total fat, 76 mg cholesterol, 185 mg sodium

sesame chicken with stir-fry vegetables

preparation time: about 35 minutes

4 chicken breast halves (about 2 lbs. *total*), skinned and boned

1 teaspoon sesame seeds vegetable oil cooking spray

4 teaspoons rice vinegar

4 teaspoons reduced-sodium soy sauce

1 ½ teaspoons Asian sesame oil

1 tablespoon grated fresh ginger

2 cloves garlic, minced or pressed ½ teaspoon sugar

1 tablespoon vegetable oil

8 ounces mushrooms, sliced

4 cups thinly sliced red cabbage

4 ounces Chinese pea pods (also called snow peas), ends and strings removed

2 cups hot cooked rice

1 Rinse chicken, pat dry, and sprinkle with sesame seeds. Spray a ridged cooktop grill pan with cooking spray. Place over medium heat and preheat until a drop of water dances on surface. Then place chicken on grill and cook, turning once, until well browned on outside and no longer pink in thickest part; cut to test (12 to 15 minutes).

2 Meanwhile, in a small bowl, stir together vinegar, soy sauce, sesame oil, ginger, garlic, and sugar; set aside. Then heat vegetable oil in a wide nonstick frying pan or wok over medium-high heat.

3 Add mushrooms and cook, stirring often, for about 3 minutes. Add cabbage and cook, stirring often, until it begins to soften (about 2 minutes). Add pea pods and cook, stirring, just until they turn bright green (1 to 2 minutes). Add vinegar mixture and stir for 1 more minute.

4 Divide vegetables among 4 warm dinner plates. Cut each chicken piece diagonally across the grain into ½-inch-wide strips. Arrange chicken over vegetables; serve with rice.

makes 4 servings

per serving: 400 calories, 40 g protein, 40 g carbohydrates, 8 g total fat, 86 mg cholesterol, 310 mg sodium

white wine turkey loaf

preparation time: about 1 hour

⅓ cup low-sodium chicken broth

⅓ cup thinly sliced green onions (including tops)

1 small green bell pepper, stemmed, seeded, and diced

½ cup dry white wine

1 cup soft whole wheat bread crumbs

1 teaspoon dry thyme leaves

1 pound fresh ground turkey

1 egg white

Freshly ground pepper

1 can (8 oz.) no-salt-added tomato sauce

1 In a small frying pan, bring chicken broth to a boil over high heat. Add onions and bell pepper and cook, stirring, until liquid has evaporated and vegetables are soft (about 5 minutes). Add wine, bring to a boil, and remove from heat. Stir in bread crumbs and thyme.

2 In a bowl, mix turkey, bread crumb mixture, and egg white; season to taste with pepper. Pat mixture into a 5- by 9-inch loaf pan. Spread half the tomato sauce over meat.

3 Bake in a 350° oven for 30 minutes. Remove pan from oven and tip to pour off fat. Spread remaining tomato sauce over loaf and continue baking until meat in center is no longer pink; cut to test (10 to 15 more minutes). Let stand for 5 minutes before slicing.

makes 4 to 6 servings

per serving: 207 calories, 19 g protein, 10 g carbohydrates, 10 g total fat, 46 mg cholesterol, 134 mg sodium

broccoli-stuffed chicken breasts

preparation time: about 1 hour

1 tablespoon salad oil

1/2 cup minced shallots

1 pound mushrooms, minced

2 cups broccoli flowerets

2 tablespoons Madeira

2 tablespoons grated Parmesan cheese

1/2 cup shredded reduced-fat Jarlsberg or Swiss cheese

6 boneless, skinless chicken breast halves (about 2 1/4 lbs. *total*)

1 Heat oil in a wide frying pan over medium heat. Add shallots and mushrooms; cook, stirring occasionally, until shallots are soft (about 5 minutes). Add broccoli and Madeira; cover and cook, stirring occasionally, until broccoli is tender-crisp to bite (about 5 minutes). Remove from heat and stir in Parmesan cheese and 1/4 cup of the Jarlsberg cheese. Let cool.

2 Rinse chicken and pat dry. Place each breast half between 2 sheets of plastic wrap and pound with a flat-surfaced mallet to a thickness of about 1/4 inch. In center of each pounded chicken piece, mound a sixth of the broccoli-mushroom mixture. Roll chicken around filling to enclose. Set chicken rolls, seam side down, in a greased 9- by 13-inch baking pan. Sprinkle evenly with remaining 1/4 cup Jarlsberg cheese.

3 Bake in a 450° oven until meat is no longer pink and filling is hot in center; cut to test (about 15 minutes). Then broil 4 to 6 inches below heat until cheese is browned (about 2 minutes).

makes 6 servings

per serving: 291 calories, 46 g protein, 9 g carbohydrates, 7 g total fat, 105 mg cholesterol, 190 mg sodium

chicken capocollo

preparation time: about 30 minutes

4 small boneless, skinless chicken breast halves (about 1 lb. *total*)

4 thin slices capocollo (or coppa) sausage or prosciutto (about 1 oz. *total*)

2 teaspoons olive oil

4 green onions, thinly sliced

2 cloves garlic, minced or pressed

1/4 cup low-sodium chicken broth or dry white wine

2 tablespoons Dijon mustard

1 tablespoon lemon juice

1/2 teaspoon dry basil

1 Rinse chicken and pat dry. Place each breast half between 2 sheets of plastic wrap and pound with a flat-surfaced mallet to a thickness of 1/3 to 1/2 inch. Lay a slice of capocollo on each pounded chicken piece, pressing lightly so that chicken and sausage stick together. Set aside.

2 Heat oil in a wide frying pan over medium heat. Add onions and garlic; cook, stirring often, until vegetables are lightly browned (about 3 minutes). Then push vegetables to one side and place chicken in pan. Cook just until edges of chicken pieces begin to brown on bottom (about 4 minutes). Turn pieces over and continue to cook until meat in thickest part is no longer pink; cut to test (3 to 4 more minutes). Transfer chicken, sausage side up, to a platter; keep warm.

3 To pan, add broth, mustard, lemon juice, and basil. Bring to a boil over high heat, stirring constantly; then pour broth mixture over chicken.

makes 4 servings

per serving: 180 calories, 29 g protein, 3 g carbohydrates, 5 g total fat, 72 mg cholesterol, 437 mg sodium

roast turkey breasts & four drumsticks

preparation time: about 45 minutes
roasting time: about 2 1/4 hours

1 boneless turkey breast half (3 to 3 1/2 lbs.)

4 turkey drumsticks (about 1 lb. *each***)**

2/3 cup apple, quince, or red currant jelly

2 tablespoons raspberry vinegar or red wine vinegar

1/2 teaspoon ground sage

Dried Tomato Couscous (recipe follows)

2 tablespoons cornstarch

about 2 cups low-sodium chicken broth

Salt and pepper

1 Trim and discard fat from turkey breast. Rinse breast and drumsticks; pat dry. Set breast skin side up and fold narrow end under to make an evenly thick piece; pull skin to cover as much of meat as possible. Using cotton string, tie breast snugly at 1-inch intervals lengthwise and crosswise. Set all turkey aside.

2 In a small pan, combine jelly, vinegar, and sage. Stir over medium heat until jelly is melted.

3 Arrange drumsticks slightly apart in an 11- by 17-inch roasting pan; brush with some of the jelly mixture. Roast in a 375° oven for 15 minutes. Set breast in pan and brush with jelly mixture. Continue to roast until a meat thermometer inserted in thickest part of breast registers 165° and until thermometer inserted in thickest part of drumsticks registers 185° (about 2 hours). If some pieces are done before others, remove them from oven and keep warm. As turkey roasts, baste it with pan drippings and jelly mixture, using all. If drippings begin to scorch, add 1/3 cup water and stir to scrape browned bits free.

4 About 30 minutes before turkey is done, prepare Dried Tomato Couscous.

5 When turkey is done, transfer it to a carving board, cover lightly, and let stand for about 10 minutes. As juices accumulate on board, drain them into roasting pan.

6 To make gravy, skim and discard fat from pan drippings. Pour drippings into a 1-quart or larger glass measure; smoothly blend in cornstarch. Then add enough broth to make 2 1/2 cups. Return mixture to roasting pan; bring to a boil over high heat, stirring. Season to taste with salt and pepper. Pour into a bowl or gravy boat. To serve, remove strings from turkey breast, then thinly slice meat across the grain. Slice drumsticks or serve whole. Arrange turkey on platter around couscous; accompany with gravy.

makes 12 to 16 servings

DRIED TOMATO COUSCOUS

Soak 1/2 cup dried tomatoes in 5 cups boiling water until very soft (about 30 minutes). Drain tomatoes, pressing out excess liquid and reserving all soaking water. Chop tomatoes coarsely and set aside. In a 3 1/2- to 4-quart pan, combine water from tomatoes and 1 can (about 14 1/2 oz.) low-sodium chicken broth. Bring to a boil over high heat. Stir in tomatoes, 1/2 teaspoon dry oregano, 1/4 teaspoon dry sage, and 3 cups couscous. Cover pan, remove from heat, and let stand for about 5 minutes. Fluff couscous with a fork; mound on a large platter, allowing room for turkey.

per serving: 465 calories, 50 g protein, 44 g carbohydrates, 8 g total fat, 127 mg cholesterol, 124 mg sodium

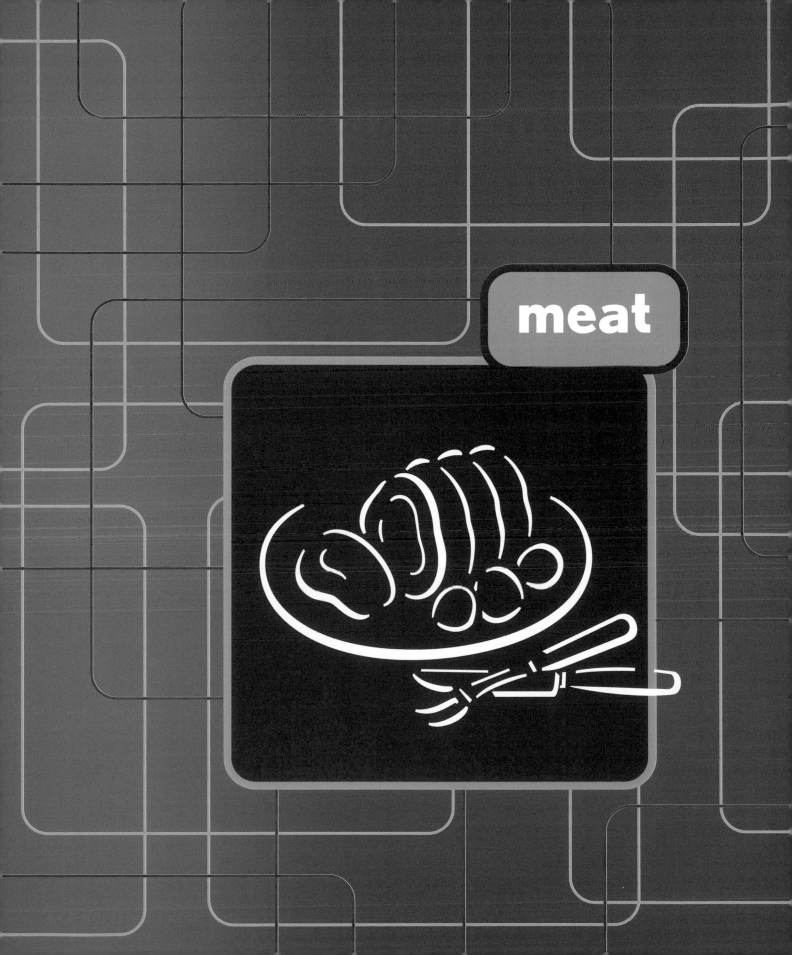

meat

pork tenderloin with bulgur

preparation time: about 40 minutes

3 cups beef broth

1 cup bulgur (cracked wheat)

½ cup sliced green onions

1½ pounds pork tenderloin (about 2 tenderloins), trimmed of fat

2 teaspoons sugar

1 tablespoon vegetable oil

1 tablespoon mustard seeds

1 tablespoon balsamic vinegar

2 teaspoons minced fresh oregano or 1 teaspoon dried oregano

½ cup dry red wine

2 teaspoons cornstarch mixed with 2 teaspoons cold water

1 pound asparagus, tough ends broken off

Salt and pepper

1 In a 2- to 3-quart pan, bring 2 cups of the broth to a boil; stir in bulgur. Cover, remove from heat, and let stand until bulgur is tender to bite (about 30 minutes). Stir in onions.

2 While bulgur is standing, sprinkle pork with sugar. Heat oil in a wide frying pan over medium-high heat; add pork and cook, turning as needed, until browned on all sides (about 4 minutes). Add ⅔ cup of the broth, mustard seeds, vinegar, and oregano. Cover, reduce heat to medium-low, and simmer just until meat is no longer pink in center; cut to test (about 12 minutes).

3 Lift pork to a warm platter and keep warm. To pan, add wine and remaining ⅓ cup. Bring to a boil over high heat; then boil until reduced to ¾ cup (about 2 minutes). Stir in cornstarch mixture; return to a boil, stirring.

4 While sauce is boiling, bring ½ inch of water to a boil in anoth-er wide frying pan over high heat. Add asparagus and cook, uncovered, just until barely tender when pierced (about 4 minutes). Drain.

5 Slice pork; mound bulgur alongside, then top with asparagus. Spoon sauce over meat. Season to taste with salt and pepper.

makes 4 servings

per serving: 442 calories, 45 g protein, 36 g carbohydrates, 11 g total fat, 111 mg cholesterol, 1,327 mg sodium

spicy pork tenderloins

preparation time: about 30 minutes
marinating time: at least 4 hours

¼ cup *each* honey and prepared mustard

¼ teaspoon *each* salt and chili powder

2 pork tenderloins (about ¾ lb. *each*), fat and silvery membrane trimmed

1 In a large bowl, stir together honey, mustard, salt, and chili powder. Add pork, turning to coat. Cover and refrigerate for at least 4 hours or until next day, turning meat several times.

2 Lift out pork and drain, reserving marinade. Place pork on a lightly greased grill 4 to 6 inches above a solid bed of medium-hot coals. Cook, basting once with reserved marinade, until no longer pink in center (cut to test) or until a meat thermometer inserted in center registers 155° (about 20 minutes). Cover with foil and let stand for 10 minutes; cut across grain into thin, slanting slices.

makes 6 servings

per serving: 201 calories, 26 g protein, 12 g carbohydrates, 5g total fat, 84 mg cholesterol, 283 mg sodium

sweet & sour pork

preparation time: about 40 minutes

1/3 cup plus 4 teaspoons cornstarch

1/4 cup white wine vinegar
   or distilled white vinegar

1/4 cup sugar

1 tablespoon catsup

1 tablespoon reduced-sodium soy sauce

1/8 teaspoon hot chili oil, or to taste

1 large egg white

1 pound pork tenderloin, trimmed
   of fat and cut into 1-inch chunks

1 tablespoon vegetable oil

1 large onion, cut into thin wedges

1 large green bell pepper, seeded and
   cut into 1-inch squares

1 or 2 cloves garlic, minced or pressed

1 large tomato, cut into wedges

1 1/2 cups fresh or canned pineapple chunks,
   drained

1 For sweet-sour sauce, in a medium-size bowl, stir together 4 teaspoons of the cornstarch and the vinegar until blended. Stir in 3/4 cup water, sugar, catsup, soy sauce and hot chile oil. Set aside.

2 In a medium-size bowl, beat egg white to blend well. Place remaining 1/3 cup cornstarch in another medium-size bowl. Dip pork chunks, a portion at a time, in egg white; then coat lightly with cornstarch and shake off excess.

3 Heat vegetable oil in a wide nonstick frying pan or wok over medium-high heat. When oil is hot, add meat and stir-fry gently until golden brown on outside and no longer pink in center; cut to test (about 8 minutes). Add water, 1 tablespoon at a time, if pan appears dry. Remove meat from pan with a slotted spoon; keep warm.

4 Add onion, bell pepper, garlic, and 1 tablespoon water to pan; stir-fry for 1 minute. Add more water, 1 tablespoon at a time, if pan appears dry. Stir reserved sweet-sour sauce well and pour into pan. Cook, stirring, until sauce boils and thickens slightly (2 to 3 minutes).

5 Add tomato, pineapple, and meat to pan. Cook, stirring gently but thoroughly, just until heated through (1 to 2 minutes). Serve immediately.

makes 4 servings

per serving: 355 calories, 27 g protein, 45 g carbohydrates, 8 g total fat, 74 mg cholesterol, 275 mg sodium

FREEZING COOKED MEAT MIXTURES: The fastest dinner of all is the one that's already cooked and tucked away in the freezer, just waiting for a busy day. Cooked meat mixtures such as sauces, stews, and chili are good choices for this kind of advance planning; make a double batch of spaghetti sauce or your family's favorite beef stew then freeze the leftovers. After cooking, let the meat mixture cool; then seal airtight in a tightly covered freezer container or in a plastic freezer bag. (Bags are especially convenient for reheating, since you can simply immerse them in boiling water; there's no need to get a pan dirty.)

smoked pork chops with ruote

preparation time: about 35 minutes

4 smoked pork loin chops, *each* about 1/4 inch thick, trimmed of fat

8 ounces dried ruote or other medium-size pasta

1 tablespoon butter or margarine

1 large onion, chopped

1 tablespoon all-purpose flour

1 1/2 cups nonfat milk

1 tablespoon Dijon mustard

1/4 teaspoon pepper

1 package (about 10 oz.) frozen tiny peas

1 cup shredded Emmenthaler or Swiss cheese

1 Place pork chops in a wide nonstick frying pan and cook over medium-high heat, turning as needed, until browned on both sides (about 10 minutes). Transfer to a platter and keep warm. Discard any pan drippings.

2 Bring 8 cups water to a boil in a 4- to 5-quart pan over medium-high heat. Stir in pasta and cook just until tender to bite (8 to 10 minutes); or cook according to package directions. Meanwhile, melt butter in frying pan over medium-high heat. Add onion and cook, stirring often, until soft (about 5 minutes). Stir in flour and remove from heat. Add milk, mustard, and pepper; mix until blended.

3 Stir peas into pasta and water; drain and set aside. Return sauce to medium-high heat and cook, stirring, until mixture comes to a boil. Add cheese and stir until melted. Remove from heat and add pasta mixture. Mix thoroughly but gently. Spoon alongside pork chops.

makes 4 servings

per serving: 593 calories, 43 g protein, 63 g carbohydrates, 17 g total fat, 86 mg cholesterol, 1,867 mg sodium

stir-fried beef & asparagus

preparation time: about 25 minutes

1/2 cup dry red wine

1/4 cup orange juice

2 tablespoons raspberry or red wine vinegar

1/4 cup finely chopped shallots

2 teaspoons chopped fresh tarragon or 1/2 teaspoon dried tarragon

1 pound lean boneless top sirloin steak (about 1 inch thick), trimmed of fat and cut across the grain into 1/8- by 2-inch strips

1 1/2 pounds asparagus

1 teaspoon olive oil

About 1/2 cup fresh raspberries

1 In a large bowl, stir together wine, orange juice, vinegar, shallots, and tarragon. Add steak and stir to coat. Set aside; stir occasionally.

2 Snap off and discard tough ends of asparagus; then cut spears into 3-inch lengths. Place asparagus and 1/2 cup water in a wide nonstick frying pan or wok. Cover; cook over medium-high heat, stirring occasionally, until asparagus is tender-crisp to bite (4 to 5 minutes). Drain asparagus, transfer to a platter, and keep warm. Wipe pan dry (be careful; pan is hot).

3 Heat oil in pan over medium-high heat. When oil is hot, lift meat from marinade and drain; reserve 1/4 cup of the marinade. Add meat to pan and stir-fry until done to your liking; cut to test (2 to 3 minutes for rare). Add the reserved 1/4 cup marinade and bring to a boil. Spoon meat mixture over asparagus; top with raspberries.

makes 4 servings

per serving: 213 calories, 27 g protein, 8 g carbohydrates, 6 g total fat, 69 mg cholesterol, 70 mg sodium

sautéed lamb with apples

preparation time: about 30 minutes

4 to 8 large radicchio leaves, rinsed and crisped

1 pound lean boneless leg of lamb, trimmed of fat and cut into 3/4-inch chunks

1/4 teaspoon salt

1/8 teaspoon pepper

1/3 cup apple jelly

1/3 cup cider vinegar

1 tablespoon cornstarch blended with 1 tablespoon cold water

1 teaspoon Dijon mustard

3/4 teaspoon chopped fresh thyme or 1/4 teaspoon dried thyme

1/3 cup dried currants or raisins

3 large Golden Delicious apples, peeled, cored, and sliced 1/2 inch thick

2 teaspoons vegetable oil

1 to 2 tablespoons chopped parsley

Thyme sprigs

1 Arrange 1 or 2 radicchio leaves on each of 4 individual plates; cover and set aside.

2 In a large bowl, mix lamb, salt, and pepper; set aside. In a small bowl, stir together jelly, 3 tablespoons of the vinegar, cornstarch mixture, mustard, and chopped thyme until well blended. Stir in currants and set aside. In a medium-size bowl, gently mix apples with remaining vinegar.

3 Heat 1 teaspoon of the oil in a wide nonstick frying pan or wok over medium-high heat. When oil is hot, add apples and stir-fry gently until almost tender when pierced (about 4 minutes). Add water, 1 tablespoon at a time, if pan appears dry. Stir jelly mixture well; pour into pan and cook, stirring, just until sauce boils and thickens slightly (1 to 2 minutes). Remove apple mixture from pan and keep warm. Wipe pan clean.

4 Heat remaining 1 teaspoon oil in pan over medium-high heat. When oil is hot, add meat and stir-fry just until done to your liking; cut to test (about 3 minutes for medium-rare). Remove from heat and stir in parsley.

5 Spoon meat into radicchio leaves; spoon apple, mixture alongside. Garnish with thyme sprigs.

makes 4 servings

per serving: 367 calories, 25 g protein, 52 g carbohydrates, 8 g total fat, 73 mg cholesterol, 114 mg sodium

eye of round in caper sauce

preparation time: about 15 minutes

4 beef eye of round steaks, *each* about 1/2 inch thick (1 lb. *total*), trimmed of fat

About 1 tablespoon all-purpose flour

Olive oil cooking spray

1 teaspoon margarine

1 teaspoon *each* Dijon mustard and drained capers

1 tablespoon *each* lemon juice and chopped chives

1 Place steaks between sheets of plastic wrap and pound with flat side of a meat mallet until about 1/4 inch thick. Dust with flour, shaking off excess.

2 Spray a wide nonstick frying pan with cooking spray and place over medium-high heat. Cook steaks, turning once, until browned on both sides (2 to 3 minutes total). Transfer steaks to plates and keep warm.

3 Remove pan from heat and add margarine; stir in mustard, capers, and lemon juice. Drizzle caper sauce over steaks; garnish with chives.

makes 4 servings

per serving: 170 calories, 25 g protein, 2 g carbohydrates, 6 g total fat, 61 mg cholesterol, 128 mg sodium

island pork with coconut couscous

preparation time: about 40 minutes

2 or 3 large mangoes

1 to 2 tablespoons lime juice

1 tablespoon cornstarch

3/4 cup mango or pear nectar

1 1/2 teaspoons sesame oil

1/4 teaspoon salt

1 cup fat-free reduced-sodium chicken broth

2/3 cup low-fat (2%) milk

1 cup couscous

1/4 cup sweetened shredded coconut

2 teaspoons olive oil

1 tablespoon minced fresh ginger

2 cloves garlic, minced or pressed

1 pound pork tenderloin, trimmed of fat and cut into 1-inch chunks

1 large red or green bell pepper, seeded and cut into thin strips

1/4 cup thinly sliced green onions

Lime wedges

1 Peel mangoes; cut fruit from pits into thin slices and place in a large bowl. Add lime juice (use 2 tablespoons juice if using 3 mangoes) and mix gently to coat. Arrange mangoes attractively on 4 individual plates; cover and set aside.

2 For sauce, place cornstarch in a small bowl. Gradually add nectar, stirring until cornstarch is smoothly dissolved. Stir in sesame oil and salt. Set aside.

3 In a 3- to 4-quart pan, bring broth and milk just to a boil over medium-high heat; stir in couscous. Cover, remove from heat, and let stand until liquid has been absorbed (about 5 minutes). Stir in coconut. Keep warm; fluff occasionally with a fork.

4 Heat olive oil in a wide nonstick frying pan or wok over medium-high heat. When oil is hot, add ginger and garlic; stir-fry just until fragrant (about 30 seconds; do not scorch). Add pork and stir-fry until lightly browned on outside and no longer pink in center, cut to test (about 8 minutes). Add water, 1 tablespoon at a time, if pan appears dry. Remove meat from pan with a slotted spoon; keep warm.

5 Add bell pepper and 2 tablespoons water to pan. Stir-fry until bell pepper is just tender-crisp to bite (about 2 minutes); add water, 1 tablespoon at a time, if pan appears dry.

6 Stir sauce well and pour into pan. Cook, stirring, until sauce boils and thickens slightly (1 to 2 minutes). Remove pan from heat and add meat and onions; mix gently but thoroughly.

7 Spoon couscous alongside mango slices; spoon meat mixture alongside couscous. Serve with lime wedges to squeeze over pork and couscous.

makes 4 servings

per serving: 541 calories, 33 g protein, 79 g carbohydrates, 11 g total fat, 77 mg cholesterol, 398 mg sodium

gingered pork with asian pears

preparation time: about 35 minutes

3 large firm-ripe Asian or regular pears, peeled, cored, and thinly sliced

3 tablespoons cider vinegar

1 teaspoon vegetable oil

1 pound pork tenderloin, trimmed of fat and cut into 1-inch chunks

2 tablespoons firmly packed brown sugar

$^2/_3$ cup dry white wine

$^2/_3$ cup fat-free reduced-sodium chicken broth

2 teaspoons minced fresh ginger

4 teaspoons cornstarch blended with 4 teaspoons cold water

$^1/_2$ to $^3/_4$ cup finely shredded spinach

1 In a large bowl, gently mix pears and 1 tablespoon of the vinegar. Set aside.

2 Heat oil in a wide nonstick frying pan or wok over medium-high heat. When oil is hot, add pork and stir-fry until lightly browned on outside and no longer pink in center; cut to test (about 8 minutes). Add water, 1 tablespoon at a time, if pan appears dry. Remove meat from pan with a slotted spoon; keep warm.

3 Add sugar and remaining 2 tablespoons vinegar to pan. Bring to a boil; then boil, stirring, for 1 minute. Add wine, broth, and ginger; return to a boil. Boil, stirring, for 3 minutes. Add pears and cook, gently turning pears often, until pears are heated through (about 3 minutes). Stir cornstarch mixture well and pour into pan. Cook, stirring, until sauce boils and thickens slightly (1 to 2 minutes).

4 Remove pan from heat; return meat to pan and mix gently but thoroughly. Gently stir in spinach.

makes 4 servings

per serving: 309 calories, 25 g protein, 34 g carbohydrates, 6 g total fat, 74 mg cholesterol, 177 mg sodium

japanese country-style pork & potatoes

preparation time: about 1 $^1/_2$ hours

8 green onions

1 tablespoon salad oil

1 $^1/_2$ pounds boneless pork shoulder, trimmed of fat and cut into $^1/_2$-inch cubes

1 large onion, sliced

$^1/_4$ cup reduced-sodium soy sauce

$^2/_3$ cup sake or dry vermouth

$^1/_2$ cup water

$^1/_2$ cup mirin (sweet rice wine) or cream sherry

1 $^1/_2$ pounds red thin-skinned potatoes, scrubbed and cut into $^1/_4$-inch-thick slices

$^1/_4$ teaspoon pepper

2 teaspoons sugar

1 Cut green onions into 1-inch lengths, keeping green and white parts separate; set aside.

2 Heat oil in a 5- to 6-quart pan over medium-high heat. Add half the pork; cook, stirring, until well browned (about 10 minutes). Remove from pan and set aside. Repeat to brown remaining pork; remove from pan.

3 Discard all but 1 tablespoon of the drippings from pan. Add sliced onion to pan and cook, stirring occasionally, until soft (about 5 minutes). Return pork to pan and add soy sauce, sake, water, and mirin. Bring to a boil; then reduce heat, cover, and simmer for 25 minutes. Add potatoes, white part of green onions, pepper, and sugar. Return to a boil; then reduce heat, cover, and simmer until pork and potatoes are tender when pierced (about 25 minutes). Skim and discard fat from stew, if necessary. Garnish with tops of green onions.

makes 6 servings

per serving: 385 calories, 26 g protein, 38 g carbohydrates, 72 g total fat, 76 mg cholesterol, 502 mg sodium

italian pork stew with polenta

preparation time: about 2 ¼ hours

1 ½ pounds lean boneless pork (cut from leg or shoulder), fat trimmed, cut into 1 ½-inch chunks

3 ½ cups water

³/₄ pound small mushrooms, halved

1 large onion, chopped

2 cloves garlic, minced or pressed

1 can (28 oz.) pear-shaped tomatoes

1 cup dry red wine

½ teaspoon *each* dry rosemary and dry marjoram, dry oregano, and dry thyme leaves

4 cups low-sodium chicken broth

2 cups polenta

½ cup chopped Italian parsley

Rosemary sprigs (optional)

1 Place pork and ½ cup of the water in a 5- to 6-quart pan. Cover and cook over medium-high heat for 10 minutes. Uncover and continue cooking, stirring, until juices have evaporated and meat is browned (about 5 more minutes). Add mushrooms, onion, and garlic; reduce heat to medium and cook, stirring often, until onion is soft (about 5 minutes).

2 Add tomatoes (break up with a spoon) and their liquid, wine, dry rosemary, marjoram, oregano, and thyme, stirring to loosen browned bits. Bring to a boil; reduce heat and simmer, partially covered, until pork is tender (about 1 ½ hours).

3 About 30 minutes before stew is done, bring chicken broth and remaining water to a boil in a heavy 3- to 4-quart pan over high heat. Stir in polenta in a thin stream. Cook, stirring, until polenta begins to thicken; reduce heat to low and continue cooking, stirring often, until no longer grainy (20 to 25 minutes).

4 Spoon onto a platter and top with stew; sprinkle with parsley. Garnish with rosemary sprigs, if desired.

makes 6 servings

per serving: 399 calories, 31 g protein, 49 g carbohydrates, 8 g total fat, 77 mg cholesterol, 321 mg sodium

pakistani beef kebabs

preparation time: about 25 minutes
marinating time: at least 8 hours

1 cup plain low-fat yogurt

1 small onion, finely chopped

1 clove garlic, minced or pressed

1 teaspoon grated fresh ginger
    or ¼ teaspoon ground ginger

1 small dried hot red chile, crushed

½ teaspoon cumin seeds, coarsely crushed

¼ teaspoon *each* ground nutmeg, ground cardamom, and salt

⅛ teaspoon *each* ground cinnamon, ground cloves, and coarsely ground pepper

1 ½ pounds boneless top sirloin steak, trimmed of fat

1 In a 2-quart bowl, combine yogurt, onion, garlic, ginger, chile, cumin, nutmeg, cardamom, salt, cinnamon, cloves, and pepper. Cut steak into 1-inch cubes; stir into yogurt mixture. Cover and refrigerate, stirring once or twice, for at least 8 hours or until next day.

2 Lift meat from marinade and thread onto 6 skewers (*each* about 9 inches long). Place on a lightly greased grill 4 to 6 inches above a solid bed of medium-hot coals. Cook, turning skewers as needed, until meat is browned on all sides (8 to 10 minutes total for rare to medium-rare).

makes 6 servings

per serving: 182 calories, 27 g protein, 2 g carbohydrates, 6 g total fat, 77 mg cholesterol, 116 mg sodium

pork & apple stir-fry

preparation time: about 6 ½ hours

½ cup orange juice

¼ cup minced fresh mint

2 tablespoons reduced-sodium soy sauce

1 tablespoon minced fresh ginger

1 clove garlic, minced or pressed

1 pound boned pork loin or shoulder (butt), trimmed of fat

2 medium-size red-skinned apples such as Red Gravenstein or Red Delicious, cored and chopped

2 tablespoons lemon juice

1 tablespoon vegetable oil

1 small onion, cut into thin wedges

3 cups hot cooked rice

1 or 2 medium-size oranges (peeled, if desired), sliced crosswise

Mint sprigs (optional)

1 To prepare teriyaki sauce, in a medium-size bowl, mix orange juice, minced mint, soy sauce, ginger, and garlic; set aside.

2 Slice pork across the grain into ⅛-inch-thick strips about 2 inches long. Add pork to teriyaki sauce in bowl; cover and refrigerate for at least 15 minutes or until next day. Mix apples with lemon juice; set aside.

3 Heat oil in a wok or wide frying pan over high heat. Add onion; cook, stirring, until soft (about 2 minutes). Add apples; cook, stirring, until hot (about 1 minute). Spoon mixture into a bowl and set aside.

4 With a slotted spoon, transfer pork to pan; reserve teriyaki sauce in bowl. Cook, stirring, until meat is lightly browned (about 2 minutes). Return apple mixture to pan, then add any remaining teriyaki sauce and bring to a boil, stirring.

5 Mound rice on a platter. Pour pork mixture over rice; garnish with orange slices and, if desired, mint sprigs.

makes 4 servings

per serving: 497 calories, 30 g protein, 69 g carbohydrates, 11 g total fat, 67 mg cholesterol, 365 mg sodium

QUICK-COOKING MEAT CUTS: If you're short on time, choose quick-cooking meat cuts—for example, those taken from the least-exercised parts of an animal (such as the middle of the back, called the loin). The loin portion of a steer yields porterhouse and T-bone steaks, the same portion of a lamb, pig, or calf produces lamb chops, pork chops, or veal loin chops. Less tender cuts, such as those from the round, flank, and chuck, can also be quick-cooked, but they'll need to be tenderized first. One popular tenderizing technique calls for soaking the meat in wine, vinegar, or citrus juice marinade; you can also break down the meat's muscle fibers by pounding the pieces out thin with a heavy, flat mallet.

garlic beef in pita bread with cool yogurt sauce

preparation time: about 30 minutes

Cool Yogurt Sauce (below)

4 to 6 cloves garlic, minced or pressed

3 tablespoons reduced-sodium soy sauce

1 1/2 teaspoons sugar

1/8 teaspoon crushed red pepper flakes

1 pound lean boneless top sirloin steak (about 1 inch thick), trimmed of fat and cut across the grain into 1/8 by 2-inch strips

3 green onions

1 teaspoon vegetable oil

1 teaspoon cornstarch blended with 1 teaspoon cold water

5 to 6 cups (5 to 6 oz.) mixed salad greens, rinsed and crisped

4 pita breads (each about 6 inches in diameter), cut crosswise into halves

1 Prepare Cool Yogurt Sauce and set aside.

2 In a large bowl, stir together garlic, soy sauce, sugar, and red pepper flakes. Add steak and stir to coat. Set aside; stir occasionally. Trim and discard ends of onions; then cut onions into 1-inch lengths and sliver each piece lengthwise. Set aside.

3 Heat oil in a wide nonstick frying pan or wok over medium-high heat. When oil is hot, lift meat from marinade and drain briefly (reserve marinade). Add meat to pan and stir-fry until done to your liking; cut to test (2 to 3 minutes for rare). With a slotted spoon, transfer meat to a bowl; keep warm.

4 Stir cornstarch mixture well; pour into pan along with reserved marinade and any meat juices that have accumulated in bowl. Cook, stirring, until sauce boils and thickens slightly (1 to 2 minutes). Remove pan from heat and stir in meat and onions.

5 To serve, divide salad greens equally among pita bread halves; then spoon in meat mixture. Drizzle Cool Yogurt Sauce over meat.

makes 4 servings

per serving: 386 calories, 34 g protein, 44 g carbohydrates, 7 g total fat, 70 mg cholesterol, 886 mg sodium

cool yogurt sauce

preparation time: about 5 minutes

1 cup plain nonfat yogurt

1 tablespoon chopped fresh mint

1 tablespoon chopped fresh cilantro

Salt

Fresh mint and cilantro leaves (optional)

In a small bowl, stir together yogurt, chopped mint, and chopped cilantro. Season to taste with salt. (At this point, you may cover and refrigerate for up to 4 hours; stir before serving.) Sprinkle with mint and cilantro leaves just before serving, if desired.

makes about 1 cup

per tablespoon: 8 calories, 0.8 g protein, 1 g carbohydrates, 0.02 g total fat, 0.3 mg cholesterol, 11 mg sodium

oregon spring stew with vegetables

preparation time: about 2 ½ hours

1 tablespoon salad oil

1 pound *each* lean boneless lamb shoulder
   and beef bottom round, fat trimmed,
   cut into 1-inch chunks

1 pound medium-size carrots, sliced

1 large onion, chopped

1 large turnip (about 10 oz.), peeled and diced

½ cup pearl barley, rinsed and drained

5 cups low-sodium beef broth

2 cups water

½ teaspoon pepper

½ pound green beans, ends trimmed,
   cut into 1-inch pieces

1 pound fresh peas, shelled,
   or 1 ½ cups frozen tiny peas

1 Heat oil in a 5- to 6-quart ovenproof pan over high heat. Add lamb and beef and cook, stirring, until browned (about 5 minutes); lift out and set aside. Reduce heat to medium-high. Add carrots, onion, and turnip and cook, stirring often, until onion is limp (about 10 minutes). Pour off fat.

2 Return meats to pan with barley, beef broth, water, and pepper. Bring to a boil over high heat. Cover and bake in a 325° oven until meat is very tender when pierced (about 1½ hours). At this point, you may cool, cover, and refrigerate for up to 2 days; lift off any fat and discard. Reheat to simmering before continuing.

3 Stir in beans and peas; continue baking until beans are tender (about 10 minutes).

makes 8 servings

per serving: 298 calories, 28 g protein, 24 g carbohydrates, 70 g total fat, 71 mg cholesterol, 720 mg sodium

mom's magic meat loaf

preparation time: about 1 ½ hours

1 cup fine dry bread crumbs

½ cup grated Parmesan cheese

1 tablespoon dry basil

½ teaspoon pepper

4 egg whites

2 cloves garlic, minced or pressed

2 cans (8 oz. *each*) no-salt-added tomato sauce

2 pounds ground lean top round

3 pounds thin-skinned potatoes
   (*each* about 3 inches in diameter)

1 large can (12 oz.) evaporated skim milk

Salt and pepper

1 In a large bowl, combine bread crumbs, cheese, basil, pepper, egg whites, garlic, and 1 cup of the tomato sauce. Add beef and mix lightly. In a rimmed shallow baking pan (about 10 inches in diameter), shape mixture into a 2-inch-thick heart. Bake in a 400° oven for 45 minutes. Remove from oven; carefully drain fat from pan, then top loaf with remaining tomato sauce. Bake for 15 more minutes.

2 While meat loaf is baking, place potatoes in a 3- to 4-quart pan and add water to cover. Bring to a boil over high heat; then reduce heat, cover, and boil gently until potatoes are tender when pierced (about 20 minutes). Drain and peel. Mash with a potato masher or electric mixer until smooth; slowly beat in milk. Season to taste with salt and pepper. Transfer meat loaf to serving plate. With a pastry bag fitted with a large star tip, pipe potatoes around meat loaf. (Or simply spoon potatoes around loaf.)

makes 8 servings

per serving: 487 calories, 34 g protein, 50 g carbohydrates, 16 g total fat, 77 mg cholesterol, 661 mg sodium

marsala beef & couscous

cooking time: about 20 minutes

1 pound lean boneless top sirloin steak (about 1 in. thick), trimmed of fat and cut across grain into 1/8-by 2-inch strips

1/4 cup marsala

3 green onions

2 1/2 cups canned beef broth

1/8 teaspoon saffron threads, or to taste

1 can (about 14 oz.) artichoke hearts in water, drained

1 cup pitted bite-size dried prunes

1 cup dried apricots

1 package (about 10 oz.) dried couscous

1 tablespoon olive oil

2 teaspoons cornstarch blended with 1 tablespoon cold water

Salt and pepper

1 In a large bowl, combine steak and marsala; set aside. Cut onions into 1-inch lengths and sliver lengthwise; set aside.

2 In a 4- to 5-quart pan, bring broth, saffron, artichokes, prunes, and apricots to a boil over high beat. Stir in couscous. Cover pan, remove from heat, and let stand until liquid has been absorbed (about 5 minutes).

3 While couscous stands, heat oil in a wide nonstick frying pan over medium-high heat. When oil is hot, lift meat from marinade and drain briefly (reserve marinade). Add meat to pan and cook, stirring, until done to your liking, cut to test (2 to 3 minutes for rare). With a slotted spoon, transfer near to a bowl; keep warm.

4 Stir cornstarch mixture well; pour into pan along with reserved marinade and any meat juices in bowl. Cook, stirring, until sauce boils and thickens slightly (about 1 minute). Remove pan from heat and stir in meat and onions. Transfer couscous to a platter, fluffing with a fork; top with meat mixture. Add salt and pepper to taste.

makes 6 servings

per serving: 456 calories, 25 g protein, 72 g carbohydrates, 6 g total fat, 46 mg cholesterol, 737 mg sodium

blackened steak with beans & greens

preparation time: about 25 minutes

3/4 pound top sirloin steak (about 1 in. thick), fat trimmed

1 tablespoon Cajun or blackening spice blend

1/2 cup salsa

1/2 cup nonfat sour cream

2 tablespoons lime juice

3/4 pound prewashed spinach leaves

1 can (about 15 oz.) black beans, rinsed and drained

1 jar (about 7.25 oz.) peeled roasted red peppers, drained and cut into thin strips

1 Pat steak with spice blend to coat both sides evenly. Heat a wide frying pan over medium-high heat. When pan is very hot, add steak. Cook, turning occasionally, until meat is well browned on the outside and done to your liking (cut to test; about 14 minutes for medium-rare.)

2 Meanwhile, in a blender or food processor, whirl salsa, sour cream, and lime juice until smooth. Arrange spinach, beans, and peppers decoratively on a large platter.

3 When meat is done, cut it into thin bite-size slices; add to platter. At the table, toss with salsa mixture. Add pepper to taste.

makes 4 servings

per serving: 247 calories, 27 g protein, 22 g carbohydrates, 5 g total fat, 52 mg cholesterol, 1,370 mg sodium

chile beef burritos

preparation time: about 30 minutes

1 fresh jalapeño or other small fresh hot chile, seeded and minced

2 cloves garlic, minced or pressed

1/4 to 1/2 teaspoon ground red pepper (cayenne)

1 tablespoon reduced-sodium soy sauce

1/2 teaspoon sugar

1 pound lean boneless top sirloin steak (about 1 inch thick), trimmed of fat and cut across the grain into 1/8- by 2-inch strips

4 to 8 low-fat flour tortillas (*each* 7 to 9 inches in diameter)

1 large onion, thinly sliced

1 teaspoon olive oil

1 In a large bowl, stir together chile, garlic, red pepper, soy sauce, and sugar. Add steak and stir to coat. Set aside.

2 Brush tortillas lightly with hot water; then stack, wrap in foil, and heat in a 350° oven until warm (10 to 12 minutes).

3 Meanwhile, in a wide nonstick frying pan or wok, combine onion and 1/4 cup water. Stir-fry over medium-high heat until onion is soft and liquid has evaporated (4 to 5 minutes). Add oil; then stir in meat and its marinade. Stir-fry until meat is done to your liking; cut to test (2 to 3 minutes for rare).

4 To serve, spoon meat mixture into tortillas. Offer a choice of condiments to add to taste.

makes 4 servings

per serving: 293 calories, 28 g protein, 34 g carbohydrates, 7 g total fat, 69 mg cholesterol, 488 mg sodium

grilled top sirloin with wine-shallot sauce

preparation time: about 30 minutes

1 to 1 1/2 pounds boneless top sirloin steak (1 1/2 to 2 inches thick), trimmed of fat

2 or 3 small red onions, unpeeled, cut in half lengthwise

1 tablespoon margarine

1/2 cup chopped shallots

3/4 cup dry red wine

1 tablespoon Dijon mustard

1 teaspoon Worcestershire

1/2 teaspoon *each* coarsely ground pepper and dry tarragon leaves

Salt

1 Place steak on a lightly greased grill 4 to 6 inches above a solid bed of medium coals. Place onions, cut sides down, on grill. Cook, turning both steak and onions after about 10 minutes, until a thermometer inserted in thickest part of steak registers 135° to 140° for rare and onions are soft when pressed (18 to 20 minutes total).

2 Meanwhile, melt margarine in a small, metal-handled frying pan on grill; add shallots and cook, stirring occasionally, until tinged with brown (6 to 8 minutes). Add wine, mustard, Worcestershire, pepper, and tarragon. Cook, stirring often, until sauce is reduced to about 1/2 cup (about 10 minutes); then move to a cooler part of grill.

3 Transfer steak and onions to a platter. Slice steak thinly across grain at a slant. If desired, stir accumulated meat juices into sauce. Season sauce to taste with salt and spoon over steak and onions.

makes 4 to 6 servings

per serving: 231 calories, 27 g protein, 9 g carbohydrates, 9 g total fat, 76 mg cholesterol, 189 mg sodium

chayote with spiced lamb filling

preparation time: about 1¼ hours

3 chayotes (about ¾ lb. *each*)

1 pound lean lamb sirloin, freshly ground

1 medium-size onion, minced

4 cloves garlic, minced or pressed

½ teaspoon *each* ground allspice and coarsely ground pepper

⅛ teaspoon ground cloves

⅓ cup raisins

1 can (6 oz.) tomato paste

2 tablespoons dry red wine

Similar in taste to zucchini, chayote is a tropical summer squash sometimes called mirliton. For an unusual entrée, serve it stuffed with a lightly spiced lamb filling.

1 In a 4- to 5-quart pan, bring 2 quarts water to a boil over high heat. Add chayotes; reduce heat, cover, and simmer until tender when pierced (about 40 minutes). Drain and let cool; halve lengthwise and discard pit. Scoop out and reserve pulp, leaving ½-inch-thick shells. Invert shells on paper towels to drain. Chop pulp.

2 Meanwhile, crumble lamb into a wide frying pan; add onion, garlic, allspice, pepper, and cloves. Cook over medium-high heat, stirring occasionally, until lamb is well browned (about 15 minutes). Stir in chayote pulp, raisins, tomato paste, and wine.

3 Spoon lamb mixture into shells. Place in a 9- by 13-inch baking pan. Cover and bake in a 350° oven for 20 minutes; uncover and continue baking until hot (about 5 more minutes).

makes 6 servings

per serving: 199 calories, 19 g protein, 23 g carbohydrates, 5 g total fat, 50 mg cholesterol, 281 mg sodium

grilled beef with soy seasoned sake

preparation time: about 40 minutes

1½ pounds boneless beef top round (about 2 inches thick), trimmed of fat

1 tablespoon Asian sesame oil or salad oil

2 cloves garlic, minced or pressed

2 tablespoons grated fresh ginger

½ cup thinly sliced green onions (including tops)

⅔ cup sake or dry sherry

3 tablespoons soy sauce

12 green onions, ends trimmed

Salt and pepper

1 Place beef on a lightly greased grill 4 to 6 inches above a solid bed of medium hot coals. Cook, turning once, until beef is browned and a meat thermometer inserted in thickest part registers 135° to 140° for rare to medium-rare (20 to 25 minutes total).

2 Meanwhile, in a metal-handled 6- to 8-inch frying pan, combine oil, garlic, ginger, and sliced green onions; place on grill over coals. Cook, stirring often, until onions are limp (5 to 8 minutes). Add sake and soy sauce. Continue cooking, stirring once or twice, until mixture boils; then move to a cooler part of the grill.

3 When beef is almost done, lay whole green onions on grill and cook, turning once, until lightly browned (2 to 4 minutes total). Transfer beef and whole onions to a serving board; slice beef thinly across grain. Top with warm green onion sauce. Season to taste with salt and pepper.

makes 6 servings

per serving: 232 calories, 28 g protein, 7 g carbohydrates, 7 g total fat, 72 mg cholesterol, 571 mg sodium

stir-fried veal piccata

preparation time: about 25 minutes

1/2 cup dry white wine

2 tablespoons lemon juice

1 1/2 teaspoons honey

1 pound veal scaloppine, cut into
   1/4- by 2-inch strips

1/2 teaspoon paprika

1/4 teaspoon grated lemon peel

1/8 teaspoon salt

1 teaspoon butter or margarine

1 teaspoon olive oil

1/2 teaspoon cornstarch blended with
   1 teaspoon cold water

2 tablespoons drained capers, or to taste

Chopped parsley and lemon wedges

Pepper

1 For the sauce, in a small bowl, stir together wine, lemon juice, and honey; set aside.

2 In a large bowl, combine veal, paprika, lemon peel, and salt. Melt butter in oil in a wide nonstick frying pan or wok over medium-high heat. When butter mixture is hot, add meat mixture; stir-fry just until meat is no longer pink on outside (1 to 2 minutes). With a slotted spoon, transfer meat to a rimmed platter; keep warm.

3 Stir reserved sauce well; pour into pan. Bring to a boil; then boil, stirring constantly, for 3 minutes. Stir cornstarch mixture well; add to pan along with capers. Cook, stirring, until sauce boils and thickens slightly (about 1 minute). Spoon sauce over meat; garnish with parsley and lemon wedges. Season to taste, with pepper.

makes 4 servings

per serving: 172 calories, 24 g protein, 3 g carbohydrates, 4 g total fat, 91 mg cholesterol, 265 mg sodium

roast pork with date and fig sauce

preparation time: about 2 hours

1 boneless pork loin roast (3 to 4 lbs.),
   trimmed of fat

1 clove garlic, peeled and halved

1/2 teaspoon dry summer savory

1 teaspoon pepper

1 cup finely chopped unpeeled tart apple

1/4 cup water

1/2 cup dry white wine

1/2 cup firmly packed brown sugar

1 cup pitted dates, cut into pieces

6 dried figs, coarsely chopped

1 Rub pork all over with garlic; discard garlic. Place pork in a 9- by 13-inch baking pan and sprinkle evenly with savory and pepper. Roast in a 375° oven until a meat thermometer inserted in thickest part registers 155° (about 1 1/2 hours). Transfer pork to a platter; keep warm.

2 While pork is roasting, combine apple and water in a 2- to 3-quart pan. Cover and cook over medium heat, stirring occasionally, until apple is tender to bite (about 5 minutes). Remove from heat; set aside.

3 Skim and discard fat from juices in roasting pan; add wine to pan. Place pan over medium heat and stir to scrape browned bits free. Add apple mixture, sugar, dates, and figs; cook, stirring, until mixture is hot and sugar is dissolved (about 3 minutes). Pour into a small bowl.

4 To serve, thinly slice pork across the grain. Accompany with fruit sauce to spoon over meat to taste.

makes 8 to 10 servings

per serving: 402 calories, 39 g protein, 37 g carbohydrates, 10 g total fat, 104 mg cholesterol, 99 mg sodium

veal with mushrooms

preparation time: about 35 minutes

1 pound veal scaloppine,
   cut into 1/4- by 2-inch strips

1/8 teaspoon salt

1/8 teaspoon pepper

8 ounces dried linguine

1 tablespoon butter or margarine

2 cloves garlic, minced or pressed

2 cups sliced mushrooms

1/2 cup marsala or cream sherry

3 tablespoons chopped parsley

1 large tomato, chopped and drained well

1/4 cup pitted ripe olives, chopped

1 In a large bowl, mix veal, salt, and pepper; set aside.

2 In a 4- to 5-quart pan, cook linguine in about 8 cups boiling water until just tender to bite (8 to 10 minutes); or cook according to package directions. Drain well, transfer to a warm rimmed platter, and keep warm.

3 While pasta is cooking, melt butter in a wide nonstick frying pan or wok over medium-high heat. Add meat and garlic; stir-fry just until meat is no longer pink on outside (1 to 2 minutes). Add water, 1 tablespoon at a time, if pan appears dry. Remove meat from pan with a slotted spoon; keep warm.

4 Add mushrooms and 3 tablespoons water to pan. Stir-fry until mushrooms are soft (about 3 minutes), gently scraping any browned bits free from pan. Add marsala and bring to a boil; then boil, stirring, until sauce is slightly thickened (about 3 minutes). Remove pan frown heat and stir in meat and parsley.

5 To serve, spoon meat mixture over pasta; sprinkle with chopped tomato and olives.

makes 4 servings

per serving: 440 calories, 33 g protein, 52 g carbohydrates, 7 g total fat, 96 mg cholesterol, 191 mg sodium

crusted lamb & potatoes

preparation time: about 1 3/4 hours

3 pounds russet potatoes, peeled and cut into
   3/4-inch-thick slices

1 1/2 cups low-sodium chicken broth

Upper thigh half (3 to 3 1/2 lbs.) of 1 leg of lamb,
   trimmed of fat

Seasoning Paste (recipe follows)

Salt and pepper

1 Arrange potatoes over bottom of a 12- by 15-inch roasting pan; pour broth into pan, then set lamb on potatoes. Roast in a 400° oven for 45 minutes. Meanwhile, prepare Seasoning Paste.

2 Spread paste evenly over lamb and potatoes. Continue to roast until crust on meat is well browned and a meat thermometer inserted in thickest part of lamb at bone registers 140° to 145° for medium-rare (about 25 more minutes). Transfer lamb and potatoes to a platter; pour any pan juices over all.

3 To serve, slice lamb across the grain; season lamb and potatoes to taste with salt and pepper.

SEASONING PASTE

In a small bowl, mash together 3 cloves garlic, minced or pressed; 1 small onion, minced; 3 tablespoons minced parsley; 1 cup seasoned stuffing mix; 3 tablespoons butter or margarine, at room temperature; 1 tablespoon grated lemon peel; and 2 tablespoons lemon juice.

makes 6 servings

per serving: 482 calories, 39 g protein, 49 g carbohydrates, 74 g total fat, 16 mg cholesterol, 357 mg sodium

barbequed sirloin with scorched corn & chile salsa

preparation time: about 35 minutes
marinating time: at least 2 hours

Cumin-Cinnamon Marinade (recipe follows)

1 pound boneless sirloin steak
(about ³/₄ inch thick), trimmed of fat

1 small tomato, seeded and finely chopped

1 medium-size fresh Anaheim (California)
green chile, seeded and finely chopped

2 cloves garlic, minced or pressed

2 tablespoons lime juice

1 tablespoon ground New Mexico
or California chiles

2 medium-size ears corn

Salt

Lime slices

1 Prepare Cumin-Cinnamon Marinade; add steak. Cover and refrigerate for at least 2 hours or until next day. Shortly before cooking steak, combine tomato, chopped chile, garlic, lime juice, and ground chiles; set aside.

2 Remove and discard husks and silk from corn. Lift steak from bowl, reserving marinade. Place steak and corn on a lightly greased grill 4 to 6 inches above a solid bed of medium-hot coals. Cook, drizzling steak several times with marinade and turning once, and turning corn as needed, until both are browned (8 to 10 minutes total for rare to medium-rare steak, about 8 minutes total for corn).

3 Place steak on a carving board and keep warm. Cut corn from cobs and stir into tomato mixture; season to taste with salt. Slice or quarter steak and garnish with lime slices; serve with salsa.

CUMIN-CINNAMON MARINADE

In a shallow glass bowl, combine ½ cup dry red wine; 1 tablespoon olive oil; 2 tablespoons finely chopped onion; 2 cloves garlic, minced or pressed; ¼ teaspoon salt; ½ teaspoon *each* ground cumin and ground cinnamon; and 1 ½ teaspoons cumin seeds.

makes 4 servings

per serving: 222 calories, 26 g protein, 13 g carbohydrates, 8 g total fat, 69 mg cholesterol, 148 mg sodium

sweet & sour flank steak

preparation time: about 25 minutes
marinating time: at least 4 hours

¹/₃ cup cider vinegar

¹/₄ cup *each* honey and reduced-sodium soy sauce

1 clove garlic, minced or pressed

¹/₈ teaspoon liquid hot pepper seasoning

1 ¹/₂ pounds flank steak, fat trimmed

Parsley sprigs (optional)

1 In a small pan, cook vinegar, honey, soy sauce, garlic, and hot pepper seasoning over medium heat, stirring often, until honey is dissolved and mixture is well blended (about 5 minutes). Let cool briefly.

2 Place steak in a shallow nonmetal bowl just large enough to hold it; pour in marinade. Cover and refrigerate for at least 4 hours or until next day, turning once or twice.

3 Lift out steak and drain, reserving marinade. Place on a lightly greased grill 4 to 6 inches above a solid bed of medium-hot coals. Cook, turning once and basting often with marinade, until done to your liking; cut to test (8 to 10 minutes total for rare).

4 Meanwhile, bring any remaining marinade to a boil in a small pan over high heat. Slice steak thinly across grain. Garnish with parsley, if desired, and offer with marinade.

makes 6 servings

per serving: 254 calories, 22 g protein, 14 g carbohydrates, 12 g total fat, 58 mg cholesterol, 473 mg sodium

garlic pork chops with balsamic vinegar

preparation time: 35 to 40 minutes

1 small head garlic, separated into cloves

6 center-cut loin pork chops (about 2 lbs. *total*), trimmed of fat

Pepper

Vegetable oil cooking spray

12 ounces dry medium-wide eggless noodles

1/4 cup sweet vermouth

1 tablespoon Dijon mustard

1/3 cup balsamic vinegar

Salt

Chopped parsley

1 In a medium-size pan, bring about 4 cups water to a boil. Add unpeeled garlic cloves and boil for 1 minute; drain. Let garlic cool slightly, then peel cloves and set aside.

2 Sprinkle pork chops generously with pepper. Coat a wide frying pan with cooking spray and place over medium-high heat. Add chops and cook until well browned on bottom (4 to 5 minutes); turn chops over, arrange garlic cloves around them, and continue to cook until chops are browned on other side (4 to 5 more minutes).

3 Meanwhile, in a 5- to 6-quart pan, cook noodles in about 3 quarts boiling water until just tender to bite (7 to 9 minutes); or cook according to package directions. Drain well, pour onto a deep platter, and keep warm.

4 While noodles are cooking, mix vermouth and mustard; pour over browned chops. Reduce heat to low, cover, and cook until chops are done but still moist and slightly pink in center; cut to test (about 5 minutes). Arrange chops over noodles and keep warm.

5 Add vinegar to sauce in pan. Increase heat to medium-high and stir to scrape browned bits free. Bring to a boil; then boil, uncovered, until sauce is reduced to about 1/2 cup (2 to 3 minutes). Season to taste with salt. Spoon sauce over chops; sprinkle chops and noodles with parsley.

makes 6 servings

per serving: 366 calories, 30 g protein, 44 g carbohydrates, 7 g total fat, 62 mg cholesterol, 155 mg sodium

PLAN AHEAD FOR LEFTOVERS: When time permits, cook a larger cut of meat—one that will yield more than enough for one meal. Roast beef, lamb, or veal can be sliced and quickly reheated; or use the meat in hot or cold sandwiches, stir-fries, or other dishes.

lentil cassoulet

preparation time: about 3 hours
marinating time: at least 6 hours

3 to 4 pounds country-style pork ribs,
   trimmed of fat

2 tablespoons *each* **salt and sugar**

1 teaspoon pepper

1 pound turkey kielbasa

About 10 cups low-sodium chicken broth

2 large onions, chopped

3 cloves garlic, minced or pressed

2 teaspoons *each* **dry thyme and coriander seeds**

1 dry bay leaf

2 pounds lentils, rinsed and drained

3 large carrots, coarsely chopped

1 cup coarse soft bread crumbs

2 teaspoons olive oil

2 tablespoons chopped parsley

1 Cut pork ribs apart between bones. Mix salt, sugar, and pepper; rub all over pork. Place pork in a large heavy-duty plastic bag; seal bag and refrigerate for at least 6 hours or up to 1 day, turning occasionally. Rinse pork well and pat dry. Place pork and whole sausage in a single layer in a 10- by 15-inch rimmed baking pan; bake in a 450° oven until browned (about 30 minutes). Discard fat from pan; set ribs and sausage aside.

2 In a 6- to 8-quart pan, combine 1 cup of the broth, onions, garlic, thyme, coriander seeds, and bay leaf. Cook over high heat, stirring often, until liquid evaporates and onions begin to brown (about 10 minutes). To deglaze, add ⅓ cup more broth and stir to scrape browned bits free. Then continue to cook, stirring occasionally, until mixture begins to brown again. Repeat deglazing and browning steps 1 or 2 more times, using ⅓ cup broth each time; onions should be well browned.

3 Add lentils, pork ribs, 8 cups of the broth, and carrots to pan. Bring to a boil; then reduce heat, cover, and simmer until lentils are tender to bite (30 to 40 minutes). Meanwhile, cut sausage into ¼-inch-thick slanting slices.

4 With a slotted spoon, lift pork ribs from lentil mixture and set aside; then pour lentil mixture into a shallow 5- to 6-quart casserole (about 12 by 16 inches). Nestle sausage slices and ribs into lentils. Cover casserole tightly. (At this point, you may let cool, then refrigerate for up to 1 day.)

5 Bake, covered, in a 350° oven until hot in center (about 35 minutes; about 1 ½ hours if refrigerated). Mix bread crumbs and oil; uncover casserole and sprinkle with crumbs. Continue to bake, uncovered, until crumbs are golden (20 to 25 more minutes). Sprinkle with parsley.

makes 8 to 10 servings

per serving: 627 calories, 55 g protein, 72 g carbohydrates, 14 g total fat, 83 mg cholesterol, 848 mg sodium

lemon-broiled flank steak with onions

preparation time: about 1 ½ hours
marinating time: at least 2 hours

1 to 1 ¼ pounds flank steak, trimmed of fat

1 large onion, thinly sliced

⅓ cup lemon juice

**1 teaspoon Italian herb seasoning
or ¼ teaspoon *each* dry basil, oregano,
thyme, and marjoram leaves**

1 teaspoon grated lemon peel

1 large clove garlic, minced or pressed

¼ teaspoon coarsely ground pepper

2 teaspoons sugar

2 tablespoons soy sauce

1 tablespoon olive oil

Lemon wedges (optional)

Chopped parsley (optional)

1 Score steak on both sides about ⅛ inch deep in a 1-inch diamond pattern. In a shallow baking dish, spread half the onion; top with steak and add remaining onion. In a small bowl, stir together lemon juice, herb seasoning, lemon peel, garlic, pepper, sugar, and soy sauce. Pour over steak and onion. Cover and refrigerate for at least 2 hours or up to 8 hours.

2 Lift steak from dish, reserving marinade and onion. Place steak on a lightly greased rack in a broiler pan. Broil 3 to 4 inches below heat, turning once until browned; cut to test (8 to 10 minutes total for rare to medium).

3 Meanwhile, heat oil in a medium-size frying pan over medium-high heat. Add marinade and onion and bring to a boil. Cook, stirring often, until onion is soft and lightly browned and most of the liquid has evaporated (6 to 8 minutes). Slice steak thinly across grain at a slant. Spoon onions over top. Garnish with lemon wedges and parsley, if desired.

makes about 4 servings

per serving: 211 calories, 22 g protein, 6 g carbohydrates, 11 g total fat, 52 mg cholesterol, 483 mg sodium

grilled orange-coriander steak

preparation time: about 20 minutes
marinating time: at least 4 hours

1 teaspoon grated orange peel

¼ cup orange juice

1 medium-size onion, minced

3 cloves garlic, minced or pressed

¼ cup white wine vinegar

1 ½ tablespoons ground coriander

1 teaspoon each cracked pepper and dry basil

**1 ½ pounds boneless beef top round
(cut about 1 inch thick), trimmed of fat**

Finely shredded orange peel

1 In a bowl, stir together grated orange peel, orange juice, onion, garlic, vinegar, coriander, pepper, and basil. Measure out ½ cup of this marinade; cover and refrigerate until serving time.

2 Pour remaining marinade into a shallow bowl; add beef and turn to coat. Cover and refrigerate for at least 4 hours or up to 1 day, turning beef over occasionally.

3 Lift beef from marinade and drain briefly; reserve marinade. Place beef on a lightly oiled grill 4 to 6 inches above a solid bed of medium coals. Cook, turning once and basting often with marinade, until done to your liking; cut to test (about 8 minutes for rare). Meanwhile, pour reserved ½ cup marinade into a small pan. Place over low heat; heat until steaming.

4 To serve, thinly slice beef across the grain. Garnish with shredded orange peel; accompany with heated marinade.

makes 6 servings

per serving: 775 calories, 28 g protein, 5 g carbohydrates, 4 g total fat, 71 mg cholesterol, 54 mg sodium

oven-braised beef in red wine

preparation time: 3 to 3 ½ hours

Vegetable oil cooking spray

1 boneless beef round tip roast (about 3 lbs.), trimmed of fat

Coarsely ground pepper

1 large onion, chopped

2 cloves garlic, minced or pressed

1 medium-size carrot, coarsely shredded

1 stalk celery, chopped

6 whole cloves

1 ½ cups dry red wine

1 tablespoon tomato paste

½ teaspoon *each* salt and dry thyme leaves

¼ cup rum (optional)

Italian parsley sprigs

1 Coat a wide nonstick frying pan with cooking spray. Add roast and brown on all sides over medium-high heat. Transfer to a 3- to 4-quart ovenproof pan or deep casserole; season to taste with pepper. Set aside. In frying pan, combine onion, garlic, carrot, celery, cloves, wine, tomato paste, salt, and thyme; bring to a boil. Pour mixture over meat and cover. Bake in a 350° oven until meat is very tender, turning once or twice (2½ to 3 hours).

2 Lift out roast and place on a warm, deep platter; cover lightly to keep warm. Skim and discard fat, if necessary, from cooking liquid; then pour into a blender or food processor. Whirl until puréed. Pour into a 2-quart pan, add rum, if desired, and bring to a boil over high heat. Add water, if needed, to make about 1¾ cups. Slice roast thinly and serve with sauce; garnish with parsley.

makes 10 to 12 servings

per serving: 168 calories, 27 g protein, 3 g carbohydrates, 5 g total fat, 74 mg cholesterol, 196 mg sodium

smoked pork chops with polenta

preparation time: about 35 minutes

3 ½ cups low-sodium chicken broth

1 cup instant polenta

1 small can (about 8 oz.) cream-style corn

4 smoked pork chops (about 1 ¼ lbs. *total*)

2 tablespoons each grated Parmesan cheese and chopped parsley

1 In a small pan, bring broth to a boil over high heat; then pour broth into a shallow 2½- to 3-quart baking dish. Gradually add polenta, stirring constantly. Stir in corn. Arrange pork chops on top of polenta mixture.

2 Bake in a 350° oven until pork chops are heated through; cut to test (25 to 30 minutes). Sprinkle chops with cheese and parsley.

makes 4 servings

Per serving: 346 calories, 28 g protein, 40 g carbohydrates, 8 g total fat, 52 mg cholesterol, 1,781 mg sodium

cuban style mini roast with black beans & rice

preparation time: about 1 1/4 hours
marinating time: at least 4 hours

1 1/2 to 1 3/4 pounds boneless fresh leg of pork, trimmed of fat

2 cloves garlic, minced or pressed

1/2 teaspoon dry oregano

1/4 teaspoon each cumin seeds (coarsely crushed) and crushed red pepper flakes

1/4 cup lime juice

Cuban Black Beans (recipe follows)

3 cups hot cooked long-grain white rice

1/4 cup thinly sliced green onions

Lime wedges

1 Roll pork compactly; then tie securely with cotton string at 1½-inch intervals. Set a large heavy-duty plastic bag in a shallow pan. In bag, combine garlic, oregano, cumin seeds, red pepper flakes, and lime juice; add pork. Seal bag and turn to coat pork with marinade; then refrigerate for at least 4 hours or up to 1 day, turning occasionally.

2 Lift pork from bag and drain briefly; reserve marinade. Place pork on a rack in a roasting pan and roast in a 350° oven, drizzling once or twice with marinade, until a meat thermometer inserted in thickest part registers 155° (35 to 55 minutes). After 25 minutes, check temperature every 5 to 10 minutes. Meanwhile, prepare Cuban Black Beans.

3 When pork is done, let it stand for about 5 minutes. Then thinly slice pork across the grain and transfer to a platter. Spoon rice alongside pork. Garnish pork and rice with green onions and lime wedges; serve with Cuban Black Beans.

CUBAN BLACK BEANS

Heat 2 teaspoons olive oil in a wide nonstick frying pan over medium heat. Add 1 medium-size onion, thinly sliced, and ½ cup finely chopped green bell pepper; cook, stirring often, until onion is soft but not browned (about 5 minutes). Stir in 1 clove garlic, minced or pressed, ½ teaspoon ground cumin, and 1 can (about 15 oz.) black beans and their liquid. Cook, stirring, until heated through (about 3 minutes). Just before serving, stir in 2 teaspoons cider vinegar.

makes 6 servings

per serving: 435 calories, 34 g protein, 43 g carbohydrates, 12 g total fat, 87 mg cholesterol, 338 mg sodium

FAT LOWERING STRATEGIES FOR HIGHER-FAT MEAT: When you're confronted with a cut of meat other than low-fat cuts for which recipes are given, here are some ways you can prepare the meat in order to reduce unwanted fat.

- **Trim surface fat scrupulously.**
- **Cook the meat in a way that renders the intramuscular fat. For example, you can pour off and discard the drippings that remain after browning meats for stew or pot roast or ground meat dishes.**
- **Skim and discard fat from the roasted meat drippings before adding liquid to roasting pan to make gravy or sauce.**
- **Make stews and soups ahead so that you can refrigerate them until thoroughly chilled. The fat that rises to the surface and hardens is then easier to lift off and discard, leaving a leaner dish to reheat.**

gingered butterflied lamb with yams

preparation time: about 1 1/2 hours
marinating time: at least 4 hours

1/3 **cup chopped fresh ginger**

8 **cloves garlic, peeled**

1/4 **teaspoon pepper**

1 1/2 **tablespoons reduced-sodium soy sauce**

3/4 **cup red wine vinegar**

2 to 2 1/2 **pounds boneless butterflied leg of lamb, trimmed of fat**

2 **teaspoons sugar**

1/4 **cup raisins**

Vegetable oil cooking spray

8 to 10 **small yams or sweet potatoes (3 1/2 to 4 lbs., *total*), scrubbed**

8 to 10 **small onions (*each* about 2 inches in diameter), unpeeled, cut lengthwise into halves**

1 **cup beef broth**

1 In a blender or food processor, combine ginger, garlic, pepper, soy sauce, and 2 tablespoons of the vinegar. Whirl until mixture forms a paste; set aside.

2 Lay lamb flat in 9- by 13-inch baking dish; spoon ginger mixture around lamb. Mix sugar, raisins, and remaining 10 tablespoons vinegar; pour over lamb. Cover and refrigerate for at least 4 hours or up to 1 day.

3 Coat a 12- by 17-inch or larger roasting pan with cooking spray. Cut unpeeled yams lengthwise into 3/4-inch-thick wedges. Arrange yams and onion halves (cut side down) in pan. Coat all vegetables with cooking spray. Roast on lower rack of a 425° oven for 15 minutes. Meanwhile, lift lamb from marinade and drain briefly; reserve marinade. Place lamb, boned side down, on a rack in a shallow baking pan.

4 After vegetables have roasted for 15 minutes, place lamb in oven on middle rack. Continue to roast both lamb and vegetables, basting lamb occasionally with marinade, for 30 minutes. Lift raisins from marinade and sprinkle over lamb. Drizzle vegetables with all but 3 tablespoons of the remaining marinade. Continue to roast until vegetables are tender when pierced and a meat thermometer inserted in thickest part of lamb registers 140° to 145° for medium-rare (10 to 15 more minutes).

5 Transfer lamb, onions, and yams to a platter; keep warm. To lamb cooking pan, add broth and reserved 3 tablespoons marinade; cook over medium heat, stirring to scrape browned bits free, until sauce is reduced to about 3/4 cup. Pour into a small bowl.

6 To serve, thinly slice lamb across the grain. Serve lamb with yams, onions, and sauce.

makes 8 to 10 servings

per serving: 328 calories, 27 g protein, 41 g carbohydrates, 6 g total fat, 73 mg cholesterol, 282 mg sodium

chile beef stir-fry on mixed greens

preparation time: about 20 minutes
marinating time: at least 30 minutes

1 pound lean boneless top sirloin steak (about 1 inch thick), fat trimmed

1 jalapeño or other small hot chile, stemmed, seeded, and minced

2 cloves garlic, minced or pressed

1/2 to 3/4 teaspoon ground red pepper (cayenne)

1 tablespoon reduced-sodium soy sauce

1/2 teaspoon sugar

1/3 cup seasoned rice vinegar; or 1/3 cup white wine vinegar mixed with 2 tablespoons sugar

3 teaspoons salad oil

8 cups bite-size pieces mixed greens, such as watercress, chicory, arugula, radicchio, butter head lettuce, and looseleaf lettuce, rinsed and crisped

Freshly ground black pepper

1 Slice steak across grain into 1/8-inch-thick strips about 3 inches long. In a medium-size bowl, mix chile, garlic, red pepper, soy sauce, and sugar. Add steak, turning to coat. Cover and refrigerate for at least 30 minutes or until next day.

2 Just before serving, stir together vinegar and 2 teaspoons of the salad oil in a large bowl. Add greens, turning to coat; arrange on individual plates and set aside.

3 Heat remaining oil in a wide nonstick frying pan over high heat. Add steak mixture and cook, stirring, until steak is browned (3 to 5 minutes). Spoon over greens and season to taste with black pepper.

makes 4 servings

per serving: 262 calories, 25 g protein, 22 g carbohydrates, 23 g total fat, 68 mg cholesterol, 226 mg sodium

curry beef in lettuce

preparation time: about 40 minutes

1 medium-size thin-skinned potato, quartered

3/4 pound lean top round, freshly ground

1 medium-size onion, chopped

2 tablespoons *each* curry powder, tomato paste, and vinegar

1/2 cup water

1/4 pound mushrooms, chopped

1 medium-size head butterhead lettuce, separated into leaves, rinsed, and crisped

1 In a 2- to 3-quart pan, bring 1 quart water to a boil over high heat; add potato and cook until tender when pierced (about 10 minutes). Drain and let cool; then dice. Set aside.

2 Crumble beef into a medium-size frying pan; add onion. Cook over medium-high heat, stirring, until meat is browned and onion is limp (about 7 minutes). Pour off any fat. Stir in curry, tomato paste, vinegar, the 1/2 cup water, and mushrooms. Reduce heat, cover, and simmer until mushrooms are soft (about 5 minutes). Uncover, increase heat to high, and cook, stirring often, until almost all the liquid has evaporated. Add potatoes; cook, stirring, until hot.

3 Spoon meat mixture into lettuce leaves and roll up.

makes 4 servings

per serving: 197 calories, 22 g protein, 17 g carbohydrates, 4 g total fat, 49 mg cholesterol, 118 mg sodium

veal curry with fruit

preparation time: about 1 hour

1 pound boneless veal loin, fat trimmed

2 tablespoons margarine

1 medium-size onion, finely chopped

1 large carrot, finely chopped

3 tablespoons all-purpose flour

1 1/2 teaspoons curry powder

1/2 teaspoon ground coriander

1/4 teaspoon *each* cardamom and white pepper

1 cup low-sodium chicken broth

1/2 cup lowfat (2%) milk

6 tablespoons dry sherry

2 small bananas

2 teaspoons lemon juice

2 cups hot cooked brown or white rice

1 cup sliced peaches, papaya, or apricots

1/2 cup golden raisins

1 Slice veal across grain into 1/2-inch-thick strips about 3 inches long. In a wide frying pan, melt margarine over medium-high heat. Add veal and cook, stirring often, until lightly browned (about 7 minutes); lift out and set aside.

2 Add onion and carrot to pan and cook, stirring, until lightly browned (about 5 minutes). Stir in flour, curry powder, coriander, cardamom, and pepper; cook for 1 minute. Stir in chicken broth, milk, and 4 tablespoons of the sherry; bring to a boil. Return veal to pan; reduce heat, cover, and simmer until veal is tender (about 25 minutes). Stir in remaining sherry.

3 Slice bananas; coat with lemon juice. Spoon rice onto individual plates. Top with curry. Offer with bananas, peaches, and raisins.

makes 4 servings

per serving: 495 calories, 30 g protein, 70 g carbohydrates, 12 g total fat, 93 mg cholesterol, 217 mg sodium

---

TOOLS FOR LIGHT COOKING:

Vegetable oil cooking spray prevents lean meat from sticking to the cooking pan or rack, whether you're cooking it in a frying pan, in a Dutch oven, or on the grill. For added flavor, use olive oil spray. Some cooks also like to spray a cooking oil on well-trimmed roasts to promote browning while adding only a whisper of fat.

A roasting rack elevates the roasting meat above any fatty drippings so that the meat doesn't reabsorb them. If you can find a rack covered with nonstick coating, it will be easier to clean.

Nonstick pans are a ready answer to the problem of how to cook lean meat in a scant amount of fat. A heavy pan is a good investment for the kitchen because it's less likely to warp, enabling meat to brown evenly. Frying pans with nonstick coatings are plentiful. Nonstick-coated roasting pans also have many advantages.

green chili with white beans

preparation time: about 2 ½ hours

3 tablespoons salad oil

2 large green bell peppers, seeded and thinly
   sliced crosswise

2 cups sliced green onions (including tops)

8 cloves garlic, minced or pressed

4 teaspoons ground cumin

6 cans (13 oz. *each*) tomatillos

4 large cans (7 oz. *each*) diced green chiles

6 cans (15 oz. *each*) Italian white kidney beans
   (cannellini), drained; or 3 cups cooked small
   white beans, drained

3 pounds lean boneless pork shoulder or butt,
   trimmed of fat and cut into ½-inch cubes

4 teaspoons dry oregano leaves

½ teaspoon ground red pepper (cayenne)

½ cup lightly packed fresh cilantro leaves

1 Heat oil in a 10- to 12-quart pan over medium-high heat; add bell peppers, onions, garlic, and cumin. Cook, stirring, until onions are soft (about 5 minutes). Mix in tomatillos (break up with a spoon) and their liquid, chiles, beans, pork, oregano, and red pepper.

2 Bring to a boil; then reduce heat and simmer, stirring occasionally, until pork is tender when pierced (about 1 ¾ hours). For a thin chili, cook covered; for thicker chili, cook uncovered to desired consistency. Reserve a few cilantro leaves; chop remaining leaves. Stir chopped cilantro into chili; garnish with reserved leaves.

makes 12 servings

per serving: 441 calories, 36 g protein, 44 g carbohydrates, 14 g total fat, 76 mg cholesterol, 1231 mg sodium

marsala & mushroom steaks

preparation time: about 20 minutes

2 teaspoons margarine

½ pound mushrooms, sliced

vegetable oil cooking spray

2 beef tenderloin steaks (about 8 oz. *total*),
   trimmed of fat

Salt and pepper

3 tablespoons Marsala

Watercress sprigs, washed and crisped

1 In a wide nonstick frying pan, melt margarine over medium-high heat. Add mushrooms and cook, stirring often, until liquid has evaporated and mushrooms are browned (6 to 8 minutes). Lift mushrooms from pan and keep warm. Coat pan with cooking spray. Add steaks and cook, turning once, until well browned (4 to 6 minutes total for rare to medium rare). Place steaks on a warm platter and season to taste with salt and pepper; then top with mushrooms.

2 Add Marsala to drippings in pan and bring to a boil, stirring to loosen any browned bits. Spoon Marsala mixture over steaks and mushrooms. Garnish with watercress.

makes 2 servings

per serving: 282 calories, 26 g protein, 8 g carbohydrates, 24 g total fat, 70 mg cholesterol, 722 mg sodium

spinach meat loaf

preparation time: about 2 hours

1 large egg white

¼ cup evaporated skim milk

1 can (about 8 oz.) tomato sauce

1½ cups soft French bread crumbs

1 small onion, finely chopped

1 large potato, scrubbed and grated

1 clove garlic, minced or pressed

2 teaspoons Dijon mustard

¾ teaspoon dry oregano

¼ teaspoon pepper

1 pound *each* extra-lean ground beef and ground
   skinless turkey breast

1 package (about 10 oz.) frozen chopped spinach,
   thawed and squeezed dry

¼ cup grated Romano or Parmesan cheese

1 tablespoon *each* firmly packed brown sugar
   and red wine vinegar

1¼ teaspoons Worcestershire

1 In a large bowl, combine egg white, milk, and ½ cup of the tomato sauce; beat until well combined. Stir in bread crumbs, onion, potato, garlic, mustard, oregano, and pepper. Add beef and turkey; mix lightly. On a large sheet of plastic wrap, pat meat mixture into a 12-inch square. Distribute spinach over meat to within ½ inch of edges; sprinkle evenly with cheese.

2 Using plastic wrap to lift meat, roll up meat jelly roll style. Pinch seam and ends closed to seal in filling. Carefully place meat loaf, seam side down, in a shallow baking pan.

3 Bake meat loaf in a 350° oven for 1¼ hours. Meanwhile, in a small bowl, stir together sugar, vinegar, Worcestershire, and remaining tomato sauce until well blended. Set aside.

4 Remove pan from oven; spoon out and discard any drippings. Spoon tomato sauce mixture over meat loaf. Return to oven and continue to bake until meat is well browned (15 to 20 more minutes). With wide spatulas, carefully transfer meat loaf to a platter. Let stand for about 5 minutes before slicing.

makes 8 servings

per serving: 259 calories, 30 g protein, 28 g carbohydrates, 7 g total fat, 73 mg cholesterol, 418 mg sodium

veal stew with caraway

preparation time: about 2 hours

1 to 1½ pounds boneless veal shoulder,
   trimmed of fat and cut into 1-inch cubes

1 tablespoon salad oil

¼ teaspoon salt

⅛ teaspoon ground white pepper

1 large onion, finely chopped

½ cup dry white wine

2 teaspoons caraway seeds

1 can (about 14½ oz.) low-sodium chicken broth

2 medium-size carrots, chopped

3 to 4 cups hot cooked eggless noodles

Chopped parsley

1 In a wide 3½- to 4-quart pan, combine veal, oil, salt, white pepper, onion, and wine. Cover and cook over medium-low heat for 30 minutes. Uncover pan and stir in caraway seeds. Increase heat to medium and continue to cook, stirring occasionally, until almost all liquid has evaporated and onion is browned (15 to 20 minutes). Add broth and carrots to pan, stirring to scrape browned bits free.

2 Reduce heat to low, cover, and simmer until veal is tender when pierced (35 to 45 minutes). Increase heat to medium and cook, uncovered, stirring often, until sauce is slightly thickened (12 to 15 minutes). To serve, spoon stew over noodles; sprinkle with parsley.

makes 4 to 6 servings

per serving: 288 calories, 28 g protein, 27 g carbohydrates, 8 g total fat, 98 mg cholesterol, 252 mg sodium

grilled beef pocket sandwiches

preparation time: about 30 minutes
marinating time: at least 30 minutes

1 ½ pounds lean tender beef steak such as top sirloin (cut about 1 inch thick), trimmed of fat

1 large clove garlic, peeled

½ small onion, cut into chunks

2 tablespoons *each* sugar, water, salad oil, and lemon juice

⅓ cup reduced-sodium soy sauce

2 large red bell peppers, seeded and cut into 1 ½-inch squares

6 pita breads (*each* about 6 inches in diameter), cut into halves

2 cups lightly packed cilantro sprigs, rinsed and crisped

1 Cut beef into long slices about ¼ inch thick. In a blender or food processor, combine garlic, onion, sugar, water, oil, lemon juice, and soy sauce; whirl until puréed. Pour into a bowl. Add beef and bell peppers; stir to coat with marinade. Then cover and refrigerate for at least 30 minutes or up to 1 day, stirring occasionally.

2 Drain marinade from beef and peppers; reserve marinade. Thread beef strips alternately with peppers on thin metal skewers. (To thread each beef strip, pierce one end of strip with skewer; then fold strip back and forth several times, piercing each time. Threaded meat will have a "rippled" look.) Place skewers on a grill 4 to 6 inches above a solid bed of medium-hot coals. Cook, turning often and basting with marinade, until beef is done to your liking; cut to test (about 4 minutes for medium-rare).

3 To eat, fill pita bread halves with beef, bell peppers, and cilantro sprigs.

makes 6 servings

per serving: 420 calories, 33 g protein, 44 g carbohydrates, 72 g total fat, 76 mg cholesterol, 911 mg sodium

szechuan beef

preparation time: about 25 minutes, plus 30 minutes to soak mushrooms

Cooking Sauce (recipe follows)

8 medium-size dried shiitake mushrooms (*each* about 2 inches in diameter)

1 pound lean top round steak

1 tablespoon salad oil

16 small dried hot red chiles

1 pound carrots, cut into thin 3-inch strips

4 cups bite-size pieces cauliflower

2 cans (about 8 oz. *each*) sliced bamboo shoots

2 cans (about 8 oz. *each*) sliced water chestnuts

1 Prepare sauce; set aside. Soak mushrooms in warm water to cover for 30 minutes; drain. Cut off and discard stems; squeeze caps dry and thinly slice. Cut steak into strips.

2 Heat oil in a wok or 12- to 14-inch frying pan over medium-high heat. Add chiles and stir until chiles just begin to char. Remove chiles from pan.

3 Add meat to pan and stir-fry until browned (1½ to 2 minutes); remove with a slotted spoon and set aside. Add carrots, cauliflower, and mushrooms; stir-fry for 1 minute, then cover and cook until carrots and cauliflower are tender-crisp to bite (about 3 minutes). Drain bamboo shoots and water chestnuts, add to pan, and stir-fry for 1 more minute.

4 Return meat and chiles to pan; stir Cooking Sauce and add. Stir until sauce boils and thickens.

COOKING SAUCE

Mix 3 tablespoons reduced-sodium soy sauce, 1½ tablespoons dry sherry, 1 tablespoon sugar, and 3/4 teaspoon cornstarch.

makes 6 servings

per serving: 300 calories, 24 g protein, 38 g carbohydrates, 9 g total fat, 43 mg cholesterol, 392 mg sodium

mediterranean veal ragout

preparation time: about 1 hour

1 pound lean boneless veal stew meat (cut from leg or shoulder), fat trimmed, cut into 1-inch chunks

2 medium-size onions, thinly sliced

1/2 cup water

1 teaspoon olive oil (preferably extra virgin)

1 cup low-sodium chicken broth

2 pound tomatoes, finely chopped

3 cloves garlic, minced or pressed

2 teaspoons dry thyme leaves

1/2 teaspoon dry rosemary

1 package (9 oz.) frozen artichoke hearts, thawed

2 tablespoons drained and rinsed capers

1/2 teaspoon anchovy paste or 1 teaspoon chopped canned anchovy fillets (optional)

1 tablespoon red wine vinegar

1 In a 5- to 6-quart pan, bring veal, onions, water, and oil to a boil over high heat; reduce heat, cover, and simmer, stirring occasionally, for 30 minutes.

2 Uncover, increase heat to medium-high, and cook, stirring often, until veal is lightly browned and onions begin to caramelize (about 5 minutes).

3 Add chicken broth, stirring to loosen browned bits. Reserve 1/4 cup of the tomatoes; add remaining tomatoes, garlic, thyme, rosemary, artichokes, capers, and, if desired, anchovy paste. Reduce heat, cover, and simmer until veal is tender and artichokes are hot (about 15 minutes). Stir in vinegar and reserved tomatoes.

makes 4 servings

per serving: 203 calories, 28 g protein, 14 g carbohydrates, 4 g total fat, 89 mg cholesterol, 236 mg sodium

steak mexicana

preparation time: about 35 minutes

2 teaspoons salad oil

1 small onion, finely chopped

1 canned California green chile, seeded and chopped

1/4 teaspoon *each* salt and ground cumin

1 1/2 cups peeled chopped tomatoes

1 pound boneless top sirloin steak (about 3/4 inch thick), trimmed of fat

1/4 cup shredded jack cheese

Lime wedges

Cilantro sprigs

1 Heat oil in a wide nonstick frying pan over medium heat. Add onion, chile, salt, and cumin. Cook, stirring often, until onion is soft and beginning to brown (3 to 5 minutes). Stir in tomato; increase heat to medium-high and cook, stirring often, until most of the liquid has evaporated (6 to 8 minutes). Keep sauce warm.

2 Cut steak into 4 portions. Place on a rack in a broiler pan. Broil about 4 inches below heat, turning once, until browned (4 to 6 minutes total). Spoon tomato sauce over steaks and top with cheese; broil until cheese is melted (1 to 2 minutes). Garnish with lime wedges and cilantro.

makes 4 servings

per serving: 234 calories, 28 g protein 5 g carbohydrates, 11 g total fat, 82 mg cholesterol, 346 mg sodium

baked polenta with veal sauce

preparation time: about 1 1/2 hours

Baked Polenta (recipe follows)

1 teaspoon olive oil

1 small onion, finely chopped

1 small carrot, shredded

4 ounces mushrooms, cut into quarters

1 clove garlic, minced or pressed

2 teaspoons Italian herb seasoning; or 1/2 teaspoon *each* dry basil, dry marjoram, dry oregano, and dry thyme

1 pound lean ground veal

1 large can (about 28 oz.) pear-shaped tomatoes

1/4 cup tomato paste

1/2 cup dry white wine

Salt and pepper

Grated Parmesan cheese (optional)

1 Prepare Baked Polenta. While polenta is baking, combine oil, onion, carrot, mushrooms, garlic, and herb seasoning in a wide nonstick frying pan. Cook over medium-high heat, stirring often, until onion is soft (about 5 minutes). Crumble veal into pan and cook, stirring often, until it begins to brown. Cut up tomatoes; then add tomatoes and their liquid, tomato paste, and wine to pan. Bring to a boil. Adjust heat so mixture boils gently; cook, uncovered, stirring occasionally, until thickened (about 20 minutes). Season to taste with salt and pepper.

2 Spoon Baked Polenta into wide, shallow bowls and top with veal sauce. Offer cheese to add to taste, if desired.

BAKED POLENTA

In an oiled shallow 2-quart baking dish, stir together 4 cups low-sodium chicken broth, 1 1/4 cups polenta, 1/4 cup finely chopped onion, and 1 tablespoon olive oil. Bake in a 350° oven until liquid has been absorbed (40 to 45 minutes).

makes 4 to 6 servings

per serving: 397 calories, 25 g protein, 43 g carbohydrates, 22 g total fat, 74 mg cholesterol, 494 mg sodium

lamb with fruited couscous

preparation time: about 2 1/4 hours

1 tablespoon olive oil

1 pound boned leg of lamb, cut into 1-inch cubes

1 large onion, chopped

1 1/2 teaspoons ground coriander

1 teaspoon ground ginger

1/2 teaspoon ground cumin

1/4 teaspoon ground allspice

1 cinnamon stick

2 cups low-sodium chicken broth

1/4 cup apricot or orange muscat dessert wine

1 cup dried apricots

10 ounces dried couscous

1 Heat oil in a 5- to 6-quart pan over medium-high heat. Add lamb and cook, turning often, until well browned (about 8 minutes). Lift out and set aside.

2 Add onion to pan and cook, stirring often, until soft (about 5 minutes). Add coriander, ginger, cumin, allspice, cinnamon stick, broth, and lamb. Bring to a boil; reduce heat, cover, and simmer until lamb is tender when pierced (about 1 1/2 hours). Discard cinnamon stick. (At this point, you may cool, cover, and refrigerate for up to a day; discard fat and reheat to continue.)

3 Lift out lamb and place on a platter; keep warm. Skim off and discard fat from pan drippings (if not already done). Measure drippings. If less than 2 1/3 cups, add water, and return to pan; if more, boil over high heat until reduced to 2 1/3 cups. Add wine and apricots; bring to a boil. Stir in couscous; cover, remove from heat, and let stand until liquid is absorbed (about 5 minutes).

4 Mound couscous beside lamb.

makes 4 servings

per serving: 606 calories, 36 g protein, 89 g carbohydrates, 10 g total fat, 73 mg cholesterol, 112 mg sodium

seafood

salmon sauté with citrus sauce

preparation time: about 40 minutes

3 or 4 medium-size oranges

1 large pink grapefruit

1 large lime

3 green onions

1 tablespoon butter or margarine

1 pound salmon fillets, skinned and cut into 1- by 2-inch strips

¼ cup dry vermouth

⅓ cup orange marmalade

1 tablespoon chopped fresh mint

Mint sprigs (optional)

Salt and pepper

1 Shred enough peel (colored part only) from oranges, grapefruit, and lime to make ½ teaspoon of each kind of peel. Combine peels in a small bowl; cover and set aside.

2 Cut off and discard remaining peel and all white membrane from grapefruit, lime, and 2 of the oranges. Holding fruit over a bowl to catch juice, cut between membranes to release segments; set segments aside. Pour juice from bowl into a glass measure. Squeeze juice from remaining oranges; add enough of this orange juice to juice in glass measure to make ½ cup (reserve remaining orange juice for other uses). Set juice aside.

3 Trim and discard ends of onions. Cut onions into 2-inch lengths, then cut each piece lengthwise into slivers; set aside.

4 Melt butter in a wide nonstick frying pan or wok over medium-high heat. Add fish. Stir-fry gently (flipping with a spatula, if needed) until fish is just opaque but still moist in thickest part; cut to test (about 4 minutes). With a slotted spoon, transfer fish to a large bowl; keep warm.

5 Add citrus juices and vermouth to pan. Bring to a boil; then boil, stirring often, until reduced to ⅓ cup (about 3 minutes). Reduce heat to low, add marmalade, and stir until melted. Add onions and citrus segments; stir gently just until heated through. Remove from heat and stir in chopped mint.

6 Spoon fruit sauce over fish; mix gently. Divide fish mixture among 4 individual rimmed plates; garnish with citrus peels and mint sprigs, if desired. Season to taste with salt and pepper.

makes 4 servings

per serving: 352 calories, 24 g protein, 39 g carbohydrates, 10 g total fat, 70 mg cholesterol, 98 mg sodium

tomato-caper sauce

preparation time: 25 minutes

1 teaspoon olive oil

1 medium-size onion, finely chopped

1 clove garlic, minced or pressed

1 can (about 14½ oz.) diced tomatoes

2 teaspoons drained capers

1 tablespoon lemon juice

2 tablespoons minced parsley

Heat oil in a wide nonstick frying pan over medium heat. Add onion and garlic; cook, stirring often, until onion is soft (about 5 minutes). Add tomatoes and capers. Bring to a gentle boil. Cook, uncovered, stirring often, until thickened (about 10 minutes). Stir in lemon juice and parsley. Serve over hot cooked fish.

makes about 2 cups

per tablespoon: 6 calories, 0.2 g protein, 19 carbohydrates, 0.2 g total fat, 0 mg cholesterol, 26 mg sodium

poached fish
with horseradish sauce

preparation time: about 45 minutes

1 ½ pounds skinless, boneless lingcod, halibut, rockfish, or sole fillets or steaks (fillets no thicker than 1 inch, steaks about 1 inch thick)

About ⅔ cup fat-free reduced-sodium chicken broth

1 tablespoon cornstarch

1 tablespoon prepared horseradish

8 to 12 hot boiled tiny potatoes (*each* about 1 inch in diameter)

3 green onions, cut into 2-inch lengths and slivered

1 Rinse fish and pat dry; fold any thin fillets in half. Arrange fish in a shallow 8-inch baking dish. Pour ⅔ cup of the broth over fish. Cover and bake in a 400° oven until fish is just opaque but still moist in thickest part; cut to test (about 15 minutes). With a slotted spatula, lift fish to a warm platter; keep warm.

2 Drain cooking liquid from baking dish into a measuring cup; you should have about 1 cup. If necessary, boil to reduce to 1 cup or add more broth to make 1 cup. In a 1 ½- to 2-quart pan, smoothly blend cornstarch, horseradish, and cooking liquid. Bring to a boil over high heat, stirring.

3 Spoon sauce evenly over fish. Arrange potatoes on platter around fish; sprinkle with onions.

makes 4 servings

per serving: 206 calories, 32 g protein, 13 g carbohydrates, 2 g total fat, 89 mg cholesterol, 218 mg sodium

whole tilapia
with onion & lemon

preparation time: about 45 minutes

1 ¼ pounds red onions, cut into ⅛-inch-thick slices

3 tablespoons lemon juice

1 tablespoon minced fresh ginger

1 whole tilapia, dressed (gutted, with head and tail attached)

1 tablespoon extra-virgin olive oil

2 large lemons

3 tablespoons minced cilantro

Salt and pepper

1 In a large bowl, mix onions, lemon juice, and ginger. Reserve a couple of onion slices; arrange remaining slices over bottom of a 9- by 13-inch or shallow 4- to 5-quart baking dish.

2 Rinse fish and pat dry. Brush both sides of fish with oil; then place fish on top of onion mixture.

3 Cut a ½-inch slice from each end of each lemon; stuff fish cavity with lemon ends, reserved onion slices, and half the cilantro. Thinly slice remaining piece of each lemon; tuck slices around fish. Sprinkle remaining cilantro over onion and lemon in baking dish. Bake in a 400° oven until a meat thermometer inserted in thickest part of fish registers 135° and flesh is just opaque but still moist; cut to test (20 to 25 minutes).

4 To serve, gently pull skin from fish; then spoon fish, onions, and lemon slices onto 2 dinner plates. Season to taste with salt and pepper.

makes 2 servings

per serving: 359 calories, 38 g protein, 40 g carbohydrates, 10 g total fat, 82 mg cholesterol, 177 mg sodium

sea bass with green beans & sesame-orange sauce

preparation time: about 35 minutes

³/₄ teaspoon grated orange peel

¹/₄ cup orange juice

2 tablespoons reduced-sodium soy sauce

1 clove garlic, minced or pressed

1 ¹/₂ teaspoons honey

1 teaspoon minced fresh ginger

¹/₂ teaspoon Asian sesame oil

1 teaspoon sesame seeds

8 ounces slender green beans (ends removed, cut diagonally into 1-inch lengths

¹/₂ cup sliced red onion

1 teaspoon vegetable oil or olive oil

1 pound Chilean sea bass, halibut, or orange roughy fillets (about ¹/₂ inch), cut into 1-inch pieces

1 To prepare sesame-orange sauce, in a small bowl, stir together orange peel, orange juice, soy sauce, garlic, honey, ginger, and sesame oil; set aside.

2 In a wide nonstick frying pan or wok, stir sesame seeds over medium heat until golden (about 3 minutes). Pour out of pan and set aside.

3 In pan, combine beans, onion, and ¹/₃ cup water. Increase heat to medium-high; cover and cook until beans are almost tender to bite (about 3 minutes). Uncover and stir-fry until liquid has evaporated. Transfer bean mixture to a rimmed platter and keep warm.

4 Heat oil in pan. When oil is hot, add fish and stir-fry gently until just opaque but still moist in thickest part; cut to test (3 to 4 minutes). Remove fish from pan with a slotted spoon; add to bean mixture and mix gently but thoroughly. Sprinkle with sesame seeds. Stir sesame-orange sauce; offer sauce to add to individual servings.

makes 4 servings

per serving: 177 calories, 23 g protein, 11 g carbohydrates, 4 g total fat, 47 mg cholesterol, 383 mg sodium

grilled soy-lemon halibut

preparation time: about 20 minutes
marinating time: 1 to 2 hours

2 pounds halibut, shark, or sea bass steaks or fillets (³/₄ to 1 inch thick)

2 tablespoons butter or margarine, melted

3 tablespoons reduced-sodium soy sauce

2 tablespoons lemon juice

1 tablespoon *each* sugar and Worcestershire

1 tablespoon minced fresh ginger or ¹/₂ teaspoon ground ginger

1 clove garlic, minced or pressed

¹/₈ teaspoon pepper

Vegetable oil cooking spray

1 Rinse fish and pat dry; then cut into 6 equal pieces, if necessary. In a shallow dish, stir together butter, soy sauce, lemon juice, sugar, Worcestershire, ginger, garlic, and pepper. Add fish and turn to coat. Then cover and refrigerate for 1 to 2 hours, turning occasionally.

2 Coat grill of a covered barbecue with cooking spray. Lift fish from marinade and drain briefly; discard marinade. Place fish on grill 4 to 6 inches above a solid bed of hot coals. Cover barbecue, open vents, and cook, turning once, until fish is just opaque but still moist in thickest part; cut to test (8 to 10 minutes).

makes 6 servings

per serving: 194 calories, 32 g protein, 2 g carbohydrates, 6 g total fat, 54 mg cholesterol, 266 mg sodium

swordfish with mango relish

preparation time: about 45 minutes

1/4 cup minced white onion

1 1/2 cups diced ripe mango

3/4 cup diced red bell pepper

1/4 cup chopped cilantro

1 tablespoon minced fresh ginger

2 tablespoons lemon juice

2 teaspoons vegetable oil

1 1/2 pounds swordfish,
   cut into 1/2- by 2-Inch strips

1/2 cup lightly packed cilantro sprigs

1 To prepare mango relish, place onion in a fine strainer; rinse with cold water. Place in a bowl, cover with ice water, and let stand for 30 minutes. Drain. Return onion to bowl; stir in mango, bell pepper, chopped cilantro, ginger, and lemon juice; set aside.

2 Heat oil in a wide nonstick frying pan or wok over medium-high heat. When oil is hot, add swordfish and stir-fry gently (flipping with a spatula, if needed) until just opaque but still moist in thickest part; cut to test (about 4 minutes). Spoon swordfish onto a platter; top with mango relish and garnish with cilantro sprigs.

makes 6 servings

per serving: 186 calories, 23 g protein, 9 g carbohydrates, 6 g total fat, 44 mg cholesterol, 106 mg sodium

crab with emerald sauce

preparation time: about 30 minutes

---

8 ounces basil sprigs

4 ounces cilantro sprigs

8 ounces dried capellini

1/4 cup seasoned rice vinegar; or
   1/4 cup rice vinegar and 1 teaspoon sugar

1 tablespoon minced lemon peel

1 tablespoon Asian sesame oil

3/4 cup fat-free reduced-sodium chicken broth

2 tablespoons vegetable oil

1/3 to 1/2 pound cooked crabmeat

1 Reserve 4 of the basil sprigs and cilantro sprigs for garnish. Bring 8 cups water to a boil in a 4- to 5-quart pan over medium-high heat. Gather half the remaining fresh basil into a bunch. Holding stem ends with tongs, dip leaves into boiling water just until bright green (about 3 seconds). At once plunge into ice water. Repeat with cilantro and remaining basil.

2 Stir pasta into water and cook just until tender to bite (about 4 minutes); or cook according to package directions. Drain well. Place in a bowl. Add vinegar, lemon peel, and sesame oil; lift with 2 forks to mix. Keep warm.

3 Drain basil and cilantro; blot dry. Cut leaves from stems, discarding stems. Place leaves in a blender or food processor with broth and vegetable oil. Whirl until smooth. Spread on individual plates. Top with pasta and crab. Garnish with reserved basil and cilantro sprigs.

makes 4 servings

per serving: 382 calories, 19 g protein, 49 g carbohydrates, 13 g total fat, 43 mg cholesterol, 485 mg sodium

baby salmon & squash with brown sugar & lime

preparation time: about 1 1/2 hours

2 pounds banana or Hubbard squash, seeded and cut into 4 equal pieces

1 1/2 cups low-sodium chicken broth

4 baby salmon fillets (about 5 oz. each)

1/2 teaspoon salad oil

1/4 cup *each* firmly packed brown sugar and lime juice

Lime wedges

Salt and pepper

1. Place squash, skin side up, in a large, shallow baking pan; pour in broth. Bake in a 350° oven until squash is tender when pierced (about 1 hour). Remove from oven; then increase oven temperature to 450°.

2. Rinse fish and pat dry. Turn squash over and push to one end of pan. Lift opposite end of pan so that any liquid runs down to mix with squash; then spread oil over exposed pan bottom.

3. Place fish fillets side by side (they can overlap slightly) in oiled part of pan. In a small bowl, mix sugar and lime juice; spoon about half the mixture over fish and squash.

4. Return pan to oven and bake until fish is just opaque but still moist in thickest part; cut to test (about 8 minutes). After fish has baked for 5 minutes, spoon remaining lime mixture over fish and squash.

5. To serve, transfer fish and squash to 4 individual plates; garnish with lime wedges. Stir pan juices to blend; season to taste with salt and pepper, then pour into a small bowl. Serve pan juices with fish and squash.

makes 4 servings

per serving: 331 calories, 32 g protein, 28 g carbohydrates, 11 g total fat, 78 mg cholesterol, 100 mg sodium

halibut with tomatoes & dill

preparation time: about 45 minutes

1 pound cherry tomatoes, cut into halves

1/2 cup thinly sliced green onions

2 cloves garlic, minced or pressed

2 tablespoons chopped fresh dill or 1/2 teaspoon dry dill weed

2 teaspoons olive oil

2 tablespoons water

1 1/2 pounds halibut fillets or steaks (or rockfish or cod fillets)

2 tablespoons lemon juice

Dill sprigs (optional)

1. Arrange tomatoes, cut side up, in a 9- by 13-inch baking pan. In a small bowl, mix onions, garlic, chopped dill, oil, and water. Distribute onion mixture over tomatoes. Bake on top rack of a 425° oven for 25 minutes.

2. Rinse fish and pat dry; then cut into 4 equal pieces, if necessary. Place fish in a baking pan large enough to hold pieces in a single layer. Drizzle with lemon juice, cover, and place in oven, setting pan on bottom oven rack.

3. Continue to bake fish and tomatoes until tomatoes are lightly browned on top and fish is just opaque but still moist in thickest part; cut to test (8 to 10 minutes).

4. Transfer fish to a platter. Add fish cooking juices to tomato mixture and stir well; spoon over fish. Garnish with dill sprigs, if desired.

makes 4 servings

per serving: 239 calories, 37 g protein, 7 g carbohydrates, 7 g total fat, 54 mg cholesterol, 106 mg sodium

salmon with creamy tomatillo sauce

preparation time: about 35 minutes

4 medium-size tomatillos, husked, rinsed, and chopped

1 tablespoon sliced green onion

1 clove garlic, peeled

¼ teaspoon grated lime peel

1 tablespoon lime juice

About ¾ teaspoon sugar, or to taste

⅛ teaspoon salt

½ cup plain low-fat yogurt (do not use nonfat yogurt) blended with 2 teaspoons cornstarch

8 low-fat flour tortillas (*each 7 to 9 inches in diameter*)

1 tablespoon butter or margarine

1 pound salmon fillets (about ½ inch thick), skinned and cut into ¾-inch pieces

1 medium-size tomato, chopped and drained well

2 tablespoons cilantro leaves

Lime wedges

Ground white pepper

1 In a blender or food processor, combine tomatillos, onion, garlic, lime peel, lime juice, sugar, and salt. Whirl until smooth. By hand, stir in yogurt mixture just until combined; do not over beat or sauce will separate. Set aside.

2 Brush tortillas lightly with hot water; then stack, wrap in foil, and heat in a 350° oven until warm (10 to 12 minutes).

3 Meanwhile, melt butter in a wide nonstick frying pan or wok over medium-high heat. Add fish and stir-fry gently until just opaque but still moist in thickest part; cut to test (about 4 minutes). Remove from pan and keep warm. Wipe pan clean (be careful; pan is hot).

4 Add yogurt-tomatillo sauce to pan. Reduce heat to medium-low and simmer gently, stirring constantly, until sauce is slightly thickened (2 to 3 minutes); do not boil.

5 Divide sauce among 4 individual rimmed plates; spread sauce out evenly, then top equally with fish. Sprinkle with tomato and cilantro leaves, garnish with lime wedges, and season to taste with white pepper. Serve with tortillas.

makes 4 servings

per serving: 370 calories, 29 g protein, 44 g carbohydrates, 12 g total fat, 72 mg cholesterol, 533 mg sodium

cool dill sauce

preparation time: about 10 minutes

⅔ cup plain nonfat or low-fat yogurt

1 tablespoon *each* white wine vinegar and minced chives

1 tablespoon minced fresh dill or 1 teaspoon dry dill weed

⅛ teaspoon liquid hot pepper seasoning

Salt and pepper

In a small bowl, stir together yogurt, vinegar, chives, dill, and hot pepper seasoning. Season to taste with salt and pepper. If made ahead, cover and refrigerate for up to 1 day. Stir before using. Serve with cold poached or grilled salmon or white-fleshed fish.

makes about ¾ cup

per tablespoon: 8 calories, 0.7 g protein, 1 g carbohydrates, 0 g total fat, 0.3 mg cholesterol, 1 mg sodium

soft crab tacos with tomatillo & lime salsa

preparation time: about 35 minutes

TOMATILLO & LIME SALSA:

8 medium-size tomatillos, husked, rinsed, and finely chopped

2 tablespoons sliced green onion

1/4 teaspoon grated lime peel

2 tablespoons lime juice

1 teaspoon sugar, or to taste

1/8 teaspoon salt, or to taste

SOFT CRAB TACOS:

6 to 12 corn tortillas (*each* about 6 inches in diameter) or 6 to 12 low-fat flour tortillas (*each* 7 to 9 inches in diameter)

2 tablespoons olive oil

1 clove garlic, minced or pressed

1 small red onion, finely chopped

1 can (about 4 oz.) diced green chiles

2 large firm-ripe tomatoes, chopped

1 pound cooked crabmeat

5 to 6 cups finely shredded lettuce

1/4 cup lightly packed cilantro leaves

1/2 cup nonfat sour cream

1 To prepare tomatillo & lime salsa, in a medium-size bowl, combine tomatillos, green onion, lime peel, lime juice, sugar; and salt; set aside. (At this point, the salsa can be covered and refrigerated for up to 4 hours; stir before serving.)

2 Brush tortillas lightly with hot water; stack, wrap in foil, and heat in a 350° oven until warm (10 to 12 minutes.)

3 Meanwhile, heat oil in a wide nonstick frying pan or wok over medium-high heat. When oil is hot add garlic and red onion; stir-fry until onion begins to brown (about 5 minutes). Add chiles and half the tomatoes; stir-fry until tomatoes are soft (about 4 minutes). Remove from heat and gently stir in crab.

4 Divide lettuce among tortillas; then top tortillas equally with crab mixture, remaining tomatoes, and cilantro. Top with tomatillo & lime salsa and sour cream. Garnish with lime wedges.

makes 6 servings

per serving: 263 calories, 21 g protein, 29 g carbohydrates, 7 g total fat, 76 mg cholesterol, 460 mg sodium

Recognizing when fish is done is essential to cooking it well—if overcooked, it rapidly loses flavor and moisture. Most recipes in this book tell you to cook fish until it's "just opaque but still moist in thickest part." To test, cut to the center of the thickest portion of the whole fish, steak, or fillet—thinner parts may appear to be done while thicker portions are still cooking and uncooked inside. As a rule of thumb, allow 8 to 10 minutes of cooking time for each inch of thickness for fish cooked by any method other than microwaving.

balsamic-broiled salmon with mint

preparation time: about 40 minutes

1 ¼ pounds small red thin-skinned potatoes, scrubbed

3 tablespoons balsamic or raspberry vinegar

1 ½ tablespoons honey

³/₄ teaspoon vegetable oil

1 to 1 ¼ pounds salmon fillets (³/₄ inch thick)

½ cup fresh mint leaves, minced

Mint sprigs

Lemon slices

1. Peel a 1-inch-wide strip around center of each potato. Steam potatoes, covered, on a rack above about 1 inch of boiling water until tender when pierced (about 25 minutes).

2. Meanwhile, in a small bowl, stir together vinegar, honey, and oil.

3. Remove and discard any skin from salmon; rinse salmon and pat dry. Cut salmon into 4 serving-size pieces; place, skinned sides down, in a lightly greased shallow rimmed baking pan. Drizzle salmon with half the vinegar mixture.

4. Broil about 6 inches below heat, brushing several times with remaining vinegar mixture, until just opaque but still moist in thickest part; cut to test (8 to 10 minutes).

5. Transfer salmon to a warm platter; drizzle with any cooking juices. Surround with potatoes. Sprinkle salmon and potatoes with minced mint; garnish with mint sprigs and lemon slices.

makes 4 servings

per serving: 332 calories, 28 g protein, 33 g carbohydrates, 9 g total fat, 71 mg cholesterol, 68 mg sodium

stir-fried tuna on spinach

preparation time: about 40 minutes

¼ cup mirin or cream sherry

6 tablespoons unseasoned rice vinegar or cider vinegar

2 tablespoons reduced-sodium soy sauce

1 teaspoon prepared horseradish

3 quarts lightly packed rinsed, crisped spinach leaves

1 tablespoon sesame seeds

1 teaspoon vegetable oil

2 tablespoons finely minced fresh ginger

12 ounces fresh tuna, cut into 2- by 2-inch strips

½ cup thinly sliced green onions

1 cup thinly sliced red radishes

Whole green onions (ends trimmed)

1. To prepare soy dressing, in a small bowl, stir together mirin, vinegar, soy sauce, and horseradish; set aside.

2. Arrange spinach on a large platter, cover, and set aside.

3. In a wide nonstick frying pan or wok, stir sesame seeds over medium heat until golden (about 3 minutes). Pour out of pan and set aside.

4. Heat oil in pan over medium-high heat. When oil is hot, add ginger and stir-fry just until light brown (about 30 seconds; do not scorch). Add tuna and stir-fry gently (flipping with a spatula, if needed) until just opaque but still moist and pink in thickest part; cut to test (about 3 minutes). Stir soy dressing and pour into pan; stir to mix, then remove pan from heat.

5. Spoon tuna mixture over spinach on platter. Sprinkle with sliced green onions, radishes, and sesame seeds. Garnish with whole green onions.

makes 4 servings

per serving: 220 calories , 24 g protein, 12 g carbohydrates, 7 g total fat, 32 mg cholesterol, 411 mg sodium

tuna & cherry tomato salsa

preparation time: about 25 minutes

1 pound red or yellow cherry tomatoes, chopped

1/2 cup lightly packed cilantro leaves, coarsely chopped

2 fresh jalapeño chiles, seeded and coarsely chopped

1 clove garlic, minced or pressed

3 green onions, thinly sliced

5 tablespoons lime juice

1 teaspoon olive oil

4 skinless, boneless tuna steaks (about 4 oz. each), 3/4 to 1 inch thick

2 medium-size cucumbers, thinly sliced

Freshly ground pepper

In a medium-size bowl, mix tomatoes, cilantro, chiles, garlic, onions, and 2 tablespoons of the lime juice. Cover and set aside.

1 Mix remaining 3 tablespoons lime juice with oil. Rinse tuna and pat dry; then brush both sides of each steak with oil mixture. Place tuna on a greased grill 4 to 6 inches above a solid bed of hot coals. Cook, turning once, until browned on outside but still pale pink in the center; cut to test (about 3 minutes).

2 Transfer tuna to a warm platter; surround with cucumber slices. Evenly top tuna with tomato salsa; season to taste with pepper.

makes 4 servings

per serving: 225 calories, 29 g protein, 12 g carbohydrates, 7 g total fat, 43 mg cholesterol, 64 mg sodium

seed-crusted fish, indian style

preparation time: about 15 minutes

1 teaspoon each coriander seeds and mustard seeds

1/2 teaspoon each coarsely ground pepper, cumin seeds, and fennel seeds

1 pound lingcod, rockfish, or orange roughy fillets (1/2 to 1 inch thick)

2 teaspoons salad oil

Cilantro sprigs

1 Mix coriander seeds, mustard seeds, pepper, cumin seeds, and fennel seeds; set aside.

2 Rinse fish, pat dry, and cut into 4 equal pieces. Brush with oil and place on a rack in a 12- by 14-inch broiler pan. Broil about 3 inches below heat for 3 minutes. Turn fish over, sprinkle with seed mixture, and continue to broil until just opaque but still moist in thickest part; cut to test (2 to 4 more minutes). Garnish with cilantro sprigs.

makes 4 servings

per serving: 125 calories, 20 g protein, 0.9 g carbohydrates, 4 g total fat, 59 mg cholesterol, 68 mg sodium

lemon shrimp over caper couscous

preparation time: about 35 minutes

1 pound large raw shrimp (31 to 35 per lb.), shelled and deveined

2 cloves garlic, minced or pressed (optional)

3/4 teaspoon chopped fresh oregano or 1/4 teaspoon dried oregano

1/2 teaspoon grated lemon peel

1/8 teaspoon pepper

2 tablespoons dry sherry

1 tablespoon cornstarch

2 cups fat-free reduced-sodium chicken broth

8 ounces asparagus

1 medium-size red bell pepper

1 cup couscous

2 tablespoons seasoned rice vinegar (or 2 tablespoons distilled white vinegar plus 3 teaspoon sugar)

1 to 2 tablespoons drained capers

1 tablespoon olive oil

Lemon wedges and oregano sprigs

1 In a large bowl, mix shrimp, garlic (if used) chopped oregano, 1/4 teaspoon of the lemon peel, and pepper. Set aside; stir occasionally.

2 To prepare sauce, in a small bowl, combine sherry and cornstarch; stir until blended. Stir in 1/2 cup of the broth; set aside.

3 Snap off and discard tough ends of asparagus; cut spears into 1/2-inch diagonal slices and set aside. Seed bell pepper, cut into thin strips, and set aside.

4 In a 3- to 4-quart pan, combine remaining 1 1/2 cups broth and remaining 1/4 teaspoon lemon peel. Bring to a boil over high heat; stir in couscous. Cover, remove from heat, and let stand until liquid has been absorbed (about 5 minutes). Stir in vinegar and capers. Keep couscous warm; fluff occasionally with a fork.

5 In a wide nonstick frying pan or wok, combine asparagus, bell pepper, and 1/3 cup water. Cover and cook over medium-high heat until asparagus is almost tender to bite (about 3 minutes). Uncover and stir-fry until liquid has evaporated. Remove vegetables from pan and set aside.

6 Heat oil in pan. When oil is hot, add shrimp mixture and stir-fry for 2 minutes. Stir sauce well and pour into pan; then return asparagus and bell pepper to pan. Cook, stirring, until sauce boils and thickens slightly and shrimp are just opaque in center; cut to test (1 to 2 more minutes). Remove from heat.

7 To serve, spoon couscous onto a rimmed platter; top with shrimp mixture. Offer lemon wedges to squeeze to taste; garnish with oregano sprigs.

makes 4 servings

per serving: 355 calories, 28 g protein, 46 g carbohydrates, 5 g total fat, 140 mg cholesterol, 696 mg sodium

cool yogurt sauce

preparation time: about 5 minutes

1 cup plain nonfat yogurt

1 tablespoon *each* chopped fresh mint and cilantro

Salt

Fresh mint and cilantro leaves (optional)

In a small bowl, stir together yogurt, chopped mint, and chopped cilantro. Season to taste with salt. If made ahead, cover and refrigerate for up to 4 hours; stir before serving. Sprinkle with mint and cilantro leaves just before serving, if desired. Serve with cold poached or grilled salmon.

makes about 1 cup

per tablespoon: 8 calories, 0.8 g protein, 1 g carbohydrates, 0 g total fat, 0.3 mg cholesterol, 11 mg sodium

shrimp with black bean sauce

preparation time: about 40 minutes

8 tablespoons fermented salted black beans, rinsed and drained

4 ounces lean ground pork

1 large red bell pepper, seeded and finely chopped

12 ounces mushrooms, thinly sliced

3 cloves garlic, minced or pressed

1 tablespoon minced fresh ginger

1 cup low-sodium chicken broth

2 tablespoons oyster sauce

2 tablespoon cornstarch

1 tablespoon salad oil

12 ounces shelled, deveined medium-size raw shrimp (about 36 per lb.)

6 green onions, thinly sliced

6 cups finely shredded papa cabbage

1 In a large bowl, mix beans, pork, bell pepper, mushrooms, garlic, and ginger. In a small bowl, stir together broth, oyster sauce, and cornstarch; set aside.

2 Heat oil in a wide nonstick frying pan over high heat. Add shrimp and cook, stirring, until just opaque in center; cut to test (2 to 3 minutes). Remove from pan and set aside.

3 Add pork-mushroom mixture to pan and cook, stirring often, until meat is lightly browned (about 5 minutes). Add broth mixture and bring to a boil, stirring. Mix in shrimp and onions. Arrange cabbage on a platter; tap with shrimp mixture.

makes 6 servings

per serving: 175 calories, 20 g protein, 12 g carbohydrates, 6 g total fat, 99 mg cholesterol, 576 mg sodium

steamed clams with garlic

preparation time: about 50 minutes

1 teaspoon butter or margarine

2 medium-size onions, thinly sliced

1/4 to 1/2 cup chopped garlic

1/4 cup water

2 medium-size tomatoes, chopped

1 teaspoon *each* paprika, dry thyme, and black pepper

1/8 teaspoon ground red pepper (cayenne)

1 cup dry white wine

36 small hard-shell clams in shell, scrubbed

1 Melt butter in a 5- to 6-quart pan over medium heat. Add onions, garlic, and water. Cook, stirring often, until liquid has evaporated and onions are soft (about 10 minutes).

2 Stir in tomatoes, paprika, thyme, black pepper, and red pepper; cook, uncovered, for 5 minutes. Add wine and bring to a boil over high heat.

3 Add clams; reduce heat, cover, and boil gently until shells pop open (about 10 minutes). Discard any unopened clams; then ladle clams and sauce into wide bowls.

makes 4 servings

per serving: 225 calories, 20 g protein, 21 g carbohydrates, 3 g total fat, 48 mg cholesterol, 102 mg sodium

cracked crab with onion

preparation time: about 25 minutes

1/3 cup dry sherry

1/3 cup water

1/4 cup oyster sauce

2 teaspoons cornstarch

14 green onions

1 tablespoon vegetable oil

3 tablespoons minced fresh ginger

3 cooked Dungeness crabs (about 6 lbs. *total*), cleaned and cracked

1 In a small bowl, stir together sherry, 1/3 cup water, oyster sauce, and cornstarch until blended; set aside. Cut onions into 2-inch lengths, keeping white and green parts separate.

2 Heat oil in a wide nonstick frying pan or wok over medium-high heat. Add ginger and white parts of onions; stir-fry until onions just begin to brown (about 2 minutes). Stir sherry mixture and pour into pan; stir until sauce boils and thickens slightly (about 1 minute). Add crab and green parts of onions; stir to coat with sauce. Reduce heat to low, cover, and cook, stirring occasionally, until crab is heated through (5 to 8 minutes).

makes 6 servings

per serving: 163 calories, 21 g protein, 8 g carbohydrates, 3 g total fat, 64 mg cholesterol, 805 mg sodium

grilled scallops with pear-ginger coulis

preparation time: about 35 minutes

4 teaspoons olive oil

1 small onion, chopped

2 tablespoons chopped fresh ginger

3 medium-size firm-ripe pears (1 1/4 to 1 1/2 lbs. total), peeled, cored, and diced

1/4 cup rice vinegar or white wine vinegar

1 pound sea scallops, rinsed and patted dry

1 Heat 1 tablespoon of the oil in a 2-quart pan over medium-high heat. Add onion and cook, stirring often, until soft but not browned (3 to 5 minutes). Add ginger; pears, and vinegar. Cook, stirring occasionally, until pears are tender when pierced (12 to 15 minutes). Transfer mixture to a food processor or blender; whirl until smoothly puréed. Return to pan and keep warm over lowest heat.

2 Meanwhile, cut scallops in half horizontally, if necessary, to make 1/2-inch-thick discs. Lightly mix scallops and remaining 1 teaspoon oil. Thread a fourth of the scallops on each of 4 metal skewers, piercing scallops horizontally (through diameter) so they lie flat.

3 Place skewers on a greased grill 4 to 6 inches above a solid bed of hot coals. Cook, turning once, until scallops are opaque in center; cut to test (5 to 7 minutes). Spoon the warm pear mixture onto 4 dinner plates; lay a skewer alongside.

makes 4 servings

per serving: 240 calories, 20 g protein, 28 g carbohydrates, 6 g total fat, 37 mg cholesterol, 184 mg sodium

pink peppercorn swordfish

preparation time: 30 minutes

¼ **cup whole pink peppercorns**

4 **swordfish or halibut steaks (***each* **about 1-inch thick and 5 to 6 oz.)**

8 **teaspoons honey**

4 **large butter lettuce leaves, rinsed and crisped**

2 **jars (about 6 oz.** *each***) marinated artichoke hearts, drained**

Lemon wedges

1 In a 1- to 1½-quart pan, combine peppercorns and about 2 cups water. Bring to a boil over high heat; then reduce heat and simmer until peppercorns are slightly softened (about 4 minutes). Drain well.

2 Rinse fish and pat dry. Arrange pieces well apart in a lightly oiled shallow 10- by 15-inch baking pan. Brush each piece with 2 teaspoons of the honey; then top equally with peppercorns, spreading them in a single layer.

3 Bake in a 400° oven until fish is just opaque but still moist in thickest part; cut to test (about 10 minutes).

4 Place one lettuce leaf on each of 4 individual plates; top lettuce with artichokes. With a wide spatula, lift fish from baking pan and arrange alongside lettuce. Season to taste with lemon.

makes 4 servings

per serving: 277 calories, 30 g protein, 21 g carbohydrates, 9 g total fat, 54 mg cholesterol, 361 mg sodium

snapper veracruz

preparation time: about 35 minutes

1 **teaspoon salad oil or olive oil**

1 **small green or red bell pepper, seeded and chopped**

1 **large onion, chopped**

3 **cloves garlic, minced or pressed (optional)**

2 **tablespoons water**

1 **small can (about 4 oz.) diced green chiles**

¼ **cup sliced pimiento-stuffed green olives**

3 **tablespoons lime juice**

1 **teaspoon ground cinnamon**

¼ **teaspoon white pepper**

1 **can (about 14 ½ oz.) stewed tomatoes**

4 **snapper or rockfish fillets (about 2 lbs. total)**

1 **tablespoon drained capers**

1 Heat oil in a wide nonstick frying pan over medium-high heat. Add bell pepper, onion, garlic (if desired), and water; cook, stirring often, until vegetables are tender-crisp to bite (3 to 5 minutes).

2 Add chiles, olives, lime juice, cinnamon, and white pepper; cook for 1 more minute. Add tomatoes to pan (break tomatoes up with a spoon, if needed); then bring mixture to a boil. Boil, stirring often, until sauce is slightly thickened (about 5 minutes).

3 Rinse fish, pat dry, and arrange in a lightly greased 9- by 13-inch baking dish. Pour sauce over fish. Bake in a 350° oven until fish is just opaque but still moist in thickest part; cut to test (10 to 15 minutes).

4 With a slotted spoon, transfer fish and sauce to four dinner plates. Sprinkle with capers.

makes 4 servings

per serving: 310 calories, 49 g protein, 16 g carbohydrates, 16 g total fat, 84 mg cholesterol, 842 mg sodium

artichokes with shrimp & cilantro salsa

preparation time: about 1 hour

$^1/_2$ **cup seasoned rise vinegar; or** $^1/_2$ **cup distilled white vinegar plus 1 tablespoon sugar**

1 tablespoon mustard seeds

1 teaspoon whole black peppercorns

4 thin quarter-size slices fresh ginger

3 large artichokes, *each* **4 to 4** $^1/_2$ **inches in diameter**

12 ounces tiny cooked shrimp

$^1/_3$ **cup minced pickled scallions**

$^1/_4$ **cup minced cilantro**

$^1/_4$ **cup minced fresh mint or 1 tablespoon dried mint**

2 tablespoons reduced-sodium soy sauce

$^1/_4$ **to** $^1/_2$ **teaspoon chili oil**

Mint or cilantro sprigs

1 In a 6- to 8-quart pan, combine $^1/_4$ cup of the vinegar, mustard seeds, peppercorns, ginger, and 4 quarts water. Cover and bring to a boil over high heat.

2 Meanwhile, remove coarse outer leaves from artichokes and trim stems flush with bases. Cut off top third of each artichoke. Trim thorny tips from remaining leaves. Immerse artichokes in cold water to clean and shake to drain.

3 Lower artichokes into boiling vinegar-water mixture. Then reduce heat and simmer, covered, until artichoke bottoms are tender when pierced (about 35 minutes). Drain, reserving cooking liquid. Let artichokes stand until they are cool enough to handle.

4 Pour artichoke-cooking liquid through a fine strainer set over a bowl; discard ginger and reserve mustard seeds and peppercorns. Place shrimp in strainer. Rinse shrimp with cool water; then drain well, place in a bowl, and mix with reserved seasoning, remaining $^1/_4$ cup vinegar, scallions, minced cilantro, minced mint, soy sauce, and chili oil.

5 Cut each artichoke in half lengthwise. Remove inner leaves and scoop out fuzzy centers. Set each artichoke half on a plate. Spoon shrimp mixture into artichokes; garnish with mint sprigs.

makes 6 servings

per serving: 122 calories, 15 g protein, 13 g carbohydrates, 2 g total fat, 111 mg cholesterol, 911 mg sodium

mussels provencal

preparation time: about 45 minutes

3 $^1/_2$ **pounds mussels in shell, scrubbed**

1 tablespoon olive oil

3 cloves garlic, minced or pressed

1 large onion, chopped

1 cup chopped celery

1 large can (about 28 oz.) tomatoes

1 cup dry white wine or low-sodium chicken broth

$^1/_2$ **cup minced parsley**

$^1/_2$ **teaspoon pepper**

1 Pull beard from each mussel with a swift tug. Set mussels aside.

2 Heat oil in a 6- to 8-quart pan over medium-high heat. Add garlic, onion, and celery. Cook, stirring often, until vegetables are soft (about 7 minutes). Cut up tomatoes; then add tomatoes and their liquid to pan. Bring to a boil; then reduce heat, cover, and simmer for 15 minutes. Add wine, parsley, and pepper. Cover and bring to a boil.

3 Add mussels, cover, and cook until shells pop open (7 to 9 minutes). Discard any unopened mussels. With a slotted spoon, transfer mussels to wide, shallow bowls; ladle sauce over each serving.

makes 4 to 6 servings

per serving: 194 calories, 13 g protein, 17 g carbohydrates, 5 g total fat, 26 mg cholesterol, 551 mg sodium

tuna steaks with roasted peppers & tuna sauce

preparation time: about 55 minutes

5 ½ cups fat-free reduced-sodium chicken broth

½ cup finely chopped dried apricots

1 pound dried orzo or other tiny rice-shaped pasta

1 can (about 6 ⅛ oz.) tuna packed in water

1 large egg yolk or 1 tablespoon pasteurized
   egg substitute

¼ teaspoon grated lemon peel

2 tablespoons lemon juice

4 teaspoons balsamic vinegar

1 teaspoon honey

½ teaspoon Dijon mustard

½ teaspoon salt (or to taste)

¼ cup *each* olive oil and salad oil

3 canned anchovy fillets, drained

1 cup nonfat sour cream

2 tablespoons fennel seeds

1 tablespoon whole white peppercorns

1 ½ teaspoons coriander seeds

2 large egg whites

4 tuna (ahi) steaks (*each* about 1 inch thick
   and about 7 oz.)

1 teaspoon olive oil

½ cup bottled clam juice

1 jar roasted red peppers (about 12 oz.),
   drained and patted dry

3 tablespoons drained capers (or to taste)

Lemon slices

Italian or regular parsley sprigs

1 In a 4- to 5-quart pan, bring broth and apricots to a boil over high heat; stir in orzo. Reduce heat, cover, and simmer, stirring occasionally, until almost all liquid has been absorbed (about 20 minutes); as liquid cooks down, stir more often and watch closely to prevent scorching. Remove from heat and keep warm.

2 While orzo is cooking, drain can of tuna, reserving ¼ cup of the liquid from can. Set tuna and liquid aside.

3 In a food processor or blender, combine egg yolk, lemon peel, lemon juice, vinegar, honey, mustard, and ¼ teaspoon of the salt (or to taste); whirl until blended. With motor running, slowly pour in the ¼ cup olive oil and salad oil in a thin, steady stream. Whirl until well blended. Add canned tuna, reserved tuna liquid, 1 tablespoon water, and anchovies; whirl until smoothly pureed. With a spoon or whisk, stir in sour cream; set aside.

4 Wash and dry food processor or blender; then combine fennel seeds, peppercorns, coriander seeds, and remaining ¼ teaspoon salt in processor or blender. Whirl until finely ground; transfer to a wide, shallow bowl. In another wide, shallow bowl, beat egg whites to blend. Rinse tuna steaks and pat dry; then cut each in half. Dip pieces, one at a time, in egg whites; drain briefly, then coat on both sides with seed mixture. Pat any remaining seed mixture on fish.

5 Heat the 1 teaspoon olive oil in a wide nonstick frying pan over medium-high heat. Add fish and cook, turning once, until browned on both sides. Add clam juice. Reduce heat and cook until fish is still pale pink in center; cut to test (about 5 minutes).

6 Spoon pasta onto a rimmed platter; fluff with a fork. With a slotted spoon, lift fish from pan and place atop pasta; arrange red peppers decoratively around fish. Top with half the tuna sauce and sprinkle with capers. Garnish with lemon slices and parsley sprigs. Offer remaining tuna sauce to add to taste.

makes 8 servings

per serving: 562 calories, 39 g protein, 60 g carbohydrates, 18 g total fat, 77 mg cholesterol, 1,201 mg sodium

lingcod with citrus almond couscous

preparation time: about 50 minutes

5 or 6 small oranges (about 2¹/₂ lbs. total)

1 large pink grapefruit

1 medium-size lemon

1 medium-size lime

¹/₄ cup slivered almonds

2 tablespoons olive oil

¹/₄ cup chopped onion

¹/₂ teaspoon almond extract

10 ounces dried couscous

2 pounds skinless, boneless lingcod or striped bass fillets (*each* about 1 inch thick)

¹/₂ cup rice vinegar

2 tablespoons minced shallots

1 Shred enough peel from oranges and grapefruit to make 1¹/₂ tablespoons each. Shred enough peel from lemon and lime to make 1 teaspoon each. Combine peels in a small bowl; set aside. Remove remaining peel and white membrane from grapefruit, lemon, lime, and 2 of the oranges. Over a bowl, cut between membranes to release segments. In a separate bowl, juice remaining oranges to make 1¹/₂ cups. Set bowls aside.

2 Toast almonds in a 2- to 3-quart pan over medium heat, shaking pan often, until golden (about 4 minutes). Remove from pan and set aside. Place 2 teaspoons of the oil in pan and heat over medium-high heat. Add onion and cook, stirring often, until soft (about 3 minutes). Add 1 cup of the orange juice, 1¹/₂ cups water, and almond extract. Bring to a boil. Stir in pasta; cover, remove from heat, and let stand until liquid is absorbed (about 5 minutes). Keep warm, fluffing occasionally with a fork.

3 Cut fish into 6 portions and brush with 2 teaspoons more oil. Place on rack of a 12- by 14-inch broiler pan. Broil about 4 inches below heat, turning once, just until opaque but still moist in thickest part; cut to test (about 10 minutes).

4 Combine remaining ¹/₂ cup orange juice and 2 teaspoons oil, vinegar, shallots, fruit, and accumulated juices in a wide nonstick frying pan. Cook over medium heat, stirring often, until warm (about 2 minutes).

5 Arrange pasta and fish on individual plates. Top fish with fruit sauce and sprinkle almonds over pasta. Garnish with citrus peel.

makes 6 servings

per serving: 455 calories, 35 g protein, 57 g carbohydrates, 10 g total fat, 79 mg cholesterol, 97 mg sodium

garlic shrimp with rice

preparation time: about 25 minutes

2 teaspoons butter or margarine

2 teaspoons olive oil

3 cloves garlic, minced or pressed

1 pound large shrimp (about 25 per lb.), shelled and deveined

About 4 cups hot cooked rice

Lemon wedges

1 Melt butter in a wide nonstick frying pan over medium-high heat.

2 Add oil, garlic, 3 tablespoons water, and shrimp. Cook, stirring, until shrimp are just opaque but still moist in center; cut to test (3 to 4 minutes).

3 To serve, spoon rice onto a platter or 4 dinner plates; Spoon shrimp and pan juices over rice. Sprinkle with parsley. Season to taste with salt and pepper, then serve with lemon wedges.

makes 4 servings

per serving: 403 calories, 24 g proteins, 59 g carbohydrates, 6 g total fat, 145 mg cholesterol, 161 mg sodium

coriander-curry shrimp

preparation time: about 30 minutes

12 ounces to 1 pound dried vermicelli or spaghetti

**²/₃ cup pineapple-coconut juice
(or ²/₃ cup unsweetened pineapple juice plus
¼ cup sweetened shredded coconut)**

2 teaspoons cornstarch

1 teaspoon vegetable oil

1 large onion, thinly sliced

1 clove garlic, minced or pressed

1 tablespoon curry powder

1 tablespoon ground coriander

⅛ teaspoon ground red pepper (cayenne)

**1 ½ pounds large raw shrimp (31 to 35 per lb.),
shelled and deveined**

2 tablespoons finely chopped parsley

Lime wedges

Salt

1 In a 6- to 8-quart pan, cook vermicelli in about 4 quarts boiling water until just tender to bite (8 to 10 minutes); or cook according to package directions. Drain well, transfer to a warm rimmed platter, and keep warm.

2 While pasta is cooking, in a small bowl, stir together pineapple-coconut juice and cornstarch until blended; set aside. Heat oil in a wide nonstick frying pan or wok over medium-high heat. When oil is hot, add onion, garlic, and 2 tablespoons water. Stir-fry until liquid has evaporated and onion is soft and beginning to brown (about 5 minutes).

3 Add curry powder, coriander, and red pepper to pan; stir to blend. Immediately add shrimp and stir-fry for 2 minutes. Stir cornstarch mixture well; pour into pan. Stir until sauce is bubbly and shrimp are just opaque in center; cut to test (1 to 2 more minutes). Add parsley and mix gently but thoroughly. Spoon shrimp mixture over pasta; garnish with lime wedges. Season with salt.

makes 6 servings

per serving: 402 calories, 28 g protein, 60 g carbohydrates, 5 g total fat, 140 mg cholesterol, 152 mg sodium

whitefish with soft cornmeal

preparation time: about 30 minutes

4 ⅓ cups low-sodium chicken broth

1 cup yellow cornmeal or polenta

½ teaspoon cumin seeds

1 small can (about 4 oz.) diced green chiles

**1 pound skinless, boneless sea bass, orange roughy,
or sole fillets, divided into 4 equal pieces**

1 red bell pepper, seeded and minced

1 tablespoon cilantro leaves

1 In a 3- to 4-quart pan, stir together broth, cornmeal, and cumin seeds until smoothly blended. Bring to a boil over high heat, stirring often with a long-handled wooden spoon (mixture will spatter). Reduce heat and simmer gently, uncovered, stirring often, until cornmeal tastes creamy (about 20 minutes). Stir in chiles.

2 When cornmeal is almost done, rinse fish, pat dry, and arrange in a single layer in a 9- by 13-inch baking man. Bake in a 475°F oven until fish is just opaque but still moist in thickest part; cut to test (about 6 minutes).

3 To serve, spoon soft cornmeal equally onto 4 dinner plates. Top each serving with a piece of fish; sprinkle with bell pepper and cilantro. Season to taste with salt and serve with lemon slices.

makes 4 servings

per serving: 279 calories, 28 g protein, 32 g carbohydrates, 6 g total fat, 47 mg cholesterol, 377 mg sodium

shrimp & avocado tostados with papaya salsa

preparation time: about 45 minutes

CRISP TACO SHELLS:

4 corn tortillas (*each* about 6 inches in diameter)

Salt (optional)

PAPAYA SALSA:

1 medium-size firm-ripe papaya, peeled, seeded, and diced

1 small cucumber, peeled, seeded, and diced

1 tablespoon chopped fresh mint, or to taste

2 tablespoons lime juice

1 tablespoon honey

AVOCADO & SHRIMP TOPPING:

1 teaspoon grated lemon peel

2 tablespoons lemon juice

1 medium-size soft-ripe avocado

1 cup low-fat (2%) cottage cheese

2 or 3 cloves garlic, peeled

1/8 teaspoon salt

2 tablespoons finely chopped cilantro

1 small fresh jalapeño or serrano chile, seeded and finely chopped

1 tablespoon thinly sliced green onion

1 large tomato, finely chopped and drained well

4 cups shredded lettuce

6 ounces small cooked shrimp

1 To prepare taco shells, dip tortillas, one at a time, in hot water; drain briefly. Season to taste with salt, if desired. Arrange tortillas, not overlapping, in a single layer on a large baking sheet. Bake in a 500° oven for 6 minutes. With a metal spatula, turn tortillas over; continue to bake until crisp and tinged with brown, about 2 more minutes. (At this point, you may let cool completely; then store airtight at room temperature until next day.)

2 To prepare papaya salsa, in a medium-size bowl, stir together papaya, cucumber, mint, lime juice, and honey; set aside. (At this point, you may cover and refrigerate for up to 4 hours.)

3 To prepare topping, place lemon peel and lemon juice in a blender or food processor. Halve and pit avocado; scoop flesh from peel into blender. Add cottage cheese, garlic, and salt. Whirl until smoothly pureed. With a spoon, gently stir in cilantro, chile, onion, and half the tomato.

4 To serve, place one taco shell an each of 4 individual plates. Evenly top taco shells with avocado mixture; then top shells equally with lettuce, shrimp, and remaining chopped tomato. Offer papaya salsa on the side to add to taste.

makes 4 servings

per serving: 308 calories, 21 g protein, 37 g carbohydrates, 10 g total fat, 87 mg cholesterol, 387 mg sodium

Always buy the freshest fish you can find. The flesh of whole fish should spring back when gently pressed, and the eyes should be clear and full, not sunken. Fillets and steaks should look cleanly cut and feel firm and moist. Avoid any fish with a strong, unpleasant odor; truly fresh seafood has a mild and delicate aroma. Uncooked fish doesn't keep well. To avoid waste, buy only as much as you need, and cook it as soon as possible after purchase—preferably on the same day, within 2 days at the most. To store fish, discard the market wrapping; rinse the fish under cold running water, place it in a container, and cover with wet paper towels. Store in the coldest part of your refrigerator.

shrimp custard

preparation time: about 45 minutes

8 ounces small cooked shrimp

1 cup nonfat milk

1 large egg

2 large egg whites

4 teaspoons dry sherry

2 teaspoons finely chopped fresh ginger

2 teaspoons reduced-sodium soy sauce

1 clove garlic, minced or pressed

1/8 teaspoon Asian sesame oil

1/8 teaspoon ground white pepper

1 teaspoon sesame seeds

1 Divide half the shrimp evenly among four 3/4-cup custard cups or ovenproof bowls; cover and refrigerate remaining shrimp. Set custard cups in a large baking pan at least 2 inches deep.

2 In a medium-size bowl, combine milk, egg, egg whites, sherry, ginger, soy sauce, garlic, oil, and white pepper; beat lightly just until blended. Pour egg mixture evenly over shrimp in custard cups.

3 Set pan on center rack of a 325° oven. Pour boiling water into pan around cups up to level of custard. Bake until custard jiggles only slightly in center when cups are gently shaken (about 25 minutes). Lift cups from pan. Let stand for about 5 minutes before serving. (At this point, you may let cool; then cover and refrigerate until next day and serve cold.)

4 Meanwhile, toast sesame seeds in a small frying pan over medium heat, stirring often, until golden (about 3 minutes). Remove from pan and set aside. Just before serving, top custards with remaining shrimp; then sprinkle with sesame seeds.

makes 4 servings

per serving: 120 calories, 18 g protein, 4 g carbohydrates, 2 g total fat, 165 mg cholesterol, 303 mg sodium

sole florentine

preparation time: about 40 minutes

6 thin sole fillets (about 3 oz. each)

2 pounds spinach, stems removed, leaves rinsed and coarsely chopped

1/4 teaspoon ground nutmeg

2 tablespoons each grated lemon peel and chopped parsley

1/4 cup each low-sodium chicken broth and dry white wine

1 small dry bay leaf

4 whole black peppercorns

1 Rinse fish and pat dry. Trim each fillet to make a 3- by 8-inch rectangle (reserve trimmings); set aside. Finely chop trimmings; place in a bowl and add 1½ cups of the spinach, nutmeg, lemon peel, and parsley. Mix well.

2 Spread spinach mixture evenly over fillets. Gently roll up fillets and secure with wooden picks.

3 Place fish rolls, seam side down, in a 9-inch baking dish. Pour broth and wine around fish; add bay leaf and peppercorns. Cover and bake in a 400° oven for 10 minutes.

4 Place remaining spinach in another 9-inch baking dish. With a slotted spoon, lift fish rolls from first baking dish; arrange atop spinach (discard poaching liquid). Cover and bake until fish is just opaque but still moist in thickest part; cut to test (about 7 minutes). Remove and discard picks from fish.

makes 6 servings

per serving: 108 calories, 79 g protein, 4 g carbohydrates, 7 g total fat, 41 mg cholesterol, 157 mg sodium

scallop & pea pod stir-fry with papaya

preparation time: about 25 minutes

2 teaspoons cornstarch

1 tablespoon honey

1 tablespoon lemon juice

1/2 teaspoon ground ginger

1/2 teaspoon Chinese five-spice (or 1/8 teaspoon *each* anise seeds, ground allspice, ground cinnamon, and ground cloves)

2 medium-size papayas

1 pound sea scallops

1 tablespoon butter or margarine

1 1/2 cups fresh Chinese pea pods (also called snow or sugar peas or sugar snap peas, ends and strings removed; or 1 package (about 6 oz.) frozen Chinese pea pods, thawed and drained

1 To prepare ginger sauce, in a small bowl, stir together cornstarch and 1/4 cup water until blended. Stir in honey, lemon juice, ginger, and five-spice; set aside.

2 Cut unpeeled papayas lengthwise into halves; remove and discard seeds. Set papaya halves, cut side up, on a platter; cover and set aside.

3 Rinse scallops and pat dry; cut into bite-size pieces, if desired. Melt butter in a wide nonstick frying pan or wok over medium-high heat. Add scallops and fresh pea pods (if using frozen pea pods, add later, as directed below). Stir-fry until scallops are just opaque in center; cut to test (3 to 4 minutes).

4 Stir ginger sauce well, then pour into pan. Stir in frozen pea pods, if using. Cook, stirring, until sauce boils and thickens slightly (1 to 2 minutes). Spoon scallop mixture equally into papaya halves.

makes 4 servings

per serving: 220 calories, 21 g protein, 26 g carbohydrates, 4 g total fat, 45 mg cholesterol, 219 mg sodium

salt-grilled shrimp

preparation time: 35 minutes

1 1/2 pounds extra-jumbo raw shrimp (16 to 20 per lb.)

About 2 tablespoons sea salt or kosher salt

5 to 6 ounces Belgian endive, separated into leaves, rinse, and crisped

8 ounces small romaine lettuce leaves, rinsed and crisped

12 ounces tiny red and/or yellow cherry tomatoes

About 1/2 cup balsamic vinegar

1 Insert a wooden pick under back of each shrimp between shell segments; gently pull up to remove vein. If vein breaks, repeat in another place. Rinse and drain deveined shrimp; then roll in salt to coat lightly.

2 Mix endive, lettuce, any tomatoes in a large bowl.

3 Place shrimp on a lightly greased grill 4 to 6 inches above a solid bed of hot coals. Cook, turning once, until shrimp are just opaque in center; cut to test (about 8 minutes). Meanwhile, divide salad among individual plates.

4 To serve, arrange shrimp atop salsas. To eat, shell shrimp any season to taste with vinegar, oil, and pepper.

makes 4 servings

per serving: 213 calories, 30 g protein, 9 g carbohydrates, 6 g total fat, 210 mg cholesterol, 1,326 mg sodium

rockfish & tiny potatoes with mustard-honey glaze

preparation time: about 50 minutes

1 tablespoon olive or salad oil

16 very small thin-skinned potatoes, scrubbed

¼ cup Dijon mustard

2 tablespoons honey

4 rockfish fillets (about 5 oz. *each*)

Salt and pepper

1 Pour oil into a 10- by 15-inch rimmed baking pan. Add potatoes and turn to coat with oil. Bake in a 425° oven until potatoes are just tender when pierced (about 25 minutes).

2 Meanwhile, in a small bowl, stir together mustard and honey. Rinse fish, pat dry, and brush with about half the mustard mixture.

3 When potatoes are tender, push them to one end of pan and brush with remaining mustard mixture. Place fish in pan in a single layer. Bake until fish is just opaque but still moist in thickest part; cut to test (8 to 10 minutes).

4 To serve, transfer fish and potatoes to 4 individual plates. Stir pan juices and season to taste with salt and pepper; pour into a small bowl. Serve pan juices with fish and potatoes.

makes 4 servings

per serving: 366 calories, 30 g protein, 45 g carbohydrates, 7 g total fat 50 mg cholesterol, 550 mg sodium

Though appetites vary, you'll still find it helpful to use the following suggested amounts per person when shopping for fish or shellfish:

Fish, fillets or steaks, ⅓ to ½ pound; hole or cleaned fish, ½ to 1 pound.
Clams, shucked, about ¼ pound; in the shell, about 1 ½ pounds.
Mussels in the shell, about 1 pound.
Lobster or crab, whole or live, 1 to 2 pounds; cooked crabmeat, about ¼ pound.
Oysters, shucked, 4 or 5 ounces, in the shell, 6 to 9 oysters.
Scallops, ¼ to ½ pound.
Shrimp, shelled, about ¼ pound; unshelled, ¼ to ½ pound.

porcini-crusted salmon

preparation time: 35 minutes

1/4 ounce dried porcini mushrooms

2 tablespoons fine dry bread crumbs

1/4 teaspoon salt

5 ounces dried farfalle (pasta bow ties)

5 ounces asparagus, tough ends snapped off,
    spears cut diagonally into thin slices

1 to 1 1/4 pounds boneless, skinless salmon fillet
    (1 inch thick), cut into 4 equal pieces

2 tablespoons olive oil

1 In a food processor or blender, whirl mushrooms to make a coarse powder. Add bread crumbs and salt; whirl to mix, then pour into a wide, shallow bowl. Set aside.

2 In a 5- to 6-quart pan, bring about 3 quarts water to a boil over medium-high heat. Stir in pasta and cook for 5 minutes; then add asparagus and cook, stirring occasionally, until pasta and asparagus are just tender to bite (3 to 5 more minutes).

3 While pasta is cooking, rinse fish and pat dry; then turn fish in mushroom mixture, pressing to coat well all over. Lay fish pieces, flatter side down and well apart, in a shallow 10- by 15-inch baking pan. Pat any remaining mushroom mixture on fish; drizzle evenly with oil. Bake in a 400° oven until fish is just opaque but still moist in thickest part; cut to test (about 10 minutes).

4 When pasta mixture is done, drain it well and divide among 4 shallow individual bowls; keep warm. With a wide spatula, lift fish from baking pan; set in bowls atop pasta. Drizzle pan juices over pasta and fish.

makes 4 servings

per serving: 483 calories, 35 g protein, 48 g carbohydrates, 16 g total fat, 71 mg cholesterol, 226 mg sodium

broiled fish dijon

preparation time: about 15 minutes

6 swordfish steaks, cut about 1 inch thick
    (5 to 6 oz. *each*)

1 1/2 pounds small zucchini, cut lengthwise
    into halves

1/4 cup lemon juice

2 tablespoons Dijon mustard

1 clove garlic, minced or pressed

Paprika

2 tablespoons drained capers

1 Rinse fish and pat dry. Then arrange fish and zucchini (cut side up) in a single layer on an oiled rack in a large broiler pan. Drizzle with lemon juice. Broil 4 to 6 inches below heat for 5 minutes. Meanwhile, in a small bowl, stir together mustard and garlic.

2 Turn fish over; spread with mustard mixture. Then continue to broil until zucchini is lightly browned and fish is just opaque but still moist in thickest part; cut to test (about 5 more minutes). Sprinkle fish and zucchini with paprika and capers.

makes 6 servings

per serving: 193 calories, 29 g protein, 5 g carbohydrates, 6 g total fat, 54 mg cholesterol, 354 mg sodium

cool salmon with radish tartar

preparation time: about 55 minutes

1 pound slender green beans, ends removed

4 salmon steaks (6 to 8 oz. *each*)

12 small red thin-skinned potatoes, scrubbed

Butter lettuce leaves, rinsed and crisped

1 pound (about 3 cups) cherry tomatoes

Radish Tartar Sauce (recipe below)

Lemon wedges (optional)

1 In a 5- to 6-quart pan, cook beans, uncovered, in about 3 quarts boiling water just until tender-crisp to bite (2 to 3 minutes). Lift out with a slotted spoon, immerse in cold water until cool, and drain. Set aside.

2 Return water in pan to a boil. Rinse fish and add to boiling water. Then cover pan tightly, remove from heat, and let stand until fish is just opaque but still moist in thickest part; cut to test (about 12 minutes). Lift out, immerse in cold water until cool, and drain. Pat dry, then set aside.

3 Return water in pan to a boil. Add unpeeled potatoes; reduce heat, partially cover pan, and boil gently until potatoes are tender when pierced (about 25 minutes). Drain, immerse in cold water until cool, and drain again. Set aside.

4 Line a platter with lettuce leaves; arrange fish atop lettuce. Arrange beans, potatoes, and tomatoes around fish. If made ahead, cover and refrigerate for up to 1 day.

5 To serve, prepare Radish Tartar Sauce. Garnish platter with lemon wedges, if desired; offer sauce with fish and vegetables.

makes 4 servings

per serving without Radish Tartar Sauce: 475 calories, 45 g protein, 43 g carbohydrates, 13 g total fat, 109 mg cholesterol, 117 mg sodium

radish tartar sauce

preparation time: about 20 minutes

3/4 cup plain nonfat or low-fat yogurt

2 tablespoons reduced-fat-sour cream

3/4 cup chopped radishes

1/3 cup thinly sliced green onions

2 tablespoons drained capers

1 tablespoon prepared horseradish

Salt

In a medium-size bowl, stir together yogurt, sour cream, radishes, onions, capers, and horseradish. Season to taste with salt. If made ahead, cover and refrigerate for up to 1 day. Stir before using. Serve with cold poached fish steaks or fillets.

makes about 1 3/4 cups

per tablespoon: 6 calories, 0.4 g protein, 0.8 g carbohydrates, 0.2 g total fat, 0.5 mg cholesterol, 22 mg sodium

fish & fennel stew

preparation time: about 1 hour

1 large head fennel

1 tablespoon olive oil

1 large onion, chopped

6 cloves garlic, minced

1 ¼ pounds pear-shaped (Roma-type) tomatoes, chopped

2 cups fat-free reduced sodium chicken broth

1 bottle (about 8 oz.) clam juice

½ cup dry white wine

¼ to ½ teaspoon ground red pepper (cayenne)

1 ½ pounds boneless, skinless firm-textured, light-fleshed fish, such as halibut, swordfish, or sea bass, cut into 1 ½-inch chunks

1 Trim stems from fennel, reserving feathery green leaves. Trim and discard any bruised areas from fennel. Finely chop leaves and set aside; thinly slice fennel head.

2 Heat oil in a 5- to 6-quart pan over medium heat. Add sliced fennel, onion, and garlic; cook; stirring often, until onion is sweet tasting and all vegetables are browned (about 20 minutes). Add water, ¼ cup at a time, if pan appears dry.

3 Add tomatoes, broth, clam juice, wine, and red pepper. Bring to a boil; then reduce heat, cover, and simmer for 10 minutes. Add fish, cover, and simmer until just opaque but still moist in thickest part; cut to test (about 5 minutes). Stir in fennel leaves.

makes 4 servings

per serving: 317 calories, 40 g protein, 16 g carbohydrates, 8 g total fat, 54 mg cholesterol, 628 mg sodium

salmon with vegetable crust

preparation time: about 45 minutes

Vegetable oil cooking spray

2 medium-size thin-skinned potatoes (about 12 oz. *total*), scrubbed and cut into ¼-inch- wide wedges

1 ounce Neufchatel cheese, at room temperature

⅛ teaspoon *each* salt and pepper

3 tablespoons lemon juice

¼ cup *each* grated carrot and chopped tomato

2 tablespoons thinly sliced green onion

1 tablespoon finely chopped parsley

2 salmon steaks, cut about 1 inch thick (about 6 oz. *each*)

1 Coat a 3- by 13-inch baking pan with cooking spray. Arrange potatoes in pan, leaving enough room for fish. Bake potatoes in a 400° oven for 20 minutes. Meanwhile, in a small bowl, mix cheese, salt, pepper, and 1 tablespoon of the lemon juice until smooth and fluffy. Stir in carrot, tomato, onion, and parsley.

2 Rinse fish, pat dry, and place in pan alongside potatoes; drizzle fish with remaining 2 tablespoons lemon juice. Mound cream cheese mixture over fish, spreading nearly to edges. Continue to bake until potatoes are tender when pierced and fish is just opaque but still moist in thickest part; cut to test (about 12 more minutes).

makes 2 servings

per serving: 409 calories, 35 g protein, 36 g carbohydrates, 14 g total fat, 93 mg cholesterol, 287 mg sodium

scallops & shells with lemon cream

preparation time: 35 minutes

2 ounces Neufchatel or cream cheese, at room temperature

2 teaspoons honey

1 teaspoon Dijon mustard

1/2 teaspoon grated lemon peel

1 pound sea scallops

8 ounces dried medium-size pasta shells

3/4 cup fat-free reduced-sodium chicken broth

1/4 cup finely chopped Italian or regular parsley

2 teaspoons dry white wine (or to taste)

1/4 cup grated Parmesan cheese

1 In a food processor or blender, whirl Neufchatel cheese, honey, mustard, and lemon peel until smooth; set aside. Rinse scallops and pat dry; cut into bite-size pieces, if desired. Set aside.

2 In a 4- to 5-quart pan, bring about 8 cups water to a boil over medium-high heat; stir in pasta and cook until just tender to bite (8 to 10 minutes); or cook pasta according to package directions. Drain well, transfer to a large serving bowl, and keep warm.

3 In a 3- to 4-quart pan, bring broth to a boil over high heat. Add scallops and cook until opaque in center; cut to test (1 to 2 minutes).

4 With a slotted spoon, transfer scallops to bowl with pasta; keep warm. Quickly pour scallop cooking liquid from pan into Neufchatel cheese mixture in food processor; whirl until smooth. With a spoon, stir in parsley and wine. Pour sauce over scallops and pasta; sprinkle with Parmesan cheese. Serve immediately.

makes 4 servings

per serving: 393 calories, 31 g protein, 49 g carbohydrates, 7 g total fat, 53 mg cholesterol, 509 mg sodium

Though prized for their special flavor, smoked fish and shellfish are too often reserved just for special-occasion buffets. Remember that smoked seafood can enliven any meal; offer it with lemon wedges and crackers or bread as an appetizer, or sliver it into quiches, egg dishes, or pasta sauces. For a salad, serve sliced or flaked smoked fish on lettuce, topped with toasted almonds and a mustard vinaigrette. With the exception of canned products, smoked seafood is perishable and must be refrigerated or frozen. Consume refrigerated varieties within a few days or purchase (or soon after opening the package); use frozen products within 6 months.

steamed trout with lettuce & peas

preparation time: about 25 minutes

3 tablespoons chopped fresh mint

1 tablespoon finely shredded lemon peel

1 clove garlic, minced or pressed

2 cups frozen tiny peas, thawed

3 cups shredded romaine lettuce

4 cleaned whole trout (about 8 oz. *each*)

8 to 12 lemon wedges

Mint sprigs

1 In a bowl, mix chopped mint, lemon peel, garlic, peas, and lettuce. Pat mixture gently into a neat mound in a heatproof, 1-inch-deep nonmetal dish that is at least ½ inch smaller in diameter than the pan you will use for steaming.

2 Rinse trout inside and out and pat dry; then arrange trout over lettuce mixture, cavity sides down and heads pointing in same direction (lean fish against each other). Arrange lemon wedges over top of fish.

3 Set dish on a rack in a pan above about 1 inch of boiling water. Cover and steam, keeping water at a steady boil, until fish is just opaque but still moist in thickest part; cut to test (about 15 minutes). If necessary, add more boiling water to pan to keep water level constant.

4 Using thick potholders, carefully lift dish from pan. Transfer trout to individual plates and spoon lettuce mixture alongside. Garnish with mint sprigs. Serve with lemon wedges.

makes 4 servings

per serving: 275 calories, 33 g protein, 15 g carbohydrates, 9 g total fat, 78 mg cholesterol, 201 mg sodium

oven-browned fish

preparation time: 20 to 30 minutes

Cheese-Crumb Coating (recipe follows)

1 to 1 ½ pounds fish steaks or fillets (½ to 1 inch thick)

3 tablespoons low-fat buttermilk

1 Prepare Cheese-Crumb Coating. Rinse fish; pat dry. Pour buttermilk into a wide bowl. Dip fish in buttermilk; then dip in coating to coat thickly on all sides.

2 Place fish pieces at least 1 inch apart in a foil-lined shallow baking pan. Bake in a 425° oven until fish is browned on outside and just opaque but still moist in thickest part; cut to test (10 to 20 minutes).

CHEESE-CRUMB COATING

On a square of wax paper, combine ¾ cup soft bread crumbs, 1 tablespoon grated Parmesan cheese, 1 teaspoon dry thyme; and ½ teaspoon paprika.

makes 4 servings

per serving (with halibut): 261 calories, 26 g protein, 5 g carbohydrates, 3 g total, fat, 38 mg cholesterol, 139 mg sodium

margarita shrimp

preparation time: about 25 minutes

¼ cup gold or white tequila

½ teaspoon grated lime peel

2 tablespoons *each* lime juice and water

2 tablespoons minced cilantro or parsley

1 tablespoon honey

⅛ teaspoon white pepper

1 pound large shrimp (about 25 per lb.),
   shelled and deveined

About 2 teaspoons orange-flavored liqueur,
   or to taste

2 large red onions

Salt

Cilantro sprigs

Lime wedges

1 In a nonmetal bowl, mix tequila, lime peel, lime juice, water, minced cilantro, honey, and white pepper.

2 Pour tequila mixture into a wide nonstick frying pan. Add shrimp and cook over medium-high heat, stirring, until shrimp are just opaque but still moist in center; cut to test (3 to 4 minutes). With a slotted spoon, transfer shrimp to a bowl and keep warm. Bring cooking liquid to a boil over high heat; boil until reduced to ⅓ cup. Remove pan from heat; stir in liqueur, if desired.

3 While cooking liquid is boiling, thinly slice onions. Arrange onion slices in a single layer on a rimmed platter. To serve, spoon shrimp and cooking liquid over onion slices. Season to taste with salt; garnish with cilantro sprigs and lime wedges.

makes 4 servings

per serving: 173 calories, 21 g protein, 19 g carbohydrates, 2 g total fat, 140 mg cholesterol, 153 mg sodium

fish & clams in black bean sauce

preparation time: about 20 minutes

1 pound rockfish fillets

1 ½ tablespoons fermented salted black beans,
   rinsed and drained

2 cloves garlic, minced or pressed

1 tablespoon reduced-sodium soy sauce

2 tablespoons dry sherry

3 green onions

3 thin slices fresh ginger

12 small hard-shell clams in shell, scrubbed

1 tablespoon salad oil

1 Rinse fish, pat dry, and place in a heatproof, 1-inch deep non-metal dish that is at least ½ inch smaller in diameter than the pan you will use for steaming.

2 In a small bowl, mash black beans with garlic; stir in soy sauce and sherry. Drizzle mixture over fish. Cut one of the onions into thirds; place cut onion and ginger on top of fish. Cut remaining 2 onions into 2-inch lengths; then cut lengths into thin shreds and set aside. Arrange clams around fish.

3 Set dish on a rack in a pan above about 1 inch of boiling water. Cover and steam, keeping water at a steady boil, until fish is just opaque but still moist in thickest part; cut to test (about 5 minutes). If fish is done before clams pop open, remove fish and continue to cook clams for a few more minutes, until shells pop open; then return fish to dish.

4 Using thick potholders, lift dish from pan. Remove and discard ginger and onion pieces, then sprinkle onion slivers over fish. Heat oil in a small pan until it ripples when pan is tilted; pour over fish (oil will sizzle). Before serving, discard any unopened clams.

makes 2 servings

per serving: 365 calories, 52 g protein, 7 g carbohydrates, 12 g total fat, 98 mg cholesterol, 799 mg sodium

couscous with berries & shrimp

preparation time: about 30 minutes

1 package (about 10 oz.) couscous

1 small cucumber

1 cup firmly packed fresh mint leaves

1/2 cup lemon juice

2 tablespoons olive oil

About 1/2 teaspoon honey (or to taste)

1 cup fresh blueberries or other fresh berries

Salt and pepper

4 to 8 large lettuce leaves, rinsed and crisped

6 to 8 ounces small cooked shrimp

Lemon wedges and mint sprigs

1 In a 2½- to 3-quart pan, bring 2 ¼ cups water to a boil over medium-high heat. Stir in couscous; cover, remove from heat, and let stand until liquid has been absorbed (about 5 minutes). Then transfer couscous to a large bowl and let stand until cool (about 10 minutes), fluffing often with a fork.

2 Meanwhile, peel, halve, and seed cucumber; thinly slice halves and set aside. Finely chop mint leaves, place in a small bowl, and mix in lemon juice, oil, and honey. Add cucumber and blueberries to couscous; then add mint dressing and mix gently but thoroughly. Season to taste with salt and pepper.

3 Line each of 4 individual plates with 1 or 2 lettuce leaves. Mound couscous mixture in center of each plate; top with shrimp. Garnish with lemon wedges and mint sprigs.

makes 4 servings

per serving: 419 calories, 21 g protein, 66 g carbohydrates, 8 g total fat, 97 mg cholesterol, 129 mg sodium

orange roughy with polenta

preparation time: about 30 minutes

1 cup polenta

4 1/3 cups low-sodium chicken broth

1/2 teaspoon cumin seeds

1 large can (about 7 oz.) diced green chiles

1 pound orange roughy fillets, cut into 4 equal pieces

1 medium-size red bell pepper, seeded and minced

1 tablespoon cilantro leaves

Salt

Lime wedges

1 Pour polenta into a 3- to 4-quart pan; stir in broth and cumin seeds. Bring to a boil over high heat, stirring often with a long-handled wooden spoon (mixture will spatter). Reduce heat and simmer gently, uncovered, stirring often, until polenta tastes creamy (about 20 minutes). Stir in chiles.

2 While polenta is simmering, rinse fish and pat dry; then arrange in a 9- by 13-inch baking pan. Bake in a 475° oven until fish is just opaque but still moist in thickest part; cut to test (about 6 minutes).

3 To serve, spoon polenta onto 4 individual plates. Top each serving with a piece of fish; sprinkle with bell pepper and cilantro. Season to taste with salt; serve with lime wedges.

makes 4 servings

per serving: 326 calories, 23 g protein, 34 g carbohydrates, 10 g total fat, 23 mg cholesterol, 434 mg sodium

mussels & millet in curry sauce

preparation time: about 1 hour

1 tablespoon salad oil

1 large onion, thinly sliced

1 tablespoon minced fresh ginger

1 teaspoon *each* mustard seeds and ground coriander

$1/2$ teaspoon *each* ground cumin and ground red pepper (cayenne)

$1/4$ teaspoon ground turmeric

3 cups low-sodium chicken broth

2 small tomatoes, chopped

1 cup millet, rinsed and drained

$1 1/2$ pounds mussels in shell, scrubbed

Salt and pepper

Plain nonfat yogurt

1 Heat oil in a 5- to 6-quart pan over medium-high heat. Add onion and ginger; cook, stirring often, until onion is soft (about 5 minutes).

2 Stir in mustard seeds, coriander, cumin, red pepper, and turmeric. Add broth and tomatoes; bring mixture to a boil.

3 Add millet to pan. Reduce heat, cover, and simmer for 15 minutes. Meanwhile, pull beard from each mussel with a swift tug.

4 Add mussels to pan; cover and simmer until millet is tender to bite and mussels pop open (7 to 9 minutes). Season to taste with salt and pepper. Discard any unopened mussels; then ladle mussels and millet into bowls. Offer yogurt to add to taste.

makes 3 servings

per serving: 435 calories, 20 g protein, 64 g carbohydrates, 11 g total fat, 79 mg cholesterol, 257 mg sodium

fish pot-au-feu

preparation time: about 45 minutes

5 cups low-sodium chicken broth

1 cup dry white wine

1 tablespoon chopped fresh tarragon leaves or $1/2$ teaspoon dry tarragon leaves

4 small red thin-skinned potatoes

8 small, slender carrots

4 medium-size leeks, roots and most of dark green tops trimmed

$1 1/2$ pounds skinless cod, rockfish, snapper, or orange roughy fillets, rinsed and patted dry

1 In a 5- to 6-quart pan, combine chicken broth, wine, and tarragon. Bring to a boil over high heat. Add potatoes and carrots and return to a boil; reduce heat, cover, and simmer for 10 minutes.

2 Meanwhile, split leeks lengthwise and rinse well. Add to pan, cover, and simmer until leeks are tender when pierced (about 10 minutes). Lift out leeks and keep warm.

3 Cut fish into 4 portions. Add to broth mixture, cover and simmer until vegetables are tender and fish looks just opaque but still moist in thickest part; cut to test (8 to 10 minutes). Carefully transfer fish, vegetables, and broth to a tureen; add leeks. Serve in wide soup bowls.

makes 4 servings

per serving: 324 calories, 37 g protein, 35 g carbohydrates, 4 g total fat, 73 mg cholesterol, 216 mg sodium

cajun scallops & brown rice

preparation time: about 55 minutes

4 1/2 cups low-sodium chicken broth

1 1/2 cups long-grain brown rice

1 1/2 pounds bay scallops

1 teaspoon paprika

1/2 teaspoon ground white pepper

1/4 teaspoon ground allspice

2 teaspoons salad oil

1 1/2 tablespoons cornstarch blended with 1/3 cup cold water

1/2 cup reduced-fat sour cream

Parsley sprigs

1 In a 3- to 4-quart pan, bring 3½ cups of the broth to a boil over high heat. Add rice; reduce heat, cover, and simmer until rice is tender to bite (about 45 minutes).

2 About 10 minutes before rice is done, rinse scallops and pat dry; then mix with paprika, white pepper, and allspice. Heat oil in a wide nonstick frying pan over high heat. Add scallops and cook, turning often with a wide spatula, until just opaque in center; cut to test (2 to 3 minutes). With a slotted spoon, transfer scallops to a bowl.

3 Bring pan juices to a boil over high heat; boil, uncovered, until reduced to ¼ cup. Add remaining 1 cup broth and return to a boil. Stir in cornstarch mixture; bring to a boil, stirring. Stir in sour cream and scallops. Serve over rice; garnish with parsley sprigs.

makes 6 servings

per serving: 350 calories, 26 g protein, 43 g carbohydrates, 8 g total fat, 44 mg cholesterol, 226 mg sodium

stir-fried scallops & asparagus

preparation time: about 30 minutes

8 ounces bay or sea scallops

1/2 cup unseasoned rice vinegar or white wine vinegar

2 tablespoons sugar

1 teaspoon *each* Asian sesame oil and reduced-sodium soy sauce

2 tablespoons salad oil

1 pound asparagus, tough ends removed, stalks cut into about 1/2-inch-thick slanting slices

3 tablespoons water

8 ounces dry vermicelli or spaghettini

1 clove garlic, minced or pressed

1 tablespoon minced fresh ginger

Lemon slices

1 Rinse scallops and pat dry. If using sea scallops, cut into ½-inch pieces. Set aside. In a small bowl, stir together vinegar, sugar, sesame oil, and soy sauce. Set aside.

2 Heat 1 tablespoon of the salad oil in a wok or wide frying pan over high heat. Add asparagus and stir to coat; then add the 3 tablespoons water. Cover and cook until asparagus is tender-crisp to bite (3 to 5 minutes). Lift asparagus from pan and keep warm. Set pan aside.

3 In a 5- to 6-quart pan, cook vermicelli in about 3 quarts boiling water until just tender to bite (8 to 10 minutes); or cook according to package directions. Drain well, pour into a large bowl, and keep warm.

4 Heat remaining 1 tablespoon salad oil in frying pan over high heat. Add garlic, ginger, and scallops. Cook, turning often with a wide spatula, until scallops are just opaque in center; cut to test (2 to 3 minutes).

5 Return asparagus to pan and add vinegar mixture; stir just until sugar is dissolved. Pour scallop mixture over pasta and mix gently. Garnish with lemon slices.

makes 4 servings

per serving: 375 calories, 19 g protein, 54 g carbohydrates, 9 g total fat, 19 mg cholesterol, 147 mg sodium

gingered chili shrimp

preparation time: about 45 minutes

1 cup long-grain white rice

1 tablespoon sugar

3 tablespoons catsup

1 tablespoon *each* cider vinegar and reduced-sodium soy sauce

1/2 to 1 teaspoon crushed red pepper flakes

1 tablespoon salad oil

1 pound large raw shrimp (31 to 35 per lb.), shelled (leave tails attached) and deveined

1 tablespoon minced fresh ginger

2 cloves garlic, minced or pressed

1/2 teaspoon Asian sesame oil

About 1/4 cup sliced green onions, or to taste

1 In a 3- to 4-quart pan, bring 2 cups water to a boil over high heat; stir in rice. Reduce heat, cover, and simmer until liquid has been absorbed and rice is tender to bite (about 20 minutes).

2 Meanwhile, in a small bowl, stir together sugar, catsup, vinegar, soy sauce, and red pepper flakes until sugar is dissolved; set aside.

3 Heat salad oil in a wide nonstick frying pan or wok over medium-high heat. When oil is hot, add shrimp. Stir-fry until just opaque in center; cut to test (3 to 4 minutes). Remove shrimp from pan with tongs or a slotted spoon; keep warm.

4 To pan, add ginger and garlic; stir-fry just until garlic is fragrant (about 30 seconds; do not scorch). Stir catsup mixture and pour into pan; bring to a boil, stirring. Remove pan from heat and add shrimp and sesame oil; mix gently but thoroughly.

5 Spoon rice onto a rimmed platter; spoon shrimp mixture over rice and sprinkle with onions.

makes 4 servings

per serving: 336 calories, 23 g protein, 46 g carbohydrates, 6 g total fat, 140 mg cholesterol, 423 mg sodium

fish with herbs

preparation time: about 40 minutes

2 pounds boneless, skinless striped bass or sole fillets

1/2 cup *each* dry white wine and low-sodium chicken broth

1/4 cup minced shallots

1 tablespoon chopped fresh tarragon, thyme, or sage

6 to 8 thin lemon slices

6 to 8 tarragon, thyme, or sage sprigs

2 teaspoons cornstarch blended with 1 tablespoon cold water

Salt and pepper

1 Rinse fish and pat dry. Then arrange fillets, overlapping slightly, in a 9- by 13-inch baking dish. Pour wine and broth over fish; sprinkle with shallots and chopped tarragon. Lay lemon slices and tarragon sprigs on fish. Bake in a 375° oven until fish is just opaque but still moist in thickest part; cut to test (about 15 minutes).

2 Keeping fish in dish, carefully spoon off pan juices into a small pan. Cover fish and keep warm. Bring pan juices to a boil over high heat; then boil, uncovered, until reduced to 3/4 cup (about 5 minutes). Stir in cornstarch mixture; bring to a boil, stirring. Season sauce to taste with salt and pepper, then pour over fish.

makes 6 servings

per serving: 178 calories, 27 g protein, 4 g carbohydrates, 4 g total fat, 121 mg cholesterol, 112 mg sodium

stuffed trout

preparation time: about 55 minutes

Toasted Bread Cubes (directions follow)

2 tablespoons finely chopped parsley

1/2 cup thinly sliced green onions (including tops)

1 medium-size red or green bell pepper, stemmed, seeded, and finely chopped

1/2 cup dry white wine or low-sodium chicken broth

1 tablespoon melted margarine

Salt and freshly ground pepper

6 boned and butterflied whole trout (about 8 oz. each), rinsed and patted dry

Nonstick cooking spray or salad oil

About 1/4 cup lemon juice

Parsley sprigs and lemon wedges (optional)

1 Prepare Toasted Bread Cubes. In a bowl, stir together bread cubes, chopped parsley, onions, bell pepper, wine, and margarine. Season to taste with salt and pepper. Lightly pack stuffing into cavities of fish; sew openings with heavy thread or close with wooden picks. (Wrap any extra stuffing in foil and bake in pan alongside fish.)

2 Lightly coat a 9- by 13-inch baking pan with cooking spray. Add fish and brush with lemon juice. Cover and bake in a 400° oven for 10 minutes. Uncover and continue baking until fish looks just opaque but still moist in thickest part; cut to test (about 10 more minutes).

3 Transfer fish to a platter and remove thread. Garnish with parsley sprigs and lemon, if desired.

TOASTED BREAD CUBES

Cut about 6 ounces French or Italian bread into 1/2-inch cubes (you should have about 4 cups). Spread in a single layer on a baking sheet and bake in a 400° oven until crisp (about 10 minutes).

makes 6 servings

per serving: 363 calories, 38 g protein, 18 g carbohydrates, 14 g total fat, 100 mg cholesterol, 279 mg sodium

dilled roughy in parchment

preparation time: about 35 minutes

1 tablespoon salad oil

3 tablespoons *each* white wine vinegar and chopped green onions (including tops)

1 teaspoon chopped fresh dill or 1/2 teaspoon dry dill weed

1 teaspoon shredded tangerine or orange peel

1 large can (about 1 lb.) mandarin oranges, drained

Nonstick cooking spray

4 orange roughy fillets (about 5 oz. *each*), rinsed and patted, dry

1 Mix oil, vinegar, onions, dill, tangerine peel, and oranges. Set aside.

2 Cut 4 pieces of parchment paper, each about 4 times wider and 6 inches longer than each fish fillet. Coat each sheet with cooking spray, starting 1 inch from long side and covering an area the size of a fish fillet. Place a fillet on sprayed area of each sheet; spoon orange mixture over each fillet.

3 Fold long edge of parchment closest to fish over fish; then roll over several times to wrap fish in parchment. With seam side down, double fold each end, pressing lightly to crease and tucking ends under packet.

4 Place packets, folded ends underneath, slightly apart on a baking sheet; spray packets lightly with cooking spray. Bake in a 500° oven until fish looks just opaque but still moist in thickest part; cut a tiny slit through parchment into fish to test (7 to 10 minutes). Slash packets open and pull back parchment to reveal fish.

makes 4 servings

per serving: 283 calories, 21 g protein, 19 g carbohydrates, 14 g total fat, 28 mg cholesterol, 97 mg sodium

baked fish & chips

preparation time: about 1 hour

1 1/2 cups yellow cornmeal

2 teaspoons sugar

1 teaspoon pepper

1/2 teaspoon salt

3 large egg whites

3 large potatoes, scrubbed

2 large zucchini

3 tablespoons salad oil

1 to 1 1/2 pounds firm-textured white-fleshed fish fillets such as rockfish or orange roughy, cut into 4 equal pieces

Malt or cider vinegar

Tartar sauce (optional)

1 In a shallow dish, mix cornmeal, sugar, pepper, and salt. In another shallow dish, lightly beat egg whites until slightly frothy.

2 Cut each potato lengthwise into 8 wedges; cut each zucchini lengthwise into 6 slices. Dip potato wedges and zucchini slices, one piece at a time, in egg whites; then roll in cornmeal mixture. Set vegetables aside, keeping potatoes and zucchini separate and arranging them in a single layer.

3 Rub 1 tablespoon of the oil over bottom of each of two 10-by 15-inch rimmed baking pans. Place pans in a 450° oven for 3 minutes. Lay potato and zucchini pieces in a single layer in separate pans, placing pieces slightly apart. Bake vegetables, turning them with a wide spatula after 15 minutes, until crust on zucchini is crisp (about 25 minutes) and potatoes are tender when pierced (about 40 minutes).

4 Meanwhile, rinse fish and pat dry. Dip fish in egg whites, then turn in cornmeal mixture to coat.

5 When zucchini is done, transfer it to a platter and keep warm. Then add remaining 1 tablespoon oil to pan; place fish pieces slightly apart in pan. Bake until crusty and golden on bottom (about 4 minutes). Turn fish over and continue to bake until golden on other side and opaque but still moist in thickest part; cut to test (4 to 6 more minutes). If fish is done before potatoes, transfer to platter with zucchini and keep warm.

6 Serve fish and vegetables with vinegar and tartar sauce (if desired) to add to taste.

makes 4 servings

per serving: 576 calories, 39 g protein, 74 g carbohydrates, 14 g total fat, 50 mg cholesterol, 417 mg sodium

citrus-horseradish cream

preparation time: about 5 minutes

1 cup nonfat sour cream

3 tablespoons orange marmalade

2 teaspoons prepared horseradish

About 1 teaspoon grated orange peel

Honey

Ground white pepper

In a small bowl, stir together sour cream, marmalade, horseradish, and 1 teaspoon of the orange peel until smoothly blended. Season to taste with honey and white pepper. If made ahead, cover and refrigerate until next day; stir before serving. Garnish with orange peel. Serve with salmon or a white-fleshed fish.

makes about 1 3/4 cups

per tablespoon: 16 calories, 0.8 g protein, 3 g carbohydrates, 0 g total fat, 0 mg cholesterol, 10 mg sodium

oven-poached lingcod

preparation time: about 45 minutes

2 medium-size onions, sliced

12 whole black peppercorns

4 whole allspice

1/3 cup lemon juice

2 dry bay leaves

1 cup dry white wine

8 cups water

3 large leeks

1 tablespoon olive oil

2 pounds lingcod fillets (about 1 inch thick)

Salt and pepper (optional)

1 In a 4- to 5-quart pan, combine onions, peppercorns, allspice, lemon juice, bay leaves, wine, and water. Bring to a boil over high heat; then reduce heat, cover, and simmer for 20 minutes. Pour liquid through a fine strainer; discard residue and return liquid to pan.

2 While poaching liquid is simmering, trim ends and all but 3 inches of green tops from leeks; remove tough outer leaves. Split leeks lengthwise; rinse well, then thinly slice crosswise. Heat oil in a wide frying pan over medium heat; add leeks and cook, stirring occasionally, until soft (about 10 minutes). Remove from heat.

3 Rinse fish, pat dry, and place in a single layer in an oiled 9- by 13-inch baking dish. Bring strained poaching liquid to a boil and pour over fish (liquid should just cover fish; if necessary, add equal parts of hot water and wine to cover fish). Cover and bake in a 425° oven until fish is just opaque but still moist in thickest part; cut to test (about 6 minutes).

4 Lift fish from baking dish, drain well, place in a serving dish, and keep warm. Measure ½ cup of the poaching liquid and add to leeks. Bring to a boil, stirring; season to taste with salt and pepper, if desired. Pour sauce over fish.

makes 6 servings

per serving: 236 calories, 28 g protein, 15 g carbohydrates, 4 g total fat, 79 mg cholesterol, 708 mg sodium

clam paella for two

preparation time: about 45 minutes

1 tablespoon olive oil

1 clove garlic, minced or pressed

1/4 teaspoon ground turmeric

2/3 cup long-grain white rice

2 tablespoons finely chopped parsley

8 ounces cherry tomatoes, cut into halves

2/3 cup dry white wine

3/4 cup bottled clam juice or low-sodium chicken broth

24 small hard-shell clams in shell, scrubbed

1 Heat oil in a wide frying pan over medium heat. Add garlic, turmeric, and rice. Cook, stirring often, until rice begins to look opaque (about 3 minutes). Stir in parsley, tomatoes, wine, and clam juice. Brig to a boil; then reduce heat, cover, and simmer for 15 minutes.

2 Arrange clams over rice. Cover and continue to cook until clams pop open and rice is tender to bite (8 to 10 more minutes). Discard any unopened clams; then spoon clams and rice into bowls.

makes 2 servings

per serving: 452 calories, 29 g protein, 61 g carbohydrates, 9 g total fat, 61 mg cholesterol, 313 mg sodium

shrimp fajitas

preparation time: about 55 minutes

1 pound medium-size shrimp (about 35 *total*), shelled and deveined

1 cup lightly packed chopped cilantro

1 clove garlic, minced or pressed

1/3 cup lime juice

4 to 6 flour tortillas

1 tablespoon salad oil

2 large green bell peppers, stemmed, seeded, and thinly sliced

1 large onion, thinly sliced

1/2 cup plain nonfat yogurt

Bottled green tomatillo salsa

1 Stir together shrimp, cilantro, garlic, and lime juice. Let stand at room temperature for 20 minutes.

2 Meanwhile, wrap tortillas in foil and place in a 350° oven until hot (about 15 minutes).

3 Heat oil in a wide nonstick frying pan over medium-high heat. Add bell peppers and onion. Cook, stirring occasionally, until limp (about 10 minutes). Remove vegetables and keep warm. Add shrimp mixture to pan, increase heat to high, and cook, stirring often, until shrimp are opaque in center; cut to test (about 3 minutes). Return vegetables to pan, stirring to mix with shrimp.

4 Spoon shrimp mixture into tortillas, top with yogurt, and roll up. Offer with salsa.

makes 4 to 6 servings

per serving: 220 calories, 17 g protein, 28 g carbohydrates, 4 g total fat, 94 mg cholesterol, 285 mg sodium

shellfish couscous

preparation time: about 45 minutes

3 slices bacon, chopped

3/4 pound large shrimp (about 18 *total*), shelled and deveined

3/4 pound bay scallops, rinsed and patted dry

1 cup dry vermouth

2 1/2 cups low-sodium chicken broth

1/2 cup orange juice

2 cups couscous

1/4 cup dried tomatoes packed in oil, drained, rinsed, and slivered

2/3 cup minced chives

2 large oranges, thinly sliced

1 In a 4- to 5-quart pan, cook bacon over medium heat, stirring often, until crisp (about 7 minutes). Discard all but 2 tablespoons of the drippings from pan. Increase heat to medium-high and add shrimp and scallops. Cook, stirring often, until opaque in center; cut to test (about 5 minutes). Lift out shellfish and bacon; keep warm.

2 Add vermouth to pan; increase heat to high and boil until reduced by about half (about 5 minutes). Add chicken broth and orange juice. Bring to a boil; stir in couscous, tomatoes, and 1/3 cup of the chives. Cover, remove from heat, and let stand until liquid is absorbed (about 5 minutes).

3 Mound couscous on a platter and top with shellfish and bacon; sprinkle with remaining chives. Tuck oranges around couscous.

makes 6 servings

per serving: 484 calories, 30 g protein, 66 g carbohydrates, 10 g total fat, 94 mg cholesterol, 477 mg sodium

grilled fish tacos

preparation time: about 55 minutes

1 ³/₄ to 2 pounds firm-textured white-fleshed fish fillets or steaks such as Chilean sea bass, swordfish, or sturgeon (1 ¹/₂ to 2 inches thick)

¹/₃ cup lime juice

3 tablespoons tequila (optional)

Cilantro Slaw (recipe follows)

6 to 12 flour tortillas (*each* 7 to 9 inches in diameter) or corn tortillas (*each* about 6 inches in diameter)

About 1 cup purchased or homemade salsa

Reduced-fat sour cream or-plain nonfat yogurt

1 Rinse fish, pat dry, and place in a wide, shallow bowl. Stir together lime juice and tequila (if used); pour over fish. Turn fish to coat; then cover and refrigerate for at least 15 minutes or up to 4 hours, turning occasionally. Meanwhile, prepare Cilantro Slaw.

2 Lift fish from marinade and drain briefly; discard any remaining marinade. Place fish on a lightly oiled grill 4 to 6 inches above a solid bed of medium-hot coals. Cook, turning once or twice, until fish is lightly browned on outside and just opaque but still moist in thickest part; cut to test (about 10 minutes).

3 Transfer fish to a platter. To assemble tacos, heat tortillas on grill, turning often with tongs, just until softened (15 to 20 seconds). Cut off chunks of fish (removing any bones and skin) and place in tortillas; add salsa, Cilantro Slaw, and sour cream to taste. Roll to enclose; eat out of hand. Also offer slaw as a side dish.

CILANTRO SLAW

In a large bowl, combine 3 cups *each* finely shredded green cabbage and red cabbage; 1 cup firmly packed cilantro leaves, minced; cup lime juice; 1 tablespoon salad oil, ¹/₂ teaspoon cumin seeds; and 1 teaspoon sugar. Season to taste with salt and pepper. If made ahead, cover and refrigerate for up to 4 hours.

makes 6 servings

per serving: 307 calories, 30 g protein, 28 g carbohydrates, 8 g total fat, 58 mg cholesterol, 518 mg sodium

soft-shell crab with ginger

preparation time: about 25 minutes

6 cleaned soft-shell blue crabs (thawed if frozen)

¹/₃ cup unseasoned rice vinegar

2 tablespoons thinly slice green onions (including tops)

1 ¹/₂ tablespoons minced fresh ginger

1 teaspoon sugar

1 Place crabs, back sides up, on a rack in a pan above 1 inch boiling water. Cover and steam over high heat until crabs are opaque in center of body; cut to test (about 8 minutes).

2 Meanwhile, stir together vinegar, onions, ginger, and sugar in a small bowl.

3 Transfer crabs to individual plates. Offer with ginger sauce.

makes 3 servings

per serving: 122 calories, 22 g protein, 3 g carbohydrates, 2 g total fat, 108 mg cholesterol, 306 mg sodium

curried fish & rice

preparation time: about 40 minutes

1 small head romaine lettuce, separated into
  leaves, rinsed, and crisped

2 tablespoons salad oil

1 cup sliced green onions

1 large red bell pepper, seeded and finely chopped

2 teaspoons curry powder

1 1/2 cups plain low-fat yogurt

1/3 cup water

2 1/2 cups cooled cooked brown or white rice

4 Chilean sea bass fillets, 3/4 to 1 inch thick
  (about 6 oz. *each*)

1 Finely shred about a third of the lettuce leaves. Cover a platter with remaining whole leaves; then mound shredded lettuce on one side of platter. Set aside.

2 Heat 1 tablespoon of the oil in a wide nonstick frying pan over medium-high heat. Add onions and bel3451 pepper and cook, stirring often, until pepper is soft (8 to 10 minutes). Add curry powder; cook, stirring, for 1 more minute.

3 Transfer vegetable mixture to a large bowl and stir in yogurt and water. Set 1 1/4 cups of the mixture aside. Add rice to remaining vegetable mixture and stir to combine well; then mound on shredded lettuce. Set aside.

4 Heat remaining 1 tablespoon oil in pan over medium-high heat. Rinse fish and pat dry. Then add to pan and cook, turning once, until just opaque but still moist in thickest part; cut to test (8 to 10 minutes). Arrange fish on lettuce leaves; spoon reserved 1 1/4 cups yogurt mixture over fish.

makes 4 servings

per serving: 450 calories, 41 g protein, 41 g carbohydrates, 13 g total fat, 75 mg cholesterol, 192 mg sodium

red snapper & shrimp

preparation time: about 1 1/2 hours

1 tablespoon olive oil

1 medium-size onion, chopped

1 medium-size green bell pepper, seeded
  and chopped

2 cloves garlic, minced or pressed

1 can (about 4 oz.) diced green chiles

1 large can (about 28 oz.) tomatoes, drained
  and coarsely chopped

1/8 teaspoon *each* salt and pepper

1 1/2 pounds red snapper fillets (1/2 inch thick)

8 ounces medium-size raw shrimp
  (about 36 per lb.), shelled and deveined

3 tablespoons lemon juice

1 Heat oil in a wide nonstick frying pan over medium heat. Add onion, bell pepper, and garlic; cook, stirring occasionally, until onion is soft (about 10 minutes). Add chiles, tomatoes, salt and pepper. Bring to a boil; reduce heat and simmer, uncovered, until sauce is thick (about 20 minutes).

2 Rinse fish and pat dry. Arrange fillets in a single layer in sauce; distribute shrimp evenly over fish. Drizzle with lemon juice. Cover and simmer until shrimp are just opaque in center and fish is just opaque but still moist in thickest part; cut to test (about 15 minutes).

3 To serve, transfer fish and shrimp to a serving dish. Bring sauce to a boil; then boil, uncovered, stirring often, until thickened (about 5 minutes). Pour sauce over fish and shrimp.

makes 8 servings

per serving: 163 calories, 24 g protein, 9 g carbohydrates, 4 g total fat, 67 mg cholesterol, 374 mg sodium

grilled tuna with teriyaki fruit sauce

preparation time: about 20 minutes

1/4 cup *each* **sugar and reduced-sodium soy sauce**

6 tablespoons sake or dry sherry

3 thin slices fresh ginger or 1/4 teaspoon ground ginger

4 boneless and skinless tuna steaks (about 6 oz. *each***), about 1 inch thick**

Vegetable cooking spray

1 medium-size papaya (about 1 lb.), peeled, seeded, and cut into 12 wedges

2 teaspoons finely chopped candied or crystallized ginger

1 large green bell pepper, seeded and cut into thin slices

1 In a 2-quart pan, combine sugar, soy, sake, and ginger slices. Bring to a boil over high heat. Boil, stirring, until sugar is dissolved; then continue to boil until reduced to 1/3 cup. Discard ginger slices, if used. Keep warm.

2 Rinse fish and pat dry. Spray both sides of each steak with cooking spray. Place fish on a grill 4 to 6 inches above a solid bed of hot coals. Cook, turning once, until just slightly translucent or wet inside; cut in thickest part to test (about 3 minutes).

4 Place fish on a platter or individual plates. Evenly top with soy mixture, papaya, and candied ginger; arrange bell pepper alongside.

makes 4 servings

per serving: 361 calories, 41 g protein, 28 g carbohydrates, 9 g total fat, 65 mg cholesterol, 673 mg sodium

grape chutney

preparation time: about 55 minutes

1 large onion, finely chopped

1 large tart apple such as Newtown Pippin or McIntosh, peeled, cored, and finely chopped

2 cups seedless red or green grapes

1/3 cup firmly packed brown sugar

1/3 cup red wine vinegar

1/8 teaspoon pepper

Salt

1 In a wide nonstick frying pan or wok, combine onion and 1/4 cup water. Cook over medium-high heat, stirring occasionally, until liquid evaporates and onion begins to brown and stick to pan bottom. To deglaze pan, add 1/4 cup more water and stir to scrape browned bits free from pan bottom. Then continue to cook, stirring often, until liquid evaporates and browned bits stick to pan again. Deglaze with 14 cup more water; then cook, stirring often, until onion is richly browned. (Total cooking time will be 10 to 15 minutes.)

2 To pan, add apple, grapes, 1/2 cup water, sugar, vinegar, and pepper. Bring to a boil; then reduce heat, cover, and simmer until grapes begin to split (about 10 minutes).

3 Uncover. Increase heat to medium-high and cook, stirring often, until mixture is thick and almost all liquid has evaporated (about 20 minutes); as mixture thickens, watch carefully and stir more often to prevent scorching. Season to taste with salt. If made ahead, let cool; then cover and refrigerate for up to 3 days. Reheat before serving, if desired.

makes about 2 1/4 cups

per 1/4 cup: 66 calories, 0.4 g protein, 17 g carbohydrates, 0.1 g total fat, 0 mg cholesterol, 4 mg sodium

sesame barbecued seafood

preparation time: about 20 to 30 minutes

Sesame-Soy Baste (recipe follows)

1 ½ to 2 pounds fish steaks or fillets
   (½ to 1 ½ inches thick), cleaned whole trout,
   sea scallops, or shelled and deveined shrimp

Vegetable oil cooking spray

1 Prepare Sesame-Soy Baste. Rinse seafood and pat dry. If using scallops or shrimp, thread on serving-size skewers.

2 Position barbecue grill 4 to 6 inches above a solid bed of hot coals; coat grill with cooking spray. Place fish or skewered shellfish on grill and brush generously with Sesame-Soy Baste. Cook, turning once and brushing often with baste, until just opaque but still moist in thickest part; cut to test. For fish, allow about 10 minutes for each inch of thickness; for scallops, allow 5 to 8 minutes; for shrimp, allow 3 to 5 minutes.

SESAME-SOY BASTE

In a small bowl, mix 1 teaspoon Asian sesame oil; ⅓ cup reduced-sodium soy sauce; 2 tablespoons minced green onion; 1 tablespoon dry sherry or sherry vinegar; 1 tablespoon minced fresh ginger; 2 teaspoons sugar; 2 cloves garlic, minced or pressed; and a dash of ground red pepper (cayenne).

makes 6 to 8 servings

per serving: 110 calories, 20 g protein, 3 g carbohydrates, 2 g total fat, 24 mg cholesterol, 542 mg sodium

simmered cod & vegetables

preparation time: about 30 minutes

12 small red thin-skinned potatoes, halved

½ pound broccoli flowerets

1 bottle (8 oz.) clam juice

1 cup dry white wine

1 pound individually frozen cod or other white- fleshed fish fillets

1 tablespoon *each* cornstarch, water, and prepared horseradish

¼ cup coarse-grained Dijon mustard

1 Place potatoes in a 3- to 4-quart pan and add enough water to cover by 1 inch. Bring to a boil over high heat; cover and cook for 15 minutes. Add broccoli; cover and continue cooking until vegetables are tender when pierced (about 5 more minutes). Drain.

2 Meanwhile, combine clam juice, wine, and fish in a wide frying pan. Bring to a boil over high heat; reduce heat, cover, and simmer until fish looks just opaque but still moist in thickest part; cut to test (about 8 minutes). Lift out fish and transfer to a platter; keep warm.

3 Boil fish liquid over high heat until reduced to 1 cup (about 5 minutes). In a small measuring cup, mix cornstarch, water, horseradish, and mustard and stir into pan. Cook, stirring, until mixture boils and thickens (about 1 minute); pour into a bowl.

4 Arrange potatoes and broccoli alongside fish. Offer with sauce.

makes 4 servings

per serving: 276 calories, 26 g protein, 38 g carbohydrates, 2 g total fat, 49 mg cholesterol, 672 mg sodium

layered cioppino

preparation time: about 1 1/2 hours

2 large cans (about 28 oz. *each*) tomatoes

1 can (about 6 oz.) tomato paste

1 cup dry white wine

1/4 cup olive oil

2 teaspoons pepper

4 cups coarsely chopped Swiss chard

2 large red bell peppers, seeded and chopped

1/2 cup chopped parsley

1/4 cup chopped fresh basil or 1 tablespoon dry basil

2 tablespoons *each* chopped fresh marjoram, rosemary, thyme, and sage; or 2 teaspoons *each* dry marjoram, rosemary, thyme, and sage

36 extra-jumbo raw shrimp (16 to 20 per lb.)

36 small hard-shell clams in shell, scrubbed

2 large Dungeness crabs (about 2 lbs. *each*), cooked, cleaned, and cracked

2 pounds firm-textured white-fleshed fish fillets such as rockfish, cut into 2-inch chunks

Salt

1 Pour tomatoes and their liquid into a large bowl; coarsely mash tomatoes. Stir in tomato paste, wine, oil, pepper, chard, bell peppers, parsley, basil, marjoram, rosemary, thyme, and sage until well blended.

2 Devein shrimp by inserting tip of a slender skewer under vein between shell segments along back of each shrimp; gently pull to remove vein. Set shrimp aside.

3 Arrange clams over bottom of a heavy 12- to 14 quart pan. Spoon a fourth of the tomato mixture over clams. Top with shrimp, a third of the remaining tomato mixture, crab, half the remaining tomato mixture, fish, and remaining tomato mixture (a 12-quart pan may be full to rim).

4 Cover pan and bring seafood mixture to a boil over high heat (10 to 20 minutes). Then reduce heat and simmer gently, covered, until fish is just opaque but still moist in thickest part; cut to test (15 to 20 minutes). Season to taste with salt.

5 To serve, ladle cioppino into wide bowls, spooning down to bottom of pan to get some of each layer; discard any unopened clams.

makes 12 servings

per serving: 299 calories, 40 g protein, 23 g carbohydrates, 8 g total fat, 165 mg cholesterol, 609 mg sodium

When you need a between-meal nibble during the day, there are a variety of snacks you can have on hand even when you are at your desk at work. Nonperishable snacks that are easy to have available are rice crackers, pretzels, graham crackers, flatbread, ginger-snaps, and animal cookies. Herb tea and instant low-sodium chicken broth make warm pick-me-ups.

crab with barbecue sauce

preparation time: about 1 hour

2 tablespoons margarine

1 medium-size onion, finely chopped

3 cloves garlic, minced or pressed

1 3/4 cups low-sodium chicken broth

1 can (8 oz.) no-salt-added tomato sauce

1 cup catsup

1/2 cup *each* white wine vinegar and firmly
   packed brown sugar

3 tablespoons Worcestershire

1 tablespoon reduced-sodium soy sauce

1 1/2 teaspoons dry mustard

1 teaspoon *each* paprika and liquid hot pepper
   seasoning

1/2 teaspoon *each* celery seeds, ground allspice,
   and dry thyme leaves

2 bay leaves

3 large cooked Dungeness crabs (5 to 6 lbs.
   total), cleaned and cracked

Sourdough bread, sliced (and toasted, if desired)

1 Melt margarine in a 5- to 6-quart pan over medium heat. Add onion and garlic and cook, stirring occasionally, until onion is soft (about 10 minutes). Add broth, tomato sauce, catsup, vinegar, sugar, Worcestershire, soy, mustard, paprika, hot pepper seasoning, celery seeds, allspice, thyme, and bay leaves. Bring to a boil over high heat; reduce heat and simmer, uncovered, until reduced to 3 cups (about 45 minutes).

2 To serve sauce with cold crab, pour into individual bowls; dip crab into sauce. Or add crab to sauce and simmer until crab is heated through (about 5 minutes), stirring gently several times. Accompany crab and sauce with bread.

makes 6 servings

per serving: 275 calories, 19 g protein, 38 g carbohydrates, 6 g total fat, 54 mg cholesterol, 987 mg sodium

ahi steaks with bacon

preparation time: about 25 minutes

2 slices bacon

4 ahi (yellowfin tuna) steaks (about 6 oz. *each*),
   about 1 inch thick, rinsed and patted dry

2 teaspoons margarine

2 tablespoons reduced-sodium soy sauce

1/2 cup dry white wine

1 In a wide frying pan, cook bacon over medium heat until crisp (about 7 minutes). Lift out and drain on paper towels. Discard all but 1 tablespoon of the drippings from pan.

2 Add fish to pan, increase heat to high, and cook, turning once, until browned on both sides (about 4 minutes total). Dot fish with margarine; add soy sauce and wine. Reduce heat to medium, cover, and cook until fish is pale pink in center; cut to test (about 4 minutes). Lift out and arrange on a platter; keep warm.

3 Increase heat to high and boil sauce until reduced to about 3 tablespoons (about 2 minutes). Meanwhile, crumble bacon. Top fish with sauce and sprinkle with bacon.

makes 4 servings

per serving: 248 calories, 41 g protein, 1 g carbohydrates, 8 g total fat 82 mg cholesterol, 453 mg sodium

swordfish with mushroom sauce

preparation time: about 25 minutes
marinating time: 30 minutes

2 pounds swordfish or shark steaks, rinsed and patted dry

6 tablespoons lemon juice, 1 cup dry white wine or water

1 clove garlic, minced or pressed

1/2 teaspoon *each* dry oregano leaves, salt, and pepper

1/4 teaspoon fennel seeds, crushed

Nonstick cooking spray

1/2 pound mushrooms, sliced

2 teaspoon salad oil

1/2 cup thinly sliced green onions (including tops)

3 cups watercress sprigs

1 Cut fish into serving-size pieces, if necessary. In a 9- by 13-inch baking pan, stir together lemon juice, wine, garlic, oregano, salt, pepper, and fennel seeds. Add fish and let stand, turning occasionally, for 30 minutes. Lift out fish and drain briefly, reserving marinade.

2 Lightly coat a broiler pan rack with cooking spray. Place fish on rack and broil 3 to 4 inches below heat, turning once or twice, until fish looks just opaque but still moist in center; cut to test (8 to 10 minutes total).

3 Meanwhile, combine mushrooms and oil in a nonstick frying pan over medium-high heat. Cook, stirring, until mushrooms are soft (about 5 minutes). Stir in reserved marinade and boil gently for 2 minutes; stir in onions and remove from heat.

4 Arrange watercress on individual plates. Add fish and top with mushroom sauce.

makes 6 servings

per serving: 210 calories, 31 g protein, 4 g carbohydrates, 7 g total fat, 59 mg cholesterol, 332 mg sodium

chinese-style steamed fish

preparation time: about 35 minutes

1 scaled and cleaned whole rockfish, snapper, or black sea bass (about 2 lbs.), head removed, if desired, rinsed, and patted dry

Salt

3 tablespoons slivered fresh ginger

3 green onions (including tops), thinly sliced lengthwise

1 dried hot red chile

1 tablespoon unseasoned rice vinegar or wine vinegar

1 tablespoon reduced-sodium soy sauce

Cilantro sprigs (optional)

1 Make 3 diagonal slashes across fish on each side. Place on a rimmed plate that will fit on a steamer rack in a pan. (If fish is too long, cut in half crosswise and place halves side by side.) Season to taste with salt. Place half the ginger and onions inside cavity; put chile and remaining ginger and onions on top. Pour vinegar and soy sauce over fish.

2 Loosely cover with foil and place plate on a rack in a pan above 1 inch boiling water. Cover and steam until fish looks just opaque but still moist in thickest part; cut to test (8 to 10 minutes per inch of thickness).

3 Arrange fish on a large platter (reassemble halves, if necessary). Garnish with cilantro, if desired. To serve, cut through fish to backbone and slide a spatula between flesh and ribs to lift off each serving. Remove backbone to serve bottom half.

makes 4 servings

per serving: 170 calories, 32 g protein, 2 g carbohydrates, 3 g total fat, 60 mg cholesterol, 254 mg sodium

scallop scampi

preparation time: about 30 minutes

1 slice sourdough sandwich bread, torn into pieces

2 teaspoons olive oil

4 cloves garlic, minced or pressed

1 tablespoon chopped parsley

2 tablespoons dry white wine

1 teaspoon lemon juice

$1/2$ teaspoon honey

1 bunch watercress, coarse stems removed, sprigs rinsed and crisped

1 pound sea scallops

$1\,1/2$ teaspoons butter or margarine

Lemon wedges

1 To prepare stir-fried crumbs, whirl bread in a blender or food processor to make fine crumbs. In a wide nonstick frying pan or wok, combine crumbs, $1\,1/2$ teaspoons water, $1/2$ teaspoon of the olive oil, and a fourth of the garlic. Stir-fry over medium heat until crumbs are crisp and golden (about 5 minutes); remove from pan and set aside.

2 Let crumbs cool slightly. Stir parsley into crumbs and set aside.

3 In a small bowl, stir together wine, lemon juice, and honey; set aside. Arrange watercress on a large rimmed platter; cover and set aside.

4 Rinse scallops and pat dry; cut into bite-size pieces, if desired. Melt butter in remaining $1\,1/2$ teaspoons oil in a wide nonstick frying pan or wok over medium-high heat. When butter mixture is hot, add remaining garlic, 1 tablespoon water, and the scallops. Stir-fry until scallops are just opaque in center.

5 Stir wine mixture well and pour into pan; bring just to a boil. With a slotted spoon, lift scallops from pan; arrange over watercress. Pour pan juices into a small pitcher. Sprinkle scallops with stir-fried crumbs and garnish with lemon wedges.

makes 4 servings

per serving: 168 calories, 21 g protein, 9 g carbohydrates, 5 g total fat, 41 mg cholesterol, 257 mg sodium

red snapper stir-fry

preparation time: about 30 minutes

1 tablespoon finely minced fresh ginger

2 tablespoons reduced sodium soy sauce

2 tablespoons unsweetened pineapple juice

2 cloves garlic, minced or pressed

1 teaspoon sugar

1 teaspoon Asian sesame oil

$1/8$ teaspoon crushed red pepper flakes

1 pound red snapper fillets, cut into 1-inch pieces

1 medium-size pineapple

1 teaspoon vegetable oil

$1\,1/2$ cups fresh Chinese pea pods

1 tablespoon cornstarch blended with 1 tablespoon cold water

$1/2$ cup thinly sliced green onions

1 In a large bowl, stir together ginger, soy sauce, pineapple juice, garlic, sugar, sesame oil, and red pepper flakes. Add fish and stir to coat. Set aside; stir occasionally.

2 Peel and core pineapple, then cut crosswise into thin slices. Arrange slices on a rimmed platter; cover and set aside.

3 Heat vegetable oil in a wide nonstick frying pan or wok over medium-high heat. When oil is hot, add fish mixture and stir-fry gently until fish is just opaque but still moist in thickest part; cut to test (2 to 3 minutes). Remove fish from pan with a slotted spoon; keep warm.

4 Add pea pods to pan and stir-fry for 30 seconds (15 seconds if using frozen pea pods). Stir cornstarch mixture well, then pour into pan. Cook, stirring constantly, until sauce boils and thickens slightly (1 to 2 minutes). Return fish to pan and add onions; mix gently but thoroughly, just until fish is hot and coated with sauce. To serve, spoon fish mixture over pineapple slices.

makes 4 servings

per serving: 278 calories, 26 g protein, 34 g carbohydrates, 5 g total fat, 42 mg cholesterol, 379 mg sodium

tuna with tomato-orange relish

preparation time: about 40 minutes

1 small orange

2 medium-size tomatoes, coarsely chopped

1 tablespoon tomato paste

1 tablespoon cider vinegar

Vegetable oil cooking spray

1 small dried hot red chile

$^1/_2$ teaspoon mustard seeds

$^1/_2$ teaspoon cumin seeds

$^1/_4$ teaspoon ground allspice

2 tablespoons firmly packed brown sugar

$^1/_4$ cup raisins

1 teaspoon olive oil

2 cloves garlic, minced or pressed

2 tablespoons lemon juice

6 skinless, boneless tuna steaks (about 6 oz. *each*), $^3/_4$ to 1 inch thick

Freshly ground pepper

Italian parsley sprigs

Orange slices

1 To prepare tomato-orange relish, grate $^1/_2$ teaspoon peel (colored part only) from orange; set grated peel aside. Cut remaining peel and all white membrane from orange; cut fruit into chunks.

2 In a food processor or blender, combine chopped orange, tomatoes, tomato paste, and vinegar. Whirl until coarsely puréed; set aside.

3 Spray a $1^1/_2$- to 2-quart pan with cooking spray. Add chile, mustard seeds, and cumin seeds; stir over medium-high heat until seeds begin to pop (about 2 minutes). Mix in allspice, brown sugar, raisins, tomato mixture, and grated orange peel. Cook, stirring, until sugar is dissolved. Reduce heat so mixture cooks at a gentle boil; cook, stirring often, until consistency is jam-like (20 to 25 minutes). Remove chile, if desired. (Relish can be served hot or at room temperature.)

4 Mix oil, garlic, and lemon juice. Rinse tuna steaks, pat dry, and brush all over with oil mixture. Place tuna steaks on a greased grill 4 to 6 inches above a solid bed of hot coals. Cook, turning once, until browned on outside but still pale pink in center; cut to test (3 to 5 minutes).

5 Transfer tuna steaks to a warm platter; season to taste with pepper. Spoon a dollop of tomato-orange relish over each piece of tuna; serve with remaining relish to add to taste. Garnish with parsley sprigs and orange slices.

makes 6 servings

per serving: 317 calories, 41 g protein, 16 g carbohydrates, 10 g total fat, 65 mg cholesterol, 97 mg sodium

cocktail sauce

preparation time: about 5 minutes

$^1/_2$ cup catsup

$^1/_4$ cup *each* tomato-based chili sauce and grapefruit juice

2 tablespoons lemon juice

1 tablespoon thinly sliced green onion

1 teaspoon *each* prepared horseradish and Worcestershire

2 or 3 drops liquid hot pepper seasoning

In a small bowl, stir together catsup, chili sauce, grapefruit juice, lemon juice, onion, horseradish, Worcestershire, and hot pepper seasoning. Serve with cold poached fish or cold shellfish.

makes about 2 cups

per tablespoon: 15 calories, 0.2 g protein, 4 g carbohydrates, 0 g total fat, 0 mg cholesterol, 151 mg sodium

oyster jambalaya

preparation time: about 1¼ hours
cooking time: about 45 minutes

2 jars (10 oz. *each*) small shucked oysters, drained and rinsed

1 tablespoon salad oil

6 ounces Canadian bacon, diced

1 large onion, chopped

3 cloves garlic, minced or pressed

2 large green bell peppers, stemmed, seeded, and chopped

1 cup chopped celery

4 large tomatoes, chopped

1 can (8 oz.) no-salt-added tomato sauce

2 bay leaves, crumbled

1 teaspoon dry thyme leaves

1½ teaspoons ground white pepper

½ teaspoon ground red pepper (cayenne)

½ cup chopped parsley

1½ cups long-grain white rice

2½ cups low-sodium chicken broth

1 Cut oysters into small pieces and set aside.

2 Heat oil in a 6- to 8-quart pan over medium heat. Add bacon and cook, stirring often, until lightly browned (about 5 minutes). Add onion, garlic, bell peppers, and celery. Cook, stirring occasionally, until vegetables are limp (about 10 minutes). Add tomatoes, tomato sauce, bay leaves, thyme, white pepper, red pepper, and parsley. Cook, stirring, until sauce boils.

3 Add rice and chicken broth. Bring to a boil; reduce heat, cover, and simmer for 20 minutes. Stir in oysters, cover, and continue cooking until rice is tender and oysters are opaque in center; cut to test (about 10 more minutes).

makes 6 servings

per serving: 388 calories, 20 g protein, 59 g carbohydrates, 8 g total fat, 66 mg cholesterol, 573 mg sodium

---

A few minutes taken to organize your menus and understand your recipes can save time and frustration. Planning menus on a day-to-day basis is inefficient; it forces you to spend extra time thinking about what to cook, and extra time in the supermarket. Instead, plot out a week's worth of menus at a time and, whenever possible, do your shopping all at once. When planning menus and when cooking, always keep simplicity in mind, but consider as well the flavor, texture, appearance, and nutritional content of the food. Remember the following tips; they'll help when you sit down to plan menus that are simple and quick to prepare, yet interesting to eat.

Provide a good variety of color, flavor, shape, temperature, and texture in foods you arrange together in a menu.

When you're planning to cook two or three dishes at once, use different cooking techniques. You wouldn't want to serve sautéed fish with stir-fried vegetables; there would be too much simultaneous activity on the range, all just before serving time. Instead, pair the stir-fried vegetables with baked fish.

Plan ahead for leftovers. If you have time to roast a chicken on Sunday, roast two; then, on Tuesday night, you might use the leftover chicken in a quick main-dish salad.

Prepare ingredients ahead of time, when possible. Shred cheese and keep it refrigerated in glass jars. Wash, dry, and store salad greens as soon as you bring them home from the market.

Schedule your meals for smooth serving, with everything ready at once. Base your schedule on the time you'll serve the meal, and then work backward from serving time, creating a workable plan.

pasta

pasta pie

preparation time: about 45 minutes

PASTA PIE:

1/2 cup nonfat milk

1 teaspoon cornstarch

2 large eggs

6 large egg whites

3/4 cup shredded part-skim mozzarella cheese

1/4 cup grated Parmesan cheese

2 tablespoons chopped fresh oregano
or 1 1/2 teaspoons dried oregano

2 cloves garlic, minced or pressed

1/4 teaspoon salt

1/8 teaspoon crushed red pepper flakes

3 cups cold cooked spaghetti

1 teaspoon vegetable oil

TOMATO CREAM SAUCE:

1 large can (about 28 oz.) diced tomatoes

1/2 cup reduced-fat sour cream

2 or 3 cloves garlic, peeled

2 teaspoons chopped fresh thyme
or 1/2 teaspoon dried thyme

1 teaspoon sugar, or to taste

Salt and pepper

GARNISH

Oregano sprigs and fresh oregano leaves

1 In a large bowl, combine milk and cornstarch; beat until smoothly blended. Add eggs and egg whites and beat well. Stir in mozzarella cheese, Parmesan cheese, chopped oregano, minced garlic, the 1/4 teaspoon salt, and red pepper flakes. Add pasta to egg mixture; lift with 2 forks to mix well. Set aside.

2 Place a 9-inch-round baking pan (do not use a nonstick pan) in oven while it heats to 500°. When pan is hot (after about 5 minutes), carefully remove it from oven and pour in oil, tilting pan to coat. Mix pasta mixture again; then transfer to pan. Bake on lowest rack of oven until top of pie is golden and center is firm when lightly pressed (about 25 minutes).

3 Meanwhile, to prepare tomato cream sauce, pour tomatoes and their liquid into a food processor or blender. Add sour cream, peeled garlic, thyme, and sugar; whirl until smoothly puréed. Season to taste with salt and pepper, set aside. Use at room temperature.

4 When pie is done, spread about 3/4 cup of the sauce on each of 4 individual plates. Cut pie into 4 wedges; place one wedge atop sauce on each plate. Garnish with oregano sprigs and leaves. Offer remaining sauce to drizzle over pie.

makes 4 servings

per serving: 411 calories, 26 g protein, 47 g carbohydrates, 14 g total fat, 133 mg cholesterol, 782 mg sodium

COOK PASTA CORRECTLY: In general, you'll need about 3 quarts of water for 8 ounces of fresh or dry pasta, about 6 quarts for a pound. Once the water has come to a boil, add the pasta; leave the pan uncovered, then begin timing after the water has resumed a full boil. Begin taste-testing before the recommended cooking time is up. Pasta should be cooked al dente—literally, "to the tooth," or tender but still firm to bite. As soon as pasta reaches that stage, drain it in a colander; then serve at once or keep warm in a warm bowl.

ravioli with gorgonzola

preparation time: about 40 minutes

2 packages (about 9 oz. *each*) fresh low-fat
   cheese-filled ravioli

1/4 cup finely chopped onion

2 cloves garlic, minced or pressed

4 teaspoons cornstarch

1 cup nonfat milk

1/2 cup half-and-half

1/2 cup vegetable broth

2 ounces Gorgonzola or other blue-veined
   cheese, crumbled

1/4 teaspoon dried thyme

1/4 teaspoon dried marjoram

1/4 teaspoon rubbed sage

1/8 teaspoon ground nutmeg

1 teaspoon dry sherry, or to taste

Finely shredded lemon peel

Salt and pepper

1 In a 6- to 8-quart pan, bring about 4 quarts water to a boil over medium high heat. Stir in ravioli, separating any that are stuck together, reduce heat and boil gently, stirring occasionally, until pasta is just tender to bite, 4 to 6 minutes. (Or cook pasta according to package directions.) Drain well, return to pan, and keep warm.

2 While pasta is cooking, combine onion, garlic, and 1 table-spoon water in a wide nonstick frying pan. Cook over medium-high heat, stirring often, until onion is soft (3 to 4 minutes); add water, 1 tablespoon at a time, if pan appears dry. Remove from heat.

3 Smoothly blend cornstarch with 2 tablespoons of the milk. Add cornstarch mixture, remaining milk, half-and-half, and broth to pan. Return to medium-high heat and bring to a boil, stirring. Reduce heat to low and add cheese, thyme, marjoram, sage, and nutmeg; stir until cheese is melted. Remove pan from heat and stir in sherry.

4 Spoon sauce over pasta; mix gently. Spoon pasta onto individual plates; sprinkle with lemon peel. Season to taste with salt and pepper.

makes 6 servings

per serving: 315 calories, 15 g protein, 40 g carbohydrates, 10 g total fat, 69 mg cholesterol, 545 mg sodium

rotini with broccoli ricotta

preparation time: about 40 minutes

12 ounces dried rotini or other
   corkscrew-shaped pasta

2 tablespoons olive oil

5 green onions, thinly sliced

1 pound broccoli flowerets,
   cut into bite-size pieces

1 1/2 cups part-skim ricotta cheese

Freshly grated Parmesan cheese

Coarsely ground pepper

1 Bring 12 cups water to a boil in a 5- to 6-quart pan over medium-high heat. Stir in pasta and cook just until tender to bite (8 to 10 minutes); or cook according to package directions. Meanwhile, heat oil in a wide nonstick frying pan over medium-high heat. Add onions and cook, stirring, for 1 minute. Add broccoli and continue to cook, stirring, until bright green (about 3 minutes). Pour in 1/4 cup water and bring to a boil; reduce heat, cover, and simmer until broccoli is tender-crisp (about 5 minutes).

2 Drain pasta well, reserving 1/4 cup of the water. Place in a serving bowl. Add vegetables and ricotta. Mix thoroughly but gently; if too dry, stir in enough of the reserved water to moisten. Offer Parmesan and pepper to add to taste.

makes 4 servings

per serving: 540 calories, 25 g protein, 75 g carbohydrates, 16 g total fat, 29 mg cholesterol, 149 mg sodium

artichoke pesto pasta

preparation time: about 30 minutes

1/4 **cup pine nuts**

1 **can (about 10 oz.) artichoke hearts in water, drained**

1/2 **cup freshly grated Parmesan cheese**

3 **ounces Neufchâtel or nonfat cream cheese**

1/4 **cup diced onion**

1 **tablespoon Dijon mustard**

1 **clove garlic, minced or pressed**

1/8 **teaspoon ground nutmeg**

3/4 **cup vegetable broth**

1 **pound dried fettuccine**

1/4 **cup minced parsley**

1/4 **teaspoon crushed red pepper flakes**

1 Toast pine nuts in a small frying pan over medium heat, shaking pan often, until golden (about 3 minutes). Remove from pan and set aside.

2 Combine artichokes, Parmesan, Neufchâtel, onion, mustard, garlic, nutmeg, and 1/2 cup of the broth in a food processor or blender. Whirl until blended. Set aside.

3 Bring 16 cups water to a boil in a 6- to 8-quart pan over medium-high heat. Stir in pasta and cook just until tender to bite (8 to 10 minutes); or cook according to package directions. Drain well and return to pan. Reduce heat to medium, add remaining 1/4 cup broth, and cook, lifting pasta with 2 forks, until broth is hot (about 30 seconds).

4 Transfer to a large serving bowl. Quickly add artichoke mixture, parsley, red pepper flakes, and nuts; lift with 2 forks to mix.

makes 8 servings

per serving: 307 calories, 13 g protein, 44 g carbohydrates, 9 g total fat, 66 mg cholesterol, 309 mg sodium

italian garden pasta

preparation time: about 40 minutes

12 **ounces Swiss chard**

1 **pound dried rotini or elbow macaroni**

3 **tablespoons olive oil or vegetable oil**

1 **pound mushrooms, sliced**

1 **medium-size onion, chopped**

3 **cloves garlic, minced or pressed**

1/2 **cup canned vegetable broth**

1/2 **cup grated Parmesan cheese**

1 1/2 **pounds pear-shaped (Roma-type) tomatoes, chopped and drained well**

1 Trim and discard discolored stem ends from chard; then rinse and drain chard. Cut stems from leaves; finely chop stems and leaves, keeping them in separate piles.

2 In a 6- to 8-quart pan, cook pasta in about 4 quarts boiling water until just tender to bite (8 to 10 minutes); or cook according to package directions. Drain well, transfer to a warm wide bowl, and keep warm.

3 While pasta is cooking, heat oil in a wide non-stick frying pan or wok over medium-high heat. When oil is hot, add chard stems, mushrooms, onion, and garlic. Cover and cook until mushrooms release their liquid and onion is tinged with brown. Add broth and chard leaves; stir until chard is just wilted (1 to 2 more minutes).

4 Pour chard-mushroom mixture over pasta, sprinkle with half the cheese, and top with tomatoes. Mix gently but thoroughly. Sprinkle with remaining Parmesan cheese.

makes 4 to 6 servings

per serving: 531 calories, 21 g protein, 84 g carbohydrates, 13 g total fat, 8 mg cholesterol, 402 mg sodium

southwestern fettuccine

preparation time: about 35 minutes

12 ounces dried fettuccine

1 can (about 15 oz.) cream-style corn

²/₃ cup nonfat milk

1 teaspoon vegetable oil

¹/₂ teaspoon cumin seeds

1 small onion, chopped

1 large red or yellow bell pepper, seeded and cut into thin strips

1 package (about 10 oz.) frozen corn kernels, thawed and drained

1 cup (about 4 oz.) shredded jalapeño jack cheese

¹/₄ cup cilantro leaves

1 ¹/₂ to 2 cups yellow or red cherry tomatoes, cut into halves

Cilantro sprigs

Lime wedges

Salt

1 In a 5- to 6-quart pan, bring about 3 quarts water to boil over medium high heat; stir in pasta and cook until just tender to bite, 8 to 10 minutes. (Or cook pasta according to package directions.) Drain pasta well and return to pan; keep warm. While pasta is cooking, whirl cream-style corn and milk in a blender or food processor until smoothly puréed; set aside.

2 Heat oil in a wide nonstick frying pan over medium-high heat. Add cumin seeds, onion, and bell pepper. Cook, stirring often, until onion is soft (about 5 minutes); add water, 1 tablespoon at a time, if pan appears dry. Stir in cream-style corn mixture, corn kernels, and cheese. Reduce heat to medium and cook, stirring, just until cheese is melted.

3 Pour corn-cheese sauce over pasta. Add cilantro leaves; mix gently but thoroughly. Divide pasta among 4 shallow individual bowls; sprinkle with tomatoes. Garnish with cilantro sprigs. Season to taste with lime and salt.

makes 4 servings

per serving: 627 calories, 25 g protein, 104 g carbohydrates, 15 g total fat, 112 mg cholesterol, 540 mg sodium.

asparagus & pasta stir-fry

preparation time: about 25 minutes

6 ounces dried vermicelli

1 pound asparagus

2 teaspoons salad oil

1 clove garlic, minced or pressed

1 teaspoon minced fresh ginger

¹/₂ cup diagonally sliced green onions

2 tablespoons reduced sodium soy sauce

¹/₈ teaspoon crushed red pepper flakes

1 In a 4- to 6-quart pan, cook pasta in about 8 cups boiling water until just tender to bite (8 to 10 minutes); or cook according to package directions.

2 Meanwhile, snap off and discard tough ends of asparagus: then cut asparagus into 1¹/₂-inch slanting slices and set aside. Heat oil in a wide nonstick frying pan sir wok over medium high heat. When oil is hot, add garlic, ginger, asparagus, and onions. Stir-fry until asparagus is tender-crisp to bite (about 3 minutes). Add soy sauce and red pepper flakes; stir-fry for 1 more minute.

3 Drain pasta well, add to asparagus mixture, and stir-fry until heated through.

makes 4 to 6 servings

per serving: 167 calories, 7 g protein, 30 g carbohydrates, 3 g total fat, 0 mg cholesterol, 248 mg sodium

goat cheese & spinach pasta

preparation time: about 35 minutes

12 ounces dried spinach fettuccine

3 quarts lightly packed rinsed, drained fresh spinach leaves, cut or torn into 2-inch pieces

²/₃ cup vegetable broth

8 ounces unsweetened soft fresh goat cheese (plain or flavored), broken into chunks, if possible (some types may be too soft to break)

2 cups ripe cherry tomatoes (at room temperature), cut into ¹/₂-inch slices

Salt and pepper

1 In a 5 to 6 quart pan, bring abut 3 quarts water to a boil over medium-high heat; stir in pasta and cook until just tender to bite, 8 to 10 minutes. (Or cook pasta according to package directions.) Stir spinach into boiling water with pasta; continue to boil until spinach is wilted (30 to 45 more seconds). Drain pasta-spinach mixture well and return to pan.

2 While pasta is cooking, bring broth to a boil in a 1-to 2-quart pan over medium-high heat. Add cheese and stir until melted; remove from heat.

3 Spoon cheese mixture over pasta and spinach; mix gently. Spoon onto a platter; scatter tomatoes over top. Season to taste with salt and pepper.

makes 4 servings

per serving: 537 calories, 30 g protein, 70 g carbohydrates, 17 g total fat, 107 mg cholesterol, 617 mg sodium

sautéed mizuna & shells

preparation time: about 25 minutes

1 pound mizuna, rinsed and drained

12 ounces medium-size dried pasta shells

2 tablespoons olive oil

¹/₄ teaspoon crushed red pepper flakes

¹/₂ cup grated Parmesan cheese

A feathery-leaved member of the mustard family, mildly tart mizuna is becoming increasingly available in well-stocked supermarkets and gourmet stores.

1 Trim off and discard bare stem ends and yellow or bruised leaves from mizuna; then chop leaves coarsely and set aside.

2 In a 5- to 6-quart pan, cook pasta in 3 quarts boiling water just until tender to bite (10 to 12 minutes); or cook according to package directions. When pasta is almost done, heat oil in a 4- to 5-quart pan over high heat. Add mizuna and stir until leaves are wilted (2 to 4 minutes).

3 Drain pasta and place in a warm serving bowl. Add mizuna; mix lightly, using 2 forks. Sprinkle with red pepper flakes and cheese; mix again.

makes 4 servings

per serving: 449 calories, 18 g protein, 69 g carbohydrates, 11 g total fat, 8 mg cholesterol, 219 mg sodium

farfalle with chard, garlic, and ricotta

preparation time: about 25 minutes

1 bunch chard, rinsed and drained

10 ounces dried farfalle (pasta bow ties)

2 tablespoons olive oil

1 medium-size onion, finely chopped

4 cloves garlic, minced or pressed

1 ½ cups part-skim ricotta cheese, at room temperature

Salt and coarsely ground pepper

Grated Parmesan cheese (optional)

1 Trim off and discard ends of chard stems; then cut off remainder of stems at base or each leaf. Thinly slice stems and leaves crosswise, keeping them in separate piles. Set aside.

2 In a 5- to 6-quart pan, cook pasta in 3 quarts boiling water just until tender to bite (8 to 10 minutes); or cook according to package directions.

3 Meanwhile, heat oil in a wide (at least 12-inch) frying pan over medium-high heat. Add onion and chard stems; cook, stirring often, until onion is soft but not browned (3 to 5 minutes). Add garlic and chard leaves and cook, stirring often, until leaves are bright green (about 3 more minutes). Add ¾ cup water and bring to a boil. Remove from heat and blend in ricotta cheese; season to taste with salt, pepper, and nutmeg.

4 Drain pasta well and place in a warm wide serving bowl. Ricotta mixture; mix lightly but thoroughly, using 2 forks to combine. If desired, serve with Parmesan cheese to add to taste.

makes 4 servings

per serving: 495 calories, 23 g protein, 67 g carbohydrates, 15 g total fat, 29 mg cholesterol, 400 mg sodium

pasta with artichokes & anchovies

preparation time: about 25 minutes

8 ounces dried linguine

1 jar (about 6 oz.) marinated artichoke hearts

2 cloves garlic, minced or pressed

1 tablespoon anchovy paste

1 can (about 2 ¼ oz.) sliced ripe olives, drained

½ cup chopped parsley

¼ cup grated Parmesan cheese

Parsley sprigs

Pepper

1 In a 4- to 5-quart pan, cook linguine in about 8 cups boiling water until just tender to bite (8 to 10 minutes); or cook according to package directions. Drain well, transfer to a warm wide bowl, and keep warm.

2 While pasta is cooking, carefully drain marinade from artichokes into a wide nonstick frying pan or wok. Cut artichokes into bite-size pieces and set aside. Heat marinade over medium heat; add garlic and stir-fry until pale gold (about 3 minutes). Add anchovy paste, olives, and artichokes; stir-fry until heated through (about 2 minutes).

3 Pour artichoke mixture over pasta. Add chopped parsley and cheese; mix gently but thoroughly. Garnish with parsley sprigs; season to taste with pepper.

makes 4 to 6 servings

per serving: 245 calories, 10 g protein, 38 g carbohydrates, 6 g total fat, 5 mg cholesterol, 499 mg sodium

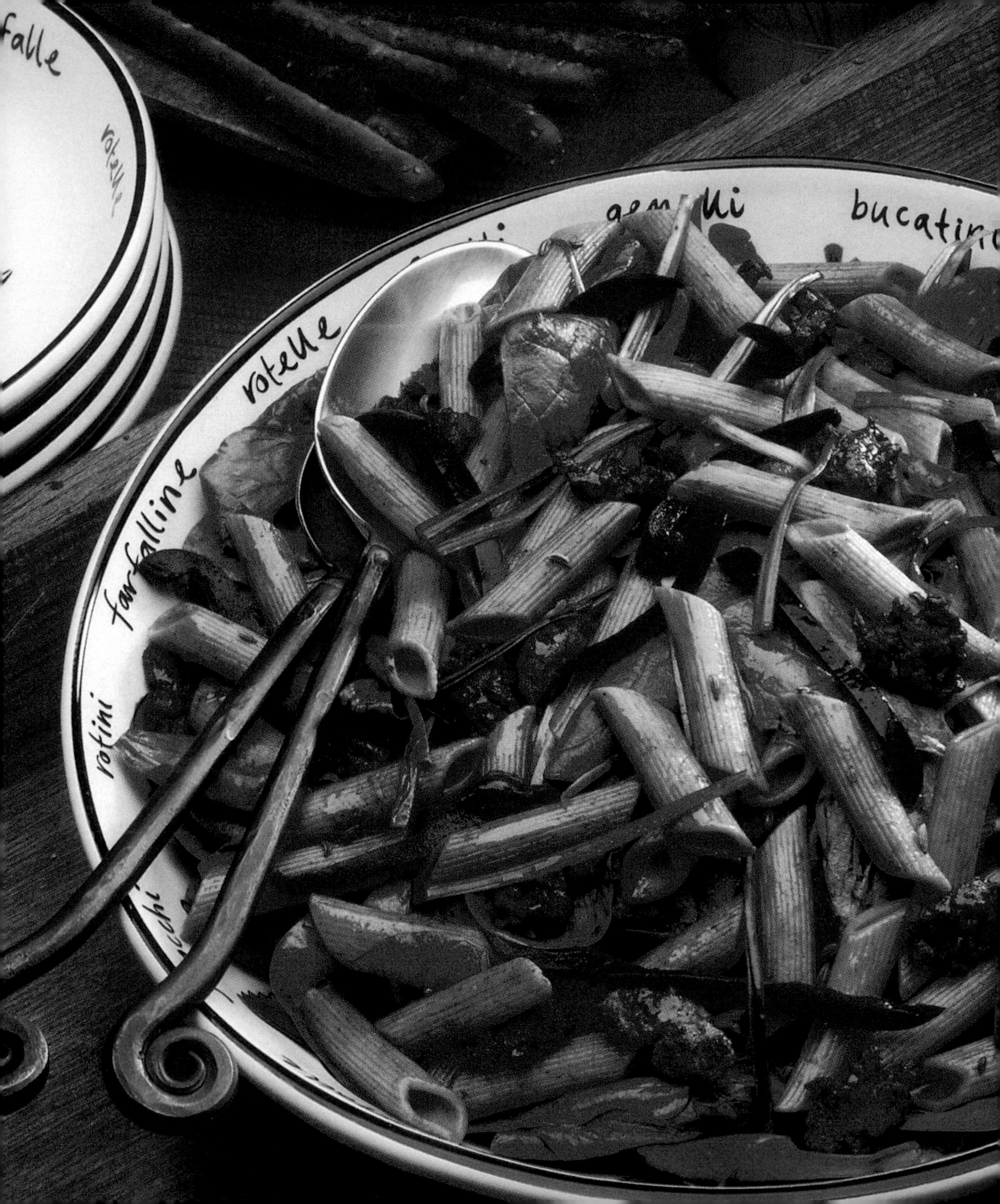
rotelle
rotelle
farfalline
rotini

vermicelli with turkey

preparation time: about 30 minutes

8 ounces dried vermicelli

1/3 cup sun-dried tomatoes packed in oil, drained (reserve oil) and slivered

2 cloves garlic, minced or pressed

1 medium-size onion, chopped

1 large yellow or red bell pepper, chopped

3 medium-size zucchini, thinly sliced

1 cup fat-free reduced-sodium chicken broth

2 cups shredded cooked turkey breast

**1/2 cup chopped fresh basil
    or 3 tablespoons dried basil**

Freshly grated Parmesan cheese

1 Bring 8 cups water to a boil in a 4- to 5-quart pan over medium-high heat. Stir in pasta and cook just until tender to bite (8 to 10 minutes); or cook according to package directions.

2 Meanwhile, heat 1 tablespoon of the reserved oil from tomatoes in a wide nonstick frying pan over medium-high heat. Add tomatoes, garlic, onion, bell pepper, and zucchini. Cook, stirring often, until vegetables begin to brown (about 8 minutes).

3 Pour broth over vegetables and bring to a boil. Drain pasta well and add to vegetables with turkey and basil. Lift with 2 forks to mix. Transfer to a platter. Offer cheese to add to taste.

makes 4 servings

per serving: 500 calories, 33 g protein, 59 g carbohydrates, 16 g total fat, 59 mg cholesterol, 85 mg sodium

penne with turkey sausage

preparation time: about 35 minutes

12 ounces spinach, coarse stems removed, rinsed and drained

1 large red or yellow bell pepper, seeded

3 green onions

8 ounces dried penne

8 to 12 ounces mild or hot turkey Italian sausages, casings removed

1/2 cup balsamic vinegar (or 1/2 cup red wine vinegar and 5 teaspoons sugar)

1/2 to 3/4 teaspoon fennel seeds

Salt and pepper

1 Tear spinach into pieces. Cut bell pepper lengthwise into thin strips. Cut onions into 3-inch lengths and sliver lengthwise. Place vegetables in a large serving bowl and set aside.

2 Bring 8 cups water to a boil in a 4- to 5-quart pan over medium-high heat. Stir in pasta and cook just until tender to bite (8 to 10 minutes); or cook according to package directions. Drain well and keep warm.

3 Chop or crumble sausages. Cook in a wide nonstick frying pan or wok over medium-high heat, stirring often, until browned (about 10 minutes). Add vinegar and fennel seeds, stirring to loosen browned bits.

4 Add pasta to vegetables and immediately pour on sausage mixture; toss gently but well until spinach is slightly wilted. Serve immediately. Offer salt and pepper to add to taste.

makes 6 servings

per serving: 238 calories, 15 g protein, 32 g carbohydrates, 6 g total fat, 36 mg cholesterol, 327 mg sodium

fresh vegetables with fettuccine

preparation time: about 45 minutes

1 tablespoon olive oil

1 large onion, chopped

3 cloves garlic, minced or pressed

³/₄ pound mushrooms, thinly sliced

3 pounds pear-shaped (Roma-type) tomatoes, thinly sliced

2 tablespoons chopped fresh basil leaves

1 pound dry eggless fettuccine or linguine

¹/₂ pound carrots, thinly sliced

³/₄ pound *each* crookneck squash and zucchini, thinly sliced

¹/₄ cup *each* grated Parmesan cheese and thin strips of lean prosciutto

1 Heat oil in a 4- to 5-quart pan over medium-high heat. Add onion and cook, stirring occasionally, until soft (about 7 minutes). Add garlic and mushrooms; cook, stirring, until all liquid has evaporated (about 5 minutes). Add tomatoes and basil; continue to cook until mixture is thickened (about 10 more minutes), stirring occasionally.

2 Meanwhile, following package directions, cook fettuccine in boiling water until barely tender to bite; drain well. Place in a large, shallow serving bowl and keep warm.

3 Add carrots to sauce and cook for 5 minutes. Add crookneck squash and zucchini; continue to cook until vegetables are barely tender to bite (about 3 more minutes).

4 Spoon sauce over pasta and top with cheese and prosciutto.

makes 8 servings

per serving: 320 calories , 13 g protein, 60 g carbohydrates, 4 g total fat, 4 mg cholesterol, 122 mg sodium

korean noodles with hot sauce

preparation time: about 20 minutes

1 tablespoon Asian sesame oil

3 tablespoons distilled white vinegar

1 to 2 tablespoons hot bean paste

2 tablespoons soy sauce

3 tablespoons sliced green onion (including tops)

1 clove garlic, minced

1 teaspoon *each* sugar and pepper

2 teaspoons minced fresh ginger

2 tablespoons sesame seeds

12 ounces dry buckwheat noodles

1 medium-size cucumber, thinly sliced

1 In a bowl, combine sesame oil, vinegar, bean paste, soy, onions, garlic, sugar, pepper, and ginger. Set aside. Toast sesame seeds in a small frying pan over medium heat until golden (about 3 minutes), shaking pan frequently. Set aside.

2 Following package directions, cook noodles in boiling water until barely tender to bite. Drain; return to pan and add vinegar mixture and sesame seeds. Mix well. Garnish with cucumber.

makes 4 to 6 servings

per serving: 265 calories, 9 g protein, 47 g carbohydrates, 5 g total fat, 0 mg cholesterol, 367 mg sodium

asian pasta primavera

preparation time: about 40 minutes, plus 30 minutes to soak mushrooms

2 tablespoons sesame seeds

8 large dried or fresh shiitake mushrooms

1/2 pound *each* asparagus and bok choy

1 can (15 oz.) miniature corn, drained

1 pound dry whole wheat spaghetti

1 tablespoon salad oil

2 cloves garlic, minced or pressed

1 tablespoon very finely chopped fresh ginger

1/2 pound Chinese pea pods (also called snow or sugar peas) or sugar snap peas, ends and strings removed

1 can (about 8 oz.) sliced water chestnuts, drained

1/4 cup dry sherry

1 cup low-sodium chicken broth

2 tablespoons reduced-sodium soy sauce

1 teaspoon *each* sugar and white wine vinegar

1 Toast sesame seeds in a small frying pan over medium heat until golden (about 3 minutes), shaking pan frequently. Pour out of pan and set aside.

2 If using dried mushrooms, soak in warm water to cover for 30 minutes, then drain. Cut off and discard stems; squeeze caps dry and thinly slice. Or trim any tough stems from fresh mushrooms; thinly slice caps.

3 Snap off and discard tough ends of asparagus. Cut asparagus spears, bok choy stems and leaves, and corn into 1/2-inch slanting slices. Set aside.

4 Following package directions, cook spaghetti in boiling water until barely tender to bite; drain well. Place in a large, shallow serving bowl and keep warm.

5 Heat oil in a 12- to 14-inch frying pan over high heat. Add garlic and ginger and cook, stirring, until lightly browned (about 30 seconds). Add mushrooms, asparagus, bok choy, corn, pea pods, water chestnuts, and sherry. Cover and cook, stirring often, until vegetables are tender-crisp to bite (about 2 minutes). Spoon vegetables over noodles.

6 Add broth, soy, sugar, and vinegar to wok; bring to a boil, stirring. Pour over noodles and vegetables. Sprinkle with sesame seeds, then mix lightly. Serve immediately.

makes 8 servings

per serving: 304 calories, 14 g protein, 55 g carbohydrates, 4 g total fat, 0 mg cholesterol, 186 mg sodium

MUSHROOMS FROM HEAVEN: To experience a true vegetable delicacy that will be a delightful addition to your pasta, look for fresh porcini mushrooms in farmers' markets during the fall. These meaty fungi, with their dark brown caps and bulbous stems, are superb strewn into pasta and risotto. Also try them thickly sliced with olive oil and garlic, and grilled. To store fresh porcini, wrap them in paper towels, place them in a paper bag, and refrigerate for up to 2 days; gently wipe clean before using.

capellini with roasted tomatoes & white beans

preparation time: about 15 minutes
cooking time: about 1 1/4 hours

1 medium-size red onion, cut into 3/4-inch chunks

1 tablespoon olive oil

6 tablespoons balsamic vinegar

14 medium-size pear-shaped (Roma-type) tomatoes, halved lengthwise

Salt

8 ounces dried capellini

2 cans (about 15 oz. *each*) cannnellini (white kidney beans)

3 tablespoons chopped fresh thyme or 1 tablespoon dried thyme

3 tablespoons chopped fresh basil or 1 tablespoon dried basil

Thyme sprigs

1 Mix onion, l teaspoon of the oil, and 2 tablespoons of the vinegar in a lightly oiled square 8-inch baking pan. Arrange tomatoes, cut sides up, in a lightly oiled 9-by 13-inch baking pan; rub with remaining 2 teaspoons oil and season to taste with salt.

2 Bake onion and tomatoes in a 475° oven, switching pan positions halfway through baking, until edges are well browned (40 to 50 minutes for onion, about 1 hour and 10 minutes for tomatoes); if drippings begin to burn, add 4 to 6 tablespoons water to each pan, stirring to loosen browned bits. Meanwhile, bring 8 cups water to a boil in a 4- to 5-quart pan over medium-high heat. Stir in pasta and cook just until tender to bite (about 4 minutes), or cook according to package directions.

3 Drain pasta well and keep warm. Pour beans and their liquid into pan. Add chopped thyme (or dried thyme and dried basil, if used). Bring to a boil; reduce heat and simmer, stirring often, for 3 minutes. Add pasta; lift with 2 forks to mix. Remove from heat; keep warm.

4 Chop 10 of the tomato halves. Add to pasta with chopped basil (if used), onion, and remaining 1/4 cup vinegar. Transfer pasta to a wide, shallow serving bowl. Arrange remaining tomato halves around edge. Garnish with thyme sprigs.

makes 4 to 6 servings

per serving: 401 calories, 17 g protein, 73 g carbohydrates, 6 g total fat, 0 mg cholesterol, 616 mg sodium

linguini with yellow tomatoes

preparation time: about 30 minutes

1 pound dried linguine

About 2 tablespoons hot chili oil

1 clove garlic, minced or pressed

1 large onion, chopped

6 cups yellow or red cherry or other tiny tomatoes (or use some of each color), cut into halves

2 cups firmly packed fresh basil leaves

Basil sprigs (optional)

Grated Parmesan cheese

Salt

1 In a 6- to 8-quart pan, cook linguine in 4 quarts boiling water until just tender to bite (8 to 10 minutes); or cook according to package directions. Drain well, transfer to a wide bowl, and keep warm.

2 While pasta is cooking, heat 2 tablespoons of the chili oil in a wide non-stick frying pan or wok over medium-high heat. When oil is hot, add garlic and onion; stir-fry until onion is soft (about 5 minutes). Add tomatoes and basil leaves; stir gently until tomatoes are heated through (about 2 minutes).

3 Pour hot tomato mixture over pasta. Garnish with basil sprigs, if desired. Offer cheese to add to taste; season to taste with more chili oil and salt.

makes 6 to 8 servings

per serving: 322 calories, 10 g protein, 59 g carbohydrates, 5 g total fat, 0 mg cholesterol, 18 mg sodium

thai tofu & tagliatelle

preparation time: 35 to 40 minutes

1 cup vegetable broth

1 cup sugar

¼ cup reduced-sodium soy sauce

2 tablespoons cider vinegar

1 tablespoon cornstarch

2 teaspoons paprika

1 teaspoon crushed red pepper flakes

1 teaspoon vegetable oil

⅓ cup minced garlic

8 to 10 ounces dried tagliatelle or fettuccine

1 pound regular tofu, rinsed and drained,
    cut into ½-inch cubes

1 large red bell pepper, cut into ½-inch pieces

1 package (about 10 oz.) frozen tiny peas, thawed

1 Combine broth, sugar, soy sauce, vinegar, cornstarch, paprika, and red pepper flakes in a small bowl; mix until well blended. Set aside.

2 Heat oil in a wide nonstick frying pan over medium-high heat. Add garlic and cook, stirring often, until tinged with gold (about 4 minutes; do not scorch); if pan appears dry, stir in water, 1 tablespoon at a time.

3 Add broth mixture. Cook, stirring often, until sauce comes to a boil. Continue to cook until reduced to about 1¼ cups (10 to 15 minutes). Meanwhile, bring 12 cups water to a boil in a 5- to 6-quart pan over medium-high heat. Stir in pasta and cook just until tender to bite (8 to 10 minutes); or cook according to package directions. Drain well and transfer to a wide, shallow serving bowl.

4 Combine tofu, bell pepper, peas, and half the sauce in a large bowl. Mix well but gently. Spoon over pasta. Offer remaining sauce to add to taste.

makes 4 servings

per serving: 634 calories, 23 g protein, 121 g carbohydrates, 8 g total fat, 0 mg cholesterol, 987 mg sodium

farfalle with fresh tomatoes & basil

preparation time: about 20 minutes

12 ounces farfalle or other dry pasta shape

1 tablespoon olive oil

2 cloves garlic, minced or pressed

1 pound ripe pear-shaped tomatoes,
    coarsely chopped

1 cup tightly packed fresh basil leaves,
    torn into pieces

Coarsely ground pepper

Grated Parmesan cheese

1 In an 8- to 10-quart pan, cook pasta in 6 quarts boiling water until al dente (7 to 9 minutes or according to package directions).

2 Meanwhile, heat oil in a wide frying pan over medium heat. Add garlic and cook, stirring, for 1 minute. Add tomatoes and cook, stirring, just until tomatoes begin to soften (about 3 minutes). Remove from heat.

3 Drain pasta and place in a large, warm bowl or platter. Add tomato mixture and basil; toss well. Season to taste with pepper and offer with Parmesan.

makes 4 servings

per serving: 382 calories, 13 g protein, 72 g carbohydrates, 5 g total fat, 0 mg cholesterol, 16 mg sodium

peanut pasta & tofu

preparation time: about 40 minutes

1/4 cup seasoned rice vinegar (or 1/4 cup distilled white vinegar plus 2 teaspoons sugar)

3 tablespoons Asian sesame oil

1 tablespoon reduced-sodium soy sauce

1 teaspoon sugar

1 package (about 14 oz.) regular tofu, rinsed, drained, and cut into 1/2-inch cubes

12 ounces dried penne

2 cups Chinese pea pods (also called snow or sugar peas), ends and strings removed

2 cloves garlic, minced

1/2 cup plum jam

1/4 cup crunchy peanut butter

1/8 teaspoon ground ginger

1/3 cup cilantro leaves

1/4 cup sliced green onions

Cilantro sprigs

Crushed red pepper flakes

1 In a shallow bowl, beat vinegar, 1 tablespoon of the oil, soy sauce, and sugar until blended. Add tofu and mix gently. Set aside; stir occasionally.

2 In a 5- to 6-quart pan, bring about 3 quarts water to a boil over medium high heat; stir in pasta and cook until almost tender to bite, 7 to 9 minutes. (Or cook pasta according to package directions, cooking for a little less than the recommended time.) Add pea pods to boiling water with pasta and cook for 1 more minute. Drain pasta mixture, rinse with hot water, and drain well again; keep warm.

3 With a slotted spoon, transfer tofu to a large, shallow serving bowl; reserve marinade from tofu.

4 In pan used to cook pasta, heat remaining 2 tablespoons oil over medium heat. Add garlic and cook, stirring, just until fragrant (about 30 seconds; do not scorch). Add jam, peanut butter, marinade from tofu, and ginger. Cook, whisking, just until sauce is smooth and well blended.

5 Remove pan from heat and add pasta mixture, cilantro leaves, and onions. Mix gently but thoroughly. Transfer pasta to bowl with tofu and mix very gently. Garnish with cilantro sprigs. Serve at once; season to taste with red pepper flakes.

makes 4 servings

per serving: 714 calories, 25 g protein, 103 g carbohydrates, 25 g total fat, 0 mg cholesterol, 558 mg sodium

fettuccine cambozola

preparation time: about 20 minutes

1 package fresh fettuccine

1 package (about 10 oz.) frozen peas

1 cup diced cambozola or Gorgonzola cheese

Freshly ground pepper

1 Bring 3 quarts water to a boil in a 5- to 6-quart pan. Add pasta and cook just until tender to bite (3 to 4 minutes); or cook according to package directions. Stir in peas. Drain well.

2 Return pasta and peas to pan over low heat. Add cheese and 2 tablespoons hot water. Mix lightly until pasta is well coated with melted cheese (2 to 3 minutes).

3 Season to taste with pepper.

makes 2 to 4 servings

per serving: 492 calories, 23 g protein, 56 g carbohydrates, 18 g total fat, 233 mg cholesterol, 918 mg sodium

stuffed shells with roasted red pepper sauce

preparation time: about 20 minutes
cooking time: about 1 hour

Roasted Red Pepper Sauce (recipe below)

1 to 2 tablespoons pine nuts

20 jumbo shell-shaped pasta

1 can (about 15 oz.) garbanzo beans

1/4 cup lightly packed fresh basil

2 tablespoons chopped parsley

2 tablespoons lemon juice

2 teaspoons Asian sesame oil

2 cloves garlic

1/4 teaspoon ground cumin

Salt and pepper

Parsley sprigs

1 Prepare Roasted Red Pepper Sauce; set aside. Toast pine nuts in a small frying pan over medium heat, shaking pan often, until golden (about 3 minutes). Remove from pan and set aside.

2 Bring 12 cups water to a boil in a 5- to 6-quart pan over medium high heat. Stir in pasta and cook just until almost tender (about 8 minutes; do not overcook).

3 Meanwhile, drain beans, reserving liquid. Combine beans, basil, chopped parsley, lemon juice, oil, garlic and cumin in a blender or food processor. Whirl, adding reserved liquid as necessary, until smooth but thick. Season to taste with salt and pepper.

4 Drain pasta, rinse with cold water; and drain well. Spoon half the red pepper sauce into a shallow 2- to 2½-quart casserole Fill shells with bean mixture and arrange, filled, sides up, in sauce. Top with remaining sauce. Cover tightly and bake in a 350° oven until hot (about 40 minutes). Sprinkle with nuts. Garnish with parsley sprigs

makes 4 servings

per serving: 467 calories, 17 g protein, 80 g carbohydrates, 9 g total fat, 4 mg cholesterol, 424 mg sodium

roasted red pepper sauce

preparation time: about 30 minutes

Roasted Red Bell Peppers (directions follow)

1 teaspoon olive oil

1 large onion, chopped

3 cloves garlic, minced or pressed

2 tablespoons dry sherry (or to taste)

1 tablespoon white wine vinegar (or to taste)

1/8 teaspoon ground white pepper

1/4 cup freshly grated

Parmesan cheese

Salt

1 Prepare Roasted Red Bell Peppers. Set aside with any drippings in a blender or food processor.

2 Heat oil in a wide nonstick frying pan over medium-high heat. Add onion and garlic. Cook, stirring often, until onion is soft (about 5 minutes); if pan appears dry or onion mixture sticks to pan bottom, add water, 1 tablespoon at a time.

3 Transfer onion mixture to blender with peppers. Whirl until smooth. Add sherry, vinegar, and pepper. Whirl until of desired consistency. (At this point, you may cover and refrigerate for up to 2 days; reheat before continuing.)

4 Add cheese. Season to taste with salt.

makes about 3 cups

ROASTED RED BELL PEPPERS

Cut 4 large red bell peppers in half lengthwise. Place, cut sides down, in a 10- by 15-inch baking pan. Broil 4 to 6 inches below heat, turning as needed, until charred all over (about 8 minutes). Cover with foil and let cool in pan. Pull off and discard skins, stems, and seeds. Cut into chunks.

per serving: 40 calories, 1 g protein, 6 g carbohydrates, 1 g total fat, 1 mg cholesterol, 33 mg sodium

fettuccine alfredo

preparation time: 40 minutes

2 cans (about 14 oz. *each*) artichoke hearts packed in water, drained and quartered

3 tablespoons chopped Italian or regular parsley

3 tablespoons thinly sliced green onions

12 ounces dried fettuccine

1 tablespoon butter or olive oil

3 cloves garlic, minced

1 tablespoon, all-purpose flour

1 1/2 cups low-fat (2%) milk

1 large package (about 8 oz.) nonfat cream cheese, cut into small chunks

1 1/2 cups (about 4 1/2 oz.) shredded Parmesan cheese

1/8 teaspoon ground nutmeg (optional)

Pepper

1 In a medium-size bowl, combine artichokes, parsley, and onions. Set aside.

2 In a 5- to 6-quart pan, bring about 3 quarts water to a boil over medium high heat; stir in pasta and cook until just tender to bite, 8 to 10 minutes. (Or cook pasta according to package directions.) Drain well, return to pan, and keep hot.

3 Melt butter in a wide nonstick frying pan over medium heat. Add garlic and cook, stirring, until fragrant (about 30 seconds: do not scorch). Whisk in flour until well blended, then gradually whisk in milk Cook, whisking constantly, until mixture boils and thickens slightly (about 5 minutes). Whisk in cream cheese, 1 cup of the Parmesan cheese, and nutmeg (if desired). Continue to cook, whisking constantly, until cheese is melted and evenly blended into sauce.

4 Working quickly, pour hot sauce over pasta and lift with 2 forks to mix. Spoon pasta into center of 4 shallow individual bowls. Then quickly arrange artichoke mixture around pasta. Sprinkle with remaining 1/2 cup Parmesan cheese, then with pepper. Serve immediately (sauce thickens rapidly and is absorbed quickly by pasta).

makes 4 servings

per serving: 641 calories, 39 g protein, 82 g carbohydrates, 17 g total fat, 126 mg cholesterol, 924 mg sodium

baked penne with radicchio

preparation time: 40 to 45 minutes

8 ounces dry penne or mostaccioli

1 tablespoon olive oil

8 ounces mushrooms, sliced

2 cloves garlic, minced or pressed

1 teaspoon dry sage

4 cups lightly packed shredded radicchio

1/4 cup grated Parmesan cheese

1/4 cup crumbled Gorgonzola or other blue veined cheese

Freshly ground pepper

1 cup evaporated skim milk

1 In a 5- to 6-quart pan, cook penne in 3 quarts boiling water just until almost tender to bite (10 to 12 minutes); or cook a little less than time specified in package directions.

2 Meanwhile, heat oil in a wide nonstick frying pan over medium heat; add mushrooms, garlic, and sage. Cook, stirring often, until mushrooms are soft and liquid has evaporated (about 10 minutes). Stir in radicchio, then remove pan from heat.

3 Drain pasta well; add to mushroom mixture along with Parmesan and Gorgonzola cheeses, then mix lightly. Season to taste with pepper. Transfer to a greased 2- to 2½-quart casserole; drizzle evenly with milk. Cover and bake in a 450° oven until bubbly and heated through (15 to 20 minutes).

makes 4 servings

per serving: 366 calories, 17 g protein, 55 g carbohydrates, 9 g total fat, 14 mg cholesterol, 263 mg sodium

orecchlette with lentils & goat cheese

preparation time: about 45 minutes

2 cups vegetable broth

6 ounces lentils, rinsed and drained

1 tablespoon chopped fresh thyme
   or 1 teaspoon dried thyme

8 ounces dried orecchiette
   or other medium-size pasta shape

1/3 cup white wine vinegar

3 tablespoons chopped parsley

2 tablespoons olive oil

1 teaspoon honey, or to taste

1 clove garlic, minced or pressed

1/2 cup crumbled goat or feta cheese

Thyme sprigs

Salt and pepper

1 Bring broth to a boil in a 1½- to 2-quart pan over high heat. Add lentils and chopped thyme; reduce heat, cover, and simmer until lentils are tender to bite (20 to 30 minutes).

2 Meanwhile, bring 8 cups water to a boil in a 4- to 5-quart pan over medium-high heat. Stir in pasta and cook just until tender to bite (8 to 10 minutes); or cook according to package directions. Drain pasta and, if necessary, lentils well. Transfer pasta and lentils to a large serving bowl; keep warm.

3 Combine vinegar, parsley, oil, honey, and garlic in a small bowl. Beat until blended. Add to pasta mixture and mix thoroughly but gently. Sprinkle with cheese. Garnish with thyme sprigs. Offer salt and pepper to add to taste.

makes 4 servings

per serving: 514 calories, 25 g protein, 75 g carbohydrates, 14 g total fat, 13 mg cholesterol, 648 mg sodium

spaghetti with beans and spaghetti squash

preparation time: about 15 minutes
cooking time: about 1 ³/₄ hours

1 spaghetti squash

1 1/2 cups vegetable broth

1 package (about 10 oz.) frozen baby lima beans

2 tablespoons fresh thyme
   or 2 teaspoons dried thyme

1 1/2 teaspoons grated lemon peel

8 cups lightly packed spinach leaves,
   cut into narrow strips

12 ounces dried spaghetti

Salt and pepper

1 Pierce squash shell in several places. Place in a shallow pan slightly larger than squash. Bake in a 350° oven until shell gives readily when pressed (1 ¼ to 1 ½ hours).

2 Halve squash lengthwise; remove seeds. Scrape squash from shell, using a fork to loosen strands, and place in a 3- to 4-quart pan. Add broth, beans, thyme, and lemon peel. Bring to a boil over high heat; reduce heat, cover, and simmer, stirring often, just until beans are tender to bite (about 5 minutes). Add spinach. Cover and cook until spinach is wilted (1 to 2 more minutes). Remove from heat and keep warm.

3 Bring 12 cups water to a boil in a 5- to 6-quart pan over medium-high heat. Stir in pasta and cook just until tender to bite (8 to 10 minutes); or cook according to package directions. Drain well; return to pan. Add squash mixture and lift with 2 forks to mix. Transfer to a serving bowl. Offer salt and pepper to add to taste

makes 8 servings

per serving: 259 calories, 11 g protein, 51 g carbohydrates, 2 g total fat, 0 mg cholesterol, 301 mg sodium

oven-baked mediterreanean orzo

preparation time: about 1 hour

2 large cans (about 28 oz.) tomatoes

About 2 cups vegetable broth

1 teaspoon olive oil

2 large onion, cut into very thin slivers

1 can (about 15 oz.) *each* black beans and
cannellini (white kidney beans, drained
and rinsed well)

1 package (about 9 oz.) frozen artichoke hearts,
(thawed and drained)

$^1/_2$ cup dried apricots, cut into halves

$^1/_3$ cup raisins

About 1 tablespoon drained capers (or to taste)

4 teaspoons chopped fresh basil
or 1 $^1/_2$ teaspoons dried basil

$^1/_2$ teaspoon fennel seeds, crushed

1 $^1/_2$ cups dried orzo or other rice-shaped pasta

$^1/_2$ cup crumbled feta cheese

Pepper

1 Break up tomatoes with a spoon and drain liquid into a 4-cup measure; set tomatoes aside. Add enough of the broth to tomato liquid to make 3 cups; set aside.

2 Place oil and onion in an oval 3- to 3½-quart casserole, about 9 by 13 inches and at least 2½ inches deep. Bake in a 450° oven until onion is soft and tinged with brown (about 10 minutes). During baking, stir occasionally to loosen browned bits from casserole bottom; add water, 1 tablespoon at a time, if casserole appears dry.

3 Remove casserole from oven and carefully add tomatoes, broth mixture, black beans, cannellini, artichokes, apricots, raisins, capers, basil, and fennel seeds. Stir to loosen any browned bits from casserole. Return to oven and continue to bake until mixture comes to a rolling boil (about 20 minutes).

4 Remove casserole from oven and carefully stir in pasta, scraping casserole bottom to loosen any browned bits. Cover tightly, return to oven, and bake for 10 more minutes; then stir pasta mixture well, scraping casserole bottom. Cover tightly again and continue to bake until pasta is just tender to bite and almost all liquid has been absorbed (about 10 more minutes). Sprinkle with cheese, cover and let stand for about 5 minutes before serving. Season to taste with pepper.

makes 6 to 8 servings

per serving: 358 calories, 35 g protein, 66 g carbohydrates, 5 g total fat, 9 mg cholesterol, 847 mg sodium

STORE BREAD IN THE FREEZER: You'll always have fresh bread if you keep a loaf in the freezer. Bread kept at room temperature must be used quickly, and refrigerated bread can dry out rapidly. To thaw frozen bread in a hurry, spread out slices in a single layer and let stand for 10 minutes. If slices are to be toasted, put them right into the toaster.

bucatini & black beans

preparation time: about 35 minutes

10 ounces dried bucatini, perciatelli, or spaghetti

²⁄₃ cup seasoned rice vinegar (or ²⁄₃ cup distilled white vinegar and 2 tablespoons sugar)

2 tablespoons honey

1 tablespoon olive oil

¹⁄₂ teaspoon chili oil

2 cans (about 15 oz. *each*) black beans, drained and rinsed

4 large pear-shaped tomatoes (about 12 oz. *total*), diced

¹⁄₃ cup finely chopped parsley

¹⁄₄ cup thinly sliced green onions

³⁄₄ cup crumbled feta cheese

Parsley sprigs

1 Bring 12 cups water to a boil in a 5- to 6-quart pan over medium-high heat. Stir in pasta and cook just until tender to bite (10 to 12 minutes); or cook according to package directions. Drain well and keep warm.

2 Combine vinegar, honey, olive oil, and chili oil in pan. Bring just to a boil over medium-high heat. Add pasta, beans, and tomatoes. Cook, stirring, until hot. Remove from heat; stir in chopped parsley and onions.

3 Spoon pasta mixture into bowls. Sprinkle with cheese. Garnish with parsley sprigs.

makes 4 servings

per serving: 564 calories, 21 g protein, 96 g carbohydrates, 11 g total fat, 23 mg cholesterol, 1,095 mg sodium

pasta with shrimp & shiitakes

preparation time: about 35 minutes

2 cups dried shiitake mushrooms

8 ounces dried capellini

2 teaspoons Asian sesame oil

6 tablespoons oyster sauce or reduced-sodium soy sauce

1 tablespoon vegetable oil

12 ounces medium-size raw shrimp (31 to 35 per lb.), shelled and deveined

1 tablespoon finely chopped fresh ginger

3 green onions, thinly sliced

1 Place mushrooms in a medium-size bowl and add enough boiling water to cover, let stand until mushrooms are softened (about 10 minutes). Squeeze mushrooms dry. Cut off and discard stems. Slice caps into strips about ¼ inch thick.

2 In a 4- to 5-quart pan, bring about 8 cups water to a boil over medium-high heat; stir in pasta and cook until just tender to bite, about 3 minutes. (Or cook according to package directions.) Drain pasta, rinse with hot water, and drain well again. Then return to pan, add sesame oil and 3 tablespoons of the oyster sauce; lift with 2 forks to mix well. Keep pasta mixture warm.

3 Heat vegetable oil in a wide nonstick frying pan over medium-high heat. Add mushrooms, shrimp, and ginger. Cook, stirring often, until shrimp are just opaque in center, cut to test (about 5 minutes). Add onions and remaining 3 tablespoons oyster sauce; mix thoroughly. Pour noodles into a wide bowl; pour shrimp mixture over noodles.

makes 4 servings

per serving: 409 calories, 25 g protein, 64 g carbohydrates, 8 g total fat, 105 mg cholesterol, 1,181 mg sodium

ziti with turkey, feta & sun-dried tomatoes

preparation time: about 30 minutes

2 to 4 tablespoons sun-dried tomatoes in olive oil

1/2 cup fat-free reduced-sodium chicken broth

2 tablespoons dry white wine

1 teaspoon cornstarch

1 small onion

8 ounces dried ziti or penne

2 turkey breast tenderloins (about 1 lb. *total*), cut into 1/2-inch pieces

1 1/2 teaspoons chopped fresh oregano or 1/2 teaspoon dried oregano

1 large tomato, chopped and drained well

2 tablespoons drained capers

1/2 cup crumbled feta cheese

Oregano sprigs

1 Drain sun-dried tomatoes well (reserve oil) and pat dry with paper towels. Then chop tomatoes and set aside.

2 To prepare sauce, in a small bowl, stir together broth, wine, and cornstarch until blended; set aside.

3 Chop onion and set aside.

4 In a 4- to 5-quart pan, cook pasta in about 8 cups boiling water until just tender to bite (8 to 10 minutes). Drain pasta well and transfer to a warm large bowl; keep warm.

5 While pasta is cooking, measure 2 teaspoons of the oil from sun-dried tomatoes. Heat oil in a wide nonstick frying pan or wok over medium-high heat. When oil is hot, add turkey and chopped oregano. Stir-fry just until meat is no longer pink in center cut to test (2 to 3 minutes). Add water, 1 tablespoon at a time, if pan appears to be dry. Remove turkey with a slotted spoon; transfer to bowl with pasta and keep warm.

6 Add sun-dried tomatoes and onion to pan; stir-fry until onion is soft (about 4 minutes). Add water if pan is dry.

7 Stir reserved sauce well and pour into pan. Cook, stirring, until sauce boils and thickens slightly (1 to 2 minutes). Remove from heat and stir in fresh tomato and capers. Spoon tomato mixture over pasta and turkey; mix gently but thoroughly.

8 Divide turkey mixture among 4 warm individual rimmed plates or shallow bowls. Sprinkle with cheese and garnish with oregano sprigs.

makes 4 servings

per serving: 489 calories, 39 g protein, 52 g carbohydrates, 13 g total fat, 83 mg cholesterol, 464 mg sodium

mixed herb pesto

preparation time: 15 minutes

2 cups lightly packed fresh basil leaves

1/2 cup thinly sliced green onions

1/3 cup lightly packed fresh oregano leaves

1/4 cup grated Parmesan cheese

1/4 cup red wine vinegar

2 tablespoons fresh rosemary leaves

2 tablespoons olive oil

1/4 to 1/2 teaspoon pepper

In a food processor or blender, whirl basil, onions, oregano, cheese, vinegar, rosemary, oil, and pepper until smoothly puréed.

makes about 1 cup

per tablespoon: 29 calories, 0.9 g protein, 2 g carbohydrates, 2 g total fat, 1 mg cholesterol, 25 mg sodium

linguine with lentils

preparation time: about 55 minutes

1 cup lentils

2 cups canned vegetable broth

1 teaspoon dried thyme

¹/₃ cup lemon juice

3 tablespoons chopped fresh basil

2 tablespoons olive oil

1 teaspoon honey (or to taste)

2 cloves garlic, minced

12 ounces dried Linguine

1 large tomato, chopped and drained

³/₄ cup grated Parmesan cheese

1 Rinse and sort lentils, discarding any debris; drain lentils. In a 1 ½- to 2-quart part, bring broth to a basil over high heat; add lentils and thyme. Reduce heat, cover, and simmer just until lentils are tender to bite (25 to 30 minutes). Drain and discard any remaining cooking liquid; keep lentils warm.

2 While lentils are cooking, combine lemon juice, chopped basil, oil, honey, and garlic in a small bowl; set aside. Also bring about 3 quarts water to a boil in a 5- to 6-quart pan over medium-high heat; stir in pasta and cook until just tender to bite, 8 to 10 minutes. (Or cook pasta according to package directions.)

3 Working quickly, drain pasta well and transfer to a large serving bowl. Add basil mixture, lentils, and tomato. Lift with 2 forks to mix. Sprinkle with cheese and serve immediately.

makes 6 servings

per serving: 426 calories, 23 g protein, 66 g carbohydrates, 9 g total fat, 8 mg cholesterol, 537 mg sodium

three-cheese lasagne with chard

preparation time: 20 minutes
cooking time: about 1 hour

12 ounces dry lasagne noodles

2 ¹/₂ cups low-fat (2%) milk

¹/₄ cup cornstarch

1 ¹/₂ teaspoons dried basil

¹/₂ teaspoon *each* dried rosemary and salt

¹/₄ teaspoon ground nutmeg

1 cup nonfat ricotta cheese

2 packages (about 10 oz. *each*) frozen chopped Swiss chard, thawed and squeezed dry

2 large ripe tomatoes, chopped

2 cups shredded mozzarella cheese

¹/₃ cup grated Parmesan cheese

1 In a 5- to 6-quart pan, bring about 3 quarts water to a boil over medium-high heat; stir in pasta and cook until just barely tender to bite, about 8 minutes. Drain pasta well and lay out flat; cover lightly.

2 In pasta-cooking pan, smoothly blend milk, cornstarch, basil, rosemary, salt, and nutmeg. Stir over medium-high heat until mixture boils and thickens slightly (about 5 minutes). Stir in ricotta cheese, chard, tomatoes, and half the mozzarella cheese. Gently stir in pasta.

3 Transfer mixture to a 9- by 13-inch baking pan; gently push pasta down to cover it with sauce. Sprinkle with remaining mozzarella cheese, then with Parmesan cheese. Bake in a 375° oven until lasagne is bubbly in center (about 40 minutes). Let stand for about 5 minutes before serving.

makes 8 servings

per serving: 362 calories, 22 g protein, 48 g carbohydrates, 10 g total fat, 33 mg cholesterol, 531 mg sodium

low-fat lo mein

preparation time: about 30 minutes

12 ounces fresh Chinese noodles or linguine

1 teaspoon Asian sesame oil

1 tablespoon vegetable oil

1 small onion, thinly sliced lengthwise

2 tablespoons oyster sauce

8 ounces ground turkey

1 pound napa cabbage, thinly sliced crosswise

4 ounces oyster mushrooms, thinly sliced

2 medium-size carrots, cut into matchstick strips

1/2 cup fat-free reduced-sodium chicken broth

2 tablespoons reduced-sodium soy sauce

1 In a 5- to 6-quart pan, cook noodles in about 3 quarts boiling water until just tender to bite (3 to 5 minutes); or cook according to package directions. Drain well, toss with sesame oil, and keep warm.

2 Heat vegetable oil in a wide nonstick frying pan or wok over medium-high heat. When oil is hot, add onion and oyster sauce; then crumble in turkey. Stir-fry until onion is soft and turkey is no longer pink (about 3 minutes). Add cabbage, mushrooms, carrots, and broth; cover and cook until carrots are just tender to bite (about 3 minutes). Uncover and continue to cook until liquid has evaporated (1 to 2 more minutes). Stir in soy sauce; add noodles and stir-fry until heated.

makes 6 servings

per serving: 295 calories, 16 g protein, 41 g carbohydrates, 7 g total fat, 69 mg cholesterol, 563 mg sodium

spinach pasta & scallops

preparation time: about 30 minutes

8 ounces dried spinach fettuccine or 1 package (9 oz.) fresh spinach fettuccine

2 tablespoons pine nuts

2 tablespoons olive oil

1 pound bay scallops, rinsed and patted dry

2 cloves garlic, minced or pressed

1 large tomato, seeded and chopped

1/4 cup dry white wine

1/4 cup chopped Italian parsley

Salt and freshly ground pepper

1 In a 5- to 6-quart pan, cook fettuccine in 3 quarts boiling water just until tender to bite (8 to 10 minutes for dry pasta, 3 to 4 minutes for fresh); or cook according to package directions. Drain well.

2 While pasta is cooking, toast pine nuts in a wide nonstick frying pan over medium-low heat until lightly browned (about 3 minutes), stirring often. Remove nuts from pan and set aside. Then heat oil in pan over medium-high heat. Add scallops and cook, turning often with a wide spatula, until opaque in center, cut to test (2 to 3 minutes). Lift from pan, place on a warm plate, and keep warm.

3 Add garlic to pan; cook, stirring, just until it begins to brown (1 to 2 minutes). Stir in tomato, then wine; bring to a full boil. Remove pan from heat and add pasta, scallops and any accumulated liquid, and parsley; mix lightly, using 2 spoons. Season to taste with salt and pepper. Sprinkle with pine nuts.

makes 4 servings

per serving: 425 calories, 29 g protein, 47 g carbohydrates, 13 g total fat, 91 mg cholesterol, 231 mg sodium

pasta with chicken & prosciutto

preparation time: about 25 minutes

1/2 cup fat-free reduced-sodium chicken broth or dry white wine

1/4 cup Dijon mustard

2 tablespoons lemon juice

1 teaspoon dried basil

8 ounces dried spinach spaghetti

2 teaspoons olive oil

4 green onions, thinly sliced

2 cloves garlic, minced or pressed

1 ounce prosciutto, cut into thin strips

1 pound skinless, boneless chicken breast, cut into 1/2- by 2-inch strips

1 In a small bowl, stir together broth, mustard, lemon juice, and basil. Set aside.

2 In a 4- to 5-quart pan, cook spaghetti in about 8 cups boiling water until just tender to bite (8 to 10 minutes); or cook according to package directions.

3 Meanwhile, heat oil in a wide nonstick frying pan or wok over medium heat. When oil is hot, add onions, garlic, and prosciutto; stir-fry until prosciutto is lightly browned (about 3 minutes). Increase heat to medium-high. Add chicken and stir-fry until no longer pink in center, cut to test (3 to 4 minutes). Add broth mixture to pan and bring to a boil. Remove from heat.

4 Drain pasta well and place in a warm wide bowl; spoon chicken mixture over pasta.

makes 4 servings

per serving: 399 calorie, 37 g protein, 45 g carbohydrates, 6 g total fat, 72 mg cholesterol, 670 mg sodium

fettuccine with shrimp & gorgonzola

preparation time: about 25 minutes

12 ounces dried spinach fettuccine or regular fettuccine

2 teaspoons butter or margarine

12 ounces mushrooms, sliced

3/4 cup half-and-half

3 ounces Gorgonzola cheese, crumbled

3/4 cup fat-free reduced-sodium chicken broth

8 ounces tiny cooked shrimp

2 tablespoons minced parsley

1 Bring 12 cups water to a boil in a 5- to 6-quart pan over medium-high heat. Stir in pasta and cook just until tender to bite (8 to 10 minutes); or cook according to package directions. Drain well and keep warm.

2 Melt butter in a wide nonstick frying pan over medium-high heat. Add mushrooms and cook, stirring often, until browned (about 8 minutes). Add half-and-half, cheese, and broth. Reduce heat to medium and cook, stirring, until cheese is melted (about 2 minutes); do not boil.

3 Add shrimp and pasta quickly. Lift with 2 forks until most of the liquid is absorbed. Transfer to a platter. Sprinkle with parsley.

makes 6 servings

per serving: 372 calories, 22 g protein, 44 g carbohydrates, 12 g total fat, 153 mg cholesterol, 366 mg sodium

farfalle with smoked salmon & vodka

preparation time: about 40 minutes

12 ounces dried farfalle

1 teaspoon olive oil

1 small shallot, thinly sliced

4 small pear-shaped (Roma-type) tomatoes, peeled, seeded, and chopped

²/₃ cup half-and-half

3 tablespoons vodka

2 tablespoons chopped fresh dill or ¹/₂ teaspoon dried dill weed, or to taste

Pinch of ground nutmeg

4 to 6 ounces sliced smoked salmon or lox, cut into bite-size strips

Dill sprigs

Ground white pepper

1 Bring 12 cups water to a boil in a 5- to 6-quart pan over medium-high heat. Stir in pasta and cook just until tender to bite (8 to 10 minutes); or cook according to package directions. Drain well and keep warm.

2 Heat oil in a wide nonstick frying pan over medium-low heat. Add shallot and cook, stirring often, until soft but not browned (about 3 minutes). Stir in tomatoes; cover and simmer for 5 minutes. Add half-and-half, vodka, chopped dill, and nutmeg. Increase heat to medium-high and bring to a boil. Cook, stirring often, for 1 minute.

3 Add pasta and mix thoroughly but gently. Remove from heat and stir in salmon. Transfer to a serving platter. Garnish with dill sprigs. Offer white pepper to add to taste.

makes 5 servings

per serving: 385 calories, 15 g protein, 54 g carbohydrates, 10 g total fat, 28 mg cholesterol, 243 mg sodium

pasta with parsley-lemon pesto

preparation time: about 20 minutes

1 pound penne, rigatoni, or other dry pasta shape

1 large lemon

2 cups lightly packed chopped fresh parsley (preferably Italian)

2 cloves garlic

3 ounces grated Parmesan cheese

3 tablespoons extra-virgin olive oil

Coarsely ground pepper

1 In an 8- to 10-quart pan, cook pasta in 6 quarts boiling water until al dente (7 to 9 minutes or according to package directions).

2 Meanwhile, use a vegetable peeler to pare zest (colored part of peel) from lemon in large strips (reserve lemon for other uses). In a food processor, whirl lemon zest, parsley, garlic, and Parmesan until finely minced, scraping down sides of bowl as needed. (Or mince lemon zest, parsley, and garlic by hand; stir in cheese.)

3 Drain pasta and place in a large, warm bowl. Add parsley mixture and oil; toss well. Season to taste with pepper.

makes 4 to 6 servings

per serving: 487 calories, 18 g protein, 71 g carbohydrates, 14 g total fat,, 12 mg cholesterol, 289 mg sodium

rotini with scallops

preparation time: about 30 minutes

1 pound dried rotini or other corkscrew-shaped pasta

1 1/2 pounds bay scallops, rinsed and drained

1 teaspoon paprika

1/2 teaspoon dried basil

1/2 teaspoon dried thyme

1/2 teaspoon dry mustard

1/2 teaspoon ground white pepper

2 teaspoons vegetable oil

1 cup fat-free reduced-sodium chicken broth

1 1/2 tablespoons cornstarch blended with 1/3 cup water

1/2 cup reduced-fat or regular sour cream

1 Bring 16 cups water to a boil in a 6- to 8-quart pan over medium-high heat. Stir in pasta and cook just until tender to bite (8 to 10 minutes); or cook according to package directions.

2 Meanwhile, place scallops in a large bowl. Add paprika, basil, thyme, mustard, and white pepper. Mix until scallops are well coated.

3 Heat oil in a wide nonstick frying pan over medium-high heat. Add scallops and cook, stirring often, just until opaque in center; cut to test (about 3 minutes). Lift out and set aside, reserving juices in pan.

4 Drain pasta well. Transfer to a serving platter and keep warm.

5 Increase heat to high and cook reserved juices until reduced to about 1/4 cup. Add broth and bring to a boil. Stir cornstarch mixture well and add to broth. Bring to a boil again, stirring constantly. Remove from heat and stir in sour cream and scallops. Spoon over pasta.

makes 6 servings

per serving: 442 calories, 31 g protein, 63 g carbohydrates, 7 g total fat, 44 mg cholesterol, 218 mg sodium

linguini with red & green sauce

preparation time: about 1 hour

8 medium-size red bell peppers

1 pound dried linguine

1 cup thinly sliced green onions

1 can (about 35 oz.) garbanzo beans, drained

3/4 cup chopped fresh basil or 1/4 cup dried basil

1 1/2 tablespoons chopped fresh tarragon or 1 1/2 teaspoons dried tarragon

3 tablespoons capers, drained

Salt and pepper

1 Place bell peppers in a 10- by 15- inch baking pan. Broil about 3 inches below heat, turning as needed, until charred all over (about 15 minutes). Cover with foil and let cool in pan. Pull off and discard skins, stems, and seeds. Chop finely in a food processor or with a knife. Set aside.

2 Bring 16 cups water to a boil in a 6-to 8-quart pan over medium-high heat. Stir in pasta and cook just until tender to bite (8 to 10 minutes); or cook according to package instructions. Meanwhile, combine bell peppers, onions, beans, basil, tarragon, and capers in a 3- to 4- quart pan. Cook over medium-high heat, stirring often, until steaming (5 to 7 minutes).

3 Drain pasta well and transfer to a wide, shallow serving bowl. Add vegetable mixture and lift with 2 forks to mix. Offer salt and pepper to taste.

makes 8 servings

per serving: 295 calories, 11 g protein, 59 g carbohydrates, 12 g total fat, 0 mg cholesterol, 151 mg sodium

sicilian pasta timbale

preparation time: 20 minutes, plus 15 minutes for eggplant to stand
cooking time: about 1 hour

MARINARA SAUCE:

1 teaspoon olive oil

3 cloves garlic, minced or pressed

1 large can (about 28 oz.) tomato purée

**¼ cup chopped fresh basil
   or 2 tablespoons dried basil**

PASTA TIMBALE:

2 small eggplants

2 teaspoons salt

4 to 6 teaspoons olive oil

1 pound dried salad macaroni

2 cups shredded provolone cheese

½ cup grated Romano cheese

**About 3 teaspoon butter
   or margarine at room temperature**

2 tablespoons fine dry bread crumbs

Garnish

Basil sprigs

1 Heat the 1 teaspoon oil in a 3- to 4-quart pan over medium heat. Add garlic and cook, stirring, just until fragrant (about 30 seconds; do not scorch). Add tomato purée and chopped basil. Bring to a boil; then reduce heat and simmer, uncovered, stirring occasionally, until sauce is reduced to about 3 cups (about 20 minutes). Season to taste with salt; set aside.

2 While sauce is simmering, cut eggplants lengthwise into ¼-inch slices; sprinkle with the 2 teaspoons salt. Let stand for 15 minutes; then rinse well and pat dry. Coat 2 or 3 shallow 10- by 15-inch baking pans with oil, using 2 teaspoons oil per pan. Turn eggplant slices in oil to coat both sides; arrange in a single layer. Bake in a 425° oven until eggplant is browned and soft when pressed (about 25 minutes; remove pieces as they brown).

3 In a 6- to 8-quart pan, bring about 4 quarts water to a boil over medium-high heat; stir in pasta and cook until just barely tender to bite (6 to 8 minutes); or cook pasta according to package directions, cooking slightly less than time recommended. Drain pasta well and mix with provolone cheese, 2 cups of the marinara sauce, and 6 tablespoons of the Romano cheese.

4 Butter sides and bottom of a 9-inch cheesecake pan. Dust pan with bread crumbs. Arrange a third of the eggplant slices in pan, overlapping them to cover bottom of pan. Cover with half the pasta mixture. Add a layer of half the remaining eggplant, then evenly top with remaining pasta mixture. Top evenly with remaining eggplant. Press down gently to compact layers and to make timbale level. Sprinkle with remaining 2 tablespoons Romano cheese. (At this point, you may cover and refrigerate until next day.)

5 Bake, uncovered, in a 350° oven until hot in center, about 30 minutes. (If refrigerated, bake, covered, for 30 minutes; then uncover and continue to bake until hot in center, about 30 more minutes.) Let stand for about 5 minutes before serving.

6 Meanwhile, pour remaining marinara sauce into a 1- to 1½-quart pan, stir over medium heat until steaming. Transfer to a small pitcher or sauce boat. With a knife, cut around edge of timbale to release; remove pan rim. Garnish timbale with basil sprigs. Cut into wedges; serve with hot marinara sauce.

makes 6 to 8 servings

per serving: 503 calories, 22 g protein, 71 g carbohydrates, 15 g total fat, 30 mg cholesterol, 994 mg sodium

green & red lasagne

preparation time: about 35 minutes
cooking time: about 1 hour and 20 minutes

Tomato-Mushroom Sauce (recipe follows)

1 egg

1 egg white

1 package (about 10 oz.) frozen chopped
    spinach, thawed and squeezed dry

2 cups low-fat cottage cheese

¹⁄₃ cup grated Romano cheese

¹⁄₄ teaspoon pepper

¹⁄₈ teaspoon ground nutmeg

8 ounces dry lasagne noodles

1 ¹⁄₂ cups shredded part-skim mozzarella cheese

1 Prepare Tomato-Mushroom Sauce. Meanwhile, in a medium-size bowl, beat egg and egg white to blend; then stir in spinach, cottage and Romano cheeses, pepper, and nutmeg.

2 Spread a fourth of the sauce in a 9- by 13-inch casserole; top with a third of the uncooked lasagne noodles. Spoon on a third of the spinach mixture.

3 Repeat layers of sauce, lasagne, and spinach mixture until all ingredients are used; end with sauce. Sprinkle with mozzarella cheese. Cover tightly with foil. (At this point, you may refrigerate until next day).

4 Bake, covered, in a 375° oven until lasagne noodles are tender to bite (about 1 hour; about 1½ hours if refrigerated). Let stand, covered, for about 10 minutes; then cut into squares to serve.

makes 6 to 8 servings

TOMATO-MUSHROOM SAUCE

Heat 1 teaspoon olive oil in a wide (at least 12-inch) nonstick frying pan over medium heat. Add 2 large onions, finely chopped; 1 large red bell pepper, seeded and finely chopped; 8 ounces mushrooms, thinly sliced; 3 cloves garlic, minced or pressed; 1 teaspoon dry oregano; and 2½ teaspoons dry basil. Cook, stirring often, until liquid has evaporated and onion is very soft (15 to 20 minutes). Stir in 1 large can (about 15 oz.) no-salt-added tomato sauce, 1 can (about 6 oz.) tomato paste, 1 tablespoon reduced-sodium soy sauce and ½ cup dry red wine. Cook, stirring, until sauce comes to a boil; use hot.

per serving: 365 calories, 25 g protein, 46 g carbohydrates, 8 g total fat, 51 mg cholesterol, 765 mg sodium

PASTA NUTRITION: Pasta is low in fat and sodium; it's a good source of complex carbohydrates, and enriched pastas provide B-vitamins and iron. The durum wheat from which most pasta is made is high in protein. Finally, pasta's calorie content is lower than you may have assumed—2 ounces of uncooked spaghetti or macaroni provide less than 210 calories.

tortellini with roasted eggplant, garlic and pepper

preparation time: about 45 minutes

2 large red bell peppers, roasted

Balsamic Vinegar Dressing (recipe follows)

3 large heads garlic, cloves peeled

2 teaspoons olive oil

1 pound slender Asian eggplants, halved lengthwise and cut into thirds

1 package (about 9 oz.) fresh cheese tortellini or ravioli

2 tablespoons chopped parsley

24 to 32 spinach leaves, coarse stems removed, rinsed and crisped

Salt and pepper

1 Prepare Balsamic Vinegar Dressing; set aside.

2 Mix garlic and 1 teaspoon of the oil in a lightly oiled 8-inch baking pan. Rub eggplant skins with remaining oil and arrange, skin sides down, in a lightly oiled 10 by 15-inch baking pan.

3 Bake garlic and eggplants in a 475° oven, switching pan positions halfway through baking, until garlic is tinged with brown (remove cloves as they brown) and eggplants are richly browned and soft when pressed (20 to 30 minutes); if drippings begin to burn, add 4 to 6 tablespoons water, stirring to loosen browned bits. Meanwhile, bring 12 cups water to a boil in a pan over medium-high heat. Stir in pasta and cook just until tender to bite.

4 Drain pasta and transfer to bowl. Add bell peppers, garlic, eggplants, parsley, and dressing. Mix thoroughly, but gently. Arrange spinach on 4 individual plates. Spoon on pasta mixture.

makes 4 servings

BALSAMIC VINEGAR DRESSING

In a small bowl, combine 2 tablespoons reduced-sodium soy sauce, 2 teaspoons balsamic vinegar, 1 teaspoon Asian sesame oil, and ½ teaspoon honey. Beat until blended.

per serving: 445 calories, 19 g protein, 75 g carbohydrates, 10 g total fat, 28 mg cholesterol, 844 mg sodium

sweet spice meat sauce

preparation time: about 20 minutes
cooking time: about 1 ²/₃ hours

Spice Blend (recipe follows)

4 slices bacon, chopped

1 pound lean ground beef

4 medium-size onions, chopped

1 cup finely chopped celery

2 cloves garlic, minced or pressed

2 tablespoons minced parsley

3 cans (about 15 oz. *each*) tomato sauce

1 can (about 6 oz.) tomato paste

2 tablespoons red wine vinegar

1 Prepare Spice Blend.

2 Combine bacon and beef in a 5- to 6-quart pan. Cook over medium-high heat, stirring often, until well browned.

3 Pour off fat. Add onions, celery, garlic, parsley, and Spice Blend. Cook, stirring often, until onions are soft (about 20 minutes).

4 Add tomato sauce, tomato paste, and vinegar; stir well. Bring to a boil; reduce heat and simmer until reduced to about 8 cups (about 1 hour). If made ahead, let cool and then cover and refrigerate for up to 2 days; reheat before using.

makes about 8 cups

SPICE BLEND

In small bowl, combine 1 tablespoon firmly packed brown sugar; ½ teaspoon *each* ground cinnamon, dried oregano, pepper, rubbed sage, and dried thyme; and ¼ teaspoon each ground cloves and ground nutmeg. Mix until blended.

per serving: 121 calories, 7 g protein, 13 g carbohydrates, 5 g total fat, 19 mg cholesterol, 616 mg sodium

penne, tofu & asparagus

preparation time: about 35 minutes
marinating time: 15 minutes

¹/₂ cup seasoned rice vinegar;
or ¹/₂ cup distilled white vinegar

4 teaspoons sugar

¹/₄ cup freshly grated Parmesan cheese

3 tablespoons finely chopped fresh basil
or 1 tablespoon dried basil

2 tablespoons olive oil

1 tablespoon Dijon mustard

1 clove garlic, minced or pressed

8 ounces regular tofu, rinsed and drained,
cut into ¹/₂-inch cubes

1 pound asparagus, tough ends removed,
cut diagonally into 1 ¹/₂-inch pieces

8 ounces (about 2 ¹/₂ cups) dried penne

1 Combine vinegar, cheese, basil, oil, mustard, and garlic in a large serving bowl. Mix well. Add tofu and stir to coat. Cover and let stand for 15 minutes.

2 Bring 12 cups water to a boil in a 5- to 6-quart pan over medium-high heat. Add asparagus and cook until tender when pierced (about 4 minutes). Lift out with a slotted spoon, add to tofu mixture, and keep warm.

3 Stir pasta into boiling water and cook just until tender to bite (8 to 10 minutes); or cook according to package directions. Drain well. Add pasta to tofu and asparagus. Mix thoroughly but gently.

makes 6 servings

per serving: 254 calories, 11 g protein, 35 g carbohydrates, 8 g total fat, 3 mg cholesterol, 524 mg sodium

food-processor pasta

preparation time: about 30 minutes

About 2 cups all-purpose flour

2 large eggs

About ¹/₄ cup water

1 Combine 2 cups of the flour and eggs in a food processor; whirl until mixture resembles cornmeal (about 5 seconds). With motor running, pour ¹/₄ cup of the water through feed tube and whirl until dough forms a ball. Dough should be well blended but not sticky. If dough feels sticky, add a little flour and whirl to blend; if it looks crumbly, add 1 or 2 teaspoons more water: if processor begins to slow down or stop (an indication that dough is properly mixed), turn off motor and proceed to next step.

2 Turn dough out onto a floured board and knead a few times just until smooth. If you plan to use a rolling pin, cover and let rest for 20 minutes. If you plan to use a pasta machine (manual or electric), roll out at once.

3 Use a rolling pin or pasta machine to roll out and cut dough.

makes 14 to 16 ounces uncooked pasta (machine-rolled dough makes about 32 pieces lasagne or about 4 cups cooked medium-wide noodles; yield off hand-rolled pasta varies).

per ounce: 71 calories, 3 g protein, 13 g carbohydrates, 0.8 g total fat, 28 mg cholesterol, 9 mg sodium

chilled asian pasta with shrimp

preparation time: about 40 minutes
chilling time: at least 1 hour

3 tablespoons salad oil

3 cloves garlic, minced or pressed

1/3 cup thinly sliced green onions (including tops)

1/8 teaspoon ground red pepper (cayenne)

1 1/2 pounds medium-size shrimp (about 35 per lb.), shelled and deveined

3 tablespoons *each* dry sherry and white wine vinegar

1 tablespoon Dijon mustard

1 tablespoon finely chopped fresh tarragon leaves or 1 teaspoon dry tarragon leaves

Asian Dressing (recipe follows)

12 ounces dry whole wheat spaghetti

2 quarts watercress sprigs, rinsed and crisped

1 Heat oil in a wide frying pan over medium-high heat. Add garlic, onions, and pepper; cook, stirring often, until onions are soft (about 3 minutes). Add shrimp and cook, stirring, until opaque in center; cut to test (about 5 minutes). Add sherry, vinegar, mustard, and tarragon; bring to a boil, stirring. Transfer mixture to a bowl and let cool; then cover and refrigerate for at least 1 hour or up to 8 hours.

2 Prepare Asian Dressing and set aside.

3 In an 8- to 10-quart pan, cook pasta in 6 quarts boiling water until al dente (about 10 minutes or according to package directions). Drain, rinse with cold water until cool, and drain again. Mix lightly with dressing. (At this point, you may cover and refrigerate for up to 8 hours.)

4 Arrange watercress on a platter. Spoon pasta over watercress and top with shrimp mixture.

makes 4 to 6 servings

ASIAN DRESSING

Mix 1/3 cup lemon juice, 3 tablespoons reduced-sodium soy sauce, 1 tablespoon each sesame oil and finely chopped fresh ginger and 2 teaspoons sugar.

per serving: 487 calories, 35 g protein, 59 g carbohydrates, 14 g total fat, 168 mg cholesterol, 647 mg sodium

cool pasta shells with scallops

preparation time: about 35 minutes
chilling time: at least 2 hours

8 ounces medium-size dry pasta shells

4 cups broccoli flowerets, cut into bite-size pieces

1 pound sea scallops, rinsed, drained, and cut in half horizontally

1/4 cup *each* lemon juice, white wine, vinegar, and olive oil

1 teaspoon *each* dry mustard and sugar

1 clove garlic, minced or pressed

1 cup finely chopped fresh basil leaves

Small inner leaves from 2 large heads romaine lettuce (about 30 *total*), rinsed and crisped

1 In a 5- to 6-quart pan, cook pasta in 3 quarts boiling water until al dente (7 to 9 minutes or according to package directions). Drain, rinse with cold water until cool, and drain again. Set aside.

2 In a wide frying pan, cook broccoli, covered, in 1/4 inch boiling water until tender-crisp (about 4 minutes). Drain, immerse in ice water until cool, and drain again. Set aside. In same pan, cook scallops, covered, in 1/4 inch boiling water until opaque in center; cut to test (about 3 minutes). Drain; set aside.

3 In a large bowl, mix lemon juice, vinegar, oil, mustard, sugar, garlic, and basil. Add pasta, broccoli, and scallops; mix gently. Cover and refrigerate for at least 2 hours or until next day.

4 Arrange lettuce on individual plates; top with pasta mixture.

makes 4 to 6 servings

per searing: 402 calories, 26 g protein, 47 g carbohydrates, 13 g total fat, 30 mg cholesterol, 182 mg sodium

homemade egg pasta

preparation time: about 45 minutes

About 2 cups all-purpose flour

2 large eggs

3 to 6 tablespoons water

1 Mound 2 cups of the flour on a work surface or in a large bowl and make a deep well in center. Break eggs into well. With a fork, beat eggs lightly; stir in 2 tablespoons of the water. Using a circular motion, draw in flour from sides of well. Add 1 tablespoon more water and continue to mix until flour is evenly moistened. If necessary, add more water, 1 tablespoon at a time. When dough becomes too stiff to stir easily, use your hands to finish mixing.

2 Pat dough into a ball and knead a few times to help flour absorb liquid. To knead, flatten dough ball slightly and fold farthest edge toward you. With heel of your hand, push dough away from you, sealing fold. Rotate dough a quarter turn and continue folding-pushing motion, making a turn each time.

3 Clean and lightly flour work surface. If you plan to use a rolling pin, knead dough until smooth and elastic (about 10 minutes), adding flour if needed to prevent sticking. Cover and let rest for 20 minutes. If you plan to use a pasta machine (manual or electric), knead dough until no longer sticky (3 to 4 minutes), adding flour if needed to prevent sticking.

4 Use a rolling pin or pasta machine to roll out and cut dough as directed on facing page.

makes 14 to 16 ounces uncooked pasta (machine-rolled dough)

makes about 32 pieces lasagne or about 4 cups cooked medium-wide noodles; (yield of hand-rolled pasta varies)

per ounce: 71 calories, 3 g protein, 13 g carbohydrates, 0.8 g total fat, 28 mg cholesterol, 9 mg sodium

noodles with cabbage & gruyère

preparation time: about 30 minutes

1 cup low-sodium chicken broth

1 head green cabbage, finely shredded

12 ounces dry whole wheat spaghetti

1 ½ teaspoons caraway seeds

2 ounces Gruyère cheese, grated

4 ounces thinly sliced prosciutto, fat trimmed, cut into slivers

1 In a 4- to 5-quart pan, combine chicken broth and cabbage. Cover and bring to a boil over high heat; reduce heat and simmer, stirring occasionally, until cabbage is very tender (about 15 minutes). Uncover, increase heat to high, and continue cooking, stirring often, until most of the liquid is absorbed (3 to 5 more minutes).

2 Meanwhile, cook pasta in 6 quarts boiling water in an 8- to 10-quart pan until al dente (9 to 12 minutes or according to package directions).

3 Drain pasta and place in a large, warm bowl. Add cabbage mixture, caraway seeds, Gruyère, and prosciutto; mix well.

makes 4 servings

per serving: 446 calories, 26 g protein, 72 g carbohydrates, 9 g total fat, 32 mg cholesterol, 696 mg sodium

pasta with lentils and oranges

preparation time: about 50 minutes

4 or 5 large oranges

8 large butter lettuce leaves, rinsed and crisped

1 tablespoon grated orange peel

³/₄ cup fresh orange juice

3 tablespoons chopped fresh basil
  or 1 tablespoon dried basil

3 tablespoons white wine vinegar

1 tablespoon *each* honey and Dijon mustard

2 to 3 cloves garlic, minced or pressed

1 ¹/₂ teaspoons ground cumin

¹/₈ teaspoon crushed red pepper flakes
  (or to taste)

2 cups vegetable broth

³/₄ cup lentils

12 ounces dried radiatorre or fusilli

Basil sprigs

1 Cut peel and all white membrane from orange. Coarsely chop one of the oranges and set aside. Thinly slice remaining 3 or 4 oranges crosswise. Arrange lettuce leaves in a wide, shallow bowl or on a rimmed platter. Top with orange slices; cover and set aside.

2 In a small bowl, stir together chopped orange, orange peel, orange juice, 2 tablespoons of the chopped basil (or 2 teaspoons of the dried basil), vinegar, honey, mustard, garlic, cumin, and red pepper flakes. Beat until blended; set aside.

3 In a 1¹/₂- to 2-quart pan, bring broth to a boil over medium-high heat. Sort through lentils, discarding any debris; rinse, drain, and add to pan along with remaining 1 tablespoon chopped basil (or 1 teaspoon dried basil). Reduce heat, cover, and simmer until lentils are tender to bite (about 25 minutes).

4 Meanwhile, in a 5- to 6-quart pan, bring about 3 quarts water to a boil over medium-high heat; stir in pasta and cook until just until tender to bite 8 to 10 minutes); or cook pasta according to package directions.

5 Drain pasta well; if necessary, drain lentils well. Transfer pasta and lentils to a large bowl. Add orange dressing and mix gently but thoroughly. Spoon pasta over orange slices. Garnish with basil sprigs.

makes 4 servings

per serving: 563 calories, 21 g protein, 115 g carbohydrates, 3 g total fat, 0 mg cholesterol, 601 mg sodium

orecchiette with sake-clam sauce

preparation time: about 30 minutes

2 cans (about 6 ¹/₂ oz. *each*) chopped clams

4 cup finely chopped onions

2 cloves garlic, minced or pressed

1 cup sake or dry vermouth

2 tablespoons capers, drained

8 ounces dried orecchiette
  or other medium-size pasta shape

¹/₄ cup finely chopped parsley

¹/₄ cup freshly grated Parmesan cheese

¹/₈ teaspoon crushed red pepper flakes

1 Drain clams, reserving juice. Set clams aside.

2 Combine ¹/₂ cup of the clam juice, onions, garlic, and ¹/₄ cup of the sake in a wide nonstick frying pan. Cook over high heat, stirring often, until about a quarter of the liquid remains (about 3 minutes). Add clams, capers, and remaining ³/₄ cup sake. Reduce heat and simmer, uncovered, for about 4 minutes. Remove from heat and keep warm.

3 Bring 8 cups water to a boil in a 4- to 5-quart pan over medium-high heat. Stir in pasta and cook just until tender to bite (8 to 10 minutes); or cook according to package directions. Drain well. Transfer to a wide serving bowl. Quickly add clam mixture and stir until most of the liquid is absorbed. Add parsley, cheese, and red pepper flakes. Mix thoroughly but gently.

makes 4 servings

per serving: 381 calories, 22 g protein, 49 g carbohydrates, 3 g total fat, 36 mg cholesterol, 266 mg sodium

pork tenderloin with peanut vermicelli

preparation time: about 55 minutes

2 pork tenderloins (about 12 oz. *each*), trimmed of fat and silvery membrane

1/4 cup hoisin sauce

3 tablespoons firmly packed brown sugar

2 tablespoons dry sherry

2 tablespoons reduced-sodium soy sauce

1 tablespoon lemon juice

12 ounces dried vermicelli

1/2 cup plum jam or plum butter

1/4 cup seasoned rice vinegar; or 1/4 cup distilled white vinegar and 2 teaspoons sugar

1/4 cup creamy peanut butter

3 tablespoons Asian sesame oil

2 cloves garlic, minced or pressed

1/8 teaspoon ground ginger

1/4 teaspoon crushed red pepper flakes

1 package (about 10 oz.) frozen tiny peas, thawed

1/3 cup cilantro

2 tablespoons chopped peanuts (optional)

Sliced kumquats (optional)

1 Place tenderloins on a rack in a 9- by 13-inch baking pan. In a bowl, stir together hoisin, brown sugar, sherry, 1 tablespoon of the soy sauce, and lemon juice. Brush over pork, reserving remaining mixture.

2 Roast pork in a 450° oven, brushing with remaining marinade, until a meat thermometer inserted in thickest part registers 155° (20 to 30 minutes; after 15 minutes, check temperature every 5 minutes); if drippings begin to burn, add 4 to 6 tablespoons water, stirring to loosen browned bits. Meanwhile, bring 12 cups water to a boil in a 5- to 6-quart pan over medium-high heat. Stir in pasta and cook just until tender to bite (8 to 10 minutes); or cook according to package directions. Drain well and keep warm.

3 Transfer meat to a board, cover loosely, and let stand for 10 minutes. Skim and discard fat from pan drippings. Pour drippings and any juices on board into a small serving container; keep warm. Meanwhile, combine jam, vinegar, peanut butter, oil, garlic, ginger, red pepper flakes, and remaining 1 tablespoon soy sauce in 5- to 6-quart pan. Bring to a boil over medium heat and cook, whisking, just until smooth. Remove from heat and add pasta, peas, and cilantro. Lift with 2 forks to mix. Mound pasta on individual plates. Thinly slice meat across grain; arrange on pasta. Garnish with kumquats, if desired. Offer juices and, if desired, peanuts to add to taste.

makes 6 servings

per serving: 631 calories, 37 g protein, 80 g carbohydrates, 18 g total fat, 67 mg cholesterol, 919 mg sodium

START PASTA WATER FIRST: When you're cooking pasta, your first step should be to heat the water—it takes time for a large quantity of water to boil. If the water comes to a rolling boil before you need to cook your pasta, reduce the heat to keep it at a simmer. Just before you want to cook, increase the heat again; the water will return to a boil fairly rapidly.

linguini with creamy shrimp

preparation time: about 35 minutes

3 tablespoons sun-dried tomatoes packed in oil, drained (reserve oil) and chopped

1 clove garlic, minced or pressed

1 pound large shrimp (31 to 35 per lb.), shelled and deveined

10 ounces dried linguine

$2/3$ cup light cream

$1/4$ cup thinly sliced green onions

2 tablespoons chopped fresh basil or 1 teaspoon dried basil

$1/8$ teaspoon ground white pepper

2 teaspoons cornstarch blended with $3/4$ cup nonfat milk

3 tablespoons dry vermouth, or to taste

Freshly grated Parmesan cheese

Salt

1 Heat 1 teaspoon of the reserved oil from tomatoes in a wide nonstick frying pan over medium high heat. Add garlic and shrimp. Cook, stirring often, just until shrimp are opaque in center, cut to test (about 6 minutes). Lift out and set aside, reserving any juices in pan.

2 Bring 12 cups water to a boil in a 5- to 6-quart pan over medium-high heat. Stir in pasta and cook just until tender to bite (8 to 10 minutes); or cook according to package directions.

3 Meanwhile, combine cream, onions, basil, tomatoes, and white pepper with juices in frying pan. Bring to a boil over medium-high heat and cook, stirring, for 1 minute. Stir cornstarch mixture and add to pan. Return mixture to a boil and cook, stirring, just until slightly thickened. Remove from heat; stir in vermouth and shrimp.

4 Drain pasta well and arrange on 4 individual plates. Top with shrimp mixture. Offer Parmesan cheese and salt to add to taste.

makes 4 servings

per serving: 546 calories, 31 g protein, 62 g carbohydrates, 17 g total fat, 167 mg cholesterol, 188 mg sodium

tortellini & peas in creamy lemon sauce

preparation time: about 35 minutes

1 large lemon (about 5 oz.)

1 tablespoon margarine

$1/4$ cup minced shallots or onion

2 tablespoons all-purpose flour

$1^1/2$ cups lowfat (2%) milk

1 cup fresh or frozen peas

1 package (9 oz.) fresh cheese-filled tortellini

2 tablespoons grated Parmesan cheese, plus additional cheese to taste

1 Grate 1 tablespoon zest (colored part of peel) from lemon. Squeeze juice. Combine in a small bowl; set aside.

2 In a 3- to 4-quart pan, melt margarine over medium heat. Add shallots and cook, stirring, until soft (about 3 minutes). Add flour and cook, stirring, for 1 minute. Add milk, increase heat to medium-high, and cook, stirring often, until sauce is thickened (about 10 minutes). Stir about $1/2$ cup of the sauce into lemon mixture; return mixture to pan and stir well. Remove from heat and set aside.

3 In a 5- to 6-quart pan, cook peas and pasta in 3 quarts boiling water until peas are tender and pasta is al dente (4 to 5 minutes or according to package directions). Drain; add to pan with lemon sauce. Cook over low heat, stirring, for 2 minutes.

4 Stir in the 2 tablespoons Parmesan and offer with additional Parmesan.

makes 4 servings

per serving: 333 calories, 18 g protein, 46 g carbohydrates, 9 g total fat, 45 mg cholesterol, 424 mg sodium

italian sausage lasagne

preparation time: about 25 minutes
cooking time: about 2 hours

Low-fat Italian sausage

3 large onions, chopped

2 large stalks celery, chopped

2 medium-size carrots, chopped

5 cups beef broth

1 can (about 6 oz.) tomato paste

1 $^1\!/_2$ teaspoons dried basil

$^1\!/_2$ teaspoon dried rosemary

$^1\!/_4$ teaspoon ground nutmeg

12 ounces dry lasagne noodles

3 tablespoons cornstarch

1 $^1\!/_2$ cups nonfat milk

2 cups shredded fontina cheese

$^1\!/_2$ cup freshly grated Parmesan cheese

1 Prepare Low-fat Italian Sausage; refrigerate, covered.

2 Combine onions, celery, carrots, and 1$^1\!/_2$ cups of the broth in a 5- to 6-quart pan (preferably nonstick). Bring to a boil over high heat and cook, stirring occasionally, until liquid has evaporated and vegetables begin to brown (12 to 15 minutes). To deglaze pan, add $^1\!/_4$ cup water, stirring to loosen browned bits. Continue to cook, stirring often, until mixture begins to brown again. Repeat deglazing step, adding $^1\!/_4$ cup more water each time, until mixture is richly browned.

3 Crumble sausage into pan; add $^1\!/_2$ cup more water. Cook, stirring occasionally, until liquid has evaporated and meat begins to brown (about 10 minutes). Add $^1\!/_3$ cup more water and cook, stirring, until meat is browned (2 to 4 more minutes). Reduce heat to medium-low and add 2$^1\!/_2$ cups more broth, stirring to loosen browned bits. Add tomato paste, basil, rosemary, and nutmeg. Bring to a boil; reduce heat, cover, and simmer, stirring occasionally, until flavors have blended (about 20 minutes). Meanwhile, bring 12 cups water to a boil in a 5- to 6-quart pan over medium-high heat. Stir in pasta and cook just until barely tender to bite (about 8 minutes). Drain well and keep warm.

4 Blend remaining 1 cup broth with cornstarch and milk until smooth. Add to meat mixture. Cook over medium-high heat, stirring, until bubbling and thickened. Stir in 1 cup of the fontina; remove from heat. Gently stir in pasta. Transfer to a shallow 3-quart baking dish; swirl pasta. Sprinkle with Parmesan and remaining 1 cup fontina. (At this point, you may cool, cover, and refrigerate for up to a day.)

5 Bake in a 375° oven until bubbling (about 30 minutes; 35 to 40 minutes if chilled).

makes 8 servings

per serving: 480 calories, 32 g protein, 53 g carbohydrates, 14 g total fat, 76 mg cholesterol, 1,625 mg sodium

chicken vermicelli carbonara

preparation time: about 55 minutes

1 large onion, finely chopped

1/2 teaspoon fennel seeds

1 3/4 cups low sodium chicken broth

12 to 14 ounces boneless, skinless chicken thighs, trimmed of fat and cut into 1/2-inch chunks

1 cup finely chopped parsley

9 egg whites (about 6 tablespoons)

1 egg

12 ounces to 1 pound dry vermicelli

1 1/2 cups (about 6 oz.) finely shredded Parmesan cheese

Salt and freshly ground pepper

1 In a wide nonstick frying pan, combine onion, fennel seeds, and 1 cup of the broth. Bring to a boil; boil, stirring occasionally, until liquid has evaporated. Continue to cook until browned bits accumulate in pan; then add water, 2 tablespoons at a time, stirring until all browned bits are loosened. Continue to cook until mixture begins to brown again; repeat deglazing, using 2 tablespoons water each time, until onions are a uniformly light golden brown color.

2 To pan, add chicken and 2 tablespoons more water. Cook, stirring, until drippings begin to brown; deglaze pan with 2 tablespoons water. When pan is dry, add remaining ¾ cup broth; bring to a boil. Add parsley; keep warm over lowest heat. In a bowl, beat egg whites and egg to blend; set aside.

3 In a 6-quart pan, cook vermicelli in 4 quarts boiling water just until tender to bite (8 to 10 minutes); or cook according to package directions. Drain well.

4 Add hot pasta to pan with chicken. Pour egg mixture over pasta and at once begin lifting with 2 forks to mix well (eggs cook if you delay mixing); add 1 cup of the cheese as you mix. Pour mixture onto a warm deep platter and continue to mix until almost all broth is absorbed. Season to taste with remaining ½ cup cheese, salt, and pepper.

makes 6 to 8 servings

per serving: 408 calories, 30 g protein, 46 g carbohydrates, 11 g total fat, 93 mg cholesterol, 491 mg sodium

orecchiette with spinach & garlic

preparation time: about 30 minutes

12 ounces orecchiette, ruote (wheels), or other dry pasta shape

3 tablespoons olive oil

6 cloves garlic, minced or pressed

1/2 teaspoon crushed red pepper flakes

1/3 cup low-sodium chicken broth

3/4 pound stemmed spinach leaves, rinsed well and coarsely chopped

Grated Parmesan cheese

1 In an 8- to 10-quart pan, cook pasta in 6 quarts boiling water until al dente (10 to 12 minutes or according to package directions).

2 Meanwhile, heat oil in a wide frying pan over medium heat. Add garlic and red pepper flakes. Cook, stirring occasionally, until garlic is slightly golden (about 2 minutes). Stir in chicken broth. Remove from heat and set aside.

3 Just before pasta is done, add spinach to pasta. Cook, stirring to distribute spinach, just until water returns to a full boil. Drain and place in a large, warm bowl.

4 Add sauce to pasta; mix well. Offer with Parmesan.

makes 4 servings

per serving: 434 calories, 14 g protein, 68 g carbohydrates, 12 g total fat, 0 mg cholesterol, 78 mg sodium

pasta with beans

preparation time: about 45 minutes

1 tablespoon olive oil

1 large carrot, finely chopped

2 celery stalks, finely chopped

1 medium-size onion, chopped

2 cloves garlic, minced or pressed

2 teaspoons dry marjoram leaves or dry oregano leaves

1 can (28 oz.) peeled tomatoes

1 can (about 15 1/2 oz.) garbanzo beans, drained and rinsed

1 can (about 15 oz.) cannellini (white kidney beans), drained and rinsed

1 cup water

8 ounces multicolored rotelle (corkscrews) or other dry pasta shape

1/4 cup minced parsley

Grated Parmesan cheese

1 Heat oil in a 4- to 5-quart pan over medium-high heat. Add carrot, celery, onion, and garlic. Cook, stirring often, until vegetables are soft (about 10 minutes). Add marjoram, tomatoes (break up with a spoon) and their liquid, garbanzos, cannellini, and water. Bring to a boil; reduce heat and simmer until slightly thickened (about 10 minutes).

2 About 5 minutes before sauce is done, cook pasta in 3 quarts boiling water in a 5- to 6-quart pan until slightly underdone (about 5 minutes or two-thirds of the cooking time indicated on package). Drain. Return to pan and stir in vegetable mixture. Bring to a boil; reduce heat and simmer, stirring often, until most of the liquid is absorbed and pasta is al dente (about 5 more minutes).

3 Transfer to a large, warm bowl. Sprinkle with parsley and offer with Parmesan.

makes 4 servings

per serving: 523 calories, 21 g protein, 98 g carbohydrates, 6 g total fat, 0 mg cholesterol, 1,069 mg sodium

spinach & tofu manicotti

preparation time: about 1 1/2 hours

2 tablespoons olive oil

1 medium-size onion, chopped

3 celery stalks, chopped

2 cloves garlic, minced or pressed

2 teaspoons dry oregano leaves

2 cans (15 oz. *each*) tomato purée

1 cup *each* dry red wine and water

1 pound soft tofu, drained and rinsed

1 package (10 oz.) frozen chopped spinach, thawed and squeezed dry

12 dry manicotti tubes

1/2 cup shredded part-skim mozzarella cheese

1 Heat oil in a 4- to 5-quart pan over medium-high heat. Add onion, celery, garlic, and oregano. Cook, stirring often, until onion is limp (about 7 minutes). Add tomato purée, wine, and water. Bring to a boil; reduce heat, cover, and simmer for 25 minutes, stirring often.

2 Meanwhile, mix tofu and spinach in a bowl. Stuff manicotti with mixture.

3 Spread 1¾ cups of the tomato sauce in a 9- by 13-inch baking pan. Set manicotti in sauce; top with remaining sauce. Cover and bake in a 375° oven until pasta is tender (about 50 minutes). Sprinkle with mozzarella.

makes 6 servings (2 manicotti each)

per serving: 293 calories, 14 g protein, 43 g carbohydrates, 9 g total fat, 5 mg cholesterol, 672 mg sodium

vermicelli with vegetable sauce

preparation time: about 1 hour and 10 minutes

2 tablespoons olive oil or salad oil

1 medium-size onion, finely chopped

1 teaspoon *each* fennel seeds and dry basil, dry tarragon, and dry oregano leaves

1 clove garlic, minced or pressed

1 small zucchini, thinly sliced

¼ pound mushrooms, thinly sliced

1 small green bell pepper, stemmed, seeded, and finely chopped

½ cup dry red wine

1 pound tomatoes, peeled, seeded, and chopped

1 can (6 oz.) tomato paste

1 teaspoon sugar

12 ounces dry vermicelli (not coiled) or spaghettini

Grated Parmesan cheese

1 Heat oil in a 4- to 5-quart pan over medium-high heat. Add onion, fennel seeds, basil, tarragon, and oregano. Cook, stirring often, until onion is soft (about 5 minutes). Stir in garlic, zucchini, mushrooms, and bell pepper. Cook, stirring often, until mushrooms begin to brown (about 10 minutes). Add wine, tomatoes, tomato paste, and sugar. Increase heat to high and bring to a boil; reduce heat, cover, and simmer until thickened (about 35 minutes), stirring occasionally.

2 About 10 minutes before sauce is done, cook pasta in 6 quarts boiling water in an 8- to 10-quart pan until al dente (7 to 9 minutes or according to package directions).

3 Drain pasta and arrange on warm plates; top with sauce. Offer with Parmesan.

makes 4 servings

per serving: 466 calories, 15 g protein, 83 g carbohydrates, 9 g total fat, 0 mg cholesterol, 355 mg sodium

turkey italian sausage sauce

preparation time: about 50 minutes

1 pound mild or hot turkey Italian sausages, casings removed, or Low-fat Italian sausage

1 large onio, chopped

3 cloves garlic, minced or pressed

1 can (about 29 oz.) tomato purée

3 tablespoons chopped fresh basil or 1 tablespoon dried basil

½ teaspoon fennel seeds

2 tablespoons dry red wine (or to taste)

Salt and pepper

1 Chop or crumble sausages. Place in a 4- to 5-quart pan with onion, garlic, and 2 tablespoons water. Cook over medium heat, stirring often, until sausage mixture is well browned (about 15 minutes); if pan appears dry or sausage mixture sticks to pan bottom, add water, 1 tablespoon at a time.

2 Stir in tomato purée, basil, and fennel seeds. Increase heat to medium high and bring to a boil; reduce heat and simmer until reduced to about 4 ½ cups (about 20 minutes).

3 Remove from heat and add wine. Season to taste with salt and pepper. If made ahead, let cool and then cover and refrigerate for up to 2 days; reheat before using.

makes about 4 ½ cups

per serving: 54 calories, 2 g protein, 12 g carbohydrates, 0.2 g total fat, 0 mg cholesterol, 366 mg sodium

capellini with cilantro pesto & white beans

preparation time: about 35 minutes

3 cups firmly packed cilantro leaves

1 cup grated Parmesan cheese

1 tablespoon grated lemon peel

1 tablespoon Asian sesame oil

3 cloves garlic, peeled

2 teaspoons honey

8 ounces dried capellini

2 tablespoons seasoned rice vinegar
(or 2 tablespoons distilled white vinegar
plus ³/₄ teaspoon sugar)

1 medium-size red onion, cut into thin slivers

1 tablespoon balsamic vinegar

1 can (about 15 oz.) cannellini (white kidney
beans), drained and rinsed

7 medium-size firm-ripe pear-shaped (Roma-
type) tomatoes (about 1 lb. total), chopped

1¹/₂ teaspoons chopped fresh thyme
or ¹/₂ teaspoon dried thyme

Thyme and cilantro sprigs

Pepper

1 To prepare cilantro pesto, in a blender or a processor, combine cilantro leaves, Parmesan, ¹/₂ cup water, lemon peel, sesame oil, garlic, and honey. Whirl until smoothly puréed. If pesto is too thick, add a little more water, set aside. (At this point, you may cover and refrigerate for up to 3 hours; bring to room temperature before using.)

2 In a 4- to 5-quart pan, cook pasta in about 8 cups boiling water until just tender to bite (about 3 minutes); or cook according to package directions. Drain well, rinse with hot water, and drain well again. Quickly return pasta to pan; add rice vinegar and lift with 2 forks to mix. Keep warm.

3 While pasta is cooking, combine onion and ¹/₃ cup water in a wide nonstick frying pan or wok. Cover and cook over medium-high heat until onion is almost soft (about 3 minutes). Uncover, add balsamic vinegar, and stir-fry until liquid has evaporated. Add beans, tomatoes, and chopped thyme to pan; stir-fry gently until beans are heated through and tomatoes are soft (about 3 minutes). Remove pan from heat.

4 Stir cilantro pesto well; spread evenly on 4 individual plates. Top with pasta, then with bean mixture. Garnish with thyme and cilantro sprigs; serve immediately. Season to taste with pepper.

makes 4 servings

per serving: 473 calories, 20 g protein, 73 g carbohydrates, 11 g total fat, 16 mg cholesterol, 786 mg sodium

INTERNATIONAL BREADS : Good bread enhances any meal, whether it encloses sandwich makings or serves as a side dish to soups, salads, or other entrées. Many traditionalists prefer crusty rolls or French bread baguettes, but a delicatessen, well-stocked supermarket, or ethnic bakery offers many tempting alternatives.If your meal has an international theme, choose a complementary bread. Try flat, chewy focaccia or seasoned breadsticks with Italian dishes, warm corn or flour tortillas with Mexican favorites; offer crisp flatbread with Scandinavian specialties, dense pumpernickel with German dishes. Armenian cracker bread or pita bread enhances Middle Eastern entrées, while challah and onion rolls go well with Jewish meals.

summertime pasta alfresco

preparation time: about 35 minutes
chilling time: at least 2 hours

3 small tomatoes, peeled and chopped

1 cup each thinly sliced green onions (including tops), finely chopped

Celery, finely chopped green bell pepper, and diced zucchini

2 cloves garlic, minced or pressed

3 tablespoons white wine vinegar

1 tablespoon sugar

$1/3$ cup chopped fresh basil leaves

1 teaspoon chopped fresh rosemary

$3/4$ teaspoon chopped fresh oregano leaves

Coarsely ground pepper

8 ounces rotelle (corkscrews), ruote (wheels), or other dry pasta shape

2 tablespoons grated Parmesan cheese

1 Combine tomatoes, onions, celery, bell pepper, zucchini, garlic, vinegar, sugar, basil, rosemary, and oregano. Season to taste with pepper; mix well. Cover and refrigerate for at least 2 hours or up to 8 hours.

2 Shortly before serving, cook pasta in 3 quarts boiling water in a 5- to 6-quart pan until al dente (7 to 9 minutes or according to package directions). Drain, rinse with cold water until cool, and drain again.

3 Transfer pasta to a serving bowl. Add tomato mixture and mix lightly. Sprinkle with Parmesan and mix again.

makes 4 servings

per serving: 283 calories, 11 g protein, 56 g carbohydrates, 2 g total fat, 2 mg cholesterol, 97 mg sodium

red pepper pesto

preparation time: 10 minutes

1 jar (12 oz.) roasted red peppers, drained, patted dry

1 cup lightly packed fresh basil leaves

1 clove garlic, peeled

$1/3$ cup grated Parmesan cheese

Salt and pepper

In a food processor or blender, whirl peppers, basil, garlic, and cheese until basil is finely chopped. Season to taste with salt and pepper.

makes about 1 $1/2$ cups

per tablespoon: 14 calories, 0.7 g protein, 2 g carbohydrates, 0.4 g total fat, 0.9 mg cholesterol, 51 mg sodium

perciatelli with turkey marinara

preparation time: about 20 minutes
cooking time: about 1 hour and 40 minutes

2 tablespoons olive oil

1 medium-size onion, finely chopped

1 medium-size green bell pepper,
   stemmed, seeded, and finely chopped

1 large carrot, finely shredded

1/4 pound mushrooms, thinly sliced

2 tablespoons chopped parsley

1 clove garlic, minced or pressed

2 teaspoons dry basil leaves

1 teaspoon *each* dry rosemary
   and dry oregano leaves

1 pound fresh ground turkey

2 cans (28 oz. *each*) peeled tomatoes

1 can (12 oz.) tomato paste

1/4 cup dry red wine

1 bay leaf

1 pound perciatelli, bucatini,
   or other dry pasta noodles

Grated Parmesan cheese

1 Heat oil in a 4- to 5-quart pan over medium-high heat. Add onion, bell pepper, carrot, mushrooms, parsley, garlic, basil, rosemary, and oregano. Cook, stirring often, until vegetables are tender (about 15 minutes). Lift out and set aside.

2 Crumble turkey into pan; cook over medium-high heat, stirring constantly, until lightly browned (about 7 minutes). Pour off fat. Return vegetables to pan. Stir in tomatoes (break up with a spoon) and their liquid, tomato paste, wine, and bay leaf. Bring to a boil; reduce heat, cover, and simmer, stirring occasionally, for 30 minutes. Uncover and continue cooking, stirring occasionally, until sauce is thickened (about 45 more minutes).

3 About 10 minutes before sauce is done, cook pasta in 6 quarts boiling water in an 8- to 10-quart pan until al dente (7 to 9 minutes or according to package directions).

4 Drain pasta and place in a large, warm bowl. Add sauce and mix lightly. Offer with Parmesan.

makes 6 to 8 servings

per serving: 497 calories, 25 g protein, 73 g carbohydrates, 13 g total fat, 33 mg cholesterol, 809 mg sodium

mint pesto

preparation time: 15 minutes

1/2 cup pine nuts

1 cup lightly packed fresh mint leaves

3 cloves garlic, peeled

3 tablespoons olive oil

1/4 cup grated Parmesan cheese

1 Stir pine nuts in a wide frying pan over medium heat until golden (about 3 minutes). Pour into a food processor or blender; let cool slightly.

2 To pine nuts, add mint, garlic, oil, and cheese. Whirl until smoothly puréed.

makes about 3/4 cup

per tablespoon: 71 calories, 2 g protein, 1 g carbohydrates, 7 g total fat, 1 mg cholesterol, 31 mg sodium

bow tie pasta with broccoli pesto

preparation time: about 35 minutes

1 pound broccoli flowerets

2 or 3 cloves garlic, minced or pressed

¹/₂ cup grated Parmesan cheese

3 tablespoons olive oil

1 ¹/₂ teaspoons Asian sesame oil

¹/₂ teaspoon salt

12 ounces dried pasta bow ties (farfalle)

1 to 2 tablespoons seasoned rice vinegar (or 1 to 2 tablespoons distilled white vinegar plus ¹/₂ to 1 teaspoon sugar)

1 small tomato, chopped

1 In a 4- to 5-quart pan, bring 8 cups water to a boil over medium-high heat. Stir in broccoli and cook until just tender to bite (about 7 minutes). Immediately drain broccoli, immerse in ice water until cool, and drain again.

2 In a food processor or blender, combine a third of the broccoli with garlic, cheese, olive oil, sesame oil, salt, and 3 tablespoons water. Whirl until smooth. Scrape down sides of container, add half the remaining broccoli, and whirl until smooth again. Add remaining broccoli; whirl until smooth. Set aside.

3 In a 5- to 6-quart pan, bring about 3 quarts water to a boil over medium high heat; stir in pasta and cook until just tender to bite, 8 to 10 minutes. (Or cook pasta according to package directions.)

4 Drain pasta well. Transfer to a large serving bowl and stir in vinegar. Add pesto and mix gently but thoroughly. Garnish with tomato and serve immediately.

makes 4 servings

per serving: 510 calories, 19 g protein, 73 g carbohydrates, 17 g total fat, 8 mg cholesterol, 604 mg sodium

sausage, basil & port fettuccine

preparation time: about 45 minutes

1 pound mild or hot pork Italian sausages (casings removed), crumbled into ¹/₂-inch pieces

2 cloves garlic, minced or pressed

1 ¹/₂ cups sliced green onions

3 cups thinly sliced red onions

1 ¹/₂ cups port

3 medium-size tomatoes, chopped

2 tablespoons balsamic vinegar

³/₄ cup chopped fresh basil

1 pound dried fettuccine

Basil sprigs

1 In a wide nonstick frying pan or wok, stir-fry sausage over medium-high heat until browned (7 to 10 minutes). Remove from pan with a slotted spoon; keep warm. Pour off and discard all but 1 teaspoon fat from pan.

2 Add garlic, green onions, and red onions to pan and stir-fry until soft (5 to 7 minutes). Add water, 1 tablespoon at a time; if pan appears dry. Add port and bring to a boil. Then boil, stirring often, until liquid is reduced by half (5 to 6 minutes). Add tomatoes, vinegar, and sausage; reduce heat and simmer for 2 minutes. Stir in chopped basil.

3 While sauce is cooking, in a 6- to 8-quart pan, cook fettuccine in about 4 quarts boiling water until just tender to bite (8 to 10 minutes); or cook according to package directions.

4 Drain pasta well and transfer to a warm bowl; top with sausage sauce. Garnish with basil sprigs.

makes 8 servings

per serving: 473 calories, 18 g protein, 58 g carbohydrates, 14 g total fat, 87 mg cholesterol, 417 mg sodium

seafood linguine

preparation time: about 50 minutes

2 pounds mussels or small hard-shell clams in shells, scrubbed

1 bottle (8 oz.) clam juice

4 tablespoons margarine

3/4 cup sliced green onions (including tops)

2 large cloves garlic, minced or pressed

1/2 cup dry white wine

1 pound medium-size shrimp (about 35 *total*), shelled and deveined

12 ounces fresh linguine

1/2 cup chopped parsley

1 If using mussels, discard any that don't close when lightly tapped. With a swift tug, pull beard (clump of fibers along side of shell) off each mussel.

2 Pour clam juice into a 5- to 6-quart pan and bring to a boil over high heat. Add mussels; reduce heat to medium, cover, and cook until shells open (about 8 minutes). Discard any unopened shells. Drain, reserving liquid. Set mussels aside and keep warm. Strain cooking liquid to remove grit; reserve 1 cup of the liquid.

3 In a wide frying pan, melt 2 tablespoons of the margarine over medium-high heat. Add onions and garlic and cook, stirring often, until onions are soft (about 3 minutes). Stir in wine and reserved cooking liquid. Increase heat to high and bring to a boil; cook until reduced by about half (about 5 minutes). Stir in remaining margarine. Add shrimp, cover, and remove from heat; let stand until shrimp are opaque in center; cut to test (about 8 minutes).

4 Meanwhile, cook pasta in 6 quarts boiling water in an 8- to 10-quart pan until al dente (3 to 4 minutes or according to package directions). Drain.

5 Add pasta and parsley to shrimp mixture and mix lightly, lifting pasta with 2 forks. Mound on a warm platter; add mussels.

makes 6 servings

per serving: 342 calories, 25 g protein, 35 g carbohydrates, 719 total fat, 247 mg cholesterol, 410 mg sodium

winter garden pasta

preparation time: about 40 minutes

3/4 pound Swiss chard, rinsed and drained

2 tablespoons olive oil

1 pound mushrooms, sliced

1 medium-size onion, chopped

3 cloves garlic, minced or pressed

1/2 cup low-sodium chicken broth

1 1/2 pounds pear-shaped tomatoes, chopped

Freshly ground pepper

1 pound penne, rigatoni, or other dry pasta shape

Grated Parmesan cheese

1 Trim off and discard discolored ends of Swiss chard stems. Cut white stalks from leaves. Finely chop leaves and stalks separately. Set leaves aside.

2 Heat oil in a wide frying pan over medium high heat. Stir in chard stalks, mushrooms, onion, and garlic; cover and cook until vegetables are soft (about 10 minutes). Uncover and cook, stirring, until liquid has evaporated (about 3 minutes).

3 Add chicken broth and chard leaves; cover and cook until leaves are wilted (about 2 minutes). Stir in tomatoes and season to taste with pepper. Cover, remove from heat, and set aside.

4 In an 8- to 10-quart pan, cook pasta in 6 quarts boiling water until al dente (7 to 9 minutes or ac cording to package directions).

5 Drain pasta and place in a large, warm bowl. Add chard mixture; mix well. Offer with Parmesan.

makes 4 to 6 servings

per serving: 455 calories, 16 g protein, 82 g carbohydrates, 8 g total fat, 0 mg cholesterol, 171 mg sodium

vegetable lasagne

preparation time: about 1 ¼ hours

1 pound firm tofu

1 package (8 oz.) dry lasagne noodles

1 pound carrots, cut into ¼-inch-thick slices

1 pound zucchini, cut into ¼-inch-thick slices

1 tablespoon olive oil or salad oil

1 large onion, chopped

1 pound mushrooms, thinly sliced

1 teaspoon *each* **dry basil, dry thyme leaves, and dry oregano leaves**

2 large cans (15 oz. *each***) no-salt-added tomato sauce**

1 can (6 oz.) tomato paste

2 packages (10 oz. *each***) frozen chopped spinach, thawed and squeezed dry**

1 cup part-skim ricotta cheese

2 cups shredded skim mozzarella cheese

1 cup grated Parmesan cheese

1 Break tofu into coarse chunks and drain in a colander. With paper towels, press tofu to remove excess liquid. Set aside.

2 In a 5- to 6-quart pan, bring 3 quarts water to a boil over high heat. Add noodles and carrots; cook for 6 minutes. Add zucchini; continue to cook until noodles are just tender to bite (about 4 more minutes). Drain well; set vegetables and noodles aside separately.

3 Heat oil in same pan over medium-high heat. Add tofu, onion, mushrooms, basil, thyme, and oregano. Cook, stirring often, until onion is soft and liquid has evaporated (about 7 minutes). Add tomato sauce and tomato paste; stir to blend, then set aside. Mix spinach and ricotta cheese; set aside.

4 Spread a third of the sauce in a 9- by 13-inch baking dish. Arrange half the noodles over sauce; sprinkle evenly with half each of the carrots, zucchini, spinach mixture, and mozzarella cheese. Repeat layers; then spread remaining sauce on top. Sprinkle with Parmesan cheese.

5 Set baking dish in a rimmed baking pan to catch any drips. Bake, uncovered, in a 400° oven until hot in center (about 25 minutes). Let stand for 5 minutes before serving.

makes 6 servings

per serving: 602 calories, 41 g protein, 70 g carbohydrates, 21 g total fat, 36 mg cholesterol, 654 mg sodium

basil pesto

preparation time: 10 minutes

2 cups lightly packed fresh basil leaves

½ cup grated Parmesan cheese

⅓ cup olive oil

¼ cup walnut pieces

2 cloves garlic, peeled

In a food processor or blender, whirl basil, cheese, oil, walnuts, and garlic until smoothly puréed.

makes about 1 cup

per tablespoon: 69 calories, 2 g protein, 2 g carbohydrates, 6 g total fat, 2 mg cholesterol, 48 mg sodium

spinach tortellini with spinach & pears

preparation time: about 50 minutes

30 to 40 large fresh whole spinach leaves,
rinsed and crisped

5 large red pears

1 tablespoon lemon juice

1 to 2 ounces prosciutto, cut into thin strips
about 1 inch long

1 package (about 10 oz.) fresh spinach, stems
and any yellow or wilted leaves discarded,
remaining leaves rinsed and drained

1 tablespoon butter or margarine

¼ cup half-and-half

½ to I teaspoon honey

About ¼ teaspoon salt (or to taste)

About ¼ teaspoon ground nutmeg (or to taste)

1 package (about 9 oz.) fresh cheese-filled
spinach tortellini

Lemon wedges

1 Divide whole spinach leaves among 4 individual plates; set aside. Peel, core, and thinly slice one of the pears. Place pear slices in a large bowl, add lemon juice, and turn to coat. With a slotted spoon, transfer pear slices to a small bowl and set aside; reserve lemon juice in large bowl.

2 Core and slice remaining pears (do not peel); add to juice in a large bowl and turn to coat. Arrange pear slices over one side of each spinach-lined plate; cover and set aside. Discard any remaining lemon juice.

3 In a wide nonstick frying pan, stir prosciutto over medium-high heat just until crisp (2 to 3 minutes). Remove from pan with a slotted spoon; set aside. Add as much of the packaged spinach as pan will hold. Reduce heat to medium and cook, stirring, just until wilted; add water; 1 tablespoon at a time, if pan appears dry. Transfer cooked spinach to a bowl; repeat to cook remaining spinach. With the back of a wooden spoon, press against spinach to remove excess liquid; discard as much liquid as possible. Keep spinach warm.

4 Melt butter in frying pan and add reserved sliced peeled pears. Sauté until almost tender when pierced (3 to 5 minutes). Working quickly, transfer pears and their juices to a blender or food processor; add cooked spinach and whirl until coarsely pureed. Add half-and-half, honey, salt, and nutmeg. Whirl until smooth; keep warm.

5 In a 5- to 6-quart pan, bring about 3 quarts water to a boil over medium-high heat. Stir in tortellini, separating any that are stuck together, and cook until just tender to bite, about 7 minutes. (Or cook pasta according to package directions.)

6 Drain pasta well and transfer to a large bowl. Add spinach-pear and mix gently but thoroughly.

7 Spoon pasta atop spinach leaves alongside pears on plates. Sprinkle prosciutto over pasta and serve immediately. Offer lemon wedges to squeeze over pasta to taste.

makes 4 servings

per serving: 430 calories, 16 g protein, 73 g carbohydrates, 2 g total fat, 62 mg cholesterol, 716 mg sodium

candy-wrap pasta with cheese & black bean sauce

preparation time: about 50 minutes

8 ounces *each* **feta cheese and part-skim ricotta cheese**

¹/₂ cup firmly packed cilantro

2 tablespoons *each* **freshly grated Parmesan cheese and milk**

18 egg roll (spring roll) wrappers

2 tablespoons all-purpose flour mixed with ¹/₄ cup water

Black Bean Sauce (recipe follows)

1 Combine feta, ricotta, ¹/₃ cup of the cilantro, Parmesan, and milk in a food processor or blender. Whirl until smooth. Lay a wrapper flat, keeping remaining wrappers covered, and place 1 heaping tablespoon of the cheese mixture in center along edge of one side (a narrow side if rectangular). Pat mixture into a log about ³/₄ inch by 1¹/₂ inches. Stir flour mixture. With your finger, lightly rub mixture along each side of filling to opposite edge of wrapper. Also rub mixture along edge opposite filling.

2 Roll wrapper up gently, starting at edge with filling; press edge to seal. Firmly squeeze dough together at ends of filling where paste is painted (pasta should look like a piece of candy twisted in paper). Lay on a lightly floured large baking sheet and cover with plastic wrap. Repeat to use all filling, arranging pasta in a single layer; use 2 baking sheets, if necessary. (At this point, you may refrigerate for up to 4 hours.)

3 Prepare Black Bean Sauce.

4 Chop remaining cilantro; set aside.

5 Pour water into a wide frying pan to a depth of 2 inches. Bring to a boil over high heat. Reduce heat to a gentle boil. Add pasta, half at a time, and cook just until tender to bite (2 to 3 minutes); if skins stick to each other or to pan bottom, stir gently to loosen. Drain well and keep warm.

6 Spoon sauce onto individual plates. Top with pasta. Sprinkle with cilantro.

makes 6 servings

BLACK BEAN SAUCE

1 Combine 1 tablespoon butter or margarine and 1 small onion, chopped, in a wide nonstick frying pan. Cook over medium heat, stirring often, until onion is lightly browned (about 8 minutes). Transfer to a food processor or blender with 1 can (about 15 oz.) black beans and their liquid and 1 cup low-sodium chicken broth. Whirl until smooth. Season to taste with salt and pepper.

2 Pour sauce into a 1 ¹/₂- to 2-quart pan. Cook over medium heat, stirring, until hot. Remove from heat and keep warm.

per serving: 547 calories, 25 g protein, 75 g carbohydrates, 16 g total fat, 62 mg cholesterol, 1,360 mg sodium

roast lamb with fettuccine alfredo

preparation time: about 1¼ hours

2 tablespoons *each* chopped parsley
  and honey

2 teaspoons Dijon mustard

1 teaspoon chopped fresh thyme
  or ½ teaspoon dried thyme

1 teaspoon chopped fresh rosemary or
  ½ teaspoon crumbled dried rosemary

1 teaspoon chopped fresh sage
  or ½ teaspoon dried sage

1 teaspoon grated lemon peel

1 clove garlic, minced or pressed

1 boned lamb loin (about 1½ lbs.),
  rolled and tied

2 cups nonfat milk

⅔ cup half-and-half

1 pound dried fettuccine

⅓ cup freshly grated Parmesan cheese

Salt

Pinch of ground nutmeg

1 or 2 lemons, cut into wedges

1 Mix parsley, honey, mustard, thyme, rosemary, sage, lemon peel, and garlic in a small bowl. Set aside.

2 Place lamb on a rack in a 9- by 13-inch pan. Roast in a 475° oven for 20 minutes; if drippings begin to burn, add 4 to 6 tablespoons water, stirring to loosen browned bits. Remove from oven, brush meat with honey mixture, and continue to roast until a meat thermometer inserted in thickest part registers 140° for rare (15 to 20 more minutes); if roast browns too quickly, drape with foil. Meanwhile, combine milk and half-and-half in a 1½- to 2-quart pan. Bring just to a boil over medium heat; reduce heat and simmer gently, stirring often, until reduced to about 2 cups (about 30 minutes). Remove from heat and keep warm.

3 Transfer meat to a board, cover loosely, and let stand for 10 minutes. Skim and discard fat from pan drippings and pour into a small serving container; keep warm. Meanwhile, bring 16 cups water to a boil in a 6- to 8-quart pan over medium- high heat. Stir in pasta and cook just until tender to bite (8 to 10 minutes); or cook according to package directions. Drain well.

4 Combine pasta, milk mixture, and cheese in a wide nonmetal bowl. Mix thoroughly but gently. Cover tightly and let stand for 5 minutes. Season to taste with salt and mix again. Cover and let stand for 5 more minutes. Meanwhile, remove and discard strings from meat; slice thinly. Add any juices on platter to pan drippings. Place meat on individual plates. Mound pasta along- side and sprinkle with nutmeg. Garnish with lemon wedges. Offer juices to add to taste.

makes 6 servings

per serving: 604 calories, 40 g protein, 66 g carbohydrates, 19 g total fat, 172 mg cholesterol, 328 mg sodium

VEGETABLES AS PASTA: Pasta of a different persuasion, spaghetti squash (with pulp that naturally separates into slender strands) and zucchini (cut into long, slim ribbons) can be fanciful subsitutes for vermicelli and linguine. Top them with sauces and butters designed to complement their mild flavor and tender-crisp nature.

pasta with roasted garlic and peppers

preparation time: about 20 minutes
baking and cooking time: about 1 1/4 hours

1 large head garlic, unpeeled

2 medium-size onions, sliced

2 large red or yellow bell peppers
(about 1 1/4 tbs. total), seeded and sliced

2 tablespoons olive oil

1/4 cup balsamic or red wine vinegar

1 tablespoon Dijon mustard

1 teaspoon dry oregano

1/8 teaspoon fennel seeds, coarsely crushed

1 pound dry penne or other tubular pasta

1/4 cup coarsely chopped Italian parsley

Grated Parmesan cheese (optional)

1 Place whole garlic, onions, and bell peppers in a 9- by 13-inch baking pan; drizzle with oil. Bake in a 425° oven, stirring several times, until vegetables are soft and edges are dark brown (about 1 hour). Keep warm.

2 Remove garlic and cut in half crosswise; squeeze cloves into a medium-size bowl. Stir in vinegar, mustard, oregano, and fennel. Set aside.

3 Bring 4 quarts water to a boil in a 6- to 8-quart pan. Add pasta and cook just until tender to bite (8 to 10 minutes); or cook according to package directions. Drain well and place in a warm wide bowl.

4 Add parsley, onion mixture, and garlic mixture to pasta; mix well. Serve with cheese to add to taste, if desired.

makes 6 servings

per serving: 383 calories, 12 g protein, 70 g carbohydrates, 6 g total fat, 0 mg cholesterol, 86 mg sodium

stuffed manicotti alla fiorentina

preparation time: about 45 minutes
cooking and baking time: about 1 1/4 hours

2 tablespoons olive oil

1 large onion, finely chopped

1 medium-size red bell pepper,
seeded and finely chopped

8 ounces spinach, coarse stems removed

3/4 cup lightly packed crumbled feta cheese

1 cup ricotta cheese

Freshly ground pepper

1 jar (about 30 oz.) Italian-style pasta sauce

1 package (about 8 oz.) large dry manicotti

1 large tomato, seeded and chopped

3 tablespoons grated Parmesan cheese

1 Heat oil in a wide frying pan over medium heat. Add onion and bell pepper. Cook, stirring often, until vegetables are soft but not browned (about 10 minutes). Let cool. Meanwhile, chop spinach finely.

2 Combine spinach, feta, ricotta, and onion mixture in a large bowl; mix well. Season to taste with pepper.

3 Spoon half the pasta sauce into a shallow 3-quart casserole. Divide spinach mixture into as many portions as there are manicotti. One at a time, rinse manicotti with cold water, shake off excess, and push spinach mixture into center of pasta tube with your fingers. Arrange in a single layer in sauce; spoon remaining sauce over pasta.

4 Cover and bake in a 400° oven for 45 minutes; uncover and continue to bake until pasta is tender when pierced (10 to 15 more minutes). Let stand for about 5 minutes.

5 Sprinkle with tomato and Parmesan.

makes 6 servings

per serving: 434 calories, 17 g protein, 51 g carbohydrates, 20 g total fat, 38 mg cholesterol, 1,190 mg sodium

black bean lasagne

preparation time: about 45 minutes
cooking and baking time: about 2 hours

3 pounds pear-shaped (Roma-type) tomatoes, halved lengthwise

1 tablespoon olive oil or salad oil

2 cloves garlic, minced or pressed

$1/2$ cup firmly packed cilantro

10 dry lasagne noodles

2 cans black beans (about 15 oz. *each*), drained and rinsed

$1/4$ cup canned vegetable broth

1 teaspoon ground cumin

$1/2$ teaspoon chili powder

2 cups part-skim ricotta cheese

$1/2$ teaspoon salt

3 cups shredded jack cheese

1 Arrange tomatoes, cut sides up, in a shallow 10- by 15-inch baking pan. Sprinkle with oil and garlic. Bake in a 425° oven until well browned (about $1\frac{1}{4}$ hours). Set aside until cool enough to handle.

2 Remove tomato skins. Place tomatoes in a colander and press lightly to drain liquid. Combine with cilantro in a food processor or blender; whirl until smooth. Set aside.

3 Bring 3 quarts water to a boil in a 5- to 6-quart pan. Add lasagne and cook just until tender to bite (about 8 minutes); or cook according to package directions. Drain; immediately immerse in cold water. Set aside.

4 Combine beans, broth, cumin, and chili powder in a large bowl. Using a potato masher or back of a large spoon, coarsely mash beans. In another bowl, mix ricotta, salt, and $2\frac{1}{2}$ cups of the jack cheese. Drain lasagne and pat dry. Arrange 5 of the noodles, overlapping slightly, in a lightly greased shallow 3-quart casserole. Layer with half each of the beans, cheese mixture, and tomato sauce. Repeat, using remaining lasagne, beans, cheese mixture, and sauce. Sprinkle with remaining jack cheese. (At this point, you may cover and refrigerate for up to a day.)

5 Bake, uncovered, in a 375° oven until top is browned and casserole is bubbly (about 40 minutes; 45 to 50 minutes if cold). Let stand for 10 minutes before serving.

makes 8 servings

per serving: 479 calories, 29 g protein, 46 g carbohydrates, 21 g total fat, 56 mg cholesterol, 522 mg sodium

COOKING WITH OLIVE OIL : How do you know which olive oil to buy? If you look closely at the labels there are some helpful clues—key words to the grade of the oil. The finest grade is "extra virgin." It comes from the first mechanical pressing of the high-quality, ripe, undamaged olives. This grade of oil is usually a light gold-green and is slightly cloudy. It has a pronounced fruity flavor. It is best in dishes where such intense flavor can be appreciated. For most ordinary cooking, though, "virgin" grade is very acceptable and much more practical. The olives used in making virgin olive oil are not as ripe or unblemished as those destined for "extra virginity."

halibut with tomato-cilantro linguine

preparation time: about 20 minutes

2 tablespoons olive oil

1 1/2 tablespoons lime juice

1 tablespoon drained capers

4 small pear-shaped (Rome-type) tomatoes, at room temperature, seeded and chopped

2 cloves garlic, minced or pressed

1/4 teaspoon ground red pepper (cayenne)

1/3 cup cilantro leaves

1 1/4 to 1 1/2 pounds halibut steaks or other white-fleshed fish steaks such as sea bass (about 3/4 inch thick)

Salt and black pepper

Olive oil cooking spray

1 package (9 or 10 oz.) fresh linguine

1 In a large bowl, stir together oil, lime juice, capers, tomatoes, garlic, red pepper, and cilantro; set aside. Remove and discard any skin from fish, then rinse fish and pat dry: Cut fish into 4 serving-size pieces; season to taste with salt and black pepper.

2 Spray a wide nonstick frying pan with cooking spray; place over medium-high heat. Add fish and cook, turning once, until lightly browned on outside and just opaque but still moist in thickest part; cut to test (6 to 8 minutes).

3 Meanwhile, in a 5- to 6-quart pan, cook linguine in 3 quarts boiling water just until tender to bite (1 to 2 minutes); or cook according to package directions. Drain pasta well. Set 2 table-spoons of the tomato mixture aside; lightly mix remaining mixture with hot pasta.

4 Divide pasta among 4 warm plates; top each serving with a piece of fish, then top fish evenly with reserved tomato mixture.

makes 4 servings

per serving: 442 calories, 42 g protein, 40 g carbohydrates, 12 g total fat, 129 mg cholesterol, 163 mg sodium

paradise pasta with pine nuts

preparation time: about 55 minutes

1/3 cup pine nuts

1 tablespoon salad oil

1 pound mushrooms, thinly sliced

1 medium-size onion, finely chopped

4 cloves garlic, minced or pressed

1 teaspoon *each* dry basil and dry oregano

4 cups broccoli flowerets

1 small red bell pepper, seeded and thinly sliced

1 1/2 cups canned vegetable broth

8 ounces dry angel hair pasta

1/2 cup grated Parmesan cheese

Salt and pepper

1 Toast pine nuts in a wide frying pan over medium heat, stirring often, until golden (6 to 8 minutes). Remove from pan and set aside.

2 Heat oil in same pan over high heat. Add mushrooms, onion, garlic, basil, and oregano. Cover and cook, stirring often, until liquid has accumulated (3 to 5 minutes). Uncover and continue to cook, stirring often, until vegetables are lightly browned (about 8 more minutes).

3 Add broccoli, bell pepper, and broth to onion mixture. Bring to a boil; cover and cook until broccoli is just tender when pierced (about 5 minutes). Meanwhile, bring 2 1/2 quarts water to a boil in a 4- to 5-quart pan. Add pasta and cook just until tender to bite (about 3 minutes); or cook according to package directions. Drain well and place in a warm wide bowl.

4 Spoon vegetable sauce over pasta. Sprinkle with pine nuts and cheese. Season to taste with salt and pepper.

makes 4 servings

per serving: 447 calories, 22 g protein, 62 g carbohydrates, 75 g total fat, 8 mg cholesterol, 607 mg sodium

vegetarian

pinto bean cakes with salsa

preparation time: about 30 minutes

1 ½ tablespoons vegetable oil

1 small onion, finely chopped

¼ cup finely chopped red bell pepper

2 cloves garlic, minced or pressed

1 medium-size fresh jalapeño chile,
    seeded and finely chopped

2 cans (about 15 oz. *each*) pinto beans,
    drained and rinsed

⅛ teaspoon liquid smoke

¼ cup chopped cilantro

½ teaspoon ground cumin

¼ teaspoon pepper

⅓ cup yellow cornmeal

Vegetable oil cooking spray, if needed

½ to 1 cup purchased or homemade salsa

1 Heat 1½ teaspoons of the oil in a wide nonstick frying pan over medium heat. Add onion, bell pepper, garlic, and chile; cook, stirring often, until onion is soft but not browned (about 5 minutes). Meanwhile, place beans in a large bowl and mash coarsely with a potato masher (mashed beans should stick together). Stir in onion mixture; then add liquid smoke, cilantro, cumin, and pepper. Mix well. If necessary, refrigerate until cool.

2 Spread cornmeal on a sheet of wax paper. Divide bean mixture into 8 equal portions; shape each into a ½-inch-thick cake. Coat cakes with cornmeal.

3 In pan used to cook onion, heat remaining 1 tablespoon oil over medium-high heat. Add bean cakes and cook, turning once, until golden brown on both sides (8 to 10 minutes); if necessary, spray pan with cooking spray to prevent sticking. Serve with salsa to add to taste.

makes 4 servings (2 cakes each)

per serving: 232 calories, 9 g protein, 34 g carbohydrates, 6 g total fat, 0 mg cholesterol, 666 mg sodium

sweet & bitter mustard greens

preparation time: about 30 minutes

¾ pound mustard greens, tough stems
    trimmed, rinsed and drained

1 tablespoon olive oil

1 large onion, thinly sliced

1 tablespoon minced fresh marjoram leaves
    or 1 teaspoon dry marjoram leaves

¾ cup golden raisins

⅓ cup low-sodium chicken broth

Salt and pepper

1 Set aside 6 large mustard green leaves. Finely chop remaining leaves.

2 Place whole leaves on a rack in a pan above 1 inch boiling water. Cover and stew over high heat just until slightly limp (about 30 seconds). Remove from pan and set aside.

3 Heat oil in a wide frying pan over medium-low heat. Add onion and marjoram and cook, stirring often, until onion is golden (about 15 minutes). Stir in raisins and cook for 30 seconds. Add chopped leaves and chicken broth and cook, stirring, until leaves are wilted (about 2 minutes).

4 Place a whole leaf on each plate and mound greens mixture on top. Season to taste with salt and pepper.

makes 6 servings

per serving: 99 calories, 2 g protein, 19 g carbohydrates, 3 g total fat, 0 mg cholesterol, 19 mg sodium

couscous bean paella

preparation time: about 30 minutes

2 teaspoons olive oil

1 large onion, chopped

1 medium-size red bell pepper,
  seeded and cut into $1/2$-inch squares

2 $1/4$ cups canned vegetable broth

$1/8$ teaspoon saffron threads, or to taste

1 package (about 9 oz.) frozen artichoke hearts,
  thawed and drained

1 cup frozen peas, thawed and drained

1 $1/2$ cups couscous

1 can (about 15 oz.) black beans,
  drained and rinsed

Lime or lemon wedges

1 Heat oil in a wide nonstick frying pan or wok over medium-high heat. When oil is hot, add onion, bell pepper, and $1/4$ cup water. Stir-fry until onion is soft (about 5 minutes); add water, 1 tablespoon at a time, if pan appears dry.

2 Add broth, saffron, artichokes, and peas to pan. Bring to a rolling boil. Stir in couscous. Cover pan, remove from heat, and let stand until liquid has been absorbed (about 5 minutes). Gently stir in beans; cover and let stand for 2 to 3 minutes to heat beans. Serve with lime wedges.

makes 4 servings

per serving: 435 calories, 17 g protein, 82 g carbohydrates, 4 g total fat, 0 mg cholesterol, 816 mg sodium

baked quesadillas

preparation time: about 25 minutes

1 can (about 15 oz.) black beans,
  drained and rinsed well

$1/4$ cup nonfat mayonnaise

2 teaspoons wine vinegar

1 teaspoon chili powder

4 nonfat flour tortillas (*each* about 7 inches
  in diameter)

1 cup shredded reduced-fat jack
  or sharp Cheddar cheese

2 small firm-ripe pear-shaped
  (Roma-type) tomatoes, chopped

$1/2$ cup chopped red onion

$1/3$ cup cilantro leaves

$1/2$ cup purchased or homemade green
  tomatillo salsa

1 In a medium-size bowl, coarsely mash beans. Add mayonnaise, vinegar, and chili powder; stir until well blended.

2 Lightly brush both sides of each tortilla with water. Spoon a fourth of the bean mixture over half of each tortilla; evenly sprinkle a fourth each of the cheese, tomatoes, onion, and cilantro over bean mixture on each tortilla. Fold plain half of tortilla over to cover filling.

3 Set quesadillas slightly apart on a lightly greased 12- by 15-inch baking sheet. Bake in a 500° oven until crisp and golden (about 7 minutes). Serve with salsa.

makes 4 servings

per serving: 323 calories, 16 g protein, 30 g carbohydrates, 8 g total fat, 20 mg cholesterol, 998 mg sodium

peanut stew with banana couscous

preparation time: about 40 minutes

1 can (about 12 oz.) banana nectar

About 1 1/4 cups low-fat (2%) milk

1 medium-size red onion, finely chopped

1 can (about 20 oz.) crushed pineapple packed in its own juice

1 medium-size very ripe banana, mashed

1 package (about 10 oz.) frozen chopped spinach, thawed and squeezed dry

1/2 cup crunchy peanut butter

About 1/8 teaspoon crushed red pepper flakes

1 package (about 10 oz.) couscous

1/4 cup coarsely chopped fresh mint

1/4 cup coarsely chopped cilantro

Lime wedges

1 Pour banana nectar into a 4-cup glass measure. Add enough milk to make 2 3/4 cups; set aside. In a wide nonstick frying pan, combine onion and 1/4 cup water. Cook over medium-high heat, stirring often, until onion is soft (about 5 minutes); add water, 1 tablespoon at a time, if pan appears dry.

2 Add undrained pineapple and mashed banana to onion mixture; bring to a boil. Stir in spinach; then reduce heat, cover, and simmer for 5 minutes. Add peanut butter and red pepper flakes. Simmer, uncovered, for 5 minutes, stirring until peanut butter is melted and smoothly blended into sauce.

3 Meanwhile, pour milk mixture into a 2- to 3-quart pan and bring just to a boil over medium-high heat. Stir in couscous. Cover, remove from heat, and let stand until liquid has been absorbed (5 to 6 minutes).

4 Spoon couscous into 4 wide individual bowls and top with spinach mixture. Sprinkle with mint and cilantro; garnish with lime wedges.

makes 4 servings

per serving: 696 calories, 23 g protein, 115 g carbohydrates, 19 g total fat, 6 mg cholesterol, 271 mg sodium

mashed potatoes & broccoli

preparation time: about 35 minutes

1 pound broccoli

2 1/2 pounds russet potatoes

3 tablespoons margarine

About 1/4 cup lowfat (2%) milk

Salt and pepper

1 Cut off broccoli flowerets; peel stalks. Finely chop stalks and all but a few small flowerets; set aside. Peel potatoes and cut into 1/2-inch cubes.

2 In a 6-quart pan, bring 3 quarts water to a boil over high heat. Add potatoes; cover and cook until tender when pierced (about 15 minutes). Add broccoli and cook, covered, until tender (about 10 minutes). Drain well. Remove whole flowerets and set aside.

3 Return potatoes and remaining broccoli to pan. Reduce heat to low, add margarine and 1/4 cup of the milk, and cook, stirring, until margarine has melted. Remove from heat. With a potato masher, mash vegetables smoothly, adding more milk, a tablespoon at a time, if mixture is too thick. Season to taste with salt and pepper. Transfer to a serving dish and top with reserved flowerets.

makes 4 to 6 servings

per serving: 258 calories, 7 g protein, 42 g carbohydrates, 8 g total fat, 2 mg cholesterol, 127 mg sodium

green potatoes with blue cheese sauce

preparation time: about 40 minutes

4 ounces soft tofu, rinsed and drained

1/3 cup low-fat buttermilk

1 tablespoon white wine vinegar

1 tablespoon honey

1 teaspoon Dijon mustard

1 or 2 cloves garlic, peeled

1/2 cup crumbled blue-veined cheese

Salt and pepper

3 to 4 cups lightly packed, rinsed, crisped spinach leaves

1 tablespoon butter or margarine

1 1/4 pounds small red thin-skinned potatoes, scrubbed and cut crosswise into 1/4-inch slices

1 medium-size red bell pepper, seeded and cut into thin strips

1 medium size onion, cut into thick slivers

1 tablespoon ground cumin

1 teaspoon ground coriander

1/8 teaspoon ground red pepper (cayenne)

1/2 to 3/4 cup lightly packed cilantro leaves

Cilantro sprigs (optional)

1 tablespoon thinly sliced green onion

1 To prepare blue cheese sauce, in a blender or food processor, combine tofu, buttermilk, vinegar, honey, mustard, and garlic. Whirl until smoothly puréed. Gently mix in cheese and season to taste with salt and black pepper. Set aside. (At this point you may cover and refrigerate for up to 3 hours.)

2 Cut 1 to 1 1/2 cups of the spinach into thin shreds about 2 inches long. Cover and set aside. Line a rimmed platter with remaining spinach leaves; cover and set aside.

3 Melt butter in a wide nonstick frying pan or wok over medium-high heat. Add potatoes, bell pepper, onion, cumin, coriander, 1/4 teaspoon salt, ground red pepper, and 1/4 cup of water. Stir-fry gently until potatoes are tinged with brown and tender when pierced (about 15 minutes; do not scorch). Add water, 1 tablespoon at a time, if pan appears dry.

4 Remove pan from heat. Sprinkle potato mixture with shredded spinach; mix gently but thoroughly. Then spoon potato mixture over spinach leaves on platter. Sprinkle with cilantro leaves; garnish with cilantro sprigs, if desired.

5 Just before serving, stir onion into blue cheese sauce. Offer blue cheese sauce to add to taste.

makes 4 servings

per serving: 279 calories, 11 g protein, 39 g carbohydrates, 9 g total fat, 21 mg cholesterol, 436 mg sodium

zucchini polenta

preparation time: about 25 minutes

1 cup polenta or yellow cornmeal

3 cups canned or homemade vegetable broth

2 cups shredded zucchini

1/2 cup shredded reduced-fat jack cheese

In a 3- to 4-quart pan, stir together polenta and broth. Bring to a boil over high heat, stirring. stir in zucchini; reduce heat to low and simmer, uncovered, stirring often, until polenta tastes creamy (about 10 minutes). Stir in cheese.

makes 4 servings

per serving: 192 calories, 8 g protein, 31 g carbohydrates, 4 g total fat, 10 mg cholesterol, 853 mg sodium

spicy chili mac

preparation time: about 40 minutes

2 large carrots, chopped

1 large onion, coarsely chopped

About 3 $\frac{1}{2}$ cups vegetable broth

1 can (about 15 oz.) tomatoes

1 can (about 15 oz.) pinto beans; or 2 cups cooked (about 1 cup dried) pinto beans

1 can (about 15 oz.) kidney beans; or 2 cups cooked (about 1 cup dried) kidney beans

3 tablespoons chili powder

8 ounces dried elbow macaroni

About $\frac{1}{2}$ cup plain nonfat yogurt

Salt

Crushed red pepper flakes

1 Combine carrots, onion, and $\frac{1}{4}$ cup water in a 4- to 5-quart pan. Cook over medium-high heat, stirring often, until liquid has evaporated and vegetables begin to brown (about 10 minutes).

2 Add 3$\frac{1}{2}$ cups of the broth and tomatoes and their liquid; break up tomatoes with a spoon. Stir in pinto and kidney beans and their liquid (if using home-cooked beans, add 1 cup more broth smoothly blended with 1 teaspoon cornstarch). Add chili powder, stirring to loosen browned bits. Bring to a boil. Stir in pasta and boil gently just until pasta is tender to bite (8 to 10 minutes). If mixture is too thick, add broth; if too thin, continue to simmer until mixture is of desired consistency.

3 Ladle into bowls. Offer yogurt, salt, and red pepper flakes to add to taste.

makes 4 to 6 servings

per serving: 399 calories, 18 g protein, 77 g carbohydrates, 3 g total fat, 0.5 mg cholesterol, 1,637 mg sodium

picadillo stuffed peppers

preparation time: about 45 minutes
baking time: about 45 minutes

6 medium-size yellow bell peppers

1 tablespoon olive oil

2 cloves garlic, minced or pressed

1 large can (about 15 oz.) tomato sauce

$\frac{1}{4}$ cup dry white wine

2 tablespoons cider vinegar

1 $\frac{1}{2}$ teaspoons ground cinnamon

1 teaspoon dry oregano

$\frac{1}{2}$ cup raisins

3 cups cooked brown rice

1 can (about 15 oz.) black beans, drained and rinsed; or 2 cups cooked black beans drained and rinsed

$\frac{1}{4}$ cup sliced almonds

2 tablespoons grated Parmesan cheese

1 Cut off stem ends of peppers and remove seeds. If necessary, trim bases so peppers will stand upright. In a 6- to 8-quart pan, bring 3 to 4 quarts water to a boil over high heat. Add peppers; cook for 2 minutes. Using tongs, lift peppers from pan and plunge into cold water to cool; drain and set aside.

2 Heat oil in a wide nonstick frying pan over medium-high heat. Add garlic and cook, stirring, just until soft (about 2 minutes). Add 1 cup of the tomato sauce, wine, vinegar, cinnamon, oregano, and raisins; cook, stirring occasionally, for 15 minutes. Stir in rice, beans, and almonds.

3 Fill peppers equally with rice mixture; set upright in a shallow 1 $\frac{1}{2}$-quart baking pan. Pour remaining tomato sauce into pan around peppers. Cover and bake in a 375° oven for 30 minutes. Uncover; sprinkle peppers evenly with cheese. Continue to bake until cheese is golden brown (about 15 more minutes).

makes 6 servings

per serving: 298 calories, 9 g protein, 55 g carbohydrates, 6 g total fat, 1 mg cholesterol, 585 mg sodium

double wheat burgers

preparation time: about 25 minutes

1 large egg plus 2 egg whites

1 1/4 cups soft whole wheat bread crumbs

1/2 cup toasted wheat germ crumbs

3 tablespoons chopped walnuts

1/2 cup sliced green onions

1/2 cup small-curd low-fat (1%) cottage cheese

2 tablespoons chopped parsley

1 teaspoon dried basil

1/2 teaspoon dried oregano

1/2 teaspoon paprika

Salt

4 thin slices reduced-fat jack cheese
(about 2 oz. *total*)

4 whole wheat hamburger buns, toasted

1/4 cup nonfat Thousand Island dressing
or mayonnaise

1 In a large bowl, beat egg and egg whites to blend. Stir in bread, wheat germ, walnuts, green onions, cottage cheese, parsley, basil, oregano, and paprika. Season to taste with salt.

2 On an oiled 12- by 15-inch baking sheet, shape mixture into 4 equal patties, each about 1/2 inch thick. Broil patties about 3 inches below heat, turning once, until deep golden on both sides (about 6 minutes). Top each patty with a slice of jack cheese and continue to broil just until cheese is melted (about 30 more seconds).

3 To serve, place patties on bottoms of buns. Top with dressing, then with tops of buns.

makes 4 servings

per serving: 346 calories, 22 g protein, 42 g carbohydrates, 12 g total fat, 64 mg cholesterol, 722 mg sodium

lentil-nut shephard's pie

preparation time: 15 minutes
cooking time: about 1 hour and 10 minutes

1 1/2 cups lentils

2 cloves garlic, minced or pressed

1 1/2 teaspoons *each* dried thyme and dried savory

1/2 teaspoon dried rubbed sage

5 1/2 cups vegetable broth

1/2 cup chopped walnuts

2 cups soft whole wheat bread crumbs

2 pounds thin-skinned potatoes,
peeled and cut into 2-inch chunks

1 cup shredded reduced-fat sharp
Cheddar cheese

1 Sort through lentils, discarding any debris. Rinse lentils, drain, and place in a 3- to 4-quart pan. Add garlic, thyme, savory, sage, and 3 1/2 cups of the broth. Bring to a boil over high heat; then reduce heat, cover, and simmer until lentils are tender to bite (about 25 minutes). Remove from heat and stir in walnuts and bread crumbs.

2 While lentils are simmering, combine potatoes and remaining 2 cups broth in a 2- to 3-quart pan. Bring to a boil over high heat; then reduce heat, cover, and simmer until potatoes mash easily when pressed (15 to 20 minutes). Drain, reserving liquid. Leaving potatoes in pan, beat or mash them until smooth. Mix in 1/2 cup of the reserved liquid; then stir in cheese.

3 Stir remaining potato-cooking liquid into lentil mixture; spoon into a 9- by 13-inch baking pan. Drop potatoes in spoonfuls onto lentil mixture. Bake in a 375° oven until potatoes are golden brown (about 35 minutes).

makes 8 servings

per serving: 340 calories, 19 g protein, 49 g carbohydrates, 9 g total fat, 10 mg cholesterol, 874 mg sodium

wheat germ burgers

preparation time: about 30 minutes

2 large eggs

³/₄ cup toasted wheat germ

¹/₂ cup shredded reduced-fat jack cheese

¹/₄ cup chopped mushrooms

3 tablespoons finely chopped onion

¹/₂ teaspoon dried thyme, crumbled

¹/₂ teaspoon dried rosemary, crumbled

1 ¹/₂ cups long zucchini shreds

Salt and pepper

1 to 2 teaspoons vegetable oil

4 kaiser rolls, hamburger buns

¹/₂ cup plain nonfat yogurt

About ¹/₄ cup catsup

About 2 tablespoons Dijon mustard

4 to 8 butter lettuce leaves, rinsed and crisped

1 large tomato, thinly sliced

1 In a large bowl, beat eggs to blend. Stir in wheat germ, cheese, mushrooms, onion, thyme, rosemary, and zucchini. Season to taste with salt and pepper.

2 On sheet of plastic wrap, shape wheat germ mixture into 4 equal patties, each about ³/₄ inch thick.

3 Heat 1 teaspoon of the oil in a wide nonstick frying pan over medium heat. Add patties and cook until deep golden on bottom (4 to 5 minutes). Turn patties over; add 1 teaspoon more oil to pan, if needed. Cook until deep golden on other side (about 4 more minutes).

4 To serve, place patties on bottoms of buns. Top with yogurt, catsup, mustard, lettuce leaves, and tomato, then with tops of buns.

makes 4 servings

per serving: 416 calories, 22 g protein, 54 g carbohydrates, 13 g total fat, 117 mg cholesterol, 885 mg sodium

roasted red & yellow potatoes

preparation time: about 10 minutes
baking time: about 55 minutes

2 pounds medium-size red thin skinned
   potatoes, quartered

3 small sweet potatoes or yams,
   cut lengthwise into 1 inch wedges

3 medium-size onions, quartered

3 tablespoons olive oil

Salt and pepper

Sherry vinegar or cider vinegar (optional)

1 Mix red potatoes, sweet potatoes, onions, and oil. Spread mixture evenly on a large rimmed baking sheet. Bake in a 425° oven until vegetables are tender and browned (about 55 minutes).

2 Transfer to a serving dish and season to taste with salt and pepper. Sprinkle with vinegar, if desired.

makes 6 servings

per serving: 315 calories, 5 g protein, 58 g carbohydrates, 7 g total fat, 0 mg cholesterol, 27 mg sodium

vegetable burritos

preparation time: about 15 minutes
chilling time: at least 20 minutes

1 teaspoon grated lime peel

1/3 cup lime juice

2 tablespoons distilled white vinegar

1 tablespoon honey

2 teaspoons Dijon mustard

1 teaspoon ground cumin

2 cloves garlic, minced or pressed

1 fresh jalapeño chile, seeded and minced

1 1/2 cups fresh-cut yellow or white corn kernels
   (from 2 medium-size ears of corn); or 1 package
   (about 10 oz.) frozen corn kernels, thawed

1 can (about 15 oz.) red kidney beans, drained
   and rinsed; or 2 cups cooked (about 1 cup dried)
   red kidney beans, drained and rinsed

1 medium-size cucumber, peeled, seeded,
   and finely chopped

1/2 cup sliced green onion

2 tablespoons minced cilantro

8 warm tortillas

1 To prepare lime marinade, in a nonmetal bowl, stir together lime peel, lime juice, vinegar, honey, mustard, cumin, garlic, and chile. Pour into a large (1-gallon) heavy-duty resealable plastic bag or large nonmetal bowl. Add corn, beans, cucumber, onions, and cilantro. Seal bag; rotate to mix vegetables (or mix vegetables in bowl, then cover airtight). Refrigerate for at least 20 minutes or up to 4 hours; rotate bag (or stir vegetables in bowl) occasionally.

2 Scoop out corn mixture with a slotted spoon; drain (discard marinade), then divide equally among tortillas. Roll up tortillas to enclose filling.

makes 8 servings

per serving: 189 calories, 7 g protein, 34 g carbohydrates, 3 g total fat, 0 mg cholesterol, 256 mg sodium

all-vegetable chili

preparation time: about 45 minutes

2 medium-size carrots (about 6 oz. total),
   chopped 1 large onion, coarsely chopped

1 can (about 14 1/2 oz.) tomatoes

1 can (about 15 oz.) pinto beans; or 2 cups
   cooked (about 1 cup dried) pinto beans

1 can (about 15 oz.) red kidney beans; or 2 cups
   cooked (about 1 cup dried) red kidney beans

2 tablespoons chili powder

About 1/2 cup plain nonfat yogurt

Salt

Crushed red pepper flakes

1 In a 4- to 5-quart pan, combine carrots, onion, and 1/4 cup water. Cook over high heat, stirring, until liquid evaporates and vegetables start to brown and stick to pan (about 10 minutes).

2 Add tomatoes and their liquid to pan; break tomatoes up with a spoon. Stir in all beans and their liquid (if using home-cooked beans, add 1 cup canned vegetable broth blended with 1 teaspoon cornstarch). Add chili powder; stir to scrape browned bits free. Bring to a boil; then reduce heat and simmer, uncovered, until flavors are blended (about 15 minutes). If chili is too thick, add a little water; if it's too thin, continue to simmer until it's as thick as you like.

3 Ladle chili into 4 individual bowls. Add yogurt, salt, and red pepper flakes to taste.

makes 4 servings

per serving: 260 calories, 15 g protein, 50 g carbohydrates, 2 g total fat, 0.6 mg cholesterol, 1,057 mg sodium

swiss chard with garbanzos & parmesan

preparation time: about 40 minutes

3 tablespoons molasses

1 ½ teaspoons dry mustard

1 ½ teaspoons Worcestershire sauce
  or reduced-sodium soy sauce

¾ teaspoon chopped fresh oregano
  or ¼ teaspoon dried oregano

1 pound Swiss chard

1 teaspoon olive oil

2 large onions, thinly sliced

½ teaspoon grated lemon peel

Salt

2 large tomatoes, chopped

1 can (about 15 oz.) garbanzo beans,
  drained and rinsed

1 teaspoon cornstarch blended
  with 1 teaspoon cold water

½ cup shredded Parmesan cheese

Oregano sprigs

1 In a small bowl, stir together molasses, mustard, Worcestershire, and chopped oregano. Set aside.

2 Trim and discard discolored stem ends from chard; then rinse chard, drain, and cut crosswise into ½-inch strips. Set aside.

3 Heat oil in a wide nonstick frying pan or wok over medium-high heat. When oil is hot, add onions, lemon peel, and 2 tablespoons water. Stir-fry until onions are soft (about 7 minutes). Add water, 1 tablespoon at a time, if pan appears dry. Add half the chard and 1 tablespoon more water to pan; stir-fry until chard just begins to wilt. Then add remaining chard and 1 tablespoon more water; stir-fry until all chard is wilted and bright green (3 to 4 more minutes). Season to taste with salt. Spoon chard mixture around edge of a rimmed platter and keep warm.

4 Stir molasses mixture and pour into pan; add tomatoes and beans. Stir-fry gently until beans are heated through and tomatoes are soft (about 3 minutes). Stir cornstarch mixture well and pour into pan. Cook, stirring gently, until mixture boils and thickens slightly (1 to 2 minutes).

5 Spoon bean mixture into center of platter; sprinkle Parmesan cheese over chard and beans. Garnish with oregano sprigs.

makes 4 servings

per serving: 264 calories, 12 g protein, 42 g carbohydrates, 7 g total fat, 8 mg cholesterol, 566 mg sodium

lemon-garlic swiss chard

preparation time: about 30 minutes

1 ½ pounds Swiss chard, rinsed and drained

¼ cup lemon juice

1 clove garlic, minced or pressed

2 teaspoons olive oil

Freshly ground pepper

4 teaspoons grated Parmesan cheese (optional)

1 Trim off and discard discolored ends of Swiss chard stems. Cut white stalks from leaves and coarsely chop; set aside. Shred leaves.

2 Place chopped stalks on a rack in a pan above 1 inch boiling water. Cover and steam over high heat for 5 minutes. Add leaves and continue steaming, covered, until leaves are tender and bright green (about 15 more minutes).

3 Transfer chard to a bowl and add lemon juice, garlic, and oil; season to taste with pepper. Toss well. Sprinkle with Parmesan, if desired.

makes 4 servings

per serving: 55 calories, 3 g protein, 7 g carbohydrates, 3 g total fat, 0 mg cholesterol, 334 mg sodium

tofu tacos with pineapple salsa

preparation time: about 35 minutes

3 tablespoons reduced-sodium soy sauce

2 tablespoons honey

1 tablespoon basil oil (or 1 tablespoon vegetable oil plus ½ teaspoon dried basil)

1 teaspoon hot chili oil

2 cloves garlic, minced or pressed

12 ounces firm tofu, rinsed, drained, and cut into ½-inch cubes

1 cup diced fresh or canned pineapple

½ cup peeled, shredded jicama

1 teaspoon grated lime peel

3 tablespoons lime juice

2 tablespoons minced fresh basil

4 low-fat flour tortillas (*each* 7 to 9 inches in diameter)

1 large red bell pepper, seeded and finely chopped

1 large onion, finely chopped

1 package (about 10 oz.) frozen corn kernels, thawed and drained

1 In a medium-size bowl, stir together soy sauce, honey, basil oil, hot chile oil, and garlic. Add tofu and stir gently to coat. Set aside; stir occasionally to blend.

2 To prepare pineapple salsa, in a large bowl, mix pineapple, jicama, lime peel, lime juice, and basil; set aside.

3 Brush tortillas lightly with hot water; then stack tortillas, wrap in foil, and heat in a 350° oven until warm (10 to 12 minutes).

4 Meanwhile, in a wide nonstick frying pan or wok, combine tofu (and any marinade), bell pepper, and onion. Stir-fry gently over medium-high heat until tofu is browned (about 15 minutes). Add water, 1 tablespoon at a time, if pan appears dry. Add corn and stir-fry until heated through.

5 Top tortillas equally with tofu mixture and pineapple salsa; roll up to enclose.

makes 4 servings

per serving: 411 calories, 20 g protein, 57 g carbohydrates, 15 g total fat, 0 mg cholesterol, 761 mg sodium

gingered asparagus

preparation time: about 15 minutes

1 pound asparagus, tough ends snapped off, cut diagonally into 2-inch pieces

1 tablespoon minced fresh ginger

3 tablespoons lemon juice

2 teaspoons sesame oil

1 Place asparagus on a rack in a pan above 1 inch boiling water. Cover and steam over high heat until tender-crisp (5 to 7 minutes).

2 Transfer to a bowl and add ginger, lemon juice, and oil. Stir well. Serve warm or at room temperature.

makes 4 servings

per serving: 37 calories, 2 g protein, 3 g carbohydrates, 2 g total fat, 0 mg cholesterol, 4 mg sodium

vegetable-bean chili

preparation time: about 30 minutes

3 tablespoons molasses

1 ½ teaspoons dry mustard

1 ½ teaspoons Worcestershire sauce
   or reduced-sodium soy sauce

1 teaspoon olive oil or vegetable oil

2 cloves garlic, minced or pressed

2 medium-size carrots (about 6 oz. total),
   cut diagonally into ¼-inch slices

1 large onion, chopped

1 tablespoon chili powder, or to taste

2 or 3 large tomatoes (1 to 1 ½ lbs. total),
   chopped

1 can (about 15 oz.) pinto beans,
   drained and rinsed

1 can (about 15 oz.) red kidney beans,
   drained and rinsed

About ½ cup plain nonfat yogurt

Crushed red pepper flakes

1 In a small bowl, stir together molasses, mustard, and Worcestershire. Set aside.

2 Heat oil in a wide nonstick frying pan or wok over medium-high heat. When oil is hot, add garlic and stir-fry just until fragrant (about 30 seconds; do not scorch). Add carrots, onion, chili powder, and ¼ cup water. Cover and cook until carrots are almost tender to bite (about 4 minutes). Uncover and stir-fry until liquid has evaporated.

3 Stir molasses mixture and pour into pan; then add tomatoes and beans. Stir-fry gently until beans are heated through and tomatoes are soft (3 to 5 minutes). Ladle chili into bowls and top with yogurt. Season to taste with red pepper flakes.

makes 4 servings

per serving: 290 calories, 14 g protein, 54 g carbohydrates, 3 g total fat, 0.6 mg cholesterol, 405 mg sodium

warm tortillas

cooking time: about 12 minutes

Warm corn or flour tortillas are obvious accompaniments for most Mexican- inspired dishes, but don't hesitate to offer them as a low-fat option to rolls or bread with any meal.

6 corn tortillas (each 6 inches in diameter) or
   6 flour tortillas (each 7 to 9 inches in diameter)

Brush tortillas lightly with hot water; then stack, wrap in foil, and heat in a 350° oven until warm (10 to 12 minutes).

makes 6 tortillas

per corn tortilla: 56 calories, 1 g protein, 12 g carbohydrates, 0.6 g total fat, 0 mg cholesterol, 40 mg sodium

per flour tortilla: 114 calories, 3 g protein, 20 g carbohydrates, 3 g total fat, 0 mg cholesterol, 167 mg sodium

green bean & tomato casserole

preparation time: about 1 hour

2 ¹/₂ pounds green beans, cut into 2-inch pieces

1 tablespoon salad oil

1 large onion, chopped

3 cloves garlic, minced or pressed

¹/₂ pound mushrooms, thinly sliced

2 pounds tomatoes, cut into wedges

¹/₄ teaspoon ground red pepper (cayenne)

1 ¹/₂ teaspoons *each* dry basil leaves
   and dry oregano leaves

1 tablespoon margarine

1 ¹/₂ cups soft whole wheat bread crumbs

¹/₄ cup grated Parmesan cheese

1 Place beans on a rack in a pan above 1 inch boiling water. Cover and steam over high heat until tender-crisp (about 10 minutes). Lift out and immerse in ice water until cool. Drain and set aside.

2 Heat oil in a wide frying pan over medium-high heat. Add onion, about two-thirds of the garlic, and mushrooms. Cook, stirring, until liquid has evaporated (about 10 minutes). Remove from heat and stir in beans, tomatoes, red pepper, and 1 teaspoon *each* of the basil and oregano. Spread mixture in a 9- by 13-inch baking pan and set aside.

3 Reduce heat to medium and melt margarine in frying pan. Add bread crumbs and remaining garlic, basil, and oregano; cook, stirring, until golden brown. (At this point, you may cool, cover, and refrigerate vegetables and topping separately for up to 2 days.)

4 Scatter bread crumb mixture over vegetables; sprinkle with Parmesan. Cover and bake in a 400° oven for 20 minutes (30 minutes if refrigerated). Uncover and continue baking until tomatoes are soft (about 15 more minutes).

makes 12 servings

per serving: 95 calories, 4 g protein, 15 g carbohydrates, 3 g total fat, 1 mg cholesterol, 87 mg sodium

zucchini carrot pizza

preparation time: about 45 minutes

1 cup fine dry bread crumbs

1 teaspoon olive oil

2 cloves garlic, minced or pressed

1 large egg

2 large egg whites

2 tablespoons all-purpose flour

¹/₄ teaspoon pepper

1 teaspoon dried basil

1 cup shredded carrots

1 cup shredded zucchini

1 teaspoon yellow cornmeal

³/₄ cup shredded reduced-fat jack cheese

1 cup very thinly sliced mushrooms

1 In a wide nonstick frying pan, combine bread crumbs, oil, and garlic. Stir over medium-high heat until crumbs are crisp (about 6 minutes). Remove from pan and set aside.

2 In a large bowl, combine egg, egg whites, flour, pepper, basil, carrots, and zucchini. Mix until evenly blended. Add crumbs and mix well. Sprinkle a 12-inch nonstick or regular pizza pan with cornmeal. Spread vegetable mixture evenly in pan and bake in a 400° oven until browned (about 20 minutes).

3 Sprinkle crust with cheese and mushrooms and continue to bake until cheese is melted (about 10 minutes).

makes 4 servings

per serving: 261 calories, 16 g protein, 32 g carbohydrates, 8 g total fat, 68 mg cholesterol, 459 mg sodium

eggplant parmesan

preparation time: 30 minutes
cooking time: about 1 hour

3 large egg whites

3 tablespoons Marsala

1 cup fine dry bread crumbs

1/2 cup shredded Parmesan cheese

1 tablespoon chopped fresh thyme
   or 1/2 teaspoon dried thyme

1/2 teaspoon salt

2 medium-size eggplants

1/4 cup yellow cornmeal

3/4 cup nonfat sour cream

2 cloves garlic, peeled

2 teaspoons cornstarch

1 teaspoon honey

3 cans (about 14 1/2 oz. *each*)
   diced tomatoes, drained well

1 tablespoon chopped fresh basil
   or 1/2 teaspoon dried basil

2 large tomatoes, very thinly sliced

1 cup shredded mozzarella cheese

Thyme sprigs

1 In a wide, shallow bowl, beat egg whites and Marsala to blend. In another wide, shallow bowl, combine bread crumbs, 1/4 cup of the Parmesan cheese, chopped thyme, and salt; set aside.

2 Cut unpeeled eggplants crosswise into slices about 1/4 inch thick. Dip slices in egg white mixture; drain briefly, then dip in crumb mixture and press to coat lightly all over. Arrange eggplant slices on 2 or 3 greased large baking sheets; pat any remaining crumb mixture on slices.

3 Bake in a 400° oven, turning once, until golden brown on both sides (about 30 minutes); switch positions of baking sheets halfway through baking. If any slices begin to brown excessively, remove them and set aside.

4 Meanwhile, sprinkle cornmeal over bottom of a greased 9- by 13-inch baking pan; set aside. In a food processor or blender, whirl sour cream, garlic, cornstarch, honey, and two-thirds of the canned tomatoes until smoothly puréed. Stir in remaining canned tomatoes and basil.

5 Spoon a third of the tomato sauce over cornmeal in pan; top evenly with a third of the tomato slices. Arrange half the eggplant slices over tomatoes; sprinkle with half the mozzarella cheese. Top evenly with half *each* of the remaining tomato sauce and tomato slices, then with remaining eggplant. Top with remaining tomato sauce, tomato slices, and mozzarella cheese. Sprinkle with remaining 1/4 cup Parmesan cheese.

6 Cover and bake in a 400° oven for 15 minutes. Then uncover and continue to bake until sauce is bubbly and casserole is golden on top and hot in center (15 to 20 more minutes). Garnish with thyme sprigs.

makes 6 servings

per serving: 337 calories, 17 g protein, 44 g carbohydrates, 10 g total fat, 20 mg cholesterol, 938 mg sodium

GETTING ENOUGH PROTEIN: Those who are new to vegetarian eating and cooking often wonder if plant foods alone can provide enough protein for a healthful diet. The answer is yes, provided that your meals contain a good variety of whole grains, legumes, and vegetables.

fruit and cheese quesadillas

preparation time: about 25 minutes

1/2 cup chopped dried apricots

1 teaspoon grated orange peel

6 tablespoons orange juice

About 2 cups part-skim ricotta cheese

About 6 tablespoons honey, or to taste

1 teaspoon ground coriander

12 flour tortillas (7- to 9-inch diameter)

3 cups chopped fresh or canned pineapple, drained well

Mint sprigs (optional)

1 In a bowl, combine apricots, orange peel, and orange juice; let stand until apricots are softened (about 10 minutes).

2 In a food processor or blender, combine apricot-juice mixture, ricotta cheese, honey, and coriander; whirl until smoothly puréed. (At this point, you may cover and refrigerate for up to 2 days.)

3 Arrange 6 tortillas in a single layer on 2 or 3 lightly oiled large baking sheets. Spread tortillas evenly with cheese mixture, covering tortillas to within 1/4 inch of edges. Evenly cover cheese mixture with pineapple, then top each tortilla with one of the remaining tortillas; press lightly.

4 Bake in a 450° oven until tortillas are lightly browned (7 to 9 minutes), switching positions of baking sheets halfway through baking.

5 Slide quesadillas onto a board; cut each into 4 to 6 wedges. Arrange on a platter and garnish with mint sprigs, if desired.

makes 8 to 10 servings

per serving: 312 calories, 10 g protein, 52 g carbohydrates, 8 g total fat, 16 mg cholesterol, 288 mg sodium

potato-onion pie

preparation time: 20 minutes
cooking time: about 1 hour and 5 minutes

---

2 slices sourdough sandwich bread, torn into pieces

4 small red thin-skinned potatoes, scrubbed

1 large onion

1 tablespoon olive oil

2 teaspoons chopped fresh rosemary or 3/4 teaspoon dried rosemary, crumbled

3 large eggs

6 large egg whites

1 cup smooth unsweetened applesauce

2/3 cup grated Parmesan cheese

About 1/4 teaspoon salt (or to taste)

1/8 teaspoon pepper

Rosemary sprigs

1 1/4 cups nonfat sour cream

1 In a blender or food processor, whirl bread to make coarse crumbs; set bread crumbs aside.

2 Cut potatoes and onion lengthwise into halves; then thinly slice potato and onion halves crosswise. Heat oil in a wide nonstick frying pan over medium-high heat. Add potatoes, onion, and chopped rosemary. Cook, stirring often, until vegetables are tinged with brown and tender when pierced (20 to 25 minutes); add water, 1 tablespoon at a time, if pan appears dry.

3 Meanwhile, in a medium-size bowl, combine eggs, egg whites, applesauce, cheese, salt, and pepper. Beat until blended; set aside.

4 Spoon potato mixture into a greased deep 9-inch pie pan. Stir crumbs into egg mixture and pour evenly over potato mixture; stir gently so egg mixture settles to pan bottom. Center of filling will be slightly above level of pan.

5 Bake in a 350° oven until top of pie is tinged with brown and a knife inserted in center comes out clean (about 40 minutes). Garnish with rosemary sprigs. Offer sour cream to add to taste.

makes 6 servings

per serving: 277 calories, 16 g protein, 31 g carbohydrates, 9 g total fat, 113 mg cholesterol, 441 mg sodium

drowned eggs

preparation time: about 35 minutes

1 can (about 14 1/2 oz.) tomatoes

2 cloves garlic, peeled

3/4 cup water

2 teaspoons chili powder

1 1/2 teaspoons dried oregano

1 1/2 teaspoons sugar

4 large eggs

1/4 cup thinly sliced green onions

4 fresh Serrano chiles, halved , and seeded

2 tablespoons cilantro leaves

Salt and pepper

Warm tortillas

1 Pour tomatoes and their liquid into a blender or food processor. Add garlic, then whirl until smoothly puréed.

2 Transfer tomato purée to a wide frying pan. Stir in water, chili powder, oregano, and sugar; bring to a boil over medium-high heat. Reduce heat so sauce is simmering.

3 Carefully crack eggs, one at a time, into sauce. Distribute onions and chile halves over sauce, disturbing eggs as little as possible. Cook, carefully basting eggs occasionally with sauce, until yolks are set to your liking (about 20 minutes for firm but moist yolks).

4 Divide eggs, onions, chile halves, and sauce equally among 4 shallow (about 1 1/2 cup) casseroles. Sprinkle with cilantro; season to taste with salt and pepper. Serve with tortillas.

makes 4 servings

per serving: 225 calories, 11 protein, 33 g carbohydrates, 7 g total fat, 213 mg cholesterol, 326 mg sodium

eggplant and cheese casserole

preparation time: 25 minutes
cooking time: about 1 hour and 40 minutes

3 small eggplants

1 large onion, chopped

1 large green bell pepper, seeded and chopped

3/4 cup fine dry bread crumbs

1 can (about 2 1/4 oz.) sliced ripe olives, drained

1 tablespoon chopped fresh oregano
 or 1 teaspoon dried oregano

1 large can (about 15 oz.) tomato sauce

1 cup nonfat ricotta cheese

1 1/2 cups shredded reduced-fat sharp
 Cheddar cheese

1 Cut unpeeled eggplants into 3/4-inch cubes and place in a deep 4-quart casserole. Add onion, bell pepper, bread crumbs, olives, oregano, and tomato sauce; stir well. Cover tightly and bake in a 400° oven for 45 minutes. Stir vegetables thoroughly and cover tightly again. Continue to bake until vegetables are very soft when pressed (about 45 more minutes); check occasionally and add water, 1 tablespoon at a time, if casserole appears dry.

2 Spoon ricotta cheese in dollops over hot vegetable mixture; sprinkle with Cheddar cheese. Continue to bake, uncovered, until Cheddar cheese is melted (about 10 more minutes).

makes 8 servings

per serving: 212 calories, 15 g protein, 27 g carbohydrates, 5 g total fat, 15 mg cholesterol, 687 mg sodium

polenta pepper torte

preparation time: 25 minutes
cooking time: about 1 hour

---

²/₃ cup all-purpose flour

1 ¹/₃ cups polenta or yellow cornmeal

¹/₄ cup sugar

¹/₂ teaspoon salt

5 tablespoons butter or margarine, cut into chunks

1 jar (about 7 oz.) roasted red peppers, rinsed and patted dry

1 large can (about 15 oz.) cream-style corn

¹/₂ cup nonfat sour cream

1 large egg

5 large egg whites

2 tablespoons cornstarch

¹/₄ cup shredded fontina or mozzarella cheese

1 tablespoon chopped fresh oregano or 1 teaspoon dried oregano

Oregano sprigs

1 In a food processor or a large bowl, whirl or stir together flour, ²/₃ cup of the polenta, sugar, and ¹/₄ teaspoon of the salt. Add butter and 1 tablespoon water; whirl or rub together with your fingers until mixture resembles coarse crumbs. If pastry is too dry, add a little more water.

2 Press pastry firmly over bottom and about 1 inch up sides of a 9-inch nonstick or well-greased regular cheesecake pan with a removable rim. Prick all over with a fork to prevent puffing. Bake in a 350° oven until crust is tinged with gold and feels slightly firmer when pressed (about 15 minutes). Let cool on a rack for 5 minutes.

3 Cut any very large pieces of red peppers into smaller pieces. Arrange peppers in baked crust. In food processor, whirl remaining ²/₃ cup polenta, corn, sour cream, egg, egg whites, cornstarch, and remaining ¹/₄ teaspoon salt until smooth. Pour egg mixture over peppers in crust. Sprinkle with cheese.

4 Return torte to oven and bake until filling is golden and a knife inserted in center comes out clean (about 45 minutes). Let cool on a rack for about 10 minutes. To serve, sprinkle with chopped oregano and garnish with oregano sprigs. Remove pan rim; then cut torte into wedges with a very sharp knife.

makes 6 servings

per serving: 498 calories, 14 g protein, 76 g carbohydrates, 15 g total fat, 80 mg cholesterol, 809 mg sodium

pepper, rice & cheese casserole

preparation time: 15 minutes
cooking time: about 1 ¹/₂ hours

---

1 ¹/₃ cups long-grain white rice

4 large red or green bell peppers

1 large onion, chopped

2 cloves garlic, minced or pressed

1 cup vegetable broth

4 large eggs

About 2 cups part-skim ricotta cheese

³/₄ cup grated Parmesan cheese

1 In a 3¹/₂- to 4-quart pan, bring 3 cups water to a boil over high heat. Stir in rice; then reduce heat, cover, and simmer until liquid has been absorbed and rice is tender to bite (about 20 minutes).

2 Meanwhile, seed peppers and chop them. Place peppers in a pan and add onion, garlic, and ¹/₄ cup of the broth. Cook over medium-high heat, stirring often, until liquid evaporates and browned bits stick to pan bottom (about 10 minutes). To deglaze pan, add water, 1 tablespoon at a time. Add ¹/₄ cup more broth, stirring to loosen browned bits from pan. Remove pan from heat.

3 Stir cooked rice into pepper mixture; then spread mixture in a deep 3-quart casserole. In a bowl, combine remaining ¹/₂ cup broth, eggs, ricotta cheese, and half the Parmesan cheese; beat until blended. Spread cheese mixture over rice mixture; sprinkle with remaining Parmesan cheese. Bake in a 375° oven until topping is golden brown (about 45 minutes).

makes 6 servings

per serving: 437 calories, 23 g protein, 55 g carbohydrates, 14 g total fat, 175 mg cholesterol, 503 mg sodium

roasted chiles with eggs

preparation time: about 30 minutes

4 fresh green poblano or Anaheim chiles

1 cup Lime Salsa (see page 67)

2 large eggs

4 large egg whites

$^1/_2$ cup nonfat cottage cheese

$^1/_2$ cup finely chopped spinach

About 1 tablespoon thinly sliced green onion

2 teaspoons cornstarch blended
    with 1 tablespoon cold water

1 $^1/_2$ teaspoons fresh thyme leaves
    or $^1/_2$ teaspoon dried thyme

$^1/_8$ teaspoon salt

$^1/_8$ teaspoon white pepper

1 teaspoon vegetable oil

Sliced fresh hot red chiles (seeded, if desired)

Thyme sprigs

About $^3/_4$ cup plain nonfat yogurt

1 To roast chiles, place chiles on a 12- by 15-inch baking sheet. Broil 4 to 6 inches below heat, turning often, until charred all over (5 to 8 minutes). Cover with foil and let cool on baking sheet; then remove and discard skins. Cut a slit down one side of each chile, but do not cut all the way to stem end and tip; be careful not to puncture opposite side of chile. Remove and discard seeds and veins from chiles; set aside.

2 Prepare Lime Salsa; refrigerate.

3 In a food processor, whirl eggs, egg whites, cottage cheese, spinach, 1 tablespoon of the onion, cornstarch mixture, thyme leaves, salt, and white pepper until smoothly puréed. Set aside.

4 Heat oil in a medium-size nonstick frying pan over medium heat. Add egg mixture to pan; stir to combine. Cook until mixture is softly set and looks like scrambled eggs (3 to 5 minutes).

5 Spoon hot egg mixture equally into chiles. Place filled chiles on a platter and garnish with red chile slices and thyme sprigs. Add yogurt, additional thinly sliced onion, and Lime Salsa to taste.

makes 4 servings

per serving: 138 calories, 14 g protein, 11 g carbohydrates, 4 g total fat, 110 mg cholesterol, 298 mg sodium

scrambled eggs & bulgur

preparation time: about 35 minutes

2 cups vegetable broth

1 cup bulgur

2 teaspoons butter or margarine

1 medium-size onion, thinly sliced

1 medium-size red bell pepper,
    seeded and thinly sliced

2 large eggs

4 large egg whites

$^1/_4$ cup grated Parmesan cheese

1 In a 1- to 1½-quart pan, bring broth to a boil over high heat. Stir in bulgur; cover, remove from heat, and let stand until liquid has been absorbed (about 10 minutes).

2 Meanwhile, melt 1 teaspoon of the butter in a wide nonstick frying pan over medium heat. Add onion and bell pepper; cook, stirring often, until onion is lightly browned (about 10 minutes). Add water, 1 tablespoon at a time, if pan appears dry. Meanwhile, in a small bowl, beat eggs, egg whites, and ¼ cup water until blended.

3 Add remaining 1 teaspoon butter to onion mixture in pan and reduce heat to medium-low. Add egg mixture; cook until eggs are softly set, gently lifting cooked portion with a wide spatula to allow uncooked eggs to flow underneath. Divide bulgur and egg mixture equally among 4 individual plates. Sprinkle with Parmesan cheese.

makes 4 servings

per serving: 254 calories, 14 g protein, 35 g carbohydrates, 7 g total fat, 116 mg cholesterol, 726 mg sodium

yellow split pea dal with brown rice & broccoli

preparation time: 30 minutes
cooking time: about 2 1/2 hours

1 cup yellow split peas

About 5 1/2 cups vegetable broth

2 large onions, chopped

2 medium-size carrots, diced

2 tablespoons finely chopped fresh ginger

2 large cloves garlic, minced or pressed

2 teaspoons *each* ground turmeric
   and chili powder

1 large can (about 28 oz.) crushed tomatoes

1 pound butternut or other gold-fleshed squash,
   peeled and cut into 3/4-inch cubes

2 cups long-grain brown rice

3 cups broccoli flowerets

1/2 cup cilantro leaves

About 1 1/2 cups plain nonfat yogurt

Lime wedges

Crushed red pepper flakes

Salt

1 Sort through peas, discarding any debris; then rinse peas, drain, and set aside.

2 In a 6- to 8-quart pan, combine 1 cup of the broth, onions, carrots, ginger, and garlic. Cook over medium-high heat, stirring often, until liquid evaporates and browned bits stick to pan bottom (about 15 minutes). To deglaze pan, add 1/3 cup more broth, stirring to loosen browned bits from pan; continue to cook until browned bits form again. Repeat deglazing step about 3 more times or until vegetables are browned, using about 1/3 cup broth each time.

3 To vegetable mixture, add peas, turmeric, chili powder, tomatoes and their liquid, and 3 cups more broth. Bring to a boil; then reduce heat, cover, and simmer for 1 hour. Add squash; cover and simmer, stirring often, until squash is tender to bite (40 to 50 more minutes).

4 Meanwhile, in a 5- to 6-quart pan, bring 4 cups water to a boil over high heat; stir in rice. Reduce heat, cover, and simmer until liquid has been absorbed and rice is tender to bite (about 45 minutes). Remove from pan and keep warm; fluff occasionally with a fork.

5 Wash pan and add broccoli and 1/3 cup water. Cover and cook over medium-high heat until broccoli is almost tender-crisp to bite (about 3 minutes). Uncover and continue to cook, stirring, until all liquid has evaporated.

6 To serve, spoon rice, broccoli, and split pea mixture onto individual plates. Offer cilantro, yogurt, lime, red pepper flakes, and salt to season each serving to taste.

makes 6 servings

per serving: 516 calories, 22 g protein, 102 g carbohydrates, 4 g total fat, 1 mg cholesterol, 1,445 mg sodium

EASY DOES IT: Never rush egg and cheese dishes. Eggs are delicate and should be cooked gently, at moderate temperatures, to avoid rubbery results. Cheese, too, becomes tough and stringy when exposed to high temperatures or prolonged cooking. If you're melting cheese atop an omelet or casserole, heat just until melted, then serve; when you're making fondue, use medium or low heat—and don't overcook.

portabella mushroom sandwiches

preparation time: 45 minutes

4 crusty rolls, split into halves

1 package (about 10 oz.) frozen chopped Swiss chard, thawed and squeezed dry

1 large package (about 8 oz.) nonfat cream cheese, at room temperature

3/4 cup shredded smoked mozzarella or smoked Gouda cheese

2 tablespoons nonfat mayonnaise

1 teaspoon Dijon mustard

1/2 teaspoon dried rubbed sage

About 1/4 cup balsamic vinegar

Pepper

3 large egg whites

3/4 cup yellow cornmeal

1/3 cup all-purpose flour

1/4 teaspoon salt

4 large portabella mushrooms, stems removed

2 tablespoons olive oil

4 to 8 green or red leaf lettuce leaves

4 to 8 large tomato slices

1 If needed, pull bread from base and top of each roll to make a shell about 1/2 inch thick; reserve bread scraps for other uses, if desired. Arrange roll halves, cut side up, in a broiler pan; broil about 6 inches below heat until lightly toasted (1 1/2 to 2 minutes). Set aside.

2 In a food processor or blender, combine chard, cream cheese, mozzarella cheese, mayonnaise, mustard, and sage. Whirl until chard is finely chopped, scraping sides of container as needed. Brush cut side of roll bottoms lightly with vinegar and sprinkle with pepper. Set aside about a fourth of the chard mixture; divide remaining mixture equally among roll bottoms (you need about 1/3 cup per roll). With a spatula, spread chard mixture to fill hollows in rolls evenly.

3 In a wide, shallow bowl, beat egg whites and 2 tablespoons water to blend. In another wide, shallow bowl, stir together cornmeal, flour, and salt. Dip mushrooms in egg white mixture; drain briefly, then dip in cornmeal mixture and press to coat well all over.

4 Heat 1 tablespoon of the oil in a wide nonstick frying pan over medium-high heat. Add 2 of the mushrooms; cook, turning once, until mushrooms are golden on both sides and tender when pierced (5 to 7 minutes). Remove from pan and keep warm. Repeat to cook remaining 2 mushrooms, using remaining 1 tablespoon oil.

5 Working quickly, place 1 or 2 lettuce leaves on each roll bottom; then top each with one hot mushroom and 1 or 2 tomato slices. Spoon reserved chard mixture over tomato slices. Brush cut side of roll tops lightly with vinegar and sprinkle with pepper; close sandwiches and serve immediately.

makes 4 servings

per serving: 709 calories, 33 g protein, 101 g carbohydrates; 19 g total fat, 36 mg cholesterol, 1,553 mg sodium

chile-cheese french toast & cherry tomato salsa

preparation time: about 45 minutes

FRENCH TOAST:

1 large egg

4 large egg whites

1 cup nonfat milk

8 diagonal slices French bread (each about 3 by 6 inches and about ¹/₃ inch)

1 cup (about 4 oz.) shredded reduced-fat jack cheese

1 can (about 4 oz.) diced green chiles

¹/₄ cup finely chopped cilantro

CHERRY TOMATO SALSA:

2 cups red cherry tomatoes, cut into halves

¹/₃ cup cilantro leaves

2 small fresh jalapeño chiles, seeded

1 clove garlic, peeled

2 tablespoons lime juice

2 tablespoons thinly sliced green onion

1 In a large bowl, beat egg, egg whites, and milk until well blended. Dip 4 slices of bread into egg mixture; turn to saturate both sides. Arrange slices in a shallow 10- by 15-inch non-stick baking pan.

2 Top bread in baking pan evenly with cheese, green chiles, and chopped cilantro. Dip remaining 4 bread slices into egg mixture, turning to coat both sides; place atop cheese-covered bread to form 4 sandwiches. Bake sandwiches in a 400° oven until bread begins to brown (about 12 minutes). Then carefully turn sandwiches over with a wide spatula; continue to bake until golden brown (about 10 more minutes).

3 Meanwhile, in a food processor, combine tomatoes, cilantro leaves, jalapeño chiles, and garlic; whirl just until tomatoes are coarsely chopped. Spoon mixture into a small bowl. Add lime juice and onion; stir to mix well.

4 To serve, transfer French toast sandwiches to individual plates. Offer salsa to add to taste.

makes 4 servings

per serving: 306 calories, 22 g protein, 37 g carbohydrates, 8 g total fat, 74 mg cholesterol, 811 mg sodium

egg, bean & potato hash

preparation time: about 45 minutes

1 tablespoon butter or margarine

1 pound thin-skinned potatoes, cut into ¹/₄-inch cubes

1 small red onion, cut into thin slivers

1 teaspoon chili powder

1 can (about 15 oz.) red kidney beans, drained and rinsed

1 large tomato, chopped

³/₄ teaspoon chopped fresh sage

4 large eggs

¹/₃ cup lightly packed cilantro leaves

³/₄ cup nonfat sour cream

1 Melt butter in a wide nonstick frying pan or wok over medium-high heat. Add potatoes, onion, chili powder, and ¹/₄ cup water. Stir-fry until potatoes are tinged with brown and tender (about 15 minutes; do not scorch). Add water, 1 tablespoon at a time, if pan appears dry.

2 Add beans, tomato, sage, and 2 tablespoons water to pan. Stir-fry gently until heated through, scraping any browned bits free from pan bottom. With a spoon, make 4 depressions in potato mixture; carefully break an egg into each depression. Reduce heat to low, cover, and cook until egg yolks are set to your liking (about 15 minutes for firm but moist yolks). Sprinkle with cilantro and top with sour cream.

makes 4 servings

per serving: 328 calories, 18 g protein, 43 g carbohydrates, 9 g total fat, 220 mg cholesterol, 280 mg sodium

quick fruit and ricotta pizza

preparation time: 35 to 40 minutes

1 package (about 10 oz.) refrigerated pizza
    crust dough

1 cup part-skim ricotta cheese

2 teaspoons grated lemon peel

2 cups shredded part-skim mozzarella cheese

2 medium-size nectarines, thinly sliced

4 ounces dried peaches, sliced

³/₄ cup halved red seedless grapes

2 tablespoons sugar

¹/₄ teaspoon ground cinnamon

3 tablespoons sliced almonds

1 Unroll dough, place on a 12- by 15-inch nonstick baking sheet, and press with your fingers to make a 10- by 15-inch rectangle. Bake on lowest rack of a 425° oven until browned (about 8 minutes).

2 In a small bowl, stir together ricotta cheese and lemon peel; spread over crust. Sprinkle with mozzarella cheese. Arrange nectarines, peaches, and grapes over cheese. In another small bowl, mix sugar and cinnamon. Sprinkle sugar mixture and almonds evenly over fruit. Return to oven and bake until fruit is hot to the touch and mozzarella cheese is melted (5 to 10 minutes).

makes 8 servings

per serving: 287 calories, 36 g carbohydrates, 14 g protein, 9 g total fat, 25 mg cholesterol, 364 mg sodium

stir-fried broccoli garlic & beans

preparation time: about 55 minutes

1 package (about ¹/₂ oz.) dried shiitake mushrooms

1 cup long-grain white rice

1 medium-size head garlic

2 teaspoons salad oil

5 cups broccoli flowerets

1 can (about 15 oz.) black beans, drained and
    rinsed

2 tablespoons reduced sodium soy sauce

1 teaspoon Asian sesame oil

¹/₂ teaspoon honey

1 Soak mushrooms in hot water to cover until soft and pliable (about 20 minutes). Rub mushrooms gently to release any grit; then lift mushrooms from water. Discard water. Squeeze mushrooms gently to remove, moisture; trim and discard tough stems. Thinly slice caps, place in a small bowl, and set aside.

2 While mushrooms are soaking, in a 3- to 4-quart pan, bring 2 cups water to a boil over high heat; stir in rice. Reduce heat, cover, and simmer until liquid has been absorbed and rice is tender to bite (about 20 minutes). Transfer to a rimmed platter and keep warm. Fluff occasionally with a fork.

3 Separate garlic into cloves; then peel and thinly slice garlic cloves. Heat salad oil in a wide nonstick frying pan or wok over medium-high heat. When oil is hot, add garlic and stir-fry gently just until tinged with brown (about 2 minutes; do not scorch). Add water, 1 tablespoon at a time, if pan appears dry. Remove garlic from pan with a slotted spoon; place in bowl with mushrooms.

4 Add broccoli and ¹/₃ cup water to pan. Cover and cook until broccoli is almost tender-crisp to bite (about 3 minutes). Uncover and stir-fry until liquid has evaporated. Add beans and stir-fry gently until heated through. Remove from heat and add mushroom mixture, soy sauce, sesame oil, and honey; mix gently but thoroughly. Spoon broccoli mixture over rice.

makes 4 servings

per serving: 352 calories, 15 g protein, 66 g carbohydrates, 5 g total fat, 0 mg cholesterol, 516 mg sodium

maple-glazed tofu in acorn squash

preparation time: 20 minutes

cooking time: about 1 hour

2 medium-size acorn squash

1 1/2 cups vegetable broth

1/2 cup dried cranberries or raisins

1/4 cup pure maple syrup

2 large Granny Smith or Newtown Pippin apples

1 tablespoon lemon juice

3/4 teaspoon ground cinnamon

1/8 teaspoon ground nutmeg

1 tablespoon chopped walnuts

1 package (about 14 oz.) firm tofu, rinsed, drained, and cut into 1/2-inch cubes

1 tablespoon balsamic vinegar

1 teaspoon cornstarch

1/3 cup thinly sliced green onions

1/2 cup nonfat sour cream

1 Cut each squash in half lengthwise; scoop out and discard seeds and fibers. Place squash halves, cut side down, in a 9- by 13-inch baking pan. Add broth. Bake in a 350° oven until squash is tender when pierced (about 1 hour).

2 Meanwhile, in a small bowl, combine cranberries and syrup. Let stand until cranberries are softened (about 10 minutes), stirring occasionally. Also peel, core, and thinly slice apples; place in a large bowl, add lemon juice, and gently turn apples to coat with juice. Stir in cinnamon and nutmeg; set aside.

3 Toast walnuts in a wide nonstick frying pan over medium heat, stirring often, until golden (about 3 minutes). Remove from pan and set aside.

4 In frying pan, combine apples, cranberry mixture, and 1/4 cup water. Cook over medium-high heat, stirring gently, until apples are almost tender when pierced (about 3 minutes). Add tofu and cook just until heated through (about 2 more minutes). In a small bowl, smoothly blend vinegar and cornstarch; add to tofu mixture. Cook, stirring, until sauce boils and thickens slightly (about 2 minutes). Remove from heat and stir in onions.

5 Arrange each squash half, skin side down, in a shallow individual bowl. Fill squash halves equally with tofu mixture; top with sour cream and sprinkle with walnuts.

makes 4 servings

per serving: 463 calories, 21 g protein, 79 g carbohydrates, 11 g total fat, 0 mg cholesterol, 421 mg sodium

zucchini burgers

preparation time: about 40 minutes

1 1/2 pounds zucchini, shredded

2 tablespoons margarine

1 large onion, finely chopped

1/4 cup fine dried bread crumbs

2 large eggs, lightly beaten

1/4 cup grated Parmesan cheese

6 onion bagels, split and toasted

1 Drain zucchini in a colander for 30 minutes; then squeeze to remove moisture. While zucchini is draining, melt 2 teaspoons of the margarine in a wide nonstick frying pan over medium head Add onion; stir often until lightly browned (about 10 minutes). Scrape into a bowl.

2 Mix drained zucchini, crumbs, eggs, and cheese with onion in bowl. In frying pan, melt remaining 4 teaspoons margarine over medium-high heat. Ladle three 1/4-cup mounds of zucchini mixture into pan, spreading each to make a 3-inch-wide patty. Cook until patties are lightly browned on bottom (about 3 minutes). With a wide spatula, turn patties over; continue to cook until browned on other side (about 3 more minutes). Remove from pan and keep warm. Repeat to cook remaining zucchini mixture, making 3 more patties. To serve, place burgers on bagels.

makes 6 servings

per serving: 282 calories, 13 g protein, 41 g carbohydrates, 8 g total fat, 73 mg cholesterol, 490 mg sodium

szechuan tofu
with eggplant

preparation time: about 45 minutes

3 tablespoons hoisin sauce

2 tablespoons seasoned rice vinegar
   (or 2 tablespoons distilled white vinegar
   plus ³/₄ teaspoon sugar)

1 tablespoon sugar

1 tablespoon chili paste with garlic

2 teaspoons Asian sesame oil

About 1 pound firm tofu, rinsed, drained,
   and cut into ¹/₂-inch cubes

10 ounces fresh Chinese noodles or linguine

1 tablespoon vegetable oil

2 medium-size eggplants, peeled
   and cut into ¹/₂-inch pieces

2 teaspoons minced fresh ginger

2 green onions, thinly sliced

¹/₂ cup lightly packed cilantro leaves

1 To prepare sauce, in a large bowl, stir together hoisin sauce, vinegar, sugar, chili paste and sesame oil. Add tofu to sauce and stir gently to coat; set aside.

2 In a 5- to 6-quart pan, cook noodles in about 3 quarts boiling water until just tender to bite (3 to 5 minutes); or cook according to package directions. Drain well, transfer to a warm rimmed platter, and keep warm.

3 While noodles are cooking, heat vegetable oil, in a wide non-stick frying pan or wok over medium-high heat. Add eggplant and ¹/₄ cup water. Stir-fry until eggplant is soft and tinged with gold (8 to 10 minutes); add more water, 1 tablespoon at a time, if pan appears dry. Add ginger and stir-fry just until fragrant (about 30 seconds; do not scorch). Add tofu mixture and cook, stirring gently, until sauce boils and tofu is heated through (about 3 minutes). Remove from heat and stir in onions.

4 Spoon tofu mixture over noodles and sprinkle with cilantro.

makes 4 to 6 servings

per serving: 476 calories, 24 g protein, 62 g carbohydrates, 16 g total fat, 54 mg cholesterol, 351 mg sodium

QUICK WAYS WITH VEGETABLES: It's easy to dress up quick-cooked vegetables—just top them off with minced parsley, grated cheese, or seasoned butters. Pesto also makes a quick and delicious topping for hot cooked vegetables.

spinach torta with fig relish

preparation time: 30 minutes
cooking time: about 1 1/2 hours

---

1 package (about 10 oz.) frozen chopped
  spinach, thawed and squeezed dry

3 large eggs

4 large egg whites

2 tablespoons cornstarch

2 cloves garlic, peeled

1 1/2 teaspoons each chopped fresh oregano,
  fresh marjoram, and fresh sage; or
  1/2 teaspoon each dried oregano, dried
  marjoram, and dried rubbed sage

2 cups half-and-half

8 slices egg or whole wheat sandwich bread,
  torn into large pieces

3/4 cup shredded fontina or mozzarella cheese

1 large firm-ripe pear such as Anjou or Bartlett,
  peeled, cored, and finely chopped

1/3 cup firmly packed brown sugar

1/3 cup red wine vinegar

1 1/2 cups dried figs, stems removed
  and fruit quartered

3/4 cup dried cranberries or raisins

3/4 cup canned vegetable broth

1/8 teaspoon each pepper, ground cinnamon,
  and ground nutmeg

2 teaspoons Marsala (or to taste)

1/4 cup thinly sliced green onions

1 In a food processor or blender, combine spinach, eggs, egg whites, cornstarch, garlic, oregano, marjoram, and sage. Whirl until smoothly puréed. Transfer to a large bowl and whisk in half-and-half. Add bread and cheese; mix gently but thoroughly. Let stand until bread is softened (about 5 minutes), stirring occasionally.

2 Transfer mixture to a square 8-inch nonstick or greased regular baking pan. Set pan in a larger baking pan; then set on center rack of a 325° oven. Pour boiling water into larger pan up to level of spinach mixture. Bake until top of torta is golden brown and center no longer jiggles when pan is gently shaken (about 1 hour and 35 minutes).

3 Meanwhile, in a wide nonstick frying pan, mix pear, sugar, and vinegar. Add figs, cranberries, broth, pepper, cinnamon, and nutmeg. Bring to a boil over medium-high heat. Then cook, uncovered, stirring often, until almost all liquid has evaporated (about 20 minutes); as mixture thickens, watch carefully and stir more often to prevent scorching. Remove pan from heat and stir in Marsala and onions.

4 To serve, spoon torta from pan; offer fig relish alongside.

makes 6 servings

per serving: 549 calories, 18 g protein, 79 g carbohydrates, 19 g total fat, 172 mg cholesterol, 570 mg sodium

mushroom bread pudding with wilted spinach

preparation time: 20 minutes
cooking time: about 1 3/4 hours

MUSHROOM BREAD PUDDING:

1 package (about 1 oz.) dried porcini

4 ounces small button mushrooms

1 teaspoon butter or margarine

4 cloves garlic, minced or pressed

**1 1/2 teaspoons chopped fresh thyme
or 3/4 teaspoon dried thyme**

1 large onion, chopped

2 large eggs

2 large egg whites

1 tablespoon cornstarch

1 1/2 cups buttermilk

1 1/4 cups nonfat milk

2 teaspoons sugar

1/4 teaspoon salt

1/8 teaspoon ground white pepper

**8 slices whole wheat sandwich bread
or egg sandwich bread (crusts removed),
cut into 1-inch squares**

WILTED SPINACH:

1 pound fresh spinach

1 tablespoon butter or margarine

1/8 teaspoon ground nutmeg (or to taste)

Salt and black pepper

GARNISH:

Thyme sprigs (optional)

1 Place porcini in a small bowl and add 1/2 cup boiling water. Let stand, stirring occasionally, until porcini are soft (about 10 minutes). Lift out porcini and, holding them over bowl, squeeze very dry; then coarsely chop and set aside. Without disturbing sediment at bottom of bowl, pour soaking liquid into a measuring cup; you should have about 1/4 cup. Set liquid aside; discard sediment.

2 While porcini are soaking, slice button mushrooms 1/4 to 1/2-inch thick; set aside. Melt the 1 teaspoon butter in a wide nonstick frying pan over medium-high heat. Add garlic and chopped thyme; cook, stirring, until fragrant (about 30 seconds; do not scorch). Add button mushrooms, onion, and 1/4 cup water; cook, stirring, until mushrooms are soft and browned bits stick to pan bottom (6 to 8 minutes). Add 2 tablespoons more water and remove pan from heat; stir to loosen any browned bits from pan. Transfer onion mixture to a small bowl and set aside.

3 In a large bowl, beat eggs and egg whites until well blended. Smoothly blend cornstarch with porcini soaking liquid; add cornstarch mixture, buttermilk, milk, sugar, the 1/4 teaspoon salt, and white pepper to eggs and whisk until blended. Stir in onion mixture and chopped porcini. Add bread and mix gently but thoroughly; let stand until softened (about 5 minutes), stirring occasionally.

4 Transfer mixture to a square 8-inch nonstick or greased regular baking pan. Set pan of pudding in a larger baking pan; then set on center rack of a 325° oven. Pour boiling water into larger pan up to level of pudding. Bake until top of pudding is golden brown and center no longer jiggles when pan is gently shaken (about 1 hour and 35 minutes).

5 When pudding is almost done, discard stems and any yellow or wilted leaves from spinach; rinse remaining leaves. Place half the spinach in a 4- to 5-quart pan. Cook over medium-high heat, stirring often, until wilted (2 to 4 minutes). Pour into a colander and drain well, then transfer to a bowl; keep warm. Repeat to cook remaining spinach. To cooked spinach, add the 1 table-spoon butter and nutmeg; season to taste with salt and black pepper and mix gently.

6 Divide spinach among 4 individual rimmed plates. Spoon pudding over spinach (or cut pudding into wedges and place atop spinach). Garnish with thyme sprigs, if desired.

makes 4 servings

per serving: 385 calories, 21 g protein, 53 g carbohydrates, 11 g total fat, 148 mg cholesterol, 716 mg sodium

sweet and sour tofu

preparation time: about 40 minutes

1 cup long-grain white rice

¼ cup white wine vinegar
or distilled white vinegar

4 teaspoons cornstarch

¼ cup sugar

1 tablespoon catsup

1 tablespoon reduced-sodium soy sauce

⅛ teaspoon hot chili oil, or to taste

1 pound firm tofu, rinsed, drained,
and cut into ½-inch cubes

1 teaspoon paprika

1 or 2 cloves garlic, minced or pressed

¼ teaspoon salt

1 teaspoon vegetable oil

1 small red onion, cut into thin wedges

1 large green, red, or yellow bell pepper,
seeded and cut into 1-inch squares

1 medium-size tomato (about 6 oz.),
cut into thin wedges

1 ½ cups fresh or canned pineapple
chunks, drained

1 In a 3- to 4-quart pan, bring 2 cups water to a boil over high heat; stir in rice. Reduce heat, cover, and simmer until liquid has been absorbed and rice is tender to bite (about 20 minutes).

2 Meanwhile, to prepare sweet-sour sauce, in a medium-size bowl, stir together vinegar and cornstarch until blended. Then stir in ¾ cup water, sugar, catsup, soy sauce, and hot chile oil. Set aside.

3 In a large bowl, gently mix tofu, paprika, garlic, and salt; set aside.

4 Heat oil in a wide nonstick frying pan over medium-high heat. When oil is hot, add tofu and stir-fry gently until heated through (3 to 4 minutes). Add water, 1 tablespoon at a time, if pan appears dry. Remove tofu from pan with a slotted spoon; keep warm.

5 Add onion, bell pepper, and 2 tablespoons water to pan. Stir-fry for 1 minute; add water, 1 tablespoon at a time, if pan appears dry. Stir sweet-sour sauce well; pour into pan. Cook, stirring, until sauce boils and thickens slightly (2 to 3 minutes). Stir in tomato, pineapple, and tofu; stir gently just until heated through (about 2 minutes).

6 To serve, spoon rice onto a rimmed platter; top with sweet and sour tofu mixture.

makes 4 servings

per serving: 482 calories, 23 g protein, 75 g carbohydrates, 2 g total fat, 0 mg cholesterol, 223 mg sodium

---

COOKING GRAINS: Rich in fiber and complex carbohydrates, grains are a great addition to almost any menu. Serve them as a bed for richly sauced meats, fish, or vegetables; or let them stand on their own as a side dish. Here are some guidelines for cooking grains:

- **Yield:** 1 cup uncooked grain yields about 3 cups cooked grain.

- **Salt:** For each cup uncooked grain, add about ¼ teaspoon salt to the cooking water.

- **Cooking option:** For some grains—bulgur, buckwheat, millet and, of course rice—one alternative to simple boiling is to cook the grain like a pilaf. Start by sautéeing the dry grain in butter, margarine, or salad oil (about 1 tablespoon per cup); then, instead of water, add boiling broth. Cover and simmer until grain is done.

- **Doneness:** Grains, like pasta, are done when they're tender to bite. Each grain should be tender, yet slightly resilient at the core.

southwestern stuffed peppers

preparation time: about 1¼ hours

2 **very large red, yellow, or green bell peppers; choose wide, squarish peppers**

¼ **cup slivered almonds**

1 **package (about 10 oz.) frozen corn kernels, thawed and drained**

1 **can (about 15 oz.) black beans, drained and rinsed well**

1 **can (about 8 oz.) tomato sauce**

½ **cup raisins or dried currants**

½ **cup sliced green onions**

2 **teaspoons cider vinegar**

2 **cloves garlic, minced**

½ **teaspoon each ground cinnamon and chili powder**

¹⁄₁₆ **to ⅛ teaspoon ground cloves**

Salt

½ **cup shredded reduced-fat jack cheese**

2 **tablespoons cilantro leaves**

1 **cup plain nonfat yogurt**

1 Using a very sharp knife, carefully cut each pepper in half lengthwise through (and including) stem; leave stem attached and remove seeds. If any of the pepper halves does not sit flat, even out the base by trimming a thin slice from it (do not pierce wall of pepper). Set pepper halves aside.

2 Toast almonds in a 5- to 6-quart pan over medium heat, stirring often, until golden (about 3 minutes). Transfer almonds to a bowl and let cool; then coarsely chop and set aside.

3 In same pan, bring 3 to 4 quarts water to a boil over medium-high heat. Add pepper halves and cook for 2 minutes. Lift out, drain, and set aside. Discard water and dry pan. In pan (off heat) or in a large bowl, combine corn, beans, tomato sauce, raisins, onions, vinegar, garlic, cinnamon, chili powder, and cloves. Mix gently but thoroughly; season to taste with salt.

4 Spoon vegetable mixture equally into pepper halves, mounding filling at top. Set pepper halves, filled side up, in a 9- by 13-inch baking pan. Cover and bake in a 375° oven for 10 minutes. Uncover and continue to bake until filling is hot in center (about 20 more minutes; if drippings begin to scorch, carefully add about ¼ cup water to pan). Remove from oven and sprinkle evenly with cheese; cover and let stand for 5 minutes. Garnish with cilantro; offer yogurt to add to taste.

makes 4 servings

per serving: 353 calories, 18 g protein, 58 g carbohydrates, 8 g total fat, 11 mg cholesterol, 678 mg sodium

LEGUMES: Low in cost, high in nutrition, and rich in good, earthy flavors, legumes are one of the best bargain foods going. To begin with, they pack in a powerhouse of protein; a navy bean, for example, is a full 20 percent protein. Legumes also contain plenty of iron, calcium, potassium, and B vitamins. They're high in fiber and low in sodium—and they're cholesterol-free.

upside-down pizza pie

preparation time: about 1 ¼ hours

FILLING:

1 cup low-fat (2%) cottage cheese

¼ cup fresh basil leaves

1 tablespoon grated Parmesan cheese

2 or 3 cloves garlic, minced or pressed

1 teaspoon Asian sesame oil

½ cup yellow cornmeal

1 teaspoon olive oil

8 ounces mushrooms, thinly sliced

1 large onion, chopped

½ teaspoon dried thyme

1 large jar (about 14 oz.) roasted red peppers, drained and rinsed

1 cup shredded part-skim mozzarella cheese

¼ teaspoon *each* dried rubbed sage and dried marjoram

1 large tomato, very thinly sliced

BATTER TOPPING:

1 ⅓ cups all-purpose flour

⅓ cup yellow cornmeal

1 tablespoon sugar

1 ½ teaspoons baking powder

¼ to ½ teaspoon dried oregano

¼ teaspoon salt

½ cup nonfat milk

2 tablespoons olive oil

2 large egg whites

1 In a blender or food processor, combine cottage cheese, basil, Parmesan cheese, garlic, and sesame oil. Whirl until smoothly puréed; set aside. Sprinkle the ½ cup cornmeal evenly over bottom of a greased deep 2½- to 3-quart casserole; set aside.

2 Heat the 1 teaspoon olive oil in a wide nonstick frying pan over medium-high heat. Add mushrooms, onion, thyme, and ¼ cup water. Cook, stirring occasionally, until vegetables are soft and almost all liquid has evaporated (about 10 minutes).

3 Spoon vegetable mixture over cornmeal in casserole. Top evenly with cottage cheese mixture, spreading to smooth top. Cover cottage cheese layer with red peppers, overlapping if necessary; sprinkle peppers evenly with mozzarella cheese, sage, and marjoram. Top with tomato slices, overlapping if necessary. Press gently to compact; set aside while you prepare batter.

4 In a large bowl, stir together flour, the ⅓ cup cornmeal, sugar, baking powder, oregano, and salt. In a small bowl, combine milk, the 2 tablespoons olive oil, 2 tablespoons water, and egg whites; beat until blended. Add egg mixture to flour mixture and stir just until dry ingredients are evenly moistened.

5 Working quickly, spoon batter over tomatoes, spreading to smooth top. Bake in a 375° oven until topping is lightly browned and firm to the touch (about 35 minutes).

makes 6 servings

per serving: 392 calories, 18 g protein, 54 g carbohydrates, 11 g total fat, 15 mg cholesterol, 645 mg sodium

mushroom & barley casserole with fila crust

preparation time: about 50 minutes
cooking time: about 35 minutes
baking time: about 45 minutes

Cheese Filling (recipe follows)

Barley Filling (recipe follows)

Mushroom Duxelles (recipe follows)

4 sheets fila pastry (*each* about 12 by 16 inches), thawed if frozen

3 tablespoons butter or margarine, melted

Reduced-fat sour cream or plain low-fat yogurt

Prepared horseradish with beets

1 Prepare Cheese Filling and Barley Filling. While barley is simmering, prepare Mushroom Duxelles.

2 Spread duxelles evenly in a 2- to 2½-quart casserole (6 by 11 by 2 inches, to 8 by 11 by 1 ½ inches). Cover evenly with Barley Filling, then Cheese Filling.

3 Work with fila sheets one at a time, keeping remainder covered to prevent drying. Lay one fila sheet flat and brush lightly with about 1½ teaspoons of the butter. Top with remaining 3 fila sheets, brushing each with butter. Then fold stack in half, bringing short ends together. Place fila stack on top of Cheese Filling; fold ends of pastry under to fit flush with casserole rim. Brush pastry with remaining butter. With a sharp knife, cut diagonally through pastry sheets every 1½ to 2 inches to make a diamond pattern. (At this point, you may cover and refrigerate for up to 1 day.)

4 Bake, uncovered, in a 350° oven until pastry is a deep golden brown and filling is hot in center (about 45 minutes; 50 to 55 minutes if refrigerated). Serve with sour cream and horseradish.

makes 6 to 8 servings

CHEESE FILLING

Pour 2 cups nonfat or low-fat cottage cheese into a fine strainer. Set strainer in a sink or over a bowl and let drain for at least 10 minutes or up to 1 hour. Transfer drained cheese to a bowl and stir in 1 tablespoon grated lemon peel and ½ teaspoon pepper.

BARLEY FILLING

In a 5- to 6-quart pan, bring 3 cups canned or homemade vegetable broth to a boil over high heat. Add 1 cup pearl barley, rinsed and drained; reduce heat, cover, and simmer until barley is tender to bite (about 30 minutes). Drain, reserving liquid for Mushroom Duxelles. To barley, add 1 tablespoon tomato paste and ¼ cup reduced-fat sour cream; mix well.

MUSHROOM DUXELLES

In a 5- to 6-quart pan, combine 2½ pounds mushrooms (minced), ½ cup minced shallots or red onions, and ½ teaspoon ground nutmeg. Cook over high heat, stirring often, until liquid evaporates and mushrooms begin to brown (about 30 minutes). Add ⅓ cup of the reserved barley liquid; stir to scrape browned bits free. Then continue to cook, stirring often, until liquid has evaporated. Use warm or cold.

per serving: 304 calories , 6 g protein, 44 g carbohydrates, 8 g total fat, 122 mg cholesterol, 795 g sodium

potato curry

preparation time: 30 minutes
cooking time: about 1½ hours

SPICE MIXTURE:

2 tablespoons ground coriander

1 tablespoon ground cumin

½ teaspoon ground turmeric

¼ to ½ teaspoon ground red pepper (cayenne), or to taste

¼ teaspoon ground cinnamon

POTATO CURRY:

About 5 cups vegetable broth

2 large onions, chopped

4 cloves garlic, minced or pressed

2 tablespoons finely chopped fresh ginger

¼ teaspoon coconut extract

3 large russet potatoes

2 very large sweet potatoes or yams

1 pound broccoli flowerets, cut into bite-size pieces

1 cup nonfat milk

1 package (about 10 oz.) frozen tiny peas, thawed and drained

ACCOMPANIMENTS:

¼ cup salted roasted cashew pieces

½ cup cilantro leaves

2 cups plain nonfat yogurt

1 To prepare spice mixture, combine coriander, cumin, turmeric, red pepper, and cinnamon in a 5- to 6-quart pan. Cook over medium-low heat, stirring, until spices are fragrant (about 5 minutes; do not scorch). Remove from pan and set aside.

2 In same pan, combine ½ of the broth, onions, garlic, and ginger. Cook over medium-high heat, stirring often, until liquid evaporates and browned bits stick to pan bottom (about 10 minutes). To deglaze pan, add ⅓ cup more broth, stirring to loosen browned bits from pan; continue to cook until browned bits form again. Repeat deglazing step about 2 more times or until vegetables are browned, using ⅓ cup more broth each time. Add spice mixture and repeat deglazing step one more time, using ⅓ cup more broth. Remove from heat.

3 Add coconut extract and 3 cups more broth to pan. Peel russet and sweet potatoes, cut into 1½- to 2-inch chunks, and add to broth mixture. Bring to a boil over high heat; then reduce heat, cover, and simmer until potatoes are tender when pierced (about 35 minutes). Add broccoli, cover, and continue to cook for 10 more minutes. Add milk and peas; simmer, uncovered, stirring occasionally, just until stew is hot (do not boil).

4 Pour stew into a serving bowl. Sprinkle with cashews and cilantro. Offer yogurt to add to taste.

makes 6 servings

per serving: 360 calories, 16 g protein, 68 g carbohydrates, 4 g total fat, 2 mg cholesterol, 1,015 mg sodium

black bean tacos

preparation time: about 15 minutes, plus 1 hour to soak beans
cooking time: about 2 ½ hours

Black Beans (recipe follows)

12 flour tortillas (*each* about 8 inches in diameter)

1 head romaine lettuce, cut into shreds

1 large tomato, chopped

1 large red bell pepper, seeded and cut into strips

6 green onions (including tops), thinly sliced
  ¼ cup red wine vinegar

1 large clove garlic, minced or pressed

1 teaspoon chili powder

½ teaspoon *each* ground cumin and salt

¼ teaspoon pepper

2 tablespoons olive oil or salad oil

¼ cup shredded extra-sharp Cheddar cheese

1 cup nonfat plain yogurt

1 Prepare beans; keep warm. Stack tortillas, wrap in foil, and heat in a 350° oven for 15 minutes.

2 Meanwhile, place lettuce, tomato, bell pepper, and onions in a large salad bowl. Then prepare dressing: combine vinegar, garlic, chili powder, cumin, salt, and pepper; add oil and blend well.

3 To serve, toss salad with dressing. To assemble a taco, spoon ¼ cup beans into a tortilla; add about ½ cup salad, 1 teaspoon cheese, and 1⅓ tablespoons yogurt.

makes 6 servings

BLACK BEANS

Sort 1 cup dried black beans to remove any debris. Rinse and drain beans, In a 3-quart pan, bring 4 cups water to a boil. Add beans; boil for 2 minutes. Remove from heat, cover, and let stand for 1 hour. Drain and rinse beans. Heat 1 tablespoon olive oil in a 3-quart pan over medium heat. Add 1 large onion, chopped; cook, stirring occasionally, until soft (about 10 minutes). Add beans, 1 clove garlic (minced), 1 small dried hot red chile (crushed), ½ teaspoon salt, and 2½ cups water. Bring to a boil over high heat. Reduce heat, cover, and simmer until liquid is absorbed and beans are very tender (about 2 hours).

per serving: 390 calories, 17 g protein, 55 g carbohydrates, 13 g total fat, 6 mg cholesterol, 719 mg sodium

roasted zucchini-mushroom sandwiches

preparation time: 1 hour, plus at least 30 minutes to chill

1 medium-size red onion

1 ¼ pounds zucchini

1 ¼ pounds mushrooms

5 teaspoons olive oil

2 tablespoons balsamic vinegar

12 slices whole wheat sandwich bread

6 thin slices reduced-fat Jarlsberg cheese

3 cups reduced-fat sour cream

1 Cut onion crosswise into ½-inch slices. Cut zucchini lengthwise into ¼-inch slices; cut mushrooms into ½-inch slices. Brush 3 shallow 10- by 15-inch baking pans with oil, using 1 teaspoon of the oil per pan. Lay onion and zucchini in a single layer in 2 of the pans; spread mushrooms evenly in third pan, overlapping slices as little as possible. Brush onion with all the vinegar; brush all vegetables with remaining 2 teaspoons oil.

2 Bake in a 475° oven for 15 minutes. Turn vegetables over and continue to bake until mushrooms are lightly browned and onion is well browned (about 15 more minutes).

3 Place onion, zucchini, and mushrooms in a food processor or blender; whirl until smoothly puréed. Before using, cover and refrigerate for at least 30 minutes or up to 3 days.

4 To make each sandwich, spread one slice of bread with about ½ cup of the vegetable spread; top with one slice of the cheese, 2 tablespoons of the sour cream, and a second slice of bread.

makes 6 servings

per serving: 286 calories, 15 g protein, 39 g carbohydrates, 9 g total fat, 7 mg cholesterol, 380 mg sodium

wild spanish rice

preparation time: about 15 minutes
cooking time: about 1 3/4 hours

2 cups canned or homemade vegetable broth

1/2 cup wild rice, rinsed and drained

1 tablespoon olive oil or salad oil

1 medium-size red onion, thinly sliced

2 cloves garlic, minced or pressed

1 cup long-grain brown rice

1 teaspoon chili powder

2 1/2 cups tomato juice

2 medium-size green bell peppers,
    seeded and chopped

2 medium-size pear-shaped (Roma-type)
    tomatoes, seeded and chopped

1/2 cup pimiento-stuffed green olives,
    cut lengthwise into halves

1/4 cup dry-roasted peanuts

1 In a wide nonstick frying pan, bring broth to a boil over high heat. Add wild rice; then reduce heat, cover, and simmer until rice is tender to bite (about 45 minutes). Drain rice, reserving broth; set rice and broth aside.

2 In same pan, heat oil over medium heat. Add onion and garlic; cook, stirring often, until onion is soft and golden (6 to 8 minutes). Add brown rice, increase heat to medium-high, and cook, stirring, until rice looks opaque (about 3 minutes). Add chili powder, tomato juice, and reserved broth.

3 Bring mixture to a boil; then reduce heat, cover, and simmer until rice is tender to bite (45 to 50 minutes). Add drained wild rice, bell pepper, tomatoes, and olives; cook, stirring gently, until heated through (about 2 minutes).

4 Transfer to a serving dish and sprinkle with peanuts.

makes 4 to 6 servings

per serving: 337 calories, 9 g protein, 56 g carbohydrates, 10 g total fat, 0 mg cholesterol, 1,188 mg sodium

vegetable curry stir-fry

preparation time: about 45 minutes

3/4 pound red thin-skinned potatoes,
    cut into chunks

2 tablespoons salad oil

1 large onion, chopped

1 medium-size head cauliflower,
    cut into flowerets

1/2 pound green beans, cut into 2-inch pieces

2 medium-size carrots, sliced

2 tablespoons curry powder

1/2 cup water

1 can (8 oz.) no-salt-added tomato sauce

1 can (about 15 1/2 oz.) garbanzo beans,
    drained and rinsed

Chopped cilantro, optional

1 Place potatoes on a rack in a pan above 1 inch boiling water. Cover and steam over high heat until slightly tender when pierced (about 10 minutes). Lift out and set aside.

2 Heat oil in a wok or wide frying pan over high heat. Add onion and cook, stirring, for 2 minutes. Add cauliflower, green beans, and carrots and cook, stirring, for 5 minutes. Add curry powder and water, stirring until vegetables are well coated. Stir in tomato sauce, garbanzo beans, and potatoes. Reduce heat, cover, and simmer until vegetables are tender (about 10 minutes).

3 Transfer to a serving dish and sprinkle with cilantro, if desired.

makes 4 to 6 servings

per serving: 280 calories, 9 g protein, 48 g carbohydrates, 7 g total fat, 0 mg cholesterol, 300 mg sodium

polenta gnocchi with dried tomato chutney

preparation time: about 1 1/4 hours, plus 15 minutes for polenta to stand

POLENTA GNOCCHI:

2 cups low-fat (1%) milk

1/2 cup vegetable broth

1 cup polenta or yellow cornmeal

1/2 teaspoon salt

1 teaspoon chopped fresh sage
    or 1/4 teaspoon ground sage

1 large egg

1 tablespoon butter or margarine

1/4 cup finely shredded Parmesan cheese

DRIED TOMATO CHUTNEY:

1 cup dried tomatoes (not oil-packed)

1 large jar (about 4 oz.) diced pimientos

1/2 cup drained capers

4 cloves garlic, peeled

2 tablespoons chopped fresh basil
    or 2 teaspoons dried basil

1 tablespoon olive oil

4 teaspoons Marsala or port (or to taste)

1 teaspoon Dijon mustard

GARNISH:

sage sprigs

1 In a 4- to 5-quart pan, bring milk and broth just to a boil over medium-high heat. Stir in polenta, salt, and chopped sage. Reduce heat and simmer, uncovered, stirring often and scraping pan bottom with a long-handled spoon (mixture will spatter), until polenta tastes creamy (about 15 minutes). Remove from heat and stir in egg and butter.

2 Working quickly, brush a 9- by 13-inch baking pan liberally with water; then spoon polenta into pan and spread to make level. Let stand in pan on a rack for 15 minutes. Then cut polenta diagonally into diamonds, making cuts about 1 1/2 inches apart. Carefully arrange polenta pieces, overlapping slightly, in a greased shallow 1 1/2- to 2-quart casserole. (At this point, you may let cool, then cover and refrigerate until next day.) Sprinkle with cheese and bake, uncovered, in a 350° oven until hot and tinged with brown (about 20 minutes; about 35 minutes if refrigerated).

3 Meanwhile, place tomatoes in a small bowl and add boiling water to cover. Let stand until soft (about 10 minutes). Drain well; squeeze out excess liquid. Transfer tomatoes to a food processor or blender. Add 1/3 cup water, pimientos, capers, garlic, basil, oil, Marsala, and mustard. Whirl until mixture is puréed and has a spoonable consistency. If chutney is too thick, add a little more water. Transfer to a small bowl.

4 Divide gnocchi among 4 individual plates; garnish with sage sprigs. Offer chutney to add to taste.

makes 4 servings

per serving: 361 calories, 14 g protein, 51 g carbohydrates, 12 g total fat, 70 mg cholesterol, 1,100 mg sodium

squash strata with cranberry chutney

preparation time: 25 minutes
cooking time: about 1 hour and 20 minutes

SQUASH STRATA:

1 large onion, very thinly sliced

1 1/2 cups canned pumpkin

2 large eggs

4 large egg whites

3/4 cup half-and-half

1/2 cup nonfat milk

1 tablespoon cornstarch

1 1/2 teaspoons chopped fresh thyme
   or 1/2 teaspoon dried thyme

1 cup grated Parmesan cheese

9 slices egg sandwich bread or whole wheat
   sandwich bread, torn into large pieces

CRANBERRY CHUTNEY:

1/2 cup currant or raspberry jelly

1/2 cup orange marmalade

1 cup fresh cranberries

1/4 cup dried cranberries or raisins

1 teaspoon balsamic vinegar (or to taste)

GARNISH:

1 to 2 tablespoons finely chopped parsley

1 In a wide nonstick frying pan, combine onion and 2 tablespoons water. Cook over medium-high heat; stirring often, until liquid evaporates and browned bits stick to pan bottom (about 10 minutes). To deglaze pan, add 1/4 cup more water, stirring to loosen browned bits from pan. Continue to cook until onion is lightly browned (about 10 more minutes); add water, 1 tablespoon at a time, if pan appears dry. Remove onion from pan and set aside.

2 In a food processor or a large bowl, combine pumpkin, eggs, egg whites, half-and-half, milk, cornstarch, and thyme. Whirl or beat with an electric mixer until smoothly puréed. Stir in three-fourths of the cheese; set aside.

3 Arrange 3 slices of bread (overlapping, if necessary) over bottom of a greased deep 2 1/2- to 3-quart casserole. Top evenly with a third *each* of the onion and pumpkin mixture. Repeat layers twice, ending with pumpkin mixture. Sprinkle with remaining cheese.

4 Cover tightly and bake in a 350° oven for 30 minutes. Then uncover and continue to bake until top is tinged with brown and a knife inserted in center comes out clean (about 30 more minutes).

5 Meanwhile, in a 1 1/2- to 2-quart pan, combine 1/4 cup water, jelly, marmalade, fresh cranberries, and dried cranberries. Bring to a boil over medium-high heat, stirring. Reduce heat and boil gently, stirring occasionally, until fresh cranberries split and are soft (about 8 minutes). Remove from heat and stir in vinegar; set aside.

6 Let casserole cool for about 5 minutes before serving. Garnish with parsley. Offer chutney to spoon over individual servings.

makes 6 servings

per serving: 462 calories, 16 g protein, 75 g carbohydrates, 12 g total fat, 93 mg cholesterol, 586 mg sodium

roasted vegetable pizzettes

preparation time: 25 minutes
cooking time: about 1 hour and 10 minutes

PIZZETTES:

1 pound mushrooms

2 medium-size onions

1 medium-size eggplant

5 teaspoons olive oil

12 ounces pear-shaped (Roma-type) tomatoes (about 4 medium-size tomatoes)

1/2 cup chopped canned roasted red peppers, drained

4 small Italian bread shells (*each* about 5 1/2 inches in diameter, about 4 oz.); or 4 pita breads (*each* about 5 inches in diameter)

DRESSING:

2 tablespoons balsamic vinegar

1 tablespoon olive oil

1 teaspoon Dijon mustard

ACCOMPANIMENTS:

4 cups lightly packed arugula leaves (tough stems discarded), rinsed and drained

3/4 cup shaved or shredded Parmesan cheese

1 Cut mushrooms into 1/2-inch slices. Cut onions into wedges about 1/2-inch thick; cut unpeeled eggplant into about 1/2-inch cubes.

2 Pour the 5 teaspoons oil into a shallow 10- by 15-inch baking pan; place in a 450° oven just until oil is hot. Remove pan from oven and add mushrooms, onions, and eggplant; return to oven and bake until vegetables are golden (about 45 minutes), turning vegetables every 15 minutes. Meanwhile, cut tomatoes crosswise into 1/4-inch slices.

3 After vegetables have baked for 45 minutes, stir in tomatoes; continue to bake until almost all liquid has evaporated, about 20 more minutes. (At this point, you may let cool, then cover and refrigerate until next day.)

5 Stir red peppers into roasted vegetables. Place bread shells in a single layer on 1 or 2 baking sheets. Spread a fourth of the vegetables evenly over each bread shell (or over each whole pita bread) to within 1/2 inch of edge.

6 Bake in a 500° oven just until bread and vegetables are heated through (about 5 minutes). Meanwhile, in a small bowl, beat vinegar, the 1 tablespoon oil, and mustard until blended; set aside.

7 To serve, transfer pizzettes to individual plates and top equally with arugula (thinly slice any large arugula pieces) and cheese. Drizzle dressing over all.

makes 4 servings

per serving: 572 calories, 25 g protein, 77 g carbohydrates, 19 g total fat, 20 mg cholesterol, 917 mg sodium

couscous with ratatouille & feta cheese

preparation time: about 35 minutes

RATATOUILLE:

1 small onion, cut into thin slivers

1 small red bell pepper seeded and thinly sliced

1 small eggplant, peeled and cut into $^1/_2$-inch cubes

1 tablespoon chopped fresh basil or $^3/_4$ teaspoon dried basil, or to taste

1 $^1/_2$ teaspoons chopped fresh thyme or $^1/_2$ teaspoon dried thyme, or to taste

$^1/_4$ teaspoon salt, or to taste

$^1/_4$ teaspoon pepper, or to taste

1 small zucchini, cut into $^1/_4$-inch slices

1 can (about 15 oz.) garbanzo beans, drained and rinsed

1 large tomato, coarsely chopped

COUSCOUS:

2 $^1/_4$ cups low-fat (1%) milk

1 package (about 10 oz.) couscous

1 cup crumbled feta cheese

GARNISH:

Basil or thyme sprigs

1 In a wide nonstick frying pan, combine onion, bell pepper, eggplant, chopped basil, chopped thyme, salt, pepper, and $^1/_2$ cup water. Cover and cook over medium-high heat until vegetables are almost tender when pierced (about 5 minutes). Uncover and add zucchini. Cook, stirring gently, until almost all liquid had evaporated. Add beans and tomato; stir gently just until heated through (about 3 minutes).

2 Meanwhile, in a 2$^1/_2$- to 3-quart pan, bring milk just to a boil (do not scald) over medium-high heat. Stir in couscous and $^3/_4$ cup of the feta cheese; cover, remove from heat, and let stand until liquid has been absorbed (about 5 minutes).

3 To serve, divide couscous equally among 4 shallow individual bowls. Top with vegetable mixture and sprinkle with remaining $^1/_2$ cup feta cheese. Garnish with basil sprigs.

makes 4 servings

per serving: 537 calories, 24 g protein, 85 g carbohydrates, 11 g total fat, 36 mg cholesterol, 714 mg sodium

STORING CHEESE: To avoid waste, wrap cheese tightly in plastic wrap and store it in the refrigerator (many varieties keep for several weeks). If you use shredded cheese often, prepare it with your food processor, then keep it refrigerated in a tightly covered container or plastic bag.

corn custard

preparation time: 10 minutes
cooking time: about 1 1/2 hours

4 teaspoons yellow cornmeal

1 can (about 15 oz.) cream-style corn

1/2 cup nonfat milk

1/4 cup half-and-half

2 teaspoons cornstarch

1/4 teaspoon salt

1/8 teaspoon ground white pepper

2 large eggs

2 large egg whites

1 package (about 10 oz.) frozen corn kernels, thawed and drained

1 jar (about 2 oz.) diced pimientos

Italian parsley sprigs

1 Sprinkle cornmeal over bottom of four 1 1/4-cup custard cups or ovenproof bowls, using 1 teaspoon of the cornmeal for each cup. Set cups in a large baking pan at least 2 inches deep.

2 In a food processor or blender, combine cream-style corn, milk, half-and-half, cornstarch, salt, white pepper, eggs, and egg whites. Whirl until smooth; stir in corn kernels and pimientos. Working quickly, divide mixture evenly among cups.

3 Set pan on center rack of a 325° oven. Pour boiling water into pan around cups up to level of custard. Bake until custard jiggles only slightly in center when cups are gently shaken (about 1 1/2 hours). Lift cups from pan. Let stand for 5 minutes before serving. Garnish with parsley sprigs.

makes 4 servings

per serving: 235 calories, 11 g protein, 41 g carbohydrates, 5 g total fat, 112 mg cholesterol, 524 mg sodium

tuscan bean stew

preparation time: about 1 hour and 10 minutes

6 slices Italian sandwich bread, cut into 1/2-inch cubes

2 teaspoons olive oil

2 large onions, chopped

4 cloves garlic, minced

1/2 teaspoon *each* dried rubbed sage, dried thyme, and dried marjoram

1/4 cup chopped fresh basil

4 large tomatoes, chopped

3 cans (about 15 oz. *each*) cannellini (white kidney beans), drained and rinsed

1 cup canned vegetable broth

1 tablespoon red wine vinegar

1/2 cup grated Parmesan cheese

1 Toast bread cubes and set aside.

2 Heat oil in a 4- to 5-quart pan over medium-high heat. Add onions, garlic, sage, thyme, marjoram, and 1/4 cup water. Cook, stirring often, until onions are soft (about 5 minutes). Add water, 1 tablespoon at a time, if pan appears dry. Stir in basil and half the tomatoes. Cook, stirring often, just until tomatoes are soft (about 3 minutes). Remove from heat and let cool slightly.

3 Transfer onion mixture to a food processor or blender; whirl until smoothly puréed. Return purée to pan and add beans, broth, and vinegar. Bring to a boil over medium-high heat; then reduce heat, cover, and simmer for 15 minutes.

4 Stir croutons into bean stew; spoon stew into individual bowls. Sprinkle remaining tomatoes around edge of each bowl. Sprinkle with cheese and serve at once.

makes 4 servings

per serving: 505 calories, 25 g protein, 89 g carbohydrates, 7 g total fat, 4 mg cholesterol, 1,716 mg sodium

broccoli cornmeal kuchen

preparation time: about 1 hour

KUCHEN:

3 ¹/₂ cups broccoli flowerets

¹/₂ cup yellow cornmeal

¹/₂ cup all-purpose flour

1 ¹/₂ teaspoons baking powder

1 cup nonfat cottage cheese

1 large egg

3 large egg whites

¹/₂ cup low-fat buttermilk

2 tablespoons butter or margarine, melted

4 teaspoons sugar

YOGURT SAUCE:

1 cup plain nonfat yogurt

¹/₄ cup white wine vinegar

2 tablespoons dried dill weed (or to taste)

1 teaspoon honey (or to taste)

¹/₄ teaspoon ground cumin

1 In a 4- to 5-quart pan, bring 8 cups water to a boil over medium-high heat. Add broccoli and cook just until barely tender-crisp to bite (about 4 minutes). Drain, immerse in ice water until cool, and drain well again.

2 In a large bowl, stir together cornmeal, flour, and baking powder. In a small bowl, beat cottage cheese, egg, egg whites, buttermilk, butter, and sugar until well blended. Add cheese mixture to cornmeal mixture and stir just until dry ingredients are evenly moistened.

3 Pour batter into a greased round 8-inch baking pan or quiche dish. Gently press broccoli decoratively into batter. Bake in a 350° oven until center of kuchen feels firm when lightly pressed (about 30 minutes).

4 Meanwhile, in a small bowl, stir together yogurt, vinegar, dill weed, honey, and cumin just until blended. Set aside.

5 Let kuchen cool slightly; then cut into wedges. Offer yogurt sauce to spoon over individual portions.

makes 4 servings

per serving: 303 calories, 14 g protein, 42 g carbohydrates, 9 g total fat, 72 mg cholesterol, 390 mg sodium

LIGHT TOUCHES: To enhance the flavor of cooked vegetables, experiment with seasonings that don't add calories in the form of fat. Try a squeeze of lemon juice from a fresh lemon, lime, or orange—it can give a boost to anything from asparagus to zucchini. Or mix minced garlic with freshly ground pepper for a little zip. Snipped fresh or crushed dried herbs contribute a fascinating array of tastes; use them singly or in combination. Thinly sliced green onions or finely chopped parsley or cilantro add flavor as well as color and make wonderful garnishes too.

spicy tofu bok choy

preparation time: 50 minutes

1 ⅓ cups long-grain white rice

1 package (about 1 lb.) firm reduced-fat tofu, rinsed and drained

1 ½ pounds baby bok choy

1 tablespoon salad oil

3 cloves garlic, minced or pressed green onions, thinly sliced

2 large red bell peppers, seeded and thinly sliced

6 tablespoons reduced-sodium soy sauce

4 teaspoons sugar

1 teaspoon liquid hot pepper seasoning (or to taste)

2 teaspoons cornstarch blended with 2 tablespoons cold water

1 Cook rice. Meanwhile, cut tofu into 1-inch slices. Place slices on paper towels and cover with more paper towels. Then set a flat pan on top layer of towels; set a 1-pound can on pan. Let tofu drain for 10 minutes. While tofu is draining, cut each bok choy in half lengthwise; if any bok choy half is thicker than 1 inch at the base, cut it in half lengthwise. Set aside.

2 Cut tofu into 1-inch cubes. Heat oil in a wide nonstick frying pan over medium-high heat. Add tofu and cook, turning gently, until golden brown (about 5 minutes). With a slotted spoon, transfer tofu to paper towels to drain.

3 Add bok choy, garlic, onions, bell peppers, and ¼ cup water to pan. Cover and cook, stirring often, until bok choy stems are just tender when pierced (about 3 minutes). Uncover pan and add tofu, soy sauce, sugar, hot pepper seasoning, and cornstarch mixture; bring to a boil, stirring gently.

4 To serve, spoon rice onto a platter or individual plates; spoon tofu mixture over rice.

makes 4 servings

per serving: 438 calories, 18 g protein, 79 g carbohydrates, 6 g total fat, 0 mg cholesterol, 1,149 mg sodium

barley casserole

preparation time: about 1 hour and 10 minutes

3 ½ cups vegetable broth

4 cloves garlic, minced or pressed

½ teaspoon dried rosemary, crumbled

¼ teaspoon fennel seeds, crushed

1 cup pearl barley, rinsed and drained

1 package (about 10 oz.) frozen baby lima beans, thawed and drained

1 large red or yellow bell pepper, seeded and finely chopped

⅓ cup thinly sliced green onions

1 tablespoon balsamic vinegar

½ cup salted roasted almonds

Rosemary sprigs (optional)

1 In a shallow 1½ to 2-quart casserole, combine 3 cups of the broth, garlic, dried rosemary, and fennel seeds. Bake, uncovered, in a 450° oven until mixture comes to a rolling boil (about 20 minutes). Remove from oven and carefully stir in barley. Cover tightly, return to oven, and bake for 10 more minutes. Stir well, cover again, and continue to bake until barley is tender to bite (about 15 more minutes).

2 Stir remaining ½ cup broth, beans, and bell pepper into barley mixture. Bake, uncovered, for 5 more minutes. Remove from oven and stir in onions and vinegar. Spoon barley mixture onto a platter and sprinkle with almonds. Garnish with rosemary sprigs, if desired.

makes 4 servings

per serving: 423 calories, 15 g protein, 66 g carbohydrates, 13 g total fat, 0 mg cholesterol, 1,070 mg sodium

chili pot pie

preparation time: 30 minutes
cooking time: about 1 hour

CHILI:

1 tablespoon chili powder (or to taste)

2 tablespoons pure maple syrup

1 1/2 teaspoons dry mustard

**1 1/2 teaspoons Worcestershire
or reduced-sodium soy sauce**

2 cloves garlic, minced or pressed

**1 can (about 15 oz.) pinto beans,
drained and rinsed**

**1 package (about 1 lb.) frozen mixed bell pepper
strips, thawed and drained; or about 4 cups
fresh yellow, red, and green bell pepper
strips (or use all of one color)**

**1 package (about 10 oz.) frozen tiny onions,
thawed and drained**

1 large tomato, chopped

1/4 cup yellow cornmeal

PASTRY:

2/3 cup low-fat (2%) cottage cheese

1/3 cup butter or margarine, cut into chunks

1 large egg

1/4 cup smooth unsweetened applesauce

1/4 teaspoon each ground cumin and salt

1 2/3 cups bread flour or all-purpose flour

2 tablespoons nonfat milk

1 In a large bowl, combine chili powder, syrup, mustard, Worcestershire, and garlic. Add beans, bell peppers, onions, and tomato. Mix gently but thoroughly. Sprinkle cornmeal over bottom of a 9-inch pie pan or dish. Spoon bean mixture over cornmeal in pan; set aside.

2 In a food processor or a large bowl, combine cottage cheese, butter, egg, applesauce, cumin, and salt. Whirl or beat with an electric mixer until smoothly puréed. Add flour; whirl or stir with a fork until dough holds together (dough will be sticky and soft). Scrape dough out onto a heavily floured board; with floured fingers, pat into a ball. Then, still using floured fingers, pat pastry into a 10-inch round. With a floured cookie cutter, cut one or more shapes (each 1 to 2 inches in diameter) from center of pastry. Set cutouts aside.

3 Carefully lift pastry and place over filling in pie pan. Fold edge under to make it flush with pan rim; flute firmly against rim. Arrange cutouts decoratively atop pastry. Set pie in a shallow 10-by 15-inch baking pan. Brush pastry (including cutouts) with milk.

4 Bake on lowest rack of a 400° oven until pastry is well browned and filling is hot in center (about 1 hour). If pastry rim or cutout begin to darken excessively before center of pastry is brown, drape rim and cover cutouts with foil. To serve, spoon filling and crust from dish.

makes 6 servings

per serving: 405 calories, 15 g protein, 58 g carbohydrates, 13 g total fat, 65 mg cholesterol, 463 mg sodium

mushroom bean pizza

preparation time: 50 minutes

1 jar (about 6 oz.) marinated quartered
    artichoke hearts

8 ounces mushrooms, thinly sliced

4 cloves garlic, minced or pressed

3 tablespoons yellow cornmeal

2 cups all-purpose flour

1 tablespoon baking powder

1/4 teaspoon salt

3/4 cup low-fat (2%) cottage cheese

1 tablespoon sugar

2 tablespoons *each* nonfat milk and olive oil

3/4 cup *each* shredded smoked Gouda
    and part-skim mozzarella cheese
    (or use all of one kind)

1 tablespoon chopped fresh oregano or
    1 teaspoon dried oregano

1 can (about 15 oz.) cannellini (white kidney
    beans), drained and rinsed

1 large firm-ripe pear-shaped (Roma-type)
    tomato, very thinly sliced lengthwise

1/4 cup very thinly sliced red onion

About 1/8 teaspoon crushed red pepper flakes
    (or to taste)

Oregano sprigs (optional)

1 Drain artichokes well, reserving marinade; you should have 1/4 cup marinade. (If necessary, add equal parts water and olive oil to marinade to make 1/4 cup liquid.) Set artichokes and marinade aside.

2 In a medium-size nonstick frying pan, combine mushrooms, garlic, and 1/4 cup water. Cook over medium-high heat, stirring occasionally, until mushrooms are soft and almost all liquid has evaporated (about 7 minutes; do not scorch). Remove from pan and set aside.

3 Sprinkle cornmeal over bottom of a lightly greased 12-inch deep-dish pizza pan; set aside. In a medium-size bowl, stir together flour baking powder, and salt; set aside.

4 In a food processor or a large bowl, combine cottage cheese, the reserved 1/4 cup artichoke marinade, sugar, milk, and oil. Whirl or beat with an electric mixer until smoothly puréed. Add flour mixture; whirl or beat just until dough holds together. Turn dough out onto a lightly floured board and knead several times; or until dough holds together (dough will be soft). Then place dough in pizza pan. Flour your hands thoroughly; then flatten dough with the heels of your hands and your fingertips to cover pan bottom evenly. (Or roll dough on board into a 12½-inch round and carefully fit into pan.)

5 Gently stretch edge of dough up sides of pan to form about a ½-inch rim. Prick dough all over with a fork; then sprinkle evenly with Gouda cheese, mozzarella cheese, and chopped oregano.

6 Arrange mushrooms, beans, artichokes, tomato, and onion over cheese. Bake pizza on middle rack of a 500° oven until crust is golden and cheese is melted (about 10 minutes). Sprinkle with red pepper flakes and garnish with oregano sprigs, if desired. Serve immediately.

makes 6 servings

per serving: 420 calories, 21 g protein, 54 g carbohydrates, 14 g total fat, 24 mg cholesterol, 855 mg sodium

vegetable scramble pockets

preparation time: about 25 minutes

1 large egg

6 large egg whites

1 teaspoon ground oregano

1 cup crumbled feta cheese

1 tablespoon olive oil

1 large onion, thinly sliced

2 large red bell peppers, seeded and thinly sliced

8 ounces mushrooms, thinly sliced

1 package (about 10 oz.) frozen chopped spinach, thawed and squeezed dry

Pepper

4 whole wheat pita breads (*each* about 6 inches in diameter), cut crosswise into halves

1 In a large bowl, lightly beat whole egg, egg whites, oregano, and cheese until blended. Set aside.

2 Heat oil in a wide nonstick frying pan or wok over medium-high heat. When oil is hot, add onion, bell peppers, and mushrooms; stir-fry until liquid has completely evaporated and mushrooms are tinged with brown (about 7 minutes). Add spinach to pan and stir-fry until heated through (about 3 minutes). Pour egg mixture over vegetables in pan; stir-fry until eggs are softly set and look scrambled (3 to 5 minutes). Season to taste with pepper. Fill pita halves equally with egg mixture.

makes 4 servings

per serving: 398 calories, 22 g protein, 54 g carbohydrates, 13 g total fat, 78 mg cholesterol, 813 mg sodium

ratatouille-topped baked potatoes

preparation time: about 25 minutes
baking time: about 1 1/2 hours

1 medium-size eggplant, unpeeled, cut into 1/2- by 2-inch sticks

8 ounces each zucchini and crookneck squash, cut into 1/2-inch-thick slices

1 1/2 pounds pear-shaped (Roma-type) tomatoes, cut into quarters

1 each large red and yellow bell pepper, seeded and thinly sliced

1 large onion, chopped

3 garlic cloves, minced or pressed

1 dry bay leaf

1/2 teaspoon *each* dry thyme and dry rosemary

1 tablespoon olive oil

6 large red thin-skinned potatoes, scrubbed

Pepper

1 In a 3- to 4-quart baking dish, mix eggplant, zucchini, crookneck squash, tomatoes, bell peppers, onion, garlic, bay leaf, thyme, rosemary, and oil. Cover and bake in a 400° oven for 1 hour. Uncover and continue to bake, stirring once or twice, until eggplant is very soft when pressed and only a thin layer of liquid remains in bottom of dish (about 30 more minutes).

2 After eggplant mixture has baked for 30 minutes, pierce each unpeeled potato in several places with a fork. Place potatoes on a baking sheet; bake until tender throughout when pierced (about 1 hour).

3 To serve, make a deep cut lengthwise down center of each potato; then make a second cut across center. Grasp each potato between cuts; press firmly to split potato wide open. Spoon eggplant mixture equally into potatoes; season to taste with pepper.

makes 6 servings

per serving: 294 calories, 8 g protein, 61 g carbohydrates, 3 g total fat, 0 mg cholesterol, 35 mg sodium

side dishes

baked fennel with gorgonzola

preparation time: 15 minutes
cooking time: about 50 minutes

½ **cup fine dry bread crumbs**

4 large heads fennel

1¾ **cups fat-free reduced-sodium chicken broth**

3 tablespoons packed crumbled Gorgonzola, cambozola, or other blue-veined cheese

Salt and pepper

1 Sprinkle three-fourths of the bread crumbs over bottom of a rectangular baking dish (about 8 by 12 inches). Set aside.

2 Trim stems from fennel, reserving about 1 cup of the feathery green leaves. Trim and discard any bruised areas from fennel; then cut each fennel head in half lengthwise. Lay fennel halves in a wide frying pan. Pour broth into pan and bring to a boil over high heat; then reduce heat, cover, and simmer until fennel is tender when pierced (about 25 minutes). With a slotted spoon, transfer fennel halves to baking dish, arranging them in a single layer with cut side up.

3 Bring cooking broth to a boil over high heat; boil until reduced to ½ cup, about 10 minutes. Stir in half the reserved fennel leaves. Spoon mixture over fennel halves in baking dish.

4 In a small bowl, mash cheese with remaining bread crumbs and 1 teaspoon water; dot mixture evenly over fennel. Bake in a 375° oven until topping begins to brown and fennel is heated through (about 15 minutes). Tuck remaining fennel leaves around fennel halves. Season to taste with salt and pepper.

makes 8 servings

per serving: 74 calories, 4 g protein, 9 g carbohydrates, 2 g total fat, 5 mg cholesterol, 416 mg sodium

green beans with sautéed mushrooms

preparation tine: 50 minutes

1 tablespoon butter or margarine

1 small onion, finely chopped

1 pound mushrooms, finely chopped

½ **cup dry sherry**

1 tablespoon reduced-sodium soy sauce

2 tablespoons balsamic vinegar

1 teaspoon *each* **cornstarch and Asian sesame oil**

3 pounds green beans, ends trimmed

1 Melt butter in a wide nonstick frying pan over medium-high heat. Add onion and cook, stirring often, until soft. Add mushrooms, ¼ cup of the sherry, and ¼ cup water; cook, stirring often, until almost all liquid has evaporated and mushrooms are lightly browned (about 15 minutes).

2 In a small bowl, stir together remaining ¼ cup sherry, ½ cup water, soy sauce, vinegar, cornstarch, and oil. Add to mushroom mixture and cook, stirring, until sauce boils and thickens slightly. Remove from heat and keep warm.

3 In a 5- to 6-quart pan, bring 3 quarts water to a boil over high heat. Add beans; cook, uncovered, until just tender to bite (4 to 6 minutes). Drain well, arrange on a platter, and top with mushroom mixture.

makes 12 servings

per serving: 70 calories, 3 g protein, 10 g carbohydrates, 2 g total fat, 3 mg cholesterol, 68 mg sodium

sweet potato stir-fry

preparation time: about 30 minutes

3 large oranges

About 24 large spinach leaves, rinsed and crisped

1/2 cup fat-free reduced-sodium chicken broth or canned vegetable broth

1/2 cup golden raisins

1/4 cup orange juice

2 teaspoons honey

1/8 teaspoon ground cloves

1/8 teaspoon ground nutmeg

2 teaspoons vegetable oil

2 large sweet potatoes or yams, peeled and cut into 1/4-inch cubes

1/4 cup sweetened shredded coconut

1/3 cup pomegranate seeds

1 Cut off and discard peel and all white membrane from oranges; then cut fruit crosswise into thin slices. Cover and set aside. Arrange spinach leaves on a rimmed platter; cover and set aside. In a bowl, stir together broth, raisins, orange juice, honey, cloves, and nutmeg; set aside.

2 Heat oil in a wide nonstick frying pan or wok over medium-high heat. When oil is hot, add sweet potatoes and 2 table-spoons water; stir-fry until potatoes begin to brown and are just tender-crisp to bite (about 7 minutes). Add some water, 1 tablespoon at a time, if pan appears dry. Add broth mixture to pan; cover and cook until potatoes are just tender to bite (about 5 minutes). Uncover and stir-fry until liquid has evaporated. Remove pan from heat and stir in coconut and 1/4 cup of the pomegranate seeds.

3 Arrange orange slices over spinach leaves on platter. Spoon potato mixture over oranges; sprinkle with remaining pomegranate seeds.

makes 4 servings

per serving: 284 calories, 4 g protein, 61 g carbohydrates, 4 g total fat, 0 mg cholesterol, 117 mg sodium

mexican rice

preparation time: about 45 minutes

1 large can (about 28 oz.) tomatoes

About 3 cups fat-free reduced sodium chicken broth

2 teaspoons butter or margarine

2 cups long-grain white rice

1 large onion, chopped

2 cloves garlic, minced or pressed

1 small can (about 4 oz.) diced green chiles

Salt and pepper

1/4 cup packed cilantro leaves

1 Drain liquid from tomatoes into a glass measure. Add enough of the broth to make 4 cups liquid. Set tomatoes and broth mixture aside.

2 Melt butter in a 4- to 6-quart pan over medium-high heat. Add rice and cook, stirring, until it begins to turn opaque (about 3 minutes). Add onion, garlic, chiles, and 1/4 cup water; continue to cook, stirring, for 5 more minutes. Add more water, 1 tablespoon at a time, if pan appears dry.

3 Add tomatoes and broth mixture to pan. Bring to a boil over medium-high heat; then reduce heat, cover, and simmer until liquid has been absorbed and rice is tender to bite (about 25 minutes).

4 To serve, season to taste with salt and pepper; garnish with cilantro.

makes 10 to 12 servings

per serving: 161 calories, 4 g protein, 33 g carbohydrates, 2 total fat, 2 mg cholesterol, 159 mg sodium

golden curried couscous

preparation time: about 25 minutes

2 ¼ cups fat-free reduced-sodium chicken broth

¼ cup golden raisins

6 tablespoonslemon juice

3 tablespoons finely chopped crystallized ginger

1 tablespoon margarine

¾ teaspoon curry powder

1 ½ cups couscous

½ cup thinly sliced celery

⅓ cup thinly sliced green onions

3 tablespoons chopped cilantro

¼ cup coarsely chopped salted roasted pistachio nuts

Cilantro sprigs

1 In a 2- to 3-quart pan, bring broth to a boil over high heat. Stir in raisins, lemon juice, ginger, margarine, curry powder, and couscous. Cover pan and remove from heat; let stand for 5 to 10 minutes. Fluff couscous with a fork (At this point, you may cover and refrigerate bring to room temperature before serving.)

2 Serve couscous warm or at room temperature just before serving, stir in celery, onions, and chopped cilantro. Mound couscous mixture in serving dish; sprinkle with pistachio nuts and garnish with whole cilantro sprigs.

makes 6 servings

per serving: 318 calories, 8 g protein, 61 g carbohydrates, 5 g total fat, 0 mg cholesterol, 330 mg sodium

asparagus sauté

preparation time: about 25 minutes

1 ½ pounds asparagus

2 teaspoons olive oil

8 ounces mushrooms, thinly sliced

1 clove garlic, minced or pressed

115 cup dry white wine

1 tablespoon grated orange peel

⅛ teaspoon crushed red pepper flakes

¼ teaspoon dried tarragon

½ cup drained canned mandarin oranges or fresh orange segments

1 Snap off and discard tough ends of asparagus. Cut spears into 1-inch diagonal slices.

2 Heat oil in a wide nonstick frying pan or wok over medium-high heat. When oil is hot, add asparagus, mushrooms, and garlic; stir-fry until asparagus is hot and bright green (about 3 minutes).

3 Add wine, orange peel, red pepper flakes, and tarragon. Cover and cook until asparagus is just tender-crisp to bite (about 3 minutes). Uncover and continue to cook until liquid has evaporated (1 to 2 more minutes). Stir in oranges.

makes 4 servings

per serving: 90 calories, 4 g protein, 12 g carbohydrates, 3 g total fat, 0 mg cholesterol, 7 mg sodium

tricolor pepper sauté

preparation time: about 40 minutes

1 cup long-grain white rice

1 to 2 teaspoons sesame seeds

3 medium-size bell peppers; use 1 *each* red, yellow, and green bell pepper

1 teaspoon vegetable oil

1 small onion, cut into thin slivers

1 tablespoon minced fresh ginger

1 clove garlic, minced or pressed

1 cup bean sprouts

2 teaspoons Asian sesame oil

Reduced-sodium soy sauce or salt

1 In a 3- to 4-quart pan, bring 2 cups water to a boil over high heat; stir in rice. Reduce heat, cover, and simmer until liquid has been absorbed and rice is tender to bite (about 20 minutes).

2 Meanwhile, in a wide nonstick frying pan or wok, stir sesame seeds over medium heat until golden (about 3 minutes). Pour from pan; set aside.

3 Seed bell peppers and cut into thin slivers, 2 to 3 inches long. Heat vegetable oil in pan over medium-high heat. When oil is hot, add onion, ginger, and garlic; stir-fry for 1 minute. Add peppers; stir-fry until tender-crisp to bite (about 3 minutes). Add bean sprouts and stir-fry until barely wilted (about 1 minute). Remove from heat and stir in sesame oil.

4 Spoon rice onto a rimmed platter; pour vegetable mixture over rice and sprinkle with sesame seeds. Offer soy sauce to add to taste.

makes 4 servings

per serving: 253 calories, 5 g protein, 48 g carbohydrates, 5 g total fat, 0 mg cholesterol, 7 mg sodium

cerveza beans

preparation time: about 25 minutes

4 slices bacon, coarsely chopped

1 large onion, chopped

2 cans (about 15 oz. *each*) pinto beans; or 4 cups cooked pinto beans

1 can (about 8 oz.) tomato sauce

½ cup regular or nonalcoholic beer, or to taste

3 tablespoons molasses

1½ teaspoons dry mustard

1½ teaspoons Worcestershire sauce

¼ teaspoon pepper

Salt

1 In a 3- to 4-quart pan, cook bacon and onion over medium heat, stirring often, until browned bits form on pan bottom and onion is soft (8 to 10 minutes). Discard any fat.

2 Drain beans, reserving ¼ cup of the liquid from cans. To pan, add beans and reserved liquid (if using home-cooked beans, use ¼ cup fat-free reduced-sodium chicken broth blended with ½ teaspoon cornstarch). Then stir in tomato sauce, ¼ cup of the beer, molasses, mustard, Worcestershire, and pepper. Bring to a boil; then reduce heat so beans boil gently. Cook, stirring occasionally, until flavors are blended, about 10 minutes. (At this point, you may let cool, then cover and refrigerate for up to 2 days; reheat before continuing.)

3 To serve, stir in remaining ¼ cup beer and season to taste with salt.

makes 4 to 6 servings

per serving: 220 calories, 10 g protein, 37 g carbohydrates, 3 g total fat, 4 mg cholesterol, 870 mg sodium

indian potatoes

preparation time: about 25 minutes

1¼ pounds small red thin-skinned potatoes, scrubbed

2 tablespoons butter or margarine

1 medium-size red bell pepper, seeded and cut into thin slivers

1 medium-size onion, cut into thin slivers

1 tablespoon ground cumin

1 teaspoon ground coriander

¼ teaspoon hot chili oil

⅓ cup chopped cilantro

½ cup nonfat sour cream

Cilantro sprigs

Salt

1 Cut potatoes crosswise into ¼-inch slices. Melt butter in a wide nonstick frying pan or wok over medium-high heat. Add potatoes, bell pepper, onion, cumin, coriander, hot chili oil, and 3 tablespoons water. Stir-fry gently until potatoes are tinged with brown and tender when pierced (about 15 minutes; do not scorch). Add water, 1 tablespoon at a time, if pan appears dry.

2 Remove pan from heat. Sprinkle potato mixture with chopped cilantro and mix gently. Spoon into a serving bowl, top with sour cream, and garnish with cilantro sprigs. Add salt to taste.

makes 4 servings

per serving: 220 calories, 6 g protein, 34 g carbohydrates, 7 g total fat, 16 mg cholesterol, 94 mg sodium

potato risotto

preparation time: about 45 minutes

1 tablespoon margarine

1 small onion, finely chopped

½ teaspoon minced fresh thyme or ¼ teaspoon dried thyme

1 clove garlic, minced or pressed

1¾ cups fat-free reduced-sodium chicken broth

3 medium-size thin-skinned potatoes

¼ cup evaporated skim milk

¼ cup grated Parmesan cheese

Freshly ground nutmeg

Thyme sprigs (optional)

1 Melt margarine in a 2- to 3-quart pan over medium heat. Add onion and minced thyme; cook, stirring often, until onion is soft but not browned (3 to 5 minutes). Stir in garlic, then add broth. Increase heat to high and bring mixture to a boil; boil until reduced to 1½ cups (about 3 minutes).

2 Peel and shred potatoes. Add to onion mixture; reduce heat to medium-low and cook, uncovered, stirring often, until potatoes are tender to bite (about 25 minutes). Remove from heat and mix in milk and cheese. Season to taste with nutmeg. Spoon into a warm serving bowl; garnish with thyme sprigs, if desired.

makes 4 to 6 servings

per serving: 147 calories, 6 g protein, 23 g carbohydrates, 4 g total fat, 4 mg cholesterol, 350 mg sodium

SHOP WISELY: Cooks who enjoy food seasoned and cooked to their own tastes aren't likely to accept completely prepared foods. Rather than searching for a frozen entrée that measures up to memories of traditional cooking, learn to identify the cuts of meat and poultry that can be cooked to your taste in a short time.

orange & rum sweet potatoes

preparation time: about 30 minutes

1 teaspoon vegetable oil

3 medium-size sweet potatoes, peeled and cut into $\frac{1}{4}$-inch-thick slices

$\frac{3}{4}$ cup fat-free reduced-sodium chicken broth

$\frac{1}{2}$ cup orange juice

1 tablespoon rum

About 2 teaspoons honey, or to taste

2 teaspoons cornstarch

$\frac{1}{8}$ teaspoon white pepper

Salt

1 tablespoon minced parsley

1 Heat oil in a wide nonstick frying pan over medium-high heat. Add potatoes and $\frac{1}{2}$ cup of the broth. Bring to a boil over medium-high heat; then reduce heat, cover, and simmer until potatoes are tender when pierced (about 10 minutes). Uncover and continue to cook, stirring occasionally, until liquid has evaporated and potatoes are tinged with brown (about 5 more minutes).

2 In a bowl, mix remaining $\frac{1}{4}$ cup broth, orange juice, rum, honey, cornstarch, and white pepper. Add cornstarch mixture to pan and bring to a boil over medium heat; boil, stirring, just until thickened. Season to taste with salt and sprinkle with parsley.

makes 4 servings

per serving: 155 calories, 2 g protein, 32 g carbohydrates, 2 g total fat, 0 mg cholesterol, 35 mg sodium

seasoned sweet corn

preparation time: about 15 minutes

6 medium-size ears corn, *each* about 8 inches long, husks and silk removed.

$\frac{1}{2}$ cup distilled white vinegar

$\frac{1}{4}$ cup lime juice

1 cup minced onion

3 tablespoons sugar

1 small jar (about 2 oz.) diced pimientos

1 teaspoon mustard seeds

$\frac{1}{4}$ to $\frac{1}{2}$ teaspoon crushed red pepper flakes

Salt and pepper

1 With a sharp, heavy knife, cut corn crosswise into 1-inch rounds. In a large pan, bring 4 quarts water to a boil over high heat. Add corn, cover, and cook until hot (3 to 4 minutes). Drain corn well and pour into a shallow rimmed dish (about 9 by 13 inches).

2 To prepare vinegar marinade, in a small pan, combine vinegar, lime juice, onion, sugar, pimientos, mustard seeds, and pepper flakes. Bring to a boil over high heat; then boil, stirring, just until sugar is dissolved. Use hot.

3 Pour hot marinade over corn; let stand, frequently spooning marinade over corn, until corn is cool enough to eat out of hand. Season to taste with salt and pepper.

makes 6 servings

per serving: 115 calories, 3 g protein, 27 g carbohydrates, 1g total fat, 0 mg cholesterol, 17 mg sodium

curry-glazed carrots

preparation time: about 30 minutes

1 tablespoon grated orange peel

³/₄ cup orange juice

2 tablespoons maple syrup

2 teaspoons cornstarch blended
  with 2 tablespoons cold water

1 teaspoon curry powder

1¼ pounds carrots, cut diagonally
  into ¼-inch slices

2 tablespoons minced parsley

Salt and pepper

1 In a bowl, stir together orange peel, orange juice, syrup, and cornstarch mixture; set aside.

2 In a wide nonstick frying pan or wok, stir curry powder over medium-high heat just until fragrant (about 30 seconds; do not scorch). Add carrots and ⅓ cup water. Cover and cook just until carrots are tender when pierced (about 4 minutes). Uncover and stir-fry until liquid has evaporated.

3 Stir orange juice mixture well; then pour into pan and cook, stirring, until sauce boils and thickens slightly. Pour carrots and sauce into a serving bowl and sprinkle with parsley. Season with salt and pepper.

makes 4 servings

per serving: 117 calories, 2 g protein, 28 g carbohydrates, 0.4 g total fat, 0 mg cholesterol, 52 mg sodium

cheese and apple hash browns

preparation time: about 45 minute

2 large Golden Delicious apples, peeled,
  cored, and finely chopped

1 tablespoon lemon juice

2 teaspoons butter or margarine

2 large russet potatoes, peeled
  and cut into ¼-inch cubes

1 medium-size onion, chopped

1 medium-size red bell pepper, seeded
  and diced

½ teaspoon cumin seeds

¼ cup chopped parsley

½ cup shredded reduced-fat sharp
  Cheddar cheese

Salt and pepper

1 In a medium-size bowl, mix apples and lemon juice. Set aside; stir occasionally.

2 Melt butter in a wide nonstick frying pan or wok over medium heat. Add potatoes, onion, and bell pepper. Stir-fry until potatoes are tinged with brown and tender when pierced (about 15 minutes). Add water, 1 tablespoon at a time, if pan appears dry.

3 Stir in apples and cumin seeds; stir-fry until apples are tender to bite (about 5 minutes). Remove pan from heat and stir in parsley; then spoon potato mixture into a serving bowl. Sprinkle with cheese. Season to taste with salt and pepper.

makes 4 to 6 servings

per serving: 178 calories, 6 g protein, 31 g carbohydrates, 4 g total fat, 12 mg cholesterol, 114 mg sodium

simply perfect eggplant

preparation time: about 45 minutes

Olive oil cooking spray

6 Japanese eggplants

¼ cup sun-dried tomatoes

2 teaspoons olive oil

1 small onion, finely chopped

8 ounces mushrooms, finely chopped

1 small red bell pepper, seeded and chopped

½ teaspoon dried oregano

½ teaspoon dried marjoram

2 cloves garlic, minced or pressed

Salt and pepper

chopped parsley

1 Spray a shallow rimmed baking pan with cooking spray. Cut eggplants crosswise into ½-inch-thick slices; arrange in a single layer in pan. Spray with cooking spray. Bake in a 425° oven until well browned and very soft when pressed (about 25 minutes).

2 Meanwhile, soak tomatoes in boiling water to cover until soft (about 15 minutes). Drain, discarding liquid; finely chop tomatoes.

3 Heat oil in a wide nonstick frying pan over medium heat. Add tomatoes, onion, mushrooms, bell pepper, oregano, marjoram, and garlic. Cook, stirring often, until mushrooms are lightly browned but mixture is still moist (10 to 15 minutes). Season to taste with salt and pepper.

4 To serve, transfer eggplant slices to a large warm serving platter; top with mushroom mixture and sprinkle with parsley.

makes 4 to 6 servings

per serving: 88 calories, 3 g protein, 15 g carbohydrates, 3 g total fat, 0 mg cholesterol, 11 mg sodium

herbed cauliflower & zucchini stir-fry

preparation time: about 25 minutes

2 teaspoons olive oil

1 large cauliflower, cut into flowerets

2 cloves garlic, minced or pressed

1 large onion, chopped

8 ounces small zucchini, cut crosswise into ¼-inch slices

⅓ cup dry white wine

3 medium-size firm-ripe pear-shaped (Roma-type) tomatoes, chopped

1 tablespoon chopped fresh basil

1 Heat oil in a wide nonstick frying pan or wok over medium-high heat. When oil is hot, add cauliflower, garlic, onion, and zucchini; stir-fry until zucchini is hot and bright in color (2 to 3 minutes).

2 Add wine, tomatoes, and basil to pan. Cover and cook until cauliflower is just tender to bite (about 4 minutes). Uncover and continue to cook until liquid has evaporated (2 to 3 more minutes).

makes 4 servings

per serving: 93 calories, 4 g protein, 13 g carbohydrates, 3 g total fat, 0 mg cholesterol, 23 mg sodium

vegetable stir-fry with soba

preparation time: about 25 minutes

2 tablespoons oyster sauce

2 tablespoons reduced-sodium soy sauce

2 tablespoons lemon juice

1 teaspoon Asian sesame oil

8 ounces dried soba noodles or capellini

1 large red or green bell pepper, seeded and cut into thin slivers

½ cup thinly sliced celery

½ cup thinly sliced green onions

½ cup salted roasted cashews

1 To prepare sauce, in a small bowl, stir together oyster sauce, soy sauce, and lemon juice. Stir in sesame oil; set aside. In a 4- to 5-quart pan, cook noodles in about 8 cups boiling water until just tender to bite (about 5 minutes for soba, about 3 minutes for capellini); or cook according to package directions. Drain well, transfer to a warm wide bowl, and keep warm.

2 In a wide nonstick frying pan or wok, combine bell pepper, celery, and ¼ cup water. Stir-fry over high heat until vegetables are tender-crisp to bite and liquid has evaporated (about 5 minutes). Stir sauce well and pour into pan; bring just to a boil. Pour vegetable mixture over noodles, then add onions and mix gently but thoroughly. Sprinkle with roasted cashews.

makes 4 servings

per serving: 329 calories, 13 g protein, 54 g carbohydrates, 10 g total fat, 0 mg cholesterol, 1,225 mg sodium

sautéed mushrooms with apple eau de vie

preparation time: about 25 minutes

8 ounces fresh chanterelle mushrooms

8 ounces large regular mushrooms

1 teaspoon butter or margarine

4 cloves garlic, minced or pressed

1½ teaspoons chopped fresh thyme or ½ teaspoon dried thyme

About ⅛ teaspoon salt, or to taste

1 tablespoon apple eau de vie or apple brandy, or to taste

1 tablespoon cream sherry, or to taste

Thyme sprigs

Pepper

1 Rinse mushrooms and scrub gently, if needed; pat dry. Cut into ¼- to ½-inch-thick slices; set aside.

2 Melt butter in a wide nonstick frying pan or wok over medium-high heat. Add garlic and chopped thyme; stir-fry just until fragrant (about 30 seconds; do not scorch). Add mushrooms and ¼ cup water; stir-fry until mushrooms are soft and almost all liquid has evaporated (about 8 minutes). Then add salt and ¼ cup more water; stir-fry until liquid has evaporated (about 2 minutes). Add eau de vie and sherry; stir-fry until liquid has evaporated. Spoon mushroom mixture into a serving bowl and garnish with thyme sprigs. Season to taste with pepper.

makes 4 servings

per serving: 58 calories, 3 g protein, 8 g carbohydrates, 1 g total fat, 3 mg cholesterol, 84 mg sodium

sautéed kale with cannellini

preparation time: about 30 minutes

1¼ pounds kale

4 slices bacon, chopped

2 large onions, thinly sliced

2 cans (about 15 oz *each*) cannellini (white kidney beans), drained and rinsed

Salt and pepper

1 Remove and discard tough stems from kale; then rinse kale, drain, and cut crosswise into ½-inch strips. Set aside.

2 In a wide nonstick frying pan or wok, stir-fry bacon over medium-high heat until crisp (about 3 minutes). Remove from pan with a slotted spoon and set aside. Add onions to drippings in pan and stir-fry until soft (about 5 minutes). Add kale and stir-fry until wilted and bright green (3 to 4 minutes). Transfer to a platter and keep warm.

3 Add beans to pan, reduce heat to medium-low, and stir until heated through (about 4 minutes). Spoon beans over kale; sprinkle beans and kale with bacon. Season to taste with salt and pepper.

makes 6 servings

per serving: 190 calories, 11 g protein, 28 g carbohydrates, 4 g total fat, 4 mg cholesterol, 276 mg sodium

lean refried black beans

preparation time: about 45 minutes

1 large onion, chopped

2 cloves garlic, minced or pressed

1½ cups fat-free reduced-sodium chicken broth

2 cans (about 15 oz. *each*) black beans, drained and rinsed

½ teaspoon ground cumin

⅓ cup packed feta cheese or queso fresco

Cilantro sprigs

1 In a wide frying pan (preferably nonstick), combine onion, garlic, and ¾ cup of the broth. Cook over high heat, stirring occasionally, until liquid evaporates and onion begins to brown. To deglaze pan, add 2 to 3 tablespoons water and stir to loosen browned bits clinging to bottom of pan. Cook, stirring occasionally, until liquid evaporates and onion begins to brown again. Repeat deglazing step, using about 2 tablespoons water each time, until onion is richly browned.

2 Stir in remaining ¾ cup broth; stir to loosen browned bits clinging to bottom of pan. Add beans and cumin. Remove from heat and coarsely mash beans with a large spoon or a potato masher. (At this point, you may cover and refrigerate for up to 2 days.)

3 Bring bean mixture to a simmer over medium heat. Then simmer, stirring often, for about 15 minutes; beans should be thick enough to hold a fork upright (push beans into a mound to test). Spoon into a serving bowl; crumble cheese over top and garnish with cilantro sprigs.

makes 6 servings

per serving: 120 calories, 8 g protein, 17 g carbohydrates, 3 g total fat, 6 mg cholesterol, 339 mg sodium

cocoa-glazed carrots & onions

preparation time: 35 to 40 minutes

10 ounces fresh pearl onions; or 1 package (about 10 oz.) frozen pearl onions

1½ pounds baby or small carrots, peeled

1 tablespoon butter or margarine

2 tablespoons lemon juice

1 tablespoon honey

1 tablespoon unsweetened cocoa powder

1 teaspoon grated fresh ginger

1 If using fresh onions, place them in a bowl and cover with boiling water. Let stand for 2 to 3 minutes. Drain; then pull or slip off skins and discard them. Also trim root and stem ends of onions.

2 Place peeled fresh onions or frozen onions in a wide nonstick frying pan. Barely cover with water and bring to a boil over high heat: Reduce heat, cover, and simmer gently until onions are tender when pierced (10 to 15 minutes). Drain onions, pour out of pan, and set aside.

3 If using baby carrots, leave whole; if using small carrots, cut diagonally into ¼-inch-thick slices. Place carrots in pan used for onions, barely cover with water, and bring to a boil over high heat. Reduce heat, cover, and simmer gently until carrots are just tender when pierced (7 to 10 minutes). Drain carrots and set aside.

4 In pan, combine butter, lemon juice, 1 tablespoon water, honey, cocoa, and ginger. Stir over medium-high heat until smooth. Add carrots and onions. Stir over high heat until sauce is thick enough to cling to vegetables (2 to 3 minutes).

makes 6 servings

per serving: 91 calories, 2 g protein, 18 g carbohydrates, 2 g total fat, 5 mg cholesterol, 61 mg sodium

stir-fried spinach with feta

preparation time: about 25 minutes

½ cup thinly sliced green onions

1 clove garlic, minced or pressed

1½ teaspoons chopped fresh dill

2 medium-size firm-ripe pear-shaped (Roma-type) tomatoes, chopped

1¼ pounds spinach, stems removed, leaves rinsed and drained

3 to 4 tablespoons crumbled feta cheese

1 tablespoon drained capers, or to taste

Pepper

1 In a wide nonstick frying pan, combine onions, garlic, dill, and ¼ cup water. Stir-fry over medium-high heat until onions are soft and almost all liquid has evaporated (about 3 minutes). Transfer to a bowl and stir in tomatoes. Keep warm.

2 Add half the spinach and 1 tablespoon water to pan; stir-fry over medium heat until spinach is just beginning to wilt. Then add remaining spinach; stir-fry just until all spinach is wilted (about 2 more minutes).

3 With a slotted spoon, transfer spinach to a platter and spread out; discard liquid from pan. Top spinach with tomato mixture, then sprinkle with cheese and capers. Season to taste with pepper.

makes 4 to 6 servings

per serving: 44 calories, 4 g protein, 5 g carbohydrates, 2 g total fat, 5 mg cholesterol, 179 mg sodium

oat pilaf with hazelnuts & scotch

preparation time: about 20 minutes
baking time: about 1 hour and 50 minutes

¾ **cup hazelnuts**

2 large onions, chopped

6½ **cups beef broth**

3 cups oat groats (uncut grains)

6 tablespoons Scotch whisky

⅓ **cup thinly sliced green onions**

1 Spread hazelnuts in a shallow 3- to 3½-quart casserole and toast in a 350° oven until pale golden beneath skins (about 10 minutes). Let nuts cool slightly; then rub off as much of skins as possible with your fingers. Chop nuts coarsely and set aside.

2 Increase oven temperature to 400°. In casserole, combine chopped onions and ½ cup water. Bake until liquid has evaporated and onions are browned at edges (about 30 minutes). To deglaze, add ¼ cup of the broth and stir to scrape browned bits free.

3 Continue to bake, stirring occasionally, until onions begin to brown and stick to casserole again (about 20 minutes). Then repeat deglazing step, using ¼ cup more broth and stirring to scrape browned bits free; continue to bake until onions begin to brown again (about 20 minutes).

4 In a 2- to 3-quart pan, combine oats and remaining 6 cups broth. Bring to a boil over high heat. Add to casserole; stir to combine with onions. Cover casserole tightly and bake until oats are tender to bite (about 30 minutes). Uncover; stir in whisky. Sprinkle with hazelnuts and green onions.

makes 6 to 8 servings

per serving: 414 calories, 16 g protein, 53 g carbohydrates, 13 g total fat, 0 mg cholesterol, 771 mg sodium

italian-style swiss chard

preparation time: about 25 minutes

2½ **pounds Swiss chard**

2 teaspoons olive oil

2 cloves garlic, minced or pressed

2 tablespoons balsamic vinegar

1 tablespoon drained capers

1 Trim and discard discolored stem ends from chard; then rinse and drain chard. Thinly slice chard stems crosswise up to base of leaves; set aside. Use a few whole leaves to line a large platter; cover and set aside. Coarsely chop remaining leaves.

2 Heat oil in a wide nonstick frying pan or wok over medium-high heat. When oil is hot, add garlic and chard stems. Stir-fry until stems are soft (about 2 minutes). Add half the chopped chard leaves to pan, cover, and cook for 2 minutes. Add remaining leaves, cover, and cook until all leaves are wilted (about 2 more minutes). Uncover pan and stir in vinegar and capers; then spoon mixture over whole chard leaves on platter.

makes 6 servings

per serving: 51 calories, 3 g protein, 8 g carbohydrates, 2 g total fat, 0 mg cholesterol, 440 mg sodium

roasted artichoke with vinaigrette

preparation time: 30 minutes
cooking time: about 1 ½ hours
chilling time: at least 2 hours

4 large artichokes

2 cups fat-free reduced-sodium chicken broth

1 teaspoon *each* **dried rosemary, dried oregano, dried thyme, and mustard seeds**

¼ cup balsamic vinegar

1 pound pear-shaped (Roma-type) tomatoes, seeded and chopped

⅓ cup sliced green onions

2 tablespoons chopped Italian or regular parsley

1 Break small, coarse outer leaves from artichokes. With a sharp knife, cut off thorny tops; with scissors, snip any remaining thorny tips from leaves. With knife, peel stems and trim bases. Immerse artichokes in water and swish up and down to rinse well; lift out and, holding by stem end, shake to remove water.

2 Place artichokes in a 9- by 13-inch baking pan. Mix broth, 1 cup water, rosemary, oregano, thyme, and mustard seeds; pour into pan. Cover very tightly with foil and bake in a 450° oven until artichoke bottoms are tender when pierced (about 50 minutes). Uncover and continue to bake until artichokes are just tinged with brown (about 8 more minutes).

3 With a slotted spoon, lift artichokes from pan. Hold briefly above pan to drain; transfer to a rimmed dish. Reserve juice in pan. When artichokes are cool enough to touch, ease center of each open; using a spoon, scoop out a few of the tiny center leaves and the choke.

4 Boil pan juices over high heat until reduced to ½ cup, about 10 minutes. Remove from heat, stir in vinegar, and pour over artichokes. Cover; refrigerate for at least 2 hours or until next day, spooning marinade over artichokes occasionally.

5 With a slotted spoon, transfer artichokes to individual plates. Stir tomatoes, onions, and parsley into artichoke marinade; spoon mixture around artichokes and into their centers.

makes 4 servings

per serving: 96 calories, 7 g protein, 19 g carbohydrates, 0.9 g total fat, 0 mg cholesterol, 441 mg sodium

sweet & sour broccoli

preparation time: about 15 minutes

About 1 pound broccoli

½ cup unseasoned rice vinegar

1 tablespoon sugar

½ teaspoon reduced-sodium soy sauce

1 Trim tough ends from broccoli stalks; peel stalks, if desired. Cut stalks into ¼-inch-thick slanting slices; cut flowerets into bite-size pieces. Arrange all broccoli on a rack in a pan above about 1 inch of boiling water. Cover and steam, keeping water at a steady boil, just until tender when pierced (5 to 8 minutes). Place broccoli in a large bowl.

2 In a small bowl, stir together vinegar, sugar, and soy sauce; pour over warm broccoli and mix well. Drain immediately and serve.

makes 4 servings

per serving: 36 calories, 2 g protein, 8 g carbohydrates, 0.2 g total fat, 0 mg cholesterol, 49 mg sodium

roasted eggplant and bell peppers

preparation time: about 1 hour

2 large red bell peppers

3 large heads garlic

1 medium-size eggplant, unpeeled, cut into 2-inch pieces

2 teaspoons olive oil

3 tablespoons balsamic vinegar

2 tablespoons chopped Italian or regular parsley

Salt and pepper

1 Cut bell peppers lengthwise into halves and arrange, cut side down, in a shallow baking pan. Broil 4 to 6 inches (10 to 15 cm) below heat until skins are charred (about 8 minutes). Cover loosely with foil and let stand until cool enough to handle (about 10 minutes).

2 Meanwhile, separate garlic heads into cloves; peel garlic cloves. Place garlic in a shallow 10- by 15-inch baking pan; add eggplant and oil. Mix to coat vegetables with oil. Bake in a 475° oven until eggplant is richly browned and soft when pressed, and garlic is tinged with brown (20 to 30 minutes). Watch carefully to prevent scorching; remove pieces as they brown and add water, 1/4 cup at a time, if pan appears dry.

3 While eggplant is cooking, remove and discard skins, seeds, and stems from bell peppers. Cut peppers into chunks, place in a large serving bowl, and set aside.

4 Add eggplant, garlic, and vinegar to bowl with peppers; mix gently but thoroughly. Sprinkle with parsley; season to taste with salt and pepper. Serve at room temperature.

makes 4 to 6 servings

per serving: 149 calories, 5 g protein, 30 g carbohydrates, 2 g total fat, 0 mg cholesterol, 16 mg sodium

broiled pineapple with basil

preparation time: about 15 minutes

1/4 cup honey

2 tablespoons cider vinegar

1 tablespoon finely chopped crystallized ginger

1 teaspoon dry basil

1 medium-size pineapple, peeled and cored

Basil sprigs (optional)

1 In a small pan, combine honey, vinegar, ginger, and dry basil. Stir over low heat until warm (about 3 minutes); set aside.

2 Cut pineapple crosswise into 1/2-inch-thick slices (or cut lengthwise into 1/2-inch-thick wedges). Arrange pineapple pieces in a single layer in a shallow baking pan; drizzle with honey mixture. Broil about 4 inches below heat until pineapple is lightly browned (3 to 4 minutes).

3 Using a wide spatula, transfer pineapple to a platter or individual plates. Spoon pan juices over pineapple; garnish with basil sprigs, if desired.

makes 4 to 6 servings

per serving: 133 calories, 0.6 g protein, 35 g carbohydrates, 0.6 g total fat, 0 mg cholesterol, 4 mg sodium

asian-style green beans

preparation time: about 35 minutes

1 medium-size onion, chopped

8 ounces mushrooms, sliced

1 medium-size red bell pepper,
   cut into 1/4-inch-wide strips

I clove garlic, minced or pressed

3 tablespoons reduced-sodium soy sauce

1 tablespoon honey

1 pound slender green beans

1/4 cup salted roasted peanuts, chopped

1 In a wide nonstick frying pan or wok, combine onion, mushrooms, bell pepper, garlic, and 1/4 cup water. Stir-fry over medium-high heat until mushrooms are soft and almost all liquid has evaporated (about 10 minutes). Add water, 1 tablespoon at a time, if pan appears to be dry.

2 Stir soy sauce and honey into mushroom mixture; then transfer to a bowl and keep warm. Wipe pan clean (be careful; pan is hot).

3 To pan, add beans and 1/3 cup water. Cover and cook over medium-high heat just until beans are tender to bite (about 3 minutes). Uncover and stir-fry until liquid has evaporated.

4 Arrange beans on a rimmed serving platter; spoon mushroom mixture over beans and then sprinkle with roasted peanuts.

makes 4 to 6 servings

per serving: 118 calories, 6 g protein, 18 g carbohydrates, 4 g total fat, 0 mg cholesterol, 400 mg sodium

snow peas with bacon & mint

preparation time: about 25 minutes

1/4 cup fat-free reduced-sodium chicken broth

1/4 cup distilled white vinegar

2 teaspoons sugar

1 teaspoon cornstarch

2 thick slices bacon, finely chopped

1 pound fresh Chinese pea pods (also called snow
   or sugar peas), ends and strings removed;
   or 3 packages (about 6 oz. *each*) frozen
   Chinese pea pods, thawed and drained

1 tablespoon chopped fresh mint

Mint sprigs

1 In a small bowl, stir together broth, vinegar, sugar, and cornstarch; set aside.

2 In a wide nonstick frying pan or wok, stir-fry bacon over medium-high heat until browned and crisp (about 3 minutes). Remove bacon from pan with a slotted spoon and set aside. Pour off and discard drippings from pan. Wipe pan clean (be careful; pan is hot).

3 Add pea pods and 1 1/3 cup water to pan. Cover and cook over medium-high heat until pea pods are tender-crisp to bite (about 1 minute for fresh pea pods, about 30 seconds for frozen). Uncover and stir-fry until liquid has evaporated. Transfer to a rimmed platter and keep warm.

4 Stir broth mixture and pour into pan. Bring to a boil over high heat; boil, stirring, until slightly thickened. Remove from heat and stir in chopped mint. Pour sauce over pea pods, sprinkle with bacon, and garnish with mint sprigs.

makes 4 to 6 servings

per serving: 73 calories, 4 g protein, 10 g carbohydrates, 2 g total fat, 4 mg cholesterol, 104 mg sodium

mediterranean squash

preparation time: about 45 minutes

2 teaspoons olive oil

1 large onion, chopped

1 pound mushrooms, thinly sliced

1½ pounds yellow crookneck squash or yellow
   zucchini, cut crosswise into ¼-inch slices

1½ tablespoons fresh thyme leaves
   or 1½ teaspoons dried thyme

3 tablespoons lemon juice

6 medium-size firm-ripe pear-shaped
   (Roma-type) tomatoes, cut crosswise
   into ¼-inch slices

½ cup thinly sliced green onions

1 ounce feta cheese, crumbled

2 oil-cured black olives, pitted and chopped

1 Heat 1 teaspoon of the oil in a wide nonstick frying pan or wok over medium-high heat. When oil is hot, add half each of the chopped onion, mushrooms, squash, and thyme. Stir-fry until squash is hot and bright in color (about 3 minutes).

2 Add ¼ cup water and 1½ tablespoons of the lemon juice to pan; cover and cook until vegetables are just tender to bite (about 3 minutes). Uncover and continue to cook, stirring, until liquid has evaporated (about 3 more minutes). Remove vegetables from pan and set aside.

3 Repeat to cook remaining chopped onion, mushrooms, squash, and thyme, using remaining 1 teaspoon oil; add ¼ cup water and remaining 1½ tablespoons lemon juice after the first 3 minutes of cooking.

4 Return all cooked vegetables to pan; gently stir in tomatoes. Transfer vegetables to a serving dish; sprinkle with green onions, cheese, and olives.

makes 8 servings

per serving: 78 calories, 3 g protein, 12 g carbohydrates, 3 g total fat, 3 mg cholesterol, 72 mg sodium

roasted garlic & broccoli

preparation time: about 35 minutes

3 large heads garlic

2 teaspoons olive oil

About 1¼ pounds broccoli flowerets

2 tablespoons reduced-sodium soy sauce

1 teaspoon Asian sesame oil

1 Separate garlic heads into cloves; then peel cloves and place in a lightly oiled 8- to 10-inch-square baking pan. Mix in olive oil. Bake in a 475° oven just until garlic is tinged with brown; do not scorch (about 20 minutes; remove smaller cloves as they brown, if needed). Set aside.

2 While garlic is roasting, in a 5- to 6-quart pan, bring 3 to 4 quarts water to a boil over high heat. Add broccoli and cook until tender-crisp to bite (about 5 minutes). Drain, immerse in ice water until cool, and drain again.

3 In a shallow bowl, mix soy sauce and sesame oil. Add garlic and broccoli; toss gently to mix.

makes 6 servings

per serving: 123 calories, 6 g protein, 22 g carbohydrates, 3 g total fat, 0 mg cholesterol, 229 mg sodium

zesty refried beans

preparation time: about 45 minutes

2 medium-size onions, chopped

2 cloves garlic, minced or pressed

2 teaspoons salad oil

2 cans (about 15 oz. *each*) pinto or other beans

2 tablespoons cider vinegar

About $^1/_8$ teaspoon ground red pepper
(cayenne), or to taste

Salt (optional)

1 In a wide nonstick frying pan, combine onions, garlic, oil, and 1 tablespoon water. Cook over medium heat, stirring often, until mixture is deep golden (20 to 30 minutes); if onions stick to pan bottom or pan appears dry, add more water, 1 tablespoon at a time.

2 Drain beans, reserving $^1/_2$ cup of the liquid from cans.

3 To pan, add beans, reserved liquid (use $^1/_2$ cup low-sodium chicken broth if using home-cooked beans), vinegar, and red pepper. Coarsely mash beans with a spoon. Season to taste with salt, if desired. Heat until steaming. If made ahead, let cool; then cover and refrigerate until next day. Reheat before serving.

makes about 3 cups

per serving: 136 calories, 7 g protein, 24 g carbohydrates, 2 g total fat, 0 mg cholesterol, 591 mg sodium

wild rice barley pilaf

preparation time: about 20 minutes
cooking time: $1^1/_2$ to $1^3/_4$ hours

1 small onion, minced

8 ounces mushrooms, sliced

1 clove garlic, minced or pressed

1 cup wild rice, rinsed and drained

$3^1/_2$ cups low-sodium chicken broth

$^1/_2$ cup pearl barley, rinsed and drained

Salt and pepper

1 In a wide frying pan or a 2- to 3-quart pan, combine onion, mushrooms, garlic, and $^1/_2$ cup water. Cook over high heat, stirring occasionally, until liquid evaporates and vegetables begin to brown (about 15 minutes). To deglaze, add 2 to 3 tablespoons water and stir to scrape browned bits free. Then continue to cook, stirring occasionally, until vegetables begin to brown again.

2 Repeat deglazing and browning steps 4 or 5 times, using 2 to 3 tablespoons water each time; vegetables should be richly browned (about 15 minutes total).

3 Stir rice and broth into mushroom mixture. Bring to a boil over high heat; reduce heat, cover, and simmer for 30 minutes. Stir in barley; cover and continue to simmer until rice and barley are tender to bite but just slightly chewy (30 to 40 more minutes). Season to taste with salt and pepper.

makes 6 servings

per serving: 189 calories, 8 g protein, 37 g carbohydrates, 2 g total fat, 0 mg cholesterol, 37 mg sodium

mediterranean spinach

preparation time: about 25 minutes

1/2 cup thinly sliced green onions

1 clove garlic, minced or pressed

1 1/2 teaspoons chopped fresh dill
   or 1/2 teaspoon dried dill weed

2 medium-size firm-ripe pear-shaped
   (Roma-type) tomatoes, chopped

1 1/4 pounds spinach, stems removed,
   leaves rinsed and drained

3 to 4 tablespoons crumbled feta cheese

1 tablespoon drained capers, or to taste

Pepper

1 In a wide nonstick frying pan or wok, combine onions, garlic, dill, and 1/4 cup water. Stir-fry over medium-high heat until onions are soft and almost all liquid has evaporated (about 3 minutes). Transfer mixture to a bowl and stir in tomatoes. Keep warm.

2 Add half the spinach and 1 tablespoon water to pan; stir-fry over medium heat until spinach is just beginning to wilt. Then add remaining spinach; stir-fry just until all spinach is wilted (about 2 more minutes).

3 With a slotted spoon, transfer spinach to a rimmed platter and spread out slightly; discard liquid from pan. Top spinach with tomato mixture, then sprinkle with cheese and capers. Season to taste with pepper.

makes 4 to 6 servings

per serving: 44 calories, 4 g protein, 5 g carbohydrates, 2 g total fat, 5 mg cholesterol, 179 mg sodium

sautéed chard with pine nuts

preparation time: 25 minutes

1 1/2 pounds Swiss chard

1 tablespoon pine nuts

1 teaspoon olive oil

2 cloves garlic, minced or pressed

1 large red bell pepper, seeded and
   cut into slivers about 2 inches long

1/3 cup dried currants

1 Cut off and discard coarse stem ends of chard. Rinse and drain chard. Then thinly slice stems crosswise up to base of leaves; set sliced stems aside. Use a few whole leaves to line a large rimmed serving dish; coarsely chop remaining leaves. Set aside serving dish and all chard.

2 Toast pine nuts in a wide nonstick frying pan over medium heat until golden (about 3 minutes), stirring often. Pour out of pan and set aside. Heat oil in pan over medium-high heat. Add garlic, chard stems, and 1 tablespoon water; cook, stirring, until stems are softened (about 2 minutes). Stir in chopped leaves, bell pepper, and currants. Cover and cook until leaves are wilted (about 5 minutes), stirring occasionally.

3 With a slotted spoon, lift chard mixture from pan and arrange in serving dish. Sprinkle with pine nuts.

makes 4 servings

per serving: 105 calories, 4 g protein, 20 g carbohydrates, 3 g total fat, 0 mg cholesterol, 336 mg sodium

sweet potato-fennel gratin

preparation time: 45 minutes
cooking time: 2 ½ hours

3 heads fennel

2 large onions, chopped

1 teaspoon fennel seeds, crushed

About 4 cups vegetable broth

¼ cup all-purpose flour

¼ teaspoon ground nutmeg

½ cup half-and-half

4 very large sweet potatoes or yams

3 cups shredded reduced-fat Jarlsberg cheese

1 Trim stems from fennel; reserve some of the feathery leaves for garnish. Discard stems. Trim and discard discolored parts of fennel. Finely chop fennel.

2 In a 5- to 6-quart pan, combine chopped fennel, onions, fennel seeds, and ½ cup of the broth. Cook over medium-high heat, stirring often, until liquid evaporates and browned bits stick to pan bottom (about 10 minutes). To deglaze pan, add ⅓ cup more broth, stirring to loosen browned bits from pan; continue to cook until browned bits form again. Repeat deglazing step about 3 more times or until vegetables are browned, using ⅓ cup more broth each time. Add flour and nutmeg to vegetables; mix well. Add half-and-half and 2 cups more broth; stir over medium heat until mixture comes to a boil (about 5 minutes). Remove from heat.

3 Peel sweet potatoes and thinly slice crosswise. Arrange a fourth of the fennel mixture in a 9- by 13-inch baking pan. Cover with a fourth of the sweet potatoes and ¾ cup of the cheese. Repeat layers 2 more times. Add remaining fennel mixture in an even layer; top evenly with remaining sweet potatoes. Reserve remaining ¾ cup cheese.

4 Cover tightly and bake in a 350° oven for 45 minutes; then uncover and sprinkle with remaining ¾ cup cheese. Continue to bake, uncovered, until potatoes are tender when pierced and top of casserole is golden brown (about 1 more hour). Garnish with reserved fennel leaves.

makes 8 to 10 servings

per serving: 294 calories, 15 g protein, 39 g carbohydrates, 8 g total fat, 25 mg cholesterol, 679 mg sodium

lemon-caper rice

preparation time: about 30 minutes

6 slices bacon

1 cup short- or medium-grain rice

1 tablespoon grated lemon peel

2½ cups water tablespoons drained capers

¼ cup seasoned rice vinegar

1 Cook bacon in a 2- to 3-quart pan over medium heat until crisp (about 5 minutes). Lift out, drain, crumble, and set aside. Discard all but 1 teaspoon of the drippings.

2 To pan, add rice, lemon peel and water. Bring to a boil over high heat. Stir; then reduce heat, cover, and simmer until liquid has been absorbed and rice is tender to bite (about 20 minutes). Uncover; stir in crumbled bacon, capers, and vinegar.

makes 6 to 8 servings

per serving: 145 calories, 4 g protein, 24 g carbohydrates, 3 g total fat, 5 mg cholesterol, 354 mg sodium

pork fried rice

preparation time: about 30 minutes

1 tablespoon vegetable oil

1 clove garlic, minced or pressed

1/2 teaspoon minced fresh ginger

1/2 cup thinly sliced green onions

4 ounces lean ground pork

8 fresh shiitake mushrooms, stems removed
and caps thinly sliced

1/2 cup frozen peas

1/2 cup frozen corn kernels, thawed and drained

1/2 cup fat-free reduced sodium chicken broth

2 tablespoons reduced sodium soy sauce

3 cups cooked, cooled long grain white rice

1 Heat oil in a wide nonstick frying pan or wok over medium-high heat. When oil is hot, add garlic, ginger, and onions; then crumble in pork. Stir-fry until pork is browned (about 5 minutes).

2 Add mushrooms, peas, corn, and 1/4 cup of the broth to pan; stir-fry until liquid has evaporated (about 2 minutes). Add remaining 1/4 cup broth; then stir in soy sauce and rice. Stir-fry until rice is heated through.

makes 6 servings

per serving: 234 calories, 8 g protein, 35 g carbohydrates, 7 g total fat, 14 mg cholesterol, 282 mg sodium

red cabbage with apple

preparation time: about 10 minutes
cooking time: about 1 hour

1 tablespoon salad oil

1 large onion, thinly sliced

1 medium-size head red cabbage, shredded

1 medium-size tart apple, peeled, cored,
and shredded

1 large clove garlic, minced or pressed

1 teaspoon caraway seeds

2 tablespoons firmly packed brown sugar

1/2 cup red wine vinegar

1 cup water

1 Heat oil in a wide frying pan over medium heat. Add onion and cook, stirring often, until soft (about 5 minutes). Add cabbage and apple; cook, stirring often, for 5 minutes. Stir in garlic, caraway seeds, sugar, vinegar, and water.

2 Bring cabbage mixture to a boil over high heat; then reduce heat, cover, and simmer, stirring occasionally, until cabbage is very tender to bite and almost all liquid has evaporated (about 45 minutes).

makes 4 servings

per serving: 151 calories, 3 g protein, 29 g carbohydrates, 4 g total fat, 0 mg cholesterol, 23 mg sodium

poached leeks with hazelnuts

preparation time: 50 minutes

¼ cup hazelnuts

3 slices sourdough sandwich bread, torn into pieces

2 cloves garlic, minced or pressed

¼ teaspoon dried thyme

1 teaspoon hazelnut oil or olive oil

8 medium-size leeks

Balsamic vinegar

1 Spread hazelnuts in a single layer in a shallow baking pan. Bake in a 375° oven until nuts are golden beneath skins (about 10 minutes). Let nuts cool slightly; then pour into a towel, fold to enclose, and rub to remove as much of loose skins as possible. Let cool; then coarsely chop and set aside.

2 While nuts are toasting, in a food processor or blender, whirl bread to form fine crumbs. Pour crumbs into a medium-size nonstick frying pan and add garlic and thyme. Drizzle with oil and 1 tablespoon water. Then stir over medium-high heat until crumbs are lightly browned (5 to 7 minutes). Remove from pan and set aside.

3 Trim and discard roots and tough tops from leeks; remove and discard coarse outer leaves. Split leeks lengthwise. Thoroughly rinse leek halves between layers; tie each half with string to hold it together.

4 In a 5- to 6-quart pan, bring 8 cups water to a boil over high heat. Add leeks; reduce heat, cover, and simmer until tender when pierced (5 to 7 minutes). Carefully transfer leeks to a strainer; let drain. Snip and discard strings; arrange leeks on a platter. Sprinkle with crumb mixture, then hazelnuts; offer vinegar to add to taste.

makes 4 to 6 servings

per serving: 185 calories, 5 g protein, 31 g carbohydrates, 5 g total fat, 0 mg cholesterol, 134 mg sodium

dried tomato pilaf

preparation time: 15 minutes
cooking time: 35 to 45 minutes

1 tablespoon olive oil

8 ounces portabella or button mushrooms, sliced

1 medium-size onion, chopped

1 cup long-grain white rice

2½ cups fat-free reduced-sodium chicken broth

¾ cup dried tomatoes (not packed in oil), chopped

¼ cup chopped cilantro

Salt and pepper

1 Heat oil in a 3- to 4-quart pan over medium-high heat. Add mushrooms and onion; cook, stirring often, until almost all liquid has evaporated and vegetables are lightly browned (10 to 12 minutes).

2 Add rice and stir until opaque (3 to 4 minutes). Add broth and tomatoes.

3 Bring to a boil; then reduce heat, cover, and simmer until rice is tender to bite (20 to 25 minutes). Stir in cilantro. Season to taste with salt and pepper.

makes 6 servings

per serving: 181 calories, 6 g protein, 34 g carbohydrates, 3 g total fat, 0 mg cholesterol, 280 mg sodium

italian greens risotto

preparation time: about 1 hour

12 ounces broccoli rabe

12 ounces asparagus, tough ends snapped off

4 teaspoons olive oil

1 large onion, finely chopped

1 cup short- or medium-grain white rice

3 cups fat-free reduced-sodium chicken broth

½ cup dry white wine

½ cup grated Parmesan cheese

1 Cut off and discard any coarse stem ends from broccoli rabe; discard any bruised or yellow leaves. If any stems are thicker than ⅜ inch, cut them in half lengthwise. Rinse and drain broccoli rabe.

2 Chop or thinly slice half each of the broccoli rabe and asparagus. Leave remaining asparagus spears and broccoli rabe leaves and flowerets whole.

3 In a wide nonstick frying pan, combine chopped broccoli rabe, chopped asparagus, and 1 tablespoon of the oil. Cook over medium-high heat, stirring, until vegetables are just tender to bite (about 4 minutes). Remove from pan and set aside. To pan, add ½ cup water, whole asparagus spears, and whole broccoli rabe leaves and flowerets. Cover and cook, turning vegetables often with a wide spatula, until vegetables are just tender to bite (about 4 minutes). Lift from pan; set aside.

4 In same pan, combine remaining 1 teaspoon oil and onion; cook over medium-high heat, stirring often, until onion is tinged with brown (5 to 8 minutes). Add rice and stir until opaque (3 to 4 minutes). Stir in broth and wine. Bring to a boil, stirring often. Then reduce heat and simmer, uncovered, until rice is tender to bite and almost all liquid has been absorbed (about 25 minutes); stir occasionally at first, more often as mixture thickens. Stir in sautéed chopped vegetables and cheese. Spoon onto a platter; surround with whole vegetables and serve immediately.

makes 6 servings

per serving: 237 calories, 10 g protein, 35 g carbohydrates, 5 g total fat, 5 mg cholesterol, 480 mg sodium

brussels sprouts with mustard glaze

preparation time: about 20 minutes

4 cups Brussels sprouts

3 tablespoons firmly packed brown sugar

2 tablespoons cider vinegar

1 tablespoon Dijon mustard

2 teaspoons butter or margarine

Salt

1 Remove and discard coarse outer leaves from Brussels sprouts. Then rinse sprouts, drain, and place on a rack in a large pan above 1 inch of boiling water. Cover and steam, keeping water at a steady boil, until sprouts are tender when pierced (about 10 minutes).

2 When sprouts are almost done, combine sugar, vinegar, mustard, and butter in a wide nonstick frying pan. Cook over medium-high heat, stirring, until mixture bubbles vigorously. Stir in sprouts; season to taste with salt.

makes 4 servings

per serving: 116 calories, 4 g protein, 22 g carbohydrates, 3 g total fat, 5 mg cholesterol, 168 mg sodium

garlic mashed potatoes

preparation time: 55 minutes

1 tablespoon olive oil

3 or 4 medium-size heads garlic

4 pounds russet potatoes

1 large package Neufchâtel cheese,
   at room temperature

3/4 to 1 cup fat-free reduced-sodium
   chicken broth

Salt

1 Pour oil into a shallow baking pan. Cut garlic heads in half crosswise through cloves; place, cut side down, in pan. Bake in a 375° oven until cut side is golden brown (about 35 minutes). Using a thin spatula, lift garlic from pan and transfer to a rack; let stand until cool enough to touch (about 10 minutes).

2 While garlic is baking, peel potatoes and cut into 2-inch chunks; place in a 5- to 6-quart pan and add enough water to cover. Bring to a boil over medium-high heat; reduce heat, cover, and boil gently until potatoes mash very easily when pressed (25 to 30 minutes). Drain potatoes well; transfer to a large bowl and keep warm.

3 Reserve 1 or 2 half-heads of garlic. Squeeze cloves from remaining garlic; add to potatoes along with Neufchâtel cheese. Mash potatoes with a potato masher or an electric mixer, adding broth as needed to make potatoes as soft and creamy as desired. Season to taste with salt and swirl into a shallow serving dish. Garnish with reserved roasted garlic.

makes 8 servings

per serving: 304 calories, 9 g protein, 48 g carbohydrates, 9 g total fat, 22 mg cholesterol, 205 mg sodium

risotto with mushrooms

preparation time: about 1 hour

1 teaspoon olive oil

8 ounces mushrooms, thinly sliced

1 large onion, chopped

1 clove garlic, minced

1 cup short- or medium-grain white rice

1/4 teaspoon *each* dried thyme, dried marjoram,
   and dried rubbed sage

3 cups fat-free reduced sodium chicken broth

1/2 cup packed crumbled Gorgonzola
   or other blue-veined cheese

1 teaspoon dry sherry (or to taste)

1 Heat oil in a wide nonstick frying pan over medium heat. Add mushrooms, onion, and garlic. Cook, stirring often, until vegetables are soft and are beginning to stick to pan bottom (about 15 minutes); add water, 1 tablespoon at a time, if pan drippings begin to scorch.

2 Add rice, thyme, marjoram, and sage; stir until rice is opaque (3 to 4 minutes). Stir in broth. Bring to a boil, stirring often. Then reduce heat and simmer, uncovered, until rice is tender to bite and almost all liquid has been absorbed (about 25 minutes); stir occasionally at first, more often as mixture thickens.

3 Remove rice mixture from heat and stir in cheese and sherry.

makes 4 to 6 servings

per serving: 230 calories, 8 g protein, 38 g carbohydrates, 5 g total fat, 10 mg cholesterol, 450 mg sodium

roasted potatoes, fennel & green beans with sherry dressing

preparation time: 25 minutes
cooking time: 50 to 60 minutes

2 large heads fennel

1 pound slender green beans, ends trimmed

2 tablespoons olive oil

2 very large russet potatoes, peeled and cut into 1-inch chunks

1 teaspoon *each* mustard seeds, cumin seeds, and fennel seeds

⅓ cup sherry vinegar

⅓ cup Gewurztraminer or orange juice

1 tablespoon grated lemon peel

1 Trim stems from fennel, reserving some of the feathery green leaves for garnish. Trim and discard any bruised areas from fennel; then cut fennel into ¾-inch chunks. Transfer to a large, shallow baking pan. Add beans and 4 teaspoons of the oil; stir to coat vegetables. In a square 9-inch baking pan, mix potatoes and remaining 2 teaspoons oil.

2 Bake all vegetables in a 475° oven, stirring occasionally, until richly browned (about 45 minutes for fennel and beans, 50 to 60 minutes for potatoes). Watch carefully to prevent scorching. As pieces brown, remove them and keep warm; add water, ¼ cup at a time, if pans appear dry.

3 While vegetables are baking, stir mustard seeds, cumin seeds, and fennel seeds in a small frying pan over medium heat until fragrant (2 to 5 minutes). Remove pan from heat and stir in vinegar, Gewurztraminer, and lemon peel; set aside.

4 Transfer fennel, beans, and potatoes to a large rimmed serving bowl; add dressing and mix gently to coat vegetables. Garnish with reserved fennel leaves.

makes 4 to 6 servings

per serving: 210 calories, 5 g protein, 33 g carbohydrates, 6 g total fat, 0 mg cholesterol, 126 mg sodium

red bell peppers stuffed with caper rice

preparation time: about 1 hour

10 to 12 very small red, yellow, or orange bell peppers

1 cup short- or medium-grain white rice

4 teaspoons grated lemon peel

8 ounces sliced bacon, crisply cooked, drained, and crumbled

¼ cup drained capers

¼ cup seasoned rice vinegar

1 Cut off the top third of each pepper. With a small spoon, scoop out seeds and white membranes from pepper bases and tops; rinse and drain both bases and tops. If needed, trim pepper bases (without piercing them) so they will sit steadily.

2 In a 2- to 3-quart pan, combine rice, lemon peel, and 2½ cups water. Bring to a boil over high heat. Reduce heat, cover, and simmer until rice is tender to bite and almost all liquid has been absorbed (about 20 minutes). Remove from heat. With a fork, stir in bacon, capers, and vinegar.

3 Set pepper bases upright, spacing them slightly apart, in a shallow 10- by 15-inch baking pan. Mound rice mixture equally in pepper bases; set pepper tops in place. Bake in a 450° oven until peppers are blistered and rice mixture is hot in center (8 to 12 minutes).

makes 10 to 12 servings

per serving: 131 calories, 4 g protein, 22 g carbohydrates, 3 g total fat, 5 mg cholesterol, 263 mg sodium

fruited basmati pilaf

preparation time: 55 minutes

1 cup orange lentils

2 teaspoons butter or margarine

1 cup basmati or long-grain white rice

4¼ cups vegetable broth

1 can (about 12 oz.) mango or apricot nectar

⅛ teaspoon ground coriander

¼ cup coarsely chopped dried apricots

4 large mangoes

3 tablespoons lime juice

½ cup dried currants or raisins

⅓ cup thinly sliced green onion tops

¾ cup coarsely chopped salted roasted
  macadamia nuts or peanuts

Lime wedges or slices

1 Sort through lentils, discarding any debris. Rinse and drain lentils; then set aside.

2 Melt butter in a 4- to 5-quart pan over medium heat. Add rice and cook, stirring often, until opaque (about 3 minutes). Add broth, mango nectar, and coriander. Increase heat to medium-high and bring mixture just to a boil. Stir in lentils and apricots; then reduce heat, cover, and simmer until liquid has been absorbed and both rice and lentils are tender to bite (about 25 minutes). If any cooking liquid remains, drain and discard it.

3 While rice mixture is simmering, peel mangoes and slice fruit from pits into a large bowl. Add lime juice and mix gently to coat. Arrange mangoes decoratively around edge of a rimmed platter; cover and set aside.

4 Remove rice mixture from heat; stir in currants and onions. Spoon pilaf into center of platter; sprinkle macadamia nuts over mangoes and pilaf. Garnish with lime wedges.

makes 6 servings

per serving: 519 calories, 14 g protein, 91 g carbohydrates, 16 g total fat, 3 mg cholesterol, 745 mg sodium

green rice
with pistachios

preparation time: about 15 minutes
cooking time: about 1 hour

2 cups long-grain white rice

5½ cups low-sodium chicken broth

½ teaspoon ground nutmeg

1½ tablespoons canned green peppercorns
  in brine, rinsed and drained

12 ounces stemmed spinach leaves, rinsed well,
  drained, and finely chopped (about 3 cups
  lightly packed)

1 cup minced parsley

Salt and pepper

½ cup shelled salted roasted pistachio nuts,
  coarsely chopped

1 Spread rice in a shallow 3- to 3½-quart baking dish (about 9 by 13 inches). Bake in a 350° oven, stirring occasionally, until rice is lightly browned (about 35 minutes). In a 2- to 3-quart pan, combine 5 cups of the broth, nutmeg, and peppercorns. Bring to a boil over high heat. Leaving baking dish on oven rack, carefully stir broth mixture into rice. Cover dish tightly with foil. Continue to bake until liquid has been absorbed and rice is tender to bite (about 20 more minutes). Stir after 10 and 15 minutes, covering dish again after stirring.

2 Uncover baking dish and stir in remaining ½ cup broth, spinach, and ¾ cup of the parsley; bake for 5 more minutes. To serve, stir rice and season to taste with salt and pepper. Sprinkle with remaining ¼ cup parsley and pistachios.

makes 8 to 10 servings

per serving: 222 calories, 7 g protein, 38 g carbohydrates, 6 g total fat, 0 mg cholesterol, 161 mg sodium

risotto cakes
with tomato purée

preparation time: 25 minutes
cooking time: about 1 1/4 hours

2 tablespoons olive oil; or 2 tablespoons butter

1 1/4 cups short- or medium-grain white rice

1 3/4 cups fat-free reduced-sodium chicken broth

5 to 6 ounces mozzarella cheese, shredded

1/4 cup grated Parmesan cheese

4 green onions, finely chopped

1 can (about 14 1/2 oz.) diced tomatoes

1/4 cup plain nonfat yogurt

1/4 cup coarsely chopped fresh basil

Basil sprigs

1 Heat 1 tablespoon of the oil in a 3- to 4-quart pan over medium-high heat. Add rice and stir until opaque (3 to 4 minutes). Stir in broth and 1 1/2 cups water. Bring to a boil, stirring often. Then reduce heat and simmer, uncovered, until rice is tender to bite and almost all liquid has been absorbed (25 to 30 minutes); stir occasionally at first, more often as mixture thickens. Remove from heat and stir in mozzarella cheese, Parmesan cheese, and onions. Let cool uncovered. (At this point, you may cover and refrigerate until next day.)

2 In a food processor or blender, combine tomatoes and their liquid, yogurt, and chopped basil. Whirl until smoothly puréed; set aside.

3 Divide rice mixture into 12 equal portions; shape each portion into a cake about 3/4 inch thick. Heat 1 teaspoon of the oil in a wide nonstick frying pan over medium-high heat. Add risotto cakes to pan, a portion at a time (do not crowd pan); cook, turning once, until golden on. both sides (about 20 minutes). Add remaining 2 teaspoons oil to pan as needed. As cakes are cooked, arrange them in a single layer in a large, shallow baking pan; cover loosely with foil and keep warm in a 300° oven until all cakes have been cooked.

4 To serve, arrange cakes on individual plates; top with tomato purée and garnish with basil sprigs.

makes 6 servings

per serving: 286 calories, 13 g protein, 38 g carbohydrates, 9 g total fat, 12 mg cholesterol, 507 mg sodium

spanish-style linguine

preparation time: about 25 minutes

8 ounces dried linguine

1 jar (about 6 oz.) marinated artichokes, quartered

2 cloves garlic, minced or pressed

1 tablespoon anchovy paste

1 can (about 2 1/4 oz.) sliced black ripe olives, drained

1/2 cup chopped parsley

Pepper

Freshly grated Parmesan cheese

1 Bring 8 cups water to a boil in a 4- to 5-quart pan over medium-high heat. Stir in pasta and cook just until tender to bite (8 to 10 minutes); or cook according to package directions. Meanwhile, drain marinade from artichokes into a 1 1/2- to 2-quart pan. Place over medium heat. Add garlic and cook, stirring often, until pale golden (about 3 minutes). Add anchovy paste, olives, and artichokes. Cook, stirring gently, until hot (about 2 minutes).

2 Drain pasta well and return to pan. Add artichoke mixture and parsley. Lift with 2 forks to mix. Transfer pasta to a large serving bowl. Offer pepper and cheese to add to taste.

makes 4 to 6 servings

per serving: 227 calories, 8 g protein, 38 g carbohydrates, 5 g total fat, 2 mg cholesterol, 424 mg sodium

sweet corn risotto

preparation time: about 1 hour

4 medium-size ears corn

4 cups finely chopped onions

1 tablespoon butter or margarine

2 cups arborio or short-grain white rice

8 cups vegetable broth

About ½ cup lime juice

2 to 4 tablespoons thinly sliced green onion tops or snipped chives

½ cup finely shaved or shredded Parmesan cheese

Salt and pepper

1 Remove and discard husks and silk from corn. In a shallow pan, hold one ear of corn upright and, with a sharp knife, cut kernels from cob. Then, using blunt edge of knife, scrape juice from cob into pan. Repeat with remaining ears of corn. Discard cobs.

2 In a wide nonstick frying pan, combine 2 cups of the chopped onions, butter, and ¼ cup water. Cook over medium-high heat, stirring often, until onions are soft (5 to 10 minutes); add water, 1 tablespoon at a time, if pan appears dry. Add rice and cook, stirring often, until opaque (about 3 minutes). Meanwhile, bring broth to a simmer in a 3- to 4-quart pan; keep broth warm.

3 Add ¼ cup of the lime juice and 6 cups of the broth to rice mixture. Cook, stirring often, until liquid has been absorbed (about 15 minutes). Add remaining 2 cups broth, corn kernels and juice, and remaining 2 cups chopped onions. Cook, stirring often, until rice is tender to bite and mixture is creamy (about 10 minutes).

4 Spoon risotto into wide individual bowls; top with green onions and cheese. Season to taste with salt, pepper, and remaining lime juice.

makes 4 servings

per serving: 628 calories, 17 g protein, 120 g carbohydrates, 10 g total fat, 17 mg cholesterol, 2,289 mg sodium

bulgur relish

preparation time: about 45 minutes

2 teaspoons olive oil or salad oil

2 medium-size carrots, shredded

2 medium-size zucchini, shredded

1 medium-size red or green bell pepper, seeded and slivered

3 cloves garlic, minced or pressed

⅓ cup bulgur

2 cups low-sodium chicken broth

2 tablespoons reduced-sodium soy sauce

1 Heat oil in a wide nonstick frying pan over medium-high heat. Add carrots, zucchini, bell pepper, and garlic; cook, stirring, until vegetables are soft (about 5 minutes).

2 Stir in bulgur, broth, and soy sauce. Bring to a boil over high heat; then cover, remove from heat, and let stand until liquid has been absorbed and bulgur is tender to bite (about 20 minutes). Serve warm or at room temperature. If made ahead, cover and refrigerate for up to 2 days.

makes about 10 servings

per serving: 50 calories, 2 g protein, 9 g carbohydrates, 2 g total fat, 0 mg cholesterol, 153 mg sodium

garbanzo beans with olive pesto

preparation time: 30 to 35 minutes

4 slices sourdough sandwich bread, cut into ½-inch cubes

5 large tomatoes, thinly sliced

1 cup pitted ripe olives, drained

3 tablespoons drained capers

4 teaspoons lemon juice

2 teaspoons *each* Asian sesame oil and Dijon mustard

1 tablespoon honey (or to taste)

2 or 3 cloves garlic, peeled

¼ cup finely chopped fresh basil

3 tablespoons grated Parmesan cheese

2 cans (about 15 oz. *each*) garbanzo beans, drained and rinsed

Basil sprigs

1 Spread bread cubes in a single layer in a shallow baking pan. Bake in a 325° oven, stirring occasionally, until crisp and lightly browned (15 to 20 minutes). Set aside.

2 Arrange tomato slices, overlapping if necessary, in a large, shallow serving bowl. Set aside.

3 In a food processor or blender, combine olives, capers, lemon juice, oil, mustard, honey, and garlic; whirl until coarsely pureed, scraping sides of container as needed. With a spoon, stir in chopped basil and cheese. Transfer olive pesto to a large bowl; add beans and two-thirds of the croutons. Mix gently but thoroughly

4 Spoon bean salad over tomatoes; sprinkle with remaining croutons. Garnish with basil sprigs.

makes 4 to 6 servings

per serving: 286 calories, 11 g protein, 41 g carbohydrates, 10 g total fat, 2 mg cholesterol, 803 mg sodium

garlic-roasted potatoes & greens

preparation time: about 25 minutes
baking time: about 1 hour

Olive oil cooking spray

2 pounds thin-skinned potatoes, scrubbed and cut into ¾-inch cubes

6 large cloves garlic, peeled and cut into quarters

3 tablespoons red wine vinegar

1 tablespoon olive oil

Salt and pepper

3 to 4 cups lightly packed watercress sprigs, rinsed and crisped

1 Coat a shallow baking pan with cooking spray. Place potatoes and garlic in pan; stir to mix, then coat with cooking spray. Bake in a 450° oven until well browned (about 1 hour), turning with a wide spatula every 15 minutes.

2 Drizzle vinegar and oil over potatoes. Turn potato mixture gently with spatula to loosen any browned bits. Season to taste with salt and pepper; transfer to a wide bowl.

3 Coarsely chop about half the watercress; mix lightly with potatoes. Tuck remaining watercress around potatoes. Serve hot or at room temperature.

makes 4 to 6 servings

per serving: 184 calories, 4 g protein, 35 g carbohydrates, 3 g total fat, 0 mg cholesterol, 27 mg sodium

asian noodles

preparation time: about 30 minutes

12 ounces fresh Chinese noodles or linguine

1 teaspoon Asian sesame oil

1 tablespoon salad oil

1 small onion, thinly sliced lengthwise

2 tablespoons oyster sauce

8 ounces ground turkey

1 pound napa cabbage, thinly sliced crosswise

4 ounces oyster mushrooms, thinly sliced

2 medium-size carrots, cut into matchstick strips

½ cup fat-free reduced-sodium chicken broth

2 tablespoons reduced-sodium soy sauce

1 In a 5- to 6-quart pan, cook noodles in about 3 quarts boiling water until just tender to bite (3 to 5 minutes); or cook according to package directions. Drain well, toss with sesame oil, and keep warm.

2 Heat salad oil in a wide nonstick frying pan or wok over medium-high heat. When oil is hot, add onion and oyster sauce; then crumble in turkey. Stir-fry until onion is soft and turkey is no longer pink (about 3 minutes).

3 Add cabbage, mushrooms, carrots, and broth; cover and cook until carrots are just tender to bite (about 3 minutes). Uncover and continue to cook until liquid has evaporated (1 to 2 more minutes). Stir in soy sauce; add noodles and stir-fry until heated through.

makes 6 servings

per serving: 295 calories, 16 g protein, 41 g carbohydrates, 7 g total fat, 69 mg cholesterol, 563 mg sodium

ravioli with mushrooms, carrots & zucchini

preparation time: about 30 minutes

1 tablespoon butter or margarine

8 ounces mushrooms, finely chopped

2 large carrot, finely shredded

2 medium-size zucchini, finely shredded

3 cloves garlic, minced or pressed

1 tablespoon minced fresh basil
  or 1 teaspoon dried basil

½ cup low-fat (1%) cottage cheese

¾ cup nonfat milk

1 package (about 9 oz.) fresh low-fat
  or regular cheese ravioli

1 Melt butter in a wide non-stick frying pan over medium-high heat. Add mushrooms, carrots, zucchini, garlic, and basil. Cook, stirring often, until liquid has evaporated (about 10 minutes).

2 Place cottage cheese and ¼ cup of the milk in a blender or food processor. Whirl until smooth. Spoon into pan with vegetables and stir in remaining ½ cup milk. Cook over medium heat, stirring often, just until sauce begins to boil (about 2 minutes). Remove from heat and keep warm.

3 Bring 12 cups water to a boil in a 5- to 6-quart pan over medium-high heat. Separating any ravioli that are stuck together, stir in pasta and cook just until tender to bite (4 to 6 minutes); or cook according to package directions. Drain well. Transfer to a large serving bowl. Add sauce and mix thoroughly but gently.

makes 6 servings

per serving: 188 calories, 11 g protein, 26 g carbohydrates, 5 g total fat, 32 mg cholesterol, 279 mg sodium

tomato, potato & eggplant gratin

preparation time: about 45 minutes
broiling time: about 15 minutes
cooking time: about 15 minutes
baking time: 1 to 1 1/4 hours

Olive oil cooking spray

1 large eggplant, unpeeled,
    cut crosswise into 1/4-inch-thick slices

3 tablespoons olive oil

1 large onion, thinly sliced

1 medium-size red bell pepper,

seeded and finely chopped

3 large tomatoes, peeled, seeded,
    and chopped

3 cloves garlic, minced or pressed

1/4 teaspoon sugar

1/2 teaspoon dry thyme

5 large russet potatoes

Salt and pepper

Chopped parsley

1 Coat a large, shallow baking pan with cooking spray. Arrange eggplant slices in a single layer in pan; coat with cooking spray. Broil about 4 inches below heat until well browned (6 to 8 minutes).

2 Turn eggplant slices over, coat other sides with cooking spray, and broil until browned (5 to 6 more minutes). Set aside.

3 Heat 2 tablespoons of the oil in a wide frying pan over medium heat. Add onion and bell pepper. Cook, stirring often, until vegetables are soft but not browned (8 to 10 minutes). Stir in tomatoes, garlic, sugar, and thyme. Cook, stirring often, until tomatoes are soft (3 to 5 minutes). Remove from heat.

4 Peel and thinly slice potatoes. Spread a third of the potatoes in an oiled shallow 3-quart casserole; sprinkle with salt and pepper. Top with half the eggplant, then half the tomato sauce. Cover with half the remaining potatoes, sprinkle with salt and pepper, and add remaining eggplant and tomato sauce. Top with remaining potatoes; sprinkle with alt and pepper. Drizzle potatoes with remaining tablespoon oil.

5 Bake in a 375° oven until potatoes are lightly browned on top and tender when pierced (1 to 1 1/4 hours). Sprinkle with parsley.

makes 6 servings

per serving: 277 calories, 6 g protein, 47 g carbohydrates, 9 g total fat, 0 mg cholesterol, 28 mg sodium

golden acorn squash

preparation time: about 5 minutes
baking time: about 50 minutes

2 tablespoons butter or margarine

2 acorn squash, cut lengthwise into halves
    and seeded

3 tablespoons each firmly packed brown sugar
    and frozen orange juice concentrate (thawed)

3 tablespoons brandy or water

Orange slices (optional)

1 Place 1 tablespoon of the butter in a 9- by 13-inch baking pan. Place pan in a 350° oven to melt butter; when butter is melted, tilt pan to coat bottom. Place squash halves, cut side down, in pan; return to oven and bake until tender when pierced (about 35 minutes).

2 Meanwhile, in a small pan, mix remaining 1 tablespoon butter, sugar, orange juice concentrate, and brandy. Bring to a boil over high heat, stirring; then remove from heat.

3 Turn squash halves cut side up. Pour brandy-butter mixture evenly into each half. Continue to bake until edges of squash halves are browned (about 15 more minutes). Transfer squash halves to a platter or individual plates, taking care not to spill sauce. Garnish with orange slices, if desired.

makes 4 servings

per serving: 224 calories, 2 g protein, 38 g carbohydrates, 6 g total fat, 16 mg cholesterol, 69 mg sodium

roasted vegetable medley

preparation time: 30 minutes
cooking time: about 45 minutes

1 large beet, peeled

2 small red thin-skinned potatoes

1 medium-size sweet potato or yam, peeled

2 large carrots

1 small red onion

5 teaspoons olive oil

2 tablespoons *each* chopped fresh oregano
   and chopped fresh basil; or 2 teaspoons *each*
   dried oregano and dried basil

1 or 2 cloves garlic, minced or pressed

¼ cup grated Parmesan cheese

Oregano and basil sprigs

Salt

1 Cut beet, unpeeled thin-skinned potatoes, and sweet potato into ¾-inch chunks. Cut carrots diagonally into ½-inch pieces; cut onion into ¾-inch wedges. Combine all vegetables in a shallow 10- by 15-inch baking pan; drizzle with oil and toss to coat vegetables evenly with oil.

2 Bake in a 475° oven until vegetables are richly browned and tender when pierced (35 to 45 minutes), stirring occasionally. Watch carefully to prevent scorching. As pieces brown, remove them and keep warm; add water, ¼ cup at a time, if pan appears dry.

3 Transfer vegetables to a platter or serving dish and sprinkle with chopped oregano, chopped basil, garlic, and a little of the cheese. Garnish with oregano and basil sprigs. Season to taste with salt and remaining cheese.

makes 6 servings

per serving: 162 calories, 4 g protein, 26 g carbohydrates, 5 g total fat, 3 mg cholesterol, 104 mg sodium

honey carrots with currants

preparation time: about 30 minutes

1½ cups water

1½ pounds large carrots, cut into
   ⅛-inch-thick, 3- to 4-inch-long sticks

2 tablespoons *each* honey and lemon juice

¼ cup dried currants

¼ cup Major Grey's chutney, minced

¼ cup orange juice

Salt

Finely slivered orange peel

1 In a 4- to 5-quart pan, bring water to a boil over high heat; add carrots, honey, and lemon juice. Cook, stirring often, until carrots are barely tender to bite (about 3 minutes). Drain carrots, reserving liquid; place carrots in a rimmed serving dish and keep warm.

2 Return cooking liquid to pan; bring to a boil over high heat. Boil, uncovered, until reduced to about ¼ cup (about 10 minutes). Add currants; stir until liquid begins to caramelize and currants look puffy. Stir in chutney. (At this point, you may let carrots and currant topping cool, then cover and refrigerate separately for up to 1 day.)

3 To serve, stir orange juice into currant topping, then spoon topping over carrots. Season to taste with salt; sprinkle with orange peel.

makes 6 to 8 servings

per serving: 108 calories, 1 g protein, 27 g carbohydrates, 0.2 g total fat, 0 mg cholesterol, 136 mg sodium

italian oven fried potatoes

preparation time: about 20 minutes
baking time: 35 to 45 minutes

2 pounds red thin-skinned potatoes, scrubbed
   and cut into 1-inch chunks

1 to 2 tablespoons olive oil

2 tablespoons *each* minced fresh oregano
   and minced fresh basil; or 2 teaspoons *each*
   dry oregano and dry basil

1 clove garlic, minced or pressed

1/3 cup grated Parmesan cheese

Salt

Oregano and basil sprigs

1 In a 10- by 15-inch rimmed baking pan, mix potatoes and oil. Bake in a 475° oven until potatoes are, richly browned (35 to 45 minutes). After potatoes have begun to brown (but not before then), turn them over several times with a wide spatula.

2 Transfer potatoes to a serving bowl and sprinkle with minced oregano and basil, garlic, and 3 tablespoons of the cheese. Stir to mix; season to taste with salt. Top with remaining cheese and garnish with oregano and basil sprigs.

makes 4 servings

per serving: 264 calories, 7 g protein, 42 g carbohydrates, 8 g total fat, 5 mg cholesterol, 141 mg sodium

baked new potatoes & apples

preparation time: about 15 minutes
baking time: about 50 minutes

2 pounds small thin-skinned potatoes,
   scrubbed

2 medium-size onions,
   cut into 1-inch-wide wedges

2 tablespoons olive oil

1 pound red-skinned apples

1¼ cups beef broth

¾ cup apple juice

2 tablespoons cornstarch

¾ teaspoon ground allspice

1 Place potatoes in a 9- by 13-inch baking pan. Separate onion wedges into layers and sprinkle over potatoes. Add oil and mix well. Bake in a 400° oven for 25 minutes, stirring occasionally.

2 Meanwhile, core apples and cut into ¾-inch-wide wedges. Also, in a small bowl, stir together broth, apple juice, cornstarch, and allspice.

3 When potatoes have baked for 25 minutes, add apples and juice mixture to pan; stir to combine. Continue to bake, spooning juices over apples and potatoes several times, until potatoes are very tender when pierced and juices begin to form thick bubbles (about 25 minutes).

makes 8 servings

per serving: 191 calories, 3 g protein, 37 g carbohydrates, 4 g otal fat, 0 mg cholesterol, 140 mg sodium

mashed parsnips & sunchokes

preparation time: about 35 minutes
cooking time: 45 to 50 minutes

3 tablespoons vinegar or lemon juice

4 cups water

1½ pounds sunchokes (Jerusalem artichokes)

2 cups low-sodium chicken broth

2 pounds parsnips, peeled and cut
   into 1-inch chunks

1¼ teaspoon *each* ground nutmeg
   and ground white pepper

1 tablespoon butter or margarine

2 tablespoons reduced-fat sour cream
   or whipping cream

Salt

Chopped parsley

1 Prepare acid water by combining vinegar and water in a large bowl. Peel sunchokes and cut them into ½-inch cubes; as you cut cubes, immediately immerse them in acid water to prevent browning.

2 Drain sunchokes and place in a 3- to 4-quart pan. Add broth, parsnips, nutmeg, and white pepper. Bring to a boil over high heat; then adjust heat so mixture boils gently. Cover and cook until parsnips are soft enough to mash easily (about 35 minutes). Uncover, bring to a boil over high heat, and boil until liquid has evaporated (10 to 15 minutes); as liquid boils down, stir often and watch mixture carefully to avoid scorching.

3 Smoothly mash vegetables with an electric mixer or a potato masher (sunchokes may retain a little texture). Mix in butter and sour cream. Season to taste with salt; sprinkle with parsley.

makes 6 servings

per serving: 193 calories, 4 g protein, 38 g carbohydrates, 3 g total fat, 7 mg cholesterol, 50 mg sodium

wine-poached carrots

preparation time: 35 to 40 minutes

1¼ cups slightly sweet, fruity wine,
   such as Sauvignon Blanc, Chenin Blanc,
   Gewurztraminer, Johannesburg Riesling,
   or white Zinfandel

¾ cup low-sodium chicken broth

1 teaspoon butter or margarine

1 pounds small carrots
   (*each* about 5 inches long)

Salt

Chervil or Italian parsley sprigs (optional)

1 In a wide frying pan, combine wine, broth, and fitter. Bring to a boil over high heat. Add carrots; reduce heat, cover, and simmer, shaking pan occasionally, until carrots are tender when pierced (10 to 15 minutes).

2 Uncover pan; bring cooking liquid to a boil over high heat. Then boil, uncovered, shaking pan ten, until liquid evaporates and carrots begin to own (about 10 minutes). Season carrots to taste with salt; garnish with chervil sprigs, if desired.

makes 6 servings

per serving: 60 calories, 1 g protein, 12 g carbohydrates, 1 g total fat, mg cholesterol, 55 mg sodium

polenta with fresh tomato sauce

preparation time: about 45 minutes

3 pounds pear-shaped (Roma-type) tomatoes, peeled (if desired) and coarsely chopped

2 large yellow bell peppers, seeded and chopped

1 cup lightly packed slivered fresh basil or ¼ cup dried basil

2 cloves garlic, minced

2 cups low-fat (2%) milk

½ cup canned vegetable broth

1 cup polenta or yellow cornmeal

1 teaspoon chopped fresh sage or teaspoon ground sage

½ teaspoon salt

½ cup grated Parmesan cheese

Basil sprigs

1 In a 3- to 4-quart pan, combine two-thirds each of the tomatoes and bell peppers, half the slivered basil, and all the garlic. Cook over medium-high heat, stirring often, until tomatoes begin to fall apart (15 to 20 minutes).

2 Meanwhile, in a 4- to 5-quart pan, bring milk and broth just to a boil over medium-high heat. Stir in polenta, sage, and salt. Reduce heat and simmer, uncovered, stirring often and scraping bottom of pan with a long-handled spoon (mixture will spatter), until polenta tastes creamy (about 15 minutes). Remove pan from heat; stir in cheese. Keep warm.

3 Working quickly, stir remaining tomatoes, bell peppers, and slivered basil into sauce. Divide polenta equally among deep individual bowls and top with sauce. Garnish with basil sprigs.

makes 4 servings

per serving: 346 calories, 16 g protein, 58 g carbohydrates, 7 g total fat, 18 mg cholesterol, 681 mg sodium

stir-fried carrots & peppers

preparation time: about 25 minutes

1 tablespoon olive oil

1½ pounds carrots, cut into matchstick pieces

1 medium-size red bell pepper, seeded and cut into matchstick pieces

2 medium-size fresh Anaheim (California) chiles, seeded and cut into matchstick pieces

2 teaspoons fresh rosemary leaves or 1 teaspoon dry rosemary

Pepper

Heat oil in a 10- to 12-inch frying pan over medium-high heat; add carrots and cook, stirring, just until lightly browned (about 6 minutes). Add bell pepper, chiles, and rosemary; cook, stirring, until pepper pieces are limp (about 2 minutes). Season to taste with pepper.

makes 6 servings

per serving: 76 calories, 1 g protein, 13 g carbohydrates, 3 g total fat, 0 mg cholesterol, 41 mg sodium

creamed spinach in a squash shell

preparation time: about 1 hour

Steamed Squash (recipe follows)

1 large onion, finely chopped

¼ cup water

1¼ cups low-sodium chicken broth

3 tablespoons all-purpose flour

1 cup reduced-fat sour cream

1 teaspoon each freshly grated nutmeg and grated lemon peel

3 packages (about 10 oz. *each*) frozen chopped spinach, thawed and squeezed dry

Salt and pepper

Finely slivered lemon peel (optional)

1 Prepare Steamed Squash. While squash is cooking, combine onion and water in a wide frying pan. Cook over high heat, stirring occasionally, until liquid evaporates and onion begins to brown (about 10 minutes). To deglaze, add ¼ cup of the broth and stir to scrape browned bits free. Then continue to cook, stirring occasionally, until onion begins to brown again. Remove from heat and stir in flour. Gradually stir in remaining 1 cup broth and ½ cup of the sour cream; add nutmeg and the 1 teaspoon lemon peel. Bring to a boil over high heat, stirring; then boil, stirring, for 3 minutes. Remove from heat and stir in spinach. Pour one-quarter to one-half of the spinach mixture into a food processor or blender; whirl until pureed. Return puree to pan. Stir in remaining ½ cup sour cream; season to taste with salt and pepper.

2 Reheat spinach, if necessary. Fill hollowed-out squash with spinach; sprinkle with slivered lemon peel, if desired. Set lid in place, if desired. To serve, remove lid; scoop squash from the shell as you spoon out spinach.

makes 8 servings

STEAMED SQUASH

1 Use 1 squat, round red kuri squash (orange in color) or kabocha squash (green in color); choose a 4-pound squash, 7 to 8 inches in diameter. Rinse squash and pierce through top to center in 2 or 3 places, using a metal skewer. For easy handling, set squash on a piece of cheesecloth large enough to enclose it. Tie cheesecloth loosely on top of squash (leave some access to squash for testing).

2 Choose a 5- to 6-quart pan at least 1 inch wider than squash. Set squash on a rack in pan above ¾ to 1 inch boiling water (water should not touch squash). Cover and steam over medium heat, keeping water at a steady boil, until squash is very tender when pierced (about 30 minutes).

3 Protecting your hands, use cheesecloth to lift squash from pan; untie cloth. Neatly slice off top quarter of squash to make a lid. With a small spoon, gently scoop out seeds and discard; take care not to tear or poke a hole in shell (some kinds are more fragile, so handle carefully).

per serving: 189 calories, 8 g protein, 34 g carbohydrates, 5 g total fat, 10 mg cholesterol, 96 mg sodium

green pea pods with red onions

preparation time: about 30 minutes

4 cups water

¹/₂ cup red wine vinegar

1 teaspoon each mustard seeds and cumin seeds

2 large red onions, thinly sliced

1 teaspoon sugar

Salt

2 pounds Chinese pea pods (also called snow or sugar peas), ends and strings removed

1 In a 5- to 6-quart pan, bring the 4 cups water to a boil over high heat. Add 5 tablespoons of the vinegar, mustard seeds, cumin seeds, and onions. Cook just until onions are limp (about 2 minutes). Pour into a fine strainer; drain well. In a medium-size bowl, stir together sugar and remaining 3 tablespoons vinegar; stir in drained onion-seed mixture. Season to taste with salt and set aside.

2 Rinse pan well. Then cook pea pods, uncovered, in pan in about 3 quarts boiling water just until they turn a brighter green (about 2 minutes). Drain pea pods well and arrange in a shallow 3- to 4-quart casserole. Let cool.

3 Just before serving, spoon onion mixture over pea pods.

makes 8 to 10 servings

per serving: 68 calories, 4 g protein, 13 g carbohydrates, 0.4 g total fat, 0 mg cholesterol, 10 mg sodium

chilled sugar snap peas with mint-bacon topping

preparation time: about 30 minutes
cooling time: at least 10 minutes

1¹/₂ to 2 pounds sugar snap peas or Chinese pea pods (also called snow or sugar peas), ends and strings removed

1 tablespoon sugar

2 teaspoons cornstarch

¹/₂ cup each low-sodium chicken broth and unseasoned rice vinegar

2 tablespoons minced fresh mint

4 or 5 thick slices bacon crisply cooked, drained, and crumbled

1 In a 5- to 6-quart pan, cook peas, uncovered, in about 3 quarts boiling water until tender-crisp to bite (about 2 minutes). Drain, immerse in cold water until cool, and drain again. Arrange in a serving bowl and set aside.

2 In a small pan, mix sugar and cornstarch; then blend in broth and vinegar. Bring to boil over high heat, stirring. Remove from heat and let stand until cool (at least 10 minutes).

3 To serve, stir mint into sauce; pour sauce over peas and sprinkle with bacon.

makes 8 servings

per serving: 77 calories, 4 g protein, 30 g carbohydrates, 2 g total fat, 3 mg cholesterol, 73 mg sodium

READ LABELS: If you're trying to avoid excessive fat, you've probably already learned to sort out the numbers that matter to you. If you prefer to avoid preservatives and additives, look at several forms of the same product and choose the one containing the fewest such ingredients.

broccoli & bell pepper with couscous

preparation time: about 30 minutes

1½ cups fat-free reduced-sodium chicken broth or canned vegetable broth

¼ to ½ teaspoon dried oregano

1 cup couscous

1 tablespoon pine nuts or slivered almonds

4 cups broccoli flowerets

1 teaspoon olive oil or vegetable oil

1 small red bell pepper, seeded and cut into thin slivers

2 tablespoons balsamic vinegar

1 In a 3- to 4-quart pan, combine broth and oregano. Bring to a boil over high heat; stir in couscous. Cover, remove from heat, and let stand until liquid has been absorbed (about 5 minutes). Transfer couscous to a rimmed platter and keep warm; fluff occasionally with a fork.

2 While couscous is standing, stir pine nuts in a wide nonstick frying pan or wok over medium-low heat until golden (2 to 4 minutes). Pour out of pan and set aside. To pan, add broccoli and ¼ cup water. Cover and cook over medium-high heat until broccoli is tender-crisp to bite (about 5 minutes). Uncover and stir-fry until liquid has evaporated. Spoon broccoli over couscous and keep warm.

3 Heat oil in pan. When oil is hot, add bell pepper and stir-fry until just tender-crisp to bite (2 to 3 minutes). Add vinegar and remove from heat; stir to scrape any browned bits from pan bottom.

4 Immediately pour pepper mixture over broccoli and couscous; sprinkle with pine nuts and serve.

makes 4 servings

per serving: 248 calories, 12 g protein, 45 g carbohydrates, 3 g total fat, 0 mg cholesterol, 278 mg sodium

garlic & rosemary green beans

preparation time: about 20 minutes

¼ to ½ ounce prosciutto or bacon, chopped

1 or 2 cloves garlic, minced or pressed

1½ teaspoons chopped fresh rosemary or ½ teaspoon

1 pound slender green beans, ends removed

Pepper

1 In a wide nonstick frying pan or wok, stir-fry prosciutto over medium-high heat just until crisp (about 1 minute). Remove from dried rosemary pan with a slotted spoon and set aside.

2 Add garlic, chopped rosemary, and 2 tablespoons water to beans, ends removed pan. Stir-fry just until garlic is fragrant (about 30 seconds; do not scorch). Add beans, ⅓ cup water, and salt. Cover and cook Rosemary sprigs just until beans are tender to bite (about 3 minutes). Uncover and stir-fry until liquid has evaporated.

3 Arrange beans on a rimmed platter, sprinkle with prosciutto, and garnish with rosemary sprigs. Season to taste with pepper.

makes 4 servings

per serving: 39 calories, 3 g protein, 8 g carbohydrates, 0.5 g total fat, 2 mg cholesterol, 125 mg sodium

almond & zucchini stir-fry

preparation time: about 35 minutes

1 cup long-grain white rice

½ cup slivered almonds

6 large zucchini, cut into ¼- by 2-inch sticks

2 cloves garlic, minced or pressed

About 2 tablespoons reduced-sodium soy sauce

1 In a 3- to 4-quart pan, bring 2 cups water to a boil over high heat; stir in rice. Reduce heat, cover, and simmer until liquid has been absorbed and rice is tender to bite (about 20 minutes).

2 Meanwhile, in a wide nonstick frying pan or wok, stir almonds over medium heat until golden (4 to 5 minutes). Pour out of pan and set aside. To pan, add zucchini, garlic, and 2 tablespoons water. Increase heat to medium-high; stir-fry until zucchini is tender-crisp to bite and liquid has evaporated (about 9 minutes). Add 2 tablespoons of the soy sauce; mix gently.

3 To serve, spoon rice into a large bowl and pour zucchini on top of it; sprinkle with almonds. Offer more soy sauce to add to taste.

makes 6 servings

per serving: 205 calories, 7 g protein, 32 g carbohydrates, 6 g total fat, 0 mg cholesterol, 207 mg sodium

broccoli with rice & pine nuts

preparation time: about 5 minutes
cooking time: about 30 minutes

¼ cup pine nuts or slivered almonds

2 teaspoons olive oil or vegetable oil

⅔ cup long-grain white rice

⅓ cup golden raisins

2 teaspoons chili powder

2 vegetable bouillon cubes dissolved in 2½ cups hot water

1¼ pounds broccoli

1 Toast pine nuts in a wide nonstick frying pan over medium-low heat until lightly browned (about 3 minutes), stirring. Remove from pan and set aside.

2 In same pan, heat oil over medium-high heat. Add rice, raisins, and chili powder. Cook, stirring, until rice begins to turn opaque (about 3 minutes). Stir in bouillon mixture; reduce heat, cover tightly, and simmer for 15 minutes.

3 Meanwhile, cut off and discard tough ends of broccoli stalks. Cut off flowerets in bite-size pieces and set aside. Thinly slice remainder of stalks.

4 Distribute broccoli flowerets and sliced stalks over rice mixture. Cover and continue to cook until broccoli is just tender to bite (7 to 10 more minutes). Mix gently, transfer to a warm serving platter, and sprinkle with pine nuts.

makes 4 servings

per serving: 247 calories, 8 g protein, 41 g carbohydrates, 8 g total fat, 0 mg cholesterol, 499 mg sodium

green & brown rice

preparation time: 25 minutes
cooking time: about 1 hour and 10 minutes

2 cups long-grain brown rice

¾ cup split peas

4 cups vegetable broth

2½ cups nonfat milk

2 tablespoons drained capers

½ teaspoon ground nutmeg

6 ounces fresh spinach, stems and any yellow
   or wilted leaves discarded, remaining leaves
   rinsed, drained, and finely chopped

½ cup grated Parmesan cheese

⅓ cup thinly sliced green onions

Whole fresh spinach leaves, rinsed and crisped

⅓ cup finely chopped parsley

½ cup salted roasted almonds, chopped

1 Spread rice in a shallow 3- to 3½-quart casserole, about 9 by 13 inches. Bake in a 350° oven, stirring occasionally, until rice is golden brown (about 25 minutes).

2 Meanwhile, sort through peas, discarding any debris; rinse and drain peas, then set aside.

3 In a 3- to 4-quart pan, combine 3½ cups of the broth, milk, capers, and nutmeg. Bring just to a boil over medium-high heat. Leaving casserole in oven, carefully stir broth mixture and peas into rice. Cover tightly and bake until almost all liquid has been absorbed (about 40 minutes); stir after 20 and 30 minutes, covering casserole tightly again each time.

4 Uncover casserole and stir in remaining ½ cup broth, chopped spinach, cheese, and onions; bake, uncovered, for 5 more minutes.

5 To serve, line 6 individual plates with whole spinach leaves. Stir rice mixture and spoon atop spinach; sprinkle with parsley and almonds.

makes 6 servings

per serving: 463 calories, 19 g protein, 70 g carbohydrates, 13 g total fat, 7 mg cholesterol, 1,049 mg sodium

pastina with peas

preparation time: about 35 minutes

2 ounces thinly sliced prosciutto or bacon,
   cut into thin strips

1½ cups dried orzo or other tiny
   rice-shaped pasta

1 package (about 1 lb.) frozen tiny peas

¼ cup thinly sliced green onions

¼ cup chopped fresh mint

¼ cup olive oil

1 teaspoon finely shredded lemon peel

2 tablespoons lemon juice

Mint sprigs

Pepper

1 In a wide nonstick frying pan, cook prosciutto over medium-high heat, stirring often, just until crisp (about 3 minutes). Remove from pan and set aside.

2 In a 5- to 6-quart (5- to 6-liter) pan, bring about 3 quarts water to a boil over medium-high heat; stir in pasta and cook until just tender to bite, about 8 minutes. (Or cook pasta according to package directions.)

3 Drain rinse with cold water until cool, and drain well again. Pour pasta into a large serving bowl; add peas, onions, and chopped mint. Mix gently.

4 In a small bowl, beat oil, lemon peel, and lemon juice until blended. Add to pasta mixture; mix gently but thoroughly. Sprinkle with prosciutto and garnish with mint sprigs. Season to taste with pepper.

makes 6 servings

per serving: 364 calories, 14 g protein, 52 g carbohydrates, 12 g total fat, 8 mg cholesterol, 282 mg sodium

asparagus with garlic crumbs

preparation times: 40 minutes

---

3 slices sourdough sandwich bread,
   torn into pieces

2 teaspoons olive oil

2 cloves garlic, minced or pressed

36 thick asparagus spears, tough ends
   snapped off

Salt and pepper

1 In a blender or food processor, whirl bread to form fine crumbs. Pour crumbs into a wide nonstick frying pan; add oil and garlic. Cook over medium-high heat, stirring often, until crumbs are lightly browned (5 to 7 minutes). Remove from pan and set aside.

2 Trim ends of asparagus spears so that spears are all the same length (reserve scraps for soups or salads). For the sweetest flavor and most tender texture, peel spears with a vegetable peeler.

3 In frying pan, bring about 1 inch water to a boil over medium-high heat. Add a third of the asparagus and cook, uncovered, until just tender when pierced (about 4 minutes). Lift from pan with a slotted spoon and place in a bowl of ice water to cool. Repeat with remaining asparagus, cooking it in 2 batches.

4 Drain cooled asparagus well; then arrange on a large platter, Sprinkle with crumb mixture; season to taste with salt and pepper.

makes 8 servings

per serving: 70 calories, 5 g protein, 11 g carbohydrates, 2 g total fat, 0 mg cholesterol, 68 mg sodium

roasted potatoes & carrots with citrus dressing

preparation time: about 15 minutes
baking time: 35 to 45 minutes

Citrus Dressing (page 155)

2 pounds small red thin-skinned potatoes,
   scrubbed and cut into 1-inch chunks

4 teaspoons olive oil or salad oil

4 medium-size carrots, cut into 1-inch chunks

Salt and pepper

Basil sprigs

1 Prepare Citrus Dressing; refrigerate.

2 In a lightly oiled 10- by 15-inch rimmed baking pan, mix potatoes with 2 teaspoons of the oil. In another lightly oiled 10- by 15-inch rimmed baking pan, mix carrots with remaining 2 teaspoons oil. Bake potatoes and carrots in a 475° oven, stirring occasionally, until richly browned (35 to 45 minutes); switch positions of baking pans halfway through baking.

3 In a shallow bowl, combine potatoes, carrots, and Citrus Dressing. Serve hot or warm. Before serving, season to taste with salt and pepper; garnish with basil sprigs.

makes 6 to 8 servings

per serving: 176 calories, 3 g protein, 35 g carbohydrates, 3 g total fat, 0 mg cholesterol, 66 mg sodium

desserts

apple-fennel tart

preparation time: 30 minutes
cooking time: about 1¼ hours

¹/₂ cup dried currants

³/₄ cup plus 2 teaspoons all-purpose flour

¹/₂ cup regular rolled oats

¹/₄ cup butter or margarine, cut into chunks

1 large egg white

¹/₃ cup granulated sugar

1 teaspoon ground cinnamon

2 cups sliced apples such as Newtown Pippin (cut slices ¹/₄ inch thick)

1¹/₂ cups sliced fennel (cut slices ¹/₄ inch thick)

2 teaspoons lemon juice

About 2 tablespoons sifted powdered sugar

1 Place currants in a small bowl and add enough water to cover. Let stand until currants are softened (about 10 minutes), stirring occasionally. Drain well; set aside.

2 In a food processor, combine ³/₄ cup of the flour, oats, and butter. Whirl until mixture resembles fine crumbs. Add egg white; whirl until dough holds together. Press dough evenly over bottom and sides of an 8-inch tart pan with a removable rim.

3 In a large bowl, mix remaining 2 teaspoons flour, granulated sugar, cinnamon, and currants. Add apples, fennel, and lemon juice; mix well. Pour fruit mixture into pan; pat to make level.

4 Bake on lowest rack of a 425° oven until top of filling begins to brown (about 45 minutes). Drape tart with foil; continue to bake until juices begin to bubble (about 30 more minutes).

5 Remove pan rim; slide a wide spatula under hot tart to release crust (leave tart in place). Serve warm or cool; dust with powdered sugar before serving.

makes 6 servings

per serving: 268 calories, 4 g protein, 46 g carbohydrates, 8 g total fat, 21 mg cholesterol, 116 mg sodium

cherry apple jubilee

preparation time: about 25 minutes

¹/₂ cup dried pitted cherries or raisins

2 tablespoons brandy

About 1 tablespoon kirsch

3 large Golden Delicious apples

1 tablespoon lemon juice

¹/₃ cup firmly packed brown sugar

2 cups vanilla nonfat frozen yogurt

Mint sprigs

1 In a small bowl, combine cherries, brandy, and 1 tablespoon of the kirsch; let stand until cherries are softened (about 10 minutes), stirring occasionally.

2 Meanwhile, peel and core apples; then cut into ¹/₄- to ¹/₂-inch-thick slices. Place in a large bowl, add lemon juice, and mix gently to coat. Set aside.

3 In a wide nonstick frying pan or wok, combine sugar and 2 tablespoons water. Add apples; stir-fry gently over medium-high heat until apples are almost tender when pierced (4 to 5 minutes). Add cherries (and any soaking liquid) and stir just until heated through.

4 Divide fruit mixture among 4 individual bowls; top equally with frozen yogurt. Garnish with mint sprigs. Offer additional kirsch to drizzle over yogurt, if desired.

makes 4 servings

per serving: 323 calorie, 2 g protein, 74 g carbohydrates, 0.5 g total fat, 0 mg cholesterol, 53 mg sodium

cream cheese blond brownies

preparation time: about 40 minutes

1 large package (about 8 oz.) nonfat
  cream cheese, at room temperature

1/2 cup granulated sugar

2 large egg whites

1/4 cup nonfat sour cream

1 1/4 cups plus 1 tablespoon all-purpose flour

1 tablespoon vanilla

1 teaspoon baking powder

1/4 cup chopped walnuts

1/3 cup pure maple syrup

1/3 cup firmly packed brown sugar

1/3 cup butter or margarine,
  at room temperature

1 large egg

1 In a small bowl, combine cream cheese, granulated sugar, egg whites, sour cream, 1 tablespoon of the flour, and 1 teaspoon of the vanilla. Beat until smooth; set aside. In another small bowl, stir together remaining 1 1/4 cups flour, baking powder, and walnuts; set aside.

2 In a large bowl, combine syrup, brown sugar, butter, egg, and remaining 2 teaspoons vanilla. Beat until smooth. Add flour mixture; beat until dry ingredients are evenly moistened.

3 Pour two-thirds of the brownie batter into a lightly greased 8-inch-square nonstick or regular baking pan; spread to make level. Pour cheese mixture evenly over batter. Drop remaining batter by spoonfuls over cheese mixture; swirl with a knife to blend batter slightly with cheese mixture.

4 Bake in a 350° oven until a wooden pick inserted in center comes out clean (about 25 minutes; pierce brownie, not cheese mixture). Let cool in pan on a rack, then cut into 2-inch squares.

makes 16 brownies

per brownie: 168 calories, 4 g protein, 25 g carbohydrates, 6 g total fat, 25 mg cholesterol, 153 mg sodium

ginger bars

preparation time: 35 to 40 minutes

1 cup whole wheat flour

1/4 cup sugar

1/2 teaspoon baking soda

3 tablespoons coarsely chopped crystallized or
  candied ginger

1/4 cup nonfat milk

1/4 cup molasses

2 large egg whites

1 In a large bowl, stir together flour, sugar, baking soda, and ginger. Add milk, molasses, and egg whites; beat until smoothly blended.

2 Spread batter evenly in a lightly greased 8-inch-square nonstick or regular baking pan. Bake in a 350° oven until center springs back when lightly pressed (20 to 25 minutes). Serve warm or cool; to serve, cut into 2-inch squares. These bars are best eaten fresh, so serve them the same day you make them.

makes 16 bars

per bar: 67 calories, 2 g protein, 15 g carbohydrates, 0.4 g total fat, 0.1 mg cholesterol, 52 mg sodium

molasses sugar cookies

preparation time: about 30 minutes

2 cups all-purpose flour

1 1/2 teaspoons baking powder

1 teaspoon ground ginger

1 teaspoon ground cinnamon

1/2 teaspoon salt

1/4 teaspoon baking soda

1/2 cup butter or margarine,
   at room temperature

1/2 cup firmly packed brown sugar

2 large egg whites

1/2 cup molasses

2 teaspoons instant espresso powder
   or coffee powder

About 2/3 cup sugar cubes, coarsely crushed

About 1/4 cup granulated sugar

1 In a medium-size bowl, stir together flour, baking powder, ginger, cinnamon, salt, and baking soda; set aside.

2 In a food processor or a large bowl, combine butter, brown sugar, egg whites, molasses, instant espresso powder, and 1/2 cup water. Whirl or beat with an electric mixer until smooth. Add flour mixture to butter mixture; whirl or beat until dry ingredients are evenly moistened.

3 Spoon rounded 1-tablespoon portions of dough onto lightly greased large nonstick or regular baking sheets, spacing cookies about 2 inches apart.

4 Bake in a 350° oven for 5 minutes. Remove from oven. Working quickly, sprinkle each cookie with about 3/4 teaspoon of the crushed sugar cubes; press in lightly. Return cookies to oven and bake until firm to the touch (about 2 more minutes). Let cookies cool on baking sheets for about 3 minutes. Transfer to racks, sprinkle with granulated sugar, and cool completely.

makes about 3 dozen cookies

per cookie: 93 calories, 0.9 g protein, 17 g carbohydrates, 3 g total fat, 7 mg cholesterol, 91 mg sodium

cherry chimichangas

preparation time: about 25 minutes

2 teaspoons berry-flavored liqueur

1 or 2 teaspoons cornstarch

1/4 cup cherry preserves

1 teaspoon grated lemon peel

2 cups pitted, chopped fresh cherries,
   or 2 cups frozen pitted dark sweet cherries,
   thawed, chopped, and drained well

6 flour tortillas

About 1/3 cup nonfat milk

Powdered sugar

1 In a bowl, combine liqueur and cornstarch until smooth (use 1 teaspoon cornstarch if using fresh cherries; use 2 teaspoons cornstarch mixed with 2 teaspoons water if using thawed frozen cherries). Stir in preserves, lemon peel, and cherries.

2 To assemble each chimichanga, brush both sides of a tortilla liberally with milk; let stand briefly to soften tortilla. Place a sixth of the filling on tortilla. Lap ends of tortilla over filling; then fold sides to center to make a packet. Place chimichanga, seam side down, on a lightly oiled 12- by 15-inch baking sheet; brush with milk. Repeat to make 5 more chimichangas.

3 Bake in a 500° oven, brushing with milk twice, until golden brown (8 to 10 minutes). Cool slightly, dust with sugar, and serve warm.

makes 6 chimichangas

per chimichanga: 203 calories, 4 g protein, 40 g carbohydrates, 3 g total fat, 0.3 mg cholesterol, 180 mg sodium

orange pudding parfaits

preparation time: about 35 minutes
chilling time: about 4 hours

3 tablespoons quick-cooking tapioca

$^1/_3$ cup sugar

2 egg whites

2 $^1/_2$ cups nonfat milk

$^1/_2$ teaspoon vanilla

1 tablespoon *each* grated orange peel
     and orange-flavored liqueur

2 large oranges

1 In a 2- to 3-quart pan, stir together tapioca, sugar, egg whites, and milk; let stand for 5 minutes. Then bring to a full boil over medium heat, stirring constantly. Remove from heat and stir in vanilla, orange peel, and liqueur. Let cool, uncovered, stirring once after 20 minutes.

2 Using a sharp knife, cut peel and all white membrane from oranges; cut segments free and lift out. Layer cooled tapioca and orange segments in four 8-ounce parfait glasses. Cover and refrigerate until cold before serving (about 4 hours).

makes 4 servings

per serving: 189 calories, 8 g protein, 40 g carbohydrates, 0.4 g total fat, 3 mg cholesterol, 105 mg sodium

bananas with pound cake & chocolate sauce

preparation time: about 25 minutes

$^1/_2$ cup firmly packed brown sugar

$^1/_4$ cup unsweetened cocoa powder

1 tablespoon cornstarch

$^1/_4$ teaspoon instant coffee powder

$^1/_2$ cup water

2 tablespoons light corn syrup

2 teaspoons light or dark rum, or to taste

$^1/_2$ teaspoon vanilla

3 large bananas

1 tablespoon lemon juice

1 tablespoon sweetened shredded coconut

3 tablespoons granulated sugar

4 slices purchased nonfat pound cake,
     each about $^3/_4$ inch thick

1 To prepare chocolate sauce, in a small pan, combine brown sugar, cocoa, cornstarch, and coffee powder. Add water and corn syrup; stir until smooth. Cook over medium-high heat, stirring until mixture boils and thickens slightly, about 4 minutes. (At this point, you may cover to prevent a film from forming on top, let cool, and refrigerate for up to 3 days.) If preparing ahead, reheat, stirring, before adding rum and vanilla. Otherwise, remove pan from heat and stir in rum and vanilla immediately. Keep warm, stirring occasionally.

2 Cut bananas diagonally into $^1/_2$-inch-thick slices; place in a large bowl, add lemon juice, and mix gently to coat. Set aside.

3 In a wide nonstick frying pan or wok, stir coconut over medium heat until golden (about 3 minutes). Remove from pan and set aside. To pan, add granulated sugar and 2 tablespoons water. Cook over medium-high heat, stirring, until sugar is dissolved. Add bananas; stir-fry gently until bananas are hot and sauce is thick and bubbly (about 2 minutes). Remove from heat.

4 Place one slice of cake on each of 4 individual plates; spoon banana mixture over cake. Just before serving, stir chocolate sauce well. Drizzle cake with sauce and sprinkle with coconut.

makes 4 servings

per serving: 410 caloriess, 4 g protein, 100 g carbohydrates, 2 g total fat, 0 mg cholesterol, 225 mg sodium

lemon poppy seed cake

preparation time: about 45 minutes

3 large eggs

2 large egg white

1 cup granulated sugar

$^1/_2$ cup smooth unsweetened applesauce

1 $^1/_2$ cups all-purpose flour

$^1/_4$ cup poppy seeds

1 tablespoons baking powder

1 tablespoon plus 1 teaspoon grated lemon peel

$^1/_2$ cup butter or margarine, melted, plus $^1/_3$ cup
   butter or margarine, at room temperature

3 cups powdered sugar

$^1/_2$ cup nonfat sour cream

$^2/_3$ cup strawberry jam

Thin strips of lemon peel

About 8 cups fresh strawberries,
   hulled and halved

1 In a food processor or a large bowl, combine eggs, egg whites, granulated sugar, and applesauce; whirl or beat with an electric mixer until mixture is thick and lemon-colored. Add flour, poppy seeds, baking powder, 1 tablespoon of the grated lemon peel, and the $^1/_2$ cup melted butter; whirl or beat until dry ingredients are evenly moistened. Divide batter equally between 2 greased, floured 8-inch-round nonstick or regular baking pans.

2 Bake in a 375° oven until cake layers just begin to pull away from sides of pans and centers spring back when gently pressed (about 15 minutes); halfway through baking, gently rotate each pan one-half turn. Let cakes cool for 10 minutes in pans on racks; then turn out of pans to cool completely.

3 Meanwhile, prepare frosting: In clean food processor or large bowl, combine powdered sugar, sour cream, the $^1/_3$ cup butter at room temperature, and remaining 1 teaspoon grated lemon peel. Whirl or beat with electric mixer until frosting is smooth and spreadable; cover and refrigerate until ready to use.

4 To assemble cake, brush all loose crumbs from sides and bottom of each cake layer. Center one layer, top side down, on a serving plate. Using a metal spatula, evenly spread jam to within $^1/_2$ inch of edge. Top with second layer, top side up.

5 Stir frosting and spread over sides and top of cake; arrange strips of lemon peel decoratively atop cake. To serve, cut cake into slices; offer strawberries alongside.

makes 10 to 12 servings

per serving: 528 calories, 6 g protein, 88 g carbohydrates, 18 g total fat, 95 mg cholesterol, 319 mg sodium

stir-fried pineapple with ginger

preparation time: about 15 minutes

1 tablespoon butter or margarine

5 cups $^1/_2$-inch chunks fresh or canned pineapple

$^1/_3$ cup firmly packed brown sugar

1 tablespoon finely chopped crystallized ginger

$^1/_4$ teaspoon grated lime peel

1 tablespoon lime juice

1 $^1/_3$ cups coarsely crushed gingersnaps

Mint sprigs

1 Melt butter in a wide nonstick frying pan or wok over medium-high heat. Add pineapple, sugar, ginger, lime peel, and lime juice. Stir-fry gently until pineapple is heated through (about 5 minutes).

2 Transfer fruit and sauce to a shallow serving bowl; sprinkle with crushed gingersnaps. Garnish with mint sprigs.

makes 4 servings

per serving: 291 calories, 2 g protein, 62 g carbohydrates, 6 g total fat, 8 mg cholesterol, 178 mg sodium

chocolate chip cookies

preparation time: about 35 minutes

1 1/2 cups all-purpose flour

1 teaspoon baking powder

1/2 teaspoon baking soda

1/2 teaspoon salt

2 tablespoons butter or margarine,
   at room temperature

2 tablespoons vegetable oil

1 cup firmly packed dark brown sugar

1 large egg

1/2 cup smooth unsweetened applesauce

1 teaspoon vanilla

2 cups regular rolled oats

1 package (about 6 oz.) semisweet
   chocolate chips

About 2 tablespoons granulated sugar

1 In a medium-size bowl, stir together flour, baking powder, baking soda, and salt; set aside.

2 In a large bowl, beat butter, oil, and brown sugar with an electric mixer until smooth. Add egg, applesauce, and vanilla; beat until blended. Add flour mixture and beat until smooth. Scrape down sides of bowl; stir in oats and chocolate chips.

3 Shape and bake dough right away; if it is allowed to sit, cookies will be dry. Working quickly, spoon 2-tablespoon portions of dough onto lightly greased large nonstick or regular baking sheets, spacing cookies evenly. Dip fingertips in granulated sugar, then pat cookies into rounds about 1/3 inch thick.

4 Bake in a 350° oven until pale golden (about 10 minutes), switching positions of baking sheets halfway through baking. Let cool for about 3 minutes on baking sheets, then transfer to racks to cool completely. Serve warm or cool.

makes about 2 dozen cookies

per cookie: 154 calories, 2 g protein, 26 g carbohydrates, 5 g total fat, 11 mg cholesterol, 109 mg sodium

frosted corinth grapes

preparation time: about 20 minutes
chilling time: about 3 hours

4 clusters (about 1 1/2 lbs. *total*) Black Corinth
   grapes (also called champagne grapes), rinsed

1 egg white, lightly beaten

3/4 cup sugar

Lemon sorbet (optional)

1 Lay clusters of grapes flat. Turning fruit with stem, gently brush all over with egg white. With a helper holding each cluster horizontally by stem and fruit ends, sprinkle with sugar, having helper turn fruit as you work.

2 Clip stems with a clothespin to a wrack in freezer, being sure nothing touches grapes (put plastic wrap beneath to catch any drips). Freeze until solid (about 3 hours) If made ahead, seal in a plastic bag and freeze for up to 2 months.

3 Offer with sorbet, if desired.

makes 4 servings

per serving: 247 calories, 2 g protein, 64 g carbohydrates, 0.5 g total fat, 0 mg cholesterol, 17 mg sodium

cocoa pepper cookies

preparation time: about 45 minutes

1 cup all-purpose flour

2 tablespoons unsweetened cocoa powder

1 teaspoon baking powder

1 cup sugar

1 teaspoon whole black peppercorns, coarsely crushed

2 tablespoons butter, melted

1/3 cup smooth unsweetened applesauce

1/2 teaspoon vanilla

1 In a food processor (or in a bowl), combine flour, cocoa, baking powder, 3/4 cup of the sugar, and peppercorns. Whirl (or stir) until blended. Add butter, applesauce, and vanilla; whirl until dough forms a compact ball. (Or stir in butter, applesauce, and vanilla with a fork, then work dough with your hands to form a smooth-textured ball.)

2 With lightly floured fingers, pinch off 1-inch pieces of dough and roll into balls. Arrange balls 2 inches apart on two 12- by 15-inch nonstick (or lightly greased regular) baking sheets. Dip bottom of a lightly greased glass into remaining 1/4 cup sugar and press each ball gently to a thickness of about 1/2 inch; dip glass again as needed to prevent sticking.

3 Bake in lower third of a 300° oven until cookies are firm to the touch and look dry on top (about 20 minutes), switching positions of baking sheets halfway through baking. Let cookies cool on baking sheets for about 3 minutes; then transfer to racks to cool completely.

makes about 1 1/2 dozen cookies

per cookie: 84 calories, 0.7 g protein, 18 g carbohydrates, 1 g total fat, 3 mg cholesterol, 41 mg sodium

mexican wedding cookies

preparation time: about 40 minutes

1 1/2 cups all-purpose flour

1 teaspoon baking powder

1/4 teaspoon salt

5 tablespoons butter or margarine, at room temperature

1/3 cup unsweetened applesauce

About 1 1/2 cups powdered sugar

1 large egg

1 teaspoon vanilla

1/4 cup chopped pecans

1 In a small bowl, mix flour, baking powder, and salt. In a food processor (or in a large bowl), whirl (or beat) butter and applesauce until well blended. Add 1/2 cup of the sugar, egg, vanilla, and pecans; whirl (or beat) until smooth. Add flour mixture to egg mixture; whirl (or stir) until blended. Dough will be stiff.

2 With lightly floured fingers, shape 2-teaspoon portions of dough into balls; you should have 24. Set balls 1 inch apart on two 12- by 15-inch nonstick (or lightly greased regular) baking sheets. Bake in a 375° oven until cookies are light golden brown (about 15 minutes), switching positions of baking sheets halfway through baking. Let cool on baking sheets until lukewarm.

3 Sift 1/2 cup of the remaining sugar onto a large sheet of wax paper. Roll each cookie gently in sugar. With your fingers, pack more sugar all over each cookie to a depth of about 1/8 inch. Place cookies on a rack over wax paper and dust with remaining sugar; let cool.

makes 2 dozen cookies

per cookie: 84 calories, 1 g protein, 14 g carbohydrates, 2 g total fat, 13 mg cholesterol, 60 mg sodium

lemon cookies

preparation time: about 40 minutes

$^1/_2$ cup all-purpose flour

$^1/_4$ teaspoon baking soda

$^1/_4$ teaspoon salt

$^1/_8$ teaspoon cream of tartar

2 tablespoons butter or margarine,
   at room temperature

6 tablespoons granulated sugar

2 teaspoons lemon peel

2 $^1/_2$ teaspoons lemon juice

$^1/_2$ teaspoon vanilla

1 large egg white

$^1/_2$ cup regular rolled oats

$^2/_3$ cup sifted powdered sugar

1 In a small bowl, mix flour, baking soda, salt, and cream of tartar. In a food processor (or in a large bowl), whirl (or beat) butter, granulated sugar, lemon peel, $^1/_2$ teaspoon of the lemon juice, vanilla, and egg white until well blended. Add flour mixture to egg mixture; whirl (or stir) until combined. Stir in oats.

2 With floured fingers, divide dough into 1$^1/_2$-teaspoon portions (you should have 18); place mounds of dough 2 inches apart on two 12- by 15-inch nonstick (or lightly greased regular) baking sheets.

3 Bake in a 350°F oven until cookies are light golden and firm to the touch (about 15 minutes), switching positions of baking sheets halfway through baking. Let cookies cool on baking sheets for about 3 minutes; then transfer to racks to cool completely.

4 While cookies are baking, prepare lemon icing: In a small bowl, combine powdered sugar, remaining 2 teaspoons lemon juice, and water. Stir until smooth.

5 Set each rack of cookies over a baking sheet to catch any drips; drizzle icing evenly over cookies. Serve; or let stand until icing hardens.

makes 1$^1/_2$ dozen cookies

per cookie: 65 calories, 0.9 g protein, 12 g carbohydrates, 1 total fat, 3 mg cholesterol, 64 mg sodium

hot papaya sundaes

preparation time: about 30 minutes

1 tablespoon margarine, melted

$^1/_2$ teaspoon grated lime peel

$^1/_3$ cup rum or water

$^1/_4$ cup lime juice

3 tablespoons honey

2 small firm-ripe papayas

2 cups vanilla low-fat frozen yogurt

1 In a 9- by 13-inch casserole, stir together margarine, lime peel, rum, lime juice, and honey.

2 Cut unpeeled papayas in half lengthwise; scoop out and discard seeds, then place papaya halves, cut sides down, in honey mixture. Bake in a 375° oven until papayas are heated through and sauce is just beginning to bubble (about 15 minutes).

3 Carefully transfer hot papaya halves, cut sides up, to dessert plates; let stand for about 5 minutes.

4 Meanwhile, stir pan juices in casserole to blend; pour into a small pitcher. Fill each papaya half with small scoops of frozen yogurt; offer pan juices to pour over sundaes to taste.

makes 4 servings

per serving: 270 calories, 4 g protein, 46 g carbohydrates, 5 g total fat, 5 mg cholesterol, 101 mg sodium

chocolate pistachio cookies

preparation time: about 40 minutes

1 cup all-purpose flour

2 tablespoons unsweetened cocoa powder

1 teaspoon baking powder

$^1/_4$ teaspoon instant espresso or coffee powder

1 cup granulated sugar

2 tablespoons butter or margarine, melted

$^1/_3$ cup smooth unsweetened applesauce

$^1/_2$ teaspoon vanilla

$^1/_4$ cup shelled pistachio nuts, chopped

$^1/_2$ cup powdered sugar

1 In a food processor or a large bowl, whirl or stir together flour, cocoa, baking powder, instant espresso, and $^3/_4$ cup of the granulated sugar. Add butter, applesauce, and vanilla; whirl until dough forms a compact ball. (Or, if not using a processor, stir in butter, applesauce, and vanilla with a fork, then work dough with your hands to form a smooth-textured ball.)

2 With lightly floured fingers, pinch off about 1-inch pieces of dough; roll pieces into balls. Set balls 2 inches apart on lightly greased large nonstick or regular baking sheets.

3 Place remaining $^1/_4$ cup granulated sugar in a shallow bowl. Dip bottom of a lightly greased glass in sugar; use glass to press each ball of dough gently to a thickness of about $^1/_2$ inch. After flattening each ball, dip glass in sugar again to prevent sticking. Sprinkle cookies evenly with pistachios.

4 Bake in lower third of a 300° oven until cookies are firm to the touch and look dry on top (about 20 minutes), switching positions of baking sheets halfway through baking.

5 Let cookies cool on baking sheets for about 3 minutes, then transfer to racks to cool completely. Meanwhile, in a small bowl, smoothly blend powdered sugar with $1^1/_2$ to 2 teaspoons water, or enough to make icing easy to drizzle. Drizzle icing over cooled cookies.

makes about 2 dozen cookies

per cookie: 83 calories, 0.9 g protein, 16 g carbohydrates, 2 g total fat, 3 mg cholesterol, 31 mg sodium

maple date bars

preparation time: 35 minutes

$^3/_4$ cup whole wheat flour

$^1/_2$ teaspoon each baking powder and baking soda

$^1/_2$ cup chopped pitted dates

$^1/_2$ cup pure maple syrup

2 large egg whites

$^1/_2$ teaspoon vanilla

1 In a large bowl, stir together flour, baking powder, baking soda, and dates. Add syrup, egg whites, and vanilla; beat until smooth.

2 Spread batter evenly in a lightly greased square 8-inch non-stick or regular baking pan. Bake in a 350° oven until center springs back when lightly pressed (about 20 minutes). Serve warm or cool; to serve, cut into 2-inch squares. These bars are best eaten fresh, so serve them the same day you make them.

makes 16 bars

per bar: 65 calories, 1 g protein, 15 g carbohydrates, 0.4 g total fat, 0 mg cholesterol, 62 mg sodium

espresso biscotti

preparation time: about 1 1/4 hours

1/2 cup hazelnuts

**5 tablespoons butter or margarine,
at room temperature**

1/2 cup granulated sugar

2 1/2 teaspoons instant espresso powder

1 large egg

2 large egg whites

1 teaspoon vanilla

2 cups all-purpose flour

2 teaspoons baking powder

1 1/2 cups sifted powdered sugar

1 Spread hazelnuts in a single layer in a shallow baking pan. Bake in a 375° oven until nuts are golden beneath skins (about 10 minutes). Let nuts cool slightly; then pour into a towel and rub to remove as much loose skin as possible. Let cool; chop coarsely and set aside. Reduce oven temperature to 350°.

2 In a large bowl, beat butter, granulated sugar, and 1 1/2 teaspoons of the instant espresso until well blended. Add egg and egg whites, beating until well blended. Stir in vanilla. In a medium-size bowl, stir together flour and baking powder; add to butter mixture and stir until well blended. Mix in hazelnuts.

3 Divide dough in half. On a lightly floured board, shape each portion into a long roll about 1 1/2 inches in diameter. Place rolls on a large nonstick or greased regular baking sheet, 3 inches apart. Flatten rolls to make loaves 1/2-inch thick. Bake in a 350° oven until loaves feel firm to the touch (about 15 minutes).

4 Remove baking sheet from oven and let loaves cool for 3 to 5 minutes; then cut crosswise into slices about 1/2 inch thick. Tip slices cut side down on baking sheet (at this point, you may need another sheet to bake biscotti all at once). Return to oven and bake until biscotti look dry and are lightly browned (about 10 minutes); if using 2 baking sheets, switch their positions halfway through baking. Transfer biscotti to racks and let cool.

5 In a small bowl, dissolve remaining 1 teaspoon instant espresso in 4 teaspoons very hot water. Stir in powdered sugar; if needed, add more hot water, 1 teaspoon at a time, to make icing easy to spread.

6 Spread icing over 1 to 1 1/2 inches of one end of each cooled cookie. Let stand until icing is firm before serving.

makes about 4 dozen cookies

per cookie: 60 calories, 1 g protein, 10 g carbohydrates, 2 g total fat, 7 mg cholesterol, 35 mg sodium

espresso chocolate cake with orange sauce

preparation time: about 1 1/4 hours

2 tablespoons butter or margarine, at room temperature

1 cup firmly packed brown sugar

1 large egg

3 large egg whites

1 cup nonfat sour cream

1 teaspoon vanilla

3/4 cup all-purpose flour

1/3 cup unsweetened cocoa powder

1 tablespoon instant espresso powder

1 1/2 teaspoons baking powder

6 or 7 large oranges

6 tablespoons granulated sugar

4 teaspoons cornstarch

1 1/2 teaspoons instant espresso powder (or to taste)

1 1/2 cups fresh orange juice

2 tablespoons orange-flavored liqueur (or to taste)

2 tablespoons unsweetened cocoa powder

Mint sprigs

1 In a food processor or a large bowl, combine butter and brown sugar; whirl or beat with an electric mixer until well blended. Add egg, egg whites, sour cream, and vanilla; whirl or beat until well blended. Add flour, the 1/3 cup cocoa, the 1 tablespoon instant espresso, and baking powder; whirl or beat just until combined. Spread batter in a greased square 8-inch nonstick or regular baking pan. Bake in a 350° oven until cake begins to pull away from pan sides and center springs back when lightly pressed (35 to 40 minutes).

2 While cake is baking, finely shred enough peel (colored part only) from oranges to make 1 to 2 teaspoons for sauce; cover and set aside. Cut off and discard remaining peel and all white membrane from oranges. Cut between membranes to release segments. Cover orange segments and set aside.

3 In a small pan, combine granulated sugar, cornstarch, and the 1 1/2 teaspoons instant espresso. Whisk in orange juice and the reserved shredded orange peel; cook over medium-high heat, stirring constantly, until sauce boils and thickens slightly (about 1 minute). Remove from heat and stir in liqueur.

4 Just before serving, sift the 2 tablespoons cocoa over cake. Cut cake into diamonds, triangles, or squares; transfer to individual plates. Arrange orange segments alongside. Drizzle sauce over oranges. Garnish with mint sprigs. Makes 8 servings.

per serving: 361 calories, 8 g protein, 74 g carbohydrates, 5 g total fat, 34 mg cholesterol, 187 mg sodium

strawberries with gingered vanilla yogurt

preparation time: about 1 1/4 hours

About 3/4 pound large strawberries with stems, rinsed and drained

3/4 cup vanilla lowfat yogurt

1/4 teaspoon ground ginger

Arrange berries on a serving platter. In a small bowl, stir together yogurt and ginger. Offer with berries for dipping.

makes 2 servings

per serving: 121 calories, 5 g protein, 23 g carbohydrates, 2 g total fat, 4 mg cholesterol, 58 mg sodium

espresso cheesecake

preparation time: 25 minutes
cooking time: 1½ to 1¾ hours
cooling and chilling time: at least 4½ hours

1 package (about 9 oz.) chocolate
    wafer cookies

¼ cup butter or margarine,
    melted and cooled slightly

1 tablespoon instant espresso powder

½ teaspoon vanilla

4 large packages (about 8 oz. *each*) nonfat
    cream cheese, at room temperature

1 cup sugar

3 large eggs

2 large egg whites

2 cups nonfat sour cream

3 tablespoons coffee-flavored liqueur

1 tablespoon sugar

1 tablespoon unsweetened cocoa powder

Chocolate-covered espresso beans
    or mocha candy beans

1 In a food processor, whirl cookies to form fine crumbs. Add butter, instant espresso, and vanilla; whirl just until crumbs are evenly moistened. Press crumb mixture firmly over bottom and about 1 inch up sides of a greased 9-inch cheesecake pan with a removable rim. Bake in a 350° oven until crust feels slightly firmer when pressed (about 15 minutes). In clean food processor or in a large bowl, combine cream cheese, the 1 cup sugar, eggs, egg whites, 1 cup of the sour cream, and liqueur. Whirl or beat with an electric mixer until smooth. Pour cheese filling into baked crust. Return to oven and bake until filling is golden on top and jiggles only slightly in center when pan is gently shaken (1¼ to 1½ hours).

2 Gently run a slender knife between cheesecake and pan rim; then let cheesecake cool in pan on a rack for 30 minutes. Meanwhile, in a small bowl, gently stir together remaining 1 cup sour cream and the 1 tablespoon sugar; cover and refrigerate.

3 Spread cooled cheesecake with sour cream topping. Cover and refrigerate until cold (at least 4 hours) or until next day. Just before serving, sprinkle with cocoa; then remove pan rim. Garnish with chocolate-covered espresso beans.

makes 12 to 16 servings

per serving: 276 calories, 15 g protein, 37 g carbohydrates, 7 g total fat, 62 mg cholesterol, 492 mg sodium

trail mix bars

preparation time: about 1 hour

1 cup all-purpose flour

1 teaspoon baking powder

¾ cup *each* golden and dark raisins

½ cup semisweet chocolate chips

⅓ cup butter or margarine,
    at room temperature

½ cup firmly packed brown sugar

½ cup smooth unsweetened applesauce

2 large egg whites

2 teaspoons vanilla

1 In a small bowl, stir together flour, baking powder, raisins, and chocolate chips. In a food processor or a large bowl, combine butter, sugar, applesauce, egg whites, and vanilla; whirl or beat with an electric mixer until smoothly blended. Add flour mixture; whirl or beat until dry ingredients are evenly moistened. Spread batter in a lightly greased square 8-inch (nonstick or regular baking pan.

2 Bake in a 325° oven until cookie is golden around edges and a wooden pick inserted in center comes out clean (about 40 minutes; do not pierce chocolate chips). Let cool in pan on a rack. To serve, cut into 2-inch squares.

makes 16 bars

per bar: 163 calories, 2 g protein, 28 g carbohydrates, 6 g total fat, 10 mg cholesterol, 81 mg sodium

cactus pear & tree pear soup

preparation time: about 45 minutes

RED PRICKLY PEAR PURÉE:

About 5 pounds despined red prickly pears (also called cactus pears or tunas)

1/3 cup lemon juice

2 tablespoons sugar

RASPBERRY PURÉE:

4 cups fresh or frozen unsweetened raspberries

1 cup orange juice

1/3 cup lemon juice

1/3 cup sugar

TREE PEAR PURÉE:

2 cans (about 1 lb. *each*) pears in extra-light syrup

1 star anise or 1 teaspoon anise seeds

1/4 cup lemon juice

1 tablespoon sugar

GARNISH:

6 to 8 star anise (optional)

Mint sprigs (optional)

1 Prepare red prickly pear purée (Step 2) or raspberry purée (Step 3), then prepare tree pear purée (Step 4).

2 To prepare red prickly pear purée, wear rubber gloves to protect your hands from hidden needles. Cut prickly pears into halves lengthwise. Using a small knife, pull off and discard outer layer (including peel) from fruit; this layer will separate easily. Place fruit in a food processor (a blender will pulverize seeds). Whirl until puréed, then pour into a fine strainer set over a bowl. Firmly rub purée through strainer into bowl; discard seeds. Add lemon juice and sugar. Pour into a small pitcher. (At this point, you may cover and refrigerate until next day; stir before using.)

3 To prepare raspberry purée, in a food processor, whirl raspberries until smoothly puréed (a blender will pulverize seeds). Pour purée into a fine strainer set over a bowl. Firmly rub purée through strainer into bowl; discard seeds. Add orange juice, lemon juice, and sugar. Pour into a small pitcher. (At this point, you may cover and refrigerate until next day; stir before using.)

4 To prepare tree pear purée, drain pears; reserving 1 1/2 cups of the syrup, discard remainder. In a small pan, combine reserved syrup and 1 star anise or anise seeds. Bring syrup to a boil over high heat; then reduce heat, cover, and simmer very gently until flavors are blended (about 10 minutes). Pour syrup through a fine strainer set over a bowl; discard star anise or seeds. In a food processor or blender, whirl pears until smoothly puréed; then add syrup (if using a blender, add syrup while you are puréeing pears). Stir in lemon juice and sugar. Pour into a small pitcher. (At this point, you may cover and refrigerate until next day; stir before using.)

5 With a pitcher in each hand, simultaneously and gently pour purées into an individual 1 1/2- to 2-cup soup bowl (wide bowls create the most dramatic effect). Repeat to fill rest of bowls, allowing a total of 1 to 1 1/2 cups purée for each serving. Garnish each with a star anise and mint sprigs, if desired.

makes 6 to 8 servings

per serving: 187 calories, 2 g protein, 46 g carbohydrates, 1 g total fat, 0 mg cholesterol, 19 mg sodium

sparkling jewels fruit soup

cooking time: about 20 minutes

1 large firm-ripe kiwi fruit, peeled and thinly sliced

¹/₂ cup diced firm-ripe nectarine or peeled peach

¹/₃ cup fresh or frozen unsweetened blueberries

¹/₃ cup thinly sliced hulled strawberries

¹/₃ cup very thinly sliced firm-ripe plums

2 tablespoons lemon juice

2 cups white grape juice

2 tablespoons minced crystallized ginger

3 tablespoons orange-flavored liqueur

Mint sprigs (optional)

1 Prepare fruit. Place fruit in a large bowl and mix gently with lemon juice. (At this point, you may cover and refrigerate for up to 2 hours.)

2 In a small pan, bring grape juice and ginger to a boil over high heat. Stir in liqueur; pour over fruit. Ladle soup into bowls; garnish with mint sprigs, if desired.

makes 4 to 6 servings

per serving: 145 calories, 0.5 g protein, 33 g carbohydrates, 0.3 g total fat, 0 mg cholesterol, 15 mg sodium

dessert nachos

preparation time: about 30 minutes

¹/₃ cup sugar

1 teaspoon ground cinnamon

10 flour tortillas

2 cups strawberries

2 large kiwi fruit

1 cup diced orange segments

1 large package (about 8 oz.) Neufchâtel or nonfat cream cheese

¹/₂ cup orange juice

3 tablespoons honey

1 To prepare nacho chips, in a shallow bowl, combine sugar and cinnamon; set aside. Dip tortillas, one at a time, in water; let drain briefly. Stack tortillas; then cut stack into 6 to 8 wedges. Dip one side of each wedge in sugar mixture. Arrange wedges in a single layer, sugar side up, on lightly oiled 12- by 15-inch baking sheets; do not overlap wedges. Bake in a 500° oven until crisp and golden, 4 to 5 minutes. (At this point, you may cool; then store airtight at room temperature for up to 3 days.)

2 To prepare fruit salsa, hull strawberries; dice into a bowl. Add kiwi fruit and orange segments. Cover and refrigerate until ready to serve or for up to 4 hours.

3 In a small pan, combine Neufchâtel cheese, orange juice, and honey. Whisk over low heat until sauce is smooth (about 3 minutes).

4 Mound chips on a platter. Offer cheese sauce and salsa to spoon onto chips.

makes 10 to 12 servings

per serving: 234 calories, 5 g protein, 37 g carbohydrates, 8 g total fat, 16 mg cholesterol, 236 mg sodium

chocolate banana cobbler

preparation time: about 1 hour

3/4 cup raisins

2 tablespoons light or dark rum

1/2 cup firmly packed brown sugar

1/4 cup half-and-half

2 tablespoons light corn syrup

1/4 teaspoon salt

2 tablespoons lemon juice

1 tablespoon cornstarch

5 large bananas, cut into slanting slices 1/2 inch thick

3/4 cup all-purpose flour

1/2 cup granulated sugar

1/2 cup unsweetened cocoa powder

1/4 teaspoon salt

1/4 teaspoon instant espresso or coffee powder

1/8 teaspoon ground ginger

1/3 cup butter or margarine, cut into chunks

1 In a small bowl, combine raisins and rum. Let stand until raisins are softened (about 10 minutes), stirring occasionally. Meanwhile, in another small bowl, mix brown sugar, half-and-half, corn syrup, and the 1/8 teaspoon salt.

2 In a shallow 1 1/2- to 2-quart casserole, blend lemon juice, cornstarch, and 2 tablespoons water; gently mix in bananas. Add brown sugar mixture and raisin mixture; stir gently to coat fruit. Spread out fruit mixture in an even layer; set aside.

3 In a food processor or a medium-size bowl, whirl or stir together flour, granulated sugar, cocoa, the 1/4 teaspoon salt, instant espresso, and ginger. Add butter; whirl or rub with your fingers until mixture resembles fine crumbs. With your fingers, squeeze mixture to form large lumps; then crumble over banana mixture.

4 Set casserole in a larger baking pan to catch any drips. Bake in a 375° oven until fruit mixture is bubbly in center and topping feels firm when gently pressed (about 35 minutes). Let cool slightly; spoon into bowls.

makes 8 servings

per serving: 385 calories, 4 g protein, 76 g carbohydrates, 10 g total fat, 23 mg cholesterol, 199 mg sodium

do-it-yourself chocolate date bars

preparation time: about 15 minutes
chilling time: about 30 minutes

---

1 package (about 6 oz.) semisweet chocolate chips

1 cup chopped pitted dates

1/4 cup light corn syrup

1/2 cup raisins

1 1/2 cups oven-toasted rice cereal

1 In a large microwave-safe bowl, combine chocolate chips, dates, and corn syrup. Microwave on high (100%) for 1 1/2 minutes; stir. Then microwave again on high (100%) for 1 to 1 1/2 more minutes or until chocolate is melted and smooth and dates are soft. Stir in raisins and cereal.

2 Line a flat tray with wax paper. Working quickly, spoon chocolate mixture onto paper into 8 bars, each about 1 inch wide and 5 inches long; smooth with 2 spoons. Refrigerate until firm to the touch (about 30 minutes). If made ahead, wrap bars individually in plastic wrap and refrigerate for up to 2 weeks.

makes 8 bars

per bar: 220 calories, 2 g protein, 46 g carbohydrates, 6 g total fat, 0.2 mg cholesterol, 62 mg sodium

banana streusel bundt cake

preparation time: 20 minutes
cooking time: 60 to 70 minutes
cooling time: 30 minutes

1/2 **cup all-purpose flour**

1/2 **cup each sweetened shredded coconut and regular rolled oats**

1/2 **cup semisweet chocolate chips**

1/4 **cup firmly packed brown sugar**

1 cup butter or margarine, cut into chunks

1 1/2 **cups coarsely mashed ripe bananas**

3/4 **cup nonfat sour cream**

3 large eggs

2 large egg whites

1 cup granulated sugar

1 1/2 **cups all-purpose flour**

1 tablespoon baking powder

1 teaspoon each ground cinnamon and vanilla

1/3 **cup butter or margarine, melted**

About 1/4 **cup powdered sugar**

1 In a medium-size bowl, stir together the 1/2 cup flour, coconut, oats, chocolate chips, and brown sugar. Add the 1/4 cup butter and 1 tablespoon water; rub with your fingers until mixture is crumbly and well blended. Set aside.

2 In a food processor or a large bowl, combine bananas, sour cream, eggs, egg whites, and granulated sugar. Whirl or beat with an electric mixer until smooth. Add the 1 1/2 cups flour, baking powder, cinnamon, vanilla, and the 1/3 cup melted butter; whirl or beat until well blended.

3 Sprinkle half the coconut streusel in a well-greased, floured 10-cup nonstick or regular fluted tube pan. Pour half the batter over coconut mixture; then sprinkle with remaining coconut streusel. Pour remaining batter over streusel.

4 Bake in a 350° oven until cake just begins to pull away from side of pan and a wooden pick inserted in center comes out clean (60 to 70 minutes). Let cool in pan on a rack for 30 minutes.

5 Invert pan onto a platter; lift off pan to release cake. If any of the streusel topping sticks to pan bottom, gently remove from pan and arrange atop cake. Sprinkle with powdered sugar.

makes 10 to 12 servings

per serving: 441 calories, 7 g protein, 71 g carbohydrates, 15 g total fat, 84 mg cholesterol, 286 mg sodium

CHEESE WITH FRUIT: For a simple, appealing dessert, serve fresh fruit and a selection of complementary cheeses. Arrange choice whole fruits in a basket, cheeses on a pretty tray; provide cheese cutters and small, sharp knives. Try blue, Gorgonzola, and Roquefort with apples, grapes, and pears; Cheddar with pears and red-skinned apples; Jarlsberg and Gouda with apples, pears, and apricots; Swiss and Emmenthaler with pears; jack or Teleme with apricots, melons, and plums.

pears and cream pie

preparation time: 35 minutes
cooking time: about 1 hour

3/4 cup raisins

3 tablespoons brandy or orange juice

Pie pastry

1 cup nonfat sour cream

1 large egg

1 large egg white

1/2 cup granulated sugar

2 tablespoons all-purpose flour

1 teaspoon vanilla

1/2 teaspoon ground cinnamon

1/4 teaspoon ground nutmeg

1/2 cup firmly packed brown sugar

2/3 cup all-purpose flour

3 tablespoons butter or margarine,
   melted and cooled slightly

2 tablespoons smooth unsweetened applesauce

4 large firm-ripe D'Anjou or Bartlett pears

1 In a large bowl, combine raisins and brandy. Let stand until raisins are softened (about 10 minutes), stirring occasionally.

2 Meanwhile, prepare pie pastry and line pie pan, but do not prick pastry after lining pan. Cover and refrigerate.

3 In a small bowl, combine sour cream, egg, egg white, granulated sugar, the 2 tablespoons flour, vanilla, cinnamon, and nutmeg. Beat until smoothly blended; set aside. In another small bowl, combine brown sugar, the 2/3 cup flour, butter, and applesauce. Stir until mixture is evenly moistened. Then, with your fingers, squeeze mixture to form large lumps; set aside.

4 Peel and core pears; cut into slices about 1/2 inch thick. As pears are sliced, add to bowl with raisin mixture and turn to coat with brandy. Add sour cream mixture to pear mixture; mix gently to coat fruit evenly.

5 Spoon pear filling into pastry shell. Crumble brown sugar mixture evenly over filling.

6 Set pie pan in a larger baking pan to catch any drips. Bake pie on lowest rack of a 375° oven until filling is bubbly in center and topping is browned (about 1 hour); if crust or topping begins to darken excessively, cover it with foil. Let cool on a rack before serving; serve warm.

makes 8 to 10 servings

per serving: 435 calories, 6 g protein, 70 g carbohydrates, 14 g total fat, 34 mg cholesterol, 137 mg sodium

oat, coconut & cocoa drops

preparation time: 20 minutes
standing time: 40 minutes to 1 hour

1/2 cup light corn syrup

1/4 cup granulated sugar

1/4 cup butter or margarine

1/4 cup milk

2 tablespoons unsweetened cocoa powder

2 1/3 cups regular rolled oats

1/2 cup sweetened shredded coconut

About 1/4 cup powdered sugar

1 In a 2-quart glass measuring cup or microwave-safe bowl, combine corn syrup, granulated sugar, butter, and milk. Microwave on high (100%) for 2 minutes; then stir until butter is melted. Microwave on high (100%) again for 30 seconds to 1 minute or until mixture bubbles; then microwave for 30 more seconds. Remove from microwave. Stir in cocoa until well blended; then stir in oats and coconut. Set mixture aside and let cool slightly.

2 To shape candies, roll 1-tablespoon portions of oat mixture into balls. Roll balls in powdered sugar to coat, then place slightly apart on a plate. Let stand or refrigerate until firm (40 minutes to 1 hour). If made ahead, wrap airtight and refrigerate for up to 4 days.

makes 24 candies

per candy: 89 calories, 1 g protein, 15 g carbohydrates, 3 g total fat, 6 mg cholesterol, 333 mg sodium

oatmeal raisin cookies

preparation time: 35 minutes

2 cups all-purpose flour

1 teaspoon *each* **baking soda
and ground cinnamon**

¹/₂ teaspoon salt

**³/₄ cup butter or margarine,
at room temperature**

1¹/₂ cups firmly packed brown sugar

**1 cup nonfat sour cream
or plain nonfat yogurt**

1 teaspoon vanilla

3 cups regular rolled oats

1¹/₂ cups raisins

1 In a medium-size bowl, stir together flour, baking soda, cinnamon, and salt; set aside.

2 In a food processor or a large bowl, combine butter, sugar, sour cream, and vanilla. Whirl or beat with an electric mixer until well blended. Add flour mixture to butter mixture; whirl or beat until dry ingredients are evenly moistened. Stir in oats and raisins.

3 Spoon rounded 1 tablespoon portions of dough onto lightly greased large nonstick or regular baking sheets, spacing cookies about 2 inches apart.

4 Bake in a 350° oven until cookies are firm to the touch (about 15 minutes), switching positions of baking sheets halfway through baking. Let cookies cool on baking sheets for about 3 minutes, then transfer to racks to cool completely.

makes about 4¹/₂ dozen cookies

per cookie: 124 calories, 2 g protein, 21 g carbohydrates, 4 g total fat, 9 mg cholesterol, 97 mg sodium

one-pan s'mores

preparation time: 35 minutes

**1¹/₂ cups graham cracker crumbs
(about twenty square 2-inch crackers)**

¹/₄ cup sugar

¹/₄ cup butter or margarine, melted

1 jar (about 7 oz.) marshmallow fluff

²/₃ cup semisweet chocolate chips

¹/₂ cup unsweetened cocoa powder

1¹/₂ cups small marshmallows

1 In a food processor or a medium-size bowl, combine graham cracker crumbs, sugar, butter, and 1 tablespoon water. Whirl or stir with a fork until mixture resembles coarse crumbs. Press crumbs firmly over bottom and about ¹/₂ inch up sides of a lightly greased square 8-inch nonstick or regular baking pan. Bake in a 350° oven until crust feels firm when pressed (about 15 minutes). Let cool completely in pan on a rack.

2 Meanwhile, in a 1¹/₂- to 2-quart pan, combine marshmallow fluff and 1 tablespoon water. Stir constantly over medium-low heat just until fluff is melted and smooth. Remove pan from heat and add chocolate chips; stir constantly until chocolate is melted and mixture is smooth. Add cocoa and stir well. Working quickly, stir in marshmallows just until combined (don't let marshmallows melt). Immediately spoon marshmallow mixture over cooled crust and spread to make level.

3 Cover and refrigerate until firm (at least 1 hour) or for up to 8 hours. To serve, cut into 2-inch squares.

makes 16 bars

per bar: 173 calories, 2 g protein, 30 g carbohydrates, 6 g total fat, 8 mg cholesterol, 105 mg sodium

apricot-amaretto torte

preparation time: 50 minutes

1 tablespoon lemon juice

5 medium-size apricots

¹/₄ cup slivered almonds

2 large eggs

1 cup sugar

4 to 5 tablespoons almond-flavored liqueur

¹/₂ teaspoon almond extract

³/₄ cup all-purpose flour

2 teaspoons baking powder

¹/₈ teaspoon salt

¹/₄ cup butter or margarine, melted and cooled slightly

4 teaspoons cornstarch

1 cup apricot nectar

¹/₂ cup fresh orange juice

¹/₂ teaspoon vanilla

1 Pour lemon juice into a medium-size bowl. Quarter and pit apricots; add to bowl and turn to coat with juice. Set aside.

2 In a food processor, whirl almonds until finely ground. (Or finely chop almonds with a knife, then place in a large bowl.) To almonds, add eggs, ¹/₂ cup of the sugar, 1 tablespoon of the liqueur, and almond extract; whirl or beat with an electric mixer until thick and well blended. Add flour, baking powder, salt, and butter; whirl or beat until well blended. Spread batter in a greased, floured 9-inch cake pan with a removable rim. Decoratively arrange apricots in batter, overlapping as needed; press fruit lightly into batter.

3 Bake in a 375° oven until cake just begins to pull away from side of pan and a wooden pick inserted in center comes out clean (about 25 minutes; pierce cake, not fruit). Let cool slightly on a rack.

4 While cake is cooling, stir together cornstarch and 6 tablespoons of the remaining sugar in a small pan. Whisk in apricot nectar and orange juice; cook over medium-high heat, whisking constantly, until mixture boils and thickens slightly. Remove from heat and stir in vanilla and remaining 3 to 4 tablespoons liqueur; keep warm.

4 Sprinkle cake with remaining 2 tablespoons sugar. Remove pan rim and cut cake into wedges; serve with apricot-orange sauce.

makes 8 servings

per serving: 340 calories, 5 g protein, 54 g carbohydrates, 10 g total fat, 69 mg cholesterol, 240 mg sodium

cantaloupe in raspberry purée

cooking time: about 15 minutes

1¹/₂ cups raspberries, rinsed and drained

3 tablespoons sugar

¹/₄ cup cream sherry

1 medium-size cantaloupe, quartered, seeded, and rind removed

1 In a blender or food processor, whirl raspberries until puréed; press through a fine sieve to remove seeds.

2 In a 1-quart pan, combine raspberry purée, sugar, and sherry. Cook over medium-high heat, stirring, until sugar is dissolved and mixture is boiling. Boil for 30 more seconds. Remove from heat and let cool. (At this point, you may cover and let stand for up to 1 hour.)

3 Thinly slice cantaloupe. Spoon raspberry purée onto individual dessert plates; arrange cantaloupe decoratively over sauce.

makes 4 servings

per serving: 131 calories, 2 g protein, 28 g carbohydrates, 0.6 g total fat, 0 mg cholesterol, 14 mg sodium

angel food cake

preparation time: about 55 minutes

1 cup sifted cake flour

1 1/4 cups granulated sugar

12 egg whites, at room temperature

1/2 teaspoon salt

2 teaspoons cream of tartar

1 1/2 teaspoons vanilla or almond extract

Powdered sugar and sliced fresh strawberries
   (optional)

1 Sift together flour and 1/2 cup of the granulated sugar; sift again and set aside.

2 In large bowl of an electric mixer, beat egg whites on high speed until foamy. Add salt and cream of tartar and continue beating until mixture holds soft peaks. Add remaining sugar, 2 tablespoons at a time, beating well after each addition, until mixture holds stiff, glossy peaks.

3 With a rubber spatula, fold in vanilla. Sprinkle in flour mixture, about 1/4 cup at a time, gently folding in each addition just until blended. Turn batter into an ungreased 10-inch tube pan with a removable bottom; gently smooth top. Slide spatula down outside edge of batter and run around pan to eliminate large air bubbles.

4 Bake in a 375° oven until cake is golden and springs back when lightly pressed (about 35 minutes). Invert pan on a funnel or pop bottle to keep cake from shrinking; let cool completely. Remove from pan and place on a cake plate or platter. Dust with powdered sugar and decorate with strawberries, if desired. Slice with an angel food cake knife or serrated knife.

makes 12 servings

per serving: 128 calories, 4 g protein, 27 g carbohydrates, 0.1 g total fat, 0 mg cholesterol, 146 mg sodium

hot cocoa-mocha fondue

preparation time: 15 minutes

1 cup firmly packed brown sugar

1/2 cup unsweetened cocoa powder

2 tablespoons cornstarch

1 teaspoon instant coffee powder

1/4 cup light corn syrup

1 teaspoon vanilla

2 tablespoons crème de cacao (optional)

Angel food cake cubes, tangerine segments,
   banana slices, pear wedges, whole strawberries,
   and sweet cherries with stems

1 In a 1 1/2-quart pan, combine sugar, cocoa, cornstarch, and instant coffee; stir to blend well. Gradually blend in corn syrup and 1 cup water, stirring until smooth. Then cook over medium-high heat, stirring constantly, until mixture boils and thickens (about 5 minutes).

2 Remove pan from heat and stir in vanilla and, if desired, crème de cacao. Pour fondue into a heatproof serving bowl over a candle warmer or into a small electric slow cooker. Spear cubes of cake and fruits with fondue forks or bamboo skewers and dip into warm fondue; stir fondue occasionally.

makes about 2 cups, 8 servings

per serving: 154 caloriess, 1 g protein, 40 g carbohydrates, 0.7 g total fat, 0 mg cholesterol, 24 mg sodium

pear cobbler with ginger crust

preparation time: 45 to 55 minutes

6 large firm-ripe D'Anjou pears, peeled, cored, and thinly sliced

2 tablespoons lime juice

$^1/_4$ cup pure maple syrup

2 cups finely crushed gingersnaps (about thirty-five 2-inch cookies)

$^2/_3$ cup firmly packed brown sugar

3 tablespoons all-purpose flour

$^1/_4$ cup butter or margarine, melted

1 teaspoon vanilla

1 In a shallow $1^1/_2$- to 2-quart casserole, combine pears and lime juice. Add syrup; mix gently to coat fruit evenly. Spread out fruit in an even layer; set aside.

2 In a food processor or a medium-size bowl, whirl or stir together crushed gingersnaps, sugar, and flour. Add butter and vanilla; whirl or stir until mixture resembles coarse crumbs. With your fingers, squeeze mixture to form large lumps; then crumble evenly over pear mixture.

3 Set casserole in a larger baking pan to catch any drips. Bake in a 325° oven until fruit is tender when pierced and topping feels firm when gently pressed (25 to 35 minutes); if topping begins to darken excessively, cover it with foil. Serve warm; to serve, spoon into bowls.

makes 8 servings

per serving: 370 calories, 3 g protein, 73 g carbohydrates, 9 g total fat, 16 mg cholesterol, 253 mg sodium

apple cobbler with oatmeal chocolate cookie crust

preparation time: 20 minutes
cooking time: about 1 hour

5 tablespoons butter or margarine, at room temperature

1 cup sugar

1 large egg white

1 teaspoon vanilla

$^3/_4$ teaspoon ground cardamom or ground cinnamon

1 cup all-purpose flour

$^3/_4$ cup regular rolled oats

$^1/_2$ cup semisweet chocolate chips

10 large tart apples such as Granny Smith or Gravenstein

$^3/_4$ cup sugar

1 tablespoon cornstarch

$1^1/_2$ teaspoons ground cinnamon

$^1/_2$ teaspoon ground allspice

1 In a food processor or a large bowl, combine butter and the 1 cup sugar; whirl or beat with an electric mixer until smooth. Add egg white, vanilla, and cardamom; whirl or beat until blended. Stir in flour, oats, and chocolate chips; set aside. (At this point, you may wrap crust mixture airtight and refrigerate until next day.)

2 peel, core, and slice apples; arrange in a shallow 3- to $3^1/_2$-quart casserole. Sprinkle with the $^3/_4$ cup sugar, cornstarch, cinnamon, and allspice; mix gently to coat fruit with sugar mixture, then spread out fruit mixture in an even layer. Crumble oat mixture over fruit mixture.

3 Set casserole in a larger baking pan to catch any drips. Bake in a 350° oven until fruit mixture is bubbly in center and topping is richly browned (about 1 hour). Serve warm or at room temperature; to serve, spoon into bowls.

makes 8 servings

per serving: 516 calories, 4 g protein, 105 g carbohydrates, 11 g total fat, 19 mg cholesterol, 82 mg sodium

chocolate cherry brownies

preparation time: 20 minutes
cooking time: 45 to 50 minutes

1 package (about 5 oz.) pitted dried cherries, chopped

4 cup kirsch or berry liqueur

¹/₂ cup butter or margarine, cut into chunks

4 ounces unsweetened chocolate, coarsely chopped

2 cups sugar

2 teaspoons vanilla

¹/₄ to ¹/₂ teaspoon instant espresso or coffee powder

2 large egg whites

2 large eggs

1 cup all-purpose flour

¹/₂ teaspoon each baking powder and salt

³/₄ to 1 cup cherry preserves

1 In a small bowl, combine dried cherries and liqueur; let stand until cherries are softened (about 15 minutes), stirring occasionally.

2 Meanwhile, melt butter in a 4- to 5-quart pan over medium-low heat. Remove pan from heat, add chocolate, and stir until chocolate is melted and mixture is smooth. Let cool for 10 minutes. Add sugar, vanilla, and instant espresso. Mix well. Beat in egg whites; then add whole eggs, one at a time, beating well after each addition. Add dried cherry mixture, flow baking powder, and salt; stir until all ingredients are evenly moistened.

3 Spoon two-thirds of the batter into lightly greased and floured 9- by 13-inch baking pan; spread to make level. Drop preserves by spoonfuls over batter and gently spread out evenly. Drop remaining batter by spoonfuls over preserves; swirl with a knife to blend batter slightly with preserves.

4 Bake in a 350° oven until a wooden pick inserted in center comes out clean (45 to 50 minutes). Let cool in pan on a rack, then cut into about 2-inch squares.

makes 24 brownies

per brownie: 200 calories, 2 g protein, 35 g carbohydrates, 7 g total fat, 28 mg cholesterol, 110 mg sodium

creamy gingered cheese dip

preparation time: 5 minutes

1 ¹/₂ cups low-fat (2%) cottage cheese

¹/₄ cup powdered sugar

1 tablespoon lemon juice

1 teaspoon vanilla

2 tablespoons chopped preserved ginger in syrup

2 tablespoons nonfat milk

Large whole strawberries, preferably with stems

1 In a food processor or blender, combine cottage cheese, sugar, lemon juice, vanilla, ginger, and milk. Whirl until smooth; scrape down side of container occasionally.

2 Transfer dip to a serving bowl. If made ahead, cover and refrigerate until next day. To serve, place bowl of dip on a tray and surround with strawberries for dipping.

makes about 1 ³/₄ cups, 6 to 8 servings

per serving: 80 calories, 7 g protein, 11 g carbohydrates, 0.9 g total fat, 4 mg cholesterol, 202 mg sodium

drunken cake

preparation time: about 30 minutes

1 1/4 cups sugar

2 tablespoons plus 1 teaspoon grated orange peel

1/2 cup orange juice

1/2 teaspoon grated lemon peel

2 tablespoons lemon juice

1/8 teaspoon ground cinnamon

2 to 3 tablespoons light or dark rum

1 teaspoon vanilla

2 large eggs

3/4 cup all-purpose flour

1 1/2 teaspoons baking powder

1/4 cup butter or margarine, melted

Mint sprigs

1 To prepare syrup, in a small pan, mix 3/4 cup of the sugar, 1 teaspoon of the orange peel, orange juice, lemon peel, lemon juice, and cinnamon. Bring to a boil over medium-high heat. Boil, stirring, just until sugar is dissolved. Remove pan from heat and let cool; then stir in rum and vanilla; set aside.

2 In a food processor, whirl eggs and remaining 1/2 cup sugar until thick and lemon-colored. Add flour, baking powder, butter, and remaining 2 tablespoons orange peel to processor; whirl until well blended. Spread batter in a greased, floured 9-inch cake pan with a removable rim. Bake in a 375° oven until cake just begins to pull away from sides of pan and center springs back when lightly pressed with a finger (about 20 minutes).

3 Set warm cake in pan on a rack; set rack over a plate to catch any drips of syrup. Pierce cake all over with a fork. Slowly pour syrup over cake; let cake cool. Just before serving, remove pan rim. Garnish cake with mint sprigs.

makes 8 servings

per serving: 259 calories, 3 g protein, 43 g carbohydrates, 8 g total fat, 69 mg cholesterol, 167 mg sodium

honeydew melon dessert bowl

preparation time: about 30 minutes

FRUIT:

2 medium-size honeydew melons

1 large can (about 20 oz.) or 2 cans (about 11 oz. *each*) litchis

10 to 16 strawberries, hulled and halved

STRAWBERRY SAUCE:

3 cups strawberries, hulled

2 tablespoons lemon juice

1 tablespoon sugar, or to taste

1 Cut off top third of each melon. Scoop out seeds; scoop fruit into balls or chunks from shells and from top slices, removing as much melon as possible. Discard top slices.

2 Place melon pieces in a bowl. Drain litchis, reserving 1/2 cup of the syrup for the Strawberry Sauce (discard remaining syrup). Add litchis and halved strawberries to melon pieces; mix gently. Spoon fruit into melon shells.

3 To prepare strawberry sauce, in a blender or food processor, combine hulled whole strawberries, the 1/2 cup reserved litchi syrup, lemon juice, and sugar. Whirl until smooth. (At this point, you may cover and refrigerate fruit salad and sauce separately for up to 4 hours.)

4 Serve fruit in melons with strawberry sauce.

makes 8 to 10 servings

per serving: 116 calories, 1 g protein, 30 g carbohydrates, 0.5 g total fat, 0 mg cholesterol, 37 mg sodium

cinnamon bread pudding with pumpkin custard

preparation time: 50 minutes

³/4 cup raisins

8 to 10 ounces unsliced day-old crusty sourdough bread

¹/4 cup butter or margarine, melted

³/4 cup sugar

2 teaspoons ground cinnamon

3 large eggs

2 ³/4 cups low-fat (2%) milk

1 can (about 1 lb.) pumpkin

¹/2 teaspoon ground nutmeg

1 teaspoon vanilla

1 In a small bowl, combine raisins and ³/4 cup hot water; let stand until raisins are softened (about 10 minutes), stirring occasionally.

2 Meanwhile, tear bread into about 1-inch chunks; you should have about 6 cups. Place bread in a large bowl and mix in butter. In a small bowl, combine ¹/4 cup of the sugar with cinnamon; sprinkle over bread, then mix gently but thoroughly. In another small bowl, beat one of the eggs with ³/4 cup of the milk until blended; gently mix into bread mixture. Drain raisins well; add to bread mixture and mix just until evenly distributed.

3 Spoon bread mixture into a greased shallow 1¹/2- to 2-quart baking dish. Bake in a 375° oven until crisp and deep brown (about 30 minutes).

4 Meanwhile, in the top of a 2- to 3-quart double boiler, combine remaining ¹/2 cup sugar, remaining 2 eggs, remaining 2 cups milk, pumpkin, nutmeg, and vanilla. Beat until blended. Then set over simmering water and cook, stirring often, until custard is steaming and thickly coats a metal spoon (about 12 minutes). Keep warm.

5 To serve, pour custard into individual bowls; spoon warm bread pudding on top.

makes 6 servings

per serving: 466 calories, 12 g protein, 74 g carbohydrates, 15 g total fat, 136 mg cholesterol, 431 mg sodium

peppermint fudge

preparation time: 20 minutes
chilling time: at least 2 hours

¹/2 cup evaporated skim milk

1 ¹/4 cups sugar

¹/4 teaspoon salt

¹/4 cup butter or margarine

1 package (about 6 oz.) semisweet chocolate chips

³/4 cup marshmallow fluff

1 teaspoon vanilla

¹/2 cup crushed hard peppermint candy

1 In a heavy 2¹/2- to 3-quart pan, combine milk, sugar, salt, and butter. Bring to a rolling boil over medium-low heat, stirring; then boil for 5 minutes, stirring constantly and reducing heat as needed to prevent scorching.

2 Remove pan from heat; add chocolate chips and stir until melted. Quickly stir in marshmallow fluff and vanilla; then mix in peppermint candy until blended. Pour into a buttered square 8-inch baking pan; spread to make an even layer. Let cool, then cover and refrigerate until firm (at least 2 hours). To serve, cut into 1-inch squares. If made ahead, wrap airtight and refrigerate for up to 2 weeks.

makes 64 pieces

per piece: 45 calories, 0.3 g protein, 2 g total fat, 8 g carbohydrates, 2 mg cholesterol, 21 mg sodium

minted poached pears

preparation time: about 40 minutes

2 cans (12 oz. *each*) unsweetened pineapple juice

4 medium-size firm-ripe Bosc, d'Anjou,
  or Cornice pears

2 tablespoons crème de menthe
  or ¹/₄ teaspoon mint extract

Mint sprigs

1 Pour juice into a 3-quart pan and place over medium heat. Peel pears, leaving some peel around stems; do not remove stems. With an apple corer, cut out blossom end and core from each pear. Place pears in juice and bring to a boil; reduce heat, cover, and simmer until pears are tender when pierced (about 20 minutes).

2 With a slotted spoon, lift out pears and place in a serving dish. Increase heat to high and boil juice, uncovered, stirring often, until reduced to about 1 cup (about 10 minutes). Stir in crème de menthe. Pour over pears. Serve warm; or cool, cover, and refrigerate until chilled and serve cold. Garnish with mint sprigs.

makes 4 servings

per serving: 229 calories, 1 g protein, 53 g carbohydrates, 0.8 g total fat, 0 mg cholesterol, 2 mg sodium

cranberry-walnut bars

preparation time: 20 minutes
cooking time: about 1 hour

1 cup dried cranberries

3 tablespoons orange-flavored liqueur or orange juice

1 ¹/₄ cups all-purpose flour

¹/₄ cup powdered sugar

¹/₈ teaspoon salt

¹/₃ cup butter or margarine, cut into chunks

1 tablespoon apple jelly, melted and cooled slightly

1 large egg

2 large egg whites

²/₃ cup light corn syrup

²/₃ cup granulated sugar

1 teaspoon vanilla

1 cup fresh or frozen cranberries, chopped

¹/₂ cup chopped walnuts

1 In a small bowl, combine dried cranberries and liqueur; let stand until cranberries are softened (about 10 minutes), stirring occasionally.

2 In a food processor or a medium-size bowl, whirl or stir together flour, powdered sugar, and salt. Add butter and jelly; whirl or rub with your fingers until mixture resembles coarse crumbs. Press crumbs firmly over bottom and about ¹⁄₁₆ inch up sides of a lightly greased square 8-inch nonstick or regular baking pan. Prick dough all over with a fork. Bake in a 350° oven until pale golden (about 15 minutes).

3 Meanwhile, in a large bowl, beat whole egg, egg whites, corn syrup, granulated sugar, and vanilla until smoothly blended. Stir in fresh cranberries, dried cranberry-liqueur mixture, and walnuts. Remove hot baked crust from oven; pour filling into crust. Return to oven and bake until filling no longer jiggles in center when pan is gently shaken (35 to 40 minutes; cover edge of crust with foil if it begins to brown excessively). Let cool in pan on a rack. Serve at room temperature or chilled; to serve, cut into 2-inch squares.

makes 16 bars

per bar: 218 calories, 2 g protein, 37 g carbohydrates, 7 g total fat, 24 mg cholesterol, 84 mg sodium

peach shortcakes

preparation time: about 35 minutes

1 cup all-purpose flour

2 teaspoons baking powder

$^1/_4$ teaspoon baking soda

3 tablespoons margarine

$^1/_3$ cup low-fat buttermilk

1 cup low-fat cottage cheese

About 3 tablespoons honey

$^1/_8$ teaspoon ground nutmeg

2 large firm-ripe peaches

1 In a medium-size bowl, stir together flour, baking powder, and baking soda until well blended. Using a pastry blender or your fingers, cut in or rub in margarine until mixture resembles coarse meal. Add buttermilk and stir just until dry ingredients are evenly moistened.

2 Turn dough out onto a lightly floured board and knead gently just until smooth (about 1 minute). Divide dough into fourths. Pat each portion into a 3-inch-diameter round; place rounds well apart on an increased baking sheet.

3 Bake in a 450° oven until lightly browned (about 15 minutes). Transfer to a rack and let cool slightly.

4 Meanwhile, whirl cottage cheese, 3 tablespoons of the honey, and nutmeg in a blender or food processor until smooth. Peel, then pit and slice peaches.

5 To serve, split each biscuit in half horizontally. Set bottom halves on 4 plates; top each with a fourth of the cottage cheese mixture and a fourth of the peach slices. Cover lightly with biscuit tops. Serve with additional honey, if desired.

makes 4 servings

per serving: 345 calories, 13 g protein, 52 g carbohydrates, 10 g total fat, 6 mg cholesterol, 663 mg sodium

hot cranberry fondue

preparation time: 25 minutes

1 cup dried cranberries

1 cup ruby port

$^2/_3$ cup sugar

1 cinnamon stick (about 3 inches long)

1 tablespoon grated orange peel

2 tablespoons orange flavored liqueur (optional)

1 In a $1^1/_2$- to 2-quart pan, combine cranberries, port, $^1/_2$ cup water, sugar, cinnamon stick, and orange peel. Bring to a boil over medium-high heat, stirring until sugar is dissolved. Then continue to cook until mixture is reduced to about $1^1/_2$ cups, about 15 minutes; stir occasionally at first, more often as mixture thickens toward end of cooking time.

2 Remove from heat and stir in liqueur, if desired. Remove and discard cinnamon stick. Transfer mixture to a blender or food processor and whirl until coarsely pureed. Pour fondue into a heatproof serving bowl over a candle warmer or into a small electric slow cooker. Pick up apple wedges with your fingers (or spear them with fondue forks or bamboo skewers) and dip into warm fondue.

makes about 1 $^1/_2$ cups, 6 servings

per serving: 209 calories, 0.01 g protein, 42 g carbohydrates, 0.3 g total fat, 0 mg cholesterol, 4 mg sodium

chocolate biscotti

preparation time: about 1 hour

1/4 cup butter or margarine,
   at room temperature

1/8 cup granulated sugar

4 large egg whites

2 cups all-purpose flour

1/3 cup unsweetened cocoa powder

2 teaspoons baking powder

1/3 cup sifted powdered sugar

About 2 teaspoons low-fat (1%) milk

1 In a large bowl, beat butter and granulated sugar until fluffy. Add egg whites and beat until well blended. In a medium bowl, combine flour, cocoa, and baking powder; add to butter mixture and stir until well blended.

2 Turn dough out onto a large nonstick or lightly greased regular baking sheet. Shape dough down length of sheet into a loaf about 2½ inches wide and 5/8 inch thick. Bake in a 350° oven until crusty and firm to the touch (about 20 minutes).

3 Remove baking sheet from oven and let loaf cool for 3 to 5 minutes; then cut diagonally into slices about 1/2 inch thick. Tip slices cut side down on baking sheet. Return to oven and bake until biscotti feel firm and dry (15 to 20 minutes). Transfer to racks and let cool.

4 In a small bowl, stir together powdered sugar and 2 teaspoons of the milk, or enough to make a pourable icing. Using a spoon, drizzle icing decoratively over biscotti. Let stand until icing is firm before serving.

makes about 1 1/2 dozen cookies

per cookie: 112 calories, 3 g protein, 19 g carbohydrates, 3 g total fat, 7 mg cholesterol, 97 mg sodium

cherry-blueberry crisp

preparation time: about 1¼ hours

1/3 cup firmly packed brown sugar

2 tablespoons all-purpose flour

1/2 teaspoon ground cinnamon

3 cups pitted fresh Bing
   or other dark sweet cherries

2 cups fresh blueberries

1 tablespoon lemon juice

1 cup quick-cooking rolled oats

1/4 cup firmly packed brown sugar

1/4 teaspoon *each* ground cinnamon
   and ground ginger

3 tablespoons butter or margarine, melted

1 In a shallow 2-quart casserole, stir together the 1/3 cup sugar, flour, and cinnamon. Add cherries, blueberries, and lemon juice; mix gently to coat fruit with sugar mixture. Spread out fruit mixture in an even layer.

2 In a small bowl, combine oats, the 1/4 cup sugar, cinnamon, and ginger; add butter and stir with a fork until mixture is crumbly. Sprinkle mixture evenly over fruit.

3 Set casserole in a larger baking pan to catch any drips. Bake in a 350° oven until fruit mixture is bubbly in center and topping is golden brown (35 to 40 minutes); if topping begins to darken excessively, cover it with foil. Serve hot, warm, or at room temperature. To serve, spoon into bowls.

makes 6 servings

per serving: 273 calories, 4 g protein, 51 g carbohydrates, 7 g total fat, 16 mg cholesterol, 71 mg sodium

tropical sherbet

preparation time: 1 hour
cooking time: about 10 minutes
chilling time: about 2 hours (for Frozen Citrus Bowls)
freezing time: about 2 ½ hours for Frozen Citrus Bowls, about 3 hours for sherbert

Frozen Citrus Bowls (recipe follows)

5 or 6 medium-size firm-ripe mangoes

6 tablespoons lime juice

1 can (about 14 oz.) mango nectar

1 jar (about 7 oz.) marshmallow fluff

2 medium-size ripe bananas

¹/₂ cup low-fat (2%) milk

Mint sprigs (optional)

1 Prepare Frozen Citrus Bowls; keep frozen.

2 Peel 1 mango; thinly slice fruit from pit into a food processor or blender. Add 2 tablespoons of the lime juice. Then add half *each* of the mango nectar, marshmallow fluff, bananas, and milk. Whirl until smooth, scraping sides of container often; transfer to a bowl. Smoothly purée remaining mango nectar, marshmallow fluff, bananas, and milk; pour into bowl.

3 Pour fruit mixture into a metal pan, 8 or 9 inches square. Cover and freeze until solid (about 3 hours) or for up to 1 week. Break into small chunks with a heavy spoon; whirl in a food processor or beat with an electric mixer until smooth. Serve; or, for firmer sherbet, freeze for up to 1 more hour. If made ahead, pack into containers, cover, and freeze for up to 1 week; before serving, whirl or beat until soft enough to scoop.

4 Just before serving, peel remaining 4 or 5 mangoes; thinly slice fruit from pits into a large bowl. Add remaining ¹/₄ cup lime juice; mix gently to coat.

5 Serve sherbet in Frozen Citrus Bowls; garnish with mint sprigs, if desired. Drain mangoes and serve alongside.

makes 6 servings

per serving: 392 calories, 4 g protein, 108 g carbohydrates, 1 g total fat, 2 mg cholesterol, 39 mg sodium

FROZEN CITRUS BOWLS

1 In a 1- to 2-quart pan, combine ¹/₂ cup sugar and ¹/₂ cup water. Bring to a boil over high heat, stirring occasionally. Remove from heat and let cool; then refrigerate until very cold (about 2 hours).

2 Meanwhile, with a sharp knife, cut 2 *each* lemons, limes, and oranges (or use all one kind of fruit) into even, paper-thin slices, ¹/₁₆ to ¹/₈ inch thick. Line six 1¹/₂- to 2-cup bowls (2 to 2¹/₂ inches deep) with plastic wrap. Selecting the prettiest citrus slices, dip them in cold sugar syrup; lift out slices and drain briefly, then use to line bottoms and sides of bowls snugly, overlapping as needed. Reserve any leftover syrup and citrus slices for other uses.

3 Wrap bowls airtight and freeze until fruit is firm (about 2¹/₂ hours) or for up to 1 week. To use, gently lift frozen citrus bowls from molds. Working quickly, peel off plastic wrap, place each bowl on a dessert plate, and fill with sherbet. Serve filled bowls immediately (they keep their shape for only about 15 minutes); or return to freezer for up to 1 hour, then serve.

makes 6 bowls

chocolate hazelnut cake

preparation time: 40 minutes
chilling time: at least 2 hours

2 tablespoons hazelnuts

1 purchased nonfat chocolate loaf cake
   (about 15 oz.)

$^1/_2$ cup purchased hazelnut-cocoa spread

1 small package (about 6 oz.) semisweet
   chocolate chips

2 cups sifted powdered sugar

1 large package (about 8 oz.)
   Neufchâtel cheese, cut into chunks

$^1/_2$ cup unsweetened cocoa powder

4 cups nonfat sour cream

2 teaspoons vanilla

1 Toast and coarsely chop hazelnuts as directed for Pear & Hazelnut Upside-down Cake (page 579). Set aside.

2 Cut cake in half horizontally. Set bottom half, cut side up, on a serving plate. Stir hazelnut-cocoa spread to soften, if necessary; then spread evenly over cake to within about $^1/_2$ inch of edges. Place top half of cake, cut side down, over filling; press lightly.

3 Place chocolate chips in a metal bowl nested over a pan of hot (not boiling) water. Stir often until chocolate is melted and smooth. Remove from heat and transfer to a food processor or blender; let stand for 2 to 3 minutes to cool slightly. Add powdered sugar, Neufchâtel cheese, cocoa, sour cream, and vanilla; whirl until smooth, scraping sides of container often. Let frosting cool slightly; it should be spreadable, but not too soft.

4 Generously spread frosting over sides and top of cake. Cover cake with a cake cover or an inverted bowl (don't let cover touch frosting); refrigerate until cold (at least 2 hours) or until next day. Sprinkle with hazelnuts, pressing them lightly into frosting. Cut into slices to serve.

makes 10 servings

per serving: 401 calories, 7 g protein, 67 g carbohydrates, 13 g total fat, 11 mg cholesterol, 324 mg sodium

raisin snack cake

preparation time: 20 minutes
cooking time: about 55 minutes

3 cups all-purpose flour

2 cups granulated sugar

2 teaspoons baking soda

1 $^1/_2$ teaspoons ground cinnamon

$^1/_2$ teaspoon *each* ground nutmeg and salt

$^1/_4$ teaspoon ground cloves

1 cup reduced-fat mayonnaise

$^1/_3$ cup nonfat milk

2 large eggs

3 large Golden Delicious apples

1 cup *each* golden and dark raisins

$^1/_4$ cup powdered sugar

1 In a large bowl, stir together flour, granulated sugar, baking soda, cinnamon, nutmeg, salt, and cloves; set aside.

2 In a food processor or another large bowl, combine mayonnaise, milk, and eggs; whirl or beat with an electric mixer until smooth. Set aside. Peel, core, and coarsely chop apples; stir apples into egg mixture. Then add flour mixture to egg mixture and whirl or beat just until dry ingredients are evenly moistened. Stir in raisins.

3 Spoon batter into a lightly greased 9- by 13-inch nonstick or regular baking pan; smooth top. Bake in a 350° oven until a wooden pick inserted in center comes out clean (about 55 minutes).

4 Let cake cool completely in pan on a rack. Just before serving, sprinkle with powdered sugar. To serve, cut into about 2-inch squares.

makes 24 servings

per serving: 213 calories, 3 g protein 45 g carbohydrates, 3 g total fat, 18 mg cholesterol, 241 mg sodium

zabaglione cream over warm fruit compote

preparation time: 15 minutes
cooking time: about 40 minutes

1 package (about 12 oz.) mixed dried fruit (whole or halved fruits, not dried fruit bits)

1 1/2 cups white grape juice

1/4 to 1/2 teaspoon ground cinnamon

3 whole cloves

6 large egg yolks

3 tablespoons sugar

1/2 cup Marsala

2 cups frozen reduced-calorie whipped topping, thawed

1 Cut large pieces of fruit into bite-size chunks; set fruit aside. In a medium-size pan, combine grape juice, cinnamon, and cloves; bring to a boil over high heat. Stir in fruit; then reduce heat, cover, and simmer until fruit is plump and tender when pierced (about 30 minutes). Remove from heat and keep warm.

2 In the top of a double boiler, combine egg yolks and sugar. Beat with an electric mixer on high speed or with a whisk until thick and lemon-colored. Beat in Marsala. Set double boiler over (not in) gently simmering water; beat mixture constantly just until it is thick enough to retain a slight peak briefly when beater or whisk is withdrawn (3 to 6 minutes).

3 Working quickly, pour warm egg mixture into a large bowl. Fold in about a third of the whipped topping to lighten egg mixture; then fold in remaining whipped topping. Serve immediately.

4 To serve, lift fruit from pan with a slotted spoon and divide among six 8-ounce stemmed glasses; discard cooking liquid or reserve for other uses. Top with zabaglione cream.

makes 6 servings

per serving: 346 calories, 4 g protein, 61 g carbohydrates, 8 g total fat, 213 mg cholesterol, 24 mg sodium

amaretti-topped raspberry-peach bake

preparation time: about 1 hour

1 tablespoon cornstarch

1/2 teaspoon ground nutmeg

1/3 cup sugar

4 cups peeled, sliced peaches

1 cup fresh raspberries

1 1/2 cups coarsely crushed crisp almond macaroons (about thirty 1 3/4-inch cookies)

1 In a shallow 1 1/2- to 2-quart casserole, stir together cornstarch, nutmeg, and sugar. Add peaches and raspberries; mix gently to coat fruit with sugar mixture. Spread out fruit mixture in an even layer; then sprinkle evenly with crushed macaroons.

2 Bake in a 375° oven until fruit mixture is bubbly in center (40 to 45 minutes); cover with foil during last 10 to 12 minutes of baking if topping begins to darken excessively. Serve warm or at room temperature; to serve, spoon into bowls.

makes 6 servings

per serving: 159 calories, 3 g protein, 32 g carbohydrates, 3 g total fat, 0 mg cholesterol, 9 mg sodium

chocolate shortbread

preparation time: about 40 minutes

1 cup chocolate graham cracker crumbs (about twelve 2-inch square crackers)

³/4 cup all-purpose flour

²/3 cup plus ¹/2 cup powdered sugar

¹/2 cup plus 1 tablespoon unsweetened cocoa powder

¹/2 teaspoon instant espresso or coffee powder

¹/4 teaspoon salt

¹/4 cup butter or margarine, cut into chunks

¹/4 teaspoon vanilla

About 1 tablespoon nonfat milk

1 In a food processor or a large bowl, whirl or stir together graham cracker crumbs and 1 tablespoon water until crumbs are evenly moistened. Press crumbs evenly over bottom of a lightly greased 9-inch nonstick or regular cheesecake pan with a removable rim; set aside.

2 In food processor or bowl, whirl or stir together flour, the ²/3 cup powdered sugar, the ¹/2 cup cocoa, 2 teaspoons water, instant espresso, and salt. Add butter; whirl or rub with your fingers until mixture resembles coarse crumbs.

3 Evenly distribute crumbly dough over graham cracker crumbs in pan. With fingers, press out dough firmly to make an even layer that adheres to graham cracker crumbs (if dough is sticky, lightly flour your fingers).

4 Bake in a 325° oven until shortbread smells toasted and feels firm in center when gently pressed (about 25 minutes). Let shortbread cool in pan on a rack for 5 minutes. Then, using a very sharp knife, cut shortbread, still in pan, into 12 equal wedges. Let cool completely in pan on rack.

5 Meanwhile, in a small bowl, stir together remaining ¹/2 cup powdered sugar, remaining 1 tablespoon cocoa, vanilla, and 1 tablespoon of the milk. Beat until smooth; if necessary, add more milk to make glaze easy to drizzle. Remove pan rim from shortbread; drizzle glaze over shortbread. Let stand until glaze is set.

makes 12 servings

per serving: 148 calories, 2 g protein, 25 g carbohydrates, 5 g total fat, 10 mg cholesterol, 137 mg sodium

chocolate taffies

preparation time: 20 to 25 minutes

1 can (about 14 oz.) sweetened condensed milk

1 cup unsweetened cocoa powder

About 1 tablespoon butter or margarine

3 ¹/2 ounces chocolate sprinkles (about ¹/2 cup)

1 In a 2- to 3-quart pan, combine milk, cocoa, and butter. Place over medium-low heat; cook, stirring, until mixture begins to bubble. Then continue to stir until mixture holds together as a soft mass when pushed to side of pan (3 to 5 minutes). Remove from heat and let stand until cool enough to touch.

2 Spread chocolate sprinkles on a plate. With lightly buttered hands, shape cocoa mixture into 1-inch balls. Roll balls, 4 or 5 at a time, in sprinkles to coat. If desired, place each candy in a small paper or foil bonbon cup. Serve at room temperature. If made ahead, cover airtight and refrigerate for up to 1 week; freeze for longer storage.

makes about 34 candies

per candy: 59 calories, 1 g protein, 11 g carbohydrates, 2 g total fat, 5 mg cholesterol, 21 mg sodium

jumbleberry crumble

preparation time: 15 minutes,
plus 15 minutes for filling to stand
cooking time: 50 to 60 minutes

²/₃ **cup granulated sugar**

3 tablespoons quick-cooking tapioca

1 ¹/₂ cups fresh blueberries

1 ¹/₂ cups fresh raspberries

3 cups hulled, halved strawberries

¹/₂ cup quick-cooking rolled oats

¹/₂ cup firmly packed brown sugar

¹/₂ cup all-purpose flour

1 teaspoon ground cinnamon

¹/₃ cup butter or margarine, melted

1 In a shallow 2-quart casserole, stir together granulated sugar and tapioca. Add blueberries, raspberries, and strawberries; mix gently to coat fruit with sugar mixture. Let stand for 15 minutes to soften tapioca, stirring occasionally; then spread out fruit mixture in an even layer.

2 In a small bowl, combine oats, brown sugar, flour, and cinnamon. Add butter and stir with a fork until mixture is crumbly. Sprinkle topping evenly over fruit mixture.

3 Set casserole in a larger baking pan to catch any drips. Bake in a 350° oven until fruit mixture is bubbly in center and topping is crisp and brown (50 to 60 minutes); if topping begins to darken excessively, cover it with foil. Serve hot, warm, or at room temperature; to serve, spoon into bowls.

makes 6 to 8 servings

per serving: 330 calories, 3 g protein, 61 g carbohydrates, 10 g total fat, 23 mg cholesterol, 117 mg sodium

panforte

preparation time: 25 minutes
cooking time: about 1 ¹/₄ hours

1 cup salted roasted almonds, coarsely chopped

1 cup dried pitted tart cherries

1 cup *each* **candied orange peel
and candied lemon peel, finely chopped**

**1 teaspoon each grated lemon peel
and ground cinnamon**

¹/₂ teaspoon ground coriander

**¹/₄ teaspoon each ground cloves
and ground nutmeg**

¹/₂ cup all-purpose flour

³/₄ cup granulated sugar

³/₄ cup honey

2 tablespoons butter or margarine

¹/₂ cup sifted powdered sugar

1 In a large bowl, combine almonds, cherries, candied orange peel, candied lemon peel, grated lemon peel, cinnamon, coriander, cloves, nutmeg, and flour. Mix until nuts and fruit pieces are thoroughly coated with flour; set aside.

2 In a deep medium-size pan, combine granulated sugar, honey, and butter. Cook over high heat, stirring often, until mixture registers 265° (hard-ball stage) on a candy thermometer. Working quickly, pour hot syrup over fruit mixture and mix thoroughly. Immediately scrape mixture into a heavily greased, floured 8- to 9-inch cake pan.

3 Bake in a 300° oven for 1 hour; if cake begins to brown excessively, drape it loosely with foil (don't let foil touch cake). Let cool completely in pan on a rack.

4 Sprinkle a work surface with half the powdered sugar. Using a slender knife and spatula, loosen sides and bottom of cake from pan, then invert cake (prying gently, if needed) onto sugared surface. Sprinkle and pat sugar over entire cake. Then dust cake with remaining powdered sugar to coat completely. Transfer to a platter. To serve, cut into wedges.

makes 12 servings

per serving: 370 calories, 4 g protein, 71 g carbohydrates, 10 g total fat, 5 mg cholesterol, 131 mg sodium

pear & hazelnut upside-down cake

preparation time: 35 minutes
cooking time: about 55 minutes
cooling time: 30 minutes

$^1/_4$ **cup hazelnuts**

$^1/_2$ **cup butter or margarine, melted**

$^1/_3$ **cup firmly packed brown sugar**

2 medium-size firm-ripe pears

1 tablespoon lemon juice

$^1/_4$ **cup all-purpose flour**

3 large eggs

2 large egg whites

$^1/_2$ **cup smooth unsweetened applesauce**

2 tablespoons hazelnut-flavored liqueur

1 cup granulated sugar

1 $^1/_2$ cups all-purpose flour

1 tablespoon baking powder

1 teaspoon ground cinnamon

$^1/_2$ **teaspoon ground ginger**

$^1/_2$ **cup firmly packed brown sugar**

$^1/_4$ **cup half-and-half**

2 tablespoons light corn syrup

1 tablespoon butter or margarine

**1 tablespoon cornstarch blended
    with 2 tablespoons cold water**

$^1/_2$ **teaspoon grated lemon peel**

$^1/_8$ **teaspoon salt**

1 $^1/_2$ teaspoons lemon juice

1 Spread hazelnuts in a single layer in a shallow baking pan. Bake in a 375° oven until nuts are golden beneath skins (about 10 minutes). Let nuts cool slightly; then pour into a towel, fold to enclose, and rub to remove as much of loose skins as possible. Let cool; then coarsely chop and set aside.

2 Pour half the melted butter into a well-greased, floured 3- to 3 $^1/_2$-quart nonstick or regular fluted tube pan. Sprinkle with the $^1/_3$ cup brown sugar; set aside. Core pears and cut into $^1/_2$-inch slices. Dip slices into the 1 tablespoon lemon juice; then coat slices with the $^1/_4$ cup flour and arrange decoratively in pan over sugar mixture (overlap slices, if necessary). Set pan aside.

3 In a food processor or a large bowl, combine eggs, egg whites, applesauce, liqueur, and granulated sugar. Whirl or beat with an electric mixer until mixture is thick and lemon-colored. Add the 1 $^1/_2$ cups flour, baking powder, cinnamon, ginger, and remaining melted butter; whirl or beat until dry ingredients are evenly moistened. Carefully pour batter over pears.

4 Bake in a 375° oven until cake just begins to pull away from side of pan and a wooden pick inserted in center of cake comes out clean (about 40 minutes). Let cake cool in pan on a rack for 30 minutes.

5 Meanwhile, in a 1- to 1 $^1/_2$-quart pan, combine the $^1/_2$ cup brown sugar, half-and-half, corn syrup, the 1 tablespoon butter, cornstarch mixture, lemon peel, and salt. Bring to a boil over medium heat. Boil gently, stirring, until slightly thickened (4 to 5 minutes). Remove pan from heat and stir in the 1 $^1/_2$ teaspoons lemon juice; let cool for about 4 minutes (glaze continues to thicken as it cools).

6 Invert cake pan onto a serving plate; carefully lift off pan to release cake. If any pears remain in pan, remove them and arrange in their original places atop cake. Drizzle cake with half the warm glaze; then sprinkle with hazelnuts and drizzle with remaining glaze.

makes 16 servings

per serving: 253 calories, 3 g protein, 42 g carbohydrates, 8 g total fat, 57 mg cholesterol, 199 mg sodium

chocolate soufflés

preparation time: 50 minutes

$^2/_3$ **cup unsweetened cocoa powder**

About $^3/_4$ **cup granulated sugar**

4 teaspoons cornstarch

1 teaspoon instant espresso or coffee powder

1 cup low-fat (2%) milk

2 ounces bittersweet or semisweet chocolate, finely chopped

2 teaspoons vanilla

7 large egg whites, at room temperature

$^1/_4$ **teaspoon cream of tartar**

$^1/_{16}$ **to** $^1/_8$ **teaspoon salt**

About 2 tablespoons powdered sugar

1 In a 1- to 2-quart pan, stir together cocoa, $^1/_4$ cup of the granulated sugar, cornstarch, and instant espresso. Whisk in milk. Cook over medium heat, whisking constantly, until mixture boils and thickens slightly (about 1 minute). Remove from heat and add chocolate and vanilla; whisk until chocolate is melted and mixture is smooth. Let cool completely.

2 While mixture cools, lightly grease six 1$^1/_2$-cup custard cups; sprinkle each lightly with granulated sugar to coat bottom. Place cups in a large baking pan and set aside.

3 In a deep bowl, beat egg whites with an electric mixer on high speed until frothy. Add cream of tartar, salt, and $^1/_2$ cup of the granulated sugar, 1 tablespoon at a time; beat until whites hold firm, moist peaks. Stir about a third of the whites into cooled chocolate mixture; then fold chocolate mixture into remaining whites.

4 Gently fill custard cups equally with batter. Position oven rack in bottom third of a 350° oven; set baking pan on rack. Pour boiling water into pan around cups up to level of batter. Bake until soufflés are puffy and feel firm when gently pressed (about 25 minutes). Carefully lift cups from pan and sprinkle soufflés with powdered sugar. Serve immediately.

makes 6 servings

per serving: 238 calories, 8 g protein, 42 g carbohydrates, 7 g total fat, 3 mg cholesterol, 122 mg sodium

port ice

preparation time: 15 minutes
chilling and freezing time: about 5 hours

$^1/_2$ **cup sugar**

1 cup port or cream sherry

$^1/_4$ **cup fresh orange juice**

1 teaspoon aromatic bitters

1 In a 1- to 2-quart pan, combine sugar and 1$^1/_2$ cups water. Bring to a boil over high heat, stirring until sugar is dissolved. Remove from heat and let cool; then stir in port, orange juice, and bitters. Cover and refrigerate until cold (about 1 hour). Pour port mixture into a metal pan 8 to 9 inches square; cover and freeze until solid (about 4 hours) or for up to 3 days.

2 To serve, break mixture into chunks with a heavy spoon, transfer to a blender or food processor, and whirl until slushy; then spoon into bowls and serve at once. (Or pour cold port mixture into container of a self-refrigerated ice cream machine and freeze according to manufacturer's instructions.)

makes 6 to 8 servings

per serving: 114 calories, 0.1 g protein, 19 g carbohydrates, 0 g total fat, 0 mg cholesterol, 3 mg sodium

amaretto soufflé

$^1/_2$ cup coarsely crushed amaretti cookies (about ten 11-inch cookies)

$^3/_4$ cup low-fat (2%) milk

3 large egg yolks

6 tablespoons granulated sugar

$^1/_4$ cup all-purpose flour

$^1/_4$ cup almond-flavored or other nut-flavored liqueur

$^1/_4$ teaspoon almond extract

5 large egg whites

1 teaspoon cream of tartar

$^1/_8$ teaspoon salt

About 1 tablespoon sifted powdered sugar

1 Sprinkle crushed cookies over bottom of a greased $1^1/_2$- to $1^3/_4$-quart soufflé dish. Place dish in a larger pan (at least 2 inches deep); set aside.

2 Bring milk to a boil in a medium-size nonstick pan over medium heat (about 5 minutes), stirring often. Remove from heat and let cool slightly.

3 In a large bowl, whisk egg yolks and 3 tablespoons of the granulated sugar until thick and lemon-colored. Add flour and whisk until smoothly blended. Whisk in a little of the warm milk, then whisk egg yolk mixture back into warm milk in pan. Return to heat and stir constantly (be careful not to scratch pan) just until mixture boils and thickens slightly. Return to large bowl and whisk in liqueur and almond extract; let cool completely.

4 In a clean large, deep bowl beat egg whites and 1 tablespoon water with an electric mixer on high speed until frothy. Beat in cream of tartar and salt. Then beat in remaining 3 tablespoons granulated sugar, 1 tablespoon at a time; continue to beat until mixture holds stiff, moist peaks. Stir about a third of the egg white mixture into yolk mixture; then fold all of yolk mixture into egg white mixture.

5 Gently spoon soufflé batter into prepared dish. Set pan with dish on middle rack of a 350° oven. Pour boiling water into larger pan up to level of soufflé batter. Bake until soufflé is richly browned and center jiggles only slightly when dish is gently shaken (about 25 minutes); if top begins to brown excessively, carefully cover dish with foil. As soon as soufflé is done, sprinkle it with powdered sugar and serve immediately.

makes 6 servings

per serving: 198 calories, 6 g protein, 29 g carbohydrates, 4 g total fat, 109 mg cholesterol, 115 mg sodium

STORING COFFEE: Heat and moisture cause coffee to go stale quickly, so store both beans and ground coffee airtight—preferably in glass jars with tight screw-on lids—in the refrigerator or freezer. When you want to brew coffee, just remove the amount you need; there's no need to thaw it or bring it to room temperature before using. Buy coffee in small quantities, since it loses its freshness after about a month even if stored properly.

mexican cocoa cake

preparation time: 40 to 50 minutes

Spiced Cream (optional; page 585)

1 cup sifted cake flour

¹/₃ cup unsweetened cocoa powder

1 teaspoon *each* baking soda, baking powder,
   and ground cinnamon

6 large egg whites

1 ¹/₃ cups firmly packed brown sugar

1 cup plain nonfat yogurt

2 teaspoons vanilla

¹/₄ teaspoon almond extract

Powdered sugar

1 Prepare Spiced Cream, if desired; refrigerate.

2 In a small bowl, mix flour, cocoa, baking soda, baking powder, and cinnamon. In a large bowl, beat egg whites, brown sugar, yogurt, vanilla, and almond extract until well blended. Stir in flour mixture and beat just until evenly moistened.

3 Pour batter into a square 8-inch nonstick (or greased regular) baking pan. Bake in a 350° oven until center of cake springs back when lightly pressed (30 to 40 minutes). Let cake cool in pan on a rack for 15 minutes; then invert it onto a serving plate. Serve warm or cool. If made ahead, wrap cooled cake airtight and store in a cool place until next day (freeze for longer storage).

4 Just before serving, sift powdered sugar over cake. To serve, cut cake into wedges or rectangles. If desired, sift more powdered sugar over each serving; then top with Spiced Cream, if desired.

makes 8 servings

per serving: 226 calories, 6 g protein, 51 g carbohydrates, 0.6 g total fat, 0.6 mg cholesterol, 297 mg sodium

campari ice

preparation time: 15 minutes
chilling & freezing time: about 5 hours

¹/₂ cup sugar

1 cup sweet vermouth or fresh orange juice

2 tablespoons Campari
   or 2 teaspoons aromatic bitters

1 tablespoon lime juice

Thin lime slices

1 In a 1- to 2-quart pan, combine sugar and 1¹/₂ cups water. Bring to a boil over high heat, stirring until sugar is dissolved. Remove from heat and let cool; then stir in vermouth, Campari, and lime juice. Cover mixture and refrigerate until cold (about 1 hour).

2 Pour mixture into a metal pan 8 to 9 inches square; cover and freeze until solid (about 4 hours) or for up to 3 days.

3 To serve, break mixture into chunks with a heavy spoon, transfer to a blender or food processor, and whirl until slushy; then spoon into bowls and serve at once. (Or pour cold port mixture into container of a self-refrigerated ice cream machine and freeze according to manufacturer's instructions.) Garnish individual servings with lime slices.

makes 6 to 8 servings

per serving: 120 calories, 0 g protein, 20 g carbohydrates, 0 g total fat, 0 mg cholesterol, 4 mg sodium

oranges with rum syrup & spiced cream

preparation time: about 35 minutes
freezing and chilling time: 45 minutes to 1 hour

Spiced Cream (recipe follows)

$^1/_2$ cup sugar

1 $^1/_2$ cups water

2 teaspoons whole cloves

2 tablespoons light rum

4 large oranges (about 3 lbs. total)

1 Prepare Spiced Cream; refrigerate.

2 In a small pan, combine sugar, water, and cloves. Bring to a boil over high heat; then boil until reduced to $^3/_4$ cup (about 20 minutes). Remove from heat, stir in rum, and let cool. (At this point, you may cover and refrigerate for up to 5 days.)

3 With a sharp knife, cut peel and all white membrane from oranges. Slice fruit into 6 dessert bowls, dividing equally. Add rum syrup and Spiced Cream to taste.

makes 6 servings

SPICED CREAM

1 Pour $^1/_4$ cup nonfat milk into small bowl of an electric mixer. Cover bowl; then freeze mixer beaters and bowl of milk until milk is slushy (30 to 45 minutes). In a small pan, sprinkle $^1/_2$ teaspoon unflavored gelatin over $^1/_4$ cup cold water; let stand until gelatin is softened (about 3 minutes). Then stir mixture over low heat just until gelatin is dissolved. Remove from heat.

2 To slushy milk, add gelatin, $^2/_3$ cup instant nonfat dry milk, 2 tablespoons sugar, 1 teaspoon vanilla, and $^1/_2$ teaspoon ground cinnamon. Beat on high speed until mixture holds soft peaks (5 to 10 minutes). Cover and refrigerate for at least 15 minutes or for up to 2 days. If needed, whisk or beat again before serving until cream holds soft peaks. Serve cold.

makes about 2 cups

per serving of oranges: 153 calories, 1 g protein, 36 g carbohydrates, 0.4 g total fat, 0 mg cholesterol, 0.6 mg sodium

per tablespoon of spiced cream: 9 calories, 0.6 g protein, 2 g carbohydrates, 0 g total fat, 0.3 mg cholesterol, 9 mg sodium

oranges in ginger champagne

preparation time: about 15 minutes

$^3/_4$ cup *each* sugar and water

2 tablespoons minced candied ginger

4 medium-size oranges

1 bottle dry champagne or 4 cups ginger ale

1 In a 2- to 3-quart pan, combine sugar, water, and ginger. Cook over medium heat, stirring, until sugar is dissolved. Increase heat to high and boil, without stirring, for 5 minutes. Transfer to a bowl; cool, cover, and refrigerate until cold or until next day.

2 Peel oranges and remove white membrane. Holding oranges over howl of ginger syrup, cut between segments to release fruit; stir. Cover and refrigerate for 3 hours.

3 Spoon orange mixture into champagne or wine glasses. Fill with champagne.

makes 8 servings

per serving: 188 calories, 0.7 g protein, 33 g carbohydrates, 0.2 g total fat, 0 mg cholesterol, 7 mg sodium

german chocolate cheesecake

preparation time: 30 minutes
cooking time: about 1 hour and 10 minutes
cooling and chilling time: at least 4 1/2 hours

1 cup chocolate graham cracker crumbs (about twelve square 2-inch crackers)

3 tablespoons apple jelly, melted and cooled slightly

3 large packages (about 8 oz. *each*) nonfat cream cheese, at room temperature

1 cup granulated sugar

3/4 cup unsweetened cocoa powder

1/3 cup all-purpose flour

1/3 cup semisweet chocolate chips, melted and cooled slightly

1/2 cup nonfat milk

2 large eggs

2 large egg whites

2 teaspoons vanilla

2/3 cup regular rolled oats

1/3 cup sweetened shredded coconut

1/4 cup finely chopped pecans

2/3 cup firmly packed brown sugar

3 tablespoons *each* half-and-half and light corn syrup

2 tablespoons butter or margarine

1 In a food processor or a large bowl, whirl or stir together graham cracker crumbs and jelly just until crumbs are evenly moistened. Press crumbs firmly over bottom of a 9-inch nonstick or regular cheesecake pan with a removable rim. Bake in a 350° oven until crust is slightly darker in color (about 15 minutes).

2 Meanwhile, in clean food processor or large bowl, combine cream cheese, granulated sugar, cocoa, flour, chocolate, milk, eggs, egg whites, and vanilla. Whirl or beat with an electric mixer until smooth.

3 Pour cream cheese filling over crust. Return to oven and bake until filling jiggles only slightly in center when pan is gently shaken (about 45 minutes). Remove pan from oven and run a slender knife between cheesecake and pan rim; let cheesecake cool in pan on a rack for 30 minutes.

4 Meanwhile, toast oats in a wide nonstick frying pan over medium heat for 5 minutes, stirring often. Add coconut and pecans; continue to cook, stirring often, until mixture is slightly darker in color (3 to 5 more minutes). Transfer oat mixture to a bowl and let cool. In same pan, combine brown sugar, half-and-half, corn syrup, and butter. Cook over medium heat, stirring, until butter is melted and mixture is smoothly blended. Stir in oat mixture. Remove pan from heat and let mixture cool for 5 minutes.

5 Gently spoon coconut topping over cheesecake; let cool completely. Then cover cooled cheesecake and refrigerate until cold (at least 4 hours) or until next day. Remove pan rim before serving.

makes 12 to 16 servings

per serving: 300 calories, 11 g protein, 51 g carbohydrates, 7 g total fat, 41 mg cholesterol, 326 mg sodium

apple & date betty

preparation time: 20 minutes
cooking time: 50 to 55 minutes

2 cups soft whole wheat bread crumbs

3 tablespoons butter or margarine, melted

1/4 cup firmly packed brown sugar

1/4 cup granulated sugar

1/2 teaspoon ground cinnamon

1/8 teaspoon ground nutmeg

4 cups peeled, sliced tart apples

1/2 cup coarsely chopped pitted dates

1 tablespoon lemon juice

1 In a medium-size bowl, lightly mix bread crumbs, butter, and brown sugar. Sprinkle half the mixture over bottom of a shallow 2-quart casserole; set aside remaining mixture.

2 In a large bowl, stir together granulated sugar, cinnamon, and nutmeg. Add apples and dates; mix gently to coat fruit with sugar mixture. Drizzle fruit mixture with lemon juice, then cover evenly over crumb mixture in casserole. Sprinkle with 2 tablespoons water; cover evenly with remaining crumb mixture.

3 Set casserole in a larger baking pan to catch any drips. Cover and bake in a 375° oven for 30 minutes. Then uncover and continue to bake until filling is bubbly in center, apples are very tender when pierced, and topping is crisp (20 to 25 more minutes). Serve hot or warm; to serve, spoon into bowls.

makes 6 servings

per serving: 242 calories, 2 g protein, 47 g carbohydrates, 7 g total fat, 16 mg cholesterol, 151 mg sodium

nectarine-blueberry cream pie

preparation time: 35 minutes, plus 15 minutes for filling to stand
cooking time: about 1 1/4 hours

Pie pastry

1 cup nonfat sour cream

1 teaspoon cornstarch

2 cups fresh blueberries

4 cups peeled, sliced firm-ripe nectarines

1 teaspoon vanilla

1/2 cup granulated sugar

3 tablespoons quick-cooking tapioca

1/2 cup firmly packed brown sugar

2/3 cup all-purpose flour

3 tablespoons butter or margarine, melted and cooled slightly

2 tablespoons smooth unsweetened applesauce

1 Prepare pie pastry and line pie pan, but do not prick pastry after lining pan. Bake pastry shell on lowest rack of a 425° oven until golden (12 to 15 minutes; pastry may puff, but filling will press it down again). Remove from oven and place on a rack. Reduce oven temperature to 350°.

2 While pastry is baking, in a large bowl, beat sour cream and cornstarch until smoothly blended. Stir in blueberries, nectarines, and vanilla. Stir together granulated sugar and tapioca; add to fruit mixture and mix gently. Let stand for 15 minutes to soften tapioca, stirring occasionally. Then pour filling into warm pastry shell and set aside.

3 In a small bowl, combine brown sugar, flour, butter, and apple-sauce. Stir until mixture is evenly moistened. With your fingers, squeeze mixture to form large lumps; then crumble evenly over filling.

4 Set pie pan in a larger baking pan to catch any drips. Bake pie on lowest oven rack until filling is bubbly in center and topping is well browned (about 1 hour); if crust or topping begins to darken excessively, cover it with foil. Let cool on a rack before serving; serve warm.

makes 8 to 10 servings

per serving: 390 calories, 6 g protein, 64 g carbohydrates, 13 g total fat, 10 mg cholesterol, 139 mg sodium

pumpkin cheesecake

preparation time: 25 minutes
cooking time: about 1 hour
cooling and chilling time: at least 4 1/2 hours

2/3 cup firmly packed brown sugar

3 tablespoons all-purpose flour

1/4 cup butter or margarine, melted

2 large packages (about 8 oz. *each*) nonfat
    cream cheese, at room temperature

1 can (about 1 lb.) pumpkin

2 large eggs

3/4 cup granulated sugar

2 tablespoons all-purpose flour

1 teaspoon ground cinnamon

1 teaspoon vanilla

1/4 teaspoon *each* ground ginger
    and ground nutmeg

1 cup nonfat sour cream

1 tablespoon granulated sugar

1/2 cup coarsely crushed gingersnaps
    (about nine 2-inch cookies)

1 In a food processor or a large bowl, whirl or stir together the 2 cups finely crushed gingersnaps, brown sugar, and the 3 tablespoons flour. Add butter; whirl or rub with your fingers until mixture resembles coarse crumbs. Press crumb mixture firmly over bottom and 1/2 inch up sides of a 9-inch nonstick or regular cheesecake pan with a removable rim. Bake in a 350° oven until crust smells toasted and feels slightly firmer in center when gently pressed (about 10 minutes).

2 Meanwhile, in clean food processor or large bowl, combine cream cheese, pumpkin, eggs, the 3/4 cup granulated sugar, the 2 tablespoons flour, cinnamon, vanilla, ginger, and nutmeg. Whirl or beat with an electric mixer until smooth.

3 Pour cream cheese filling into baked crust. Return to oven and bake until filling jiggles only slightly in center when pan is gently shaken (about 50 minutes). Let cool in pan on a rack for 30 minutes. Meanwhile, in a small bowl, gently stir together sour cream and the 1 tablespoon sugar; cover and refrigerate.

4 Spread cooled cheesecake with sour cream topping. Cover and refrigerate until cold (at least 4 hours) or until next day. Just before serving, remove pan rim; sprinkle cheesecake with the 1/2 cup coarsely crushed gingersnaps.

makes 12 servings

per serving: 317 calories, 10 g protein, 54 g carbohydrates, 7 g total fat, 50 mg cholesterol, 404 mg sodium

anise poofs

preparation time: about 35 minutes
standing time: 8 to 24 hours

About 2 cups sifted powdered sugar

1 cup all-purpose flour

1 teaspoon baking powder

1/4 teaspoon ground cinnamon

1 tablespoon olive oil

1 large egg, beaten

2 tablespoons anisette liqueur;
    or 1 teaspoon anise extract (or to taste)
    blended with 5 teaspoons water

1 teaspoon vanilla

1 In a large bowl, stir together 2 cups of the powdered sugar, flour, baking powder, and cinnamon. Add oil, egg, liqueur, and vanilla; stir until well blended. Turn dough out onto a board lightly dusted with powdered sugar; knead until smooth, about 4 turns.

2 Cut dough into 6 pieces. Roll each piece into a rope 20 inches long and about 1/2 inch wide.

3 Cut each rope into 2-inch lengths. Place pieces about 1 1/2 inches apart on lightly oiled large baking sheets. Let cookies stand, uncovered, for 8 to 24 hours. (Do not omit standing time; if dough does not stand, cookies will not puff.) Then bake in a 325° oven until pale golden (about 8 minutes). Immediately transfer cookies to racks and let cool.

makes 5 dozen cookies

per cookie: 27 calories, 0.3 g protein, 5 g carbohydrates, 0.5 g total fat, 4 mg cholesterol, 9 mg sodium

lime cheesecake

preparation time: 20 minutes
cooking time: 45 to 55 minutes
cooling and chilling time: at least 4 1/2 hours

1 1/2 cups graham cracker crumbs (about eighteen square 2-inch crackers)

1 cup plus 1 tablespoon sugar

1/4 cup butter or margarine, at room temperature

2 large packages (about 8 oz. *each*) nonfat cream cheese, at room temperature

2 cups nonfat sour cream

2 large eggs

2 large egg whites

1 tablespoon grated lime peel

1/4 cup lime juice

3 tablespoons all-purpose flour

Lime slices

1 In a food processor or a large bowl, whirl or stir together graham cracker crumbs, 2 tablespoons of the sugar, and butter until mixture resembles coarse crumbs. Press mixture firmly over bottom and 1/2 inch up sides of a 9-inch nonstick or regular cheesecake pan with a removable rim. Bake in a 350° oven until lightly browned (about 10 minutes).

2 Meanwhile, in clean food processor or large bowl, combine 3/4 cup plus 2 tablespoons of the sugar, cream cheese, 1 cup of the sour cream, eggs, egg whites, lime peel, lime juice, and flour. Whirl or beat with an electric mixer until smooth.

3 Pour cream cheese filling into crust. Return to oven and bake until filling jiggles only slightly in center when pan is gently shaken (35 to 45 minutes). Let cool in pan on a rack for 30 minutes. Meanwhile, in a small bowl, gently stir together remaining 1 cup sour cream and remaining 1 tablespoon sugar; cover and refrigerate.

4 Spread cooled cheesecake with sour cream topping. Cover and refrigerate until cold (at least 4 hours) or until next day. Before serving, remove pan rim and garnish cheesecake with lime slices.

makes 12 to 16 servings

per serving: 211 calories, 9 g protein, 31 g carbohydrates, 5 g total fat, 43 mg cholesterol, 305 mg sodium

peach cobbler with almond topping

preparation time: 35 minutes, plus 15 minutes for filling to stand
cooking time: about 1 hour

1 cup almond paste

1/2 cup sugar

1/4 cup cornstarch

9 medium-size firm-ripe peaches

2 tablespoons sugar

2 tablespoons lemon juice

1 Crumble almond paste into a medium-size bowl. Add the 1/2 cup sugar and 2 tablespoons of the corn starch. Rub together with your fingers until well blended. With your fingers, squeeze mixture to form large lumps; set aside.

2 Peel and pit peaches; then slice them into a shallow 1 1/2- to 2-quart casserole. Add the 2 tablespoons sugar, lemon juice, and remaining 2 tablespoons cornstarch; mix gently. Spread out fruit mixture in an even layer; then crumble almond topping over top.

3 Set casserole in a larger baking pan to catch any drips. Bake in a 350° oven until fruit mixture is bubbly in center and topping is browned (45 to 50 minutes); if topping begins to darken excessively, cover it with foil. Let cool slightly; spoon into bowls.

makes 6 to 8 servings

per serving: 277 calories, 4 g protein, 51 g carbohydrates, 8 g total fat, 0 mg cholesterol, 4 mg sodium

amaretto cheesecake

preparation time: 20 minutes
cooking time: about 1 1/2 hours
Cooling and chilling time: at least 4 1/2 hours

2 cups graham cracker crumbs

1/4 cup butter or margarine, melted

1/4 teaspoon almond extract

2 tablespoons slivered almonds

4 large packages (about 8 oz *each*) nonfat
   cream cheese, at room temperature

1 cup granulated sugar

3 large eggs

2 large egg whites

1 cup nonfat sour cream

2 tablespoons almond-flavored liqueur

2/3 cup firmly packed brown sugar

3 tablespoons each half-and-half
   and light corn syrup

2 tablespoons butter or margarine

1 teaspoon almond-flavored liqueur, or to taste

1 In a food processor or a large bowl, whirl or stir together graham cracker crumbs, the 1/4 cup melted butter, and almond extract just until crumbs are evenly moistened. Press crumbs firmly over bottom of a 9-inch nonstick or regular cheesecake pan with a removable rim. Bake in a 350° oven until crust is slightly darker in color (about 15 minutes).

2 Meanwhile, toast almonds in a small frying pan over medium heat until golden (3 to 5 minutes), stirring often. Transfer almonds to a bowl and set aside. In clean food processor or large bowl, combine cream cheese, granulated sugar, eggs, egg whites, sour cream, and the 2 tablespoons liqueur. Whirl or beat with an electric mixer until smooth.

3 Pour cream cheese filling over baked crust. Return to oven and bake until filling jiggles only slightly in center when pan is gently shaken (about 1 hour and 5 minutes). Let cheesecake cool in pan on a rack for 30 minutes.

4 Meanwhile, in a 1- to 1 1/2-quart pan, combine brown sugar, half-and-half, corn syrup, and the 2 tablespoons butter. Bring mixture just to a boil over medium heat, stirring constantly. Remove pan from heat and let cool for about 4 minutes; glaze thickens as it cools. Stir in the 1 teaspoon liqueur; set aside.

5 Run a slender knife between cheesecake and pan rim, then remove pan rim. Stir glaze and drizzle over cheesecake; let cool completely. Then lightly cover cooled cheesecake and refrigerate until cold (at least 4 hours) or until next day.

makes 12 to 16 servings

per serving: 321 calories, 14 g protein, 47 g carbohydrates, 8 g total fat, 67 mg cholesterol, 505 mg sodium

apricot slims

preparation time: 15 minutes
chilling time: at least 30 minutes

1 package (about 6 oz.) dried apricots

4 cup sweetened shredded or flaked coconut

1 tablespoon orange juice

2 tablespoons finely chopped almonds

3 tablespoons powdered sugar

1 In a food processor, combine apricots, coconut, and orange juice. Whirl until mixture begins to hold together in a ball.

2 Divide apricot mixture into 4 equal portions and wrap each in plastic wrap. Refrigerate until cold (at least 30 minutes).

3 In a small bowl, mix almonds and powdered sugar. Sprinkle a fourth of the almond mixture on a board. Place one portion of the apricot mixture atop almond mixture; roll apricot mixture back and forth with your palms to form a 16-inch rope. Repeat to make 3 more ropes, using remaining almond and apricot mixtures. To serve, cut ropes diagonally into 2-inch pieces.

makes 32 pieces

per piece: 20 calories, 0.3 g protein, 4 g carbohydrates, 0.3 g total fat, 0 mg cholesterol, 2 mg sodium

index